NEW APPROACHES FOR SECURITY, PRIVACY AND TRUST IN COMPLEX ENVIRONMENTS

IFIP – The International Federation for Information Processing

IFIP was founded in 1960 under the auspices of UNESCO, following the First World Computer Congress held in Paris the previous year. An umbrella organization for societies working in information processing, IFIP's aim is two-fold: to support information processing within its member countries and to encourage technology transfer to developing nations. As its mission statement clearly states,

> *IFIP's mission is to be the leading, truly international, apolitical organization which encourages and assists in the development, exploitation and application of information technology for the benefit of all people.*

IFIP is a non-profitmaking organization, run almost solely by 2500 volunteers. It operates through a number of technical committees, which organize events and publications. IFIP's events range from an international congress to local seminars, but the most important are:

- The IFIP World Computer Congress, held every second year;
- Open conferences;
- Working conferences.

The flagship event is the IFIP World Computer Congress, at which both invited and contributed papers are presented. Contributed papers are rigorously refereed and the rejection rate is high.

As with the Congress, participation in the open conferences is open to all and papers may be invited or submitted. Again, submitted papers are stringently refereed.

The working conferences are structured differently. They are usually run by a working group and attendance is small and by invitation only. Their purpose is to create an atmosphere conducive to innovation and development. Refereeing is less rigorous and papers are subjected to extensive group discussion.

Publications arising from IFIP events vary. The papers presented at the IFIP World Computer Congress and at open conferences are published as conference proceedings, while the results of the working conferences are often published as collections of selected and edited papers.

Any national society whose primary activity is in information may apply to become a full member of IFIP, although full membership is restricted to one society per country. Full members are entitled to vote at the annual General Assembly, National societies preferring a less committed involvement may apply for associate or corresponding membership. Associate members enjoy the same benefits as full members, but without voting rights. Corresponding members are not represented in IFIP bodies. Affiliated membership is open to non-national societies, and individual and honorary membership schemes are also offered.

NEW APPROACHES FOR SECURITY, PRIVACY AND TRUST IN COMPLEX ENVIRONMENTS

Proceedings of the IFIP TC-11 22nd International Information Security Conference (SEC 2007), 14-16 May 2007, Sandton, South Africa

Edited by

Hein Venter
University of Pretoria, South Africa

Mariki Eloff
University of South Africa, South Africa

Les Labuschagne
University of Johannesburg, South Africa

Jan Eloff
University of Pretoria, South Africa

Rossouw von Solms
Nelson Mandela Metropolitan University, South Africa

Library of Congress Control Number: 2007925686

New Approaches for Security, Privacy and Trust in Complex Environments

Edited by H. Venter, M. Eloff, L. Labuschagne, J. Eloff, and R. von Solms

p. cm. (IFIP International Federation for Information Processing, a Springer Series in Computer Science)

ISSN: 1571-5736 / 1861-2288 (Internet)
ISBN: 13: 978-0-387-72366-2
eISBN: 13: 978-0-387-72367-9
Printed on acid-free paper

9 8 7 6 5 4 3 2 1
springer.com

Foreword

This book contains the Proceedings of the 22nd IFIP TC-11 International Information Security Conference (IFIP/SEC 2007) on "New Approaches for Security, Privacy and Trust in Complex Environments" held in Sandton, South Africa from 14 to 16 May 2007. The IFIP/SEC conferences are the flagship events of TC-11. In May 1995 South Africa for the first time hosted an IFIP/SEC conference in Cape Town. Now, twelve years later, we are very pleased to have succeeded in our bid to once again present the IFIP/SEC conference in South Africa.

The current IT environment deals with novel, complex approaches such as information privacy, trust, digital forensics, management, and human aspects. This modern environment challenges the whole information security research community to focus on interdisciplinary and holistic approaches, whilst retaining the benefit of previous research efforts. Papers offering research contributions that focus both on access control in complex environments and on other aspects of computer security and privacy were solicited for submission to IFIP/SEC 2007. A total of 107 submissions were received, which were all reviewed by at least three members of the international programme committee.

At a one-day meeting the programme committee discussed the submitted papers, after which 36 papers were selected for presentation at the conference (implying an acceptance rate of 33.6%). IFIP/SEC 2007 places special emphasis on access control, which is addressed by 14 of the 36 accepted papers. Further topics addressed include information privacy, digital forensics for pervasive environments, human aspects of security, computer-based trust, intrusion detection and network security.

These proceedings also include the papers of two other workshops that are associated with IFIP/SEC 2007, namely the workshop on "Security and Control of Identity in Society (SCITS 4)" organised by IFIP Working Group 9.6/11.7 and the workshop on "Fostering Knowledge and Skills for Manageable Information Security", organised by IFIP Working Group 11.1/11.8. These working groups had their own call for papers, programme committees and selection processes with acceptance rates of papers similar to that of the main IFIP/SEC 2007 conference. A paper by one of the keynote speakers, Bill Caelli, entitled "Modernising MAC: New Forms for Mandatory Access Control in an Era of DRM" is also included in the proceedings. The paper is aimed at being not too technical but rather at posing questions and investigating current directions in this field.

IFIP/SEC 2007 is organised in cooperation with the University of Pretoria, the University of South Africa, the University of Johannesburg, the Nelson Mandela Metropolitan University and SBS Conferences, under the auspices of the Computer Society of South Africa. We are grateful to all authors and members of the programme committees for contributing to the scientific quality of this conference and the two workshops. Last but not least, our sincere thanks are extended to the organising committee for their efforts in preparing for this conference.

February 2007

Jan Eloff (Programme Committee Chair)
Hein Venter (Publication Chair and Programme Committee member)

Organization

IFIP/SEC 2007 is hosted by The Computer Society South Africa and organized by IFIP TC-11 (Technical Committee on Security & Protection in Information Processing Systems) and SBS Conferences, South Africa in cooperation with the University of Pretoria, the University of South Africa, the University of Johannesburg, and the Nelson Mandela Metropolitan University.

Conference Chairs

Conference General Chair
Rossouw von Solms, Nelson Mandela Metropolitan University, South Africa

Programme Committee Chair
Jan Eloff, Universtiy of Pretoria, South Africa

Local Organizing Committee Co-Chairs
Rossouw von Solms, Nelson Mandela Metropolitan University, South Africa
Les Labuschagne, University of Johannesburg, South Africa
Peter Aspinal, SBS Conferences, South Africa

Publication Chair
Hein Venter, Universtiy of Pretoria, South Africa

Programme Committee

Helen Armstrong, Curtin University, Australia
Tuomas Aura, Microsoft Research, UK
Richard Baskerville, Georgia State University, USA
Rolf Blom, Ericsson Research, Sweden
Reinhard Botha, Nelson Mandela Metropolitan University, South Africa
Caspar Bowden, Microsoft EMEA Technology Office, UK
Bill Caelli, Queensland University of Technology, Australia,
Jan Camenisch, IBM Zurich Research Laboratory, Switzerland
Bruce Christianson, University of Hertfordshire, UK
Roger Clarke, Xamax Consultancy, Australia
Richard Clayton, University of Cambridge, UK
Frédéric Cuppens, ENST Bretagne, France
Mads Dam, Royal Institute of Technology, Sweden
Bart De Decker, Katholieke Universiteit Leuven, Belgium
Yves Deswarte, LAAS-CNRS, France
Ronald Dodge, United States Military Academy, USA
Paul Dowland, Plymouth University, Plymouth, UK

Hanne Riis Nielson, Technical University of Denmark, Denmark
Pierangela Samarati, Universita` di Milano, Italy
David Sands, Chalmers University of Technology, Sweden
Ryoichi Sasaki, Tokyo Denki University, Japan
Ingrid Schaumüller-Bichl, ITSB Linz, Austria
Matthias Schunter, IBM Zurich Research Laboratory, Switzerland
Anne Karen Seip, Kredittilsynet (FSA), Norway
Andrei Serjantov, The Free Haven Project, UK
Nahid Shahmehri, Linköping University, Sweden
Leon Strous, De Nederlandsche Bank, The Netherlands
Masato Terada, Hitachi Ltd., Japan
Stephanie Teufel, University of Fribourg, Switzerland
Hein Venter, University of Pretoria, South Africa
Basie von Solms, University of Johannesburg, South Africa
Rossouw von Solms, Nelson Mandela Metropolitan University, South Africa
Teemupekka Virtanen, Helsinki University of Technology, Finland
Jozef Vyskoc, VaF, Slovak Republic
Matthew Warren, Deakin University, Australia
Tatjana Welzer, University of Maribor, Slovenia
Gunnar Wenngren, Swedish Defence Research Agency (FOI), Sweden
Felix Wu, University of California, USA
Louise Yngström, Stockholm University/KTH, Sweden
Hiroshi Yoshiura, The University of Electro- Communications, Japan
Albin Zuccato, Karlstad University, Sweden

IFIP WG 9.6/11.7 – IT Misuse and the Law & the NoE "Future of Identity in the Information Society" (FIDIS) – Workshop on Security and Control of Identity in Society

Programme Committee Chair
Kai Rannenberg, Goethe University Frankfurt, Germany
Albin Zuccato, TeliaSonera, Sweden

Programme Committee
Reinhardt Botha, Nelson Mandela Metropolitan University, South Africa
Caspar Bowden, Microsoft, UK
Arslan Brömme, ConSecur GmbH, Meppen, Germany
Simone Fischer-Hübner, Karlstad University, Sweden
Mark Gasson, University of Reading, UK
Marit Hansen, Independent Centre for Privacy Protection, Germany
David-Olivier Jaquet-Chiffelle, VIP - Berne University of Applied Sciences & ESC - Lausanne University, Switzerland
Bert-Jaap Koops, Tilburg University, Netherlands
Javier Lopez, University of Malaga, Spain
Vijay Masurkar, Sun, USA
Morton Swimmer, IBM Research, Switzerland

Jozef Vyskoc, VaF, Slovakia
Gunnar Wenngren, AB Wenngrens, Sweden
Louise Yngström, Stockholm University KTH, Sweden

IFIP WG 11.1/11.8 Workshop on Fostering Knowledge and Skills for Manageable Information Security

Programme Committee Chair
Steven Furnell, University of Plymouth, UK
Colonel Daniel Ragsdale, United States Military Academy, USA

Programme Committee
Helen Armstrong – Curtin University, Australia
Andrzej Bialas - Instytut Systemów Sterowania, Poland
Matt Bishop - University of California, Davis, USA
Nathan Clarke - University of Plymouth, UK
Jeimy José Cano Martínez - Universidad de los Andes, Colombia
Ronald Dodge – United States Military Academy, USA
Neil Doherty - Loughborough University, UK
Paul Dowland - University of Plymouth, UK
Lynn Futcher - Nelson Mandela Metropolitan University, South Africa
Dimitris Gritzalis – Athens University of Economics & Business, Greece
Brian Hay - University of Alaska Fairbanks, USA
Lech Janczewski – The University of Auckland, New Zealand
Jorma Kajava – University of Lapland, Finland
Vijay Masurkar - Sun Microsystems, USA
Vaclav (Vashek) Matyas - Masaryk University, Czech Republic
Kara Nance - University of Alaska Fairbanks, USA
Reijo Savola - VTT Technical Research Centre of Finland, Finland

Table of Contents

Digital Forensics

Human-Computer Interaction I

Computer-Based Trust

Information Security Management I

Network Security I

Information Security Management II

Network Security II

Access Control I

Human-Computer Interaction II

Intrusion Detection Systems

Access Control II

Information Privacy I

Access Control III

Information Privacy II

Access Control IV

Security Services

Access Control V

Trust and Intrusion Detection Systems

Keynote paper

IFIP WG 9.6/11.7 – IT Misuse and the Law & the NoE "Future of Identity in the Information Society" (FIDIS) – Workshop on Security and Control of Identity in Society

IFIP WG 11.1/11.8 Workshop on Fostering Knowledge and Skills for Manageable Information Security

FORSIGS: Forensic Signature Analysis of the Hard Drive for Multimedia File Fingerprints

John Haggerty and Mark Taylor
Liverpool John Moores University, School of Computing & Mathematical Sciences, Byrom Street, Liverpool, L3 3AF. E-mail: {J.Haggerty, M.J.Taylor}@ljmu.ac.uk

Abstract. Computer forensics is emerging as an important tool in the fight against crime. Increasingly, computers are being used to facilitate new criminal activity, or used in the commission of existing crimes. The networked world has seen increases in, and the volume of, information that may be shared amongst hosts. This has given rise to major concerns over paedophile activity, and in particular the spread of multimedia files amongst this community. This paper presents a novel scheme for the automated analysis of storage media for digital pictures or files of interest using forensic signatures. The scheme first identifies potential multimedia files of interest and then compares the data to file signatures to ascertain whether a malicious file is resident on the computer. A case study of the *forsigs* application presented within this paper demonstrates the applicability of the approach for identification and retrieval of malicious multimedia files.

1 Introduction

Due to the increased use of computer and network technologies in certain types of criminal activity, computer forensics is emerging as an important tool in the fight against crime. Computer forensics is defined as the application of computer investigation and analysis techniques to determine potential evidence [1]. Crime involving computers and associated technologies may be classified in three ways [2]; the computer is the target of the crime, a repository of information used or generated during the commission of a crime, or as a tool in committing a crime. Therefore, the investigation and analysis techniques are wide and varied, and often rely on the context surrounding the activity under scrutiny.

A major advantage within the networked world is the speed and volume of information that may be shared between hosts. This has given rise to major concerns over paedophile activity and the spread of multimedia files, in particular indecent

Please use the following format when citing this chapter:

Haggerty, J. and Taylor, M., 2007, in IFIP International Federation for Information Processing, Volume 232, New Approaches for Security, Privacy and Trust in Complex Environments, eds. Venter, H., Eloff, M., Labuschagne, L., Eloff, J., von Solms, R., (Boston: Springer), pp. 1–12.

images of children amongst this community. As with many types of computer crime, whilst an investigation may begin with one suspect, it is rare that it will end with only the same suspect. In addition, due to the greater capacity of today's hard drives (upwards of 200 Gigabytes) and the amount of multimedia information that may be held on a suspect's computer, a large volume of data must be analysed. A major challenge facing law enforcement and national security is accurately and efficiently analysing this growing volume of evidential data [3].

The current practice of searching a hard drive for evidence is a time-consuming, manual process. An image of the hard drive is taken to replicate the original evidence source, and this itself may take 24 – 48 hours to make a robust copy. A forensics tool is then used to recreate the logical structure of the underlying file system. A computer forensic analyst views the files, both extant and deleted, and files of interest are reported with supporting evidence, such as time of investigation, analyst's name, the logical and actual location of the file, etc. As the investigation of the hard drive relies on the analyst viewing files as if part of the file system, this process is laborious. Therefore, attempts by practitioners have been made to improve the speed of the search within the constraints of the tools at their disposal. Some practitioners achieve this by comparing MD5 file checksums from the files on the hard drive under investigation to MD5 checksums of known malicious files recorded from previous investigations.

This paper presents a novel scheme for the forensic application of signature analysis, and in particular, the search of raw data for evidence of illegal or suspicious multimedia files[1] resident or deleted on the hard drive. This approach focuses on the the speed of search and robust identification of multimedia files of interest. It is recognised that other pieces of information would be gained from a manual search using the logical file structure, such as time of file creation, access or modification, etc., once these files are identified and located.

The advantages of the forensic signature approach are fourfold. First, the speed of analysing a suspect's machine may be reduced by automating the search process. This is not to say that a manual inspection may not be required later, but it can direct the forensic analyst to the relevant areas of the hard drive. However, this approach may be used to detect data not discovered by more traditional computer forensic techniques [2]. Second, the application can be extended to investigate related data types other than multimedia files, such as searching for text strings or evidence produced by other applications, e.g. Word, e-mail, etc. Third, current practice by some practitioners of analysing data for known files of interest utilises searches for MD5 checksums produced during previous investigations. Recent research has questioned the reliability of MD5 and SHA-1 hash functions in producing digital signatures [4], and this will have serious ramifications within the legal arena. In addition, a suspect may avoid detection by altering just one byte within the multimedia file of interest which will alter the MD5 checksum produced. Finally, the analyst is not required to look at any images that they may find disturbing and which may have an adverse psychological effect on them.

The remainder of this paper is organised as follows. In section two, related work is discussed. Section three first provides an overview of the way in which

[1] In this paper, the term multimedia file(s) refers to a digital picture(s).

multimedia files are organised on the hard drive that aids forensic signature analysis. It then provides an overview of the digital fingerprint signature analysis approach. Section four presents the results of a case study to demonstrate the applicability of the approach. Finally, section five discusses further work and we make our conclusions.

2 Related Work

A number of computer forensic tools and approaches are used for the detection of suspicious images located on the hard drive. These can be generally divided into *file analysis* and *format specific* approaches.

Commonly used computer forensic tools, such as *Forensic Toolkit* (*FTK*) [5] and *EnCase* [6], provide examples of *file analysis* approaches. These tools are used for storage media analysis of a variety of files and data types in fully integrated environments. For example, *FTK* can perform tasks such as file extraction, make a forensic image of data on storage media, recover deleted files, determine data types and text extraction. *EnCase* is widely used within law enforcement and like *FTK* provides a powerful interface to the hard drive or data source under inspection, for example, by providing a file manager that shows extant and deleted files. These tools have in common the ability to read the data source as a whole, irrespective of the underlying logical structure of the operating system. Whilst these applications provide a robust forensic analysis, they are often time consuming in building a case due to the analyst having to manually read the data, e.g. looking at file contents, recovering deleted files, etc., to determine the relevance of the files to the investigation.

Format specific approaches specifically look for data belonging to particular applications or data types. For example, *Jhead* [7] is an application to extract specific Joint Photograph Experts Group (JPEG) image data, such as time and date a picture was taken, camera make and model, image resolution, shutter speed, etc. Tools such as *Data Lifter* [8] are able to extract files of a multitude of types. These tools support data carving to retrieve files of specific types by searching the disk for file preambles. The main problem with these tools is that they are not designed for robust forensic analysis. For example, *Jhead* enables the user to alter JPEG files. Whilst *DataLifter* extracts files of particular types, it does not differentiate between suspicious, malicious or benign files. Therefore, the user must still manually trawl through the extracted files to determine the nature of the file and its relevance to the investigation.

Recent research has recognised the disadvantages of current practice and has therefore proposed alternative approaches. These approaches attempt to not only identify file types, but also known files of a particular type by utilising statistical data derived from file analysis. For example, [9] posit a method based on intrusion detection to identify files of interest. This method models mean and standard deviation information of individual bytes to determine a *fileprint*, or identification of a specific file. This method is dependent on file header data for file categorisation, and therefore requires that the files are not fragmented and for the file system to be intact [10]. As such, [11] propose the Oscar method, which determines probable file types from data fragments. This approach, unlike the previous one, aims to identify files based on fragmented data, such as that in RAM, and therefore does not require header information or an extant file system. A disadvantage of this approach is that it uses a more computationally exhaustive statistical measure than [9] with not much advantage in detection rate, in order to achieve the identification of data fragments.

3 Digital Fingerprints Using Signature Analysis

Within this section the properties of data resident on a hard drive or other storage media that are relevant to this approach are described and an overview of the digital fingerprint method is provided. The scheme for the *forsigs* (forensic signature) analysis for multimedia files is also posited.

3.1 Organisation of Files on the Hard Drive

The hard drive typically consists of a set of data structures organised into layers for access. At the highest level is the *hard drive* itself, which can be configured into one or more *partitions*. Partitions allow a single hard drive appear to be a number of individual drives and are referenced by the underlying operating system and partition tables. At the next level sits the *filesystem*. The filesystem determines how data is stored on the disk and provides a logical map to the data resident within the partition. A filesystem is typically organised into a set of *directories*. Directories provide a hierarchical organisation and referencing system for *files*. The file is a data structure, created by a person or system, that holds relevant information for both the user and the operating system.

The underlying hard drive on which data resides is organised into a series of memory locations, called *sectors*, which are typically 512 bytes long. The operating system organises these memory locations, 'blocks' in Linux or 'clusters' in Windows, to hold a finite amount (512 bytes to 4,096 bytes) of information. As files are normally much larger than this size, data is segmented and stored in a series of blocks, which may or may not be sequentially ordered. The relevant blocks associated with a file are then referred to by a master file table to allow the file to be seamlessly recreated when accessed by the user in the associated application. As a file is rarely an exact multitude of available bytes, the last block will contain as much information as required before placing an *end of file* (EOF) indicator for the operating system. The operating system reads the data up to the EOF indicator but no further. This gives rise to the condition known as 'slack space'. As this last block may have been used previously, data from the previous file using that block not overwritten for the new file will remain extant after the EOF indicator. Thus, partial file fragments of deleted files may be retrieved.

Signature analysis of multimedia files on the storage media relies on the premise that a significant number of files that may be of interest to the forensic examiner follow a relatively simple structure [2]. The *file header* contains information specific to the file format, for example, whether it is a JPEG, Graphic Interchange Format

(GIF), Microsoft Office, etc., file. The *file body* contains the data pertinent to the file itself. This data is used to reconstruct the multimedia file on the computer, thus enabling the user to view the data as a picture within an application. However, additional information is also stored within this file section that may have a direct impact on the investigation when analysing image files. For example, camera make and model, photograph time, application used, font types, etc. This information may be used with other forms of evidence, such as physical seizure of a camera at the scene of a crime or existence of a particular user application, to help the forensic analyst build their case. The *file footer* indicates information such as EOF.

3.2 Digital Fingerprint Approach

Previous work focused on identifying the file type, for example through the JPEG header, and then comparing the entire block to a signature block [12]. Whilst this approach proved successful, three principal problems remain. First, only the first block of any file is used for signature comparison. Much of this first block reveals supporting evidence such as the application used to create the file, camera make and model, time and date a picture was taken, setting up fonts, etc. The image itself starts later in the block, thus leaving much redundant information to be searched. This is particularly pertinent when looking at Linux blocks, which are substantially smaller than Windows clusters, and therefore the first block holds less picture information. Second, knowing that the approach focuses on matching the entire first block of a file of interest to a signature block requires that the suspect only changes one byte within this data to avoid detection. This is a similar problem to that faced by practitioners today relying on MD5 checksum comparisons. Third, the entire evidence file[2] is loaded into the application leading to additional computational load on the application, and therefore search time. In addition, the application is bounded by the size of the evidence data and in experiments could only read evidence files up to 500 Mb in size.

[2] The term evidence file refers to the entire sequential contents of a hard drive transformed into a file.

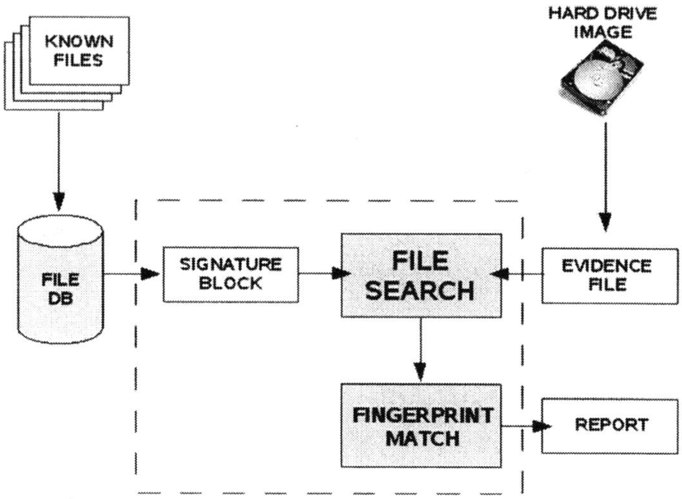

Fig. 1. Application overview.

Figure 1 provides an overview of the signature analysis approach. The dashed line represents the application and its internal components. Known multimedia files collected from previous investigations are collected in raw data form, and are stored in a database. This database views file data in hexadecimal form rather than as an image. Thus, anyone interrogating the database is not confronted with indecent images of children, just hexadecimal values. In this way the analyst does not have to view disturbing images, thereby alleviating psychological pressures involved in this type of investigation. This also has the advantage that signatures, as partial fragments of hexadecimal data, may be shared by authorities without the legal restrictions of disseminating the entire image.

The hard drive seized from the suspect's computer is copied, or *imaged*, in a robust manner in order to protect the original data. This is a requirement of current practice, whereby the analyst does not interrogate the original hard drive, as this may alter evidence located there. Every byte is copied across to a replica hard drive to provide an exact duplicate of the original to protect the integrity of the evidence. The raw data on the imaged hard drive at byte level forms an evidence file which is analysed by the fingerprint application.

The file database provides a signature block(s), which is used by the application for comparison to data in the evidence file. The signature is formed from a single block from the original multimedia file held on the file database and obtained using the *siggrab* application developed by the authors. This may be any part of the file, and the size of the block alters depending on the underlying operating system used by the suspect. By focusing on a single block, the search does not rely on a file being sequentially ordered on the suspect's computer; this block could reside anywhere on the hard drive, and data prior to or after this block may be related to the same file, or not. The choice of signature block will be discussed in section 3.3.

The *forsigs* application reads in both the signature block(s) and the evidence file to conduct the signature search. The file is searched for evidence of known multimedia files of interest. Once the search is complete, a report is generated for the analyst. This process is described in the next sub-section.

3.3 Digital Fingerprint Signature Search

The signatures on which we search will have an impact on the effectiveness of the approach. If we were to search for a whole digital image file, there are four factors that will affect the search. First, digital images may be in the region of Megabytes, thereby requiring a large signature to be transferred from the file database. Second, only one byte in the original data need be altered to give rise to a large number of false negatives. Third, clusters allocated to a digital image are not necessarily sequentially ordered on the underlying storage media. As the data is not sequentially stored, searches using large signatures may be defeated due to fragmentation of the picture in the evidence file. Finally, as has been found in intrusion detection, large signatures can be computationally exhaustive [13], and this is also assumed to be the case with searches of storage media.

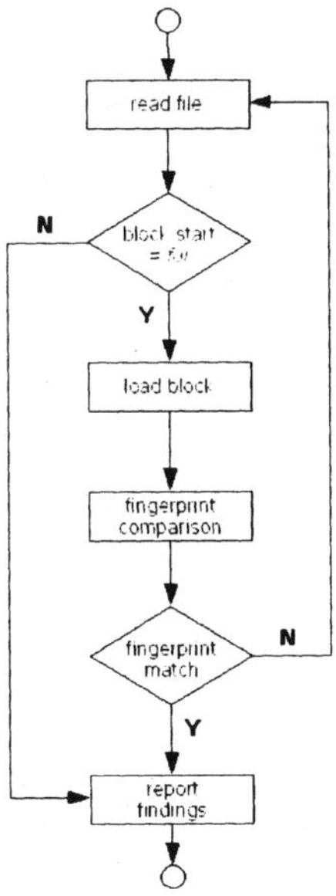

Fig. 2. Digital fingerprint signature search process.

Figure 2 provides an overview of the digital fingerprint signature search process. The application reads in the evidence file. This is conducted a character at a time to ensure that all bytes are analysed. Whilst this may add some computational overhead, this ensures the robustness of the data collection by the application. The beginning of each block within the evidence file is compared to the first byte of the file of interest's signature block. If none of these are found within the file, the application reports that no signatures are matched, and therefore, no multimedia files of interest are resident on the hard drive. If, however, there is a match, the remainder of the block is loaded for comparison. A fingerprint comparison is conducted, and if a match is confirmed, a report is generated. If the fingerprint is not confirmed, the application continues to search the data until the end of the evidence file.

For the signature search, an *ad hoc* block within the original multimedia file is chosen. With many multimedia files being upwards of hundreds of kilobytes in size, the file itself will use many blocks. This ensures that a suspect would be required to alter the start of every block of data stored on the hard drive as they will not know which block is used for the signature. Whilst this scheme has been used as the basis for the case study to demonstrate the applicability of the fingerprint approach, anywhere in the block can be used as the basis for identification of files of interest. This would further complicate attacks on the scheme.

The first and last block of a file are not provided for the signature search. As discussed earlier, the first block may hold generic but redundant data, such as setting up fonts, and therefore is less robust for analysis. The last block will include slack space data, and therefore cannot provide a reliable signature. Using either of these two blocks will lead to false postitives.

The application loads suspected blocks from the evidence file and compares them to the signature block. In order to defeat the possible attack of a suspect altering bytes, 16 points of reference within the signature block are compared to the corresponding points of reference in the evidence block. The positions that are compared can be randomised. If a match is found, it is reported to the analyst.

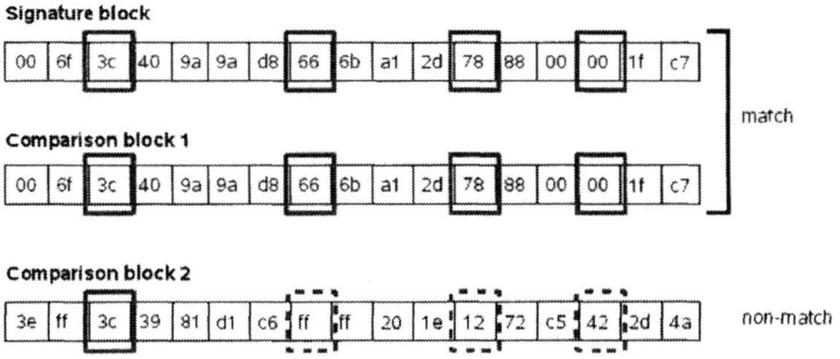

Fig. 3. Digital fingerprint signature matching.

Figure 3 illustrates the digital fingerprint search process. The signature block refers to a signature read into the application from the signature file, as illustrated in figure 1. Suspicious blocks from the evidence file that potentially could be from a file of interest are placed into a comparison block. Sixteen points within the block are compared to the corresponding points within the signature block. Highlighted in boxes in figure 3 are the points at which comparisons are made. Comparison block 1 reveals that all points of comparison match, and therefore a fingerprint is found. Comparison block 2 shows that only the first comparison value is matched, whereas the rest do not, as indicated by dashed boxes. All 16 points within the file must be matched to identify a signature.

The probability that all sixteen points within a block will match that of the fingerprint taken from an *ad hoc* block is remote. A single byte can take any one of $2^8 = 256$ distinct values. The probability that a byte triggering a fingerprint comparison will match in arbitrary file with an even distribution of independent values will therefore be 1/256. The probability that all sixteen values will present a perfect match is approximately 2.29×10^{-1532}.

4 Case Study and Results

The previous section presented an overview of the novel *forsigs* scheme; the forensic application of signature analysis, and in particular, the search of raw data for evidence of illegal or suspicious multimedia files resident or deleted on the hard drive. This section provides a case study to demonstrate the fingerprint signature approach and presents its results.

Experiments were undertaken on a 2 Ghz AMD Athlon host with 256 Mb RAM running Suse Linux 10. This represents a similar set up to that which would be deployed in the field on a laptop by a forensic analyst, and therefore provides a useful benchmark for speed and efficiency tests. More computational power could be provided within the forensics lab.

Four files, ranging from 250 Mb to 2 Gb data sets, are used as the basis of the evidence search. These files are images taken from real computer data to form a single evidence (or search) file. The filetypes in the evidence data are wide and varied, including MP3, system files (dat, swf, dll, and Master File Table information, etc.), exe, ogg, pdf, ppt, doc, and jpg files. Amongst this data are a wide range of digital picture files other than the specific file(s) of interest. This ensures that the *forsigs* application has many opportunities to return false positives by incorrectly identifying a digital picture. In addition, many of these pictures were taken with the same camera, of a similar subject and in similar lighting conditions. It should be noted that no malicious images are used in the tests, only benign pictures and consist of images of historical manuscripts from archives. In all the data sets, a single file of interest was placed amongst the data. In all cases, the *forsigs* application successfully identified the signature and location of the file of interest and no false positives were returned.

Figure 4 illustrates the time *forsigs* takes to search evidence files for a single signature ranging from 250 Mb to 2 Gb in size. The time is recorded as both real and user time and returned by the system. Real time represents the actual time between invocation and termination of the program, whereas the user time records the actual CPU time of the application. The real time measure is used to represent a maximum search time. The search and correct identification of a single signature within 250 Mb of data takes approximately 11.5 seconds, as opposed to 95 seconds for 2 Gb. With a 1 Gb search taking approximately 45 seconds, it can be assumed that it may take 75 minutes to search all bytes on a 100 Gb hard drive, which is significantly faster than a manual search of the same scale.

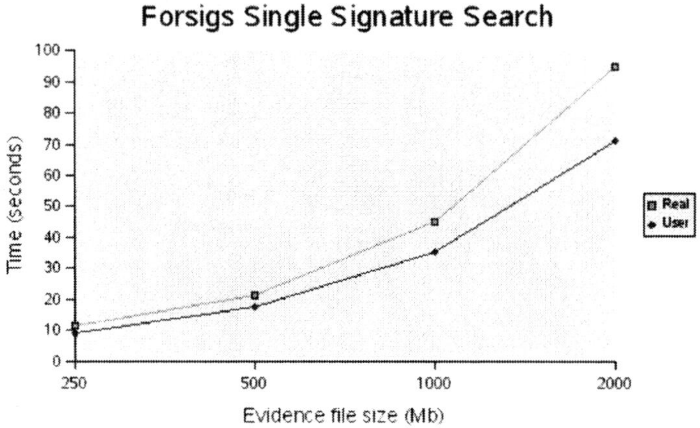

Fig. 4. Digital fingerprint signature matching over time.

In order to evaluate the impact of searching for more than one signature, between one and five signatures are simultaneously searched for within a 250 Mb evidence file. The application reports the detection of any of the signatures, if found. Again, real and user times are recorded, as illustrated in figure 5. Interestingly, the results show that it takes slightly more time (both real and user) to search for a single signature than for multiple signatures. This is despite the number of comparison indicators identifying the possibility of a block of interest. The real times recorded ranged from 12.1 seconds for three signatures (the fastest) to 12.9 seconds for a single signature (the slowest). However, this efficiency may be demonstrated by the average search time per signature; 12.9 seconds for a single signature but just over 2 seconds per signature when searching for five signatures.

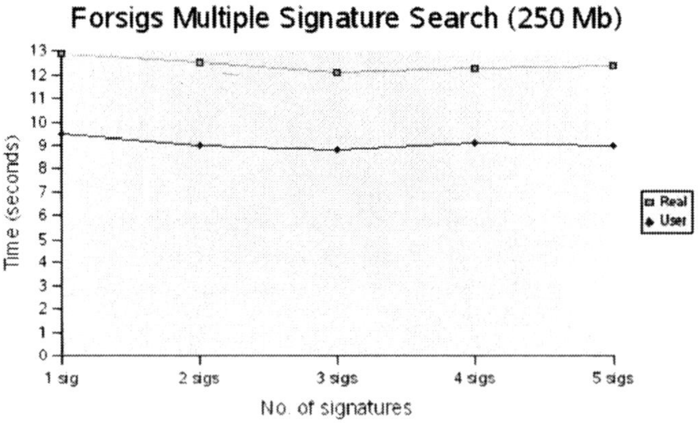

Fig. 5. Impact on search time of multiple signature search.

The efficiency of the *forsigs* approach is also demonstrated by the increased number of comparisons that multiple signature searches require. Figure 6 illustrates the number of comparisons on the 'trigger' byte that indicates the possibility of a block of interest and therefore will be compared to a signature. The similarity in comparisons between three and four signatures is due to the comparison indicator being the same for both signature blocks. However, *forsigs* still correctly identifies the correct signature in both these cases. Therefore, the number of comparisons that the application must make does not have an adverse effect on the time of search, as indicated above.

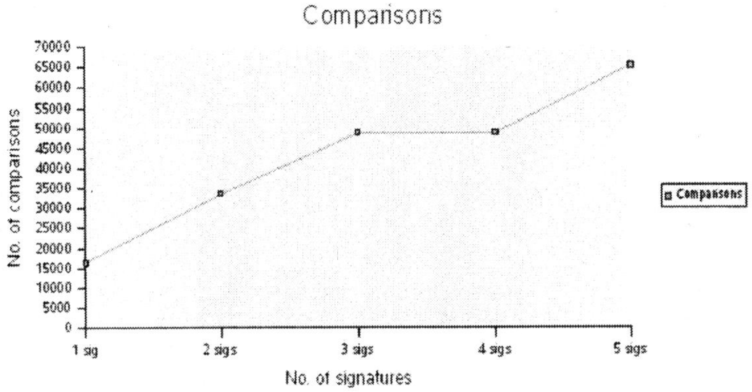

Fig. 6. Number of *forsigs* comparisons on a 'trigger' byte.

The case study demonstrates the applicability of the *forsigs* approach. Despite the number of signatures, and therefore comparisons, the program identifies and locates the signature, and therefore file of interest, correctly and efficiently.

5 Conclusions and Further Work

Further work aims to extend the tests to include larger data sets and wider signature searches to build on the work in this paper. In addition, work is being conducted into the position within a file that provides the optimum signature for *forsigs* searches. Whilst this paper has focused on digital pictures, other file types are of interest to the forensic examiner and the application of the *forsigs* approach to these will be investigated. Finally, compression, resizing or encryption of files of interest has an adverse effect on this approach. Therefore, future work will attempt to address the prediction of these algorithms on a file of interest, and the signature that may be produced.

This paper has presented the novel *forsigs* approach for forensic signature analysis of the hard drive for multimedia file fingerprints. The widespread use of computer and network technologies has given rise to concerns over the spread of digital picture files containing indecent images of children. Current forensic analysis techniques are time consuming and laborious, as well as raising the psychological burden on the forensic analyst by viewing such images. Therefore, the *forsigs* approach provides a means by which hard drives may be searched automatically and efficiently for evidence of malicious images. The approach identifies potential files of interest and compares them to known images to determine whether data contained on a hard drive is malicious or benign. The case study presented in this paper demonstrates the applicability of this approach.

References

1. Li, X. & Seberry, J., "Forensic Computing", *Proceedings of INDOCRYPT*, New Delhi, India, 8-10 Dec 2003, LNCS 2904, Springer, 2003, pp.18-35.
2. Mohay, G., Anderson, A., Collie, B., De Vel, O. & McKemmish, R., *Computer and Intrusion Forensics*, Artech House, MA, USA, 2003.
3. Chen, H., Chung, W., Xu, J.L., Wang, G., Qin, Y. & Chau, M., "Crime Data Mining: A General Framework and Some Examples", *Computer*, April 2004, pp. 50-56.
4. Burr, W.E., "Cryptographic Hash Standards Where Do We Go from Here?", *IEEE Security and Privacy*, March/April, 2006, pp. 88-91.
5. The Forensics Toolkit, available from http://www.accessdata.com, accessed October 2006.
6. Guidance Software Encase, available from http://www.guidancesoftware.com, accessed October 2006.
7. Jhead, available from http://www.sentex.net/~mwandel/jhead/ , last updated April 2006, accessed October 2006.
8. DataLifter Computer Forensic Software, available from http://datalifter.com/products.htm, accessed October 2006.
9. Li, W. J., Wang, K., Stolfo, S. & Herxog, B., "Fileprints: Identifying File Types by n-gram Analysis", *Proceedings of the 6th IEEE Systems, Man and Cybernetics Assurance Workshop*, West Point, NY, USA, June, 2005.
10. Karresand, M. & Shahmehri, N., "Oscar – File Type Identification of Binary Data in Disk Clusters and RAM Pages", *Proceedings of IFIP SEC 2006*, Karlstadt, Sweden, 22 – 24 May, 2006.
11. Karresand, M. & Shahmehri, N., "File Type Identification of Data Fragments by their Binary Structure", *Proceedings of the 2006 IEEE Workshop on Information Assurance*, US Military Academy, West Point, NY, 21-23 June, 2006.
12. Haggerty, J., Berry, T. & Gresty, D., "Forensic Signature Analysis of Digital Image Files", *Proceedings of the 1st Conference on Advances in Computer Security and Forensics*, Liverpool, UK, 13-14 July, 2006.
13. Zhang, Y. & Paxson, V., "Detecting Backdoors", *Proceedings of USENIX Security Symposium*, Denver, CO, USA, 2000.

Digital Forensic Readiness as a Component of Information Security Best Practice

CP Grobler[1], CP Louwrens[2]

1 University of Johannesburg, Department of Business IT, Bunting Road Auklandpark, Johannesburg, South Africa
tgrobler@uj.ac.za,

2 Nedbank, South Africa
buksl@nedbank.co.za

Abstract. In a world where cyber crime is constantly increasing, pervasive computing is on the rise and information is becoming the most sought after commodity making an effective and efficient Information Security (IS) architecture and program essential. 'With this improved technology and infrastructure, ongoing and pro-active computer investigations are now a mandatory component of the IS enterprise' [16]. Corporate governance reports require that organizations should not only apply good corporate governance principles, but also practice good IT governance and specially IS governance. Organizations develop their security architectures based on current best practices for example IS017799 [21] and Cobit [12]. These best practices do not consider the importance of putting controls or procedures in place that will ensure successful investigations. There is a definite need to adapt current Information Security (IS) best practices to include for example certain aspects of Digital Forensics (DF) readiness to the current best practices to address the shortcomings. Whilst IS and DF are considered as two different disciplines, there is a definite overlap between the two [29]. The aim of this paper is to examine the overlap between DF and IS, to determine the relevance of DF readiness to IS and propose the inclusion of certain aspects of DF readiness as a component for best practice for IS.

1 Introduction

The Information Security (IS) program of an organization is only as strong as its weakest link. Incidents will occur, but it is essential to link the attacker or source of

Please use the following format when citing this chapter:

Grobler, T. and Louwrens, B., 2007, in IFIP International Federation for Information Processing, Volume 232, New Approaches for Security, Privacy and Trust in Complex Environments, eds. Venter, H., Eloff, M., Labuschagne, L., Eloff, J., von Solms, R., (Boston: Springer), pp. 13–24.

the attack to the attack so that management can make the appropriate decision as to what action to take.

Most of the security incidents do not proceed to legal action, as companies want to proceed with normal business activities as soon as possible [9]. Statistics from the CSI/FBI computer crime survey of 2006 [7] indicate that only 25% of all cases were reported to law enforcement, 15% to legal or regulatory authorities and 70% of the respondents deal with security incidents by patching the holes. Although the ratio is still very high, there has been an improvement in the way organizations deal with the breaches [7]. Reasons for this are that companies want to prevent negative publicity and do not want their competitors to use the incident to gain a competitive advantage.

According to von Solms [28], we are experiencing the fourth wave of IS: Information Security Governance. He defines it as the 'process of the explicit inclusion of IS as an integral part of good Corporate Governance and the maturing of the concept of Information Security Governance'. The result of this wave is that management must take the responsibility and are personally responsible for the security health of their IT systems. These IT systems are the foundation which provide accurate information that managers use to substantiate their every day decisions. There is therefore a need to prove that the IS systems are healthy and should an incident occur, that management must deal with the incident in an appropriate way.

The CSI/FBI 2006 computer crime survey [7] indicates that more than 60% of the respondents have indicated the need to improve the IS posture of the organization as a result of the Sarbarnes–Oxley [26] report. The report has changed the focus of IS from managing technology and people to Corporate Governance and specifically IS Governance.

Many organizations have an Information Security (IS) strategy in place to protect the information and information assets of the organization. This strategy will determine how the organization manages all IS activities in the organization. Computer crime is a very lucrative activity that continues to grow in prevalence and frequency [14]. More and more commercial organizations are using DF technologies to investigate for example fraud, accessing pornography or harassment.

The increase in cyber related criminal activity places a strain on law enforcement and governments. Courts no longer require only document-based evidence but also digital/electronic-based evidence. Criminal investigations require solid, well documented, acceptable procedures and evidence. Normal forensic investigations are no longer suitable or applicable and digital forensic investigations need to be undertaken.

Digital evidence is becoming increasingly prominent in court cases and internal hearings. Network administrators and system administrators want to analyze activities on the networks and applications. Organizations should look at the evidence required so that security programs and architectures can be adapted to provide the evidence when required.

The format of the paper will be to

1 define IS and DF;
2 discuss the overlap between IS and DF;
3 discuss DF readiness;

4 discuss the overlap between DF readiness and IS and
5 propose DF readiness as a best practice for IS.

The next part of the paper will define IS and DF and discuss the overlap between DF and IS.

2 Digital Forensics and Information Security

Information Security can be defined as the process of protecting information and information assets from a wide range of threats in order to ensure business continuity, minimize business damage, maximize return on investments and business opportunities by preserving confidentiality, integrity and availability of information [21].

Forensics is the use of science and technology to investigate and establish facts in criminal and civil courts of law [1]. The goal of any forensic investigation will be to prosecute the criminal or offender successfully, determine the root cause of an event and determine who was responsible.

The environment in which digital crimes are committed has changed drastically with the emergence of digital devices e.g. digital fax, the internet and wireless devices. It is no longer sufficient to only investigate the hard drive of the victim's PC (computer forensics), as there will be additional evidence required for a successful prosecution. With the emergence of new technologies e.g. wireless communications, PDA's, flash disks and the internet, computer forensics has become a subset of DF. DF is more comprehensive than computer forensics. Cyber-trained defense attorneys require the chain of evidence that must link the attacker to the victim [24].

DF can be defined as the efficient use of analytical and investigative techniques for the preservation, identification, extraction, documentation, analysis and interpretation of computer media which is digitally stored or encoded for evidentiary and / or root-cause analysis and presentation of digital evidence derived from digital sources for the purpose of facilitation or furthering the reconstruction of events found to be criminal, or helping to anticipate unauthorized actions shown to be disruptive to planned operations [14, 4, 18, 23, 20].

DF is a new discipline that will become more relevant and essential as it becomes the vehicle for organizations to assess the effectiveness of controls implemented and to determine the root-cause of an incident. These controls can be typically security controls.

Traditionally an organization will conduct a DF investigation once a security breach is encountered, but DF can be conducted in a pro-active as well as a re-active manner. Re-active forensic investigations will occur after an incident has taken place. Most of the current investigations are re-active. Typically an investigation will focus upon the legal and law enforcement aspects of an incident or it will be used to determine the root-cause that instigated the incident [24].

Pro-active DF will enable an organisation to become DF ready. DF readiness can be defined as the ability of an organization to maximise its potential to use digital evidence whilst minimising the costs of an investigation [20].

It is essential to determine what evidence is required should an incident occur. The authors propose that organizations have pro-active evidence. Pro-active evidence can be defined as evidence that will have evidentiary weight in a court of law and contain all the evidence necessary (relevant and sufficient) to determine the root-cause of the event, link the attacker to the incident and will result in a successful prosecution of the perpetrator.

The Electronic Communications and Transactions Act of South Africa (ECT) [25] have the following requirements for determining the admissibility of a digital document or digital evidence in a court of law: The reliability of the manner in which the record was communicated and stored, how the integrity of the data was maintained, and the manner in which the originator / author of the record is identified.

IS can also be pro-active and re-active. Pro-active IS will ensure that appropriate controls e.g. policies are in place to prevent attacks or security breaches. Re-active IS will ensure that organizations can resume operations as soon as possible whilst minimising the damage.

The authors have compared IS and DF in

Table 1. The aim of this comparison will be to identify potential areas where DF and IS overlap.

Table 1 Comparison of IS and DF

	Information Security	**Digital Forensics**
Pro-active	**Purpose:** Prevent damage to information and information resources by applying the most effective and efficient controls for the identified threats by the organization	**Purpose: (two fold)** Ensure that all processes, procedures, technologies and appropriate legal admissible evidence is in place to enable a successful investigation, with minimal disruption of business activities Use DF technology to determine the 'holes' in the security posture of the organization
	How: IS policies, e.g. incident recognition, Implement IS procedures and mechanisms Determine legal requirements IS Awareness and training	**How:** DF policies, e.g. evidence preservation DF readiness, e.g. prevent anonymous activities, secure storage of logs, hashing etc. Determine legal requirements DF awareness and training
Re-active	**Purpose:** Ensure that the damage that has occurred from a breach is minimised and prevent further damages	**Purpose:** To investigate an event in a way that the evidence gathered can used to determine the root-cause of an event and successful prosecution of the perpetrator
	How: Incident response plan (IRP) Disaster Recovery Plan (DRP) Business Continuity Plan (BCP)	**How:** Incident response plan (IRP) Disaster recovery plan (DRP) Business Continuity plan (BCP)

	Fix security loophole	Adequate DF processes and techniques

From
Table 1 the authors have identified similar areas between the two disciplines e.g. IRP's, policies and staff training. Both disciplines demonstrate the need for policies, but it may not be the same policy. DF policies may augment some IS policies for example the IS policy for the identification of an incident will be influenced by the DF policy for the preservation of evidence.

DF awareness training will link with IS awareness training for example with first incident response training.

During the IR, DRP and BCP of organizations, the DF process and procedural requirements will influence the way IS plans (IRP, DRP, BCP) are developed. The main aim from a IS perspective will be to resume business as soon as possible and minimise the damage, whereas the DF requirement is to capture and preserve all relevant evidence for prosecution. This can cause a conflict, as normally business does not want to wait for evidence gathering before they resume the operations. Pro-active evidence can allow business to continue with minimal interruption.

DF will influence all stages of the IS management lifecycle: planning, developing, implementing, monitoring and assessing the security posture of the organization. DF techniques are currently used to assess the security posture of the organization, by using for example penetration testing and audits. DF readiness will add the missing controls and procedures to perform a successful investigation to the security posture of the organization.

The relationship between IS and DF is also identified by a study done by Endicott-Popovsky [5]. According to the authors a survivable system consists of 3 R's: *Resistance, Recognition and Recovery.*

- Resistance is defined as the ability to repel attacks. It will deal with firewalls, user authentication, diversification;
- Recognition is defined as the ability to detect an attack coupled with the ability to react or adapt during an attack. It will deal with IDS and internal integrity tests;
- Recovery is defined as the ability to provide essential services during an attack and restore services after an attack. It will deal with incident response, replication, back-up systems and Fault tolerant designs. All 3 R's should be taken care of by the ISA of an organization.

Endicott-Popovsky [5] suggests that a fourth R, *Redress* must be included in the IS Security strategy:

- Redress is defined as the ability to hold intruders accountable in a court of law and the ability to retaliate. It will consider DF techniques, legal remedies and active defense.

The outcome of a 3R strategy will be to recover from the incident as soon as possible by for example applying a suitable patch, whereas the outcome of a 4R strategy will be to gather evidence, restore the system and pursue legal consequences. The 4R strategy therefore includes DF, as you will not be able to take legal action without following the appropriate DF processes.

There is a definite overlap between IS and DF from the discussion above and studies done by Louwrens and von Solms [29]. IS architectures concentrate on preventing incidents from happening and should an incident occur, the incident response, disaster recovery and business continuity plans focus on recovering as quickly as possible from the incident so that the interruption is minimized and the business can continue. IS will concentrate on confidentiality, integrity and availability of information and information assets and does not consider the preservation of evidence.

DF will ensure that the organization will have the adequate evidence, processes and policies in place to ensure that a successful investigation can be done with minimal disruption in business processes.

DF investigations will enable the organization to find the source of the attack, preserve the evidence and to take appropriate action. DF is concerned with the integrity of the information and processes of the investigation. The result of a DF investigation should be used as input into the security strategy of an organization so that the security posture can improve.

DF must have an influence on the way security is planned, implemented and measured in an organization. DF is perceived as a very expensive exercise [20], but thoughtful planning can combat the costs, for example: an inexpensive way will be to define adequate policies and processes to capture applicable evidence [30, 17].

DF is not only important for the IS management of the organization, but also vital for good Corporate Governance and specifically IS Governance. Corporate Governance reports such as Sarbarnes-Oxley and King II as well as best practices for example ISO17799 and Cobit [27] requires that adequate controls are in place. DF tools and techniques are being used to assist with the assessment of controls.

In the next part of the paper the authors will define DF readiness and discuss the role and importance of DF readiness for an organization.

3 Digital Forensic Readiness

As discussed in the first part of the paper, DF consists of pro-active and re-active components. DF is transforming from an investigation and response mechanism to include a powerful pro-active measure. DF tools are currently used to: collect digital evidence in a legally acceptable format, audit an organization's networks and structure, validate policies and procedures, assist in identifying major risks, prioritize protection of and access to an organization's most valuable data during and investigation and provide training in first response to avoid the contamination of evidence [11].

Management is often wary of the cost implication to become DF ready in an organization. It is essential to convince them of the benefits of DF processes in the organization. These benefits can include the demonstration of due diligence for good corporate governance, useful for data retention and provide protection for the organization against litigation risks.

Pro-active DF management must ensure that all business processes are structured in such a way that essential data and evidence will be retained to ensure successful DF investigations, should an incident occur. Proper pro-active DF management should minimize interruption to the business processes while conducting an investigation. It is essential that the organization become DF ready.

DF readiness was defined in paragraph 2 of the paper. Another definition is the 'art of maximizing the environment's ability to collect credible evidence' [6].

The organization must identify all possible evidence sources and ways to gather evidence legally and cost-effectively. It will not help just to identify and capture the evidence, but organizations must implement a digital evidence record management system and electronic document management system. The ECT Act [25] prescribes the following conditions for electronic records retention:

- The retained records should be accessible;
- the electronic version should accurately represent the original format and
- meta-data such as author and date should be retained with the record.

The digital evidence management system must enable organizations to identify and manage applicable evidence in an organised way.

According to Rowlingson [20] the goals of forensic readiness are as follows:

- To gather admissible evidence legally and without interfering with business processes;
- To gather evidence targeting the potential crimes and disputes that may adversely impact an organization;
- To allow an investigation to proceed at a cost in proportion to the incident;
- To minimize interruption to the business from any investigation;
- To ensure that evidence makes a positive impact on the outcome of any legal action [20].

The authors want to add the following goals to DF readiness:

- To ensure that the organization practices good corporate governance, specifically IS governance;
- To 'enrich' / augment the security program of the organization to ensure that adequate evidence, processes and procedures are in place to successfully determine the source of an attack;
- Use of DF tools to enhance the IS management of an organization, for example to recover data from a crashed hard drive and
- To prevent the use of anti-forensic strategies for example data destruction or manipulation and data hiding.

The above discussion has indicated that DF readiness is a business requirement in any organization.

4 The overlap: DF readiness and IS

According to Rowlingson [20], DF readiness will concern itself with incident anticipation - instead of incident response - and enabling the business to use digital evidence. Information security will concern itself with ensuring the business utility of information and information assets is maintained – excluding the requirement for digital evidence.

From the discussion in paragraph 3 and Rowlingson's activities for DF readiness [20], the overlap of DF readiness and IS will be in:

- IS and DF awareness training. All IS training programs must be revised to include aspects of DF training. Caution must be taken on what should be included in the IS awareness training, as the curriculum must maintain a balance between necessary awareness and unnecessary information sharing. The result of badly planned curriculums can result in criminals manipulating or tampering with evidence to prevent successful investigations ;
- IS and DF policies. Determine all the IS policies that will need inputs from DF – for example: evidence identification and preservation;
- IS Risk Management where it will include:
    - Assessing the risks by identifying all the business scenarios that will require digital evidence;
    - Determine the vulnerabilities and threats during risk assessment, but also determine what evidence will be required to determine the root–cause of the event, also for more unlikely threats;
    - Determine what information is required for evidence (the format and exactly what is required);
    - Determine how to legally capture and preserve the evidence and integrate it into the legal requirements for the organization. Consider the other legal requirements for example monitoring of activities, interception of communications and privacy;
    - Ensure that monitoring is targeted to detect and deter incidents;
    - Augment the IRP to specify when to escalate to a full investigation;
    - Define the first response guidelines to the IRP to preserve evidence and
    - Determine when and how to activate DRP and BCP;
- Establish an organizational structure with roles and responsibilities to deal with DF in the organization. There should be a clear segregation of duties between the DF and IS teams;
- Establish a digital evidence management program;
- Incorporate DF techniques in the IS auditing procedures, this will enable a more accurate audit that can for example determine the efficiency of a control;
- Access controls should be reviewed to prevent anonymous activities;
- Establish a capability to securely gather admissible evidence by considering technology and human capacity.
- Use DF tools and processes to demonstrate good corporate governance so that for example management can prove that they have tested the adequacy of IS controls;
- Use DF tools for non-forensic purposes to enhance the ISA, for example data recovery if a hard disk crashes;
- Developing a preservation culture in the organization to preserve all processes and activities should an investigation arise;
- Design all security controls to prevent any anti-forensic activities. Typically no password crackers, key-loggers, steganography software etc. should be allowed in the organization and
- Removable / portable devices must be monitored and preferably controlled so that potential cyber crimes can be minimized, for example Intellectual Property theft.

In this part of the paper the authors have identified that there is a big overlap and coherence of activities of DF readiness and IS. This overlap is not necessarily the same activity that takes place, but the way 'how' and 'what' should be done from an IS perspective is influenced by the 'what' that is required of the DF perspective. For example: when setting a policy on first incident response, the policy should not only include the elements to identify an incident and what should be done, but the preservation of evidence must be included in the policy so that no contamination of evidence can take place.

In the next part of the paper the authors will propose DF readiness as a component of an IS best practice.

5 DF Readiness as a component if of IS Best Practice

A best practice is defined as the 'most broadly effective and efficient means of organizing a system or performing a function' [3]. Von Solms et al [19] conclude that 'best practice can possibly serve as a reference to the care that an ordinarily reasonable and prudent party should apply in the case of the protection of valuable company information resources' [19].

IS governance and management models, must include a way to prove that the controls in place are the most broadly efficient and effective for the specific organization. According to the CSI/FBI computer crime survey 2006, 82% of organizations assess their security posture by performing internal audits and 62% using external audits [7]. Other means of assessing is penetration testing, e-mail monitoring and web activity monitoring tools. Assessing the security posture of the organization will not be sufficient as the IS architectures do not consider the requirement for the preservation of digital evidence. Organizations will not be able to determine the source of an event in a legally acceptable way as admissible evidence is not in place.

By including some aspects of DF readiness into the IS architecture of the organization, it will be possible to link the source of the attack to the incident and the perpetrator. It will also enable management to assess the current controls so that they have proof that the controls in place are efficient and effective.

The following Sarbarnes–Oxley [26] sections require DF readiness in an organization:

- Section 302 stipulates that CEO's and CFO's (CIO's) are responsible for signing off the effectiveness of internal controls. DF readiness can assist by looking at information on the corporate network as part of compliance. CIO's will be able to use DF processes to prove that regular checks have been performed;
- Section 802 indicates that there are criminal penalties if documents are altered. DF procedures adhere to legal requirements for evidence, therefore it will be possible to prove that the information is original and not altered;
- Section 409 requires rapid response and reporting. DF readiness will enable rapid response and
- Finally, the report also requires a whistle blowing policy. Remote network forensics is good at doing an analysis without tipping off the perpetrator [9].

In a study done by Spike Quinn [17] in New Zealand he has proved that:

- internal policies and procedures for dealing with evidence recovery is often insufficient for admissible evidence in court;
- management can also not plan for events that may need forensic investigation as they often do not sufficiently comprehend the requirement for admissible evidence required for successful prosecution and lastly;
- where management expect IT staff to deal with events that may require DF investigations, often the evidence will not be admissible in court as the staff are not properly trained [17].

This is not a country specific example, but many organizations are still not ready for successful prosecution of a perpetrator should an event take place [11].

It is therefore clear that DF and specifically DF readiness can not be treated as a separate issue from IS. DF readiness should also not only be included in the security awareness programs and incident response plans of the organizations, but in all aspects of planning, implementing, monitoring and assessment of IS in an organization. DF readiness must therefore be included as a component of best practice for IS.

6 Summary

Most organizations have accepted IS as a fundamental business requirement. Protecting the information and information assets is no longer sufficient as corporate governance reports require full responsibility and accountability from management, also in terms of IS governance.

This paper has indicated that the current IS architectures, strategies and best practices are lacking in the sense that successful prosecution of an event can seldom occur due to the lack of admissible evidence and poor procedures. Management will not be able to prove that the security controls are effective and efficient.

DF readiness will demonstrate due diligence and good corporate governance of a company's assets. It will provide guidelines of the legal admissibility of all processes and evidence, identify the misuse or illegal use of resources, and provide guidance on the legal aspects of logging data and monitoring of people's activities using IT systems in an organization

DF readiness as discussed in the paper will enhance the security strategy of an organization by providing a way to prepare an organization for an incident, whilst gathering sufficient digital evidence in a way that minimizes the effect on normal business processes. This can help to minimize system downtime and the cost of the investigation if an incident occurs.

DF readiness is a component of an IS best practice, as it will provide the IS manager and top management the means to demonstrate that reasonable care has been taken to protect valuable company information resources.

References

1. American Heritage Dictionary (4th Edition), (New York, NY: Houghton Mifflin, 2000).
2. Cullery A, *Computer Forensics: Past Present And Future, Information Security Technical Report,* Volume 8, number 2, (Elsevier, 2003), p 32-35.
3. Dictionary.Com, (June 31, 2006), http://dictionary.reference.com.
4. Digital Forensic Research Workshop, *A Roadmap for Digital Forensics Research,* (2001), www.dfrws.org.
5. Endicott-Popovsky B, Frincke D, *Adding the 4th R: A Systems Approach to Solving the Hackers Arms Race*, Proceedings of the 2006 Symposium 39th Hawai International Conference on System Sciences, (2006).
6. Garcia J, 2006, *Pro-Active and Re-Active Forensics,* (September 5, 2006), http://jessland.net.
7. Gordon La, Loeb M, Richardson R, Lucyshyn W, 2006 *CSI/FBI Computer Crime and Security Survey,* (Computer Security Institute, 2006).
8. Grobler CP, Von Solms SH, *A Model To Assess The Information Security Status of an Organization with Special Reference to the Policy Dimension* , Master's Dissertation, (2004).
9. Hilley, 2004, *The Corporation: The Non-Policed State*, (September 24, 2006), http://www.infosecurity-magaqzine.com/features/novdec04/corp_novdec.htm.
10. Hoffman T, 2004, *Sarbanes-Oxley Sparks Forensics Apps Interest,* (March 29, 2004), http://www.computerworld.com/action/article.do?command=viewarticlebasic&articleid=91676.
11. Inforenz, 2006, *Are You Ready For Forensics*?, (September 14, 2006), http://Inforenz.com/press/20060223.html.
12. Cobit: Control Objectives for Information and related technologies, (IT Governance Institute, 3rd edition, 2000)
13. King II Report on Corporate Governance, (August, 2003), http://iodsa.co.za/lod%20draft%20king%20report.pdf.
14. Kruse II, Warren G, Jay G Heiser JG, *Computer Forensics Incident Response Essentials*, (Addison Wesley, Pearson Education 2004).
15. Louwrens B, Von Solms SH, Reeckie C, Grobler T, *A Control Framework for Digital Forensics*, Advances in Digital Forensics, (Springer, 2006).
16. Patzakis J, *Computer Forensics as an Integral Component of Information Security Enterprise*, Guidance Software, (October 24, 2005), www.guidancesoftware.com.
17. Quinn S, *Examining The State of Preparedness of IT Management in New Zealand for Events that may require Forensic Analysis*, Digital Investigation, December 2005, Volume 2, Issue 4, (Elsevier, 2005), p. 276-280.
18. Reith M, Varr V, Gunch G, *An Examination of Digital Forensic Models*. International Journal Of Digital Evidence Volume 1, Issue 3, (Elsevier, 2002), (February 15, 2005), http://www.ijde.org/docs/02 art2.pdf.
19. Rosseau Von Solms, SH (Basie) Von Solms, *Information Security Governance: Due Care*, Computers And Security, (August 13, 2006), doi:10:1016/Jcose.
20. Rowlingson, *A Ten Step Process for Forensic Readiness*, International Journal of Digital Evidence, Volume 2 Issue 3, Winter 2004, (Elsevier, 2004).

21. SABS ISO/IEC17799. SABS Edition 11/iso/iec Edition1, South African Standard, Code of Practice for Information Security Management, (South African Bureau of Standards, 2001).
22. Sheldon A, Forensic Auditing, *The Role of Computer Forensics in the Corporate Toolbox*, (March 25, 2004), http://www.itsecurity.com/papers/p11.htm.
23. Sinangin D, *Computer Forensics Investigations in a Corporate Environment*, Computer Fraud and Security Bulletin, Volume 8, p.11-14, June 2002, (Elsevier, 2002).
24. Stephenson P, *Conducting Incident Post Mortems*, Computer Fraud and Security, April 2003, (Elsevier, 2003).
25. The Electronic Communications and Transactions Act, (2003), http://www.gov.za/gazette/regulation/2003/24594a.pdf.
26. Sarbarnes-Oxley Act of 2002, (October 20, 2006), http://frwebgate.access.gpo.gov/cgi-bin/getdoc.cgi?dbname=107_cong_bills&docid=f:h3763enr.txt.pdf.
27. Von Solms SH, *Information Security Governance: Cobit or ISO17799 or both,* Computers and Security, Volume 24, Issue2, March 2005, (Elsevier, 2005).
28. Von Solms SH, *Information Security: The Fourth Wave*, Computers and Security, Volume 25, Issue3, May 2006, (Elsevier, 2006), p. 165-168.
29. Von Solms SH, Louwrens CP. *Relationship between Digital Forensics, Corporate Governance, Information Technology and Information Security Governance* ,(Information Security Of South Africa Conference 2005 Proceeding , 2005).
30. Wolfe H, *The question of organizational forensic policy*, Computer Fraud and Security, Volume 6, June 2004, (Elsevier, 2004), p. 13-14.

Value creation and Return On Security Investments (ROSI)

Christer Magnusson, Josef Molvidsson and Sven Zetterqvist
Department of Computer and System Sciences
Stockholm University/Royal Institute of Technology
Forum 100, SE-164 40 Kista, Sweden
Tel: +46 (0)8 674 72 37
Fax: +46 (0)8 703 90 25
E-mail: cmagnus@dsv.su.se

Abstract. This paper investigates if IT security is as a part of value creation. The first part of the commentary focuses on the current theoretical conditions for IT security as a part of value creation. Different Return On Security Investment (ROSI) models are studied to investigate if they can calculate value creation with regard either to efficiency or to effectiveness. The second part of the paper investigates empirical evidence of a ROSI or any indication of a shareholder value perspective on IT security in three large, listed companies from different business segments. What they have in common is their first priority: value creation. The commentary begins by describing the "Productivity Paradox". It is followed by the most well-known ROSI models. Then, it explains the models applicability in value creation. Next, the three companies in the study are investigated. In the following section conclusions are drawn. Finally, the results of the research are discussed.

1 Introduction

To promote shareholder value every measure taken by the management should maximize value creation, from strategic investments to procedures for managing the daily operations. Since a cornerstone in shareholder value is free cash flow, "...the underlying value drivers of the business must also be the drivers of free cash flow" [1]. No other strategies are accepted than those linked to the creation of shareholder value:

"Value based strategic planning upholds no particular orthodoxy. For instance, if more market share, more customer service, more quality, or re-engineering the manufacturing process to increase efficiency will create more value for the business, it is a good thing. If the effort does not create

Please use the following format when citing this chapter:

Magnusson, C., Molvidsson, J. and Zetterqvist, S., 2007, in IFIP International Federation for Information Processing, Volume 232, New Approaches for Security, Privacy and Trust in Complex Environments, eds. Venter, H., Eloff, M., Labuschagne, L., Eloff, J., von Solms, R., (Boston: Springer), pp. 25–35.

higher value, further investment in share, service or quality is unjustified". [2].

According to this principle, Net Present Value (NPV) calculations for IT security investments should be drawn up to "compete" with other investments on the same conditions and to be a part of the value creation. The first objective of this study is to investigate the current theoretical conditions for IT security as a part of the value creation. Secondly, we are interested in finding out the empirical indications of a shareholder value perspective on IT security. Finally, conclusions are drawn.

This paper is directed towards researchers and practitioners in the field of security and risk management. However, the commentary may also interest Chief Financial Officers, controllers, line managers, and providers of security products and services.

The commentary begins by describing the "Productivity Paradox". It is followed by the most well-known ROSI models. Then, it explains the models applicability in value creation. Next, the three companies in the study are investigated. In the following section conclusions are drawn. Finally, the results of the research are discussed.

2 Methodology

In order to start reasoning on how IT security could be managed more rationally as an investment category, it should be investigated how the category is being used today. Our ambition is to elucidate this. In order to make the area comprehensible, we will start with "The Productivity Paradox", which will provide the necessary basis before we continue going through different models for "Return On Security Investments" (ROSI) and to try to assess their applicability. We will then make an empirical study on security investments.

In the empirical study we are interested in finding out if security investments are an integrated part in value creation, or at least calculated, or if they are decided on without estimating their financial value? We approached three subjectively chosen companies to try to find, if not an answer, at least an indication of answer to these questions. A prerequisite for the participation in the study was that the company in question was listed at a stock exchange, since we then could assume that it had a shareholder value perspective on value creation. Moreover, the company should be in different business segments to reduce the risk with segments specific behavior.

3 The Productivity Paradox

There are at least two ways IT security can create business value:

Firstly, it can increase a company's efficiency. This means a company will decrease operational expenses due to investments in IT security. A security service (or product), for example, will execute controls, previously carried out by back office personnel, thus increasing back office productivity. IT security investments can also increase efficiency by reducing costs for business interruption, fraud, embezzlement, etc. Secondly, IT security can increase a company's effectiveness. This means that IT security functionality will enable new, superior products or processes, thus providing a competitive advantage in the market. Banks, insurance services and air carriers with reengineered business models, completely based on Internet, are examples of businesses were IT security is a business enabler; without security these services would not sustain Internet hostilities [3, 4].

The major problems with IT security investments is however often the difficulty to identify and quantify its benefit, especially to translate it into economic terms and thus show its potential profitability [5, 6].

The problem to motivate IT security investments economically, is partly a consequence of the difficulties to generally produce correct calculations for IT investments, compared to traditional investments. Reasons for this are:

- The lack of a uniform working method to establish profitability
- IT investments will often carry their expenses, but not their benefits
- The general difficulty to identify and quantify the yield of IT investments

This originates in an "unjust" picture of IT projects; they bear all of their expenses, since these are easily quantified, but may not include their benefit, since these "cannot be identified". The noted economist Robert Solow quipped that computers are everywhere - except in "the productivity statistics" [7], and the economic historian Paul A. David invented "The Modern Productive Paradox" (Robert Solow) to describe the phenomenon. The Productive Paradox indicates the experienced loss of a positive correlation between investments in IT and an improvement of the companies' productivity due to these investments [8]. In 1996, a Swedish study established, that it was a paradox that there were almost no economical models to calculate the *benefit* from IT, although IT investments amount to several per cents of Sweden's BNP [8]. For some time now some attempt has been made to calculate the benefit from IT security. This will be studied more closely in the following sections.

4 Return On Security Investments

The investment category IT security inherits many of the problems which arise when valuating IT investments, but has also its "own" problems, e.g.

- How can the argument be overcome that security investments do not generate any revenue?
- How can an IT security investment be established as cost-effective, when the best that could happen is that "nothing" happens
- How can the optimal level of the total IT security investments be determined

A number of attempts have been made to adapt the existing economic profitability models to the special requirements for IT security in order to value IT security correctly. This kind of models was only recently developed. They have been able to quantify the earning capacity from IT security investments on a more scientific basis instead of merely "listing" the various abstract benefit from these investments.

ROSI is an acronym for Return On Security Investments, referring to research results from different directions in the US. It is however emphasized that this research is more or less in its infancy. The results published so far are however starting to gain acceptance in the academic world and to some extant also within the trade and industry.

The problem that the ROSI models are trying to bridge is the validity on, or even the lack of, statistics and data on various security incidents and attacks. When there is no information available showing what can be regarded as for example an extreme or medium number of attacks of a certain kind, it will be very difficult for different actors to assess their optimal level of security. One cannot ask oneself the question "are we in a good position" or "what does it mean for us if we would invest another million in security".

The quality of statistics on information security incidents has been criticized. Even Computer Security Institute (CSI) admits that their annual reports on data related crime were not done scientifically, but only intended to give a hint on the situation and the very best they could do in the present situation [9].

4.1 The Hummer model

Under the management of Hua Qiang Wei [10] a scientific team from the University of Idaho has developed the Hummer model. It consists principally of a "box", which in a network logs suspected incoming traffic which has passed through a firewall. To establish what can be regarded as "suspected" traffic, certain special patterns are stored. When an attack is suspected, reports will be sent to the administrative staff who can investigate the matter.

The model shows that it is more cost-efficient to discover and handle attacks using intrusion detection systems than using other preventive IT security mechanisms. Questions that the scientific team had to decide on with regards to costs and profitability were to try to establish the costs to discover an incident, the operational security costs and financial consequences if an attack would remain undiscovered.

To carry out this valuation the work was initiated by valuing the assets that could be reached through the network. Software could be valued in the same way as information. The valuation was also graded to define that, e.g. information A was three times as valuable as information B. Then different forms of attacks are associated with different costs in accordance with the standard of the U.S. Department of Defense.

In that way the ratio Annual Loss Expectancy (ALE) could be calculated in accordance with the normal procedure as a measure of the economic damage an attack causes multiplied with its likeliness. Consequently, an attack that would cost 100.000 dollar and occur every second year has an ALE of 50.000 dollar.

Accordingly, the Hummer model uses the ratio ALE as an important component when valuating intrusion detection systems. According to Wei the economic basis of the Hummer model is a "cost-benefit analysis", the objective of which is to weigh the pro and cons of intrusion detection systems with one another.

4.2 The Hoover model

The Hoover model has been developed by the Massachusetts Institute of Technology and the company @Stake in Boston, U.S., under the management of Kevin Soo Hoo [11]. The model's foremost objective is to calculate how companies who develop software can achieve the maximum yield on their security functionality investments. Hoover is principally database managing detailed information on security problems and vulnerabilities in software. The information has been obtained from companies that develop software and participated in the research work trying to understand how they could develop their products with a higher security level.

To be able to calculate yield due to IT security functionality investment in the different programming development processes one starts, for example, from the motto "A one dollar investment to manage a bug in the designing process will save 99 dollar compared to managing a bug later in the implementation phase".

The Hoover model's most important aspect from the historic information in the database is that the earlier one includes security into the software process, the higher the yield. The general result that the model generates is that security functionality investment in the designing phase results in the highest yield, 21 per cent. To add security functionality later in the development phase lower the yield, 15 per cent in the implementation phase and 12 per cent in the testing phase.

The Hoover model illustrates thus two ordinary construction mistakes in the development of software: to include security functionality "at last minute" and to let the users (or hackers) discover the security problems before one takes (tries to take) measures to correct these. The model shows that the earlier security aspects are considered in the development phase, the higher is the yield. The model shows this by applying Net Present Value (NPV) based calculations [11].

4.3 The CMU model

This quantitative study by Carnegie Mellon University shows how a system's ability to survive attacks increases if investment increases; it shows when the optimal investment level takes shape.

The study is primarily a regression analysis on "attack data" obtained from CERT [12]. The CMU model managed data between 1988 and 1995. It investigated which attacks occurred and how often, the odds for a certain type of attack affecting a certain company, the caused damage and the available defense including functionality [13].

This data was utilized to develop a model that could generate attacks in simulated companies. Consequently, one could get a picture of the frequency and grade of seriousness in the different attacks in practical terms. Afterwards the reaction of different networks was studied, during the attack and under various conditions. For instance, the grade of security (grade of cost) and the probability for attacks were varied to learn how these would affect the ability to resist attacks.

The absence of a "binomial view" on security was one of the news in the CMU model. The model no longer presumed that a company would be either attacked or not, but introduced a scale on how many times a company had been attacked. The systems ability to resist the attack (survivability) was measured between 0 and 1; 0 signified that the company was completely "eliminated" by an attack and 1 that the company remained completely unaffected by an attack.

By plotting data from these simulations, a model of the system's ability to survive depending on the security investment costs could be obtained. The cost was calculated in absolute terms ($) and the grade of survival between 0 and 1. The regression line shows a connection that is strongly increasing for low costs, but decreasing for high costs. Consequently, there is a decreasing marginal benefit when increasing the cost for security investments.

Accordingly, the CMU model can establish that the yield that can be delivered by security investments will be the highest in the initial stage and then gradually decrease when more money is invested in security.

By combining an imaginary curve, representing yield, with a curve representing the benefit that a company experiences due to increased security investments, the "optimal security" can be identified by using the CMU model. It is depicted in the diagram when the two curves intersect.

The CMU model concludes that if one can proof the need for a security investment, the model can deliver optimal security.

5 Applicability in Value Creation

It is important to observe that the three ROSI models studied are to a different extent "economically correct" with regard to the valuation of IT security. Their most important contribution is to formulate practical procedures how IT security investments may be evaluated. However, it can be noted that the basic economic models, which have been used, are not always explicitly specified.

With regard to the Hummer model it can be noted that the advantage of using an intrusion detection system is calculated by deducting the generated reduction in ALE from the annual cost for the system. The asset valuation, which the ALE calculation is based on, is done by using the present (capitalized) value. The model takes also as one's starting point that certain assets are more difficult to value in monetary terms than others. That is the reason why the company's assets are divided into "tangible assets" (principally physical assets as working stations and servers) and "intangible assets" (principally assets as stored data and information). It is only the first category that can be valued in economic terms. The value of the latter asset type is estimated in terms of "points" [10].

In the Hoover model Soo Hoo tries to calculate the benefit security functionality provides by using the function called "net benefit". The benefit is quantified in monetary terms. Soo Hoo points also out that the valuation of "intangibles" can generate controversial values. He tries therefore to consider this by only focusing on ALE. This value if calculated from relatively concrete losses in connection with the implementation of different security policies. According to Soo Hoo an investment decision can often be made based on the relatively concrete consequences that can be estimated, since these are generally big enough to prove profitability in a potential security investment [9]. Finally, Soo Hoo calculates a "net benefit" consisting of ALE minus "added cost" plus "added profit". By "added cost" one refers to the cost that can arise because of introduced security functionality, e.g. the staff is dissatisfied with circumstantial security routines. "Added profit", on the other hand, represents new business opportunities (IT security effectiveness) because of the new security investments, e.g. increased customer trust after the implementation of a PKI system.

The CMU model is not primarily about producing a monetary measurement of the value in a security investment. The model focuses rather on measuring each company's individual risk aversion in order to determine the company's optimal grade of investment. The decision criterion for this model will be directly affected by the investments costs, but unlike other investments it will not directly be affected by the revenues or monetary profits from a security investment. It is rather the subjective benefit vs. the cost that arises.

After this further accounting of the ROSI models' economic basis it can be established that it is neither easy to verify whether the models claim to be economically correct, nor if they claim to develop a valuation model for ex post or ex ante perspective. A common feature of the models is that they all value advantage in terms of net benefit. This term cannot not without difficulty be translated into cash flows. Therefore it is difficult to establish to what degree the ROSI models could be utilized in a Net Present Value (NPV) or Return On Investment (ROI) calculation and accordingly in value creation.

6 The study

To be able to carry out our empirical study we needed some large, listed companies with different business portfolios but with one unifying objective – a clear focus on shareholder value. Three companies were chosen for and accepted to participate in the study. They have completely different business portfolios. One company is the global leader (based on revenue) in white goods. The second company is one of the largest banks (by volume) in the Nordic region. The third company is a major Nordic telecom operator (measured in revenue).

All three companies have strong balance sheets. However, all of them have experienced financial stress and the bear market. One of the companies was not far from bankruptcy in the beginning of the nineties. Another has seen its shares dropping substantially over the last years (even though currently it has recovered somewhat). The third company faced the challenge with integrations costs after massive acquisitions around the globe.

After we had studied the companies' annual reports, it became obvious that shareholder value is on the agenda in all three companies. This gave us the opportunity to find an answer to our second research question, i.e. if there are any empirical indications of a value creation perspective on IT security, at least in these companies? We put forward to following questions to the companies.

- Do you have internal measures for controlling value creation?

- What is your business' appetite for risk?
- What internal measures do you have for controlling the IT risks, as for example the ROSI formulas?

The questions mentioned above were discussed with senior controllers on Group level in each corporation. Their positions were "Head of Group Controller and Finance" or "Head of Group Business Control". Even though they formally had slightly different positions, they had in common that they were responsible for overlooking the processes of value creation and investments in the companies.

6.1 Measures for controlling value creation

According to the senior controllers, the primary target of the companies is to deliver the highest possible shareholder returns (change in share price and dividends relative local market index or industry peer group). However, there were some differences in the methods for governing and controlling the business units in their effort to create shareholder value.

The bank had three value drivers for their business units: the key figure "Costs/Revenue" (excluding credit losses); Return On Equity (ROE); and a qualitative measure to estimate employee satisfaction. When being asked a question about the balance between the financial measures and the qualitative measure, the Senior Vice President made clear, that "the bottom line is always the most important".

The Telco had a concept named "Wanted Positions" covering customers, services, personnel, and growth (turnover and ROE). Priority number one was growth in turnover. The white goods giant had one single value driver: their internally developed version (Operative income – (Weighted Average Cost of Capital x Net assets)) of Economic Value Added. The Group Business Controller made it absolutely clear that the financial goals, expressed in the Groups value creation figures for the business units, were the first and only priority.

6.2 Risk appetite

A corporation can decide on its aggregated risk appetite and express it in percentage of some key figures, as for example:

- 1-5% on Working Capital
- 5-10% on Cash Flow
- 1-3% on EBITDA (Earnings Before Interest, Taxes, Depreciation, and Amortization)
- 3-5% on Earnings Per Share

The reasons behind deciding on risk key figures are twofold. Firstly, a corporation decides on a risk level estimated to sustain any impact on its share value due to incurred losses. Secondly, the figures allow the company to actively take on calculated risks and not to avoid them at any price.

None of the companies in the study had any financial key figures for IT risk appetite. All three companies had individual and aggregated credits limits for there customers and financial risk management systems. The Telco came closest to some sort of (qualitative) key figure of risks with a list of 20 risks that could threaten the "Wanted Positions" for the Group. The controllers of the companies explained that the IT risk was not an integrated part of their value creation systems. Consequently, management of the IT risk had no impact on the bonus systems, either.

6.3 Measures for controlling risk

None of the companies' controllers had any knowledge of the three ROSI models, or of any other methods or models (quantitative or qualitative). The controller of the Telco thought that maybe locally, in the business units and subsidiaries, some kind of NPV calculation (or similar) was carried out. The others had not heard of any unit in their corporations that had made any calculation whatsoever of investments in security.

All of the controllers underlined that the reason for neither having focused on risk analyses nor made calculations on IT security investments was that risk costs were not a part of their companies' value creation (and bonus) systems.

7 Conclusion

The first objective in this study was to investigate the current theoretical conditions for IT security to become a part of value creation. The ROSI models in our study are of limited value to help us calculate value creation neither with regard to efficiency nor to effectiveness. A fundamental reason is that the basic economic models, which were used, are not stated explicitly. This reduces obviously their practical usefulness.

Moreover, it is neither easy to verify whether the models claim to be economically correct, not if they claim to develop a value model for ex post or ex ante perspective. One further difficulty to apply the models is that they all value advantage in terms of net benefit. This concept cannot be easily transformed into cash flow. Therefore, it is not easy to establish to what degree the ROSI models' result could be utilized in a NPV or ROI calculation and accordingly in value creation. These difficulties may be a reason for the result in our empiric study.

According to the senior controllers participating in the study, the primary target of the companies is to deliver highest possible total shareholder returns. Despite that, made the result of the study it absolutely clear that there are no empirical evidence what so ever of a shareholder value perspective on IT security in these companies; there are no models in place for calculation the value contribution of IT security investments. As a matter of fact, there aren't any calculations done at all (at least not that the senior controllers are aware of).

8 Discussion

Straub et. al. in [14] discussed (information) security as "back-burner issue" for managers as well as employees, and the difficulties to change such a perception.

Sherwood et. al. [15] concluded that "[IT] Security has a bad reputation for getting in the way of real business". A study conducted by Nalla et. al. [16], underlined that the need for management and communication skills is critical to the security function.

A question arises why don't IT risk and security managers take the opportunity to integrate their work tasks with value creation and get senior management attention? Is it possible that Angell's "pathology of consciousness" in [17] gives an explanation; are they trapped within a mode of the traditional social organization (the IT security community) where the (traditional technology oriented security) assignments are created and supported in their everyday lives?

Another question may be if the IT risk and security managers are qualified enough in general management to be aware of the drivers behind value creation. Without these qualifications, it is difficult to navigate with the IT security and risk management function; the risk the IT security profession runs is to be left behind in the corporate world of yesterday.

Nevertheless, one thing we know is that cost for IT security is increasing; according to a CSI/FBI survey, 34% of respondents said security accounted for more than 5% of their organizations' total IT budgets and 13% spent more than 10% [18]. Another thing we know is that increasing cost is usually a reliable way to get senior management attention. Then, IT security may go the same route as many costly IT projects – the outsourcing and offshore route. The value creation in such a context is fairly easy to calculate.

Acknowledgement

We would like to take this opportunity to express our gratitude to the Executive Management in the companies who gave us this opportunity to gain some insight in value creation in their companies. We are especially grateful to the Chief Security Officers for their support during the project.

The opinions expressed in this paper are the author's opinions and do not necessarily represent the views of the companies in the study.

References

1. T. Copeland, T. Koller, and J. Murrin, Valuation, Measuring and Managing the value of companies, second edition, McKinsey & Company, Inc. (John Wiley & Sons, Inc, 1995).
2. J. McTaggart, P. Kontes, M. Mankins, in: Shareholder Value, I. Cornelius and M. Davies (FT Financial Publishing, Pearson Professional Limited, London, 1997), p. 223.
3. C. Alberts and A. Dorofee, Managing Information Security Risks, The OCTAVE Approach, Carnegie Mellon Software Engineering Institute, USA (Addison Wesley, 2003).

4. A. Granova and J.H.P. Eloff, Who Carries The Risk? Proceedings of the 4TH Annual International Information Security South Africa conference, July 2004, (ISBN 1-86854-522-9).
5. B. V. Solms and R. V. Solms, The 10 deadly sins of information security management, in: Computers & Security, Vol.23 No 5 (ISSN 0167 -4048, 2004), pp. 371-376.
6. J.H.P. Eloff, Tactical level - an overview of the latest trends in risk analysis, certification, best practices and international standards, Information Security Architectures Workshop, Fribourg, Switzerland, February 2002.
7. P.A. David, The Dynamo and the Computer: An Historical Perspective on the Modern Productivity Paradox, (American Economic Review, 1990).
8. T. Falk and N-G. Olve, IT som strategisk resurs (Liber-Hermods, 1996).
9. K.J. Soo Hoo, How Much Is Enough? A Risk Management Approach to Computer Security, Ph.D. Thesis, University of Stanford, 2000.
10. H. Wei, D. Frinke, O. Carter, and C. Ritter Wei, Cost-Benefit Analysis for Network Intrusion Detection, Centre for Secure and Dependable Software, University of Idaho, Proceedings of the 28th Annual Computer Security Conference October, 2001.
11. K.J. Soo Hoo, A.W. Sudbury, A.R. Jaquith, Tangible ROI through Secure Software Engineering (Secure Business Quarterly, 4th Quarter 2001).
12. The CERT® Coordination Center (April 30, 2003); http://www.cert.org.
13. S.D. Moitra and S.L. Konda, A Simulation Model for Managing Survivability of Networked Information Systems, Technical Report CMU/SEI-2000-TR-020, Carnegie Mellon Software Engineering Institute, 2000.
14. D.W. Straub and R.J. Welke, Coping With Systems Risk: Security Planning Models for Management Decision Making (MIS Quarterly, December 1998).
15. J. Sherwood, A. Clark, A, and D. Lynas., Enterprise Security Architecture: a business driven approach (CMP Books, USA, 2005).
16. M. K. Nalla, K. Christian, M. Morash, and P. Schram, Practitioners' perceptions of graduate curriculum in security education (Security Journal, 6, 1995), pp. 93-99.
17. I. O. Angell, Computer security in these uncertain times: the need for a new approach, Proceedings of the Tent World Conference on Computer Security, Audit and Control, COMPSEC, London, UK, 1993, pp. 382-388.
18. Eleventh Annual CSI/FBI Computer Crime and Security Survey, Computer Security Institute, 2006; www.gocsi.com.

Usability and Security of Personal Firewalls

Almut Herzog[1] and Nahid Shahmehri[1]

Dept. of Computer and Information Science, Linköpings universitet,Sweden
{almhe, nahsh}@ida.liu.se

Abstract. Effective security of a personal firewall depends on (1) the rule granularity and the implementation of the rule enforcement and (2) the correctness and granularity of user decisions at the time of an alert. A misconfigured or loosely configured firewall may be more dangerous than no firewall at all because of the user's false sense of security. This study assesses effective security of 13 personal firewalls by comparing possible granularity of rules as well as the usability of rule set-up and its influence on security.

In order to evaluate usability, we have submitted each firewall to use cases that require user decisions and cause rule creation. In order to evaluate the firewalls' security, we analysed the created rules. In addition, we ran a port scan and replaced a legitimate, network-enabled application with another program to assess the firewalls' behaviour in misuse cases. We have conducted a cognitive walkthrough paying special attention to user guidance and user decision support.

We conclude that a stronger emphasis on user guidance, on conveying the design of the personal firewall application, on the principle of least privilege and on implications of default settings would greatly enhance both usability and security of personal firewalls.

1 Introduction

In times where roaming users connect their laptops to a variety of public, private and corporate wireless or wired networks and in times where more and more computers are always online, host-based firewalls implemented in software, called *personal firewalls*, have become an important part of the security armour of a personal computer. Typcially, personal firewalls control both incoming network connections—to defeat unsolicited connection attempts and host explorations—and outgoing network connections—to contain network viruses and spyware and to thwart distributed denial of service attacks by zombie machines.

Most of the time, a personal firewall runs silently in the background, but at times, it alerts its unsuspecting user of ominous, security-critical events and demands instant attention and an instant decision. This is the moment where security and usability meet. If the user, at this moment, does not take in the alert message, the firewall ends up with an ad-hoc configuration that the user will rarely take time to revise and which may be more dangerous than no firewall at all because of the user's false sense of security.

From this anecdotal scenario, one can identify a number of security and usability issues that make personal firewalls special and interesting to study:

Please use the following format when citing this chapter:

Herzog, A. and Shahmehri, N., 2007, in IFIP International Federation for Information Processing, Volume 232, New Approaches for Security, Privacy and Trust in Complex Environments, eds. Venter, H., Eloff, M., Labuschagne, L., Eloff, J., von Solms, R., (Boston: Springer), pp. 37–48.

- Personal firewalls target end users that are not security experts, yet
- the effective security of personal firewalls depends to a great extent on the correctness and level of detail of a lay user decision.
- At decision time, the lay user is typically busy with other tasks.
- A wrong decision by the user can compromise the user's privacy and computer.

However, *if* personal firewalls can address these difficult issues successfully, they could potentially serve as guiding examples of how to warn and inform user of security events, and, consequentially, also of how to explain security features to lay users. Therefore we have conducted a usability study of personal firewalls that takes the pulse of applications that must unite security and usability under the rather adverse conditions described above.

We have studied the following 13 personal firewalls for the Windows XP platform: BlackICE PC Protection 3.6, Comodo Personal Firewall 2.0, F-Secure Internet Security 2006 6.13-90, LavaSoft Personal Firewall 1.0, McAfee Personal Firewall Plus 7.0, Microsoft Windows Firewall (SP2), NetVeta Safety.Net 3.61.0002, Norman Personal Firewall 1.42, Norton Personal Firewall 2006, Sunbelt Kerio Personal Firewall 4.3.268.0, Tiny Desktop Firewall 2005 (6.5.126) (gone out of business in autumn 2006) and the free and professional versions of ZoneAlarm 6.1.744.001. According to the firewall portal `firewallguide.com`, these are the most popular personal firewalls for the Windows platform that are either available for free or as time-limited but full-featured evaluation versions.

2 Method

For the evaluation, we have defined two common use cases that typically require user interaction with the firewall, namely (1) setting up an application so that it has access to the Internet and (2) setting up a server on the local host so that it accepts incoming connections from exactly one host. We have also evaluated firewall behaviour for the misuse cases of port scanning and replacing a legitimate, network-allowed application with another application.

The evaluation method is the method of cognitive walkthrough [11]. Cognitive walkthrough means that the evaluator uses the program as prescribed by use and misuse cases and notes usability problems as they arise.

During the cognitive walkthrough, we have paid special attention to user guidance, user help and whether the created firewall rule grants the minimally necessary set of permissions. The firewall design with its default settings and user guidance features are the focus of this work, rather than the meticulous listing of each and every usability problem encountered.

3 Use cases

In this section we describe the findings from performing the tasks of enabling an application to access hosts on the Internet and to set up a server that can receive connections from only one host.

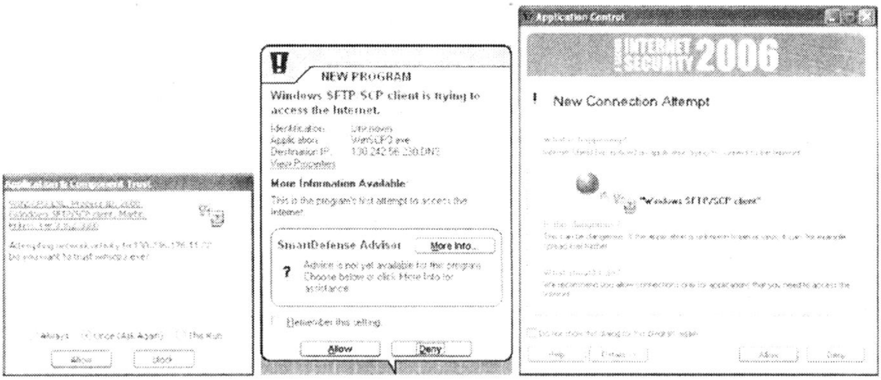

NetVeda Zone Alarm Pro F-Secure

Fig. 1. Alerts for outgoing connections ranging from very technical (left) to non-technical (right), from no help (left) to full help (right).

Detailed results from our study with screenshots and additional information on the firewalls' installation process, help system and log viewing capabilities can be found at `www.ida.liu.se/~iislab/projects/firewall-comparison`.

3.1 Allowing outgoing connections

Setup A personal firewall should only allow trusted applications to access the network. WinSCP (`winscp.net`) is a small application for connecting to SCP (secure copy protocol) or SFTP (secure file transfer protocol) servers. We used WinSCP to connect to a host. If necessary, we responded to the alerts of the firewall. In an alert window, we would follow the path of least resistance, choosing those answers that the interface suggested or, if no default indicated, we would choose the seemingly securest answer.

Findings 9 of 13 firewalls pop up an alert when WinSCP tries to open a network connection to the SCP server to ask the user whether to allow the network connection or not. In the alert—some example alerts are shown in figure 1—, the user can typically choose between allowing and denying the connection and whether to remember this setting for this application i.e. to automatically create a rule for this application (Comodo, F-Secure, ZoneAlarms). Some firewalls offer a greater variety of user choices. Answer alternatives for all examined firewall products are shown in table 1.

However, there are four firewall products (BlackICE, Win XP, Norton, Sunbelt) that by installation default allow any outgoing connection, either silently (BlackICE, Win XP, Sunbelt) or with an unobtrusive float alert informing the user (Norton). By design, the Windows XP firewall does not monitor outgoing connections. However, as all other firewall products do this, one wonders how many users assume that the Windows XP firewall does so, too, and feel protected even though there is no protection.

Table 1. Information available in alerts and default rule created when allowing an outgoing connection. The darker the cell background the less secure or usable is the firewall behaviour.

Product	How dangerous is it?	What shall I do?	Choice in Popup Dialog	Typical Rule When Allowing Outgoing Connection
BlackICE	Not applicable. BlackICE never alerts.			Full out and listen permissions for local applications
Comodo	Signalled by slider	"No advice available" for WinSCP. No help. Open choice.	Allow, Deny–Once, Always	Full in/out permissions. In-permission needed for the return data connection (!).
F-Secure	Generic text, see figure 1	Help and details available. Default: Allow once	Allow, Deny–Once, Always	Full out permissions
LavaSoft	No indication	No advice. No help. Default: Guesses default rules.	Allow all, Stop all, Create custom rules	Guessed custom rule
McAfee	"McAfee does not recognize this application." may be perceived as dangerous.	Help me choose-button as help. Open choice.	Grant Access, Grant Access Once, Block All	Full out and listen permissions.
MS Win XP	*No indication (only incoming)*	*Generic text, link to documentation, open choice (only incoming)*	*Allow, Deny–Ask me later (only incoming)*	Full out permissions.
NetVeda	No indication	No advice, only technical details. No help. Default: Allow once	Allow, Deny–Once, Session, Always	Full in/out permissions
Norman	No indication	"Tip: None" for WinSCP. General help available. Default: Allow always	Allow, Deny–Once, Session, Always	Wizard guides to rule for this port and any host.
Norton	Learn: N/A, Manual: "Medium Risk"	Learn: N/A, Manual: Alert assistant, suggested: allow always	Learning mode: no popup but informative float. Manual mode: Allow, Deny, Manual rule–Once, Always.	Notifies user that it has learnt the app with needed permissions or app-specific defaults. In manual mode, suggests full in/out permissions.
Sunbelt	Green background signals harmless to user but is only contrast to red for incoming connections.	No advice. No help. Open choice.	Default: No prompt. After change: Allow, Deny–Once, Always	Full out permissions.
Tiny	Red header signals dangerous, but the header is always red.	Limited and technical help available. Open choice between allow or deny always.	Allow, Deny–Once, Session, Always	Tight rule with host and port
Zone-Alarms	Colourcoding of alerts: yellow—outgoing, violet—listening, orange—changed application	Smart Defense Advisor has no advice for WinSCP. Default: Allow once	Allow, Deny–Once, Always	Full out permissions

The same request and what would seem to be the same user answer may result in the creation of very different rules. Some firewalls, often those aimed at technical users (LavaSoft, Norman, Tiny), create rather tight rules. Other firewalls, often those aimed at lay users, create a rule that gives full permission to the application to initiate (F-Secure, Sunbelt, ZoneAlarms) and sometimes even to listen for socket connections (BlackICE, Comodo, McAfee) and, still worse, to also accept connections (NetVeda, Norton's suggestion in manual mode).

3.2 Allowing software to receive incoming requests

Setup A firewall should not allow any host to connect to a local server. We tested this by running the Cerberus FTP (file transfer protocol) Server, and trying to set up the firewall so that Cerberus could accept connections and FTP commands from only one, named host.

Findings From the overview presented in table 2, one can roughly identify four ways of handling server applications and incoming traffic to them.

1. Some firewalls generate *alerts when applications start listening* for connections. By default, this is done by Comodo, F-Secure, the ZoneAlarms and Norton. In a default installation Norton does not alert but announces with a float that it has learnt that the FTP server is listening.
2. Those firewalls that do alert when an application starts listening, often also *allow any host to connect* as a default behaviour. The user decision to allow an application to listen also implies for these applications the permission to let any host connect. However, NetVeda, without showing a specific listen alert, also allows connection by any host. This comes from the peculiarity of the Cerberus server that it first does a DNS lookup. This lookup is caught by NetVeda and if allowed by the user, who only sees this as a simple outgoing connection, implies full permissions for Cerberus, i.e. not only to connect out, but also to listen for and accept connections from any host.
3. Firewalls that *silently drop incoming connections to open ports* are BlackICE, Comodo, McAfee and Sunbelt. For users that rarely interact with their firewall it may be unclear why clients cannot connect since the firewall usually runs silently in the background. In misuse cases, this is good; but when the user cannot determine why an authorised client cannot connect, the firewall has become a hinder for the user's primary task of setting up an FTP server.
4. The fourth strategy is to *generate an alert for incoming connection attempts.* Norman alerts upon connection attempts to *any* port. If the computer is exposed to port scanning, the user is swamped by alerts. By default, LavaSoft and Tiny alert upon a connection attempt to an open port. From this alert, the user can create a fine-grained rule. The Windows XP firewall normally alerts upon connection attempts to open ports but Cerberus modifies the XP firewall rules so that Cerberus is trusted by the firewall and no alert is caused. That an application can modify firewall rules and grant itself additional permissions renders the firewall useless. However, all Windows applications that run from an administrator account can change firewall rules if only they know where and for which product.

Application-specific rules that restrict which host can connect on which port can be set up with LavaSoft, Norman, Norton, Sunbelt, Tiny and ZoneAlarm Pro. The other firewalls have coarser rule granularity, the worst case being to

Table 2. Personal firewall default behaviour when trying to set up an FTP server that should allow only one host to connect to it. The darker the cell shading the less secure or usable is the firewall.

Product	Type	Listen Alert	Default Behaviour (if Listening Allowed)	How to allow only one host to connect	User Guidance
BlackICE	3	N	Silently blocks all incoming traffic also to open ports	Manually open port for host.	None
Comodo	1, 3	Y	Silently blocks all incoming traffic also to open ports	Manually open port for host.	None
F-Secure	1, 2	Y	Any host can connect.	Manually open port for host and deny for others. App-based rules should be possible but did not work for us.	None
LavaSoft	4	N	Alerts upon connection attempt to open port.	From alert, open port for host to app.	Alert guides through creation but by default uses ephemeral port in rule.
McAfee	3	N	Silently blocks all incoming traffic also to open ports	Either manually open port (for any host) or trust host (with any connection).	Last event hint in main interface.
MS Win XP	4	N	Creates alert upon connection attempt to an open port.	Either manually open port for host or open app for host.	None
NetVeda	2	N	If outgoing connection is allowed, also incoming is silently allowed and any host can connect (!).	Not possible. Interface is prepared for setting up finer-grained rules but the choices are so limited that our case could not be set up.	None
Norman	4	N	Alerts upon connection attempt to *any* port.	From alert, open port for host.	Wizard guides through rule creation from alert.
Norton	1, 2	*y*	*Learns* and informs (not alerts) with float that server is listening. Any host can connect.	Open port for host to app.	None
Sunbelt	3	N	Silently blocks all incoming traffic also to open ports.	Open port for host to app from alert after changing the default for this app, so that incoming connections cause an alert.	By default: None; after default change: From alert
Tiny	4	N	Alerts upon connection attempt to open port.	Restriction to one host is default behaviour.	None
Free Zone-Alarm	1, 2	Y	Any host can connect	Not possible	None
Zone-Alarm Pro	1, 2	Y	Any host can connect	Manually open port for host to app and deny for others.	None

either fully trust or distrust an application (free ZoneAlarm). Table 3 contains the details of the possible rule granularities.

We found that the most usable and most secure way to achieve the goal of setting up an FTP server and letting only one host connect to it, is presented by LavaSoft, Norman, Sunbelt and Tiny. These firewalls display an alert if an FTP client tries to connect, and from this alert, it is possible to directly create a fine-grained rule. Of these four firewalls, Tiny creates the tightest rule with the least amount of user interaction.

User guidance for this task was nonexistent in many firewall products. By 'nonexistent' we mean that to find out how to allow the connection and only from one host, one had to either resort to exploring the firewall interface or to reading the documentation—all this under the assumption that the user would understand that it was the firewall that caused the problem! However, all firewalls that prompted for an incoming connection attempt showed good guidance by allowing the set-up of fine-grained rules from the alert.

4 Information in alerts

When the user is confronted with an alert from the firewall, there is often a surprising lack of information and guidance from the software. The user typically needs to know how dangerous the current situation is and what he or she should do.

Of the 9 firewalls that show an alert, the alerts of two firewalls (NetVeda and Tiny) do not contain the product name or the word 'firewall', thus leaving the user clueless as to which application caused the message.

Firewalls spend little effort on classifying and explaining the severity of an alert. Of those 12 firewalls that can be made to raise alerts, only three (Comodo, F-Secure, Norton in manual mode) attempt to classify the severity. Comodo shows a slider, F-Secure some generic text under the heading "Is this dangerous?" (see figure 1); Norton classifies the risk as low, medium and high. The other firewalls identify whether it is an incoming or outgoing connection by way of colour coding, symbols or text in the window but do not indicate whether this particular connection attempt is dangerous.

Astonishingly, no firewall attempts to explain the port number to the user other than possibly translating the port number into a—for many people—equally cryptic service name such as '22' to 'ssh' and '80' to 'http', but with no explanation whether 'ssh' or 'http' are potentially dangerous services or are to be expected from an application. Only Norton in manual mode makes a distinction in response alternatives if the outgoing connection is a DNS connection for resolving host names.

Also the host *name* is not readily available in alerts that display that information, even though we entered the host name for the SSH connection using a name, not an IP address. This makes it practically impossible for a user to verify whether the application is connecting to the desired host or not.

The firewalls Comodo, LavaSoft, NetVeda and Sunbelt do not provide access to any help from the alert (Tiny provides some limited help). If details are given in the alert, these are often technical such as paths, IP addresses, protocols and/or ports. Other firewalls keep technical details deliberately away from users (F-Secure, McAfee, Win XP for incoming, Norton in learning mode). User guidance is usually available in the form of online help and context-sensitive help (not in NetVeda, Comodo only partially, Tiny accesses online help over the Internet and has limited context-sensitive help). Some firewalls (BlackICE, especially McAfee) use guiding or explanatory texts in windows and alerts so that the user finds the necessary information without consulting the help system.

5 Misuse cases

We created two misuse cases to test the default reaction of the firewall. It was not our purpose to seriously test the security solution of the firewall, but to see the firewall's presentation of the situation to the user. In-depth security testing of personal firewalls with tools such as `grc.com` is documented on e.g. `firewallguide.com` and we refer to that site for more details on possible security flaws in the blocking behaviour of firewalls.

5.1 Stealth

Setup: A personal firewall should block connection attempts to all ports unless stated otherwise by a firewall rule. To test how the firewalls reacted to incoming packets, we used Netcat (`netcat.sourceforge.net`). For the basic tests we ran sequential port scans on the low port ranges. In this test, we were interested in the default behaviour for unsolicited incoming connection attempts.

Findings By default, 12 of the 13 firewall products block all closed ports. Of the 12, only Norman shows prompts on every connection attempt. With Norman, this behaviour is difficult to change. One is either prompted for everything or for nothing, or one must create rules. Other firewalls can be configured to alert on certain types of incoming traffic. Upon port scanning, LavaSoft and Sunbelt blocked our attacking host. Tiny is the only firewall that failed to block incoming connection attempts by default because it had automatically put all network interface cards (NIC) in its so-called "safe zone", where port blocking is not default behaviour. Had it correctly placed the NICs in the Internet zone, port blocking would have been the default.

5.2 Fooling the firewall

Setup: Firewalls that base their security rules on trusted software are vulnerable to malicious programs that masquerade as trusted software. We replaced a legitimate firefox.exe with a renamed version of winscp.exe, making sure that no firewall rules for WinSCP existed and that Firefox was allowed to connect to the Internet.

Findings Only the Sunbelt Kerio firewall was fooled by this simple masquerading attempt. Norton and Tiny show the spoofed Firefox as a new application, thus they do not recognise (or verbalise clearly) that they have a rule for the genuine Firefox application. The remaining 10 firewalls detect that Firefox has changed and show a special alert saying that a program which has changed is trying to access the network.

User guidance in this issue is very difficult and not handled satisfactorily. Users of Norton and Tiny could easily believe that the Firefox rules had somehow gone amiss and must be reset. Users of other firewalls are faced with an alert that announces the change but still could easily believe that Firefox was updated and that the rule must be reconfirmed.

6 Summary and recommendations

In this section, we highlight findings, suggest products for certain user groups as shown in table 3 and present recommendations that would render firewalls more usable and secure.

Some firewalls—Comodo, LavaSoft, NetVeda, Norman, Sunbelt—target technical users that are not deterred by IP and port numbers in alert windows. Of these firewalls, Tiny is the one that guides the technical user to the strictest rule with least overhead and also allows additional, advanced application monitoring.

Some firewalls—F-Secure, McAfee, Norton, ZoneAlarm—are part of a product suite and specifically target users with little or no knowledge about network security. Their drawback is that they do not always support the possibility of fine-grained rules and may only be partially of interest for risk-taking Internet users.

This evaluation has shown that there are many different design alternatives and default settings for personal firewalls. One clean design is shown by the LavaSoft and Tiny firewalls. They alert on outgoing connections as well as on incoming connection attempts to open ports. They do not alert when a service starts listening as this is not security-critical in their design. From an alert, they guide the user through the creation of a fine-grained rule (LavaSoft) or create a tight rule by default (Tiny) and thus achieve tight security.

There are a number of guidelines, e.g. [8, 4, 16], which deal with security and usability. Also more traditional usability guidelines such as [11, 13, 10] must be considered. For the firewall domain we could identify the following specific issues that should be addressed for increased usability and security.

- *Firewalls must make themselves more visible.* This can be achieved through the animation of their logo in the system tray (as shown by Sunbelt and ZoneAlarm). But it may also mean showing small informative floating windows close to the system tray indicating certain actions of the firewall that did not trigger user interaction and displaying the firewall name and logo in every alert that it creates.
- *Encourage learning.* Firewalls spend very little effort in teaching users about network security. All firewalls could be made to show IP address and port; some translate the port number into a service name. But no firewall tries to explain the specific service or shows the host name together with the IP address.
- *Give the user a chance to revise a hasty decision later.* Users that are busy with a primary task take security chances to get the primary task done. However, they may need a reminder, maybe by using a floating window or bubble, of their security settings.

Table 3. Summary of the firewalls including the supported granularity of rules, suitable user group and a concluding comment. The darker the cell shading the less secure or appealing is the firewall.

Product	Product Type	Granularity	User Group	Comment
BlackICE	Commercial	Coarse–medium	Tech user that wants a network monitor rather than a firewall	After installation, scans for and adds all applications on the local host with Allow-permissions to its rule base.
Comodo	Free	Medium	Tech user that wants an appealing user interface	Needs permission for back connection on high ports, prompts for all Windows default applications.
F-Secure	Commercial, part of suite	Medium-fine	Lay user	Tidy alert window with few choices. Application-based rules difficult.
LavaSoft	Commercial	Fine	Tech user with time to set up fine-grained rules	Guesses application type from connection attempt. Ephemeral port numbers in suggested rules.
McAfee	Part of suite	Medium	Playful lay or tech user	High fun factor with tracing events, good informational text in windows.
MS Win XP	Built-in	Medium(in), None (out)	Better than nothing but not good enough	Allows only user control for incoming traffic, not outgoing.
NetVeda	Free	Coarse–medium	Tech user	Fine-grained rules do not work satisfyingly yet. Yes to outgoing implies that the application can listen and respond to incoming events.
Norman	Commercial	Fine	Tech user with a lot of time	Longish wizard is default for all connection attempts.
Norton	Commercial, part of suite	Fine	Lay user or tech user with patience to explore interface	Difficult to access and modify rules.
Sunbelt	Commercial	Fine	User that can change default setting	Default after installation allows all local applications to access the network, fooled by replaced legitimate application.
Tiny	Commercial	Fine	Tech user that wants to learn more about applications	Allows also fine-grained monitoring of other security-critical actions. Alert info very technical, little help.
Free ZoneAlarm	Free, part of suite	Coarse	Lay, low-risk user	Simple user interface, good as a first contact.
ZoneAlarm Pro	Commercial, part of suite	Fine	Lay or tech user	Fine-grained rules not possible from alert: User must remember to refine rule later.

- *Prefer handling security decisions at once.* In order to set up tight rules or set up the Cerberus server, some firewalls require their users to access the firewall main interface. This is a burden to the workflow of the user and should be avoided if possible.
- *Enforce least privilege* wherever possible. The firewalls of Tiny and LavaSoft show that fine-grained rule set-up is feasible without much user burden.
- *Indicate severity, indicate what to do and show the created rule.* In an alert, users need to know how dangerous the attempted action is, what they can and should do, and receive feedback as to which rule was actually created by the firewall.

7 Related work

While usability evaluations of security applications abound—e-mail software with encryption [14, 5], Internet banking [6, 12], Internet Explorer [1], Outlook Express [3], setting up security policies for Java applications [7]— the evaluations that fit best into our context are two previous evaluations of firewalls. Johnston and others [8] have evaluated the first version of the Windows XP firewall and arrive at specific usability issues that may deter users from building trust in the firewall. The authors believed that the following version, roughly the version that we had in our test, would remedy many of the problems they had identified, but the XP firewall still does not rate high on our evaluation. Professional firewall products for network administrators also exhibit usability problems [15]. Technical terms are not explained and terms such as 'inbound' and 'outbound' can be used in confusing ways—we found such a mix-up in Comodo and Norman. In fact, if the target user is a security professional, usability issues may be even more neglected by designers than if the target user is a security novice [2].

Plenty of firewall reviews can be found online, e.g. through the portal `firewallguide.com`. However, many of these are only short reviews, test the firewall for security only using the e.g. web-based firewall tests like ShieldsUp (`grc.com`) or other automated tools or ask their audience for ratings. A vulnerability test for firewalls is described in [9].

8 Conclusion

In this article, we have presented the evaluation of 13 free and commercial personal firewall products. We have evaluated the products by means of a cognitive walkthrough of the use cases of allowing a local application to access the network and setting up a local server and allowing it to receive connections from only one host. Two misuse cases—port scanning and replacing a legitimate version of an application with a faked one—showed how the firewalls react to potential attack situations.

A winning firewall could not be identified; all firewalls had one or more shortcomings. Personal firewalls are generally good at protecting ports of the local host from unsolicited connection attempts from the Internet. However, they are generally poor at informing users and creating security awareness.

More than half of the evaluated firewalls do not support the set-up of truly fine-grained rules.

If a user switches between firewall products, she cannot anticipate what the default behaviour and its security implications will be. User guidance could remedy this but firewalls spend little effort on conveying their design, default settings or concepts of network security to their users. We conclude that this failure is a notable obstacle to usable and secure personal firewalls.

References

1. S. M. Furnell. Using security: easier said than done. *Computer Fraud & Security*, 2004(4):6–10, April 2004.
2. S. M. Furnell and S. Bolakis. Helping us to help ourselves: Assessing administrators' use of security analysis tools. *Network Security*, 2004(2):7–12, February 2004.
3. S. M. Furnell, A. Jusoh, and D. Katsabas. The challenges of understanding and using security: A survey of end users. *Computers & Security*, 25:27–35, 2006.
4. S. L. Garfinkel. *Design Principles and Patterns for Computer Systems That Are Simultaneously Secure and Usable.* PhD thesis, Massachusetts Institute of Technology, May 2005.
5. D. Gerd tom Markotten. *Benutzbare Sicherheit in informationstechnischen Systemen.* Rhombos Verlag, Berlin, 2004. ISBN 3-937231-06-4.
6. M. Hertzum, N. Jørgensen, and M. Nørgaard. Usable security and e-banking: Ease of use vis-à-vis security. In *Proceedings of the Annual Conference of CHISIG (OZCHI'04).* http://webhotel.ruc.dk/nielsj/research/papers/eBanking-ajis.pdf (visited 3-Aug-2005), November 2004.
7. A. Herzog and N. Shahmehri. A usability study of security policy managment. In S. Fischer-Hübner, K. Rannenberg, and S. L. Louise Yngström, editors, *Security and Privacy in Dynamic Environments, Proceedings of the 21st International Information Security Conference (IFIP TC-11) (SEC'06)*, pages 296–306. Springer-Verlag, May 2006.
8. J. Johnston, J. H. P. Eloff, and L. Labuschagne. Security and human computer interfaces. *Computers & Security*, 22(8):675–684, December 2003.
9. S. Kamara, S. Fahmy, E. E. Schultz, F. Kerschbaum, and M. Frantzen. Analysis of vulnerabilities in Internet firewalls. *Computers & Security*, 22(3):214–232, April 2003.
10. N. Leveson. *Safeware: System Safety and Computers.* Addison Wesley, 1995.
11. J. Nielsen. *Usability Engineering.* Morgan Kaufmann Publishers, Inc, 1993.
12. M. Nilsson, A. Adams, and S. Herd. Building security and trust in online banking. In *Proceedings of the Conference on Human Factors in Computing Systems (CHI'05)*, pages 1701–1704. ACM Press, April 2005.
13. B. Shneiderman and C. Plaisant. *Designing the User Interface.* Addison Wesley, 4th edition, 2004.
14. A. Whitten and J. D. Tygar. Why Johnny can't encrypt: A usability evaluation of PGP 5.0. In *Proceedings of the 8th USENIX Security Symposium (Security'99).* Usenix, August 1999.
15. A. Wool. The use and usability of direction-based filtering in firewalls. *Computers & Security*, 23(6):459–468, September 2004.
16. K.-P. Yee. User interaction design for secure systems. In *Proceedings of the International Conference on Information and Communications Security (ICICS'02)*, pages 278–290. Springer-Verlag, December 2002.

Trusted Ticket Systems and Applications

Nicolai Kuntze[1] and Andreas U. Schmidt[1]

Fraunhofer–Institute for Secure Information Technology SIT
Rheinstraße 75, 64295 Darmstadt, Germany
{andreas.u.schmidt,nicolai.kuntze}@sit.fraunhofer.de

Abstract. Trusted Computing is a security base technology that will perhaps be ubiquitous in a few years in personal computers and mobile devices alike. Despite its neutrality with respect to applications, it has raised some privacy concerns. We show that trusted computing can be applied for service access control in a manner protecting users' privacy. We construct a ticket system, a concept at the heart of Identity Management, relying solely on the capabilities of the trusted platform module and the Trusted Computing Group's standards. Two examples show how it can be used for pseudonymous, protected service access.

1 Introduction

In a ticket based authentication and authorisation protocols like Kerberos [1] software tokens are used to prove the identity of a single entity. Based on this tokens access to certain systems is restricted to entities producing appropriate tokens. Additionally data embodied in the token can be used to implement also an authorisation control enabling a token based access control scheme beside the mere authentication. These tokens are an electronic analog to physical tickets. They can have a limited validity period ore be used a specified number of times. For the adept, some base concepts of Trusted Computing (TC) look very similar to Identity Management (IDM). We exploit the analogy between TC and IDM and construct a ticket system using TC functionality, thus obtaining a cornerstone of IDM systems. The applicability of such a *trusted ticket system* is shown in the context of a reputation system and a push service.

Section 2 provides necessary background on TC. Section 3, developing the trusted ticket system, is subdivided in 3.1, explaining how to use Attestation Identity Keys (AIKs) for the realisation of tickets, and 3.2 detailing the proceedings for their acquisition and redemption. Section 3.3 outlines a general service access architecture utilising trusted tickets, with a high degree of separation of duties, providing pseudonymity, accountability, and charging functionality. Section 4 embeds trusted ticket systems in the two mentioned application contexts and discusses the benefits. Conclusions are drawn in Section 5.

2 Trusted Computing Essentials

Trusted Computing uses a hardware anchor as a root of trust and is now entering the mobile domain with the aim to provide a standardised security infrastructure. Trust as defined by the Trusted Computing Group (TCG) means that an entity always behaves in the expected manner for the intended purpose. The trust anchor, called Trusted Platform Module (TPM), offers various functions

Please use the following format when citing this chapter:

Kuntze, N. and Schmidt, A.U., 2007, in IFIP International Federation for Information Processing, Volume 232, New Approaches for Security, Privacy and Trust in Complex Environments, eds. Venter, H., Eloff, M., Labuschagne, L., Eloff, J., von Solms, R., (Boston: Springer), pp. 49–60.

related to security. Each TPM is bound to a certain environment and together they form a trusted platform (TP) from which the TPM cannot be removed. Through the TPM the TP gains a cryptographic engine and a protected storage. Each physical instantiation of a TPM has a unique identity by an Endorsement Key (EK) which is created at manufacture time. This key is used as a base for secure transactions as the Endorsement Key Credential (EKC) asserts that the holder of the private portion of the EK is a TPM conforming to the TCG specification. The EKC is issued as well at production time and the private part of the key pair does not leave the TPM. There are other credentials specified by the TCG which are stating the conformance of the TPM and the platform for instance the so called platform credential. Before a TPM can be used a take ownership procedure must be performed in which the usage of the TPM is bound to a certain user. The following technical details are taken from [2].

The TPM is equipped with a physical random number generator, and a key generation component which creates RSA key pairs. The key generator is designed as a protected capability, and the created private keys are kept in a *shielded capability* (a protected storage space *inside* the TPM). The shielded capabilities protect internal data structures by controlling their use. Three of them are essential for applications. First, *key creation and management*, second the ability to create a *trust measurement* which can be used to assert a certain state toward a, remote party, and finally *sealing* methods to protect arbitrary data by *binding* it (in TCG nomenclature) to TP states and TPM keys.

For the TPM to issue an assertion about the system state, two *attestation* protocols are available. As the uniqueness of every TPM leads to privacy concerns, they provide pseudonymity, resp., anonymity. Both protocols rest on Attestation Identity Keys (AIKs) which are placeholders for the EK. An AIK is a 1024 bit RSA key whose private portion is sealed inside the TPM. The simpler protocol Remote Attestation (RA) offers pseudonymity employing a trusted third party, the Privacy CA (PCA, see [3]), which issues a credential stating that the respective AIK is generated by a sound TPM within a valid platform. The system state is measured by a reporting process with the TPM as central reporting authority receiving measurement values and calculating a unique representation of the state using hash values. For this the TPM has several Platform Configuration Registers (PCR). Beginning with the system boot each component reports a measurement value, e.g., a hash value over the BIOS, to the TPM and stores it in a log file. During RA the communication partner acting as verifier receives this log file and the corresponding PCR value. The verifier can then decide if the device is in a configuration which is trustworthy from his perspective. Apart from RA, the TCG has defined Direct Anonymous Attestation. This involved protocol is based on a zero knowledge proof but due to certain constraints of the hardware it is not implemented in current TPMs.

AIKs are crucial for applications since they can not only be used, according to TCG standards, to attest the origin and authenticity of a trust measurement, but also to authenticate other keys generated by the TPM. Before an AIK can testify the authenticity of any data, a PCA has to issue a creden-

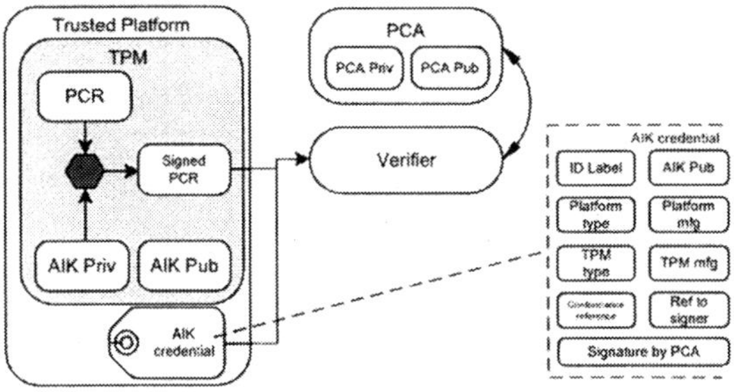

Fig. 1. Remote Attestation process.

tial for it. This credential together with the AIK can therefore be used as an identity for this platform. The protocol for issuing this credential consists in three basic steps. First, the TPM generates an RSA key pair by performing the `TPM_MakeIdentity` command. The resulting public key together with certain credentials identifying the platform is then transferred to the PCA. Second, the PCA verifies the correctness of the produced credentials and the AIK signature. If they are valid the PCA creates the AIK credential which contains an identity label, the AIK public key, and information about the TPM and the platform. A special structure containing the AIK credential is created which is used in step three to activate the AIK by executing the `TPM_ActivateIdentity` command. So far, the TCG-specified protocol is not completely secure, since between steps two and three, some kind of handshake between PCA and platform is missing. The existing protocol could sensibly be enhanced by a challenge/response part to verify the link between the credentials offered in step one and used in step two, and the issuing TPM. The remote attestation process is shown in figure 1.

Beside the attestation methods TC offers a concept to bind data blobs to a single instantiation and state of a TPM. The `TPM_unbind` operation takes the data blob that is the result of a `Tspi_Data_Bind` command and decrypts it for export to the user. The caller must authorise the use of the key to decrypt the incoming blob. In consequence this data blob is only accessible if the platform is in the namely state which is associated with the respective PCR value.

A mobile version of the TPM is currently being defined by the TCG's Mobile Phone Working Group [4]. This Mobile Trusted Module (MTM) differs significantly from the TPM of the PC world and is in fact more powerful in some respects. In particular, it contains a built-in verifier for attestation requests, substituting partly for an external PCA. Both TPM and MTM are a basis for application architectures. Trusted Computing affects the world of networked PCs but also heavily impacts the mobile industry. Accordingly, one of our applications, see section 4.2, is a mobile one. The concept for ticket system we present in section 3 is in fact network agnostic and can be applied to the Internet as well the mobile world. Further mobile scenarios can be found in [6, 7].

3 A TC-based Ticket System

The basic idea is to establish a (pseudonymous) ticket system using the identities embodied in the PCA-certified AIKs. Specific about our design is that tickets are generated locally on the (mobile) user device. Ticket acquisition an redemption rests solely on trusted computing methods implemented in the TPM chip embedded in the users platform. We first describe how AIKs can be turned into tickets that can be used in a ticket-based service access or IDM architecture, and then develop the processes for their acquisition and redemption.

3.1 AIKs as Tickets

For security considerations the TPM restricts the usage of AIKs. It is not possible to use AIKs as signing keys for arbitrary data and in particular to establish tickets in that way. It is therefore necessary to employ an indirection using a TPM generated signing key and certify this key by signing it with an AIK — *viz certify* it in the parlance of the TCG. Creation of a key is done by executing the `TPM_CMK_CreateKey` command, which returns an asymmetric key pair where the private portion is encrypted by the TPM for use within the TPM only. The resulting key pair is loaded into the TPM by `TPM_LoadKey` and thereafter certified by `TPM_CertifyKey`. By certifying a specific key the TPM makes the statement that "this key is held in a TPM-shielded location, and it will never be revealed". For this statement to have veracity, a challenger or verifier must trust the policies used by the entity that issued the identity and the maintenance policy of the TPM manufacturer.

This indirection creates to each AIK a certified key (by the namely AIK) that can be used for signing data, in particular the payload data of a ticket to be submitted to, and accepted by, a service. We call this key pair the *certified signing key* (CSK). CSK, AIK, together with a certificate by the PCA (see below) attesting the validity of that AIK, are the ingredients that realise a ticket for a single operation, e.g., a service access.

3.2 Ticket Acquisition and Redemption

Tickets are acquired by a *trusted agent* (TA), i.e., the user of a ticket system and associated services operating with his trusted platform, from the PCA. They are then redeemed at the *(ticket) receiving system* (RS). In both processes, a *charging provider* (CP) may occur as a third party, depending on application architectures. We now describe how these operations proceed.

Note that we do not distinguish between public and private key portions of a certificate establishing a credential. As a notation, the credential of some certified entity Cert(*entity*, *certificate*) means the union of the public key Pub(*certificate*) and the entity signed with the certificate's private key, $entity_{\mathrm{Priv}(certificate)}$. Verifying a credential means to check this digital signature.

An interesting option is that the credentials issued by the PCA for a AIKs can be designed as *group credentials*, i.e., they do not identify a single AIK *viz* ticket but rather its price or value group g chosen from a predetermined set indexed by the natural numbers $g \in \{1, \ldots, G\}$. The group replaces an individual identity of a platform and many TAs will get the same group certificate. Only the PCA can potentially resolve the individual identity of a platform. This allows combination of a value proposition with privacy protection, as the groups are used to implement price and value discrimination of tickets. The PCA is free in the choice of methods to implement group certificates, e.g., by simply using the same key pair for the group or by sophisticated group signature schemes [5].

If a TA wants to acquire a rating ticket from group g, he first generates an AIK using the `TPM_MakeIdentity` command. Next, TA requests from the PCA a credential for this AIK, belonging to group g, by sending AIK, group identifier and supplementary data as required by TCG protocols, to the PCA. The PCA now knows the identity of the TA. This can be used to perform a charging for the ticket, either by contacting CP or by the PCA itself (how charging actually works is not in the scope of this paper). It is important that, at this stage, an authorisation decision on the ticket generation can be made by the PCA, for instance to blacklist misbehaving participants. If the authorisation succeeds (and not earlier, to save bandwidth and resources), the PCA performs a handshake operation with the TA to ensure that the AIK has actually been generated by the particular TPM in question. Upon success, the PCA generates the credential Cert(AIK, g) certifying that the AIK belongs to group g. The credential is transferred back to TA, where finally the `TPM_ActivateIdentity` command is executed to enable subsequent usage of this AIK. The process is shown on the left hand side of Figure 2.

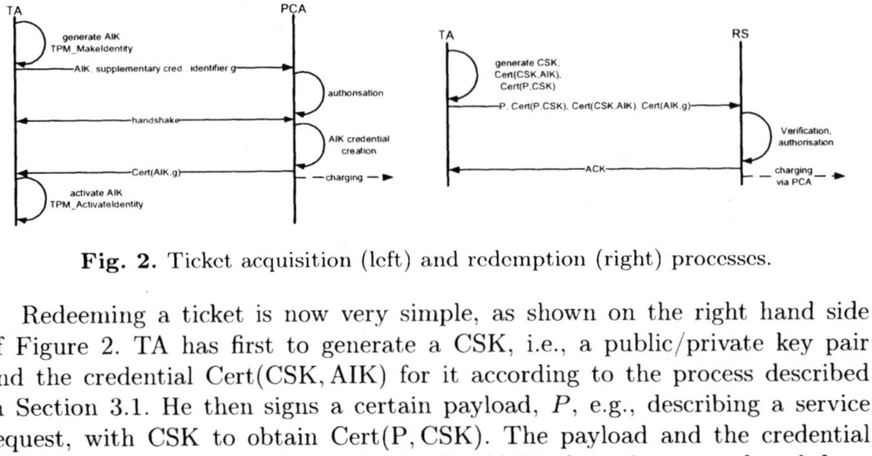

Fig. 2. Ticket acquisition (left) and redemption (right) processes.

Redeeming a ticket is now very simple, as shown on the right hand side of Figure 2. TA has first to generate a CSK, i.e., a public/private key pair and the credential Cert(CSK, AIK) for it according to the process described in Section 3.1. He then signs a certain payload, P, e.g., describing a service request, with CSK to obtain Cert(P, CSK). The payload and the credential chain Cert(P, CSK), Cert(CSK, AIK), Cert(AIK, g) is then transferred from TA to RS and this set of data embodies the ticket proper (we do not discuss a particular data format for the ticket). RS verifies this chain and makes an authorisation decision, for instance to implement a protection against multiple spending. Finally, RS acknowledges receipt of P and optionally initiates another charging operation (ex post charging) via PCA.

3.3 A Generic Architecture for Service Access

The embedding of the described ticket acquisition and redemption into an application system and business context offers many variants. A very basic scenario is shown in Figure 3. Here, a trusted agent (user) would like to access some service, and buys a ticket of a certain value from the PCA. The ticket belongs to a certain group which can represent statements such as "for usage with Service n", and a certain value, monetary or intangible, e.g., in a rebate scheme. The user then issues a service request as payload in the ticket redemption toward RS. The TA pays for the ticket at the CP at the time of redemption of the ticket and the CP distributes revenue shares between himself, PCA, and RS, according to service level agreements. RS, in turn, remunerates the service (an acknowledgement of service processing is omitted for simplicity).

This realises an access control scheme to multiple services mediated by PCA and RS, yielding three essential benefits: 1. non-repudiation by the chain of credentials, 2. accountability by resolution of the TA's identity through PCA, and 3. pseudonymity by separation of duties. The PCA/RS combination plays a very central role for the control of identities embodied in the pseudonymous tickets that PCA issues. It is in fact an embodiment of the role of an identity provider in a ticket-based identity management (IDM) system. That TC can be used to model IDM was outlined in [6, 7].

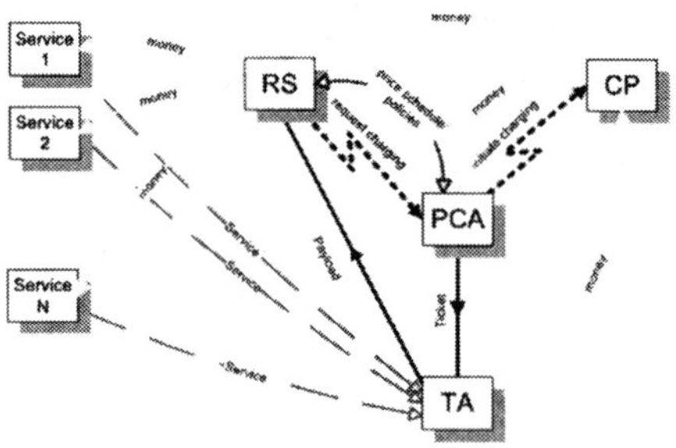

Fig. 3. A generic architecture using TC-based tickets.

Though the separation of duties between PCA and CP allows in principle even for anonymity of the person using a TA, since only upon charging this person must be identified by credit card account or other means, this may not be the best option. In fact this would loose some accountability of the TA users. While RS may be able to obtain personal identities from PCA if pertinent contractual relationships are in place, e.g., if fraud by a TA user is suspected, data protection regulations may prevent a CP from unveiling personal identities. A second role played by the PCA is the initiation of charging. With respect to the revenues from ticket sales, a natural approach is a sharing between RS and PCA (and CP for its service). RS and PCA negotiate and implement policies for authorisation within the ticket acquisition and redemption processes, e.g., to prevent double spending or to blacklist misbehaving users. In collaboration between PCA and RS, practically any price schedule can be realised. This architecture naturally extends to an arbitrary number of receiving systems to which PCA offers ticket management and pricing as services. An extension would be to let TA express values of tickets by using different (groups of) CSKs. In this way tickets can be associated with additional certified attributes, e.g., priorities.

3.4 Security and Privacy

The presented method for the management of tickets provides for perfect pseudonymity of the participants toward the system. In fact, only PCA is able to de-anonymise users. For the namely reason only PCA can initiate a charging, since only he knows (or is able to know) the identity of a TA and can link it to the identity of the corresponding participant. To keep this pseudonymity strength, it is essential that our concept relies only on genuine TPM functionality, and in particular avoids the usage of trusted software. If there was a trusted software managing tickets in some way at the side of TA, then this software, and the state of the platform would have to be attested both in ticket acquisition and redemption. To this end the TC protocols for remote attestation transfers trust measurements and measurement logs to the corresponding verifier (PCA or RS in our case). These data can however — and this is a principal problem with remote attestation — be used to individualise the trusted platform, if, as in the PC domain, the number of system states and different measurement logs created at boot time, is very large in relation to the number of users of a TC-based service. Besides, avoiding remote attestation saves bandwidth and resources consumption. Since in this case no trust can be laid in the TA for ticket management, some kind of double, or multiple, spending protection or usage authorisation is needed at RS upon ticket redemption.

On the other hand security necessitates additional means of protection of content in transit. In many applications, for instance if confidentiality of transported payload is a protection target, trusted software usage cannot be avoided We show in Section 4.2 how TC can be used to establish end-to-end protection for P, but this definitely requires trusted software clients at both ends.

4 Two Applications

4.1 Price Scheduling in Pseudonymous Rating Systems

This application has been outlined in [8]. Electronic market places are increasingly occupied by self-organising communities and exhibit the characteristics of the so-called long tail economy [9]. That is, the classical asymmetry between suppliers and consumers is lifted. Buyers and sellers are often even in numbers and may change their roles dynamically. Information and physical goods are offered in large numbers and diversity and with potentially small demand for each single one. Matchmaking and orientation of buyers is difficult in a long tail economy, long term relationships are hard to build, and trust between trade partners must be established somehow [10]. Common approaches let market players provide the necessary guidance. This is mostly embodied in reputation systems by which buyers and sellers rate each other and the goods sold, or recommendation systems attempting to predict items that a user may be interested in, given some information about the user's profile. Reputation systems, according to Paul Resnick *et al.* [11] "seek to establish the shadow of the future [the expectation of reciprocity or retaliation in future interactions, cf. [12]] to each transaction by creating an expectation that other people will look back on it". The goal is to establish a homogeneous market for honest participants.

Existing reputation systems are fragile, in that they can easily be distorted or abused even within the frame of laws governing them. 'Attacks' of this kind threaten the integrity of the informational content of the system. Calsses of unfair behaviour are [13]: 1. *Ballot stuffing*: A seller colludes with a group of buyers to be given unfairly high ratings. 2. *Bad-mouthing*: Sellers and buyers collude to rate other sellers unfairly low to drive them out of the market. 3. *Negative discrimination*: Sellers provide good services only to a small, restricted group of buyers. 4. *Positive discrimination*: Sellers provide exceptionally good service to some buyers to improve their ratings. A situation of controlled anonymity in which the market place knows the identity of participants and keeps track of all transactions and ratings, but conceals the identity of buyers and sellers, is identified as essential to avoid unfair behaviour. E.g., anonymity is an effective protection against bad-mouthing, but cannot work for ballot stuffing as sellers can give hidden indications of their identities to colluders.

The best known individual attack on reputation systems uses Sybils to obtain a disproportionately large influence [14]. Friedman and Resnick [15] point to the general problem of 'cheapness' of pseudonyms in reputation systems, since with name changes dishonest players easily shed negative reputation, as corroborated theoretically in [16]. However, an indiscriminate pricing of identities for the submission of ratings poses an undesired entry deterrent. It seems therefore plausible that reputation systems should be based on pseudonyms which allow for a flexible forward pricing.

While related work addresses particular vulnerabilities [17], or proposes general frameworks to ensure accountability in reputation systems while maintaining anonymity [18, 19], we here propose a simple mechanism to introduce arbitrary costs for pseudonyms. The separation of duties between PCA and RS in our ticket system implements here precisely the controlled anonymity desired for reputation systems through the properties 1.–3. mentioned in Section 3.3.

Again, the generic ticket system can be embedded in various ways into a (commercial) reputation system. If a TA user wants to express a rating about another user (for example, a buyer about a seller, a seller about a buyer), he buys a *rating ticket* from the PCA. The group attribute of the ticket expresses a value proposition for the rating, e.g., an impact factor used by the rating system to calculate weighted overall ratings, as well as an attribution to a particular rating system. The user then formulates the rating and sends it to RS as ticket payload, and charging is executed. The result would be a rating statement about another participant of the rating system which is trustworthy, accountable, but protected as a pseudonym. This enables the resolution of one important problem in reputation systems, namely accountability of users, i.e., the possibility to trace back malicious ones and threaten them with consequences. Based on the trusted ticket system, price schedules can be adapted to the requirements of rating systems as laid out above. On the extreme ends of the spectrum are cost-free registration of ratings by PCA, ensuring only accountability, and increasing charges with the number of ratings (or, e.g., their frequency). Even reverse charging, i.e., paying incentives for ratings, e.g., such of good quality, is possible.

4.2 Content Protection for Push Services

Workers occupied with 'nomadic' tasks depend on infrastructures for easy and swift access to required data. E-Mail push services like RIM's Blackberry conquer this market with huge success, and aim at high availability and ease of use. Push services are characterised by the ability to notify end users of new content. For an e-mail service the end user device is activated by the mail server, gets new mail, and notifies the user. The basic method for this has been formulated for instance in the standards of the Open Mobile Alliance (OMA, see [21]). Some providers have extended their range to enable access to company databases and implement loosely coupled work-flows incorporating nomadic workers.

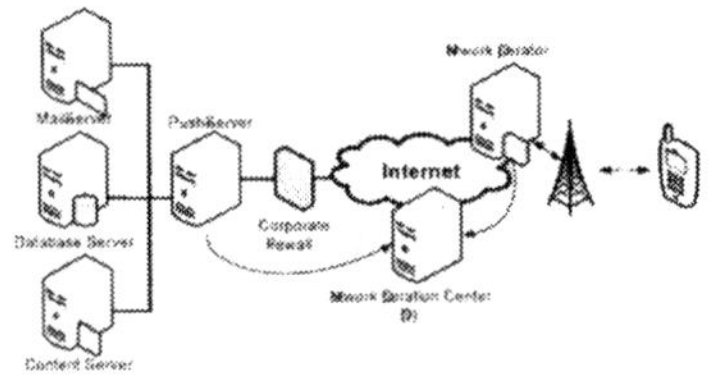

Fig. 4. A centralised architecture

Due to the high value of the exchanged data these systems are threatened by, even professional, attackers, raising the requirement to protect the distribution of pushed data. Security concerns can be grouped in two main areas. First, data has to be protected in transit to the device, and confidentiality is to be maintained. Second, after the data is delivered it has to be protected against unauthorised access. The latter problem is of practical importance in use cases like the mentioned e-mail push, but also for SMS delivery, and other data synchronisation processes between a central data base and a mobile device. Current approaches to this challenge are predominantly using software tokens, e.g., PKCS#7, to secure message transport and storage. Such solutions however suffer from the drawback that an attacker can extract keys from memory during encryption or decryption of a data block. Smart cards are a more evolved approach, but in the mobile domain no standard has become prevalent.

Figure 4 illustrates the widely used, centralised push architecture. In its centre a Network Operation Center (NOC) performs all tasks regarding the communication to the mobile devices. The data destined for the mobile devices are stored in sources like mail servers. These sources excite the push server and deliver the data. Due to this activation the push server either requests a channel to the mobile device managed by the NOC or delivers the data to the NOC which in turn stores them until they are handed to the mobile device. From a company's view the management costs are low as there is no additional effort needed to maintain, e.g., a special firewall configuration. The decentralised counterpart includes direct communication between push server and mobile device, requiring access over, e.g., the Internet to servers behind a company firewall, in turn necessitating special protection of the internal infrastructure. Taking a malicious service provider into consideration privacy concerns are added to the general ones regarding transport security. Potentially the NOC can access every message which is sent. Thus, the message content could be extracted and disclosed by the NOC operator. Moreover, analysis of the collaboration between active users becomes possible. Both attacks have to be treated in the protocol design to enable end-to-end security and to conceal all sensitive information.

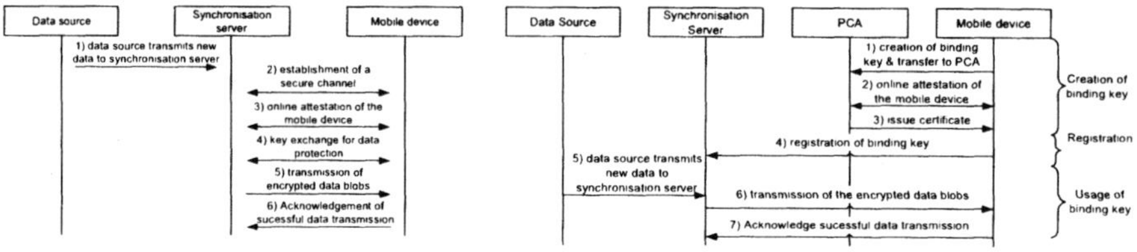

Fig. 5. Scenarios based on blob sealing (left) resp. key sealing (right)

Protection of content is a major use case for trusted computing [20]. We first present basic options to protect push content, and then describe the integration with th trusted ticket system of Section 3. Based on blob binding (see Section 2) the simplest scenario see the left diagram in Figure 5. First, the data source signals the synchronisation server (SyncS) which then locates the target device, establishes communication, and controls the synchronisation relying on, e.g., OMA data synchronisation. Channel security can be realised using Transport Layer Security. Remote attestation of the device and key exchange for payload encryption are performed. The data is transferred to the device and stored in sealed blobs, see [2, Chapter 12], only accessible in the determined state of this unique device. This approach suffers from latency produced by the Steps 2-4, in particular attestation creates computational load and produces some traffic.

An approach to meet this challenge is shown on the right hand side of Figure 5. SyncS encrypts the data with a public part of a key pair. The use of the corresponding private part is restricted by a PCR value. To grant trust in this public key the SyncS requires a certificate issued by a PCA, and a certified PCR value, signifying, e.g., the presence of an e-mail application in a certain configuration and a well defined environment. The PCA which certifies the platform keys can actually be used here to issue certificates augmented by the information of the PCR value. This variant of an AIK is further called a *binding key*. Step 1 transmits the public portion of a key pair to the designated PCA for content encryption keys. Remote attestation is performed and a certificate is created stating that the key originates from a TP and is usable if and only if the platform is in a certain state. This certificate is transmitted to the mobile device, and then, together with the binding key, to SyncS. Steps 1 to 4 only have to be performed once during roll out of the device or take ownership by its user. In Step 5 the data is transmitted to SyncS, which can now encrypt the data with the binding key or with a hybrid scheme. Data transmission is executed in Steps 5–7. Note that the first presented method is much more flexible than the second one, since in the former the server can decide each time if the particular device can be considered as trustworthy.

The combination of the ticket system with the content protection system proceeds as follows. After it has been activated, the mobile device uses a ticket obtained from the PCA as a token to access SyncS which can either be the RS itself or an associated service. The ticket AIK cannot be used for data encryption, but the ticket payload can carry the mentioned public key for content encryption, *and* its certificate. The ticket PCA can act concurrently as the CA certifying the binding key or in separation from it. Ticket grouping or prioritising can be used advantageously in such a scheme, e.g., for attribution of bandwidth to a request and load balancing.

5 Conclusions

We have shown how to generate and use tickets based on TC, and have provided theoretical proof-of-concept in two independent application scenarios employing trusted tickets. What we have constructed is essentially a payment system with a trusted third party guaranteeing pseudonymity. It is therefore worthwhile to compare our method with the use case scenario "Mobile payment" of TCG's Mobile Phone Working Group Use Case Scenarios [20, Section 8]. There, the focus lies on device-side support of payment operations on a mobile phone which is turned into a trusted platform. This always involves a trusted software on the device which is not required in our approach. On the other hand this is only possible through the introduction of a trusted third party, the PCA with its extended duties. Thus we lack the universality of client-side solutions. Yet we have shown that a very simple ticket system with strong pseudonymity can be established resting solely on the most basic TPM functions.

It should be noted that our applications use TC in a way very different from Digital Rights Management (DRM), which is often considered as the sole use for TC. Both applications bind the economic value to a particular instantiation of the TPM. If this trust anchor breaks, only a limited damage can occur as the damage is restricted in space and time, e.g., to a single data synchronisation in a push service or submission of a single reputation. In contrast, if a single TPM in a DRM system breaks, the protected digital good can be converted into an unprotected version which can be freely distributed on a large scale, causing heavy monetary losses to its owner. It is interesting to note that introducing TC yields a secondary user bound identification token. Due to the take ownership procedure of the TPM it is bound to a certain user. Therefore it is in its function very similar to a SIM as it is also possible to migrate the relevant parts from one TPM to the next. One may ask whether two different identification tokens will survive in future TC-enabled mobile devices.

References

1. Massachusetts Institute of Technology: Kerberos: The Network Authentication Protocol. http://web.mit.edu/kerberos/
2. Trusted Computing Group: TCG TPM specification version 1.2 revision 94. Technical report, TCG (2006)
3. Trusted Computing Group: TCG Infrastructure Working Group Reference Architecture for Interoperability (Part I) V. 1.0 Rev. 1. TCG (2005)

4. Trusted Computing Group: TCG Mobile Trusted Module Specification. Specification version 0.9 Revision 1. Technical report, TCG (2006)
5. Chaum, D., van Heyst, E.: Group signatures. In Davies, D., ed.: Advances in Cryptology - EUROCRYPT '91. Volume 547 of Lecture Notes in Computer Science, Berlin, Heidelberg, Springer-Verlag (1991) 257–265
6. Kuntze, N., Schmidt, A.U.: Transitive trust in mobile scenarios. In Müller, G., ed.: Proceedings of the International Conference on Emerging Trends in Information and Communication Security (ETRICS 2006). Volume 3995 of Lecture Notes in Computer Science (LNCS), Springer-Verlag (2006) 73–85
7. Kuntze, N., Schmidt, A.U.: Trusted computing in mobile action. In Venter, H.S., Eloff, J.H.P., Labuschagne, L., Eloff, M.M., eds.: Proceedings of the Information Security South Africa (ISSA) Conference (2006)
8. Kuntze, N., Schmidt, A.U.: Employing Trusted Computing for the forward pricing of pseudonyms in reputation systems. Workshop Virtual Goods at the Conference AXMEDIS 2006, Leeds, UK, 13.–15. Dec. 2006
9. Anderson, C.: The Long Tail. Wired. October 2004. http://web.archive.org/web/20041127085645/http://www.wired.com/wired/archive/12.10/tail.html
10. Bakos, Y.: The emerging role of electronic marketplaces on the internet. Commun. ACM **41** (1998) 35–42
11. Resnick, P., Kuwabara, K., Zeckhauser, R., Friedman, E.: Reputation systems. Communications of the ACM **43** (2000) 45 – 48
12. Axelrod, R.: The Evolution of Cooperation. Basic Books, New York (1984)
13. Dellarocas, C.: Immunizing online reputation reporting systems against unfair ratings and discriminatory behavior. In: ACM Conference on Electronic Commerce. (2000) 150–157
14. Douceur, J.R.: The sybil attack. In Druschel, P., Kaashoek, F., Rowstron, A., eds.: Peer-to-Peer Systems: First InternationalWorkshop, IPTPS 2002 Cambridge, MA, USA, March 7-8, 2002. Volume 2429 of Lecture Notes in Computer Science, Springer-Verlag (2002) 251–260
15. Friedman, E.J., Resnick, P.: The social cost of cheap pseudonyms. Journal of Economics & Management Strategy **10** (2001) 173–199
16. Dellarocas, C.: Sanctioning reputation mechanisms in online trading environments with moral hazard. MIT Sloan Working Paper No. 4297-03 (2004)
17. Cheng, A., Friedman, E.: Sybilproof reputation mechanisms. In: P2PECON '05: Proceeding of the 2005 ACM SIGCOMM workshop on Economics of peer-to-peer systems, ACM Press (2005) 128–132
18. Buttyan, L., Hubaux, J.P.: Accountable anonymous access to services in mobile communication systems. In: Proceedings of the 18th IEEE Symposium on Reliable Distributed Systems. (1999) 384–389
19. Zieglera, G., Farkas, C., Lõrincz, A.: A framework for anonymous but accountable self-organizing communities. Inform. and Software Technol. **48** (2006) 726–744
20. Trusted Computing Group: Mobile Phone Working Group Use Case Scenarios - v 2.7. Technical report, TCG (2005)
21. Open Mobile Alliance: Push architecture. draft version 2.2 - 20 jan 2006. oma-ad-push-v2_2-20060120-d. Technical report, Open Mobile Alliance (2006)

Trust Evaluation for Web Applications based on Behavioral Analysis

Luiz Fernando Rust C. Carmo, Breno G. de Oliveira and Augusto C. Braga
Computer Center (NCE) – Federal University of Rio de Janeiro (UFRJ)
Caixa Postal 2324 – 20.010-974 – Rio de Janeiro – RJ – Brasil
{rust,breno,augustocesar}@nce.ufrj.br

Abstract. This paper deals with a joint use of a trust evaluation approach and access control mechanisms for improving security in Web-usage. Trust evaluation is achieved by means of both behavioral evaluation and credentials exchange, in such way that transitions among different access policies are automatically fired whenever a user behavior is validated. Behavioral analysis uses machine-learning techniques to gain knowledge about users navigation tracks, creating a user signature to be compared with a current behavior of the respective user. This mechanism is validated through experimental evaluation.

1 Introduction

Nowadays there is a huge concern for Web application security. The public key infrastructure (PKI) is definitely a great ally in solving many security issues, especially those related to authentication. The difference between authentication and authorization is discussed in [1]: (i) an authentication service proves that the identity of an object/subject is in fact the one it claims to have; while (ii) authorization means the grant of permission based on the authenticated identification. This latter definition can be altered with the introduction of the "trust" concept: usually an entity can say that it "trusts" another one whenever it assumes that the second entity will behave exactly as it expects. This way authorization can be rewritten as the "grant of permission based on the deposited trust". The fact is that, maybe more important than knowing who you are relating to, is knowing how this person/object will behave. On the other hand, a fraudless authentication is still the best way to foresee an announced behavior profile, and the combination of authentication with continuous behavioral analysis enables a gradual verification of the coherence between both factors, generating a trust consolidation.

It has been seen recently a sensitive increase in proposals to incorporate trust based mechanisms in Web applications, Web services and ubiquitous computing. Most of those mechanisms propose the use of digital credentials for an effective

Please use the following format when citing this chapter:

da Costa Carmo, L., de Oliveira, B., and Braga, A., 2007, in IFIP International Federation for Information Processing, Volume 232, New Approaches for Security, Privacy and Trust in Complex Environments, eds. Venter, H., Eloff, M., Labuschagne, L., Eloff, J., von Solms, R., (Boston: Springer), pp. 61–72.

management in the establishment of trust. The goal is to, after an initial authentication stage, manage the user's demands and increase the level of trust through the exchange of credentials in predetermined moments. In order to do that, trust management is linked to an access control mechanism in a granular way (i.e. RBAC [1]) so the evolution of the trust relationship implicates an alteration of the access privileges given to this user.

A classic example of this kind of approach is the relationship between a user and a shopping *website* [2]: after the authentication, the user (i) browses the *site* and selects a given object to buy; at this time there is a need of more access privileges to (ii) consolidate the payment; this transition is controlled by a credit card number (credential example) that, in case of success, implies a trust level increase and the attribution of a new "role" in the access policy, providing the necessary privileges for the (iii) continuity of the operation.

This paper basically proposes a trust evaluation strategy guided not only by the gradual disclosure of credentials, but also by a behavioral evaluation mechanism based on the continuous analysis of the current conduct of a user vis-à-vis with its past activities, generating the grounds for a possible evolution in the trust level. In the previous shopping *website* example, if the user is an identified client, it is possible to gradually establish a certain signature for his browsing habits in a way that the browsing trajectory is analyzed against this signature in each new operation, promoting an automatic increase in the trust level, without the need for an exchange of credentials.

The basic idea is to develop a continuous user behavioral evaluation system, where trust and access restrictions can be inflicted automatically in Web applications. However, the mechanism is not restricted to Web applications, and the ubiquitous computing seems to enforce even more the role of trust, not only for the inherently high decentralization, but also for the propagated non-intrusive *modus operandi*. In this kind of application, trust would completely replace traditional authentication methods, supporting the concept of free users (without certificates, logins or passwords).

Web services are also gaining increased importance as technologies enabling the development of service oriented distributed applications. And, along with the crescent number of services, specially in corporate networks, there is also a growth in the complexity required to authenticate and administrate user privileges, creating a favorable environment for the use of the trust concept [3].

2 Related Work

Approaches bringing together access control policy models and trust managers are relatively new and seek the establishment of trust in a gradual and interactive way, to dynamically update access privileges [4].

In [2] it is proposed a trust negotiation *framework* (*Trust-Serv*) for Web services. The trust relationship evolves through the exchange of credentials controlled by a state machine associated with the application. Some examples of credentials are credit cards, passports and membership documents. The credential attributes are evaluated in order to enable, or not, a state movement and the corresponding alteration in the user's access profile. [5] proposes an adaptive access control and trust negotiation *framework* that combines an access control and authorization API and a trust manager (*TrustBuilder*), in order to control when, and how, sensitive information can be revealed. This proposal is based on a reactive analysis in face of a failure event, i.e, wrong credentials, implicates a greater suspicion level on a user, which in turn implicates in access privilege restrictions.

Both previous works use credentials to inflict security: the difference is that the former is proactive — increasing trust upon success, and the latter is reactive — increasing the suspicion (lowering trust) upon failure. This article's approach does not discard the use of credentials, but suggests a joint use of behavioral analysis for trust evolution.

[3] proposes a trust evaluation mechanism in Web services based in behavioral analysis through continuous tracking of a user. The goal is to provide a self-manageable mechanism for access control in an environment of Web services federations. The trust level is exponentially modeled as a function of the services required by the user: increases for certain classes of expected services and decreases for others.

One of the main differences between this approach and the proposed work is in the way that the user's behavior is evaluated. Basically, previous proposal start from an initial mapping of services/functions available in the provider in predetermined paths that, if followed, enables one to increase the trust on the user. Our proposal evaluates the user's behavior in function of his past (usage *logs*) with the purpose of increasing the trust on a user's identity (if he is really who he claims to be), using a learning based behavioral analysis technique.

Security systems based on behavioral analysis by learning can be classified in two categories according to the kind of "behavior" studied: (i) *Physical behavior* – attempts to learn some personal characteristic of a user, i.e: patterns in keyboard typing or mouse use; and (ii) *contextual behavior* – attempts to learn a user's service utilization profile, i.e: UNIX commands, Web navigation, etc. The first category is strongly related to complementary authentication mechanisms, while the latter is disseminated in the Intrusion Detection domain.

A heavily explored approach in literature, in the "physical behavior" category, consists of generating a signature from the individual dynamics of keyboard use [6, 7, 8]. Basically, this method does not use the information being typed, but the rhythm in which it is typed — time gap between two key strokes and duration of a key stroke. Collected data are modeled in fixed length arrays and, for each new authentication, a new array is created and compared to the initial one, generating a similarity index. This method offers as its main disadvantage the current tendency for the obsolescence of text-based interfaces over mouse-driven ones.

[9] proposes a re-authentication mechanism based on mouse movements. This mechanism captures mouse information (instant position, click, double click, etc) and, after creating a regular behavior model, uses a decision tree classifier to validate the current behavior and re-authenticate the user.

An example of contextual behavioral analysis approach is the work of [10] for anomaly detection, comprising both intrusion detection and the identification of hostile behavior of authenticated users. The focus of this work is the analysis of command lines against the history of commands issued by the user, through *Instance-based Learning* (IBL) [11]. Unlike the proposal of this article, there is no concern in characterizing a user's individual behavior, but only in classify it as "normal".

Another kind of user's behavioral analysis approach, directly related to Web applications, is directed to the customization of a website's navigability. [12] propose the use of data mining techniques on *Web logs*, in order to inflict upon different user's access profiles and, automatically, adapt a *website*'s navigation options.

In conclusion, the innovative character of the approach presented in this work is supported by two main factors:

1. the use of a learning based behavioral evaluation mechanism to offer grounds for the evolution of trust;
2. proposal of a behavioral evaluation mechanism based on Web navigation path analysis, superimposed to a historical contextual signature.

3 Trust Evaluation

The concept of trust used in this work can be informally defined as a measurement of how sure the application provider is about the identity of a user and, consequently, of the way in which the user will behave.

In [2] the evolution of trust is controlled by a finite state machine (*Trust-Serv* model) previously specified, where the states represent the current level of trust in a relationship. Each state is associated to a specific access policy (i.e.: a role in a RBAC model), while the state transition is controlled by exchange of credentials, predictions/obligations (services that need to be executed first) and *timeouts*. Figure 1 describes a small excerpt of a state machine example used in the trust negotiation in *Trust-Serv*. This machine has two states, Client and Reviewer, each with its own required level of trust and controlled by a specific access policy (A & B). The transition between these two states is safeguarded by the exchange of credentials address and credit card.

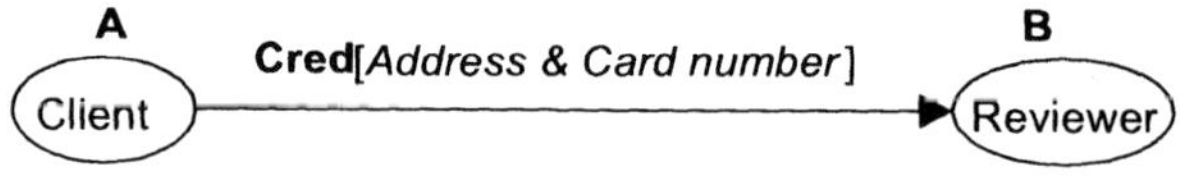

Fig. 1: Trust negotiation model

The concept of trust level/access policy is captured by the definition of a macro-state, while states represent the pages of a web application. A change from one macro-state to another (implying a change in the access policy) is performed automatically by the result of a behavioral evaluation or, in case of insucccess, by an explicit negotiation via exchange of credentials (figure 2).

Definition 3.1. A trust evaluation scenery C is defined by the 6-tuple:
$$(MacroStates^C, States^C, Transitions^C, Profiles^C, \varphi^C, \omega^C)$$

- *MacroStates*^{C} is the set of macro-states of *C*, where each *macro-state* M is a subset of *States*^{C}
- *States*^{C} is the set of states of *C* (pages)
- *Transitions*^{C} is the set of transitions of *C*
- *Profiles* is the set of access profiles (roles) associated to *C*
- φ^C transition attribution function, that associates every transition to a state of origin and to a states of destination

  φ^C: *Transitions* → *States*^{C} x *States*^{C}
- ω^C is the access profile attribution function, that associates each profile to a set of macro states

  ω^C: *Profiles*^{C} → *Set of the parts of Macro-States*^{C}

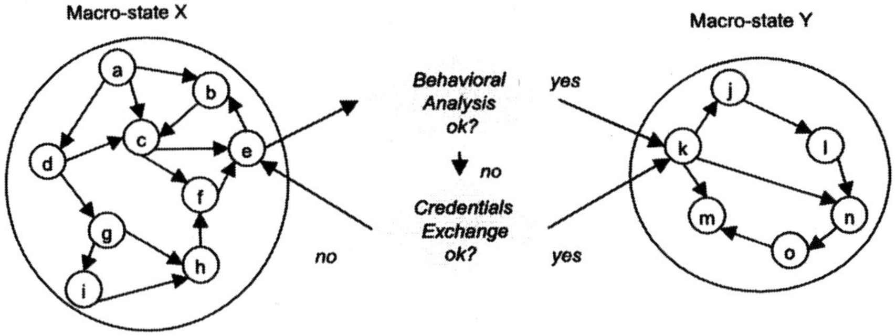

Fig.2: Macro-states x Trust evaluation

Definition 3.2. The specific transitions between the macro states may be captured by the set denominated:

$$MacroTransitions^C = \{t \in Transitions^C \mid \varphi(t) = (a,b) \wedge (a \in m_1, b \in m_2 : m_1 \neq m_2)\}$$

Definition 3.3. Let V^C be the subset of *MacroTransitions*^{C} experimented during the user's section in a *C* scenario, let the *BehaviouralTrust* and the *Credential* be function with V^C domain and boolean range, the user's section is set according to the evaluation strategy proposed if the following condition is satisfied :

$$\forall t \in V^C : BehavioralTrust\ (t) \vee Credential(t) = true$$

It is important to stand out that there is a dependence relationship between the result of the evaluation of the behavioral trust and the execution of the evaluation through credentials; the second one goes only in the case of a negative evaluation of the first (figure 2). This kind of approach, practically establishing the credentials switch as a redundancy, has significant impacts in the requirements imposed to the behavioral analysis' mechanisms. The concern with false negatives almost disappears since the non-identification of a user's behavior doesn't cause any degradation in the section in course, it only leads to the solving of the redundant step of credentials' exchange.
On the other hand, a single use of behavioral evaluation would make possible to find out the following anomalous conducts: (i) a system's authenticated user that makes a legitimate use to abuse of the system's resources, (ii) the sporadic use by a colleague at work "that asks to borrow" a workstation, (iii) an automated attack launched by a

relatively naive user through a typical sequence of attacks. With the combined use of a credentials' exchange mechanism, the condition (i) naturally looses its' effectiveness, since it is very probable that an authenticated user be also successful in an exchange of credentials.

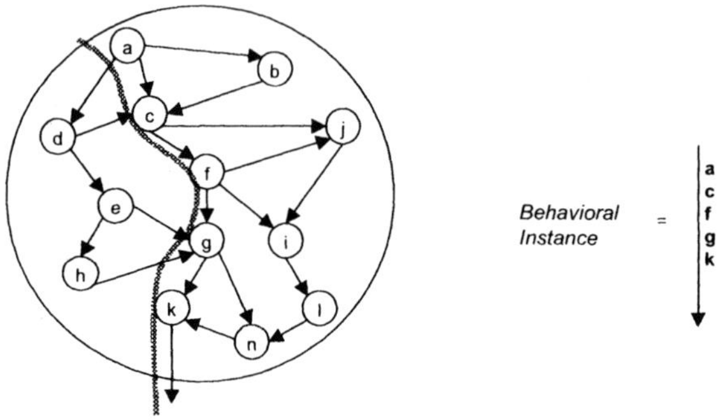

Fig. 3: Example of behavioral instance

4 Behavioral evaluation

This section analyzes the problem of behavioral evaluation through learning, in a way that characterizes and differentiates each individual/system's behavior in terms of a discrete data sequence. The characterization of a user's typical behavior is a great challenge, because, besides the inherent variability, there is a change in the regular used pattern as a natural consequence of the user's absorption of new knowledge. The use of a learning machine allows training a classifier with a user's historical data, so that it is possible to distinguish different behaviors, considering both variability and the evolutive aspect. In this section we examine methods to collect a user's behavioral signature based on learning, and the appropriate definition of similarity according to the required context.

4.1 Behavioral Signature Collecting

Many of the traditional learning approaches is not suitable for behavioral differentiation due to the class of data being processed, i.e. discrete elements with nominal values. Neural networks [13] have proved to be useful to continuous series of numerical values, typically using *Euclidean Distance* for similarity computation, but there is a major limitation for using it in behavioral differentiation: the necessity of retraining for every new user [6]. A very popular and generic class of learning machine techniques is the *Instance-based Learning* (IBL). In this model, a concept is represented implicitly by a set of instances that exemplify it (dictionary). In our situation, it is possible to directly apply a very simple method of the IBL learning model, in which every behavioral instance is directly classified according to the generating user. This way, the behavioral signature is represented by a set of a specific user's behavioral instances (figure 3), generated in every macro-transition.

Definition 4.1. Let I be a set of indexes; the behavioral instance concept *ic* and the behavioral signature *ac* may be defined as:

$$ic = \{e_i \in States^C \mid i \in I\}$$
$$ac = \{ic_i \mid i \in I\}$$

4.2 Behavioral Trust Measure

The degree of similarity S is a function of two behavioral instances which expresses a measure of how alike those behaviors are. We examined several measures for computing the similarity between two discrete-valued temporal instances. Here we describe the measure that we found performs the best on average in empirical evaluations. Basically, this procedure must pinpoints pairs of identical elements and uses a cumulative calculation to give a bigger weight to identical enchained pairs (isentical subsequences). A fundamental requirement for this calculation is no restriction about different sizes between *ic* sequences (i.e.: {a,b,c,d} & {a,g,d}).

Definition 4.2. Let *a* and *b* be two behavioral instances; a preprocessing procedure is captured by the function:

$$\tau(a,b) = (\{z_0, z_1, \ldots z_{m-1}\}, \{w_0, w_1, \ldots w_{n-1}\})$$

Where $\{z_0, z_1, \ldots z_{m-1}\}$ *is the set of the length of identical subsequences between a and b;* $\{w_0, w_1, \ldots w_{n-1}\}$ *is the set of the length of different subsequences between a and b; and the behavior of the function* τ *is expressed by the pseudocode of fig.4.*

```
τ(a,b)
Let p be any position of an array i
Let w, z  be arrays of variable length
Let p_a, p_b, p_w, p_z equals the first position of
   a, b, w, z respectively
For each p_a in {p_a until last position of a}, do
   If p_a equals p_b , then
      If p_w > 0, then
         Advances p_w to the next position of w
      Add 1 to p_z
   Else, then
      If p_z > 0, then
         Advances p_z to the next position of z
      Let p_b  equals the first position of b
      Let found  equals FALSE
      For each p_b in {p_b until last position of b},
      do
         If p_a equals p_b, then
            Let p_a equals  p_b
            If p_w > 0, then
               Advances p_w to the next position of w
            Let found - TRUE
            Add 1 to p_z
            Leave the inner loop
      If found equals TRUE
         Add 1 to p_w
   Advances p_a to the next position of array b
Return arrays z e w
```

Fig. 4: Pseudocode of τ(a,b) function

For example: considering an *ic* pair *{a,g,b,c,d} and {a,b,c,d},* the application of the preprocessing function returns: *(i)* the set {1,3} meaning two identical subsequences: one of 1 element (a) and other of 3 elements (b,c,d); and (ii) the set {1} meaning one different subsequence of 1 element (g).

Definition 4.2. Let $(X,Y) = \tau(a,b)$, the similarity degree *S* between $a = (a_0, a_1, \ldots a_{m-1})$ and $b = (b_0, b_1, \ldots b_{m-1})$ is given by the following trio of functions:

$$\delta(X,Y) = Sum(X) - Sum(Y) \mid Sum(c_0, c_1, \ldots c_{m-1}) = \sum_{i=0}^{m-1} 2c_i - 1 \qquad (1)$$

$$S'(a,b) = \begin{cases} \dfrac{\delta(\tau(a,b))}{\delta(\tau(a,a))} & if \quad card(a) \geq card(b) \\ \dfrac{\delta(\tau(b,a))}{\delta(\tau(b,b))} & if \quad card(a) < card(b) \end{cases} \tag{2}$$

$$S(a,b) = \frac{S'(a,b) + 1}{2} \tag{3}$$

The advantage of this type of calculation lies on the possibility to adjust the importance given to sequential states by just exchanging the *Sum* function. Figure 5 shows a comparison between the similarity values obtained from the set of behavioral instances pairs from table 1 for both the linear equation given in (1) and the exponential one defined in (4). It is clear that the linear formula is more sensitive to small differences among sequences, which is the behavior we were looking for.

$$Sum(c_0, c_1, \ldots c_{m-1}) = \sum_{i=0}^{m-1} 3^{c_i - 1} \tag{4}$$

Table 1. Similarity for linear and exponential function Sum

a	*a g b c d*	*a g b c d*	*a g a b d d*	*a b c d e f g h*	*a a b a b c d*
b	*a b c d*	*g a b c d*	*a b c d*	*d e f g h*	*a b c d*
Linear	*0.7775*	*0.8885*	*0.7272*	*0.6330*	*0.9230*
Exponential	*0.5555*	*0.5679*	*0.5102*	*0.5164*	*0.5212*

Using *S* (similarity) is possible to calculate three independent factors that need to be considered in trust : *Comparative similarity*, *Intra-similarity* and *Inter-similarity.*

Comparative Similarity (*Scomp*) – represents the similitude between the current collected instance and the set of instances that form the signature. Essentially, its value mirrors how close this behavior is from the previously captured ones. To perform this calculation, a *similarity* function is applied between the current behavioral instance and every instance that form the signature, retaining the maximum value obtained:

$$Scomp^M = \max\{S(ic_{cur}^M, ic_i^M), \forall ic_i^M \in ac^M\} \tag{5}$$

where ic_{cur} denotes the current computational instance, and ac^M denotes the behavioral signature of the macro-transition M.

Intra-Similarity (Sintra) – is related to the quality of the user's signature, being completely independent of the current behavioral instance sample. This represents if a user has a well-formed behavior (when signature instances are repeated, or slightly different), or the opposite (when all signature instances are very different amongst themselves). Naturally, a bad-formed signature makes the user's behavioral validation process difficult. To calculate *Sintra*, we calculate the mean among every resulting values of the similarity function between all 2 to 2 arrangements of the signature instances:

$$Sintra^M = \frac{\displaystyle\sum_{\forall ic_n^M \in ac^M} \sum_{\forall ic_m^M \in ac^M} S(ic_m^M, ic_n^M)}{A_{card(ac^M),2}} \tag{6}$$

Inter-Similarity (Sinter) – represents the quality of a user signature in function of the complete set of signatures (from different users) associated to the same macro-transition. A given behavioral instance can be extremely similar to a well-formed signature, and even so, not be trusted due to a possible similarity with other existent signatures (from several users from the same scenery). Signature similarity makes the user differentiation process difficult. *Sinter* reflects the similarity between a given signature and the signature most "alike" from the full set of signatures, and is expressed by the following pair of functions:

$$\Phi(ac^M, ac_i^M) = \frac{\sum_{\forall ic_n^M \in ac^M} \max\{S(ic_n^M, ic_m^M), \forall ic_m^M \in ac_i^M\}}{card(ac^M)} \quad (7)$$

$$Sinter(ac^M) = 1 - \max\{\Phi(ac^M, ac_i^M), \forall ac_i^M \in U^M - \{ac^M\}\} \quad (8)$$

where U^M denotes the full set of signatures associated to M from a scenario C.

Finally, trust calculation (*Trust*) is expressed by the product of these three factors:

$$Trust^M = Scomp^M * Sintra^M * Sinter^M \quad (9)$$

Given that *trust* can be quantified, all there is left is to establish a minimal acceptance level *TrustRef* to evaluate the function *BehavioralTrust* (definition 3.3):

$$BehavioralTrust(M) = \begin{cases} True & if \quad Trust^M \geq TrustRef \\ False & if \quad Trust^M < TrustRef \end{cases} \quad (10)$$

5 Experimental evaluation

The performance of a mechanism such as this is strongly influenced by the kind of application and the variety of intrinsic behaviors. Empirical analysis, performed on concrete usage examples as test environments, have been largely used for testing purposes in similar proposals, as [9, 13]. The major problem of this kind of approach is the danger of selecting an extremely inappropriate environment, generating a possible false negative evaluation of the mechanism; or, on the other hand, an extremely appropriate one, which would also lead to a false conclusion of a questionable effectiveness, certainly unadvisable to be generalized. We chose not to develop a perfectly suitable website model for the simulation, but rather to perceive how the mechanism would behave in different environments that were not initially devised to support macrostates or trust evaluation systems.

The first step was to find ways to adjust the requirements of the trust evaluation model in a regular website log. The following items had to be assessed consistently: (i) States and Macrostates definition and (ii) Users and user's behavioral instances

Each possible state *e* of the website was defined as a HTML or PHP web page, logged via a HTTP GET requests. Other requests, mostly for images and stylesheets, were discarded. As no user authentication was provided, an user *u* was defined as any known static IP address. Also, since no macrostate boundaries were available, every state *e* was defined as part of the same macrostate *M* and the following conventions were adopted: (i) behavioral instances with less than 5 states would not be considered; and (ii) a behavioral instance is said to have ended when more than 30 minutes have passed from the last state included in the instance until the next state entered by the same user. Those rules suffice the need to distinguish between behavioral instances of the same user and prevent the model from analyzing instances too small to be meaningful.

We have experimented with our approach on logs collected at the Computing Center Department, Federal University of Rio de Janeiro. We examined the Web-server logs of different applications through the trust model perspective to see what kind and quality of usage patterns were available.

The first website collected (UFRJ virtual library - www.bibvirtuais.ufrj.br) was not appropriate for not showing the actual IP addressess of the machines that made the HTTP requests. The second one (UFRJ Architecture and Urbanism school - www.fau.ufrj.br), although well structured (for macrostate adaptation), has a poor navigation diversity to generate different signatures (very low *Sint*er value). The last website (UFRJ Libraries and Information System - www.sibi.ufrj.br) showed none of the above problems and therefore was chosen for the model evaluation. We collected access logs from march 31st to september 6th 2006 (160 days), and then devised a parser to (i) anonymize all entries, replacing IP addresses and webpages by index numbers; (ii) remove all but those IP addresses known to be unique to a single user's computer; (iii) remove any sequential state repetitions (page reloads), as the model does not predict state transitions to itself; (iv) ignore requests to non-existent webpages, considering only the ones with a server return status of 200 (OK) or 304 (Not Modified); (v) ignore instances with less than 5 states; and (vi) ignore signatures with less than 5 instances, the empirical minimum value established for the evaluation. The result was 42 valid behavioral signatures files ready to be tested by the model prototype. The *SIntra* values (figure 5) give a clear understanding of whether the signatures are good or not, for example: user 34 has little difference between its internal behavioral instances, while user 38 had most of its instances remarkably differentiated among them.

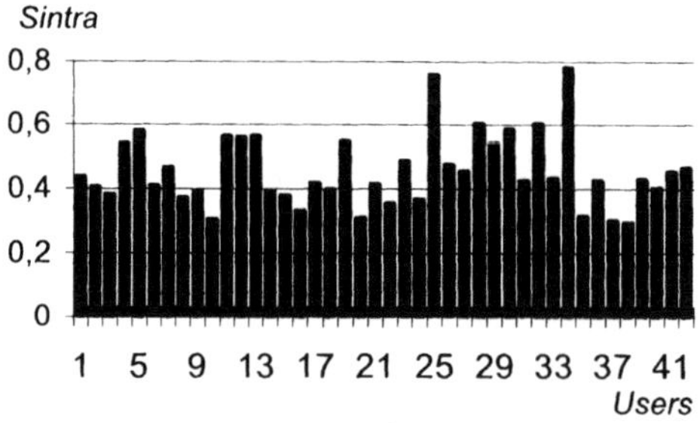

Fig.5: *Sintra* measures

Trust Ref	*Users Accepted*	*False Pos*	*False Neg*
0.070	42 (100%)	39 (93%)	0 (0%)
0.120	29 (69%)	3 (7%)	13 (31%)
0.150	16 (38%)	1 (2%)	26 (62%)

Table 2. *TrustRef* Evaluation

To simulate the user's input, we retrieved a random behavioral instance from inside each user's own signature database, leaving it with $n - 1$ instances, with n being the original number of instances inside the signature. The simulation evaluated every user's input against each signature, and calculated the Trust value for each case. The purpose was to see whether the highest Trust value was indeed from the same user as the signature in question.

Figure 6 shows a comparison between the mean values of the actual *Trust* evaluation obtained for each signature against the best false positive result for that signature (i.e. input from a different user that achieved the best Trust result against that signature). It is relevant to notice that, of all simulations performed with those 42 signatures, absolutely none held a user whose Trust evaluation was higher than the actual owner of the signature being tested. Another pertinent issue lies on the significantly low Trust values obtained, mostly because the experiment had rather low Sinter values, with a mean value of 0.365, indicating little difference between signatures. Even so, it was still possible to differentiate behaviors from the Trust results and establish possible positions for a TrustRef mark to be set, considering the desired amount of false positives and false negatives, as shown in Table 2.

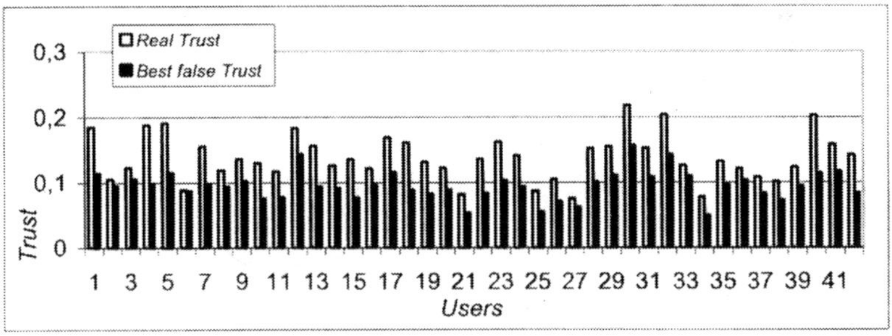

Fig. 6: Real Trust x Best false Trust

5 Conclusions and Future Work

This paper described a proposal for an integrated use of the concept of trust and access control management in secure Web applications. The originality of the approach lies on the employ of a user's behavioral evaluation mechanism (via Web navigation track) through a learning machine. The result of this analysis is used in the trust evolution process to replace, or complement, the classic use of mechanisms for credentials exchange. An important contribution of this work is the similarity measure between two representative samples of a user's behavior that, unlike the usual, compares behavioral sequences of different lengths.

It is also noticeable the extent of the proposed heuristics in the calculation of the trust level of a behavioral instance, which takes into account three different factors: (i) comparative similarity – relationship between the current behavioral instance and the signature (behavior resemblance), (ii) intra-similarity – relationship between behavioral instances that form the signature (quality of the signature) and (ii) inter-similarity – relationship between the different existing signatures (signature differentiability).

The performance of the proposed mechanism is well characterized by experimental evaluation that, besides attesting the viability of its utilization in the behavioral differentiation context, give some important subsides for the establishment of a minimal trust level *TrustRef*.

An open question in the proposed approach, and subject of ongoing works, concerns the necessity of the use of data reduction techniques, once the signatures store all of a user's past behavioral instances. For certain applications, that allow a great variability of behaviors, the signature size may grow considerably. It is under study the viability of the replacement of a set of similar behavioral instances for generic models that capture a certain degree of variability. Another work in progress tries to characterize a timetable of the behavior of a certain user, allowing the removal of old behaviors from his signature that should not reoccur.

References

1. J. Lopez, R. Oppliger and G. Pernul, Authentication and authorization infrastructures (AAIs): a comparative survey, *Computers & Security*, 23 - 2004, Elsevier, pp. 578-590.
2. H. Skogsrud, B. Benatallah and F. Casati, Model-Driven Trust Negotiation for Web Services, *IEEE Internet Computing*, 1089-7801/03, Nov/Dec 2003, pp. 45-52.
3. C. Platzer, Trust-based Security in Web Services, Master's Thesis, Information Systems Institute, Technical University of Vienna, Austria, 2004.
4. J. Bacon, K. Moody and W. Yao, Access Control and Trust in The Use of Widely Distributed Services, *Software-Practice Experience*, 33, 2003, pp. 375–394.
5. R. Tatyana, L. Zhou, C. Neuman, T. Leithead and K.E. Seamons, Adaptive trust negotiation and access control, In tenth ACM symposium on Access control models and technologies, ACM Press, Stockholm, Sweden, 2005.
6. F. Monrose and A. Rubin, Authentication via Keystroke Dynamics, In Fourth ACM Conference on Computer and Communication Security - CCS 97, Zurich, Switzerland, 1997, pp. 48-56,
7. A. Guven, and I. Sogukpinar, Understanding Users' Keystroke Patterns for Computer Access Security, *Computers & Security*, Elsevier, Vol. 22-8, 2003, pp. 695-706.
8. A. Peacock, X. Ke and M. Wilkerson, Typing Patterns: A Key to User Identification, *IEEE Security & Privacy*, September/October, 2004, pp. 40-47.
9. M. Pusara and C.E. Brodley, (2004). "User Re-Authentication via Mouse Movements, In CCS Workshop on Visualization and Data Mining for Computer Security -VizSEC/DMSEC'04, ACM press, Washington, DC, USA, October, 2004.
10. T. Lane, and C. Brodley, Temporal Sequence Learning and Data Reduction for Anomaly Detection, *ACM Transactions on Information and System Security*, Vol. 2, No. 3, August, 1999, pp. 295–331.
11. D.W. Aha, D. Kibler and M.K Albert, Instance-based learning algorithms", *Machine Learning*, Kluwer Academic Publishers, Vol. 6, No 1, January, 1991, pp. 37–66.
12. M. El-Ramly and S. Stroulia, Analysis of Web-usage behavior for focused Web sites: a case study", *Journal of Software Maintenance and Evolution: Research and Practice*, No. 16, 2004, pp. 129–150.
13. T. Lane, "Machine learning techniques for the computer security". Ph.D. thesis, Purdue University, 2000.

Improving the Information Security Model by using TFI

Rose-Mharie Åhlfeldt[1], Paolo Spagnoletti[2] and Guttorm Sindre[3]
1 University of Skövde, Box 408, S-542 28 Skövde, Sweden
rose-mharie.ahlfeldt@his.se
2 CeRSI – Luiss Guido Carli Unversity, Roma, Italy pspagnoletti@luiss.it
3 NTNU, Trondheim, Norway guttors@idi.ntnu.no

Abstract. In the context of information systems and information technology, information security is a concept that is becoming widely used. The European Network of Excellence INTEROP classifies information security as a non-functional aspect of interoperability and as such it is an integral part of the design process for interoperable systems. In the last decade, academics and practitioners have shown their interest in information security, for example by developing security models for evaluating products and setting up security specifications in order to safeguard the confidentiality, integrity, availability and accountability of data. Earlier research has shown that measures to achieve information security in the administrative or organisational level are missing or inadequate. Therefore, there is a need to improve information security models by including vital elements of information security. In this paper, we introduce a holistic view of information security based on a Swedish model combined with a literature survey. Furthermore we suggest extending this model using concepts based on semiotic theory and adopting the view of an information system as constituted of the technical, formal and informal (TFI) parts. The aim is to increase the understanding of the information security domain in order to develop a well-founded theoretical framework, which can be used both in the analysis and the design phase of interoperable systems. Finally, we describe and apply the Information Security (InfoSec) model to the results of three different case studies in the healthcare domain. Limits of the model will be highlighted and an extension will be proposed.

1 Introduction

In the information society, security of information plays a central role in several domains with different scopes and objectives: Privacy of personal data in healthcare; Integrity of transaction and business continuity in the business domain; Safeguard of citizens in the infrastructure domain; and Defence of democracy in the e-government

---

Please use the following format when citing this chapter:

Åhlfeldt, R.-M., Spagnoletti, P., and Sindre, G., 2007, in IFIP International Federation for Information Processing, Volume 232, New Approaches for Security, Privacy and Trust in Complex Environments, eds. Venter, H., Eloff, M., Labuschagne, L., Eloff, J., von Solms, R., (Boston: Springer), pp. 73–84.

domain, are some examples of such objectives. In the last decades, due to the spread of Information and Communication Technologies (ICT), governmental organisations and communities of academics and practitioners have developed security models for evaluating products, and setting up security specifications in order to prevent incidents and reducing the risk of harm.

Many different terms have been used to describe security in the IT/IS area. *Information security* has become a commonly used concept, and is a broader term than data security and IT security [1]. Information is dependent on data as a carrier and on IT as a tool to manage the information; hence, information security has an organizational focus [2].

The Swedish National Encyclopedia [3] states that information security is focused on information that the data represent, and on related protection requirements. The U.S. National Information Systems Security Glossary [4] defines information system security as: "the protection of information systems against unauthorized access to or modification of information, whether in storage, processing or transit, and against the denial of service to authorized users or the provision of service to unauthorized users, including those measures necessary to detect, document, and counter such threats". Four characteristics of information security are: availability, confidentiality, integrity and accountability, simplified as "the right information to the right people in the right time" [5]. The Swedish Standardization of Information Technology (SIS) advocates that information security concerns the protection of information assets, aiming to maintain confidentiality, integrity, availability and accountability of information [6].

Availability concerns the expected use of resources within the desired time frame. *Confidentiality* relates to data not being accessible or revealed to unauthorized people. *Integrity* concerns protection against undesired changes. *Accountability* refers to the ability of distinctly deriving performed operations from an individual. Both technical and administrative security measures are required to achieve these four characteristics. *Administrative security* concerns the management of information security; strategies, policies, risk assessments, education etc. Planning and implementation of security requires a structured way of working. This part of the overall security is at an organizational level and concerns the business as a whole.

Technical security concerns measures to be taken in order to achieve the overall requirements, and is subdivided into physical security and IT security. *Physical security* is about physical protection of information, e.g. fire protection and alarm systems. *IT-security* refers to security for information in technical information systems and can be subdivided into computer- and communication security. *Computer Security* relates to the protection of hardware and its contents, e.g. encryption and backup techniques. *Communication Security* involves the protection of networks and other media that communicate information between computers, e.g. firewalls.

In order to provide a more understandable view of how information security characteristics and security measures relate to one another, an information security model (Fig. 1) has been created based on the common characteristics of information security and SIS classification of information security measures [6]. The aim of the model is to describe what information security represents both in terms of characteristics and measures, combining the definitions and descriptions mentioned above.

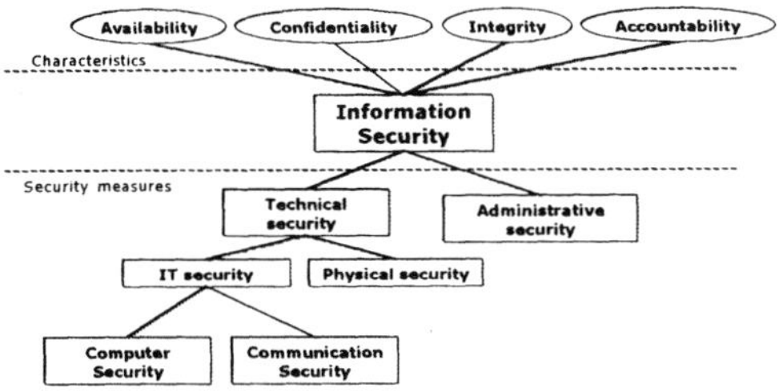

Fig. 1. Information Security Model (InfoSec model)

The main concept "information security" is presented in the middle. The four characteristics together represent information security, and are placed at the top of the figure. All requirements from the organizations concerning these characteristics must be fulfilled for information security to be achieved. The lower part of the model presents the different security measures, divided in a hierarchical order and these are gathered directly from the SIS conceptual classification [6]. Since the term "information security" includes several parts of security measures, the model has been useful both in the research and the educational area, in order to get an understanding of information security and its content. Furthermore, the model has been used as a tool in the research area to express where the problems and needs exist in the information security area [7].

In Figure 1, administrative security is not subdivided, but a case study in the distributed healthcare domain has shown that there is a need to improve the model with a more fine-grained understanding of administrative issues [7]. One way to improve the InfoSec model is to look at other security standards, methods and models in order to discover solutions to extend the InfoSec model.

The aim of the paper is to present the suggested extended InfoSec model by using concepts derived from a semiotic model (TFI) in order to increase the understanding of the information security domain and to develop a well founded theoretical framework which can be used both in the analysis and the design phase of interoperable systems. The results from three different case studies have been drawn upon in order to show the limitations of the current model and to validate the extended model.

Our contribution aims to provide a theoretically founded and empirically tested information security model for the analysis of Information Systems and its context. In this model both the IT infrastructure and the more contextual related aspects related to organizational culture and human behavior are taken in to account in order to enlarge the scope of the analysis and to select countermeasures with a holistic view on information security.

The next section presents related work, describes the TFI-model and argues for its appropriateness. In section 3 the results from three case studies are described, highlighting the limitations of the information security model. In section 4 we present a suggestion for an extended InfoSec model and the same results from the case studies are compared with the model in order to validate its extension. Finally, section 5 concludes the paper.

2 Related work

The harmonisation of the North American (TCSEC commonly known as Orange Book) and European (ITSEC) criteria for IT security evaluations led, at the end of the 1990s, to the definition of a common set of criteria (Common Criteria) for use in evaluating products and systems and for stating security requirements in a standardised way. The International Standard Organisation accepted these criteria in the ISO15408-1999. These standards define the IT product or system under evaluation as a Target of Evaluation (TOE). TOEs include, for example, operating systems, computer networks, distributed systems, and applications.

Additional standards and models were developed by other national and international organizations taking into account the abovementioned works and more context specific issues. The European Computer Manufacturers Association, ECMA, wanted to achieve a widely accepted basic security functionality class for commercial applications, defining the "Commercially Oriented Functionality Class" (COFC) and afterwards the Extended Commercially Oriented Functionality Class (E - COFC), which extends the application of ECMA's class of commercial security functions to an environment of interconnected IT systems.

These standards consider "administrative security measures" outside the scope of security evaluation criteria "because they involve specialized techniques or because they are somewhat peripheral to IT security" (CC, Introduction and general model). Despite they recognize that a significant part of the security of a TOE can often be achieved through administrative measures such as organizational, personnel, physical, and procedural controls, they chose to focus on IT security measures and they start from the assumption of a secure use of IT systems and products.

A different approach to the security of information can be found in the Code of Practice BS7799, recently accepted by the ISO in the ISO/IEC 27000 family In this case the processing of information assumes a central role and the focus is on the management of information security instead of the design of secure IT systems and products. This approach considers security of information as a quality sub-factor and provides a set of controls to be put in place in order to deploy an information security management system based on a "plan-do-check-act" cycle similar to the ISO 9000 for quality management. Another quality management based approach to information security comes from Firesmith [8] who defines taxonomy of security-related requirements based on the safety requirements of a system.

This brief overview of security standards shows that the focus of security models, standards and best practices, has moved from considering security as an intrinsic feature of IT systems and products towards a wider vision including the processing of information and the related management issues such as roles and responsibilities. Starting from well-known principles and standards, some authors [9] use layered models to classify security controls and to describe security models. For instance at the top level there is the organization policy with respect to security, followed by specific corporate programs to promote security and finally technical controls. A step forward with respect to these approaches can be to focus on more context-related aspects such as organizational culture and human behavior instead of technology and processes. To this end, starting from the above mentioned InfoSec model, we propose an extension based on concepts derived from a semiotic model. Adopting this view makes it possible to better understand all those context specific aspects that can be difficult to analyze using generalized risk management techniques.

2.1 The TFI model

Adopting the view of an information system as constituted of the technical, formal and informal (TFI) parts which are in a state of continuous interaction [10], the need for an holistic approach to the study of IS security becomes apparent. Using the words of Stamper et al [11] is possible to illustrate this interrelation of abstracted layers explaining that, "Informal norms are fundamental, because formal norms can only operate by virtue of the informal norms needed to interpret them, while technical norms can play no role…unless embedded within a system of formal norm." In other words, the informal ways of managing information in organisations are critical and not always they can be replaced by rules or embedded in technical systems. With this view the informal elements (i.e. perception of risks, awareness, beliefs, culture, etc.), which are very context related, should drive the design and the selection of formal (policies, business processes, standards, procedures, etc.) and technical solutions (i.e. software and hardware platforms, network infrastructures, devices, etc.). In the context of information systems crossing the boundaries of a single organization (i.e. virtual organizations and other interoperable systems), the relationship among these three levels is even more complex and requires to address additional issues such as trust and privacy by the means of new formal and informal mechanisms (i.e. Circle of Trust, federated Identity Management Systems, etc.).

The above mentioned conceptual framework, based on semiotic theory, will be one of the assumptions behind all the subsequent discussion on IS security management. Furthermore we agree with Dhillon's [12] assumption by viewing problems as an emergent property of reflexive interaction between a system and its context, instead of considering them as a consequence of a system's function.

These premises give an idea of the complexity implicit in preventing, detecting, investigating and responding to incidents, using deterministic methods, when different organizational contexts are involved. This complexity is a serious challenge for the design phase of Information Security Management Systems (ISMS) when organizations with different security models in terms of people, rules and technology need to cooperate. Indeed information security can be considered a critical non-functional requirement when inter-organizational interoperability is pursued.

IS security is a wide field and contributions come from several disciplines such as mathematics, engineering, and social and management sciences. In this section we briefly introduce some of the contributions to the IS security literature in order to clarify the differences among the three levels [13]: *(1) technical*: automating and standardizing parts of formal systems such as computers helping in operational tasks; *(2) formal*: organizational level security mechanisms like governance, policies or processes, such as establishing controls in structure of organization and *(3) informal*: individual level security mechanisms, like shaping the norms, beliefs, values, and attitudes of employees, such as establishing normative controls.

Technical level security. From a technical perspective, the preservation of confidentiality, integrity availability and accountability requires the adoption of IT security solutions such as encryption of data and communication, physical eavesdropping, access control systems, secure code programming, authorisation and authentication mechanisms, database security mechanisms, intrusion detection systems, firewalls, etc. At this level it is possible to introduce models and methods for the selection of the appropriate technological solution depending on the needs for a particular application.

Formal level security. The formal level of IS security is related with the set of policies, rules, controls, standards, etc. aimed to define an interface between the technological subsystem (Technical level) and the behavioural subsystem (Informal level). According with Lee's definition of an IS [14], this is the level where much of the effort of the IS management is concentrated. An interesting review of the security literature identifies a trend in information system research moving away from a narrow technical viewpoint towards a socio-organisational perspective [15]. In fact the first methods for addressing security at this level are checklist, risk analysis and evaluation. At the beginning such methods have been grounded in particular well-defined reality (i.e. military), focusing on a functionalist view of reality. However Dhillon and Backhouse [15] show that the definition of rules, standards and controls becomes more complicated than the design of technical systems.

Informal level security. In the domain of the informal level of IS security, the unit of analysis is individual and the research is concerned about behavioural issues like values, attitude, beliefs, and norms that are dominant, and influencing an individual employee regarding security practices in an organization. The solutions suggested in this domain are more descriptive than prescriptive in nature and the findings at this level need to be effectively implemented through other levels (i.e. formal and technical). An interesting review of research papers in the behavioural domain, looking at used theories, suggested solutions, current challenges, and future research has been presented by Harris and Mishra [13].

This approach helps in the management of insider threats. Numerous studies [16-20] have indicated that there is a problem in managing information security especially with respect to controlling the behavior of internal employees. Research has also shown that many times internal employees subvert existing controls in order to gain undue advantage essentially because either an opportunity exists to do so or they are disgruntled [21]. The problem gets compounded even further when an organization is geographically dispersed and it becomes difficult to institute the necessary formal controls [22].

Also the prevention of social engineering attacks deals with the informal level of information security. According with Jones [23], while the typical hacker "takes more advantage of holes in security," the social engineer manipulates personnel to gain information that would not normally be available, such as passwords, user IDs, or even corporate directories. In effect, social engineering is typically employed by hackers as a means to acquire information that would be extremely difficult to obtain through strictly technical means. Unlike hacking, social engineering taps into the psychology of what people expect from others and their natural tendency to be helpful. Therefore technical barriers and rigid rules are not sufficient to contrast these threats if people are not aware of the security risks.

3 Extended InfoSec model based on TFI

One way to extend the InfoSec model in its administrative part is to use the elements of the TFI-model; formal and informal. Administrative security concerns information security management, which can be both formal and informal. According to chapter 2, the formal element includes policies, rules controls, standards etc aimed to define an interface between the technological subsystems while the informal element includes the aspects related to the human behaviour. This seems to be in conjunction with the security area too. Also Björck [24] has declared this division of information security when he classifies some written papers from the security areas. He divides them into technical, formal and informal parts. He also concludes that information security papers mostly concern technical aspects while there is a further need of research in the formal level but above all, the informal level has been neglected. One important element in this level is to make the users security aware. Concerning the formal part it seems to be natural to subdivide this part into external and internal levels. Each organisation is subject to external regulations concerning security issues, for instance, laws, regulations and agreements with other companies. Furthermore, there is internal formalism for information security management, such as IT-strategies, security polices, educational programs etc. According to Lee [14] this is the level where much of the effort of the information security management is concentrated. Hence, we have extended the InfoSec model as depicted in Figure 2.

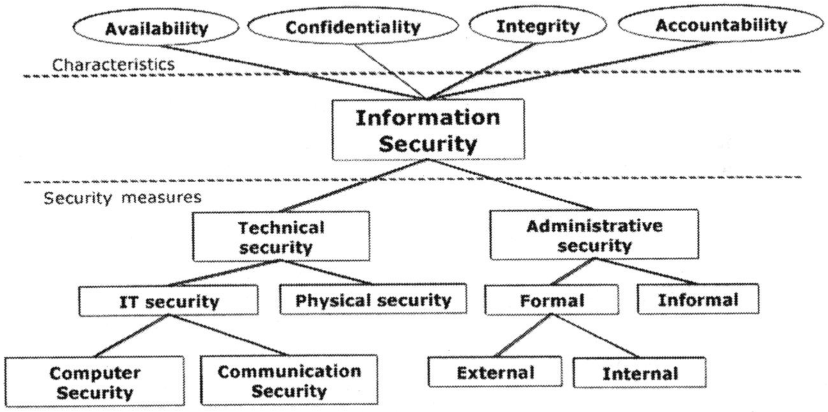

Fig. 2. Suggestion for an extended InfoSec model

4 Evaluating the new InfoSec Model

In this section we present the case studies and apply a summary of the results to the new extended model in order to illustrate its usefulness. It is beyond the scope of this paper to describe the specific case studies in huge detail, this can be found in referenced papers. However, a brief description is presented in this section.

4.1 The applied case studies

The first case study [25] was conducted in the home healthcare of two municipalities. The focus in this case study was patient privacy and information from the Swedish Data Inspection Board (DIB) was used as a basis for the interviews with the responsible persons and the healthcare staff working in home healthcare. Observations were also carried out in order to obtain an idea of how personal data is managed by following the healthcare staff in their work.

The second case study [26] includes observations and interviews with healthcare staff at a hospital in the western region of Sweden. The aim of the study was to determine how users of EHR are affected by the requirements of information security, as well as how the users themselves affect information security and in what way they follow the recommendations and advice of the Swedish DIB.

The third case study was performed as part of the VITA Nova Hemma research project [27]. In this research project different healthcare providers participated in order to investigate how a process manager can be used to support a leg ulcer process. This process connects different healthcare actors: primary care, secondary care and municipalities [28, 29]. Part of the case study included a system analysis of different security aspects for the involved healthcare systems. Interviews were held with administrators for the respective healthcare systems. A second part included further studies of the healthcare organizations' systems and networks. The suppliers of the patient record systems and the people responsible for the communication networks in the included healthcare organizations were interviewed. The basis for the questions in the security analysis was the ISO-standard ISO/IEC 17799 Information Security Management [30].

The results are briefly summarized: *IT-security* - inadequate logon functions in both systems and networks. *Computer Security* - inadequate access profiles levels. *Communication security* - facsimiles as a communication transmitter, interruptions in the networks, inadequate authentications techniques and security measures concerning mobility. *Administrative security* - missing IT-strategies and information security polices, inadequate education in information security, no compliance and follow up, inadequate security awareness and attitudes, inadequate security routines, and missing security requirements.

The results from the case studies are presented in Figure 3a and show a number of problems and needs in the different levels of security. The symbols refer to the results for specific case studies, for instance, 1a refers to case study 1 and the results noted a in that particular case. It is out of the scope of this paper to analyse the particular result. Instead we focus on the structure of the problems and needs. The results show that there is a cluster of problems and needs in the administrative security area. In comparison with the technical security this part will be hard to express in more detail, and there is no balance concerning the graphical illustration between the technical and administrative level. One reason could be that technical measures have got higher priority and have been in focus for a longer period of time. Therefore it is necessary to further detail the administrative part of the information security model as well, and thus get an improved view of where problems and needs are located within administrative security.

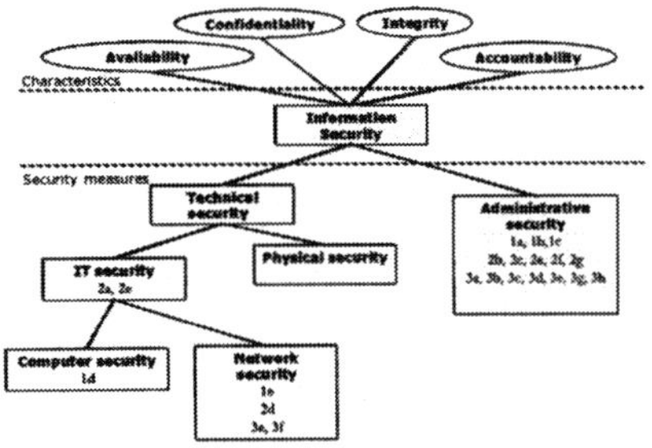

Fig. 3a: Needs in healthcare.

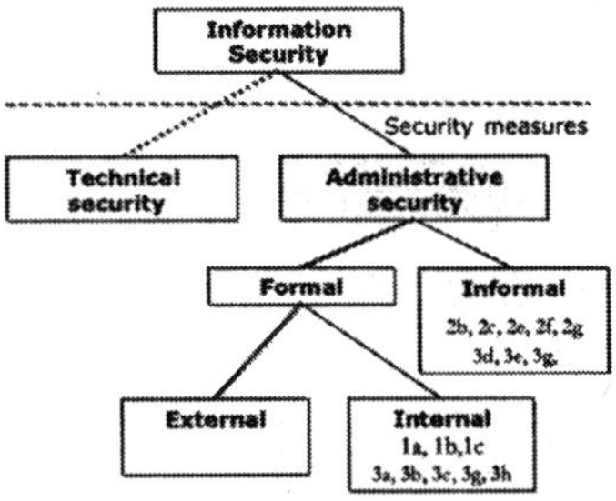

Fig. 3b: Corresponding results in the extended InfoSec model

One approach is to apply the results shown in Figure 3a to the extended InfoSec model. The result at the administrative security level has been classified according to the new levels of administrative security: formal and informal. The formal issues have been further classified as external and internal. The result of this classification is shown in Figure 3b and should be compared with results from Figure 3a.

The result shows that our case studies exhibit both formal and informal problems and needs. However, in the formal part, there are no reported problems in the formal external level. This does not imply that there are no problems in this area, however. Other investigations reveal problems at this level, concerning for instance legislation contradiction [31]. It is reasonable to assume that the problem was not mentioned in our case studies since other more internal problems impact the respondents' daily work more directly. Another formal external problem could be e-contracting. In the healthcare area, no such contracting is applied yet, and therefore no such problems have been identified. In the future when different healthcare performers will exchange patient information, some kind of contracting may very well be implemented, and may hence also become a security problem in this level.

An interesting finding is that if the InfoSec model had included external administrative security from the beginning, the interviewer could have asked more direct questions for the formal external purposes. Instead, the administrative part alone was in focus, causing the questions to be rather abstract. This also shows that the extended model could be of great use in order to emphasize the whole of the information security area, and the administrative security level in particular.

In the informal part we find problems like inadequate security awareness and attitudes but also missing measures for compliance and follow up activities. Technical solutions are quite easy to implement. Formal administrative solutions can be considered a rigid task to perform but is in fact attainable. The main challenge for information security in the future is to implement useful methods to achieve security awareness in organisations. According to Valentine: "Employee security awareness programs need to begin growing out of their infancy and be treated with as much attention to detail as any other information security engagement" [32].

5 Discussion and Conclusion

We have shown how the InfoSec model can be extended by using elements from the TFI model. The administrative part in the InfoSec model has been subdivided into formal and informal security. The formal part has been further subdivided into external and internal parts. Our main contributions include showing how the extended InfoSec model can be of great use in order to emphasize a more holistic view of the information security area, and the administrative security level in particular. The model also visualises more specifically within what areas information security measures need to be taken into account.

The case studies presented in this paper, indicated no external problems and needs in the formal part of information security. We do not claim that all external regulations and legalisation issues have been taken to account or that there are no problems concerning the external part. This investigation of external issues has just not been in focus. In the internal formal part, there is a need for information strategies and information security policies strongly related to context or the type of domains such as healthcare, military and business sectors. The internal rules, instructions and education should emerge after defining the policies. In the informal part there is also a need for measures to support the organisation in implementing information security awareness. This is not a simple task, but is very important in order to reach sufficient information security within the whole organisation.

One weakness in this paper is that only one single investigation has been used to evaluate the extended InfoSec model. Future work must evaluate the model in other studies as well, both theoretically and practically, in order to establish its usefulness.

Furthermore, we need to investigate how to construct context-related strategies and polices. A risk management methodology which takes behaviour and cultural aspects into account is needed to improve security awareness. The extended Info Sec model has a holistic approach and can therefore be a helpful tool to bring informal issues into account, why such a risk management methodology should be based on our model, especially in the asset identification phase (physical asset but also value of information for the stakeholders) and also in the control selection phase.

The need for formalisation in the design phase of information systems development is moving towards the use of semantic technologies and ontologies. Future research should therefore evaluate the extended model in other domains. In the INTEROP project and the task group of non-functional aspects in particular, some related work is on-going which may enable a broader evaluation. The extended model should be seen as a semantic model in order to be a useful support in different areas to include the information security issues.

References

1. Björck, F., 2005a. Knowledge Security [on line]. Available from: http://www.bjorck.com/3.htm [Accessed 1 November, 2005].
2. Oscarsson, P., 2002. Information Security, Data Security, IT Security, Computer Security, IS Security ... - What Makes the Difference? In Proceedings of Promote IT, pp. 649-655. Skövde, Sweden. 22-24 April 2002.

3. NE 2005. National Encyclopedia [on-line]. Available from: http://www.ne.se [Accessed 28 October 2005].
4. U.S. National Information Systems Security Glossary, 2006. Available from: http://security.isu.edu/pdf/4009.pdf [Accessed 25 October 2006].
5. Wikipedia, 2006. Information Security. Available from: http://www.wikipedia.com [Accessed 29 May, 2006].
6. SIS, 2003. SIS Handbok 550. Terminologi för informationssäkerhet. SIS Förlag AB. Stockholm (in Swedish).
7. Åhlfeldt, R-M., 2006. Information Security in a Distributed Healthcare Domain – Exploring the Problems and Needs of Different Healthcare Providers. Licentiate Dissertation. Report series No. 06-003. ISSN 1101-8526.
8. Firesmith D.G., 2005. “Analyzing the Security Significance of System Requirements,” Requirements Engineering’2005 (RE’05) Symposium on Requirements Engineering for Information Security (SREIS), IEEE Computer Society, Washington, D.C., September 2005.
9. Jain, A. & Raja, M K 2006. An Exploratory Assessment of Information Security Principles & Practices: An Insight from a Financial Services company, Proceedings of the 5th Security Conference, Las Vegas.
10. Liebenau and Backhouse 1990 Understanding Information: an Introduction, Macmillan, London
11. Stamper R., Liu K., Hafkamp M. and Ades Y. 2000 Understanding the Roles of Signs and Norms in Organisations - A semiotic approach to information systems design. Journal of Behaviour & Information Technology, vol. 19 (1), pp 15-27.
12. Dhillon, G. 1997. Managing information system security. London: Macmillan.
13. Harris, M. & Mishra, S. 2006 Human Behavior Aspects in Information Systems Security. Proceedings of the 5th Security Conference, Las Vegas.
14. Lee, A.S. (1999). Inaugural Editor’s Comments, MIS Quarterly, 23(1), v-xi.
15. Dhillon, G. and Backhouse J. 2001 Current Directions in IS Security Research: Toward Socio-Organisational Perspectives. Information Systems Journal 11(2): 127-153.
16. Siponen M.T. 2000 “A Conceptual Foundation for Organizational Information Security Awareness”, Information Management & Computer Security, 11 (1), pp. 31-41.
17. Whitman, M. 2003. "Enemy at the Gate: Threats to Information Security." Communications of the ACM 46(8): 91-95.
18. Bottom, N. 2000. "The human face of information loss." Security Management 44(6):50-56.
19. Magklaras, G. and S. Furnell 2005. "A preliminary model of end user sophistication for insider threat prediction in IT systems." Computers & Security 24: 371-380.
20. Schultz, E. 2002. A framework for understanding and predicting insider attacks. Compsec, London.
21. Dhillon, G., & Backhouse, J. 1997. Managing for secure organizations: a review of information systems security research approaches. In D. Avison (Ed.), Key issues in information systems: McGraw Hill.
22. Dhillon, G. 2000 Challenges in Managing IS Security in the new Millennium, Chapter 1 of Challenges in Managing Information Security, Idea Group Publishing.

23. Jones, C. 2003 The Social Engineering: Understanding and Auditing [Online]. SANS Institute. Available from: http://www.sans.org/rr/whitepapers/engineering/1332.php [Accessed Nov 01 2005].
24. Björck, F. 2005b Discovering Information Security Management. PhD Dissertation. University of Stockholm. Report series No. 05-010, Stockholm.
25. Åhlfeldt, R. 2002. Information Security in Home Healthcare: A Case Study, In the *Conference Proceedings of the Third International Conference of the Australian Institute of Computer Ethics (AiCE) 2002*. Sydney, Australia, 30 September 2002, pp. 1-10. Eds. M. Warren and J. Barlow. Australian Institute of Computer Ethics. ISBN 0-7300-2560-8.
26. Åhlfeldt, R. and Ask, L. 2004. Information Security in Electronic Medical Records: A case study with the user in focus. In *Proceedings of the 2004 Information Resources Management Association International Conference*, New Orleans, USA, May, pp 345 – 347.
27. Åhlfeldt, R. and Nohlberg, M. 2005. System and Network Security in a Heterogeneous Healthcare Domain: A Case Study. In *CD-ROM Proceedings of the 4th Security Conference, Las Vegas, USA, 30–31 March 2005*. ISBN 0-9729562-5-5.
28. Perjons, E., Wangler, B., Wäyrynen, J. and Åhlfeldt, R. 2005a. Introducing a process manager in healthcare: an experience report, *Health Informatics Journal*, Vol 11(1), 45-61, March 2005. ISSN 1460-4582.
29. Johannesson, P., Perjons, E., Wangler, B. and Åhlfeldt, R-M. 2005. Design Solutions for Interoperability using a Process Manager. In Proceedings of the 1th International Conference on Interoperability of Enterprise Software and Applications (INTEROP-ESA'2005), Geneva, Switzerland, 23 – 25 February 2005, pp 397-408. ISBN 13-978-1-84628-151-8
30. ISO/IEC 17799 Part 1: Code of practice for information security management.
31. Nationell IT-strategi för vård och omsorg. 2006. ISBN 91-631-8541-5 (in Swedish).
32. Valentine, A., 2006 "Enhancing the employee security awareness model", Computer Fraud & Security, June 2006, pp 17-19.

Ontological Mapping of Common Criteria's Security Assurance Requirements

Andreas Ekelhart[1], Stefan Fenz[1], Gernot Goluch[1], and Edgar Weippl[1]

Secure Business Austria, 1040 Vienna
{ekelhart,fenz,goluch,weippl}@securityresearch.at

Abstract. The Common Criteria (CC) for Information Technology Security Evaluation provides comprehensive guidelines for the evaluation and certification of IT security regarding data security and data privacy. Due to the very complex and time-consuming certification process a lot of companies abstain from a CC certification. We created the CC Ontology tool, which is based on an ontological representation of the CC catalog, to support the evaluator at the certification process. Tasks such as the planning of an evaluation process, the review of relevant documents or the creating of reports are supported by the CC Ontology tool. With the development of this tool we reduce the time and costs needed to complete a certification.

1 Introduction

The Common Criteria for Information Technology Security Evaluation (CC) describes an international standard regarding the criteria for the evaluation and certification of IT products and systems pertaining to data security and data privacy. Requirements for the security functions of IT products and systems as well as requirements for assurance measures applied to the security functions during a security evaluation are provided by the CC [1]. The security functions of such products and systems and the applied assurance measures have to meet defined requirements to obtain a certain level of confidence during the evaluation process. With the results of the evaluation process the costumer should be able to estimate the actual security risks regarding the evaluated IT product or system. One of its major strengths is that the CC process offers a standardized approach for product and system evaluation. Raskin [2] is one of the first to introduce ontological semantic approaches to information security. He implies that one of the ultimate goals is the inclusion of natural language data sources to facilitate the specification and evaluation of information security certification by organizing and unifying the terminology.

Despite being a standard, the CC offer the flexibility to certify only requirements that are important to the customer. Protection Profiles state the desired requirements of a particular community in almost any combination desired [3]. Other standards such as the Orange Book follow an "all-or-nothing" approach. If a product or system misses even just a single and for the customer irrelevant

---

Please use the following format when citing this chapter:

Ekelhart, A., Fenz, S., Goluch, G., and Weippl, E., 2007, in IFIP International Federation for Information Processing, Volume 232, New Approaches for Security, Privacy and Trust in Complex Environments, eds. Venter, H., Eloff, M., Labuschagne, L., Eloff, J., von Solms, R., (Boston: Springer), pp. 85–95.

requirement, it cannot be certified at the desired level. The CC's flexibility makes it harder both for the developer and evaluator to keep track of what is required for a certain level and which security functions are to be included.

The drawback of such a comprehensive standard is the fact that it is very time-consuming and expensive to evaluate a certain product or system against a specific CC evaluation assurance level. Little commercial interest is driving the CC market; most evaluations and certifications result from government regulation or government purchase [4].

Katzke suggested several ways to deal with CC's problems and shortcomings [5]. The suggestions include better administration and management processes, long-term planning and budget processes, and accountability for meeting goals, milestones, and deliverables. We concentrate on the first of Katzke's points because sophisticated support tools for management and administration of CC processes are still not available; both the evaluator and on the developer would certainly benefit from such a tool. Furthermore the CC include rather abstract verbalizations: e.g. "ALC_DVS.1.1C: The development security documentation shall describe all the physical, procedural, personnel, and other security measures that are necessary to protect the confidentiality and integrity of the TOE design and implementation in its development environment" [6]. Such abstract definitions do not provide sufficient information on the concrete measures a company has to fulfill and therefore often leads to conflicts during the evaluation process. To counter the abstract verbalizations, we align the CC ontology with the Security Ontology [7, 8, 9], and thus are able to offer concrete threat and countermeasure terminology for demanded security requirements.

We eliminated the aforementioned flaws by creating a CC ontology which comprises the entire CC domain [1, 10, 6]. In comparison to the available PDF or paper version of the CC, the ontology is easily browseable with any standard RDF [11] - or OWL [12] (ontology) visualization tool and thus easier to handle, especially pertaining to relationships. Furthermore, due to the OWL representation the CC domain is now available in a machine readable format and can be utilized in computer programs. Another important advantage of our approach is the option to query the data structure in an efficient way, taking advantage of the well known RDF- or OWL-based query languages such as SPARQL [13]. Due to the complexity of these languages it is nonetheless necessary to create an intermediate layer, which translates the user input into a valid query and thus the ontology has to be designed in a way that easy query transformations are feasible. Additionally, utilizing a standardized ontology language, such as OWL (Web Ontology Language) [12], not only provides a syntax for semantic knowledge representation but further is the basis to integrate already established reasoning engines, facilitating a movement towards the paradigm of rule based expert systems.

Following this, based on the CC ontology and the SPARQL query language stated above, we developed a tool to support the CC evaluation process in several ways. Our contribution is:

The CC Ontology covers the entire domain of the CC. It can be used to query the data structure in an efficient way using SPARQL.
The CC Ontology Tool takes the CC ontology as input and supports the evaluation process in several novel and useful ways such as tagging and linking.

The previous pages already mentioned "ontology" as a central term in this paper. Even though ontologies are widely used in research of semantic systems, this subsection provides some definitions and defines the scope of an ontology in the context of this paper. The term ontology has its origin in the philosophical discipline, where it means a systematic explanation of being. One of the first ontology definitions regarding to the computer science's sector, was published 1991 by Neches:

> *'An ontology defines the basic terms and relations comprising the vocabulary of a topic area as well as the rules for combining terms and relations to define extensions to the vocabulary.'* [14]

This definition shows already the basic elements of an ontology in the sense of computer science: a set of defined terms, their interrelations, rules for combining terms and the scope of the ontology. The main components of an ontology are: (1) Classes: represent concepts (e.g. trees, animals,) (2) Relations: represent an association between concepts (3) Functions: special case of relations in which the n-th element of the relation is unique for the n-1 preceding elements [15] (4) Formal axioms: model sentences that are always true (5) Instances: represent elements or individuals in an ontology.

2 Common Criteria Ontology

A machine-readable ontology representing the CC is required for two reasons: First, users can easily navigate the ontology with a standardized tool and have a better overview of the entire process. Second, the ontology is the knowledge base upon which our CC ontology tool builds. This tool automatically configures the list of required certification documents and customizes the checklists to fit the specific needs of the certification process.

Common Criteria Terms and Definitions: The following list of CC terms and definitions explains the main terms used in the following sections. For a complete list please refer to [1], Chapter 3.

The *evaluation assurance level* is a set consisting of assurance components from CC security assurance requirements (compare [6]) representing a level on the predefined assurance scale.
A *class* is a package of *families*, sharing a common focus. Families are sets of *components*, which are the smallest selectable group of elements, sharing security objectives.

Developer action elements are activities which should be performed by the developer.
Content and presentation of evidence elements encompass several required aspects of the evidence: (1) what the evidence should demonstrate; (2) what information the evidence should convey; (3) when the evidence is considered appropriate and (4) specific characteristics of the evidence that either the TOE or this assurance must possess [6].
Evaluator action elements are activities that should be performed by the evaluator, which explicitly include confirmation that the requirements prescribed in the content and presentation of evidence elements have been met.

The Common Criteria Security Assurance Ontology: The evaluator's view on the CC focuses on the security assurance requirements. We therefore concentrated on modeling them since they are used by the evaluator as a mandatory statement of evaluation criteria when determining the assurance of the TOE and when evaluating protection profiles and security targets. This information is clearly also of vital value for developers as a reference when interpreting statements of assurance requirements and determining assurance approaches for the TOE. We used Protege [16] to maintain, visualize and navigate the ontology. Table 1 shows all concept relations including their range and special characteristics. Due to the size of the CC security assurance ontology it is not possible to show the entire knowledge base. Following this we extracted relevant parts, which we are going to discuss in this section.

Table 1. Concept Relations

Domain	Relation	Range
Activity	evaluates_component	Component
Class	has_family	Family
Component	has_content_and_...*	Content_and_...*
Component	has_developer_action_element	Developer_Action_Element
Component	has_input	Evidence_Element
Component	has_evaluator_action_element	Evaluator_Action_Element
Component	has_dependency	Component
Content_and_...*	has_workunit	Workunits
Developer_Action_Element	has_workunit	Workunits
EAL_Evaluation	has_activity	Activity
Evaluator_Action_Element	has_content_and_...*	Content_and_...*
Evaluator_Action_Element	has_developer_action_element	Developer_Action_Element
Family	has_component	Component

*...presentation_of_evidence_element

With the ontology it is possible to reconstruct the complete CC security assurance evaluation process taking the used evaluation assurance level into account by the following relations (see Figure 1 for EAL4 and configuration

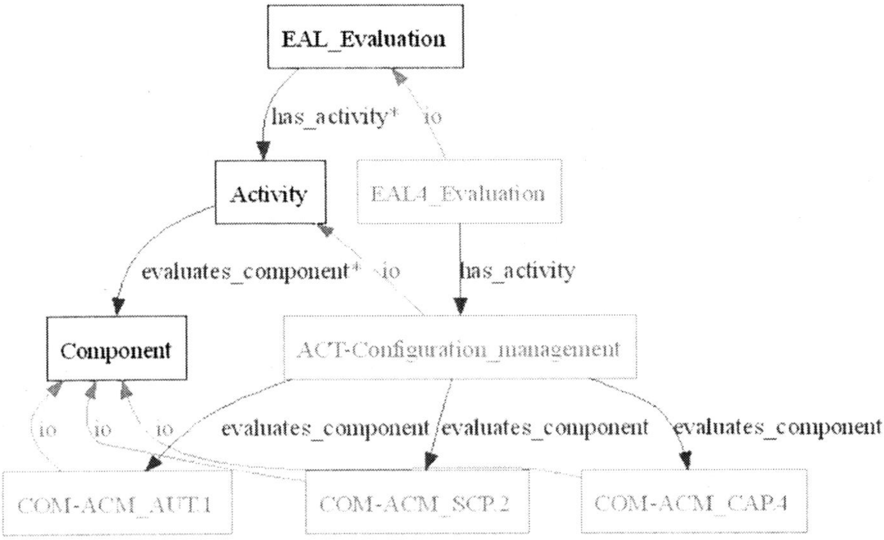

Fig. 1. Evaluation Activities

management activity): (1) *has_activity* describes which activities are necessary for the needed evaluation assurance level (e.g. configuration management activity) and (2) *evaluates_component* defines which specific component has to be evaluated to comply to the evaluation activity (e.g. ACM_CAP.4 for configuration management activity on EAL4).

Furthermore the dependencies and relationships between CC classes, families and components, including cross references of assurance component dependencies, are shown by the (1) *has_family* and (2) *has_component* relations (see Figure 2 for Class ACM, Family CAP and Component 4).

Additionally every component is refined with the following relations and their corresponding items (1) *has_content_and_presentation_of_evidence_element* links to the corresponding content and presentation of evidence elements (2) *has_developer_action_element* links to the corresponding developer action elements and (3) *has_evaluator_action_element* links to the corresponding evaluator action elements (e.g. Component 4 in Family CAP from Class ACM [abbr.: ACM_CAP.4] has content and presentation of evidence Element 5C, developer action element 2D and evaluator action element 1E). Workunit elements, which optionally refine the elements stated above, are linked to content and presentation of evidence elements, developer action elements and evaluator action elements (e.g. Workunit ACM_CAP.4-8 is linked to content and presentation of evidence Element ACM_CAP.4.5C).

Specific evidence elements are linked to their corresponding components through a *has_input* relationship (e.g. Component ACM_CAP.4 needs evidence

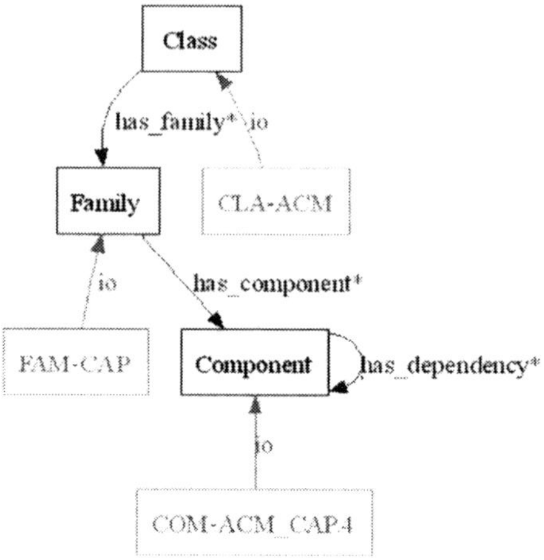

Fig. 2. Class, Family, Component

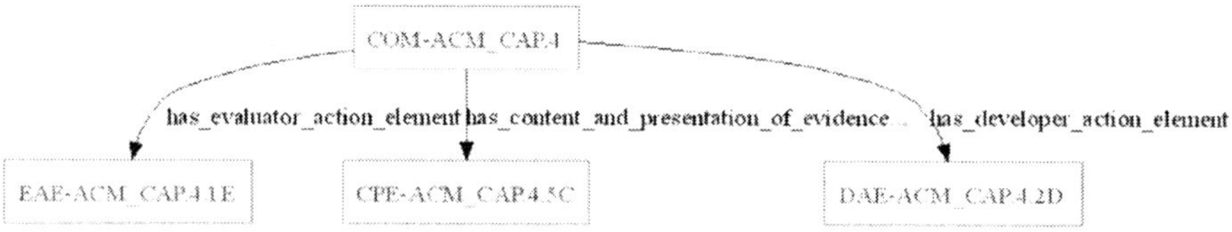

Fig. 3. Class, Family, Component

input configuration management documentation and the TOE suitable for testing).

Using our ontology, the following knowledge about the aforementioned elements can be derived: E.g. evaluation assurance level 4 needs several security assurance activities [6]. Among them is the activity "configuration management". This activity evaluates specific components, such as Component 4 (generation support and acceptance procedures) in Family CAP (configuration management capabilities) from Class ACM (configuration management). Further drilling down shows that this component has specific dependencies (e.g. to ALC_DVS.1: Identification of security measures), developer action elements (e.g. "The developer shall provide CM documentation."[6]), content and presentation of evidence elements (e.g. "The CM documentation shall include a configuration list, a CM plan, and an acceptance plan" [6]) and evaluator action elements (e.g. "The evaluator shall confirm that the information provided meets all requirements for content and presentation of evidence" [6]). These elements can be refined optionally by specific workunits (e.g. "The evaluator shall examine the configuration list to determine that it identifies the configuration items that comprise the TOE" [6]) for the content and presentation of evidence element stated above.

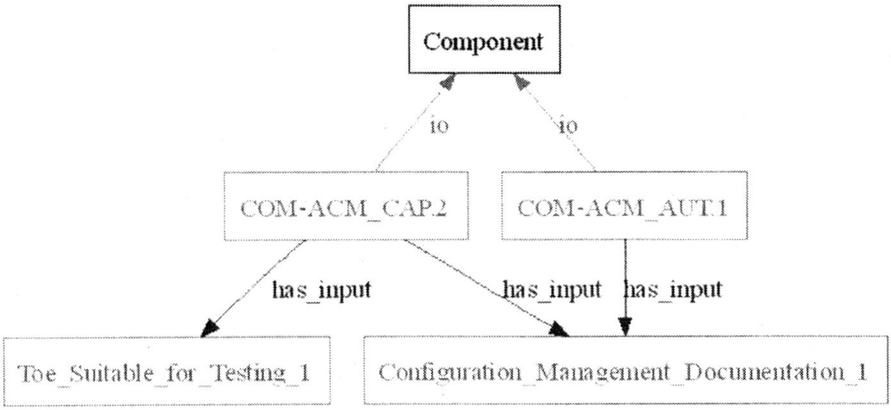

Fig. 4. Evidence Elements

3 Common Criteria Ontology Tool

Based on the Common Criteria Ontology, introduced in section 2, we created an evaluation tool to support the CC certification process. Figure 5 shows the main user interface. It enables the user to augment each certification sub-process with comments and the progress status. The tool is also useful to mitigate the "composition problem". These conflicts may arise when combining different protection profiles or security targets [17].

3.1 Document Preparation and Linking

Besides the simple listing of all CC classes, including their families and concepts, the tool is able to filter only those components which are necessary for a certification against a specific EAL level. Due to the hiding of unnecessary components this feature eases the work for the evaluator and enhances the quality and efficiency of the certification process. The bulk of preparatory work for a typical Common Criteria certification consists of checking documents against a certain target state required by the certification level; we thus implemented a feature to link relevant documents with certain components to enhance the clarity for the evaluator. Vetterling et al. [18] identified the increased need for documentation and the interdependencies between the documents as one of the major causes for the additional costs of a certification. Keeping all documents current and maintaining consistency can be achieved easier by using the previously described approach: (1) hiding of currently not relevant documents, and (2) linking of relevant documents.

The status of each developer and evaluator action element is indicated by a status symbol; the tool provides the evaluator with the option to augment component instances with comments to document the evaluation process. Using comments and linking relevant documents enables the user to generate reports

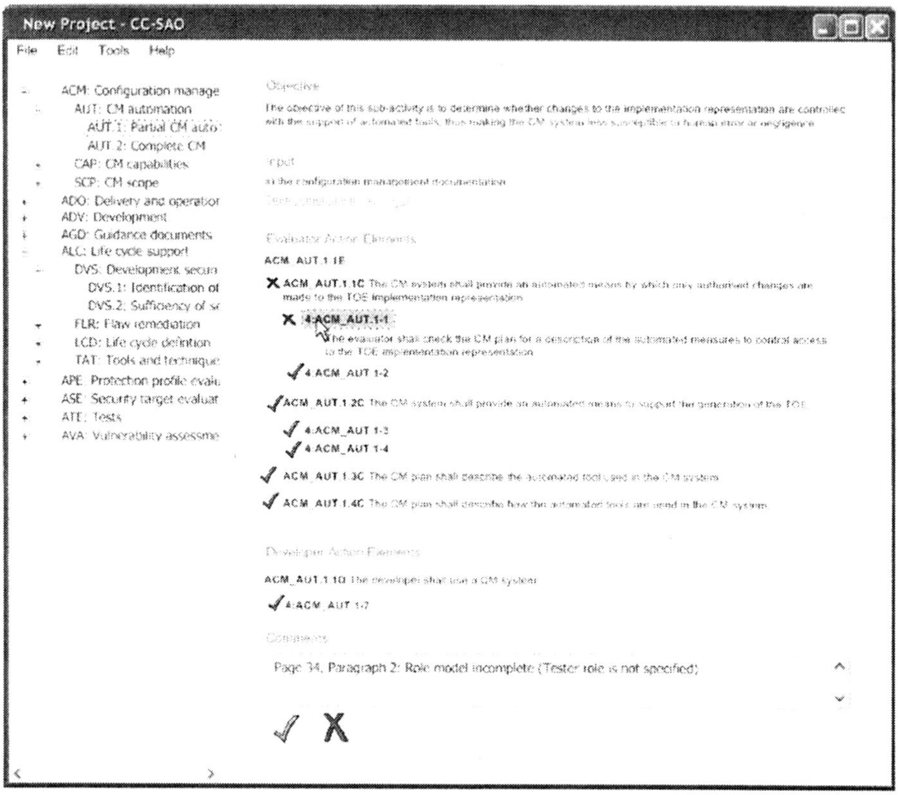

Fig. 5. Common Criteria Ontology Tool - main user interface

including a history of the evaluation process. By storing the entire evaluation history it is possible to generate various report types, specifically tailored to different target groups. The tool creates a concise executive summary of the evaluation results and, in addition, a detailed comparison (including comments and progress status) of different evaluation process states. Such reports are invaluable in review cycles, both for the evaluator and the developer.

So far we described a tool that supports the work for the evaluator by preparing, storing and organizing the evaluation data in a single repository. The "Tagging" approach (Subsection 3.1) enriches every component with relevant keywords to enhance the evaluation process.

3.2 The "Tagging" approach

By linking documents with the corresponding Common Criteria components and tagging each component with specific keywords we established the basis to support the evaluator in the document review.

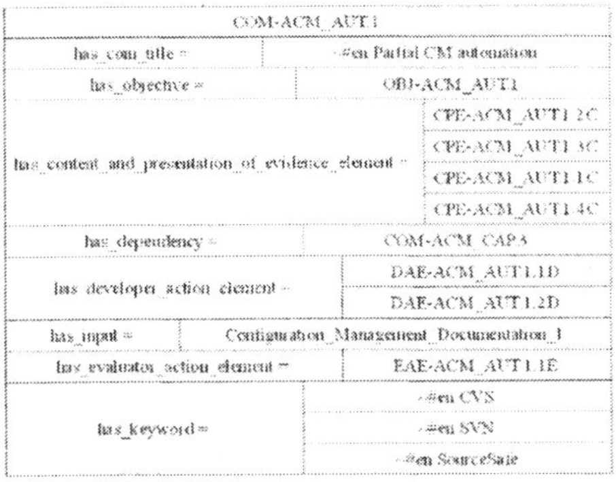

Fig. 6. Component instance with keyword tags

Based on our experience we believe that certain components and the corresponding documents often contain similar keywords and concepts. Figure 6 visualizes a typical component instance with its keywords and the input document reference. The keywords represent concepts which can be evidence for the compliance with the connected action elements. For example the keyword "CVS" in Figure 6, appearing in the Configuration Management Documentation, may be an indication that a configuration management system is used. Moreover, the text parts are visually highlighted in the input document, so the evaluator can check the corresponding information.

Obviously the keywords have to be entered into the ontology; this process can be done either manually by the evaluator or automatically supported by the following approach: In our previous research work on security ontologies [7, 8, 9] we presented an ontology which comprises infrastructure components as well as security related concepts (threats and countermeasures). The goal of this work was to run a risk analysis and threat simulations against corporate assets. Our security ontology (i.e. a knowledge base) can be used to extract keywords for the Common Criteria Ontology by querying it with SPARQL [13].

In the following this approach is described in detail in connection with the Life Cycle Support Activity - Evaluation of Development security (ALC_DVS.1). One point of Action ALC_DVS.1.1E states that the evaluator shall search for security measures: "physical, for example physical access controls used to prevent unauthorized access to the TOE development environment (during normal working hours and at other times)". Figure 7 shows an abridgement of biometric access control systems (Category sec:PhysicalThreatPrevention), taken from the Security Ontology.

To fill the Common Criteria automatically with keywords we have to query the ontology - in the following listing a SPARQL query is shown that lists all biometric system instances (the keywords we need):

```
SELECT ?biometricKeyword
WHERE {?biometricKeyword rdf:type sec:Biometric}
```

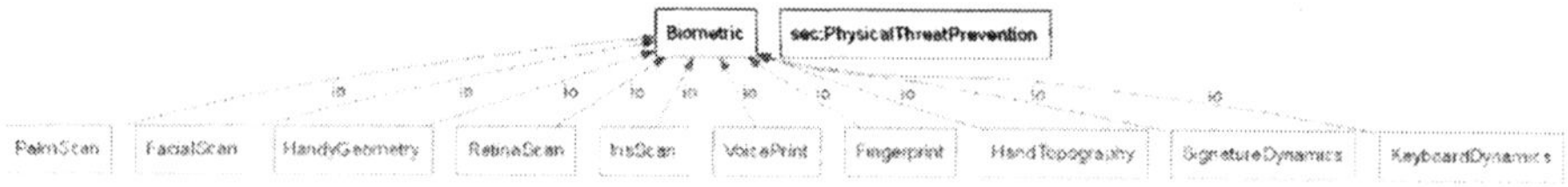

Fig. 7. Biometric access control systems

An example will clarify our approach: if the evaluator wants to examine the Action Element "Action ALC_DVS.1.1E", the system automatically searches for the keywords listed in Figure 7 (and corresponding notation variants) to present the evaluator evidence for biometric access control systems. Combining various keywords increases the hit possibility of the demanded section. On the other hand, if no keywords are found, it is unlikely that a biometric access control is in place. The tagging approach has similar goals as the method proposed by Razzazi et. al [19], i.e. to speed up the entire process. In contrast, however, we do not propose to decompose the entire CC process into smaller subtasks as this tighter framework will impede experienced developers and evaluators.

4 Conclusion

To conquer the very time-consuming and expensive Common Criteria evaluation process for a specific CC evaluation assurance level, we first presented a CC ontology, comprising the entire CC domain with special focus on security assurance requirements relevant for the evaluation. The ontology is easily browseable with any standard RDF or OWL visualization tool - unlike the already available PDF or paper version of the CC standard. Second, our approach provides the possibility to query the data structure in an efficient way using SPARQL. Our third contribution is the CC Ontology Tool; this tool takes the CC ontology as input and supports the evaluation process in several novel ways such as tagging and linking. Several CC certifications showed us that certain components and the corresponding documents often contain similar keywords and concepts, hence we introduced the "Tagging" approach in our CC ontology, which supports the evaluator in the document review by reusing information produced in earlier CC evaluation certification processes.

5 Acknowledgment

This work was performed at the Research Center Secure Business Austria funded by the Federal Ministry of Economics and Labor of the Republic of Austria (BMWA) and the federal province of Vienna.

References

1. CC, "Common criteria for information technology security evaluation. part 1: Introduction and general model, version 2.3," 2005.
2. V. Raskin, C. F. Hempelmann, K. E. Triezenberg, and S. Nirenburg, "Ontology in information security: a useful theoretical foundation and methodological tool." in *In Proceedings of the 2001 Workshop on New Security Paradigms, NSPW '01, ACM Press, New York*, 2001.
3. K. Olthoff, "A cursory examination of market forces driving the use of protection profiles." in *In Proceedings of the 1999 Workshop on New Security Paradigms, NSPW '99, ACM Press*, 2000.
4. J. Hearn, "Does the common criteria paradigm have a future?" *Security & Privacy Magazine, IEEE*, vol. 2, p. 6465, 2004.
5. S. Katzke, "The common criteria years (19931998): Looking back and ahead." Presentation, 4th International Common Criteria Conference, 2003.
6. CC, "Common criteria for information technology security evaluation. part 3: Security assurance requirements, version 2.3," 2005.
7. A. Ekelhart, S. Fenz, M. Klemen, and E. Weippl, "Security ontologies: Improving quantitative risk analysis," in *in Proceedings HICCS*, 2007.
8. A. Ekelhart, S. Fenz, M. Klemen, A. Tjoa, and E. Weippl, "Ontology-based business knowledge for simulating threats to corporate assets," in *in Proceedings of the International Conference on Practical Aspects of Knowledge Management PAKM, Springer Lecture Notes in Computer Science*, 2006.
9. S. Fenz and E. Weippl, "Ontology based it-security planning," in *in IEEE Proceedings on IEEE International Symposium Pacific Rim Dependable Computing PRDC*, 2006.
10. CC, "Common criteria for information technology security evaluation. part 2: Security functional requirements, version 2.3," 2005.
11. RDF, "Resource description framework. www.w3.org/rdf/," 2006.
12. OWL, "http://www.w3.org/tr/owl-features/," 2004.
13. SPARQL, "Sparql query language for rdf. http://www.w3.org/tr/rdf-sparql-query/," 2006.
14. R. Neches, R. Fikes, T. Finin, T. Gruber, R. Patil, T. Senator, and W. Swartout, "Enabling technology for knowledge sharing." *AI Magazin 12*, vol. 3, pp. 36–56, 1991.
15. A. Gmez-Prez, M. Fernndez-Lpez, and O. Corcho, *Ontological Engineering*. Springer, London, first edition, 2004.
16. Protege, "The protege ontology editor and knowledge acquisition system. http://protege.stanford.edu/," 2005.
17. F. Keblawi and D. Sullivan, "Applying the common criteria in systems engineering," *Security & Privacy Magazine, IEEE*, vol. 4, pp. 50–55, 2006.
18. M. Vetterling, G.Wimmel, and A.Wisspeintner, "Secure systems development based on the common criteria: the palme project," in *In Proceedings of the 10th ACM SIGSOFT Symposium on Foundations of Software Engineering, SIGSOFT '02/FSE-10, ACM Press, New York*, 2002.
19. M. Razzazi, M. Jafari, S. Moradi, H. Sharifipanah, M. Damanafshan, K. Fayazbakhsh, and A. Nickabadi, "Common criteria security evaluation: A time and cost effective approach." in *in Procedings Information and Communication Technologies, ICTTA*, vol. 2, 2006, pp. 3287– 3292.

Management of Exceptions on Access Control Policies*

J. G. Alfaro[1,2], F. Cuppens[1], and N. Cuppens-Boulahia[1]

[1] GET/ENST-Bretagne, 35576 Cesson Sévigné - France,
{frederic.cuppens,nora.cuppens}@enst-bretagne.fr

[2] Universitat Oberta de Catalunya, 08018 Barcelona - Spain,
joaquin.garcia-alfaro@uoc.edu

Abstract. The use of languages based on positive or negative expressiveness is very common for the deployment of security policies (i.e., deployment of permissions and prohibitions on firewalls through single-handed positive or negative condition attributes). Although these languages may allow us to specify any policy, the single use of positive or negative statements alone leads to complex configurations when excluding some specific cases of general rules that should always apply. In this paper we survey such a management and study existing solutions, such as ordering of rules and segmentation of condition attributes, in order to settle this lack of expressiveness. We then point out to the necessity of full expressiveness for combining both negative and positive conditions on firewall languages in order to improve this management of exceptions on access control policies. This strategy offers us a more efficient deployment of policies, even using fewer rules.

1 Introduction

Current firewalls are still being configured by security officers in a manual fashion. Each firewall usually provides, moreover, its own configuration language that, most of the times, present a lack of expressiveness and semantics. For instance, most firewall languages are based on rules in the form $R_i : \{condition_i\} \rightarrow decision_i$, where i is the relative position of the rule within the set of rules, $decision_i$ is a boolean expression in $\{accept, deny\}$, and $\{condition_i\}$ is a conjunctive set of condition attributes, such as *protocol* (p), *source* (s), *destination* (d), *source port* (sport), *destination port* (dport), and so on. This conjunctive set of conditions attributes, i.e., $\{condition_i\}$, is mainly composed of either positive (e.g., A) or negative (e.g., $\neg A$) statements for each attribute, but does not allow us to combine both positive and negative statements (e.g., $A \wedge \neg B$) for a single attribute, as many other languages with

* This work was supported by funding from the French ministry of research, under the *ACI DESIRS* project; and the Spanish Government (CICYT) project *SEG2004-04352-C04-04*.

Please use the following format when citing this chapter:

Garcia-Alfaro, J., Cuppens, F., and Cuppens-Boulahia, N., 2007, in IFIP International Federation for Information Processing, Volume 232, New Approaches for Security, Privacy and Trust in Complex Environments, eds. Venter, H., Eloff, M., Labuschagne, L., Eloff, J., von Solms, R., (Boston: Springer), pp. 97–108.

full expressive power, such as SQL-like languages [8], do. The use of more general access control languages, such as the eXtensible Access Control Markup Language (XACML) [10], also present such a lack of expressiveness. This fact leads to complex administration tasks when dealing with exclusion issues on access control scenarios, i.e., when some cases must be excluded of general rules that should always apply.

Let us suppose, for instance, the policy of a hospital where, in general, all doctors are allowed to consult patient's medical records. Later, the policy changes and doctors going on strike are not allowed to consult medical records; but, as an exception to the previous one, and for emergencies purposes, doctors going on strike are still allowed to consult the records. Regarding the use of a language with expressiveness enough to combine both positive and negative statements, one may deploy the previous example as follows. We first assume the following definitions: *(A)* "*Doctors*"; *(B)* "*Doctors going on strike*"; *(C)* "*Doctors working on emergencies*". We then deploy the hospital's policy goals, i.e., *(1)* "*In Hospital, doctors can access patient's medical records.*"; *(2)* "*In Hospital, and only for emergency purposes, doctors going on strike can access patient's medical records.*"; through the following statement: "*In Hospital,* $(A \wedge (\neg B \vee C))$ *can access patient's medical records*".

The use of languages based on partial expressiveness may lead us to very complicated situations when managing this kind of configurations on firewalls and filtering routers. In this paper, we focus on this problem and survey current solutions, such as first and last matching strategies, segmentation of condition attributes, and partial ordering of rules. We then discuss how the combination of both negative and positive expressiveness on configuration languages may help us to improve those solutions. This strategy allows to perform a more efficient deployment of network access control policies, even using fewer rules, and properly manage exceptions and exclusion of attributes on firewall and filtering router configurations.

The rest of this paper is organized as follows. Section 2 recalls our motivation problem, by showing some representative examples, surveying related solutions, and overviewing their advantages and drawbacks. Section 3 then discusses our approach. Section 4 overviews some related work, and, finally, Section 5 closes the paper.

2 Management of Exceptions via Partial Expressiveness

Before going further in this section, let us start with an example to illustrate our motivation problem. We first consider the network setup shown in Figure 1(a), together with the following general premise: "*In Private, all hosts can access web resources on the Internet*". We assume, moreover, that firewall FW_1 implements a closed default policy, specified in its set of rules at the last entry, in the form $R_n : deny$. Then, we deploy the premise over firewall FW_1 with the following rule:

$$R_1 : (s \in Private \wedge d \in any \wedge p = tcp \wedge dport = 80) \rightarrow accept$$

Regarding the exclusion issues pointed out above, and according to the extended setup shown in Figure 1(b), let us assume that we must now apply the following three exceptions over the general security policy:

1. *The interfaces of firewall FW_1 (i.e., Interf-fw = {111.222.1.1, 111.222.100.1}) are not allowed to access web resources on the Internet.*
2. *The hosts in Admin are not allowed to access web resources.*
3. *The hosts in Corporate do not belong to the zone Internet.*

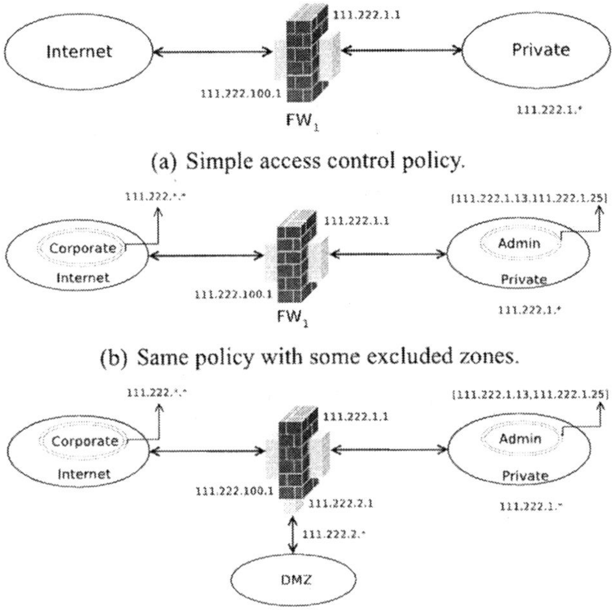

(a) Simple access control policy.

(b) Same policy with some excluded zones.

(c) Extended access control policy.

Fig. 1. Sample access control policy setups.

According to the first exception, we should exclude the IP address 111.222.1.1 from the hosts of *Private*. Similarly, we must exclude the whole set of hosts in zone *Admin* from the zone *Private*, and the whole set of hosts in zone *Corporate*, i.e., the range 111.222.$*$.$*$, from *Internet*. The use of a language with expressiveness enough to combine both positive and negative statements may allow us to deploy the previous policy goal, i.e., "*All the hosts in (Private $\wedge$ ¬Admin $\wedge$ ¬Interf-fw) are allowed to access web resources on (Internet $\wedge$ ¬Corporate)*", as the following single rule:

R_1 : ($s \in$ (Private $\wedge$ ¬Admin $\wedge$ ¬Interf-fw) $\wedge$ $d \in$ (any $\wedge$ ¬Corporate) $\wedge$ $p = tcp \wedge dport = 80) \rightarrow accept$

However, the lack of semantics and expressiveness of current firewall configuration languages (specially the impossibility for combining both positive and negative statements on single condition attributes) forces us to use different strategies to make up for this lack of expressiveness. We overview in the following sections some possible solutions for applying the previous example by means of such languages.

2.1 First Matching Strategy

Most firewalls solve the managing of exceptions by an ordering of rules. For instance, the configuration language for IPTables, the administration software used to configure GNU/Linux-based firewalls through the Netfilter framework, is based on a *first matching* strategy, i.e., the firewall is parsing the rules until a rule applies. When no rule applies, the decision depends on the default policy: in the case of an open policy, the packet is accepted whereas if the policy is closed, the packet is rejected. Other languages, like the configuration language of IPFilter, the administration software for configuring FreeBSD-, NetBSD- and Solaris 10-based firewalls, apply the opposite strategy, called *last matching*. Similar approaches have also been proposed in other security domains, such as the formal access control proposed in [9] to specify protection policies on XML databases. Through a first matching strategy, one may specify the handling of exceptions in the form $R_1 : (s \in (A \wedge \neg B)) \rightarrow accept$ by means of the following ordering of rules:

$$\begin{array}{l} R_1 : (s \in B) \rightarrow deny \\ R_2 : (s \in A) \rightarrow accept \end{array}$$

Regarding the access control setup shown in Figure 1(b), together with the set of policy goals and exceptions defined above, i.e., "*All the hosts in (Private ∧ ¬Admin ∧ ¬Interf-fw) are allowed to access web resources on (Internet ∧ ¬Corporate)*", a possible solution for such a motivation example through a first matching strategy shall be the following set of rules:

$$\begin{array}{l} R_1 : (s \in 111.222.1.0/24 \wedge d \in 111.222.0.0/16 \wedge p = tcp \wedge dport = 80) \rightarrow deny \\ R_2 : (s \in [111.222.1.13, 111.222.1.25] \wedge d \in any \wedge p = tcp \wedge dport = 80) \rightarrow deny \\ R_3 : (s \in 111.222.1.1 \wedge d \in any \wedge p = tcp \wedge dport = 80) \rightarrow deny \\ R_4 : (s \in 111.222.1.0/24 \wedge d \in any \wedge p = tcp \wedge dport = 80) \rightarrow accept \\ R_5 : deny \end{array}$$

Although this strategy offers a proper solution for the handling of exceptions, it is well known that it may introduce many other configuration errors, such as *shadowing* of rules and *redundancy* [1, 2], as well as important drawbacks when managing rule updates, specially when adding or removing new general rules and/or exceptions. For example, if we consider now the extended access control policy shown in Figure 1(c), together with the insertion of the following general rule: "*In Private, all hosts can access web resources on the zone DMZ*"; and the insertion of the following exception to the previous rule: "*The interfaces of firewall FW_1 (i.e., Interf-fw = {111.222.1.1, 111.222.2.1, 111.222.100.1}) are not allowed to access web resources on the zone DMZ*"; we shall agree that the resulting rules according with these two new premises are the following ones: $R_i : (s \in 111.222.1.1 \wedge d \in 111.222.2.0/24 \wedge p = tcp \wedge dport = 80) \rightarrow deny$; $R_j : (s \in 111.222.1.0/24 \wedge d \in 111.222.2.0/24 \wedge p = tcp \wedge dport = 80) \rightarrow accept$. Such new rules must be inserted in the previous set of rules as shown in Figure 2.

Notice that, in the previous example, the only possible ordering of rules that guarantees the defined assumptions forces us to place the new general rule in the second

$R_1 : (s \in 111.222.1.1 \wedge d \in any \wedge p = tcp \wedge dport = 80) \rightarrow deny$
$R_2 : (s \in 111.222.1.0/24 \wedge d \in 111.222.2.0/24 \wedge p = tcp \wedge dport = 80) \rightarrow accept$
$R_3 : (s \in [111.222.1.13, 111.222.1.25] \wedge d \in any \wedge p = tcp \wedge dport = 80) \rightarrow deny$
$R_4 : (s \in 111.222.1.0/24 \wedge d \in 111.222.0.0/16 \wedge p = tcp \wedge dport = 80) \rightarrow deny$
$R_5 : (s \in 111.222.1.0/24 \wedge d \in any \wedge p = tcp \wedge dport = 80) \rightarrow accept$
$R_6 : deny$

Fig. 2. Set of rules for our second motivation example.

position of the set of rules as $R_2 : (s \in 111.222.1.0/24 \wedge d \in 111.222.2.0/24 \wedge p = tcp \wedge dport = 80) \rightarrow accept$. Let us also notice that the related rule to the local exception "*The interfaces of firewall FW_1 are not allowed to access web resources on the Internet*", i.e., the former rule $R_3 : (s \in 111.222.1.1 \wedge d \in any \wedge p = tcp \wedge dport = 80) \rightarrow deny$, is now a global exception, and it must be placed in the first position of the set, i.e., it must be placed as $R_1 : (s \in 111.222.1.1 \wedge d \in any \wedge p = tcp \wedge dport = 80) \rightarrow deny$.

As we can observe, the use of this strategy will continously increase the complexity of the firewall's configuration as the combination of rules will also do. Furthermore, we can even propose combinations of rules that will not be possible to implement by simply ordering the rules. For instance, let us consider the following two condition attributes A and B, such that $A \cap B \neq \emptyset$, and the following two rules: $R_1 : (s \in (A \wedge \neg B)) \rightarrow accept$; $R_2 : (s \in (B \wedge \neg A)) \rightarrow accept$. As we have seen in this section, the use of a first matching strategy should easily allow us to separately implement these two rules as follows:

$R_{1.1} : (s \in B) \rightarrow deny$ $R_{1.2} : (s \in A) \rightarrow accept$	$R_{2.1} : (s \in A) \rightarrow deny$ $R_{2.2} : (s \in B) \rightarrow accept$

However, the simple ordering of rules for such an example will not allow us to find out any appropriate combination of rules R_1 and R_2. Instead, we should first compute $A \cap B$ and then transform the previous rules as follows:

$R_{1.1} : (s \in (A \cap B)) \rightarrow deny$ $R_{1.2} : (s \in A) \rightarrow accept$	$R_{2.1} : (s \in (A \cap B)) \rightarrow deny$ $R_{2.2} : (s \in B) \rightarrow accept$

and finally deploy the following set of rules:

$R_1 : (s \in (A \cap B) \rightarrow deny$
$R_2 : (s \in A) \rightarrow accept$
$R_3 : (s \in B) \rightarrow accept$

We can thus conclude that through this strategy the handling of exceptions can lead to very complex configurations and even require additional computations and transformations processes. The administration of the final setup becomes, moreover, an error prone difficult task. Other strategies, like the segmentation of condition attributes or the use of a partial order of rules, will allow us to perform similar managements with better results. We see these other two strategies in the following section.

2.2 Segmentation of Condition Attributes

A second solution when managing exceptions on access control policies is to directly exclude the conditions from the set of rules. In [6, 5], for example, we presented a rewriting mechanism for such a purpose. Through this rewriting mechanism, one may specify the handling of exceptions in the form $R_1 : (s \in (A \wedge \neg B)) \rightarrow accept$ by simply transforming it into the following rule:

$$\boxed{R_1 : (s \in (A - B)) \rightarrow accept}$$

The deployment of our motivation example, i.e., "*All the hosts in (Private* $\wedge \neg$*Admin* $\wedge \neg$*Interf-fw) are allowed to access web resources on (Internet* $\wedge \neg$*Corporate)*", through this new strategy, will be managed as follows. We first obtain the set of exclusions, i.e., (*Private – Admin – Interf-fw*) and (*Internet – Corporate*):

*Private = 111.222.1.**
Admin = [111.222.1.13, 111.222.1.25]
Interf-fw = {111.222.1.1, 111.222.100.1}
Private – Admin – Interf-fw → *[111.222.1.2, 111.222.1.12]* ∪ *[111.222.1.26, 111.222.1.254]*
*Internet = *.*.*.**
Corporate = 111.222..**
Internet – Corporate → *[0.0.0.1, 111.222.255.254]* ∪ *[111.223.1.1, 255.255.255.254]*

Then, we must deploy the following rules:

$$\begin{array}{l}
R_1 : (s \in [111.222.1.2, 111.222.1.12] \wedge d \in [0.0.0.1, 111.222.255.254] \quad \backslash \\
\qquad \wedge\, p = tcp \wedge dport = 80) \rightarrow accept \\
R_2 : (s \in [111.222.1.26, 111.222.1.255] \wedge d \in [0.0.0.1, 111.222.255.254] \quad \backslash \\
\qquad \wedge\, p = tcp \wedge dport = 80) \rightarrow accept \\
R_3 : (s \in [111.222.1.2, 111.222.1.12] \wedge d \in [111.223.1.1, 255.255.255.254] \quad \backslash \\
\qquad \wedge\, p = tcp \wedge dport = 80) \rightarrow accept \\
R_4 : (s \in [111.222.1.26, 111.222.1.255] \wedge d \in [111.223.1.1, 255.255.255.254] \quad \backslash \\
\qquad \wedge\, p = tcp \wedge dport = 80) \rightarrow accept \\
R_5 : deny
\end{array}$$

The main advantage of this approach, apart from offering a solution for the management of exceptions, is that the ordering of rules is no longer relevant. Hence, one can perform a second transformation in a positive or negative manner: positive, when generating only permissions; and negative, when generating only prohibitions. Positive rewriting can be used in a closed policy whereas negative rewriting can be used in case of an open policy. After this second rewriting, the security officer will have a clear view of the accepted traffic (in the case of positive rewriting) or the rejected traffic (in the case of negative rewriting). However, it also presents some drawbacks. First, it may lead to very complex configuration setups that may even require a post-process of the different segments. Second, it may involve an important increase of the initial number of rules[2]. Nevertheless, such an increase may only degrade the performance of the firewall whether the associated parsing algorithm of the firewall depends on the number of rules. Third, the managing of rule updates through this strategy may also be very complex, since the addition or elimination of new exceptions may require a further segmentation processing of the rules. Some firewall implementations, moreover, are not able to directly manage ranges (e.g., they can require to transform the range $[111.222.1.2, 111.222.1.12]$ into $\{111.222.1.2/31 \cup 111.222.1.4/29 \cup 111.222.1.12/32\}$), and should require the use of third party tools.

2.3 Partial Ordering of Rules

To our knowledge, the most efficient solution to manage the problem of exceptions on access control policies would be by means of a strategy based on partial ordering of rules. Notice that in both first and last matching approaches (cf. Section 2.1), the interpretation of the rules depends on the total order in which the rules are specified, i.e., a total order describes the sequence of rules from a global point of view. However, this ordering of rules can also be implemented in a partial manner, where a set of local sequences of rules are defined for a given specific context.

In the case of NetFilter-based firewalls, for instance, a partial ordering of rules may be achieved through the chain mechanism of IPTables. In this way, we can group sets of rules into different chains, corresponding each one to a given exception. These rules are, moreover, executed in the same order they were included into the chain, i.e., by means of a first match strategy. When a specific traffic matches a rule in the chain, and the decision field of this rule is pointing out to the action $return$, the matching of rules within the given chain stops and the analysis of rules returns to the initial chain. Otherwise, the rest of rules in the chain are considered until a proper match is found. If no rule applies, the default policy of the chain does. Thus, through this new strategy, one may specify the handling of exceptions in the form $R_1 : (s \in (A \wedge \neg B)) \rightarrow accept$ as follows:

$$R_1 : (s \in A) \rightarrow jump\_to\ chain_A$$

$$R_2^{chain_A} : (s \in B) \rightarrow return$$
$$R_1^{chain_A} : accept$$

Regarding the scenario shown in Figure 2, i.e., "*(1) All the hosts in (Private* $\wedge$ *¬Admin* $\wedge$ *¬Interf-fw) are allowed to access web resources on (Internet* $\wedge$ *¬Corporate)*; *(2) All the hosts in (Private* $\wedge$ *¬Interf-fw) are allowed to access web resources on DMZ*", we can now implement such premises via two chains, *private-to-internet* (or *p2i* for short) and *private-to-dmz* (or *p2d* for short), as follows:

[2] This increase is not always a real drawback since the use of a parsing algorithm independent of the number of rules is the best solution for the deployment of firewall technologies [14].

$R_1 : (s \in 111.222.1.0/24 \wedge d \in any \wedge p = tcp \wedge dport = 80) \rightarrow jump\_to\ p2i$
$R_2 : (s \in 111.222.1.0/24 \wedge d \in 111.222.2.0/24 \wedge p = tcp \wedge dport = 80) \rightarrow jump\_to\ p2d$
$R_3 : deny$

$R_1^{p2i} : (s \in 111.222.1.1) \rightarrow return$
$R_2^{p2i} : (s \in [111.222.1.13, 111.222.1.25]) \rightarrow return$
$R_3^{p2i} : (d \in 111.222.0.0/16) \rightarrow return$
$R_4^{p2i} : accept$

$R_1^{p2d} : (s \in 111.222.1.1) \rightarrow return$
$R_2^{p2d} : accept$

Let us now consider the same rules specified in the syntax of NetFilter. The first two rules create a chain called "private-to-internet" (or *p2i* for short) and a chain called "private-to-dmz" (or *p2d* for short). The third rule corresponds to the positive inclusion condition for the first general case (this way, when a given packet will match this rule, the decision is to jump to the chain *p2i* and check the negative exclusion conditions). Similarly, the fourth rule corresponds to the positive inclusion condition for the second general case. We shall observe that in order to deploy this example over a firewall based on Netfilter we should first verify whether its version of IPTables has been patched to properly manage ranges. We must also correctly define in the final IPTables script those variables such as $PRIVATE, $DMZ, etc.

```
iptables -N p2i
iptables -N p2d

iptables -A FORWARD -s $PRIVATE -p tcp –dport 80 -j p2i
iptables -A FORWARD -s $PRIVATE -d $DMZ -p tcp –dport 80 -j p2d
iptables -A FORWARD -j DROP

iptables -A p2i -s $INTERF_FIREWALL -j RETURN
iptables -A p2i -s $ADMIN -j RETURN
iptables -A p2i -d $CORPORATE -j RETURN
iptables -A p2i -j ACCEPT

iptables -A p2d -s $INTERF_FIREWALL -j DROP
iptables -A p2d -j ACCEPT
```

The main advantages of this strategy (i.e., partial ordering of rules) are threefold. First, it allows a complete separation between exceptions and general rules; second, the ordering of general rules is no longer relevant; and third, the insertion and elimination of both general rules and exception is very simple. We consider, moreover, that a proper reorganization of rules from a total order strategy to a partial order one may also help us to improve not only the handling of exception, but also the firewall's performance on high-speed networks [15, 11]. In [15], on the one hand, the authors propose a refinement process of rules which generates a decision-like tree implemented through the chain mechanism of IPTables. Their approach basically reorganizes the set of configuration rules into an improved setup, in order to obtain a much flatter design, i.e., a new set of configuration rules, where the number of rules not only decreases but also leads to a more efficient packet matching process. In [11], on the other hand, the authors also propose a reorganization of rules in order to better deploy the final configuration. Nevertheless, both authors in [15] and [11] do not seem to address the handling of exceptions, neither expressiveness aspects of their configuration language – that seems to rely upon partial expressiveness languages.

3 Use of Full Expressiveness

Notice that the solutions above overviewed are always based on partial expressiveness, i.e., they implement security policies by means of security rules whose condition attributes are mainly composed of either positive (e.g., A) or negative (e.g., $\neg A$) statements, but they do not allow us to combine both positive and negative statements (e.g., $A \wedge \neg B$) for a single attribute at the same time. Although we have seen in the previous section that these languages may allow us to specify any possible security policy, they can can lead to very complex configurations when dealing with the management of exceptions. However, the use of both negative and positive statements for each condition attribute may allow us to specify filtering rules in a more efficient way. The use of a structured SQL-like language [8], for example, will allow us to manage the handling of exceptions in the form $R_1 : (s \in (A \wedge \neg B)) \rightarrow accept$ through the use of queries like the following ones:

select decision **from** $firewall$ **where** $(s \in A) \wedge (s \notin B)$	**select** decision **from** $firewall$ **where** $(s \in A)$ **minus** **select** decision **from** $firewall$ **where** $(s \in B)$

However, these kind of languages are not currently being used for the configuration of firewalls or similar devices – at least not for managing exceptions on access control policies, as defined in this paper. We consider that they will allow security officers to deploy the security policies in a more efficient manner, as well as to properly manage the handling of exceptions on access control policies. Let us for example assume that the configuration language we have been using along the examples of this paper allows us the combination of either positive (e.g., A) and negative (e.g., $\neg A$) statements for each attribute of a single filtering rule. For the sake of simplicity, let us just assume the use of a 2-tuple for specifying both positive and negative values of each attribute (e.g., $R_i : (s \in (A \wedge \neg B)) \rightarrow accept$ becomes $R_i : (s[+] \in A \wedge s[-] \in B) \rightarrow accept$). Let us also assume that both positive and negative values are initialized to $\emptyset$ by default. Let us finally assume that we rewrite the matching algorithm implemented in our hypothetical firewall FW_1 into Algorithm 1. In this case, we can easily deploy the first motivation example based on Figure 1(b)'s setup, i.e., "*All the hosts in (Private $\wedge$ $\neg$Admin $\wedge$ $\neg$Interf-fw) are allowed to access web resources on (Internet $\wedge$ $\neg$Corporate)*", as follows:

Algorithm 1: `MatchingAlgorithm`

---

input : (1) firewall's filtering rules: $r_1 \ldots r_n$;
(2) firewall's default policy: *policy*;
(3) packet: p

output: *decision*

$decision \leftarrow policy$;

$H \leftarrow$ `GetPacketHeaders` (p);

/* Let $r_i = (A_1^i[+] \in V_1^+) \wedge (A_1^i[-] \in V_1^-) \cdots (A_p^i[+] \in V_p^+) \wedge (A_p^i[-] \in V_p^-) \rightarrow d_i$. */

/* where $A_{1..p}^i[+]$ and $A_{1..p}^i[-]$ are, respectively, the set of positive and negative */

/* attribute conditions of rule r_i; and $V_{1..p}^+$ and $V_{1..p}^-$ are, respectively, the set */

/* of positive and negative attribute values of rule r_i; */

for $i \leftarrow 1$ **to** n **do**

  if $(H_1 \cap V_1^+ \neq \emptyset) \wedge (H_1 \cap V_1^- = \emptyset) \cdots (H_p \cap V_p^+ \neq \emptyset) \wedge (H_p \cap V_p^- = \emptyset)$ **then**

    $decision \leftarrow d_i$;

    break; /* Leave the loop */

return *decision*;

$R_1 : (s[+] \in 111.222.1.0/24 \ \wedge \ s[-] \in \{[111.222.1.13, 111.222.1.25] \ \backslash$
$\cup \ 111.222.1.1\} \ \wedge \ d[+] \in any \ \wedge \ d[-] \in 111.222.0.0/16 \ \wedge \ p[+] = tcp \ \backslash$
$\wedge \ dport[+] = 80) \rightarrow accept$
$R_2 : deny;$

Regarding the second motivation example, i.e., "(1) *All the hosts in (Private ∧ ¬Admin ∧ ¬Interf-fw) are allowed to access web resources on (Internet ∧ ¬Corporate)*; (2) *All the hosts in (Private ∧ ¬Interf-fw) are allowed to access web resources on the zone DMZ*", we can now properly specify the resulting set of rules as follows:

$R_1 : (s[+] \in 111.222.1.0/24 \ \wedge \ s[-] \in \{[111.222.1.13, 111.222.1.25] \ \backslash$
$\cup \ 111.222.1.1\} \ \wedge \ d[+] \in any \ \wedge \ d[-] \in 111.222.3.0/24 \ \wedge \ p[+] = tcp \ \backslash$
$\wedge \ dport[+] \in 80) \rightarrow accept$
$R_2 : (s[+] \in 111.222.1.0/24 \ \wedge \ s[-] \in \ 111.222.1.1\} \ \wedge \ d[+] \in 111.222.2.0/24 \ \backslash$
$\wedge \ p[+] = tcp \ \wedge \ dport[+] \in 80) \rightarrow accept$
$R_3 : deny;$

As we can observe, the use of a language based on both positive and negative statements, when specifying the condition attributes of the security rules of a firewall, allows us a more efficient deployment of policies, even using fewer rules. We therefore consider that the little modification we must perform to improve the expressiveness of current firewall configuration languages may allow us to better afford the managing of exceptions on network access control policies. To verify such an assumption, we implemented a proof-of-concept by extending the matching algorithm of IPTables through a Netfilter extension. Due to space limitation, we do not cover in the paper this first proof-of-concept. However, a report regarding its implementation and performance is provided at the following address `http://www.crim-platinum.org/fex/report.pdf`.

4 Related Work

To our knowledge, very little research has been done on the use of full expressiveness languages for the management of firewall configuration as we address in this paper. In [12], for instance, a SQL-like query language for firewalls, called Structured Firewall Query Language is proposed. The authors do not seem to address, however, whether such a language can be used for examining incoming and outgoing traffic, neither to accept nor discard such traffic. The language seems to only be used for the understanding and analysis of firewall's functionality and behavior, rather than be used to perform packet matching or for expressiveness improvement purposes. Similarly, the authors in [13] propose a firewall analysis tool for the management and testing of global firewall policies through a query-like language. However, the expressiveness power of such a language is very limited (just four condition attributes are allowed), and we doubt it may be useful to address our motivation problem.

Some other approaches for the use of formal languages to address the design and creation of firewall rules have been proposed in [4, 7, 3]. However, those approaches aim at specifying and deploying a global security policy through a refinement process that automatically generates the configuration rules of a firewall from a high level language. Thus, the problem of managing exceptions is handled in those works at a high level, rather than a concrete level, and so, the proper configuration once solved the managing issues shall be implemented through one of the strategies already discussed in Section 2. Finally, some proposals for the reorganization of filtering rules have been presented in [15, 11]. However, and as we already pointed out in Section 2, those approaches do not seem to address the handling of exceptions, neither expressiveness aspects of their configuration languages. Their reordering process aim at simply improve the firewall's performance on high speed networks, rather than to offer an easier way to manage the exclusion of condition attributes.

5 Conclusions

In this paper we have studied current strategies in order to manage and deploy policy exceptions when configuring network security components, such as firewalls and filtering routers. As we have discussed, those components are still being configured by security officers in a manual fashion through partial expresssiveness based languages. We have also discussed how the use of these languages can lead to very complex configurations when dealing with exclusions of general rules that should always apply. We finally pointed out to the necessity of full expressiveness for combining both negative and positive conditions on firewall languages in order to improve this management of exceptions on access control policies. As we have seen, the simple modification of a general packet matching algorithm can allow us to perform a more efficient deployment of policies by using almost always fewer rules.

As work in progress, we are actually evaluating the implementation of the strategy presented in this paper over NetFilter-based firewalls. For the moment, we have slightly modified its matching process according to the algorithm shown in Section 3, through the rewriting of a new matching process for IPTables. This first proof-of-concept demonstrates the practicability of our approach. However, we must conduct more experiments to study the real impact on the performance of Netfilter through real scenarios when using our proposal. We plan to address these evaluations and report the results in a forthcoming paper.

References

1. Alfaro, J. G., Cuppens, F., and Cuppens-Boulahia, N. Analysis of Policy Anomalies on Distributed Network Security Setups. In *11th European Symposium On Research In Computer Security (Esorics 2006)*, pp. 496–511, Hamburg, Germany, 2006.
2. Alfaro, J. G., Cuppens, F., and Cuppens-Boulahia, N. Towards Filtering and Alerting Rule Rewriting on Single-Component Policies. In *Intl. Conference on Computer Safety, Reliability, and Security (Safecomp 2006)*, pp. 182–194, Gdansk, Poland, 2006.
3. Alfaro, J. G., Cuppens, F., and Cuppens-Boulahia, N. Aggregating and Deploying Network Access Control Policies. In *Symposium on Frontiers in Availability, Reliability and Security (FARES), 2nd International Conference on Availability, Reliability and Security (ARES 2007)*, Vienna, Austria, 2007.
4. Bartal, Y., Mayer, A., Nissim, K., Wool, A. Firmato: A novel firewall management toolkit ACM Transactions on Computer Systems (TOCS), 22(4):381–420, 2004.
5. Cuppens, F., Cuppens-Boulahia, N., and Alfaro, J. G. Detection and Removal of Firewall Misconfiguration. In *Intl. Conference on Communication, Network and Information Security (CNIS05)*, pp. 154–162, 2005.
6. Cuppens, F., Cuppens-Boulahia, N., and Alfaro, J. G. Misconfiguration Management of Network Security Components. In *7th Intl. Symposium on System and Information Security*, Sao Paulo, Brazil, 2005.
7. Cuppens, F., Cuppens-Boulahia, N., Sans, T. and Miege, A. A formal approach to specify and deploy a network security policy. In *2nd Workshop on Formal Aspects in Security and Trust*, pp. 203–218, 2004.
8. Date, C. J. A guide to the SQL standard. Addison-Wesley Longman Publishing Co., Inc. Boston, MA, USA, 1989.
9. Gabillon, A. A formal access control model for XML databases. Lecture notes in computer science, 3674, pp. 86-103, February 2005.
10. Godik, S., Moses, T., and et al. eXtensible Access Control Markup Language (XACML) Version 2. Standard, OASIS. February 2005.
11. Hamed, H. and Al-Shaer, E. On autonomic optimization of firewall policy organization, Journal of High Speed Networks, 15(3):209–227, 2006.
12. Liu, A. X., Gouda, M. G., Ma, H. H., and Ngu, A. H. Firewall Queries. In *Proceedings of the 8th International Conference on Principles of Distributed Systems (OPODIS-04)*, pp. 197–212, 2004.
13. Mayer, A., Wool, A., Ziskind, E. Fang: A firewall analysis engine. *Security and Privacy Proceedings*, pp. 177–187, 2000.
14. Paul, O., Laurent, M., and Gombault, S. A full bandwidth ATM Firewall. In *Proceedings of the 6th European Symposium on Research in Computer Security (ESORICS 2000)*, pp. 206–221, 2000.
15. Podey, B., Kessler, T., and Melzer, H.D. Network Packet Filter Design and Performance. *Information Networking*, Lecture notes in computer science, 2662, pp. 803–816, 2003.

Security Analysis of Two Ultra-Lightweight RFID Authentication Protocols

Tieyan Li and Guilin Wang

Systems and Security Department
Institute for Infocomm Research (I^2R)
21 Heng Mui Keng Terrace, Singapore 119613
{litieyan, glwang}@i2r.a-star.edu.sg

Abstract. In this paper, we analyze the security vulnerabilities of two ultra-lightweight RFID mutual authentication protocols: LMAP and M^2AP, which are recently proposed by Peris-Lopez *et al.* We identify two effective attacks, namely *De-synchronization attack* and *Full-disclosure attack*, against their protocols. The former attack can break the synchronization between the RFID reader and the tag in a single protocol run so that they can not authenticate each other in any following protocol runs. The latter attack can disclose all the secret information stored on a tag by interrogating the tag multiple times. Thus it compromises the tag completely. Moreover, we point out the potential countermeasures to improve the security of above protocols.

1 Introduction

Radio Frequency Identification (RFID) systems have been aggressively deployed in a variety of applications, but their further pervasive usage is mainly limited by a number of security and privacy concerns [2, 7]. Since RFID tags are generally low cost with extremely limited resources, traditional security primitives can not be incorporated well. But when they are deployed in pervasive environment, where threats are not uncommon, security and privacy issues must be addressed before their massive deployment.

In this paper, we analyze the security of two ultra-lightweight RFID mutual authentication protocols, *w.r.t.*, LMAP [12] and M^2AP [13], which are recently proposed by Peris-Lopez *et al.* Different from the majority of existing solutions [15, 11, 9, 10, 1] of using classic cryptographic primitives, those two protocols are *ultra-lightweight*, since they use only simple bitwise operations to achieve mutual authentication between the RFID reader and the tags. Consequently, only about 300 gates are required to implement such an RFID tag. The protocols are very practical to be implemented on low-cost tags (with price $0.05 - 0.1$ US dollar), where less than $1K$ (out of totally $5K$) gates are allowed for security operations. Moreover, both LMAP and M^2AP protocols are claimed to be secure in sense of "Man-in-the-middle attack prevention" and "forgery resistance". However, we identify some vulnerabilities in those two protocols. Specifically,

---

Please use the following format when citing this chapter:

Li, T. and Wang, G., 2007, in IFIP International Federation for Information Processing, Volume 232, New Approaches for Security, Privacy and Trust in Complex Environments, eds. Venter, H., Eloff, M., Labuschagne, L., Eloff, J., von Solms, R., (Boston: Springer), pp. 109–120.

we first show that the protocols suffer from *De-synchronization attack.* The attack is very effective by only eavesdropping a single protocol run and then can destroy the "synchronization" between the database [1] and the tag. Thus, the tag cannot be further authenticated by the database. Then we present a more serious attack - *Full-disclosure attack.* By interacting with the reader ($O(1)$ times) and the tag ($O(m)$ times), this attack enables an attacker to compromise the ID of the tag, as well as all other secret information stored on a tag. Thus, all security properties claimed by above protocols are destroyed. Finally, to defend against the above attacks, we propose several potential countermeasures. One of them addresses the stateless property of the original protocols, which could be enhanced by adding status information into the protocols. As a result, additional ($\sim 40\%$) memory space is needed to implement such a tag.

The rest of this paper is organized as follows. Section 2 generally reviews the related work on RFID authentication protocols. Then, we review LMAP and M^2AP in Section 3 and analyze their vulnerabilities in Section 4. Section 5 points out several countermeasures. At last, we conclude the paper.

2 RFID Authentication Protocols

Authentication normally involves the use of secret data. Note that not all RFID tags are able to be authenticated since their inabilities of storing the secret data, *e.g.*, EPC class I tags. In the literature, one widely adopted assumption is using hash function within a tag. Weis *et al.* propose a randomized "hash lock" based mutual authentication protocol in [15]. Ohkubo *et al.* proposed a hash chain model embedding two hash functions in a tag [11]. Some solutions assume Pseudo-Random Function (PRF) in a tag. Molnar and Wagner use a tree scheme for authentication [9]. They further propose a scalable pseudonym protocol for ownership transfer [10]. Other assumptions includes using symmetric cipher, like [1], in which Feldhofer *et al.* proposed a simple two way challenge-response mutual authentication protocol with AES encryption algorithm. The other work [4] even assume public key cryptographic primitive, in which tags update their IDs with re-encryption scheme.

To reduce the gate numbers in RFID tags, some approaches have been proposed without assumptions on classic cryptographic primitives. In [16], Weis introduced the concept of human computer authentication protocol due to Hopper and Blum, adaptable to low-cost RFID tags. Further on, Weis and Juels proposed a lightweight symmetric-key authentication protocol named HB^+ [6]. The security of both the HB and the HB^+ protocols is based on the Learning Parity with Noise (LPN) Problem, whose hardness over random instances still remains as an open question. In [14], the authors proposed a set of extremely-lightweight challenge-response authentication protocols that are suitable for

[1] As in [12] and [13], the protocols make no difference on the database and the reader. Thereafter, we use either the reader or the database to indicating the counterpart of a tag in the authentication protocols.

authenticating tags, but their protocols can be broken by a powerful adversary [3]. In [5], Juels proposed a solution based on pseudonyms without using hash functions at all. The RFID tags store a short list of random identifiers or pseudonyms (known by authorized verifiers). When tag is queried, it emits the next pseudonym in the list. However, the list of pseudonyms should be reused or updated via an out-of-band channel after a number of authentications. Due to those reasons, Peris-Lopez et al. proposed two mutual authentication protocols for low-cost RFID tags: LMAP [12] and M^{2}AP [13], in which only simple bitwise operations are used. Their schemes are extremely lightweight and claimed to be secure against many attacks. However, we shall show the vulnerabilities of those protocols in the following sections.

3 Review of LMAP and M^{2}AP

In LMAP [12] protocol, simple operations such as: bitwise XOR ($\oplus$), bitwise OR ($\vee$), bitwise AND ($\wedge$), and addition mod 2^m ($+$), are used. Costly operations such as multiplications and hash evaluations are not required at all, and random number generation is only done by the reader. The scheme uses index-pseudonyms (IDSs). An index-pseudonym (96-bit length) is the index of a table (a row) where all the information about a tag is stored. Each tag is associated with a key, which is divided in four parts of 96 bits ($K = K1||K2||K3||K4$). As the IDS and the key (K) must be updated, it needs 480 bits of rewritable memory (EEPROM) in total. A ROM memory to store the 96-bit static identification number (ID) is also required. The protocol is shown in Table 1.

Tag identification: Reader $\longrightarrow$ Tag: *hello* Tag $\longrightarrow$ Reader: $IDS^{(n)}_{tag(i)}$	*where:*
LMAP mutual authentication: Reader $\longrightarrow$ Tag: $A\|\|B\|\|C$ Tag $\longrightarrow$ Reader: D	$A = IDS^{(n)}_{tag(i)} \ominus K1^{(n)}_{tag(i)} \oplus n1$ $B = (IDS^{(n)}_{tag(i)} \vee K2^{(n)}_{tag(i)}) + n1$ $C = IDS^{(n)}_{tag(i)} + K3^{(n)}_{tag(i)} + n2$ $D = (IDS^{(n)}_{tag(i)} + ID_{tag(i)}) \oplus n1 \oplus n2$
M^{2}AP mutual authentication: Reader $\longrightarrow$ Tag: $A\|\|B\|\|C$ Tag $\longrightarrow$ Reader: $D\|\|E$	*where: A, C same as in LMAP.* $B = (IDS^{(n)}_{tag(i)} \wedge K2^{(n)}_{tag(i)}) \vee n1$ $D = (IDS^{(n)}_{tag(i)} \vee ID_{tag(i)}) \wedge n2$ $E = (IDS^{(n)}_{tag(i)} + ID_{tag(i)}) \oplus n1$

Table 1. LMAP and M^{2}AP Protocol

The protocol has three main stages: tag identification, mutual authentication and then index-pseudonym updating and key updating. We repeat the updating equations here.

Index-Pseudonym and Key Updating: After the reader and the tag authenticated each other, they carry out the index-pseudonym and key updating by the following equations.

$$IDS^{(n+1)}_{tag(i)} = (IDS^{(n)}_{tag(i)} + (n2 \oplus K4^{(n)}_{tag(i)})) \oplus ID_{tag(i)}$$
$$K1^{(n+1)}_{tag(i)} = K1^{(n)}_{tag(i)} \oplus n2 \oplus (K3^{(n)}_{tag(i)} + ID_{tag(i)})$$
$$K2^{(n+1)}_{tag(i)} = K2^{(n)}_{tag(i)} \oplus n2 \oplus (K4^{(n)}_{tag(i)} + ID_{tag(i)})$$
$$K3^{(n+1)}_{tag(i)} = (K3^{(n)}_{tag(i)} \oplus n1) + (K1^{(n)}_{tag(i)} \oplus ID_{tag(i)})$$
$$K4^{(n+1)}_{tag(i)} = (K4^{(n)}_{tag(i)} \oplus n1) + (K2^{(n)}_{tag(i)} \oplus ID_{tag(i)})$$

LMAP [12] has a sister protocol called M^2AP [13], which is a very similar lightweight RFID mutual authentication protocol. The index-pseudonym updating equation in M^2AP is changed to $IDS^{(n+1)}_{tag(i)} = (IDS^{(n)}_{tag(i)} + (n2 \oplus n1)) \oplus ID_{tag(i)}$, slightly different from LMAP. All key updating operations are the same as LMAP. The table 1 describes M^2AP, too.

The authors of [12, 13] presented some security analysis and claimed that both LMAP and M^2AP are secure against the followings: *tag anonymity, mutual authentication, man-in-the-middle attack prevention, replay attack prevention, forgery resistance*. In the next section, we identify effective attacks that can break above protocols and show the flaws with all of their claims.

4 Vulnerabilities of LMAP and M^2AP

First of all, we remark that the above protocols are not robust in the sense of cryptographic protocols, because the tag doesn't know if D is indeed received or verified by a legitimate reader. If D is not received or verified successfully, the reader will not update its storage relating to the tag, while the tag will update its storage since it has already authenticated the reader. Obviously, the storages at the tag and the reader are not synchronized. But this issue is more about an assumption problem, not as a serious security problem. To patch it implicitly, we suppose there is a completion message being sent to each other to indicate a successful completion of the protocol. This completion message will enable the updating operations at both the reader and the tag side. All the following attacks assume that the protocols have above completion message to trigger the updating. Follow on, we will present the security problems of LMAP as well as M^2AP.

4.1 *De-synchronization Attack*

To provide privacy for an RFID tag, most RFID authentication protocols update a tag's ID after a successful protocol round. Typically, the database has to update the tag's ID accordingly so that a legitimate reader can still authenticate the tag later on. So the synchronization of secret information between the database and the tag is crucial for their following successful protocol runs. A flawed protocol, as discussed above, might leave the protocols uncomplete and cause the asynchronization at both sides. Additionally, an intended attack, like the *De-synchronization attack* introduced below, may also destroy the authentication protocols.

Attack 1: Changing message C. We now present the simplest *de-synchronization attack*: without any previous knowledge of any former protocol, a man-in-the-middle can first eavesdrop on the on-going protocol, and then change $A||B||C$ to $A||B||C'$, where $C' = C \oplus [I]_0$ and $[I]_0 = [000 \cdots 001]$ (set the first 95 most significant bits of I as 0 and the least significant bit as 1). Similarly, the attacker changes the reply D from the tag to $D' = D \oplus [I]_0$. This procedure is drawn in Table 2.

LMAP mutual authentication:	*where:*
	$n2' \leftarrow - - n2$
Reader $\longrightarrow$ Tag: $A\|\|B\|\|C'$	$C' = C \ominus [I]_0$
Tag $\longrightarrow$ Reader: D'	$D = (IDS^{(n)}_{tag(i)} + ID_{tag(i)}) \oplus n1 \oplus n2'$
	$D' = D \oplus [I]_0$

Table 2. *De-synchronization Attack* against LMAP

At the tag side, the attack doesn't affect the first round of interaction protocol: "tag identification". But in the second round, when the tag receives the message $A||B||C'$, it can still authenticate the reader as A and B are retained. But, the tag will get a wrong random number $n2' \leftarrow - - n2$ (where $n2'$ depends on $n2$, but is not necessarily expressed as a function of $n2$, according to equations 1-4). The tag will accept this value and compute its reply according to $n2'$, $D = (IDS^{(n)}_{tag(i)} + ID_{tag(i)}) \oplus n1 \oplus n2'$. In this simplest attack, the attacker can now provide the reader with a reply D'. If the reader accepts the value D', we say the attack is successful; otherwise, the attack is failed. Now we analyze the success rate as follows: the operation on C is actually toggling the least significant bit of C (denoted as $[C]_0$).

$$If \;\; [C]_0 = 1; \Rightarrow [C']_0 = 0; \rightarrow If \;\; [n2]_0 = 0, HW(n2 \oplus n2') \geq 2 \qquad (1)$$

$$\rightarrow If \;\; [n2]_0 = 1, n2' = n2 \oplus [I]_0 \qquad (2)$$

$$If \;\; [C]_0 = 0; \Rightarrow [C']_0 = 1; \rightarrow If \;\; [n2]_0 = 0, n2' = n2 \oplus [I]_0 \qquad (3)$$

$$\rightarrow If \;\; [n2]_0 = 1, HW[n2 \oplus n2'] \geq 2 \qquad (4)$$

Here, $HW(a)$ is the hamming weight of a, so $HW(a \oplus b)$ denotes the number of bit differences between a and b. Note that $n2' = n2 - 1$ for cases (1) and (2); and $n2' = n2 + 1$ for cases (3) and (4). For cases (2) and (3), the reader will accept D' since $D' = D \oplus [I]_0 = (IDS^{(n)}_{tag(i)} + ID_{tag(i)}) \oplus n1 \oplus n2' \oplus [I]_0 = (IDS^{(n)}_{tag(i)} + ID_{tag(i)}) \ominus n1 \oplus n2$. For cases (1) and (4), the reader will not accept it due to the mismatch on corresponding (more than one) bit positions. Suppose $n2$ is randomly generated, there is 50% success rate of the simplest attack.

Once the reader accepts the value, the reader needs to update the tag's secret information with the pair $(n1, n2)$. However, the tag uses another pair $(n1, n2')$ to update its secrets. *E.g.*, $IDS^{(n+1)}_{tag(i)} = (IDS^{(n)}_{tag(i)} + (n2' \oplus K4^{(n)}_{tag(i)})) \oplus ID_{tag(i)}$. It is obvious that there is a mismatch of secret storage for both tag and reader (refer to Table 3). To this end, the simplest attack assumes that there is only one (least significant) bit change on the message C. The attack is efficacious as it will succeed once for two trials. In fact, the simplest attack can be extended to toggle a single bit of C at any location i, so that it can be a general attack with the same (50%) success rate.

Generalized de-synchronization attack: For any on-going LMAP protocol, an adversary can intercept the message C and toggle any bit of C to get C' as $C' = C \oplus [I]_j$ $(0 \leq j \leq 95)$. The new message $A||B||C'$ is then sent to the tag. Upon receiving a reply D from the tag, the adversary change it to $D' = D \oplus [I]_j$ and send it to the reader. As per analysis above, the success rate of the attack is 50%. A successful attack may change the tag's secret status on a reader; or say, it de-synchronizes the reader and the tag.

With this attack, some claims in [12] are not true. Noted that the authors introduces an extension LMAP$^+$ in Section 5 of [12], our attack can also be applied on this version directly.

Attack 2: Changing messages A and B. Further on, the attack can also target on $n1$ similarly. In this case, the attacker intercepts the messages $A||B||C$ and sends $A'||B'||C$ to the tag, where $A' = A \oplus [I]_j$ and $B' = B \oplus [I]_j$, i.e., we toggle the j-th bit of A and B. Since $A = IDS^{(n)}_{tag(i)} \oplus K1^{(n)}_{tag(i)} \oplus n1$, we set $n1' = n1 \oplus [I]_i$. For B, we obtain

$$If\ \ [B]_j = 1; \Rightarrow [B']_j = 0; \rightarrow If\ \ [n1]_j = 0, HW(n1 \oplus n1') \geq 2 \quad (5)$$
$$\rightarrow If\ \ [n1]_j = 1, n1' = n1 \ominus [I]_j \quad (6)$$
$$If\ \ [B]_j = 0; \Rightarrow [B']_j = 1; \rightarrow If\ \ [n1]_j = 0, n1' = n1 \oplus [I]_j \quad (7)$$
$$\rightarrow If\ \ [n1]_j = 1, HW(n1 \oplus n1'] \geq 2 \quad (8)$$

in which, $n1' = n1 - 2^j$ for cases (5) and (6); and $n1' = n1 + 2^j$ for cases (7) and (8). For cases (6) and (7), the tag will authenticate the reader by accepting $n1'$. For cases (1) and (4), the tag will not authenticate the reader. Suppose $n1$ is randomly generated, the attacker has 50% success rate to cheat the tag. Suppose the tag accepts the manipulated message (A', B'), it will produce the message D to complete the protocol. The attacker needs to send $D' = D \oplus [I]_j$ to the reader with any valid reply from the tag. And this message D' will be verified by the reader successfully. Upon a successful attack, both reader and tag need to update their secret information. The reader will update with the pair $(n1, n2)$, while the tag uses $(n1', n2)$ that will cause the mismatch in the next execution of authentication protocol (refer to Table 3).

Attack Analysis. Compared with attack 1, where the target is on the partial protocol of the reader authenticating the tag, attack 2 is targeting on the procedure of the tag authenticating the reader. Above attack can be extended to attack 3: if we change $n1$ and $n2$ simultaneously, we do not need to change D anymore. In this case, the attacker intercepts the message and sends $A'||B'||C'$. Success rate is about 25%. The effects on updating at both the reader and tag side are summarized in Table 3.

Attacks	Success rate	Reader storage	Tag storage
Attack 1	50%	$[IDS\ K1\ K2\ K3\ K4]$	$[IDS'\ K1'\ K2'\ K3\ K4]$
Attack 2	50%	$[IDS\ K1\ K2\ K3\ K4]$	$[IDS\ K1\ K2\ K3'\ K4']$
Attack 3	25%	$[IDS\ K1\ K2\ K3\ K4]$	$[IDS'\ K1'\ K2'\ K3'\ K4']$

Table 3. Updated storages at the reader and the tag after the attacks

4.2 *Full Disclosure Attack*

Given above attacks, we can further disclose the original ID of a tag, which is much more serious. Suppose the tag has no memory for status information (therefore, it is considered stateless), but a legitimate reader is stateful (as to remember all status information regarding the protocol with a specific tag). That means we can repeatedly run the uncomplete protocol many times at the tag side. The assumption is reasonable as the tag has to answer any request by legitimate or illegitimate readers, and the protocol is not complete if the reader didn't receive final message D.

The attack is illustrated in Fig. 1. Step 1, an attacker impersonates a legitimate reader and gets the current IDS of a tag. Step 2, using this valid IDS the attacker impersonates a tag to get a valid message $A||B||C$ from a legitimate reader. Step 3, the attacker tries to send all possible $A'||B'||C$ to the tag, where A' and B' are obtained by changing the j-th bit of A and B respectively ($0 \leq j \leq 95$). According to whether a proper D or an error message is received (the attacker doesn't need to know the value, an error indicator is enough for an attacker to make his decision), the attacker concludes that the j-th bit of n_1 is equal or not equal to the j-th bit of B. In this way, with merely 96 trials, the attacker can get full bit values of $n1$. Then, from A, B, IDS and $n1$, the attacker can calculate $K1$ and $K2$.

Now, the unknown parameters are $n2$, $K3$, $K4$, and ID. Obviously, we can use above method to obtain the value of $n2$, but to interact with the reader m times. However, the repeating trials by the attacker are easily identified by a stateful reader and countered by limiting the interactions by a constant (*e.g.*, up to 10) times. With this assumption, we have to devise another way to derive the secrets. Thus, in Step 4, the attacker pretends to be a legitimate tag and sends the IDS to the readers again (the 2nd interaction with the reader). The

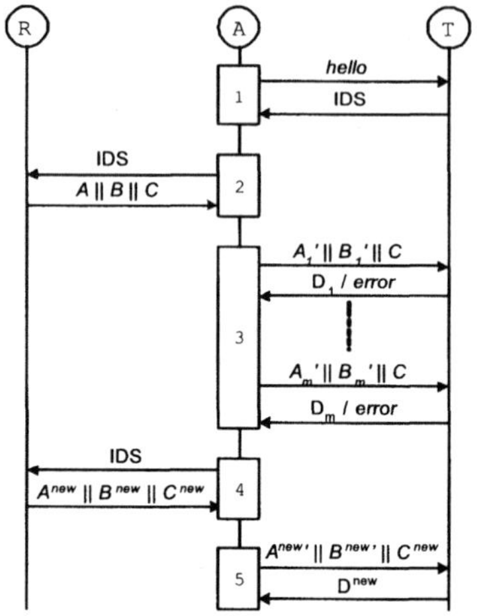

Fig. 1. *Full Disclosure Attack*

reader will response as $A^{new}||B^{new}||C^{new}$. Then, in Step 5, the attacker can set $n1^{new} = 0$ (using the currently known parameters IDS, $K1$ and $K2$) and sends $A^{new'}||B^{new'}||C^{new}$ to the tag. The tag will reply with D^{new}. Note that in the above steps, there are totally 2 interactions between the reader and the attacker, and $m+2$ interactions between the attacker and the tag.

To this point, the attacker has the following equations:

$$C = (IDS^{(n)}_{tag(i)} + K3^{(n)}_{tag(i)}) + n2 \tag{9}$$

$$D = (IDS^{(n)}_{tag(i)} + ID_{tag(i)}) \oplus n1 \oplus n2 \tag{10}$$

$$C^{new} = (IDS^{(n)}_{tag(i)} + K3^{(n)}_{tag(i)}) + n2^{new} \tag{11}$$

$$D^{new} = (IDS^{(n)}_{tag(i)} + ID_{tag(i)}) \oplus n2^{new} \tag{12}$$

After that, the attacker can solve the $ID_{tag(i)}$ as follows. First, by eliminating $n2$ from equations (9) and (10), and $n2^{new}$ from equations (11) and (12), we get the equations with unknown parameters ID and $K3$:

$$C - IDS^{(n)}_{tag(i)} - K3^{(n)}_{tag(i)} = (IDS^{(n)}_{tag(i)} + ID_{tag(i)}) \oplus n1 \oplus D \tag{13}$$

$$C^{new} - IDS^{(n)}_{tag(i)} - K3^{(n)}_{tag(i)} = (IDS^{(n)}_{tag(i)} + ID_{tag(i)}) \oplus D^{new} \tag{14}$$

We further eliminate $K3$ from the above two equations and get

$$C^{new} - C = (IDS^{(n)}_{tag(i)} + ID_{tag(i)}) \oplus D^{new} - (IDS^{(n)}_{tag(i)} + ID_{tag(i)}) \oplus n1 \oplus D$$

Now, we discuss how to solve $ID_{tag(i)}$ from above equation. Let $a = D^{new}$, $b = n1 \oplus D$, $c = C^{new} - C \mod 2^{96}$, and $x = (IDS^{(n)}_{tag(i)} + ID_{tag(i)}) \mod 2^{96}$.

Since $IDS^{(n)}_{tag(i)}$ is already known, the problem is equivalent to find $x \in \{0,1\}^{96}$ for given (a,b,c) such that

$$x \oplus a = x \oplus b + c \mod 2^{96}. \tag{15}$$

To solve x in equation (15), we just need to note that x's more significant bits do not affect the computation involving its less significant bits. So, we can try to determine x from its less significant bits to its higher significant bits. For example, we can divide the 96 bits into 24 parts so that each part has 4 bits. After that, by exclusively searching we can find all possible solutions for the first 4 less significant bits of x, then the next 4 less significant bits of x, and so on. This procedure involves no more than $(2^{24}-1)$ times of exclusively searching all 4-bit strings, due to the possible carries at all $(4k+1)$-th bit locations $(1 \le k \le 23)$. This means that such a naive algorithm can be carried out by a PC in several minutes. Actually, employing efficient algorithms proposed in [8], equation (16) can further be solved in complexity $O(m)$ ($m = 96$ in the protocols). Note that from one given triple (a,b,c), one may not uniquely determine the value of x. In this scenario, the attacker can interact with the reader several times [2] to attain a few instances of equation (15). By intersecting the solution sets of those different instances, the value range of x can be significantly narrowed down. In addition, since $ID_{tag(i)}$ is not a truly random number but has fixed format, some bits of x are almost predefined. Combined with this techniques, it is likely that the value of x can be uniquely determined with enough but not so many interactions with the reader and tag. Once the value of x is fixed, the attack can easily derive the rest secret information $(ID, K3, K4)$ stored on the tag. This completes our full disclosure attack against LMAP.

Note that the above full disclosure attack against LMAP protocol can also be adapted for attacking M^{2}AP protocol. Actually, the attack only needs the attacking steps from 1 to 3, from which we can get $n1$. Further on, with a valid E, we obtain ID directly. This implies that the full disclosure attack against M^{2}AP is much more efficient than that on LMAP, since the attacker has only 1 interaction with the reader and $m+1$ interactions with the tag.

5 Countermeasures

5.1 Re-synchronization

In fact, in a naif extension - LMAP$^+$ of [12], the authors did mentioned a method on re-synchronization between the reader and the tag. The tag will have a state associated in the database: synchronized or uncertainty. Furthermore, each tag

[2] Not necessarily in a single protocol run, that means the attacker can launch the attack for an arbitrary protocol run, perhaps after several successful protocol executions, and no matter how many times the tag has updated its secret information. Even a stateful reader is not able to detect the subtle attack.

will have $l + 1$ database records, instead of only 1 record. The first record is the actual index-pseudonym (IDS) and the others are the potential next index-pseudonyms $(IDS + 1, IDS + 2, ..., IDS + l)$. The parameter l is decided by the size of the database, thus it can not be too large for all records being stored in a database. The extension can help re-synchronize some situations of asynchronization. Unfortunately, the method can only affect only a small percent on the efficacy of our attack. Suppose $l \leq 2^L$, for all $[I]_i, (L < i \leq m)$, our attack can still succeed with 95% [3] trials. One natural remedy against the *de-synchronization attack* is to build bit level error correcting mechanisms at the database. However, the bit errors between mismatched IDSs as well as other secrets, like $K1, K2, K3, K4$, are not easily corrected in this way. Since the combination usage of bitwise operations (*e.g.*, $\oplus$, $+ \bmod 2^m$) broke the algebraic property of their functions. A single bit flip on $n1$ or $n2$ may cause different bit error patterns on updated secret values, where an adaptive error correction mechanism should be deployed. Hence, additional costs on computation and storage at the database are incurred.

5.2 Sending $\widetilde{D}$

One of the trick we did in our *Full-disclosure attack* is to try all possible $A'||B'||C$ and observe the replies from the tag (in step 3). If the tag sends a valid message D, that means the trial is successful; if not, the trial is not successful. Suppose the tag always sends a message $\widetilde{D}$ implicitly whatever the reader is authenticated or not ($\widetilde{D} = D$, if the reader is authenticated; Or $\widetilde{D} \in_R \{0,1\}^m$, if the reader is not authenticated). Then, the attacker can not get any clue on distinguishing a valid message D or an arbitrary message. The attacker has to send it to a legitimate reader and expects a reply. As it might not be possible for a tag to generate a random value $\{0,1\}^m$, the tag can assign $\widetilde{D} = (IDS^{(n)}_{tag(i)} + ID_{tag(i)}) \oplus n2$, if the reader is not authenticated. As long as $\widetilde{D}$ is distinguishable for the reader and indistinguishable for the attacker, any other (secure) mechanism will work.

5.3 Storing Status

Storing some addendum at the database alone might not be helpful, but storing some status information at both the reader and the tag sides could be useful to counter our attacks. The intuition is that our attack targets on the tag's inability to distinguish the requests from a legitimate reader or the trials from an attacker. To counter our attack, it is necessary for a tag to have some status information stored, to indicate the trials of some on-going sessions. To this end, we assign an additional status bit s, and set $s = 0$, if the protocol is completed

---

[3] The success rate is about $(m - \log_2 l)\ m$, for all $(0 \leq l \leq 2^m)$. Set $l = 32\ m = 96$, we get $91\ 96 \approx 95\%$.

(or synchronized) successfully; or $s = 1$, if the protocol is uncompleted (or asynchronized) due to some reason.

The protocol status bit is set for the purpose of indicating the completion of a protocol execution. Only a successful completed protocol can trigger the updating operations at both the reader and the tag sides. That means an attacker can not learn the bit values of $n1$ or $n2$ within a single (incomplete) protocol by launching multiple (failed) trials.

Therefore, the stateful protocol needs both the reader and the tag to store two random numbers in the last (incomplete) protocol round $(n1, n2)$, in case of asynchronization. Given an incomplete protocol, the tag will expect a completion message E (*e.g.*, $E = (IDS_{tag(i)}^{(n+1)} + ID_{tag(i)}) \oplus n1 \oplus n2)$ from the reader. The reader, already updated, needs to search the database to calculate a former IDS of the tag with the stored values $(n1, n2)$. If a former IDS is found, the reader further composes the completion message E and sends it to the tag to complete the protocol. If not, a tag is considered compromised permanently.

With only 1 bit added to present the protocol status and two additional random numbers $(2 * 96 = 192$ bits) stored in EEPROM, the new protocol increases a tag's memory size by 40% (193 96$*$5), while nearly all other hardware implementations for algorithm logic units or control units are not changed.

Above we proposed several countermeasures against different attacks. While there must be some other ways on attacking the protocols, the current countermeasures might not guarantee the security due to attacks discovered later on. Some of the countermeasures can be combined to provide stronger security for the protocols. However, the new mechanisms have some limitations to be deployed in some real situations. For example, the stateful protocol is not suitable for ubiquitous environment, where distributed readers can not retrieve the tags' information efficiently online so as to authenticate a tag.

6 Conclusions and Future Work

In this paper, we demonstrated two effective attacks against two ultra-lightweight RFID mutual authentication protocols, which are recently proposed in [12, 13]. The severity of the attacks indicates the insecure design of the protocols. Our work shows that it may be quite dangerous on using only simple bitwise operations to achieve secure RFID mutual authentication under powerful adversarial model. The security of such protocols must be proved with elaborated cryptanalysis. To counter those attacks, some countermeasures were also presented to deal with disruptive attacks. Taken these attacks and countermeasures in mind, our next step is to design secure (ultra) lightweight RFID mutual authentication protocol and to apply it on low-cost RFID tags.

7 Acknowledgement

The author would like to thank Mr. Hongjun Wu for the discussion on drafting this paper.

References

1. M. Aigner and M. Feldhofer. Secure Symmetric Authentication for RFID Tags. *Telecommunication and Mobile Computing*, March 2005.
2. G. Avoine. Security and Privacy in RFID Systems. `http://lasecwww.epfl.ch/~gavoine/rfid/`
3. B. Defend, K. Fu and A. Juels. Cryptanalysis of Two Lightweight RFID Authentication Schemes. In: *Proc. of PERSEC'07*, March 2007.
4. A. Juels and R. Pappu. Squealing euros: Privacy protection in RFID-enabled banknotes. In: *Proc. of FC'03*, LNCS 2742, pp. 103-121. Springer-Verlag, 2003.
5. A. Juels. Minimalist Cryptography for Low-Cost RFID Tags. In: *Proc. of SCN'04*, LNCS 3352, pp. 149-164. Springer-Verlag, 2004.
6. A. Juels and S. Weis. Authenticating pervasive devices with human protocols. In: *Proc. of CRYPTO'05*, LNCS 3126, pp. 293-308. Springer-Verlag, 2005.
7. A. Juels. RFID Security and Privacy: A Research Survey. *IEEE Journal on Selected Areas in Communications*, 24(2): 381-394, Feb. 2006.
8. H. Lipmaa and S. Moriai. Efficient Algorithms for Computing Differential Properties of Addition. In: *Proc. of FSE '01*, LNCS 2355, pp. 336-350. Springer-Verlag, 2001.
9. D. Molnar and D. Wagner. Privacy and Security in Library RFID: Issues, Practices, and Architectures. In: *Proc. of CCS'04*, pp. 210-219. ACM Press, 2004.
10. D. Molnar, A. Soppera, and D. Wagner. A Scalable, Delegatable Pseudonym Protocol Enabling Ownership Transfer of RFID Tags. In: *Proc. of SAC'05*, LNCS 3897, pp. 276-290. Springer-Verlag, 2005.
11. M. Ohkubo, K. Suzuki, and S. Kinoshita. Cryptographic approach to privacy-friendly tags. In: *Proc. of RFID Privacy Workshop*, 2003.
12. P. Peris-Lopez, J. C. Hernandez-Castro, J. M. Estevez-Tapiador, and A. Ribagorda. LMAP: A Real Lightweight Mutual Authentication Protocol for Low-cost RFID tags. In: *Proc. of 2nd Workshop on RFID Security*, July 2006. `http://events.iaik.tugraz.at/RFIDSec06/`.
13. P. Peris-Lopez, J. C. Hernandez-Castro, J. M. Estevez-Tapiador, and A. Ribagorda. M^2AP: A Minimalist Mutual-Authentication Protocol for Low-cost RFID Tags. In: *Proc. of International Conference on Ubiquitous Intelligence and Computing UIC'06*, LNCS 4159, pp. 912-923. Springer-Verlag, 2006.
14. I. Vajda and L. Buttyan. Lightweight authentication protocols for low-cost RFID tags. In: *Proc. of UBICOMP'03*, 2003.
15. S. Weis, S. Sarma, R. Rivest, and D. Engels. Security and privacy aspects of low-cost radio frequency identification systems. In: *Proc. of 1st Int. Conf. on Security in Pervasive Computing*, LNCS 2802, pp. 201-212. Springer-Verlag, 2003.
16. S. Weis. Security parallels between people and pervasive devices. In: *Proc. of PERSEC'05*, pp. 105-109. IEEE Computer Society Press, 2005.

Exploratory survey on an evaluation model for a sense of security

Natsuko Hikage [1*], Yuko Murayama [1] and Carl Hauser [2]

[1] Graduate school of Software and Information Science,
Iwate Prefectural University
152-52, Sugo, Takizawa-mura, Iwate 020-0193 JAPAN
n.hikage@comm.soft.iwate-pu.ac.jp, murayama@iwate-pu.ac.jp

[2] School of Electrical Engineering and Computer Science,
Washington State University
PO Box 642752, Pullman, WA 99164-2752 USA
hauser@eecs.wsu.edu

Abstract. Research in information security is no longer limited to technical issues: human-related issues such as trust and the sense of security are also required by the user. In this paper, we use a Japanese word for such feelings, Anshin; "An" means to ease, and "Shin" is to mind. One feels Anshin when he is free from worry and fear. We try to identify the factors of Anshin so that we can construct a framework of the evaluation of Anshin. We present an initial Anshin model, and report our recent research results from user survey with factor analysis. We derive the following factors from the analysis; 1) user expectation of trust and confidence, 2) satisfaction with user interface and 3) understanding of risk and threats from user experience as well prior knowledge.

1 Introduction

This paper presents our initial work on the sense of security. Security technology usually has been evaluated in terms of theoretical and engineering feasibility and mostly from service providers' viewpoints, e.g.[1-3]. What has been missing is evaluation from users' viewpoints. Usability is one of the factors, but not only in engineering terms, but in terms of the users' subjective feeling in use of security tools --i.e., the sense of security. Indeed, the term, "security" includes objective viewpoints of security engineering as well as such subjective factors as

[*] Currently affiliated with NTT Corporation.

Please use the following format when citing this chapter:

Hikage, N., Murayama, Y., and Hauser, C., 2007, in IFIP International Federation for Information Processing, Volume 232, New Approaches for Security, Privacy and Trust in Complex Environments, eds. Venter, H., Eloff, M., Labuschagne, L., Eloff, J., von Solms, R., (Boston: Springer), pp. 121–132.

sense of security. We use the Japanese word, Anshin, for the latter throughout this paper. Anshin is a Japanese noun which is composed of two words, viz. An and Shin. "An" is to ease, and "Shin" indicates mind. Anshin literally means to ease one's mind. In this research, we have constructed our initial Anshin model incorporating several factors and conducted a preliminary experiment with users to understand how effective those factors are in the model.

The more we enjoy the network-based web services, the more risk and threats we encounter such as compromise and phishing. Such destabilizing factors on the security may prevent the users from using network-based service. The users need to get Anshin to use such services extensively. The objective of our research is to produce the Anshin model for evaluating security tools in order to provide better interfaces for users. However, it's still not clear model and framework for evaluation it. This study attempts to look into this problem and propose an initial model of evaluating security systems in terms of the sense of security. Additionally, we try to analyze the factors contributing to Anshin and to produce an Anshin model with which one can get a quantitative score on how secure users feel.

This paper proposes our Anshin model with social-scientific viewpoints rather than technical security issues. The next section presents related work with a focus on trust model. Section 3 proposes our evaluation model based on some previous work, later sections describe result of experimental survey including factor analysis. The final section gives some conclusion and presents future work.

2 Related Work

2.1 Trust and Security

Trust has been studied in various disciplines such as sociology, psychology and economics. From psychological viewpoint, Deutsch defined trust in an interpersonal context [4]. Later he introduced confidence in trust so that one will find what is desired from another [5]. Gambetta defined trust as a particular level of one's subjective probability that another's action would be favorable to oneself [6]. Marsh proposed the first computational trust model with quantized trust values in the rage of -1 to +1 [7].

According to Friedman, "people trust people, not technology" [8]. In contrast with Friedman's view of trust, our perspective is that *security* is intimately connected with technology. Trust and security are interdependent concepts. Lamsal illustrates this using cryptography as an example: one's secure communication with another requires a key obtained via trusted key distribution [9]. If the key distribution was not worthy of that trust the communication is not secure. Dimmock incorporates trust as a part of access control security [10]. Recently, new trust models in security research have proposed [11,12].

2.2 Anshin and emotional trust

As we see it, trust is a belief based on an expectation of others' behavior. In other words, it is to do with the *relationship* between the trustor and trustee. On the other hand, Anshin, the sense of security, is a personal emotion. In other words, it is a subjective feeling towards an object, such as security measures.

As we point out in section 2.1, trust has been studied in various disciplines such as sociology, psychology and economics. A lot of it is concerned primarily with *cognitive trust.* Firstly, Lewis as sociologist defined the type of trust as follows; *Trusting behavior may be motivated primarily by strong positive affect for the object of trust (emotional trust) or by "good rational reasons" why the object of trust merits trust (cognitive trust), or more usually some combination of both* [13]. Popularly, the latter nature, viz. cognitive trust is defined as a trustee's rational expectation that a trustee will have the necessary competence, benevolence, and integrity to be relied upon. On the other hand, the emotional aspect of trust is defined as an emotional security, or feeling secure, or comfortable [14]. Xiao also mentioned that emotional trust is feeling, while cognitive trust is cognition [15]. In like wise, more recent work by Chopra [16], Kuan [17] etc points out multidimensionality of trust. Also from a sociological viewpoint, Yamagishi [18] gives a distinct definition on Anshin and trust. Anshin is the belief that we have no social uncertainty, whereas trust is needed when we have high social uncertainty. Trust is expectations of others' intentions based on trustor's judgment of others' personalities and feelings. From the viewpoint of communication about the risks of nuclear power plants, Kikkawa introduces two Anshin states, viz. one *with* knowledge and the other *without* knowledge [19]. Kikkawa suggests that it is necessary for users to study and obtain information in an active way to get more Anshin feeling. To create Anshin experts on technology need to provide information to users as well as reducing technological risks.

2.3 Human Interface

From a human interface viewpoint, Whitten and Tygar point out that user interfaces in security systems need special interfaces [20]. Stephens gives design elements, such as page layout, navigation, and graphics which affect the development of trust between buyers and sellers in e-commerce [21]. Pu also reports that how information was presented affected trust building in user interfaces [22]. According to Riegelsberger [23], quantitative studies on trust in e-commerce, such as [24], and other consumer research confirm that affective reactions influence consumer decision-making.

3 The Anshin Model

3.1 Overview

In this paper, in terms of Anshin, we take a different approach from Yamagishi in that we incorporate trust as a factor of Anshin. Anshin, in our work, is attached more to computer security technology than to the general term of security. Anshin could be derived from some factors including knowledge. We incorporate the viewpoints of both Kikkawa and Xiao into our model in that knowledge could be a factor of Anshin. Yamagishi presented an empirical study on how positive and negative reputations would affect trust. Yamagishi's definition of trust and Anshin is slightly different from ours, as we try and incorporate trust as a factor of Anshin. We take reputation as one type of information which affects our trust factor. We include the intuitive user interface factor as Riegelsberger suggested.

3.2 An Anshin Model

Based on the discussions in previous section, we construct an Anshin model. The model is based on Beck's cognitive model [25] so that the emotion factor, Anshin, is produced from factors such as *trust* in providers, services and systems, *knowledge* of security technology and the intuitively sensed *quality of the user interface*. Those factors are expressed as subjective functions which take cognitive factors as an argument. The cognitive factors, combined using an appropriate weight function, produce the degree of Anshin. Additional factors, experience of the use of the service and system, give feedback to each factor.

Figure 1 depicts the model. A user takes an exterior cognitive factor, information, r, on system providers such as an implementor, as an argument of the *Trust* function, T. System cognitive factors such as security technology and the quality of user inter face are also taken as arguments for the *Knowledge* and *Intuitive* functions, K and I. Output of each function is substituted for assessable value quantitatively. For example, evaluated value about cognitive factors in "r" becomes confidence in society, feeling of trust, and expectations for ability by user's subjective assessment. All function together with experience information, e_i, and weight parameters, w_i the emotion value, Anshin, A, is calculated as:

$$A = w_0 * T(r+e_0) + w_1 * K(s+e_1) + w_2 * I(u+e_2)$$

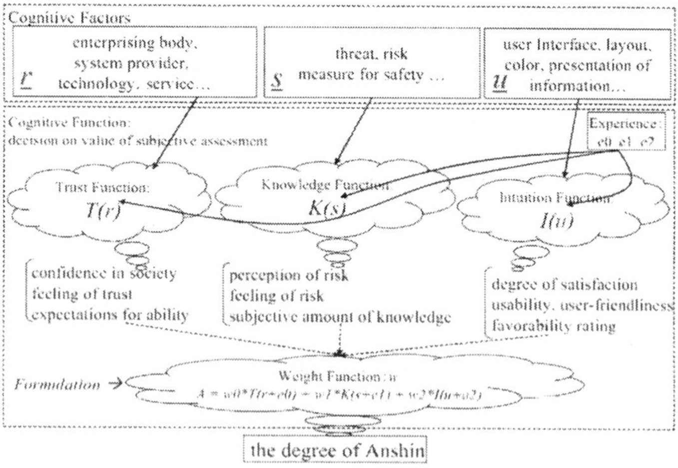

Figure.1: Anshin model

4 Study Design

We tried a variety of approaches to grasp the structure of "sense of security". To assess the validity of the hypothesis in Anshin model, we conducted two types of a user survey. The former is empirical examination as preliminary study (pre-test) that we tried a quantitative assessment of "sense of security" using framework of anshin model. 18 participants were asked a question about a sense of security when they sent a file including their own personal information by file transfer system over the Internet. The latter is that we apply questionnaire method to 140 participants to make a statistical survey using factor analysis, whether hypothesis of three factor; trust in provider, knowledge of technology and risks, quality of user interface, is meaningful factor.

4.1 Preliminary study

We conducted a preliminary study (pre-test) of users to see how the three factors, trust in providers, knowledge of technology and risks, and quality of user interface, affect users' perceptions in the Anshin Model [26]. We used two versions of a file store system on the world-wide web called the under-the-door communication system [27], viz. an insecure version and a secure version. In the former, a password and information were transferred as a plain text over the network, whereas in the latter they were transferred using of the secure shell, SSH. The experimental subjects were asked to use both systems without explanation for the first run, and then were given information including basic knowledge about security and the reputation of the provider of the system. The former was to measure the knowledge factor and the latter was for the trust factor.

For the trust factor, we prepared two cases: one with a good reputation and another with a bad reputation. The bad reputation says that the system was created by a student using unknown free software available on a dubious site. On the other hand, the good reputation says that the system was created by a well-known researcher and evaluated highly by an academic society. In addition, for the quality of the interface, we change the color of the user interface of the system. According to the psychology of colors [28], black gives an anxious feeling and green gives Anshin. The neutral color between them is blue. For the first run, both groups used the systems whose interfaces are blue. For the second run, we prepared two interfaces, one for Group 1 and the other for Group 2. The interfaces of the systems for Group 1 are green whereas those for Group 2 are black. Using only color differences to study the importance of the user interface factor is a considerable oversimplification.

There were 18 experimental subjects divided into two equal-sized groups. The subjects were mainly freshman in faculty of software and information science in our university, and they did not previously know much about security. Each group performed two runs of the experiment. In each run the subjects first used the system without SSH and then with SSH. After the first run each group was given different information: group 1 received positive information and group 2 received negative information. Then the second run was performed as before, first without SSH and then with SSH (see Table 1)

Table 1. The conditions in the experiment

Time axis	The First Run		The Second Run	
factors	Group1	Group2	Group1	Group2
Knowledge: information about security	No previous knowledge		Fundamental information on security and SSH	
Trust: reputation about the system provider	No previous knowledge		with *positive* information: highly evaluated researcher	with *negative* information: unknown student using the dubious codes

The experiment was conducted for the cases listed in Table 2. Each case includes the first and second runs as in Table 1. The first run without any knowledge and information and the second one with knowledge of security as well as the biased information: positive information for Group 1 and negative for Group 2. The arrows in Table 2 indicate the sequences a subject of each group went though. For instance, after a subject of Group 1 went through the first run of Cases 1 and 2, he filled in the questionnaire. He was given the security knowledge and reputation information and went on to the second run of Cases 1 and 2, finally answering the questionnaire once again. In the beginning, the subjects were not told the difference, but the display of the system with SSH showed "with SSH". Only one of eighteen subjects noticed the difference; the others did not because they did not know what SSH was. One of them knew about SSH before the experiment. The subjects are not associated with the researchers' laboratory. The researchers are graduate students whom the subjects had never met before. Presumably, they had no subconscious motivation or intention to help the researchers but this pre-test experiment did not explicitly control for that possibility. The manipulation check has been done by introspection.

Table 2.Cases of the experiment

	System Option	*1stRun*	*2ndRun*	
Case 1	without SSH			Group 1
Case 2	with SSH			Group 1
Case 3	without SSH			Group 2
Case 4	with SSH			Group 2

Legend: ▬ indicates the timing that a subject filled in a questionnaire

Principal results are as follows. The results for Case 2, in which the subjects were provided with the positive information in the second run as well as knowledge of security, show that the degree of fear has been reduced with most of the subjects --- i.e., they felt more Anshin after they learned the positive reputation of the system implementor and the security fundamentals with SSH as in Figure 2. Almost all the subjects felt fear in Case 3 after receiving negative information and security knowledge when they used the system without SSH (see Figure 3).

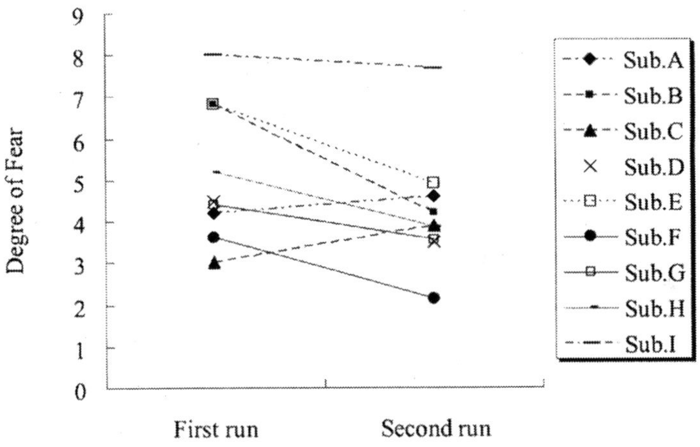

Figure 2. The change of fear in Case 2 (with SSH and with positive information)

We found noticeable change with the trust factor which indicates how much trust one would put on the system provider. If SSH was being used, when subjects were given positive reputation information, the degree of trust went up. If SSH was not being used when the reputation information was negative, trust went down. For additional result and questionnaire details, it is shown on our previous paper [26].

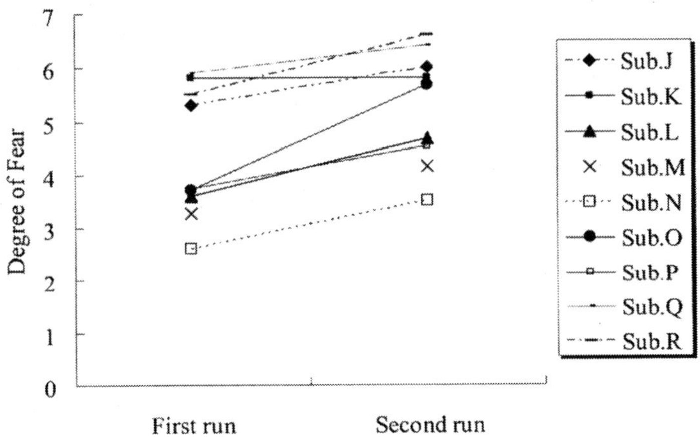

Figure 3. The change of fear in Case3 (without SSH and with negative information)

Our findings from this preliminary study were as follows. After obtaining knowledge about security and positive reputation information about the system implementor, the subjects increased Anshin when they used a secure system, and decreased it when they used an insecure system. Also after obtaining knowledge about security and negative reputation information, the subjects felt fear when they used an insecure system. With security knowledge and negative reputation information, subjects' feelings varied when they used the secure system. When one learns some technology, he may well learn its risks as well; he will be more aware of such risks. The alternative view is that the secure feeling changes depending on what one's experience or knowledge. The very simple user interface color change in this experiment did not result in any noticeable difference in the subjects' Anshin.

4.2. Factor Analysis

Previous section 4.1 suggests the impact of knowledge and trust on Anshin. But, user interface factor did not show statistically-useful difference because of lack of sample number. Hence this preliminary experiment would go but a little way to show validity of our model. Therefore, we planned to carry out a questionnaire survey to grasp the structure of "sense of security" in a statistically optimal fashion.

The purpose of this survey conducted by factor analysis was to confirm the structure of Anshin, and to verify a validity of our anshin model. We expected three subscales based on above discussion and our previous work. The 27 items from Q1 to Q27 were adapted from previous research and revised to fit context of this study. Most study used a 7-point Likert scale system ranging from "strongly disagree"(1) to "strongly agree"(7), e.g.[29]. 140 students in the faculty of Software and Information Science, Iwate Prefectural University, took part in the survey. After eliminating incomplete responses, there were 122 valid entries used for the analysis. Of the 122 participants, 81 were male, and 41 were female. The age range of participants was from 19 to 36, average age 20.

Main results were as follow: The explanatory factor analysis(EFA) with principal factor method and promax rotation found that three factors are present in Table 3. Several repeated analysis led to a statistically-meaningful 22 items, and resulted in following factor structure; 1) *trust and security by user expectation*, 2) *satisfaction of user interface*, and 3) *understanding of risk and threat by user experience and prior knowledge*. All items has factor loading above 0.338. The three factors were explained by 43.5%(Cumulative) of the total. To confirm reliability of measurement, Cronbach's coefficient alpha of subscale is summarized in Table 3. According to this, it shows relatively high value of alpha more than 0.7.

I. Factor 1 (27.9% of the variance)

The first factor consists of 11 items (Q1,3,4,5,6,7,8,9,10,11,27) about trust and security. Mainly, it has feeling confidence in society and trust by user expectation for one's ability, security, safety, etc. The results tends to confirm that this factor suggest validity of trust function in an Anshin model.

II. Factor 2 (9.3% of the variance)

The second factor consists of 5 (Q17,18,19,20,21) items about satisfaction of user interface(UI). Especially, it has subjective assessment of the quality of UI; for example, usability, attractive design and user-friendliness. This results tends to confirm that this factor support hypothesis of intuition function in an Anshin model.

III. Factor 3 (6.2% of the variance)

The third factor consist of 6 items (Q12,13,14,15,25,26) about knowledge in measure for safety. Particularly, it shows perception of risk, understanding of risk and threat by user experience and prior knowledge. The findings suggest that hypothesis of knowledge function is significant in an Anshin model.

Table 3. Three-factor solution in EFA

No.	Items	i	ii	iii
Q8.	In case of trouble, the system provides help.	**0.82**	-0.05	-0.18
Q7.	In case of trouble, the system recovers perfectly.	**0.77**	-0.01	-0.22
Q9.	It assures adequate security.	**0.73**	-0.08	0.08
Q6.	In case of trouble, the company provide gives assurance.	**0.70**	0.04	-0.14
Q3.	I have a sense of security as the company is a giant.	**0.53**	0.09	0.07
Q4.	The company has good privacy management policy.	**0.53**	-0.01	0.17
Q1.	I trust the company / enterprising body providing the services.	**0.45**	0.11	0.24
Q27.	I just feel secured but I don't have a concrete ground.	**0.41**	0.14	0.04
Q5.	I don't have trust in the company but the technology and the system.	**0.40**	0.17	0.06
Q11.	If it not secure, be saved.	**0.37**	-0.08	0.06
Q10.	I can really feel secure.	**0.36**	-0.01	0.06
Q17.	Terminal device or the system provides user a good impression.	-0.10	**0.98**	-0.07
Q18.	Terminal device or the system has attractive design.	-0.01	**0.93**	-0.09
Q19.	Terminal device or system interface has a neat layout or use of color.	-0.03	**0.92**	-0.10
Q21.	Terminal device or the system interface has user-friendliness.	0.13	**0.62**	0.15
Q20.	Terminal device or the system interface has a good usability.	0.11	**0.55**	-0.05
Q14.	I know well about information technology.	-0.05	-0.12	**0.67**
Q12.	I understand the way the system or technology works.	-0.02	-0.18	**0.64**
Q13.	I pay attention to safety measures.	0.21	-0.12	**0.55**
Q25.	I am expressed because I use quite often.	-0.02	0.38	**0.48**
Q15.	I user it with the full knowledge of risk and threat.	-0.17	0.14	**0.48**
Q26.	I am not afraid as I am quite experienced.	0.11	0.26	**0.34**
	Cumulative(%)	27.93	37.27	43.52
	Cronbach's coefficient alpha	0.84	0.90	0.72

4.3 Discussion

Based on the above result, the results of factor analysis provide strong support for the hypotheses in our Anshin that three factors contribute to a sense of security. To enhance the reliability of the result, confirmatory factor analysis (CFA) are needed. However, for the first experimental attempt in section 4.1, difference in color of user interface does not show significant difference. Presumably, this is attributed to the reason that impression of color is susceptible to cultural background or personal taste, so pre-test by the small number of subjects does not show significant difference statistically. Consequently, there is a possibility that color factor was not appropriate as experimental condition. As the related literature points to the UI as being a significant factor in trust [21-23], we try to validate empirically by some sort of factors related UI.

5 Conclusion and Future Work

Security has long been looked at from an engineering viewpoint. Information security is no longer limited to technical issues but human factor issues such as trust and a sense of security are required by the user. This paper introduced an initial study on the sense of security as new concept; Anshin. This study proposed an initial model of evaluating security systems in terms of the sense of security, and tried a variety of approaches to grasp the structure of "sense of security"

Our recent study results using factor analysis showed the following factors contribute to a sense of Anshin: 1) trust and security by user expectation, 2) satisfaction of user interface, and 3) understanding of risk and threat by user experience and prior knowledge. In terms of factor analysis, this survey showed that theoretical three factors in the structure of a sense of security were significant statistically. Further analyses are needed to determine what effects other factors including subjective amount of knowledge, feeling of risk, feelings of trust and computer anxiety, have on the sense of security.

However, Anshin model have new threats as exploited by a scam, e.g. phishing. Another way of saying, it is that the factor people feel security is made bad use of deceit. As future work, we plan a case study to focus on phishing. Especially, we are planning the evaluation of phishing site using our framework how secure a victim feels incorrectly. For example, Dhamija shows that phishing sites exploit lack of knowledge, visual deception, and lack of attention [30]. According to this, in ether case, human property is made wrong use as social engineering. Therefore, it's believed that ensuring security as system including "human" is one of the important issues from social-scientific and ergonomics approaches.

ACKNOWLEDGMENT This research was supported by Strategic International Cooperative Program, Japan Science and Technology Agency (JST). Special thanks to Ryuya Uda of Tokyo University of Technology, Mizuki Yamazaki of the Research Institute of Science and Technology for Society, Basabi Chakraborty, Yukinori Goto, Norihisa Segawa and Hisayoshi Ito of Iwate Prefectural University, and Makiko Matsumura of National Institute of Public Health. Without their help this research was not possible.

REFERENCES

1. D. Basin, S. Mödersheim and L. Viganò: CDiff: a new reduction technique for constraint-based analysis of security protocols, *Proc. of the 10th ACM conference on Computer and Communications Security*, pp.335-344 (2003).
2. W. Shi, H.S. Lee, C. Lu and T. Zhang: Attacks and risk analysis for hardware supported software copy protection systems, *Proc. of the 4th ACM workshop on Digital rights management*, pp. 54–62 (2004).
3. J.J. Yan: A note on proactive password checking, *Proc. of the 2001 workshop on New Security Paradigms*, pp. 127-135 (2001).
4. M. Deutsh: The effect of motivational orientation upon trust and suspition, *Human Relation*, 13, pp. 123-139 (1960).
5. M. Deutsh: The resolution of conflict (Yale University Press, 1973).
6. D. Gambetta: Can we trust trust?, *Making and Breaking Cooperative Relations,* electronic edition, Department of Sociology, University of Oxford, chapter 13, pp. 213-237 (originally published from Basil Blackwell, 1988). Available at : http://www.sociology.ox.ac.uk/papers/gambetta213-237.pdf (Last Access: 9 Feb 2007)
7. S.P. Marsh: Formalising trust as computational concept, PhD Thesis, Department of Mathematics and Computer Science, University of Stirling (1994).
8. B. Friedman, P.H. Khan and D.C. Howe: Trust online, *Communication of ACM,* Vol. 43, No.12, pp. 34-40 (2000).
9. P. Lamsal: Understanding Trust and Security, Available at : http://www.cs.helsinki.fi/u/lamsal/asgn/trust/UnderstandingTrustAndSecurity.pdf (Last Access: 9 Feb 2007).
10. N. Dimmock, A. Belokosztolszki, D. Eyers, J. Baconand and K. Moody: Access management for distributed systems: Using trust and risk in role-based access control policies, *Proc. of the ninth ACM symposium on Access Control Models and Technologies*, pp. 156-162 (2004).
11. L.J. Hoffman, K. Lawson-Jenkins, J. Blum: Trust beyond security: an expanded trust model, *Communications of the ACM,* Vol. 49, No.7, pp.94-101 (2006).
12. Stephen Flowerday, Rossouw von Solms: Trust: An Element of Information security, *Proc. of the IFIP TC-11 21st International Information Security Conference (SEC2006)*, pp.87-98 (2006).
13. J.D. Lewis. and A. Weigert: Trust as a Social Reality, *Social Forces*, Vol.63, No.4, pp.967-985 (1985).
14. S. Xiao. and I. Benbasat: The formation of trust and distrust in recommendation agents in repeated interactions: a process-tracing analysis, *Proc. of the 5th international conference on Electronic commerce (ICEC'03)*, pp.287-293 (2003).
15. S. Xiao and I. Benbasat: Understanding Customer Trust in Agent-Mediated Electronic Commerce, Web-Mediated Electronic Commerce, and Traditional

Commerce, *Information Technology and Management*, Vol.4, No.1-2, Kluwer Academic Publishers, pp.181-207 (2004).
16. K. Chopra, W.A. Wallace: Trust in Electronic Environments, *Proc. of the 36th Hawaii International Conference on System Science (HICSS'03)*, pp.331-340 (2003).
17. H.H Kuan. and G.W. Bock: The Collective Reality of Trust: An Investigation of Social Relations and Networks on Trust in Multi-Channel Retailers, *Proc. of the 13th European Conference on Information Systems* (ECIS 2005), Available at: http://is2.lse.ac.uk/asp/aspecis/20050018.pdf (Last Access: 9 Feb 2007)
18. Yamagishi, T.: *The structure of trust: The evolutionary games of mind and society* (Tokyo University Press, 1998). English version is available at : http://lynx.let.hokudai.ac.jp/members/yamagishi/english.htm (Last Access: 9 Feb 2007) .
19. T. Kikkawa, S. Shirato, S. Fujiiand and K. Takemura: The pursuit of informed reassurance ('An-Shin' in Society) and technological safety('An-Zen'), *Journal of SHAKAI-GIJUTSU* , Vol. 1, pp.1-8 (2003). in Japanese.
20. A. Whitten and D. Tygar: Why Johnny Can't Encrypt: A Usability Evaluation of PGP 5.0, *Proc. of the 9th USENIX Security Symposium*, pp.169–184 (1999).
21. R.T. Stephens: A framework for the identification of electronic commerce design elements that enable trust within the small hotel industry, *Proc. of ACMSE'04*, pp.309 – 314 (2004).
22. P. Pu, L. Chen: Trust building with explanation interfaces, *Proc. of the 11th international conference on Intelligent user interfaces (IUI'06)*, pp.93-100 (2006).
23. J. Riegelsberger, M.A. Sasse and J.D. McCarthy: Privacy and trust: Shiny happy people building trust?: photos on e-commerce websites and consumer trust, *Proc. of the SIGCHI conference on Human factors in computing systems (CHI'03)*, Vol. 5, No. 1, pp. 121-128 (2003).
24. Sapient & Cheskin: eCommerce Trust, 1999
25. Beck, A.T.: *Cognitive Therapy of Depression* (Guilford Press 1979).
26. Y. Murayama, N. Hikage, C. Hauser, B. Chakraborty and N. Segawa: An Anshin Model for the Evaluation of the Sense of Security, *Proc. of Hawaii International Conference on System Science (HICSS'06)*, Vol.8, p.205a (2006).
27. T. Tomita, K. Suzumura and Y. Murayama: Proposal for Under the Door Communication on the network, *Human-Computer Interaction: Theory and Practice(Part II)*, pp. 1019-1023 (2003).
28. R.H. Alschuler and H.L. Berta: Painting and Personality, University of Chicago Press, Vol.1 (1947).
29. D.J. Kim, C. Steinfield and Y. Lai: Revisiting the Role of Web Assurance Seals in Consumer Trust, *Proc. of the 6th international conference on Electronic Commerce*, pp.280-287 (2004).
30. R. Dhamija, J.D Tygar. And M. Hearst: Why phishing works, *Proc. of the SIGCHI conference on Human Factors in computing systems (CHI'06)*, pp.581-590 (2006).

Employees' Adherence to Information Security Policies: An Empirical Study

Mikko Siponen[1], Seppo Pahnila[1], and Adam Mahmood[2]
1 Department of Information Processing Science, The University of Oulu, Finland, {mikko.siponen, seppo.pahnila}@oulu.fi
2 Department of Information and Decision Sciences, University of Texas at El Paso, mmahmood@utep.edu

Abstract. The key threat to information security is constituted by careless employees who do not comply with information security policies. To ensure that employees comply with organizations' information security procedures, a number of information security policy compliance measures have been proposed in the past. Prior research has criticized these measures as lacking theoretically and empirically grounded principles to ensure that employees comply with information security policies. To fill this gap in research, this paper advances a new model that explains employees' adherence to information security policies. In this model, we extend the Protection Motivation Theory (PMT) by integrating the General Deterrence Theory (GDT) and the Theory of Reasoned Action (TRA) with PMT. To test this model, we collected data (N = 917) from four different companies. The results show that threat appraisal, self-efficacy and response efficacy have a significant impact on intention to comply with information security policies. Sanctions have a significant impact on actual compliance with information security policies. Intention to comply with information security policies also has a significant impact on actual compliance with information security policies.

1 Introduction

Up to 90% of organizations confront at least one information security incident within any given year [5, p. 684]. To cope with the increase in information security threats, not only technical solutions, but also information management methods and policies have been proposed. Employees, however, seldom comply with these information security procedures and techniques, placing the organizations' assets and business in danger [32, p. 125]. To address this concern, several information security compliance approaches have been proposed. Aytes and Connolly [3], Siponen [29] and Puhakainen [24] have criticized these extant approaches as lacking not only

---

Please use the following format when citing this chapter:

Siponen, M., Pahnila, S., and Mahmood, A., 2007, in IFIP International Federation for Information Processing, Volume 232, New Approaches for Security, Privacy and Trust in Complex Environments, eds. Venter, H., Eloff, M., Labuschagne, L., Eloff, J., von Solms, R., (Boston: Springer), pp. 133–144.

theoretically grounded methods, but also empirical evidence on their effectiveness. In fact, only three approaches [4], [34], [35] meet these important criteria. This paper fills this gap in research by first building a new theoretical model, explaining how employees' compliance with information security policies and guidelines can be improved. In this model, we combine PMT with the modern GDT and TRA. The model is then validated using an empirical study.

The results of this study are of relevance to researchers and practitioners. Since the extant studies on information security policy compliance present only anecdotal information on the factors explaining employees' adherence to information security policies with three exceptions mentioned above, it is of utmost importance to study this issue. This information is also useful for practitioners who want to obtain empirically proven information on how they can improve their employees' adherence to information security policies, and hence improve the information security of their organizations.

The paper is organized as follows. The second section reviews previous works. The third section proposes the research model and the fourth discusses the research methodology. The results are presented in the fifth section. The sixth section discusses the implications of the study.

2 Previous work on information security policy compliance

To understand the fundamental limitations of the extant works on information security policy compliance, these works have been divided into three categories: (1) conceptual principles without an underlying theory and empirical evidence; (2) theoretical models without empirical support; (3) empirical support grounded upon theories. These categories are discussed next.

Conceptual principles present practical principles and suggestions for improving employees' compliance with information security polices. These studies include generic information security awareness training programs by Sommers and Robinson [30], McCoy and Fowler [20 p. 347], Thomson and von Solms [36], McLean [21], Spurling [31, p. 20], and Parker [22, p. 464].

Perry [23, pp. 94-95] offers practical principles for the improvement of information security behavior: highlighting information security violations, sending managers to information security seminars, and getting consultants to evaluate the information security state of the organization. Gaunt [11], Furnell, Sanders and Warren [10] and Katsikas [16] all propose information security awareness programs for improving information security behavior in healthcare contexts. Furnell et al. [9] propose the use of information security training software that helps users to become aware of potential risks and the corresponding information security countermeasures. Finally, Wood [39] suggests 53 means for ensuring that employees comply with information security procedures, such as information security advertisements on coffee mugs.

While all the above propose interesting principles for increasing information security awareness, none of them are theoretically grounded or offer empirical evidence to support their principles in practice.

Theoretical models without empirical support contain studies that contribute to the creation of theoretical insights on how employees' information security policy compliance can be increased. Aytes and Connolly's [3] study suggests that the perceived probability and desirability of the outcomes of the individuals' choices explains users' security behavior. Lee and Lee [17] use the social bonds theory, the theory of planned behavior, the social learning theory, and GDT to explain computer crimes, while Siponen [29] suggests the use of the theory of planned behavior, the theory of intrinsic motivation, and need-based theories to ensure that employees follow information security policies and guidelines. Thomson and von Solms [37] suggest the use of social psychology to improve employees' information security behavior.

To summarize, while these works contribute to the creation of theoretical insights on how employees' information security compliance can be increased, they are lacking empirical evidence on their practical usefulness.

Empirical works grounded upon theories include Aytes and Connolly [4], Straub [34], Straub and Welke [35] and Woon et al. [40]. Aytes and Connolly [4] use the Rational Choice Model to explain why workers violate information security procedures. Straub [34] and Straub and Welke [35] use the GDT to investigate whether investment in information security measures reduces computer abuse. Weekly hours dedicated to information security, dissemination of information security polices and guidelines, stating penalties for non-compliance, and the use of information security software were found to be most effective deterrents [34, p. 272-273]. Finally, Woon et al. [40] found that the perceived severity of the information security threat, effectiveness of response, perceived capability to use the security features (self-efficacy) and the cost of using the security features (response cost) affect home users' decisions on whether or not to use security features.

To summarize the literature review, while several information security awareness, education and enforcement approaches exist, only four approaches are theoretically and empirically grounded. Of these three, Woon et al. [40] study wireless network users, while Straub [34] and Straub and Welke [35] focus on classical deterrence theory, and Aytes and Connolly [4] apply the Rational Choice Model. Thus, excluding Straub [34], Straub and Welke [35], and Aytes and Connolly [4], the prior approaches do not offer an exploratory model or evidence of what factors affect employees' information security policy compliance. This study aims to fill this gap.

3 The research model

The theoretical model combines PMT, TRA and GDT. PMT is best known for its use in health science: it has been used to motivate people to avoid unhealthy behavior. PMT is divided into two components: threat appraisal and coping appraisal. The former is further divided into threat and coping appraisal, while the latter consists of self-efficacy, response efficacy and response costs. PMT emphasizes the changes produced by persuasive communications [27]. Persuasive communications is based on interacting, aiming to alter the way people think, feel or behave. Thus, the goal of persuasion is to motivate or to influence an individual's attitude or behavior in a predetermined way.

'Intention to comply with information security policies' and 'actual compliance with information security policies' are based on TRA [8]. Attitude indicates a person's positive or negative feelings toward some stimulus object [2]. According to Ajzen [2], 'intentions' captures the motivational factors that influence a behavior, and they indicate how hard people are willing to try to perform the behavior in question. According to TRA, the stronger the intention to engage in a behavior, the more likely the behavior is to be carried out. According to our model, the stronger the intention to comply with information security policies is, the more likely it is that the individual will actually comply with the information security policies.

Threat appraisal consists of two dimensions: perceived vulnerability and perceived severity. Perceived vulnerability means conditional probability that a negative event will take place if no measures are taken to encounter it [25]. In the context of our study, the negative event is any information security threat. Therefore, in the context of our study, perceived vulnerability refers to employees' perceived assessment of whether their organization is vulnerable to information security threats, which will take place if no measures are taken to counter them.

Perceived severity, on the other hand, refers to the degree of both physical and psychological harm the threat can cause [25]. In our study, it refers to potential harm caused by information security breaches in the organization context. Here our assumption is that if organizations' employees do not realize that they are really confronted by information security threats (threat appraisal) and if they do not feel that these threats can cause consequences with a destructive impact on the organization (perceived severity), they will not comply with information security policies. Therefore, we hypothesize:

H1: Threat appraisal affects employees' intention to comply with information security policies.

Coping appraisal is a measure consisting of three dimensions: response efficacy, self-efficacy, and response cost [26], [27]. Response efficacy relates to the belief in the perceived benefits of the coping action [26], that is, belief that carrying out the coping action will remove the threat. In our study, it means that adherence to information security policies is an effective mechanism for detecting an information security threat. Self-efficacy emphasizes the individual's ability or judgment of their capabilities to perform the coping response actions [6]. Placing self-efficacy theory in the context of our study, it refers to workers' beliefs in whether they can apply and adhere to information security policies; this belief will lead to compliance with these policies. Maddux and Rogers [19] found in their study that self-efficacy was the most powerful predictor of intention. In our study, the response costs were not studied.

Therefore, we hypothesize:

H2: Self-efficacy affects employees' intention to comply with information security policies.

H3: Response efficacy affects employees' intention to comply with information security policies.

Sanctions. The concept of deterrence has been a key focus of criminological theories for more than thirty years. One of the leading theories in the field is GDT, which was originally developed for controlling criminal behavior [14]. Traditionally, the classical deterrence theory suggests that certainty, severity, and celerity of punishment affect people's decisions on whether to commit a crime or not [14]. Certainty means that an individual believes that his or her criminal behavior will be detected, while severity means that it will be harshly punished. Celerity signifies that the sanctions will occur quickly. Straub [34] found that stating penalties for information security policy non-compliance increases proper information security behavior. However, studies by Straub [34] and Straub and Welke [35] employ what Higgins et al. [14] refer to as the classical deterrence theory. Therefore, these seminal studies by Straub [34], [35] do not address three important components of contemporary GDT: social disapproval, self-disapproval and impulsivity. Social disapproval refers to the degree to which family members, friends and co-workers disapprove of the action. Self-disapproval refers to an individual's feeling of shame, guilt, and embarrassment about an action, while impulsivity means low self-control, that is, the inability of an individual to resist a temptation toward criminal behavior when an opportunity for it exists. This leads to the following hypothesis:

H4. Sanctions affect employees' actual compliance with information security policies.

Intentions indicate people's willingness to try to perform the behavior in question [2], adherence to information security policies in this case. Rogers and Prentice-Dunn [27] suggest that the intentions are the most applicable measure of protection motivation. Previous research on technology acceptance, for instance, shows that intentions are good predictors of actual behavior [38], which, in the context of our study, is adherence to information security policies. Moreover, in our study, behavioral intention is an indicator of the effects of persuasion related to information security policies. Thus we can hypothesize:

H5. Employees' intention to comply with information security policies affects actual compliance with information security policies.

4 Research methods and results

According to Straub [33] and Boudreau et al. [7], using validated and tested questions will improve the reliability of constructs and results. Accordingly, we used items that have been tried and tested by previous studies, when available (Table 1).

Table 1. Constructs and their theoretical background

Construct	Theoretical background	Adapted from
Intention to comply	TRA	[1]
Actual compliance	TRA	[18]
Threat and copying appraisal	PMT	[27]
Sanctions	GDT	[14]

All the items are measured using a standard seven-point Likert scale (strongly disagree – strongly agree). Since the measures presented in Table 1 are not previously tested in the context of information security policy compliance, the present research tests these measures in the information security context. Hence, the questions were pilot tested using 15 people. Based on their feedback, the readability factor of the questions was improved. The data was collected from four Finnish companies. A total of 3130 respondents were asked to fill out the web-based questionnaire. The distribution of the respondents was quite geographically spread all over Finland. Taking into consideration missing data and invalid responses we had a total sum of reliable responses of 917, the response rate being 29.3%. 56.1% were males and 43.9% females.

Reliability and validity. The data analysis was conducted using SPSS 14.0 and AMOS 6.0 structural equation modeling software (SEM). The mean, standard deviation and correlations of the constructs are shown in Table 2. The content validity of the instrument was ensured by the pilot test as discussed above. Convergent validity was ensured by assessing the factor loadings and by calculating variance extracted. We conducted a single confirmatory factor analysis for each of the constructs. As Table 2 shows all the model items loaded well, exceeding 0.50 [12]. Divergent validity was assessed by computing the correlations between constructs. Correlations between all pairs of constructs were below the threshold value of 0.90. The variance extracted of all the constructs exceeded 0.5 [13]. Internal consistency reliability among the items was assessed by calculating Cronbach's alpha. As Table 3 shows, Cronbach's alpha exceeded the suggested value of 0.60 for all constructs [12]. Hence, the reliability and validity of the constructs in the model are acceptable.

Table 2. Mean, standard deviation and correlations of the constructs.

Construct	Mean	Standard deviation	1.	2.	3.	4.	5.	6.
1. Actual compliance	6.16	0.98	1					
2. Intention to comply	6.35	0.88	0.848	1				
3. Threat appraisal	5.72	0.99	0.374	0.351	1			
4. Response efficacy	4.75	1.43	0.203	0.193	0.215	1		
5. Self-efficacy	5.89	1.02	0.407	0.402	0.322	0.256	1	
6. Sanctions	3.80	1.58	0.217	0.132	0.333	0.156	0.140	1

Table 3. Convergent validity and internal consistency and reliability.

Construct	Items	Factor loading	Variance extracted	Cronbach's alpha
Actual compliance	Actcomp1	0.65	0.81	0.84
	Actcomp2	0.88		
	Actcomp3	0.89		
Intention to comply	Intcomp1	0.71	0.80	0.85
	Intcomp2	0.86		
	Intcomp3	0.84		
Threat appraisal	Thrappr1	0.54	0.62	0.76
	Thrappr2	0.65		
	Thrappr3	0.60		
	Thrappr4	0.61		
	Thrappr5	0.70		
	Thrappr6	Dropped		
Response efficacy	Respeffi1	0.73	0.75	0.80
	Respeffi2	0.88		
	Respeffi3	0.66		
Self-efficacy	Selfeffi1	Dropped	0.85	0.83
	Selfeffi2	0.89		
	Selfeffi3	0.80		
Sanctions	Sanctio1	0.91	0.83	0.90
	Sanctio2	0.96		
	Sanctio3	0.89		
	Sanctio4	Dropped		
	Sanctio5	0.59		
	Sanctio6	Dropped		

The model was assessed using the maximum likelihood method. The fitness of the model was tested in structural equation modeling using goodness-of-fit criteria, which in practice indicate the degree of compatibility between the proposed model and the observed covariances and correlations.

Table 4. Convergent validity and internal consistency and reliability.

Model		Criteria
χ^2	8.361	
df	3	
p	0.039	
CMIN/DF	2,787	2-3
CFI	0.997	>0.9
NFI	0.995	>0.9
RMSEA	0.044	<0.05

The fit indexes (Table 4) chosen for this study are based on the literature, and represent three different fit characteristics: absolute fit, comparative fit measures and global fit measures. The chi-square test ($\chi 2$) with degrees of freedom, p-value and sample size is commonly used for absolute model fit criteria [15, 28]. Root mean square error of approximation fit index (RMSEA) is used to assess the error due to the simplifying of the model. The Comparative Fit Index (CFI) and Normed Fit Index (NFI) are recommended for model comparison, for comparison between the hypothesized and independent models [15, 28]. Overall goodness of fit was assessed with relative chi-square; $\chi 2$/degree of freedom (CMIN/DF). The fit indices indicate that the research model provides a good fit with the data.

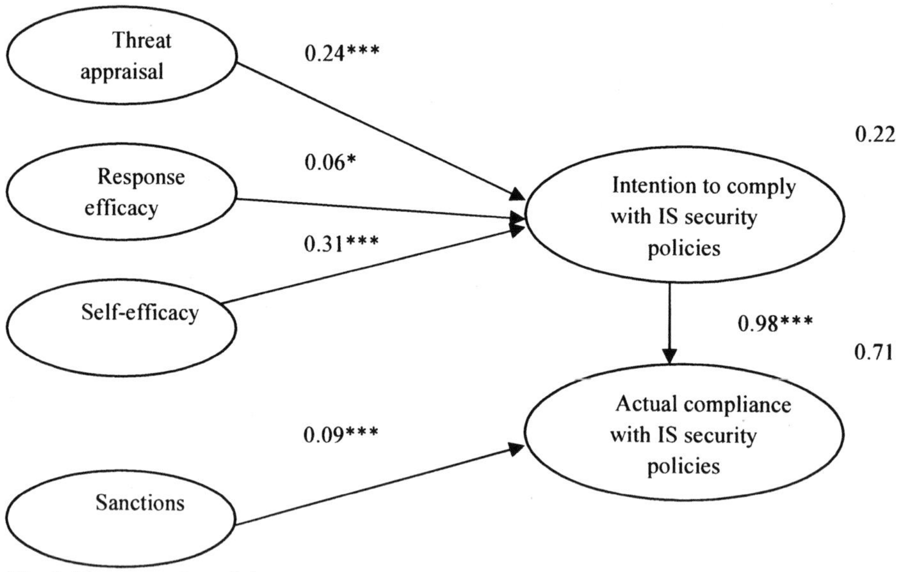

Fig. 1. The research model.

The research model yielded a $\chi 2$ value of 8.361 with 3 degrees of freedom, with a p value of 0.039 (Fig. 1). The findings indicate that the direct path from threat appraisal (ß = 0.24) to intention to comply with IS security policies is significant. The correlation (Table 2) between threat appraisal and intention to comply with IS security policies was quite high (0.351), explaining alone about 12.3% of the variance in intention to comply with IS security policies. Response efficacy (ß = 0.06) and self-efficacy (ß = 0.31) also have a significant effect on intention to comply with IS security policies. Sanctions (ß = 0.09) have a significant effect on actual compliance with IS security policies. Intention to comply with IS security policies (ß = 0.98) has a significant effect on actual compliance with IS security policies. In all, the research model accounts for 71% (R2 = 0.71) of the variance in actual compliance.

5 Conclusive discussion

The literature agrees that the major threat to information security is constituted by careless employees who do not comply with organizations' information security policies and procedures. Hence, employees have not only to be aware of, but also to comply with organizations' information security policies and procedures. To address this important concern, different information security awareness, education and enforcement approaches have been proposed. Prior research on information security policy compliance has criticized these extant information security policy compliance approaches as lacking (1) theoretically and (2) empirically grounded principles to ensure that employees comply with information security policies. To address these two problems in the current research, this study first put forward a new model in order to explain employees' information security compliance. This model combined the Protection Motivation Theory, the Theory of Reasoned Action and the General Deterrence Theory. Second, to validate this model empirically, we collected data (N = 917) from four companies.

We found that threat appraisal has a significant impact on intention to comply with information security policies. Hence, it is important that employees are made aware of the information security threats and their severity and celerity for the organization. To be more precise, our findings suggest that practitioners should emphasize to the employees that not only are information security breaches becoming more and more serious for the business of organizations, but their severity to the business of the organization is also increasing.

Self-efficacy, referring to employees' beliefs in whether they can apply and adhere to information security policies, will lead to compliance with these policies in the context of our study, and has a significant impact on intention to comply with information security policies. This finding stresses the perceived relevance of information security policies. If employees do not perceive information security policies as relevant and sufficiently up-to-date for their work, they will not adhere to the policies. Yet it also suggests that it is important to ensure through information security education or verbal persuasion, for example, that employees really can use information security measures.

Our results show that response efficacy has a significant effect on intention to comply with information security policies. In order to minimize IS security breaches, first it is important that the organization's IS security personnel is aware of IS security threats and knows how to react them. Second, IS security policy should be clear and up-to-date, and third, employees should comply with IS security policies.

Sanctions have a significant impact on actual compliance with information security policies. This means in practice that practitioners need to state the sanctions for information security policy non-compliance in a visible manner. In particular, it is important to get employees to believe that their non-compliance with information security policies will be detected and severe legal sanctions will take place. The findings also suggest that the detection must occur quickly. Also, on the basis of our findings, information security practitioners should realize that social pressure (sanctions: social disapproval) towards information security policy compliance from top management, the employee's immediate supervisor, peers and information security staff is important for ensuring employees' information security policy compliance. This is consistent with the findings that social environment has an effect on individuals' behavior [2]. To create and ensure such verbal persuasion, top management, immediate supervisors and information security staff should clearly and explicitly explain the importance of complying with information security polices to their employees. This finding has implications for the information security education strategy of organizations. In the light of our finding, organizations should pay special attention to educating top management, supervisors and information security staff in order that they can spread the word on the importance of adherence to information security policies, and hence create social pressure towards information security policy compliance. This is good news for large corporations who may face difficulties educating all their employees.

Finally, intention to comply with information security policies has a significant impact on actual compliance with information security policies. Intention is a motivational factor that influences a behavior by indicating how hard people are willing to try and how much of an effort they are planning to exert in order to perform the behavior. The stronger the intention to engage in the behavior, the more likely it is to be performed [2].

6 References

1. Agarwal, R. and J. Prasad, Conceptual and Operational Definition of Personal Innovativeness in the Domain of Information Technology. *Information Systems Research*, 1998. 9(2): p. 204-215.
2. Ajzen, I., "The Theory of Planned Behavior", *Organizational Behavior and Human Decision Processes* 50,2, 1991, 179-211.
3. Aytes, K. and Connolly, T., "A Research Model for Investigating Human Behavior Related to Computer Security", Proceedings of the 2003 American Conference On Information Systems, Tampa, FL, August 4-6. 2003.
4. Aytes, K. and Connolly, T., "Computer and Risky Computing Practices: A Rational Choice Perspective", *Journal of Organizational and End User Computing*, 16,2, 2004, 22-40.
5. Bagchi, K. and Udo, G., "An analysis of the growth of computer and Internet security breaches", *Communications of AIS* 12, 2003, 684–700.
6. Bandura, A., "Self-Efficacy: Toward a Unifying Theory of Behaviour Change", *Psychological Review* 84, 2, 1977, 191-215.

7. Boudreau, M.-C., Gefen, D. and Straub, D. W., "Validation in information systems research: A state-of-the-art assessment." *MIS Quarterly* 25, 1, 2001, 1-16.
8. Fishbein, M. and Ajzen, I., Belief, Attitude, Intention and Behavior: An Introduction to Theory and Research. MA, Addison-Wesley. 1975.
9. Furnell, S. M., Gennatou, M. and Dowland P. S., "A prototype tool for information security awareness and training", *International Journal of Logistics Information Management*, 15, 5, 2002, 352-357.
10. Furnell, S., Sanders, P. W. and Warren, M. J., "Addressing information security training and awareness within the European healthcare community", in Proceedings of Medical Informatics Europe '97. 1997.
11. Gaunt, N., "Installing an appropriate information security policy in hospitals", *International Journal of Medical Informatics*, 49, 1, 1998, 131-134.
12. Hair, J.F.J., Anderson, R.E., Tatham, R.L., and Black, W. C., Multivariate data analysis. 5 ed: Upper Saddle River, New Jersey, Prentice Hall Inc. 1998.
13. Hair, J.F.J., Black, W.C, Babin, B.J, Anderson, R.E., Tatham, R.L., Multivariate data analysis. Sixth ed. 2006: Pearson Prentice Hall.
14. Higgins, G.E., Wilson, A.L. and Fell, B.D., "An Application of Deterrence Theory to Software Piracy", *Journal of Criminal Justice and Popular Culture*, 12, 3, 2005, 166-184.
15. Hoyle, R.H., Structural Equation Model. Conceprts, Issues, and Applications., ed. H. Rick, Hoyle. 1995: SAGE publications, Inc.
16. Katsikas, S. K., "Health care management and information system security: awareness, training or education", *International Journal of Medical Informatics*, 60, 2, 2000, 129-135.
17. Lee, J. and Lee, Y., "A holistic model of computer abuse within organizations", *Information management & computer security*, 10, 2, 2002, 57-63.
18. Limayem, M., and Hirt, S.G., "Force of Habit and Information Systems Usage: Theory and Initial Validation", *Journal of Association for Information Systems*, 4, 2003, 65-97.
19. Maddux, J.E. and R.W. Rogers, Protection Motivation and Self-Efficacy: A Revised Theory of Fear Appeals and Attitude Change. *Journal of experimental social psychology*, 1983. 19: p. 469-479.
20. McCoy, C. and Fowler, R.T., "You are the key to security": establishing a successful security awareness program. In the proceedings of the SIGUCCS'04, Baltimore, Maryland, October 10-13, 2004, 346-349.
21. McLean, K., "Information security awareness - selling the cause", in Proceedings of the IFIP TC11, Eighth International Conference on information security, IFIP/Sec '92. 1992.
22. Parker, D. B., Fighting Computer Crime: A new Framework for Protecting Information, John Wiley & Sons, USA. 1998.
23. Perry, W. E., Management Strategies for Computer Security, Butterworth Publishers, USA. 1985.
24. Puhakainen, P. Design Theory for Information Security Awareness, 2006. Ph.D Thesis, the University of Oulu, Finland.
25. Rippetoe, S. and Rogers, R. W., "Effects of Components of Protection - Motivation Theory on Adaptive and Maladaptive Coping with a Health Threat", *Journal of Personality and Social Psychology*, 52, 3, 1987, 596-604.
26. Rogers, R. W., "Cognitive and Physiological Processes in Fear Appeals and Attitude Change: A Revised Theory of Protection Motivation Theory", in Social Psychophysiology, J. Cacioppo and R. Petty (Eds.), Guilford, New York, 1983.
27. Rogers, R. W. and Prentice-Dunn, S., "Protection motivation theory", In D. S. Gochman (Ed.), Handbook of Health Behavior Research I: Personal and Social Determinants, New York, NY: Plenum Press, 1997, 113-132.
28. Schumacker, R.E. and R.G. Lomax, A Beginner's Guide to Structural Equation Modeling. 1996, Mahwah, New Jersey: Lawrence Erlbaum Associates. 288.

29. Siponen, M., "A Conceptual Foundation for Organizational Information Security Awareness", *Information Management & Computer Security*, 8, 1, 2000, 31-41.
30. Sommers, K. and Robinson, B., "Security awareness training for students at Virginia Commonwealth University", In the proceedings of the SIGUCCS'04, Baltimore, Maryland, October 10-13, 2004, 379-380.
31. Spurling, P., "Promoting security awareness and commitment", *Information Management & Computer Security*, 3, 2, 1995, 20-26.
32. Stanton, J. M., Stam, K. R., Mastrangelo, P. and Jolton, J., "An analysis of end user security behaviors", *Computers & Security*, 24, 2005, 124-133
33. Straub, D. W., "Validating Instruments in MIS Research", *MIS Quarterly*, 13, 2, 1989, 147-169.
34. Straub, D.W., "Effective IS Security: An Empirical Study", *Information Systems Research*, 1, 3, 1990, 255-276.
35. Straub, D.W. and Welke, R.J., "Coping with Systems Risk: Security Planning Models for. Management Decision-Making", *MIS Quarterly*, 22, 4, 1998, 441-469.
36. Thomson, M.E. and von Solms, R., "An effective information security awareness program for industry", in proceedings of the WG 11.2 and WG 11.1 of the TC-11 IFIP, 1997.
37. Thomson, M. E. and von Solms, R., "Information security Awareness: educating your users effectively", *Information Management & Computer Security*, 6, 4, 1998, 167-173.
38. Venkatesh, V., Morris, M. G., Davis, G. B. and Davis, F. D., "User Acceptance of Information Technology: Toward a Unified View", *MIS Quarterly*, 27, 3, 2003, 425-478
39. Wood, C. C., "Information Security Awareness Raising Methods", *Computer Fraud & Security Bulletin*, Elsevier Science Publishers, Oxford, England, June 1995, pp 13-15.
40. Woon, I. M. Y., Tan, G. W. and Low, R. T., "A Protection Motivation Theory Approach to Home Wireless Security", Proceedings of the Twenty-Sixth International Conference on Information Systems, Las Vegas, 2005, 367-380.

Phishing in the Wireless: Implementation and Analysis

Ivan Martinovic, Frank A. Zdarsky, Adam Bachorek, Christian Jung, and Jens B. Schmitt

disco | Distributed Computer Systems Lab
University of Kaiserslautern, Germany
{martinovic,zdarsky,a_bacho,c_jung82,jschmitt}@informatik.uni-kl.de

Abstract. Web-based authentication is a popular mechanism implemented by Wireless Internet Service Providers (WISPs) because it allows a simple registration and authentication of customers, while avoiding high resource requirements of the new IEEE 802.11i security standard and backward compatibility issues of legacy devices. In this work we demonstrate two different and novel attacks against web-based authentication. One attack exploits operational anomalies of low- and middle-priced devices in order to hijack wireless clients, while the other exploits an already known vulnerability within wired networks which, in dynamic wireless environments, turns out to be even harder to detect and protect against.

1 Introduction

Taking into consideration the tremendous growth of public Internet access, one can easily see that IEEE 802.11 [1] networks have played a major role during recent years. High transmission rates, low costs, and simple deployment have all resulted in a high number of *hotspots* that are now offering wireless Internet access in coffee shops, airports, libraries, conferences, hotels, etc. For example, one of the major German WISP states that it operates more than 25,000 domestic and international hotspots that customers may use in order to roam and access the Internet worldwide.

Parallel to the popularity of wireless LAN technology, the topic of its security gained a similar, although rather negative publicity. The tragic end of Wired Equivalent Privacy (WEP) [8, 4] and the simplicity of various DoS attacks on a wireless medium have resulted in giving up security at the logical-link layer and shifting it to upper layers (or in the best case leaving it within virtual private networks (VPNs)).

Although WLAN's new security standard IEEE 802.11i [2], which was ratified in 2004, provides mechanisms for strong mutual authentication, data integrity, and data confidentiality, its deployment and utilization have not followed the same growth. Therefore, IEEE 802.11i is still not widely utilized, its strong security services often require new hardware and extension of the already existing infrastructure, while most of the handhelds have not yet been certified according to the standard. As a result, WISPs incorporate proprietary security solutions that can easily be implemented within their infrastructure and business models, providing a higher usability and lower complexity for customers, but on the other hand customers are expected to take care of the security themselves.

Please use the following format when citing this chapter:

Martinovic, I., Zdarsky, F., Bachorek, A., Jung, C., and Schmitt, J., 2007, in IFIP International Federation for Information Processing, Volume 232, New Approaches for Security, Privacy and Trust in Complex Environments, eds. Venter, H., Eloff, M., Labuschagne, L., Eloff, J., von Solms, R., (Boston: Springer), pp. 145–156.

In a popular scenario of public hotspots provided by WISPs most security services are reduced to a simple access control mechanism which is implemented through a web-based authentication. For example, in most of the WISPs that we have analyzed, the only requirement placed upon a customer is to have a "wireless-enabled mobile device, BSSID set to a WISP, and Internet-ready web browser". No additional software is required. Every user can associate himself with the WISP's access point and by launching his Internet-browser he will be redirected to a login page. A customer can use that page to either authenticate or create a new account by paying for wireless access with his credit card. Upon a successful login, his Ethernet address (MAC address) will be authenticated and allowed to access the Internet. This simple solution does not require any knowledge of digital certificates, signatures, or any other security mechanisms. Yet, as we will show in this work, there is a price to pay for this simplicity.

We show and analyze two different attacks on web-based authentication. The goal of both attacks is to impersonate a legal AP and to inject a fake web page asking the user for his credentials. The first attack targets the access points and can in certain cases result in operational anomalies allowing the attacker to "steal" new clients. This attack is described and discussed in Section 2. The second attack focuses on the wireless clients and is based on a well-known vulnerability within wired networks. Unlike in wired networks, however, it shows to be still fully exploitable today and fatal on every wireless client, especially in conjunction with web-based authentication. The second attack as well as various countermeasures are discussed in Section 3. The related work on this subject is presented in Section 4. Section 5 concludes this work.

2 Flooding-based Client Hijacking

By executing a DoS attack, the aim of the attacker is to exhaust the server's resources which would then result in the server's inability to provide any service at all. On one hand, this can remain the main goal of the attacker and on the other hand, it can serve as a starting point for the execution of even more sophisticated attacks. A similar attack can also be started against web-based authentication provided that the attacker is able to disrupt an original service offered by a WISP's AP and during the attack a fake service is provided to wireless users. IEEE 802.11 networks have been subject to this type of attack from the beginning of their deployment. A common wireless attack based on rouge AP is traditionally executed by installing the rouge AP with a stronger signal and disguising it with the same BSSID as the legal one. The fact that a wireless client automatically connects to the AP with a stronger signal would then be abused so as to hijack the wireless station. Back in 2001/2002 various tools were enabling a DoS attack based on flooding an AP with authentication requests. In most cases the AP would crash or freeze and only a hard reset would help. Today, most access points provide a "DoS protection mechanism" based on a reduced rate of allowed authentication requests and should no longer be vulnerable to this type of attack.

2.1 IEEE 802.11 Association Process

Before going into more detail, we briefly summarize the functionality of IEEE 802.11 networks operating in infrastructure mode.

The infrastructure mode of IEEE 802.11 contains an access point which provides certain control and management functionalities. An access point takes care of accepting only the data traffic of wireless stations that are in a valid connection state. A wireless station can be in three different connection states: *initial* state, *authenticated but not associated* state, and *authenticated and associated* state. In order to send or receive data frames, the wireless client must be in the third state, i.e. in the authenticated and associated state.

A successful authentication is realized by sending an authentication frame in which one of two different authentication algorithms can be chosen: Open-System authentication (meaning no authentication at all) or Shared-Key authentication. Since the introduction of IEEE 802.11i and as a consequence of WEP being completely broken, Open-System authentication is now the only mandatory IEEE 802.11 authentication algorithm. Therefore, an authentication frame can no longer provide any authentication functionality but mainly serves to bring the wireless station into the second state. After a successful authentication, the wireless station proceeds by sending an association frame by which the association procedure is being finalized. From that moment onward, a wireless client is able to receive and send data.

On the other side, if an AP detects frames coming from a wireless client that is not in a valid state (with respect to the frames it is sending), the AP will respond with either a deauthentication frame or a disassociation frame, depending on the state the client managed to reach. This mechanism is important for two reasons; the first is to help a wireless station to re-authenticate itself in case it is in the wrong state and the second is to mitigate the possibility of an AP impersonation. For example, if a fake AP uses the same MAC address of a legal AP to steal wireless clients, the legal AP will then respond with a deauthentication frame to every client that starts to communicate with the fake AP.

2.2 Exploiting Operational Vulnerability

Although no real authentication takes place during the association process, an AP still needs to reserve resources to keep state about every wireless client. Common DoS attacks make use of this fact to fill up authentication table by flooding the AP with fake authentication requests. Eventually, this results in a total crash of the AP after which only a physical reset could help. An attacker may then use its own fake AP to impersonate a legal one. One should assume that this kind of DoS attack should no longer be feasible on modern equipment. With the aim of investigating this matter we have collected 6 different access points dating from 2003 to 2006 that were chosen based on their popularity and price (all of them with the latest firmware upgrade as provided by the manufacturer). For legal purposes, we shell keep the vendor and product names of the selected APs anonymous and therefore only describe price classes:

- Class 1: low-priced access points ($\leq$50 USD). Two APs, produced in 2003, 2004.

- Class 2: middle-priced access points (from 50 USD to 100 USD). Two APs, produced in 2004, 2006.
- Class 3: high-priced access-points (from 350 USD and higher). Two APs, produced in 2004, 2006.

To analyze the AP's behaviour we have flooded each AP with approximately 50 authentication requests per second. Since no significant differences in the operation of APs within the same class were detected, we select one AP from each class to describe it in more detail.

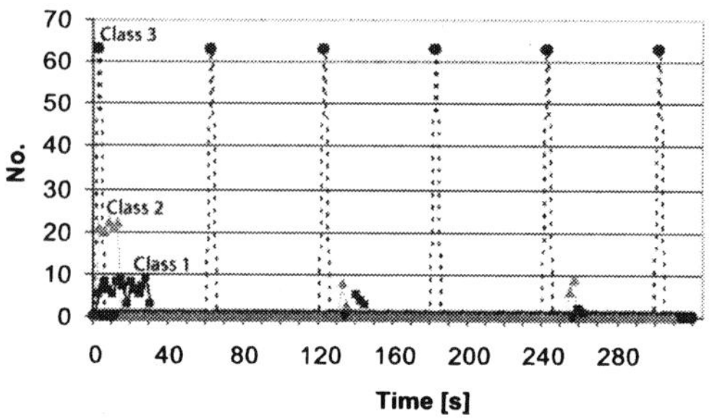

Fig. 1. Time Trace of Successful Authentications

Figure 1 shows the behaviour of one representative of each class under the flooding attack. As it can be seen, the most expensive AP (Class 3) allows 63 new authentication requests every 60 seconds. It is interesting to mention that both APs from Class 3, after allowing a certain number of requests, refuse to send any further response. This violates the IEEE 802.11 standard which mandates replies with appropriate reason codes to notify wireless client of unsuccessful authentications. This minor deviation from the standard introduces a certain performance degradation for wireless clients, because clients wait for the maximal response timeout before trying to authenticate again (we have observed that certain clients wait up to 7 seconds before retrying to authenticate).

In contrast to Class 3, both other classes accept various numbers of requests approximately every 2 minutes. Furthermore, they notify wireless clients if the authentication request has not been accepted by sending an "unsuccessful authentication" response. On the other hand, both classes have a high decrease in the number of accepted requests after initial admission, thus it seems that the flooding attack still impacts their resource management. Especially interesting is the longer period of time during which both other classes accept authentication request (e.g. one of the Class 2 APs accepts 126 authentication requests within the first 12 seconds and one of the Class 1 APs accepts 95 new requests within the first 30 seconds).

To analyze these phenomena in more detail, we have measured the delay between authentication requests and responses before and during the flooding attack. The attack rate remains the same with approximately 50 authentication requests per second, which implies an attacker throughput of about 1.5 KByte/s. The flooding attack started after 20 seconds of normal operation. We have found that both Class 1 and Class 2 APs suffer from an operational anomaly that causes an exceptionally high delay between the authentication request and the authentication response (see Figure 2). After only 8 seconds of flooding, the response delay increases to 12 seconds. This is in contrast to all Class 3 APs where the authentication response delay remains stable with a mean of 1.6 ms and a standard deviation of 3 ms.

From a security perspective all three classes of APs have a potential vulnerability. Class 3 APs only respond to accepted authentication requests, leaving all other wireless clients to wait for authentication responses for a client-dependent period of time. This fact can be exploited by an attacker who uses a fake AP with the same MAC address to answer authentication and association requests as successfully. As a result, wireless clients associate with the fake AP instead of the legal one.

The two other classes, although answering all requests, suffer from a high delay during the flooding attack by which only after 12 seconds an authentication response reaches a wireless client. Similarly, the attacker can also answer those requests before the legal AP.

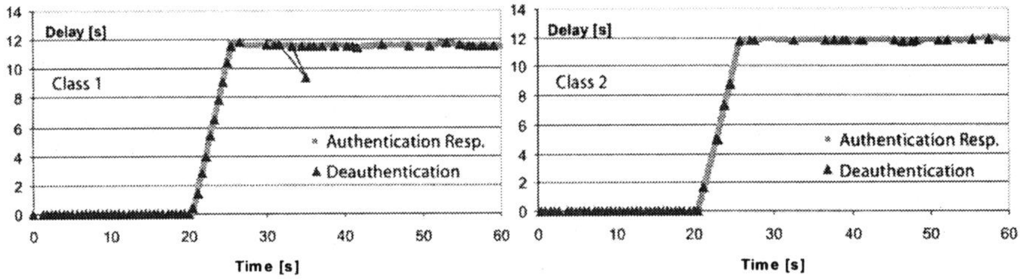

Fig. 2. Authentication and Deauthentication Delay

One last barrier for the attacker is the Deauthentication frame which is sent every time a data frame from an unauthenticated client is detected by the AP (as explained in subsection 2.1). We have measured the delay for this frame under the same experimental settings and only Class 3 APs are able to send the Deauthentication frame on time, meaning without any significant delay (mean response time for Deauthentication frame is 1.04 ms with a std.dev. of 1.7 ms). Both other classes have an increased Deauthentication delay which follows the Authentication delay as depicted in Figure 2. These results show that Class 3 APs, although deviating from the IEEE 802.11 standard, do not appear to have a security vulnerability due to their prompt response with a Deauthentication frame in case of their impersonation. This, regrettably cannot be said for their cheaper relatives.

2.3 Attack Implementation

In this subsection we are particularly interested in exploiting the aforementioned anomalies in order to implement an AP impersonation attack. The scenario remains the same as described in the motivation. The attacker's objective is to impersonate a WISP's access point and to inject a fake web page to a wireless client.

Discovered delays of Class 1 and Class 2 APs enable us to fully disguise the fake AP as a legal one. In the following steps we describe our implementation:

1. An attacker consists of a laptop running a web server and two wireless interfaces. One of the interfaces is set to a master mode in order to enable the access point's functionality (called a fake AP) while another one is used to start the flooding attack. The web server responds to all HTTP requests sent by a user and contains the same web page as the one of the WISP.
2. The MAC address of the fake AP is set to correspond to the MAC address of the legal AP using the same BSSID. The attacker starts flooding the legal AP.
3. After the legal AP has increased its authentication and deauthentication delay, the fake AP starts answering every request sent by wireless clients.
4. The attacker captures HTTP requests and responds with a fake web page (it can also choose to respond to any other control packet like ARP, DNS, DHCP,...).

As a result of this attack, we were able to authenticate and associate every wireless client with the fake AP. As assumed, all Class 1 and 2 APs did not detect the impersonation and the wireless clients successfully established a connection with a fake AP before first Deauthentication frames from a legal AP arrived and deauthenticated the client. In order to analyse the quality of the connection between a wireless client and the fake AP, we have measured both UDP and TCP throughputs (shown in Figure 3). The UDP sender rate was set to 5 Mb/s.

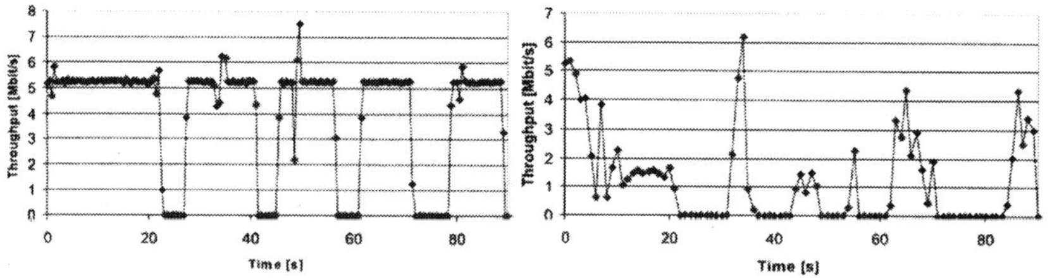

Fig. 3. UDP (left) and TCP (right) Throughput

Figure 3 shows that during the first 22 seconds the communication between the fake AP and the wireless client is undisturbed by the legal AP. We were able to intercept all requests and successfully redirect the wireless client to the fake web page without noticing any quality loss or other indication of the attack. Following that, the channel was influenced by Deauthentications frames sent from a legal AP. By receiving a Deauthentication frame, the wireless client would disconnect and immediately try to reconnect. Again, the fake AP was the first to react and the connection was re-established. This can clearly be seen in the UDP traffic where the connection is disrupted by slots where the client is not connected. Although this frequent re-connection disturbs the link-layer connection, the transport layer still provides a connection. The TCP throughput on the right shows a trace of SSL traffic between the wireless client and the fake web-server which was used to present a fake authentication login page similar to those from WISPs.

Table 1. Various UDP Rates and Measured delay

UDP Throughput [Mbit/s]	1	2	3	5
delay (mean) [s]	13.23	14.40	20.17	32.97
std. dev.	1.75	1.96	7.07	12.20

Another interesting question that occurs is why the delay presented in Figure 3 is higher then the one initially measured between authentication request and response (12 seconds). The reason is that the delay strongly depends on the traffic sent to the AP. In Table 1, we have used different UDP sender rates and 15 repetitions for each level of UDP throughput. It turned out that increased traffic highly incresed AP's response delay and delay variance.

2.4 Discussion

In this attack we have shown how simple it is for an attacker to fully impersonate a legal AP. It also shows that web-based authentication is highly vulnerable, meaning that the users but also providers should be more careful in using and providing such an authentication method. This attack was possible on all low-priced and middle-priced access points. Only the most expensive class of access points was immune to this kind of attack. In our opinion, this is an important fact because a low price of IEEE 802.11 technology is often considered to be one of its most mentioned advantages.

Another question that arises is how realistic this attack can be? On one hand, an attacker is able to spoof a web page, but on the other hand he still cannot fake an original WISP's digital certificate. This is a well known issue and although most of today's attacks, from fake emails to phishing web-sites, are technically solved, it is also well-known that the most effective and successful attacks are the ones based on abusing human naivety [13].

3 Wireless ARP Attack

In contrast to the attack described in the previous section which is based on attacking APs, in this section we describe an attack which focuses directly on wireless clients. It is based on the well-known idea of ARP spoofing, which although considered to be solved within wired networks, can be fully exploited within wireless networks. We show that by tweaking certain IEEE 802.11 frame parameters, a novel wireless ARP spoofing attack can be mounted which is hard to detect. Moreover, even a well-administrated infrastructure with ARP spoofing protection based on packet analysis cannot help in securing the wireless part of the network. As a result, the simplest solution against this attack is to abandon web-based authentication and to use the logical-link layer protection provided, e.g., by the IEEE 802.11i security standard.

3.1 Good Old ARP Poisoning

The Address Resolution Protocol (ARP) is used to resolve an IP address to a 48 bit Ethernet address (MAC address). It is a simple protocol consisting of the sender's IP address and sender's MAC address as well as the target's IP address (which is known to the sender) and MAC address (which is unknown). Since the ARP request is being sent as broadcast, it will therefore be received by every host on the same network. The host with the target IP address will then respond with an ARP reply containing his Ethernet address as a target MAC address.

By replying to ARP requests with an ARP replay containing a fake target MAC address, an attacker can simply redirect client's traffic to itself. This is why the ARP protocol has served as the basis for many different Man-In-The-Middle and DoS attacks mostly focused on switched (wired) networks.

The simplicity and frequency of ARP spoofing attacks in wired networks has resulted in a wide-spectrum of solutions that can detect and avoid the problem of fake ARP replies (existing solutions against ARP spoofing will be discussed later in subsection 3.3). Nevertheless, in contrast to a wired infrastructure, wireless environments are considerably different in their nature. Most importantly, public hotspots are characterized by clients which dynamically join and leave the wireless network.

3.2 Attack Implementation

At first sight, in order for the attacker to mount an ARP spoofing attack, he can simply choose to impersonate either the already associated stations or the AP itself by using their MAC addresses as sender's address. Although still effective, both of these approaches can be successfully detected. For every frame that the attacker sends (using either the address of an associated client or of the AP) the receiving station will send an acknowledgment. As a result, by receiving many acknowledgment frames, the legal station can identify that someone is using the same MAC address to send frames. Another problem that arises from impersonation of an already existing wireless client is that any frame received by the AP can be forwarded to a wired network in which traffic monitoring tools or intrusion detection systems can easily detect this kind of attack.

Therefore, to avoid being monitored and analyzed by more sophisticated systems, an attacker prefers to attack wireless clients only. Hence his goal is to keep fake ARP packets only within the wireless network. Furthermore, in order to avoid being detected by acknowledgements sent to existing clients, the attacker requires the possibility of using unknown MAC addresses as the source address for his attack.

In the following section we show that only by tweaking certain 802.11 frame characteristics an attacker can successfully send fake ARP packets with fully unknown MAC addresses, keep them undetectable by the AP and thus limit their propagation to wireless participants only.

Figure 4 shows a generic frame control field which is a part of every 802.11 frame.

Protocol Version	Type	Subtype	To DS	From DS	More Frag	Retry	Pwr Mgt	More Data	WEP	Order

Fig. 4. 802.11 Frame Control Field

The two one-bit flags `ToDS` and `FromDS` are used to indicate whether the frame is sent from the distribution system to a wireless station or the other way around. In infrastructure mode, any frame sent from a wireless client will have `ToDS` bit set and `FromDS` bit cleared. Those frames are checked by AP to assure that a sender is an authenticated and associated station (as described in subsection 2.1).

On the other side, if the frame has the `FromDS` bit set, the AP believes that the frame was sent from a different AP (one distribution system can contain several APs). The AP does not know all the stations within the distribution system and cannot check if the sender's MAC belongs to a known and associated station. As a result, by setting `FromDS` bit an attacker can send arbitrary frames, even with an unknown MAC address without the frame being intercepted by the AP. These fake frames will therefore not be forwarded to the distribution system which renders protection mechanisms inside the networks.

The very last problem that the attacker has to overcome in order to successfully disguise his attack is the fact that although pretending to come from a wired network, the replies are received by an AP over the wireless medium. Although this could be used by AP to detect a fake frame, the mentioned situation is valid within IEEE 802.11 networks in case of a wireless bridge (valid ToDS and FromDS configurations and their meaning are shown in Table 2). Thus, the AP will neither see it as security vulnerability nor will react to it.

Table 2. ToDS and FromDS Flags and Their Meaning

	`ToDS = 0`	`ToDS = 1`
`FromDS = 0`	IBSS (ad hoc mode)	Frames from stations to DS
`FromDS = 1`	Frames exiting the DS	Frames from AP to AP (wireless bridge)

As a proof of concept we have created *smartspoof* tool which implements and executes the attack described above (the tool can be made available upon request). It is an event-based tool that monitors the wireless medium for ARP requests and then immediately answers with a fake ARP inside a manipulated IEEE 802.11 frame. From our experiments in which we have used various wireless clients (both Linux-based and Windows-based) we can state that this attack was successfully executed on every tested client and after only a few minutes, all wireless clients had a poisoned ARP cache and the traffic was diverted to the attacker.

3.3 Discussion

Among the most common protections against ARP spoofing is a static ARP where the MAC-to-IP mapping can only be changed manually. Although very efficient within small infrastructures, this solution is not suitable for more dynamic environments. Especially in wireless environments where joining clients are new and initially do not know the network configuration, this solution cannot be implemented without introducing additional complexity. Furthermore, we have seen that different monitoring and traffic analyzing tools that are used inside the wired network to check if ARP replies provide valid MAC addresses are not effective. These mechanisms focus on networks in which traffic can be physically controlled. In contrast, a wireless environment with its broadcast nature makes neither of these solutions practical.

A more successful approach would be to monitor and analyze the wireless traffic. The difficulty in this approach lies in the operating mode of an access point. To be able to capture all traffic and still provide management and control functions, an AP must operate simultaneously in both, monitoring mode and master mode. However, this still imposes certain operational problems because in this case all the traffic should be analyzed by the AP itself. A more simple protection based on this approach would be to have additional access points or wireless stations for monitoring the traffic which consequently increases operational costs.

However, in contrast to a wireless enterprise network where all clients are known in advance and where the network is centrally administrated, the implementation of 802.11i within public, easily accessible wireless networks seem still to present a problem (although according to our measurements the performance tradeoff of introducing IEEE 802.11i does not represent a significant performance decline [11]). As a matter of fact, the usability-related problems of enforcing such security policies within public WLAN hotspots have already resulted in abandoning PKI-based solutions in favour of more light-weight proprietary solutions like web-based authentication which are the aim of the attacks as motivated at the beginning of this work.

4 Related Work

In 2003 the WLAN's security was a centre of various attacks against all security objectives. The unprotected management and control frames allowed fast and effective attacks on availability [3]. The poor security of WEP allowed attacks on confidentiality and integrity [5, 8, 4]. Various tools enabled simple flooding attacks, wireless client impersonation and injections of different frames directly on a wireless medium. In [3] the authors showed how simple it is to mount different DoS attacks on IEEE 802.11 networks. There were several research activities coping with that problem and proposing cryptography based solution [6, 12]. Furthermore, in 2005 the IEEE 802.11 Task Group w (TGw) was established with the aim of creating a standard for authentication of management and control frames with an expected draft due in 2008.

The ratification of IEEE 802.11i standard helped to gain more trust into providing confidentiality, but due to still unprotected management frames, attacks on availability of IEEE 802.11i were fast to follow [9, 10].

In contrast to previous research, in this work we have introduced a novel attack based on performance decrease of a certain APs. This attack does not focuses on any of vulnerabilities based on IEEE 802.11 itself but shows that low- and middle-priced access points feature an operational anomaly that although intended to protect against DoS attacks can be abused to implement a new attack. This, in contrary to a reputation of WLAN as a low-cost technology shows that to provide a secure and reliable service more attention should be made on a choice of a hardware.

On the other hand, the second attack introduced in this work has its roots within a well known ARP cache poisoning attack [14] but it is used in a novel way within a wireless network. Probably the most similar work describing ARP poisoning attack within wireless networks is described in [7]. The author shows how a wireless network can be used to attack the wired infrastructure of an enterprise. This attack does not concentrate on the wireless network itself but uses it to attack the wired network.

5 Conclusion

In this work we have presented two different attacks within IEEE 802.11 wireless environments. Although both attacks have known ancestors, we have developed novel way to show that even a new generation of APs is prone to such kind of attacks. The first attack, based on extensive measurements of various APs abuses an operational anomaly of low- and middle-priced APs to hijack wireless clients and intercept their traffic. Although we cannot state that this attack can be applicable on every AP, our measurements let us assume that cheaper devices do introduce certain performance degradation which can also represent a security vulnerability. While the first attack can be avoided by using more expensive equipment, in our second attack we showed simple and yet effective client-based attack applicable in every scenario which sacrifices link-layer security. More importantly, we showed that one of the frequently used authentication methods within WISPs perfectly assists the attacker in hijacking the wireless clients.

6 Acknowledgement

We would like to thank Steffen Reithermann from Transkom Ltd. for many fruitful discussions and information from a WISPs perspective and for making various APs available to analyze.

References

1. IEEE 802.11. IEEE Standard for Local and Metropolitan Area Networks - Part 11: Wireless LAN Medium Access Control (MAC) and Physical Layer (PHY) Specifications. IEEE Standard, July 1999.
2. IEEE 802.11i/D10.0. Security Enhancements, Amendment 6 to IEEE Standard for Information Technology. IEEE Standard, April 2004.
3. J. Bellardo and S. Savage. 802.11 Denial-of-Service attacks: real vulnerabilities and practical solutions. In *Proceedings of the USENIX Security Symposium*, pages 15–28, August 2003.
4. A. Bittau, M. Handley, and J. Lackey. The Final Nail in WEP's Coffin. In *SP '06: Proceedings of the 2006 IEEE Symposium on Security and Privacy (S&P'06)*, pages 386–400, Washington, DC, USA, 2006. IEEE Computer Society.
5. N. Borisov, I. Goldberg, and D. Wagner. Intercepting Mobile Communications: The Insecurity of 802.11. In *MobiCom '01: Proceedings of the 7th Annual International Conference on Mobile Computing and Networking*, pages 180–189, July 2001.
6. D. Faria and D. Cheriton. DoS and authentication in wireless public access networks. In *Proceedings of the 2004 ACM Workshop on Wireless Security*, pages 47–56, September 2002.
7. B. Fleck and Dimov J. Wireless Access Points and ARP Poisoning: Wireless vulnerabilities that expose the wired network. `www.packetnexus.com/docs/arppoison.pdf` (last access: 2006-10-30).
8. S. Fluhrer, I. Mantin, and A. Shamir. Weaknesses in the key scheduling algorithm of RC4. In *SAC '01: Revised Papers from the 8th Annual International Workshop on Selected Areas in Cryptography*, pages 1–24, August 2001.
9. C. He and J. C. Mitchell. Analysis of the 802.11i 4-way handshake. In *Proceedings of the 2004 ACM Workshop on Wireless Security*, pages 43–50, October 2004.
10. C. He and J. C. Mitchell. Security analysis and improvements for IEEE 802.11i. In *Proceedings of the 12th Annual Network and Distributed System Security Symposium (NDSS'05)*, pages 90–110, February 2005.
11. I. Martinovic, F. A. Zdarsky, A. Bachorek, and J. B. Schmitt. Introduction of IEEE 802.11i and Measuring its Security vs. Performance Tradeoff. In *Proceedings of the 13th European Wireless Conference, Paris, France.* accepted for publication, April 2007.
12. I. Martinovic, F. A. Zdarsky, and J. B. Schmitt. On the Way to IEEE 802.11 DoS Resilience. In *Proceedings of IFIP Networking 2006, Workshop on Security and Privacy in Mobile and Wireless Networking, Coimbra, Portugal.* Springer LNCS, May 2006.
13. B. Schneier. *Secrets & Lies: Digital Security in a Networked World.* John Wiley & Sons, Inc., New York, NY, USA, 2000.
14. S. Whalen. Introduction to ARP Spoofing. `http://www.node99.org/projects/arpspoof/arpspoof.pdf` (last access: 2006-10-24).

Secure Path-Key Revocation for Symmetric Key Pre-distribution Schemes in Sensor Networks

Tyler Moore and Jolyon Clulow

Computer Laboratory, University of Cambridge
15 JJ Thomson Avenue, Cambridge CB3 0FD United Kingdom
{Tyler.Moore,Jolyon.Clulow}@cl.cam.ac.uk

Abstract. Path keys are secrets established between communicating devices that do not share a pre-distributed key. They are required by most key pre-distribution schemes for sensor networks, because topology is unknown before deployment and storing complete pairwise-unique keys is infeasible for low-cost devices such as sensors. Unfortunately, path keys have often been neglected by existing work on sensor network security. In particular, proposals for revoking identified malicious nodes from a sensor network fail to remove any path keys associated with a revoked node. We describe a number of resulting attacks which allow a revoked node to continue participating on a network. We then propose techniques for ensuring revocation is complete: universal notification to remove keys set up with revoked nodes, path-key records to identify intermediaries that are later revoked, and blacklists to prevent unauthorized reentry via undetected malicious nodes. Path keys also undermine identity authentication, enabling Sybil attacks against random pairwise key pre-distribution.

1 Introduction

A number of symmetric key management and distribution schemes have been proposed to address the trust bootstrapping problem for sensor networks. Most notable are the seminal papers of Eschenauer and Gligor [1] proposing pools of keys and Chan et al.'s [2] random key pre-distribution scheme. These papers have inspired many subsequent proposals balancing storage, computational and communication overhead while retaining reasonable security levels [2, 3, 4, 5, 6].

Most key distribution schemes pre-load a limited number of secret keys into permanent memory so that nodes can either communicate directly using a shared key or, failing that, set up a *path key* using intermediaries they do share keys with. Path keys are a necessity for any scheme that minimizes storage costs prior to deployment. But path keys must also be considered in the later stages of credential revocation. Existing revocation proposals [1, 2, 7] fail to remove path keys established during operation. This oversight enables attackers to wreak havoc in a number of ways: rejoining the network after dismissal, issuing spoofed revocation messages, and retaining access to path keys established for others. Safeguarding revocation mechanisms from these attacks is essential.

Please use the following format when citing this chapter:

Moore, T. and Clulow, J., 2007, in IFIP International Federation for Information Processing, Volume 232, New Approaches for Security, Privacy and Trust in Complex Environments, eds. Venter, H., Eloff, M., Labuschagne, L., Eloff, J., von Solms, R., (Boston: Springer), pp. 157–168.

To our knowledge, this is the first paper in the literature of key pre-distribution schemes and revocation mechanisms for sensor networks to identify the need for and difficulty in revoking path keys. We demonstrate that existing proposals used in conjunction with path keys are vulnerable to number of attacks, defeating attempts to revoke bad nodes and enabling Sybils [8] where one node pretends to be many. We propose *path-key records*, which detail the identifiers of proxy nodes that help establish each path key. These records are used to identify and remove path keys tainted by a bad node. We show that the combined use of path-key records and blacklisting can secure a centralized revocation mechanism such as Eschenauer and Gligor's. We also show how to modify decentralized revocation schemes to make revocation decisions verifiable to the entire network. Finally, we show that naïve instantiations of Sybil detection mechanisms where results are not verifiable to third parties leave the network vulnerable to path-key-enabled Sybil attacks.

2 Background

There are four basic events in the life cycle of a distributed, wireless, sensor network: *pre-deployment*, *initialization*, *operation* and *revocation*. In pre-deployment, the network owner programs nodes with keys and authentication values. This is regarded as a secure operation occurring away from the attacker under the owner's control. Nodes are then deployed into the environment where attackers may be present and initialized by establishing keys with their neighbors. When nodes are mobile, key setup is ongoing as they establish links with new neighbors and break links with old ones. At any stage, one or more nodes may find another node misbehaving, prompting a decision mechanism to determine whether the node should be removed from the system. Revocation makes invalid any credentials shared between the revoked node and honest nodes.

In the pre-deployment phase, keys and authentication values are computed by the owner and stored on the nodes. The keys assigned to nodes are effectively also their identities. As a result, the uniqueness of a node's identity is tied to the secrecy of the keys it has been assigned. A message encrypted under a symmetric key assigned to a group of nodes could have originated from any node in the group. Encrypting under a pairwise unique key, by contrast, unambiguously demonstrates a node's identity to the other node that shares the key.

2.1 Key pre-distribution schemes

The simplest architecture is a single shared key known to all nodes. This scheme is vulnerable to the compromise of a single node, and revocation is impossible. At the other extreme is the *complete pairwise scheme*, where every node stores a unique pairwise key for each of the $n-1$ other nodes in the network. Here all nodes can confidentially communicate with each other, and any individual node can be revoked. However the scheme is infeasible when considering large networks of low cost nodes with limited storage space. We now review a number of proposals seeking a middle ground where a limited number of keys are assigned to nodes while maintaining a high likelihood of node confidentiality.

Eschenauer and Gligor [1] propose two related techniques for reducing the number of keys pre-loaded onto nodes: *key pools* and *random key assignment*. Here each node is randomly assigned m keys from a large pool P of l keys (where $m << n$ and $l >> n$). Nodes determine which keys are shared between them by querying each other for the identifiers of keys held. These *link keys* are used to secure and authenticate messages between nodes. Using results from random graph theory to identify suitable choices of l and m, the network is probabilistically guaranteed to be connected, with nodes sharing a link key with an average of d neighbors in communication range. This pooling mechanism and random key assignment have inspired several extensions and variations. [2] generalizes the scheme to require q shared secrets to establish a link key. In [4, 5], the authors propose creating a large polynomial pool to offer threshold secrecy.

Eschenauer and Gligor randomly assign keys to nodes; thus the only way for nodes to determine whether they share keys is to exchange lists of key identifiers, or by challenge-response. Zhu et al. [3] propose a deterministic algorithm that calculates the key identifiers known to a node from the node identifier. This increases efficiency, but it also helps an attacker obtain any desired keys by targeting nodes for compromise. To counter this, [9] describes a way for nodes to check whether they share keys without revealing all keys held by every node.

While undoubtedly reducing storage requirements, key pools also introduce a new set of security challenges. First, it is impossible to authenticate identity based on the keys held by a node, since several nodes may legitimately possess the same keys. Second, pool keys make it hard to revoke a misbehaving node's keys without negatively impacting legitimate nodes. Removing compromised keys is onerous since many nodes across the network could be assigned some keys in common with a revoked node; yet removing too many keys could deplete the key pool, causing inadvertent denial-of-service attacks. Finally, pool keys make harvesting attacks attractive, where an attacker compromises enough nodes to increase the chance of reusing keys to eavesdrop other nodes' communications.

Chan, Perrig and Song propose a *random pairwise* scheme [2] as an alternative to key pools combining aspects of the complete pairwise scheme with the storage-saving random distribution approach of [1]. Nodes are pre-loaded with pairwise unique keys, but rather than allocate $n - 1$ keys per node, a fraction of the keys are randomly assigned. Pre-distributing pairwise unique keys prevents a key-harvesting attacker from compromising the confidentiality of any pre-assigned key shared between uncompromised nodes. It also enables mutual authentication between nodes sharing a key. This forms the basis of a revocation scheme whose details we describe below. One disadvantage of the random pairwise scheme is increased storage cost: nodes are pre-loaded with keys totaling a significant fraction of n (e.g., $\frac{1}{5}$ to $\frac{1}{3}$). Since very few keys are used for neighbors in communication range, a small number of colluding nodes can set up many fake link keys across the network to drown out legitimate links [10].

2.2 Path-key establishment

In all of the schemes outlined above, there must exist neighboring nodes that are not pre-assigned a common key but wish to communicate. These nodes must discover a path between each other using a number of intermediate nodes, where each hop is secured by a link key. One of the nodes chooses a new *path key* and sends it to the other node, encrypted using link keys between intermediaries.

Intermediate nodes are selected for setting up path keys in two ways. In *random* path-key establishment, nodes discover paths to other nodes using locally broadcast messages. The average path length depends on the scheme used. In random pool-key deployment with plausible values for l, m and n, path keys to most neighboring nodes can be established within three hops [1]. Path keys to distant nodes are more expensive, however, requiring an average of eleven link keys for the simulations in [1]. Random path-key establishment is simple but has relatively high communication costs. Schemes using random path-key establishment include [1, 2, 4, 5]. Alternatively, in *deterministic* path-key establishment, link keys are assigned based on a node's identifier so that nodes can unilaterally select the intermediaries used to set up path keys. This eliminates the communication cost of searching for suitable intermediate nodes. Schemes using deterministic path-key establishment include [6, 3].

Path-key establishment is also vulnerable to malicious intermediaries, since only link-level encryption is used to establish an end-to-end key. Several papers explore multi-path key reinforcement for strengthening path keys [11, 2, 3].

2.3 Revocation mechanisms

Few papers on sensor networks consider the revocation phase at all. Eschenauer and Gligor describe a centralized scheme [1] where the base station determines which keys are tied to a compromised node and instructs all nodes holding these keys to delete them. In [2], Chan, Perrig and Song propose a distributed revocation mechanism for the random pairwise scheme, where nodes sharing pre-assigned pairwise keys vote to remove a node. Their scheme is extended and generalized in [7]. Here, each node B that shares a pairwise key with A is assigned to the set of *participants of* A, V_A. Every node A is assigned a unique revocation secret rev_A, which is divided into secret shares and given to every $B \in V_A$ along with an authentication value for the revocation secret, $h^2(\text{rev}_A)$. Nodes vote for another's removal by revealing their share. If enough shares are revealed, then rev_A is reconstructed and $h(\text{rev}_A)$ broadcast across the network. Every node $B \in V_A$ deletes its key shared with A upon verifying the broadcast.

2.4 The Sybil attack and countermeasures

Sybil identities [8], where a malicious node pretends to be multiple distinct nodes in the network, can facilitate attacks against routing, voting, misbehavior detection, distributed storage, resource allocation and data aggregation in sensor networks. As discussed earlier, a node's identity is determined by the the keys it holds. So key pool schemes, for example, are especially vulnerable to Sybil attacks: an attacker can create many fake identities from a few known pool keys since many nodes would be expected to hold these keys.

Newsome et al. propose a Sybil detection mechanism where honest nodes challenge each other for the expected pre-loaded keys associated with claimed identities [12]. Two nodes that share a common key can directly challenge each other to prove they have knowledge of the key. As more nodes challenge a given node in this way, confidence increases that this node is not a Sybil identity. However, the authors do not specify how to aggregate the results of a number of direct challenges in a manner verifiable to other nodes in the network. This they term *indirect validation* and describe as a challenging problem in the absence of a trusted central authority because malicious nodes must be prevented from vouching for each other. Potential approaches to indirect validation include reputation or voting schemes. However, both are prone to manipulation and increase the computational and communication overhead significantly.

3 Path-key-enabled attacks

In this section we describe two classes of attack that exploit path keys: circumventing revocation mechanisms and Sybil attacks.

We use the following threat model. Honest nodes adhere to their programmed strategy including algorithms for routing and revocation. The attacker can compromise a small minority of nodes $M_1, M_2, \ldots, M_i$ since devices may be unprotected and deployed in hostile environments. All such malicious nodes can communicate with each other and with honest nodes. Malicious nodes have access to any secret information, including keys, of all other malicious nodes, and can use their identifiers if desired. They do not have to correctly execute revocation mechanisms to identify misbehavior or delete keys shared with revoked nodes. Notably, we do not assume active node compromise is immediately detected. In fact, node compromise may never be detected.

In particular, we consider two threat models:

T.0 We assume a global passive adversary upon deployment. However, no nodes are actively compromised until path-key establishment is complete.

T.1 Again, we assume a global passive adversary upon deployment. Here we allow the adversary to actively compromise a small minority of nodes prior to path-key establishment. This threat model is adopted by most key distribution schemes for sensor networks [1, 2, 4, 5, 6].

3.1 Path-key attacks on revocation mechanisms

Incomplete revocation of path keys In a centralized revocation scheme, the base station issues revocation orders verifiable by all other nodes which then delete any paths keys shared with the revoked node. However, under the

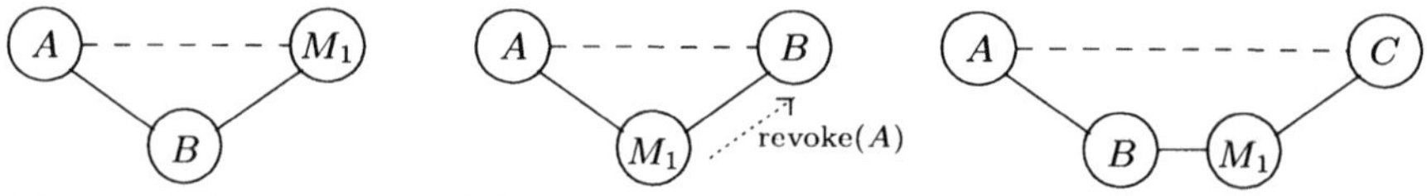

(a) Unrevoked path key (b) Spoofed revocation (c) Revoked intermediary

— Pre-distributed key - - Path key

Fig. 1. Path-key attacks on revocation mechanisms.

distributed schemes described above, the only nodes that can verify votes are those that can participate in a revocation vote. Therefore, only these nodes, which have been pre-assigned keys, know to revoke keys; therefore, only the pre-assigned keys are removed during revocation. Notably, *nothing is done to remove any path keys established with the revoked node.*

Any revocation scheme that does not remove path keys is vulnerable to the attacks in Figure 1. Consider the network in Figure 1(a). Suppose a malicious node M_1 has been identified and a revocation order issued to all nodes sharing pairwise keys with M_1. B knows to remove the key shared with M_1, but A does not so the path key established between M_1 and A continues to function.

It is not possible to counter this attack by allowing A to accept forwarded revocation claims from B, since A cannot verify the veracity of the claim from B of M_1's revocation (apart from that B made it). This lack of authentication would enable the attack shown in Figure 1(b) where the undetected malicious node M_1 could lie to B, falsely claiming that honest A had been revoked.

Malicious intermediaries and path keys The threat of malicious intermediaries during the establishment of path keys has been investigated by a number of authors [11, 2, 3]. These authors have focused on making the path key establishment mechanism as robust as possible under threat model T.1 and include techniques such as using multiple disjoint paths. These methods make it harder, but not impossible, for an attacker to compromise a path key, requiring that more intermediary nodes be compromised.

However, these papers do not consider what to do if, as a result of such an attack, a path key is, or might be, compromised. For example, suppose that M_1 has served as an intermediary to establish a path key between A and C as in Figure 1(c). Suppose further that M_1 is subsequently identified as malicious and revoked from the network. While C could observe a revocation order for M_1, it is unaware that its path key to A was set up via M_1. M_1 could use its knowledge of the path key to eavesdrop on or rejoin the network. Clearly, the path key should also be revoked.

The use of multiple disjoint paths during path key establishment simply changes the threshold at which the path key should be revoked. Once an intermediary on each path has been compromised, the resulting path key should also be revoked. A conservative network may require this to happen earlier (e.g., once half of the paths are compromised or when just one path remains secure).

Note that both threat models T.0 and T.1 are relevant. In the latter case, the attacker has actively compromised M_1 prior to path-key setup and can immediately determine k_{AC}. However, a path-key recovery attack is still possible under threat model T.0, where an adversary eavesdrops traffic during path-key setup but does not compromise the intermediary until after path-key setup. Suppose A establishes a path key to C, using M_1 as an intermediary. Here, A sends $\{k_{AC}\}_{k_{AM_1}}$ to M_1 , which then transmits $\{k_{AC}\}_{k_{M_1C}}$ to C. When the attacker subsequently compromises M_1, she can recover k_{AM_1} or k_{M_1C} and decrypt the message containing k_{AC}.

Compromised but unrevoked pool keys The centralized revocation scheme of Eschenauer and Gligor [1] is susceptible to an additional path key attack. Since generating truly random noise is hard for sensor nodes to do, the authors advocate that nodes select unused keys from their key rings as path keys. These keys are, of course, pool keys. A malicious node can establish as many path keys with neighbors as possible, requiring them to provide an unused pool key (and therefore, a key that the attacker does not already possess).

However, the network owner is never informed that the node knows additional pool keys. Therefore, should the network owner subsequently revoke the node, none of the path keys are removed. The malicious node retains not only the path-key-enabled links to its neighbors, but also the pool keys for establishing communications back into the system. However, addressing this attack by tracking and removing path keys (and thus pool keys) could enable a denial-of-service attack whereby the adversary deliberately depletes the key pool by setting up many unused pool keys as path keys prior to revocation.

Unauthorized reentry of revoked nodes One problem with implementing revocation by simply deleting shared keys is that it is not permanent when multiple undetected compromised nodes are present. Suppose malicious nodes M_1 and M_2 both share link keys with honest node A, and a revocation order is issued for M_1 but not M_2. A deletes its link key with M_1, as do all honest neighbors of M_1. Yet M_1 can rejoin the network by establishing path keys using M_2 as an intermediary. Unless honest nodes are required to maintain a network-wide blacklist of all revoked nodes, A does not remember that M_1 has already been revoked. Under random path-key establishment, M_1 can rejoin via any colluding node. For deterministic path-key establishment schemes, M_1 can only rejoin via colluding nodes pre-assigned a key.

3.2 Path-key-enabled Sybil attacks

Pool-key-based pre-distribution schemes are susceptible to Sybil attacks since shared keys are not guaranteed to be unique. Pairwise-key-based pre-distribution schemes, by contrast, should be Sybil-resistant since the keys are unique, which enables authentication between nodes sharing keys. However, consider the scenario given in Figure 2. Node M_1 shares a pairwise key with A but creates several fake nodes $M_2..M_k$ and requests path keys for each of them. Under Chan et

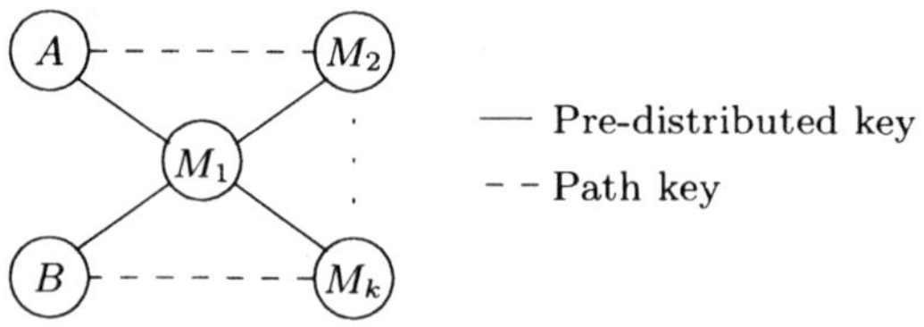

Fig. 2. Path-key-Sybil attacks on revocation mechanisms.

al.'s distributed revocation protocol, these Sybil nodes are unrevokable! Their sets of voting members, $V_{M_2} \ldots V_{M_k}$, are all empty since the identities are fake, yet A has no way of knowing this. Node M_1 can use each of these fake identities to carry out attacks, while otherwise behaving honestly to its real neighbors.

The fact that path keys enable Sybil attacks is important because it has been claimed in [12] that 'an adversary cannot fabricate new identities' under the random pairwise scheme, making it immune to Sybil attack. As we have demonstrated, Sybil attacks remain viable under the random pairwise scheme due to the use of path keys. So a scheme such as Newsome et al.'s must be employed to detect Sybils for random pairwise schemes. But their direct key validation Sybil defense [12] cannot detect these path-key-Sybil attacks for the random pairwise scheme. What we require is the missing indirect validation protocol (that is, a protocol that allows nodes which don't share keys with the target node to be able to verify claims from nodes that do share keys). So while Chan et al.'s revocation scheme [7] assumes the existence of adequate Sybil attack detection and refers to Newsome et al.'s techniques as an example, path-key-enabled Sybil attacks remain an unaddressed impediment to effective revocation, and to pairwise key pre-distribution in general.

Note also that the degree-counting mechanism proposed in [2] cannot detect Sybil attacks. It detects attackers using more pairwise keys than allowed, but these attacks create path keys without using any pre-assigned pairwise keys.

4 Secure path-key revocation

We now present three techniques for securing revocation mechanisms from the path-key attacks outlined above: (1) complete notification of node revocation, (2) path-key records to identify malicious intermediaries and (3) blacklists to prevent unauthorized reentry via path keys. We propose both centralized and decentralized solutions where appropriate.

4.1 Complete notification of node revocation

Every node eligible to establish a path key with a revoked node must be notified of its compromise. In sensor networks where the topology is unknown before deployment, path keys could conceivably be established between any two nodes. Thus, every node must be notified of every revocation.

A centralized revocation mechanism for removing pre-distributed keys, similar to the one proposed by Eschenauer and Gligor, can be trivially augmented to revoke path keys. Here, the central authority unicasts a message to every node (signed by the pairwise key shared between the authority and the node) instructing them to remove any path keys established with the node.

For a decentralized revocation mechanism, nodes must verify revocation messages sent by other nodes even when they do not necessarily trust them. To do so, each node is loaded with an authentication value for the revocation secrets of all n nodes in the network. (Recall from Section 2.3 that revocation secrets are reconstructed from voting shares broadcast by nodes eligible to decide when it is best to revoke a node.) This is in contrast to Chan et al.'s distributed revocation mechanism, which equips nodes with only the ability to verify the revocation of nodes sharing pre-assigned keys. This $O(n)$ storage cost could impede deploying revocation with symmetric keys for large networks. While costs may be reduced by storing authentication values as leaves in a Merkle tree [13], one must be careful in distributing the $\log n$ path-authentication values. We cannot rely on the node being revoked to provide the information to verify its own removal; a safer alternative is for every voting member to keep a copy of the path-authentication values for each node it might revoke.

4.2 Path-key records to identify malicious intermediaries

Recall that under threat model T.0, an attacker may collect traffic that passes through a node, then compromise it and determine all path keys established with the node as intermediary (Figure 1(c)). However, if nodes periodically update their link keys using a one-way function, e.g., $k'_{AB} = h(k_{AB})$, then an attacker cannot recover any path keys established prior to node compromise.

To address the case where nodes are compromised during path-key establishment (under threat model T.1), nodes must keep track of the intermediate nodes used to establish each path key so that affected path keys can be removed once node compromise is detected. To do so, nodes can build a list of all node identifiers used as intermediaries in conjunction with path-key establishment. When node A establishes a path key with node B, it stores a *path-key record*

$$B, K_{AB}, N_1, N_2, \ldots, N_l$$

where K_{AB} is the path key, and $N_1, N_2, \ldots, N_l$ are the identifiers for the l intermediate nodes. Whenever a revocation order is issued, nodes must check their path-key records for the revoked nodes, discard affected path keys and reinitiate transmission to discover a new path key.

Path-key record generation and verification should remain decentralized, even when access to a central authority is used for other components of path-key revocation. Because path-key records are constructed every time a path key is established, it is unreasonable to always consult a base station. If this frequency of communication with base stations is allowed, then nodes are better off using the base station to set up the path keys in the first place.

When undetected malicious nodes exist during path-key establishment, constructing the record becomes much harder. Nodes along the path cannot be allowed to help build the record since an undetected malicious node M_1 can trivially modify the record's contents to its own end. For instance, M_1 could replace its identifier with that of an honest neighbor C so that if M_1 is subsequently removed its path key will not be. Random path-key establishment techniques are inappropriate for this reason. Instead, we advocate using a deterministic key-discovery technique (e.g., [3, 9]) to remove the potential for manipulation during path-key record construction. Whenever a node must set up a path key, it can unilaterally decide which nodes to use as intermediaries and build the path-key record without consulting other nodes. Deterministic key-discovery techniques provide a degree of authentication to the identifiers selected for the path; we exploit this when constructing a secure path-key record.

Suppose A wants to establish a path key with D. A determines that it shares a link key with B, which shares a key with C, which in turn shares a key with D. A stores this information in the path-key record and sets up the path key. Now suppose that one of the nodes A selects happens to be malicious (say B). B cannot add or remove identities, including its own, to the path-key record.

Minimizing the number of intermediaries used to establish path keys reduces the likelihood of selecting a malicious node as an intermediary. Furthermore, using multiple disjoint paths for establishing path keys [11, 2, 3] makes compromised path keys less likely. Here, path-key records can be modified to include sets of node identifiers for each of the k paths:

$$\begin{aligned} B, K_{AB}, &\{N_{11}, N_{12}, \dots, N_{1l}\}, \\ &\{N_{21}, N_{22}, \dots, N_{2l}\}, \\ &\vdots \\ &\{N_{k1}, N_{k2}, \dots, N_{kl}\}. \end{aligned}$$

4.3 Blacklists to prevent reentry via path keys

As described in Section 3.1, a previously revoked node can reenter the network by setting up path keys via an undetected malicious intermediary. To counter this, nodes must maintain an up-to-date blacklist of all revoked nodes.

A centralized blacklist maintained by the base station is undesirable, since nodes set up path keys without first consulting the base station. However, a consistent distributed blacklist is easy to construct. Since nodes already observe every revocation order, they simply store the identifiers of each removed node.

So long as revocations are infrequent, keeping such a blacklist is not a problem. An alternative to maintaining a blacklist that still identifies unauthorized reentry via path keys is to combine reentry detection with node replication detection. In [14], nodes periodically transmit signed copies of their identifiers and locations across the network. Nodes check these messages for multiple claims originating from different places. Similarly, nodes could be required to remember only a subset of revoked nodes (e.g., each node remembers nodes it has decided to revoke). Nodes check the identifiers transmitted in the node replication detection messages against their own subset of the blacklist. If detected, nodes forward the message to the base station, which issues a new revocation order. This scheme can be less expensive than requiring nodes to maintain a complete blacklist when node replication detection is already in frequent use.

4.4 Cost summary

In summary, path keys impose the following additional costs to those outlined in [7] for revocation to be effective:

- Authenticated revocation secrets for all nodes in the network
- Maintain path-key record listing all intermediaries on every path key
- Maintain blacklist of all revoked nodes in network

These previously unaccounted costs reflect the difficulty in designing efficient revocation mechanisms using pre-distributed symmetric-key cryptography. We believe these costs are unavoidable whenever anything less than complete pairwise keys are used. Furthermore, path keys necessitate Sybil attack detection using indirect validation [12] to secure pairwise key pre-distribution schemes.

5 Conclusions

Any symmetric key management scheme pre-distributing less than complete pairwise keys necessarily weakens notions of identity. Complications inevitably ensue. In this paper we identified problems with revocation mechanisms and Sybil identities caused by path keys. We proposed effective countermeasures to ensure that keys shared with or exposed to revoked nodes are removed, and blacklists to prevent the unauthorized reentry of revoked nodes. We note that exposure to path-key attacks may be limited by employing deterministic path-key establishment mechanisms and minimizing the number of intermediaries used. We also showed that, contrary to prior understanding, path keys make incomplete pairwise key-distribution schemes vulnerable to Sybil attacks. Pairing key pre-distribution schemes with Newsome et al.'s Sybil detection scheme is not convincing; the authors themselves note they do not provide a practical way to detect Sybils by nodes not sharing pre-distributed keys, the case for path keys. It remains an open problem whether an efficient Sybil detection mechanism can be created for this scenario.

More generally, the efficiency gains made at one stage in the life cycle of a network may cause unforeseen problems that are expensive to remedy at other stages. We have shown that trade-offs made to improve the efficiency of bootstrapping keys to sensor nodes open the door to devastating attacks that are costly to handle during the maintenance phase of revocation, counteracting the gain from the earlier trade-offs. This resonates with Anderson's argument that protocol designers have long underestimated the maintenance costs of security mechanisms [15]. One could continue to layer on patchwork mechanisms for mitigating these attacks, accepting the costs as unavoidable. In contrast, we question whether efficient key establishment coupled with inefficient or insecure revocation is desirable. Instead, we should perhaps consider selective uses of asymmetric cryptography or develop more innovative revocation mechanisms.

References

1. L. Eschenauer and V. D. Gligor, A Key-Management Scheme for Distributed Sensor Networks, *ACM Conference on Computer and Communications Security*, 2002, pp. 41–47.
2. H. Chan, A. Perrig, and D. X. Song, Random Key Predistribution Schemes for Sensor Networks, *IEEE Symposium on Security and Privacy*, 2003, pp. 197–213.
3. S. Zhu, S. Xu, S. Setia, and S. Jajodia, Establishing Pairwise Keys for Secure Communication in Ad Hoc Networks: a Probabilistic Approach, *IEEE International Conference on Network Protocols*, 2003, pp. 326–335.
4. W. Du, J. Deng, Y. S. Han, and P. K. Varshney, A Pairwise Key Pre-distribution Scheme for Wireless Sensor Networks, *ACM Conference on Computer and Communications Security*, 2003, pp. 42–51.
5. D. Liu and P. Ning, Establishing Pairwise Keys in Distributed Sensor Networks, *ACM Conference on Computer and Communications Security*, 2003, pp. 52–61.
6. H. Chan and A. Perrig, PIKE: Peer Intermediaries for Key Establishment in Sensor Networks, *IEEE INFOCOM*, 2005, pp. 524–535.
7. H. Chan, V. D. Gligor, A. Perrig, and G. Muralidharan, On the Distribution and Revocation of Cryptographic keys in Sensor Networks, *IEEE Trans. Dependable Secur. Comput.* **2**(3), 233-247 (2005).
8. J. R. Douceur, in: Lecture Notes in Computer Science 2429, edited by P. Druschel, M. Kaashoek, and W. Rowstron (Springer, Heidelberg, 2002), pp. 251–260.
9. R. Di Pietro, L. V. Mancini, and A. Mei, Energy Efficient Node-to-Node Authentication and Communication Confidentiality in Wireless Sensor Networks, *Wireless Networks* **12**(6), 709–721, 2006.
10. T. Moore, A Collusion Attack on Random Pairwise Key Predistribution Schemes for Distributed Sensor Networks, *IEEE International Workshop on Pervasive Computing and Communications Security*, 2006, pp. 251 255.
11. R. J. Anderson, H. Chan, and A. Perrig, Key Infection: Smart Trust for Smart Dust, *IEEE International Conference on Network Protocols*, 2004, pp. 206–215.
12. J. Newsome, E. Shi, D. X. Song, and A. Perrig, The Sybil Attack in Sensor Networks: Analysis and Defenses, *Information Processing and Sensor Networks*, 2004, pp. 259–268.
13. R. C. Merkle, Protocols for Public-Key Cryptosystems, *IEEE Symposium on Research in Security and Privacy*, 1980, pp. 122–134.
14. B. Parno, A. Perrig, and V. D. Gligor, Distributed Detection of Node Replication Attacks in Sensor Networks, *IEEE Symposium on Security and Privacy*, 2005, pp. 49–63.
15. R. Anderson, The Initial Costs and Maintenance Costs of Protocols, *International Workshop on Security Protocols*, 2005.

A Credential-Based System for the Anonymous Delegation of Rights

Liesje Demuynck*, Bart De Decker, and Wouter Joosen

Katholieke Universiteit Leuven, Department of Computer Science,
Celestijnenlaan 200A, 3001 Heverlee, Belgium
{Liesje.Demuynck,Bart.DeDecker,Wouter.Joosen}@cs.kuleuven.be

Abstract. An anonymous delegation system enables individuals to retrieve rights and to delegate different subparts of these rights to different entities. The delegation procedure is anonymous, such that no collusion of entities can track an individual's delegation behavior. On the other hand, it is ensured that a user cannot abuse her delegation capabilities. This paper introduces a general delegation model and presents an implementation. Our implementation is based on credential systems and provides both anonymity for the individual and security for the organizations.

1 Introduction

The concept of authentication and authorization has long been studied in computer science. Intuitively, all solutions follow the same procedure: the user first retrieves her access rights from a trusted authority and afterwards shows it to a service provider. For security reasons, the retrieval protocol will typically be performed in an identified or pseudonymous manner. The showing protocol, on the other hand, may be performed in an anonymous but controlled fashion: users are anonymous but can still be held accountable for their actions [2, 4].

In many applications, the owner of a right may need to delegate (part of) her right to a different entity. Consider, for example, a doctor having access to a medical database. When she is absent from the hospital, she may grant one of her assistants access to some specific files in the database. She may prefer this delegation procedure to be anonymous, such that no central authority can monitor her delegation behavior. On the other hand, it should be ensured that she cannot abuse her delegation capabilities in any way.

Wohlgemuth et al. [12] present a privacy-preserving delegation system in the context of business processes with proxies; a user delegates some of her rights to a proxy, who may then use these rights to access services on the user's behalve. The authors do not assume a delegate to be anonymous. In addition, a lot of trust is put in a central certification authority, who knows what subrights are issued and to which proxies. Finally, re-delegation is not achieved.

* Ph. D. fellowship of the Research Foundation - Flanders (FWO).

Please use the following format when citing this chapter:

Demuynck, L., De Decker, B., and Joosen, W., 2007, in IFIP International Federation for Information Processing, Volume 232, New Approaches for Security, Privacy and Trust in Complex Environments, eds. Venter, H., Eloff, M., Labuschagne, L., Eloff, J., von Solms, R., (Boston: Springer), pp. 169–180.

This paper introduces a formal model for a delegation system and presents an implementation based on anonymous credentials. Our model can be used in various applications and achieves, among others, controlled re-delegation and the revocation of rights. Anonymity is provided for the delegator as well as for the delegate. At the same time, the security of individuals and service providers is protected and users can be held accountable for their actions.

The outline of this paper is as follows. Section 2 presents a formal model for the delegation system. Section 3 introduces the basic building blocks for the implementation: commitments, anonymous credentials and verifiable encryptions. The system itself is described in Section 4 and evaluated in Section 5. We conclude in Section 6.

2 General delegation model

We first present a general model for the anonymous delegation of rights. Section 2.1 gives a global overview of the system's entities and protocols. Section 2.2 then states some assumptions on the behavior of these entities and Section 2.3 describes a general set of requirements on the system's behavior.

2.1 Roles and protocols

Roles. An entity in the system is either a *user* U or an *organization* O.

An organization must at all times be identifiable. It is either a *registrar* RG, an *issuer* I, a *verifier* V or a *revocation manager* RM. A registrar registers users to the system and an issuer issues rights to these users. A right contains a set of specifications and a validity period. It can be shown to a verifier or it can be used to issue sub-rights. These sub-rights can in turn be used to issue sub-rights of themselves. As such, a *delegation tree* of a right is constructed. The root of this tree is the right itself, while all other nodes are sub-rights of their parent-node. When abuse of a right is detected, or when it is no longer needed, the right as well as all other rights in its delegation tree, are revoked by the revocation manager.

In contrast to an organization, a user may be anonymous within the system. It can be either a *delegator* Do or a *delegate* De. Do delegates part of her right to De. We will refer to Do's right as the main-right and to De's new right as the corresponding sub-right. Note that a right can be both a main-right w.r.t. one right and a sub-right w.r.t. another right. (e.g. an access right to sections $\{A, B\}$ of a database may be a sub-right w.r.t. an access right to sections $\{A, B, C\}$, and a main-right w.r.t an access right to section $\{A\}$). Similarly, a user can be both a delegator and a delegate with respect to different users in the system.

Protocols. A summary of the system protocols is given in Table 1.

U registers to the system by performing the *Registration* protocol with RG. She retrieves a right $\mathtt{R}$ satisfying specifications $\mathtt{RSpecs}$ by performing the *IssueRight* protocol with issuer I. As a result, I receives a transcript $\mathtt{IssueTrans}$.

Table 1. general delegation model - protocol overview.

$U \leftrightarrow RG$	: *Registration*(certifications)
$I \leftrightarrow U$	: *IssueRight*(RSpecs) returns R ; IssueTrans
$Do \leftrightarrow De$	: *DelegateRight*([I], MR, SRSpecs) returns SR; IssueTrans
$U \leftrightarrow V$	: *ShowRight*(R, showProperties)
RM	: *RevokeRight*(revTag)

The *DelegateRight* protocol takes as input both a main-right `MR` and a specification `SRSpecs` of the new sub-right. It outputs a transcript `IssueTrans` for delegator *Do* and a sub-right `SR` for delegate *De*. Potentially, an additional issuer *I* may be involved in the protocol.

A right `R` can be shown to *V* by means of the *ShowRight* protocol. Attribute `showProperties` specifies the right's properties which are revealed to *V*. Note that this may be only a subpart of the entire right. As an example, consider a right granting full database access to *U*. When showing this right to *V*, *U* may decide to only reveal her access rights for a particular subpart of the database.

Finally, a right can be revoked by means of the *RevokeRight* protocol. The input to this protocol is a revocation tag `revTag`. This tag can be found as a unique subpart of the `IssueTrans` transcript.

2.2 Assumptions

We employ the following assumptions concerning the entities in the system.

- System registrar and organizations can be trusted to perform their tasks correctly, i.e. they follow the protocols. This is a reasonable assumption and can, for example, be enforced by collecting secure logs of the parties' activities.
- All entities in the system can freely exchange their information. In particular, users may exchange information about the rights they have received. Note, however, that entities will not give away any information of which the secrecy is important to themselves. Examples of such information are secret keys and revocation information of sub-rights issued by themselves.

2.3 Requirements

We consider anonymity and security requirements. Anonymity requirements are optional and provide the user with a set of privacy guarantees. Security requirements are mandatory and protect the organization from malicious users.

Anonymity and linkability requirements.

A1. *Privacy preserving show protocol.* The *ShowRight* protocol should not reveal more information than what is absolutely necessary to gain access to *V*'s services. In particular, the following requirements should be satisfied.
   (a) *Anonymity.* Service access is anonymous.
   (b) *Unlinkability.* Different service accesses based on the same right cannot be linked to each other.

(c) *Right indistinguishability.* The access protocol does not reveal any information on how the access right was obtained.

A2. *Sub-right unlinkability.* Different sub-rights deduced from the same main-right must not be linkable to each other, even when all parties in the system (except for the main-right owner) share their information. This ensures that a user's delegation behavior cannot be tracked by other entities.

Security requirements.

S1. *Unforgeability.* Users may not successfully show a right which was not retrieved by means of an *IssueRight* or of a *DelegateRight* protocol.

S2. *Correct sub-rights.* The set of rights which are encoded in a sub-right must be a subset of the set of rights encoded in its corresponding main-right. In addition, the validity periods of a sub-right must fall within the validity period of its corresponding main-right.

S3. *Non-transferability.* The legitimate owner of a right must not be able to pass on the digital tokens constituting her right. Note that this requirement does not forbid to pass on a right by the delegation of a sub-right identical to the original right.

S4. *Consistency of rights.* Users may not be able to pool their rights in order to gain an asset (e.g. the access to a service or a new right), which each of them separately could not have obtained by correctly executing the protocols.

S5. *Correct revocation.* Rights must be revocable and the revocation of a right must include the revocation of all the rights in its delegation subtree. In addition, users must be prohibited to request the revocation of rights which are not issued or owned by themselves.

S6. *Conditional deanonymization.* In case of abuse of a right, appropriate measures should be taken against its owner. We distinguish two types of actions.
- retrieval of the owner's identity.
- retrieval of the right's issue transcript, enabling the right's revocation.

3 Basic building blocks

Our construction is based on commitments, credential systems and verifiable encryptions. We briefly introduce these concepts and their primitives. All communication is performed over anonymous communication channels.

Commitments. A commitment [11, 7] can be seen as the digital analogue of a "non-transparent sealed envelope". It enables a committer to hide a set of attributes (non-transparency property), while at the same time preventing her from changing these values after commitment (sealed property). The primitive

$$E: \mathit{Comm}, \mathit{OpenInfo} = \mathit{Comm}(\{\texttt{attrName} := \mathit{attrValue}, \ldots\})$$

enables an entity E to create a commitment *Comm* on a set of attributes. Additionally, she retrieves a secret key *OpenInfo* containing, among others, the attributes encoded into *Comm*. This key can be used to prove properties concerning the attributes.

$$E_1 \rightarrow E_2 : ComProps(Comm, P(\texttt{attr1}, \ldots))$$

The public input to this protocol is both a commitment *Comm* and a boolean predicate P concerning *Comm*'s attributes. For example, P may be the predicate $(\texttt{attr}_1 > 0)$. If E_2 accepts, she is convinced that E_1 knows the *OpenInfo* belonging to *Comm*, and that *Comm*'s attributes satisfy predicate P. She does not find out any other information concerning *Comm* or *Comm*'s attributes.

Credentials. A credential system [2, 4] allows for anonymous yet accountable transactions between users and organizations. In the remainder of the paper, we employ the system proposed by Camenisch et al. [4, 1, 6].

A credential *Cred* is retrieved from I by means of the *CredGet* protocol.

$$U \leftarrow I : Cred = CredGet(\{\texttt{attr}_1 := G(.), \ldots\})$$

It consists of a set of attributes as well as a secret key for showing it to a verifier.

Each attribute is constructed as a separate function $G(.)$ of public values and attributes encoded into previously shown credentials or commitments. As an example, $\texttt{attr}_1$ may be constructed as $\texttt{attr}_1 := Cred_x.\texttt{a}_1 + 5$, where $Cred_x.\texttt{a}_1$ refers to attribute $\texttt{a}_1$ of a previously shown credential $Cred_x$. Issuer I cannot find out any information concerning the credential's attributes, apart from the fact that they are constructed correctly based on $G(.)$.

During the *CredShow* protocol, U shows her credential *Cred* to V.

$$U \rightarrow V : CredShow(Cred, P(\texttt{attr}_1, \ldots))$$

Additionally, U reveals a boolean predicate P concerning public values, attributes occurring in *Cred* and attributes occurring in previously shown credentials or commitments. For example, P may be the predicate $(\texttt{attr}_1 > C_x.\texttt{a}_1 \ \wedge \ \texttt{attr}_1 < C_x.\texttt{a}_2)$, where $C_x.\texttt{a}_1$ and $C_x.\texttt{a}_2$ refer to attributes $\texttt{a}_1$ and $\texttt{a}_2$ encoded into a previously shown commitment C_x. V cannot learn any new information from the execution of the protocol, apart from the fact that U has a valid credential which is issued by I and of which the attributes satisfy P.

Different show-protocols of the same credential cannot be linked to each other, nor can they be linked to their issue protocol.

Using the *CredSign* protocol, a credential can be used to sign a message.

$$U : Sig = CredSign(Cred, P(\texttt{attr}_1, \ldots), msg)$$

The properties of this protocol are exactly the same as for the *CredShow* protocol, except for the additional fact that a message *msg* is signed using the credential. For ease of representation, we assume that output *Sig* contains the signature as well as the signed data.

Verifiable encryptions. Verifiable encryptions [5] have all the characteristics of regular encryptions. Based on a public key *pk*, any user U can encrypt a message. In addition, U can demonstrate properties of the encrypted plaintext. For example, U can prove to V that the encrypted plaintext is encoded as an attribute in a previously shown credential or commitment. This is denoted as a predicate $c = VE(\mathtt{x})$, where c refers to the ciphertext and where $\mathtt{x}$ refers to the credential's (or commitment's) attribute.

Note that c is created using a public key *pk* of which the corresponding secret key *sk* may not be known by V. For ease of representation we omit the specifications of *pk* and its owner. We merely assume its owner to be an entity T which can be contacted when decryption is needed. Additionally, T is trusted not to perform any unwanted decryptions.

The use of credentials, commitments and verifiable encryptions offers numerous advantages in the construction of privacy-sensitive applications. Credentials are unforgeable and allow for service accesses which are anonymous and unlinkable. By combining them with commitments and verifiable encryptions, additional properties such as non-transferability, consistency of credentials, conditional deanonymization and revocation can easily be added using standard techniques [2, 4]. These properties will turn out to be very handy in our final construction.

4 The delegation system

We first give a general outline of the system and its components. Afterwards, the system and its protocols are described in more detail.

4.1 General outline of the system

All rights in the system are represented as digital credentials. In particular, main-rights and sub-rights have an identical credential structure. The credential's attributes consist of a tuple $(id, e, RSet)$, where id is the owner's identity, e is the right's revocation tag and $RSet$ is a specification of the right. A sub-right is issued by constructing a new tuple $(id', e', RSet')$ and by signing a commitment on this tuple. Note that we sign a commitment rather than the actual tuple $(id', e', RSet')$. This way the tuple is hidden from any third parties. The signature is created by the main-right's credential and by using the *CredSign* protocol. In a final step, this signature is exchanged with I for a new credential.

To achieve correct revocation, the sub-right's revocation tag e' may not be arbitrarily chosen by *Do*. Instead, it must be requested from *RM* through an auxiliary *IssueRevTags* protocol. During the protocol, *Do* retrieves a credential $Cred_{rev}$ containing e and a list of random revocation tags. *RM* does not know the values of these tags, but she is able to recover them as soon as the corresponding main-right is revoked. Furthermore, by means of the attribute value

e occurring in both credentials, $Cred_{rev}$ is invisibly bound to the main right's credential.

An example is given in Figure 1. Doctor Jones has access to sections A, B and C of the hospital's database. This is represented by a credential $Cred_{ABC}$ containing a revocation tag e. In addition, she owns a credential $Cred_{rev}$ which is retrieved during an *IssueRevTags* protocol. $Cred_{rev}$ encodes $Cred_{ABC}$'s revocation tag e. As such, it can only be used to delegate sub-rights based on $Cred_{ABC}$. In addition, $Cred_{rev}$ contains a set $(e_1, \ldots, e_n)$ of random revocation tags. Whenever a sub-right is issued, its new revocation tag must be one of these values e_i encoded into $Cred_{rev}$. In our example, Dr. Jones has delegated two sub-rights based on $Cred_{ABC}$. Due to the randomness of the e_i's, their corresponding credentials cannot be linked to each other.

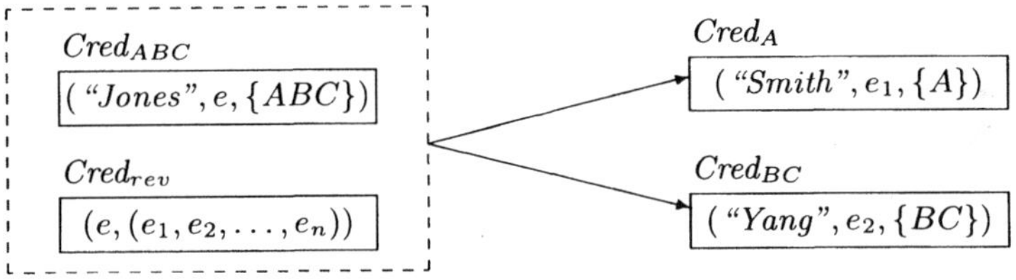

Fig. 1. Example credential structures

4.2 Protocol description

The delegation system is depicted in Figures 2 and 3. We now give a detailed description of the protocols.

Registration. U registers to the system by authenticating to RG. She then receives a credential $Cred_u$ containing her global identifier id_u. In the remainder of the paper, we will refer to this credential as $Cred_{do}$, $Cred_{de}$ or $Cred_u$, depending on its owner's role as a delegator, a delegate or a user.

IssueRight. U first proves to be registered to the system. If successful, she retrieves a credential $Cred_{right}$ containing three attributes: a copy of attribute id in $Cred_u$, an issuer-chosen revocation tag e and a specification $RSet$ of rights. We will refer to this credential as $Cred_{right}$, $Cred_{main}$ or $Cred_{sub}$, depending on its function as a general right (which can be both a main-right or a sub-right), a main-right or a sub-right.

IssueRevTags. This protocol can be executed multiple times for the same value e. It provides Do with n additional revocation tags for her sub-rights. First, Do creates a commitment C_{rev} containing random values $e_{1u}, \ldots, e_{nu}$. This commitment, together with the main-right's revocation tag e and a verifiable encryption $encr$ of $(e_{1u}, \ldots, e_{nu})$ are sent to RM. Do also proves that $encr$ is constructed correctly. After receiving random values $e_{1i}, \ldots, e_{ni}$ from RM, Do proves that value e is the same revocation tag as is encoded in her main-right. For this, she creates a credential-based signature Sig_{rev}. This ensures that RM is provided with sufficient evidence of the transaction. Finally, when

- **Registration.**

$U \xrightarrow{\textit{user authentication}} RG$

$U \xleftarrow{Cred_u \;=\; CredGet(\{\mathtt{id} := id_u\})} RG$

- **IssueRight.**

$U \xrightarrow{CredShow(Cred_u,\ null)} I$

$U \xleftarrow{Cred_{right} \;=\; CredGet(\{\mathtt{Owner} := Cred_u.\mathtt{id},\ \mathtt{revTag} := e,\ \mathtt{rights} := RSet\})} I$

- **IssueRevTags.**

Do: choose random values $e_{1u}, \ldots, e_{nu}$
$C_{rev}, O_{rev} = Comm(\{\mathtt{e_{1u}} := e_{1u}, \ldots, \mathtt{e_{nu}} := e_{nu}\})$
$encr = VE(e_{1u}, \ldots, e_{nu})$

$Do \xrightarrow{e,\ encr,\ C_{rev},\ ComProps(C_{rev}, \{encr == VE(\mathtt{e_{1u}}, \ldots, \mathtt{e_{nu}})\})} RM$

RM: choose random values $e_{1i}, \ldots, e_{ni}$

$Do \xleftarrow{e_{1i}, \ldots, e_{ni}} RM$

Do: $Sig_{rev} = CredSign(Cred_{right}, \{\mathtt{revTag} == e\}, (e, e_{1i}, \ldots, e_{ni}, encr))$

$Do \xrightarrow{Sig_{rev}} RM$

$Do \xleftarrow{Cred_{rev} \;=\; CredGet(\{\mathtt{revTag} := e,\ \mathtt{e_1} := C_{rev}.\mathtt{e_{1u}} + e_{1i}, \ldots, \mathtt{e_n} := C_{rev}.\mathtt{e_{nu}} + e_{ni}\})} RM$

Fig. 2. Credential-based implementation of the delegation model (1/2)

e has not been revoked, a credential $Cred_{rev}$ is issued by *RM*. The attributes of this credential consist of e and of the new revocation tags $e_1, \ldots, e_n$ which are constructed as $e_k = e_{ki} + e_{ku}$ for $k = 1, \ldots, n$. Note that the resulting e_k's are unknown to RM; she only knows that they are constructed correctly as $e_k = C_{rev}.\mathtt{e_{ku}} + e_{ki}$. Moreover, their values cannot be manipulated by *Do*.

DelegateRight. This protocol consists of two phases which can be separated in time. It may be preceded by an optional identification step from *De* to *Do*.

During the first phase, *De* creates a commitment C_{de} on her global identifier id_{de}. She sends it to *Do* and proves that it is constructed correctly. Upon success, *Do* creates two commitments C_{do} and C_{sub}. C_{do} encodes her main-right's revocation tag e, while C_{sub} contains both the revocation tag e_i and the right-specifications *SRSet* of the prospective sub-right. Commitments C_{do}, C_{de} and C_{sub} are then signed by means of the *CredSign* protocol for credentials $Cred_{main}$ and $Cred_{rev}$. This results in a signature tuple (Sig_{sub1}, Sig_{sub2}) which is sent with the key O_{sub} to *De*. The signatures ensure the following properties:

- The signer owns credentials $Cred_{main}$ and $Cred_{rev}$.
- The same revocation tag e is encoded in both $Cred_{main}$ and $Cred_{rev}$.
- The rights encoded into C_{sub} are a subset of the rights encoded into $Cred_{main}$.
- C_{sub}'s attribute `subRevTag` is one of the revocation tags encoded in $Cred_{rev}$.

- **DelegateRight.**

De: $C_{de},\ O_{de} = Comm(\{\mathtt{id} := id_{de}\})$

$Do \longleftarrow$ $C_{de},\ CredShow(Cred_{de}, \{\mathtt{id} == C_{de}.\mathtt{id}\})$ $\longleftarrow De$

Do: $C_{sub},\ O_{sub} = Comm(\{\mathtt{subRevTag} := e_i,\ \mathtt{rights} := SRset\})$
$C_{do},\ O_{do} = Comm(\{\mathtt{revTag} := e\})$
$Sig_{sub1} = CredSign(Cred_{main}, \{\mathtt{revTag} == C_{do}.\mathtt{revTag} \wedge \mathtt{rights} \supset C_{sub}.\mathtt{rights}\}, (C_{do}, C_{de}, C_{sub}))$
$Sig_{sub2} = CredSign(Cred_{rev}, \{\mathtt{revTag} == C_{do}.\mathtt{revTag} \wedge C_{sub}.\mathtt{subRevTag} \in \{\mathtt{e}_1, \ldots, \mathtt{e}_n\}\}, (C_{do}, C_{de}, C_{sub}))$

$Do \longrightarrow$ $O_{sub},\ Sig_{sub1},\ Sig_{sub2}$ $\longrightarrow De$

De: retrieve e_i and *SRset* from O_{sub}
$Sig_{de} = CredSign(Cred_{de}, \{\mathtt{id} == C_{de}.\mathtt{id}\},\ (Sig_{sub1},\ Sig_{sub2}))$

$I \longleftarrow$ Sig_{de} $\longleftarrow De$

$I \longrightarrow$ $Cred_{sub} = CredGet(\{\mathtt{owner} := C_{de}.\mathtt{id},\ \mathtt{revTag} := C_{sub}.\mathtt{subRevTag}, \mathtt{rights} := C_{sub}.\mathtt{rights}\})$ $\longrightarrow De$

- **ShowRight.**

$Do \longrightarrow$ $CredShow(Cred_{right}, \{\mathtt{revTag} \notin BL\ \wedge\ \mathtt{rights} \supset NSet\})$ $\longrightarrow V$

- **RevokeRight.**

$E \longrightarrow$ *request revocation of the right with revocation tag revTag* $\longrightarrow RM$

RM. set $L = \{revTag\}$, while $L \neq \{\}$ do the following
1. remove value e from L, add e to blacklist BL
2. check archive for Sig^j_{rev} on tuple $(e, e^j_{1i}, \ldots, e^j_{ni}, encr^j)$
3. for each Sig^j_{rev} found do the following
   a. decrypt $encr^j$ and retrieve tuple $(e^j_{1u}, \ldots, e^j_{nu})$
   b. add values $e^j_k = e^j_{ku} + e^j_{ki}$ to L, for all $k \in \{1, \ldots, n\}$

Fig. 3. Credential-based implementation of the delegation model (2/2)

During the second phase, *De* sends a signature Sig_{de} to *I*. This signature includes tuple (Sig_{sub1}, Sig_{sub2}) and additionally proves that *De* is the owner of identifier id_{de} encoded into C_{de}. If Sig_{de} is accepted by *I*, and if (Sig_{sub1}, Sig_{sub2}) has not been shown to *I* before, *De* retrieves a new credential of which the attributes are based on the values encoded into C_{sub}.

ShowRight. During the *ShowRight* protocol, *U* shows her credential $Cred_{right}$ to *V*. Additionally, she proves that it contains sufficient rights for accessing *V*'s services and that it has not been revoked. The latter can be achieved using the efficient privacy-friendly blacklisting techniques of [9, 3].

RevokeRight. Revocation manager *RM* revokes a right by adding its revocation tag to a public blacklist *BL*. If *revTag* belongs to a main-right, all rights in its revocation tree are iteratively revoked by retrieving the signatures Sig^j_{rev} on *revTag* and by decrypting the encryptions $encr^j$. Note that *RM* will generally not be aware of the correct decryption key. In this case, decryption requires the interaction with a trusted third party.

Before performing a revocation, *RM* receives a revocation request from an entity *E* in the system. Requests from identified entities such as issuers or verifiers generally pose no problem, as they can easily be held accountable for their actions. Care must be taken, however, when requests are made by unidentified entities. These requests will only be granted if the requester can prove to be the owner of a credential $Cred_{rev}$ containing revocation tag *revTag*. The proof protocol is given in Figure 4. During the protocol, *Do* can either request the revocation of a sub-right issued by herself, or of a right owned by herself.

$$Do \xrightarrow{Sig_{rev} = CredSign(Cred_{rev}, \{revTag \in \{\mathsf{e}, \mathsf{e}_1, \ldots, \mathsf{e}_n\}\}, revTag)} RM$$

Fig. 4. Revocation request for anonymous users

5 Evaluation

Anonymity and linkability requirements.

A1. Service access is anonymous and unlinkable, even if multiple entities collaborate and freely exchange their information. Since main-rights and sub-rights have an identical structure, right indistinguishability is also achieved.

A2. Provided that no revocations are performed, subright unlinkability is trivially achieved. When a right is revoked, all revocation tags of this right and of its sub-rights are retrieved and linked. A "skeleton" of the right's delegation tree can then be reconstructed. This skeleton contains as its nodes the revocation tags of possible sub-rights, but not the sub-rights themselves. Users who are willing to display the specifications of their revoked sub-rights, may place it at the correct position in the tree. As such, limited but nevertheless additional information concerning a user's delegation behavior may be retrieved.
One way to avoid these unwanted linkabilities is by not allowing any revocations. This is however not a reasonable solution. A good compromise is the adoption of "medium-size" validity periods. These time periods should be short enough to avoid most revocations on the one hand but long enough to avoid burdensome renewals on the other hand.

Security Requirements.

S1. All rights are unforgeable thanks to the unforgeability of credentials and the unforgeability of the *CredSign* signature scheme.

S2. Sub-rights are issued correctly. During the *DelegateRight* protocol, *Do* explicitly proves that the sub-right's validity periods and right specifications are more strict than or equal to what is specified in the main-right. Note that *Do* is not prohibited to issue revoked sub-rights. Issuing such rights would be useless, however, as they would be refused by *V* anyway.

S3. Transferability of rights can be discouraged by using non-transferable user secrets [2, 10]. For this, value id_u is constructed as a secret key or a credit card number. An exception to this adaptation is credential $Cred_{rev}$, which does not contain id_u. Here, transferring is discouraged by the fact that it may only harm its original owner *Do*. This is because (1) transferring $Cred_{rev}$ does not enable another user to employ its encoded revocation tags e_i, and (2) transferring $Cred_{rev}$ does enable other users to revoke the sub-rights issued by *Do*.

S4. When showing multiple rights to the same verifier. Consistency of these rights can be demonstrated by an additional proof that the `Owner` attribute is the same in all credentials.

S5. Rights are revocable and the revocation of a main-right implies the revocation of all the rights in its delegation tree. In addition, users cannot request the revocation of rights which are not issued or owned by themselves.

S6. Conditional deanonymization can easily be added using standard techniques [4]. During the *showRight* protocol, *U* simply provides *V* with a verifiable encryption of either her identity or of her right's revocation tag.

Extensions and adaptations.
In our construction, every right has a validity period and a set of right specifications. All types of sub-right can be issued, provided that their encoded constraints are a subset of what is specified in the main-right. In many applications, however, these system specifications are too limited. We now give some examples of extensions to the system. A detailed discussion on these and other extensions and on how to achieve them can be found in our technical report [8].

By employing limited-show credentials, it is possible to limit the number of times that a right can be shown to a verifier. Note that in this case, the issuing of a sub-right which can be shown t times must imply the loss of t show instances for the main-right.

The maximal depth of a right's revocation tree can be set to a fixed number. As an example, this depth may be set to 1 in the situation where a doctor may delegate sub-rights to her assistants, but where her assistants are not allowed to issue sub-rights of themselves.

Our system has the obvious drawback that *I* needs to be involved in every delegation. In applications with less strict privacy and functionality requirements, this dependability on *I* can be alleviated by a small transformation of the system [8]. First, we note that signature tuple (Sig_{sub1}, Sig_{sub2}) contains sufficient proof that *De* is entitled to a sub-right. Hence *De* can show her right by simply showing (Sig_{sub1}, Sig_{sub2}) and by proving some additional statements about the signed values. As an example, in order to prove that her right has not yet been revoked and that it is sufficient for accessing *V*'s services. *De* can prove the predicates $(C_{sub}.\texttt{subRevTag} \notin BL)$ and $(C_{sub}.\texttt{rights} \supseteq Nset)$. Note that this procedure does not maintain the unlinkability of service access, the indistinguishabilty of rights or the delegation capability of the sub-right. If one of these features is needed by *De*, she gets back to the original protocol and contacts *I* for a credential.

Finally, our system can easily be extended to allow sub-rights which are created as a combination of rights situated in different main-rights.

6 Conclusion

This paper introduced a formal model for a delegation system and presented a credential-based implementation. The system provides both anonymous delegation for the individual as well as security for the organizations. A trade-off has been made between the security requirement of correct revocation and the anonymity requirement of the delegation process. It is an interesting problem to investigate whether this conflict can be solved, such that both revocation and sub-right unlinkability can be achieved.

References

1. Michael Backes, Jan Camenisch, and Dieter Sommer. Anonymous yet accountable access control. In *WPES*, pages 40–46, 2005.
2. S. A. Brands. *Rethinking Public Key Infrastructures and Digital Certificates: Building in Privacy.* MIT Press, Cambridge, MA, USA, 2000.
3. Stefan Brands, Liesje Demuynck, and Bart De Decker. A practical system for globally revoking the unlinkable pseudonyms of unknown users. Technical Report CW472, Katholieke Universiteit Leuven, 2006.
4. J. Camenisch and A. Lysyanskaya. An efficient system for non-transferable anonymous credentials with optional anonymity revocation. In *EUROCRYPT*, pages 93–118, 2001.
5. Jan Camenisch and Victor Shoup. Practical verifiable encryption and decryption of discrete logarithms. In *CRYPTO*, pages 126–144, 2003.
6. Jan Camenisch, Dieter Sommer, and Roger Zimmermann. a general certification framework with applications to privacy-enhancing certificate infrastructures. Tech. Rep. RZ 3629, IBM Zurich Research Laboratory, July 2005.
7. Ivan Damgård and Eiichiro Fujisaki. A statistically-hiding integer commitment scheme based on groups with hidden order. In *ASIACRYPT*, pages 125–142, 2002.
8. Liesje Demuynck and Bart De Decker. Credential-based systems for the anonymous delegation of rights. Technical Report CW468, K.U. Leuven, 2006.
9. Liesje Demuynck and Bart De Decker. How to prove list membership in logarithmic time. Technical Report CW470, Katholieke Universiteit Leuven, 2006.
10. Anna Lysyanskaya, Ronald L. Rivest, Amit Sahai, and Stefan Wolf. Pseudonym systems. In *Selected Areas in Cryptography*, pages 184–199, 1999.
11. Torben P. Pedersen. Non-interactive and information-theoretic secure verifiable secret sharing. In *CRYPTO*, pages 129–140, 1991.
12. Sven Wohlgemuth and Günter Müller. Privacy with delegation of rights by identity management. In Günter Müller, editor, *ETRICS*, volume 3995 of *Lecture Notes in Computer Science*, pages 175–190. Springer, 2006.

Development and Application of a Proxy Server for Transparently, Digitally Signing E-Learning Content

Christian J. Eibl[1], SH Basie von Solms[2], and Sigrid Schubert[1]

[1] Didactics of Informatics and E-Learning, University of Siegen, Germany
{eibl,schubert}@die.informatik.uni-siegen.de
[2] Academy for Information Technology, University of Johannesburg, South Africa
basie@rau.ac.za

Abstract. Integrity as minimal requirement for successful protection of the learning process is neglected by most learning management systems. To implement integrity protection independent of existing e-learning systems we present the concept of a proxy server that digitally signs outgoing messages to the learning management systems and verifies the signature of incoming messages accordingly. We illustrate the architectural design and give specification details. Realization deliberations are outlined with respect to the hypertext transfer protocol. Finally, we discuss the approaches on the case study of the open-source learning management system MOODLE.

1 Motivation

E-learning as well as many other computer based services were concerned by the growing interconnection, i.e., security has become a major topic in this field. Even more, security as a quality factor is vital to the reputation and further existence of institutes, companies or similar being interconnected to thousands of users over the Internet. Security issues in learning management systems (LMS) that are already in extensive use will undoubtedly lead to discouragement of participating learners. That means that especially in commercial offerings or at distance universities that demand fees for their e-learning material the quality of such provided material and the e-learning system itself has to be best possible. Such quality must be due in courses one pays for.
Regarding different e-learning systems, it becomes obvious that security cannot be considered uniformly. We have to cope with different system types and their security requirements accordingly. Exemplified the following system types will be distinguished and described more in detail below:

1. simulation system,
2. virtual university,
3. assessment system.

Please use the following format when citing this chapter:

Eibl, C.J., von Solms, S.H.B., and Schubert, S., 2007, in IFIP International Federation for Information Processing, Volume 232, New Approaches for Security, Privacy and Trust in Complex Environments, eds. Venter, H., Eloff, M., Labuschagne, L., Eloff, J., von Solms, R., (Boston: Springer), pp. 181–192.

In *simulation systems*, for example, learning material is read-only. There is no need for learners to be able to store data on the e-learning server. In *virtual universities*, on the other hand, all aspects of real universities get mapped to this piece of software, and therefore, it demands write-access on the e-learning server, e.g., for communication capabilities. As third type, an *assessment system* describes facilities that are used to assess learners in a computer-based way. Such a system requires a lot of security mechanisms to prevent learners from cheating or denying their participation. This type of system, of course, is the one with the highest security requirements in order to be incontestable.
For being able to ensure integrity, e.g., of learning content, as well as parts of non-repudiation, e.g., for proving the participation of some student, the digital signature gives an appropriate means – it even allows multiple signing of learning content to signalize consensus among teachers. But although digital signatures have a mainly accepted value for security, the application of such methods demands a lot of interaction with users. Especially when thinking ahead, i.e., if we would like to sign all messages sent to an LMS even those for chats and other communication capabilities, then digital signatures will become a weary load for users. Learners must not be disturbed more than necessary in their learning process by the system's security mechanisms in order to increase a positive learning outcome. Hence, we need an automatism that can cope with these aspects, i.e., the increased security by digital signatures and the automatic application of those methods.
This paper will present a proxy server running locally on every client machine that automatically appends digital signatures to messages sent to the LMS and, of course, evaluates incoming messages again according to their embedded signature.

2 Security in E-Learning

E-learning has become more and more focus of security investigations. An exhaustive security examination is given by the doctoral dissertation of Graf [6]. Graf considers different security issues concerning e-learning systems and focuses on secure assessment systems in WWW-based learning environments, i.e., using the World Wide Web (WWW). His approaches mostly depend on Java programs that establish communication between client and server instead of using the Hypertext Transfer Protocol (HTTP) which can be easier manipulated and eavesdropped. Weippl [14] as well as Graf provide an overview over the area of information security in e-learning, but Weippl also considers risk analysis approaches. He regards the security requirements from different points of view according to the corresponding role in the system. As roles he proposes authors, teachers, managers, and students. Teachers and authors, although in other literature often combined into the same person, are distinguished in that way, that authors are the ones who write the learning content, and therefore, are concerned with security of this material. Teachers, on the other hand, take place while the system is already running. They coach students and manage different tasks like supporting students in their courses, administering resources, and doing exams. Managers have nothing (directly) to do with learning content and the learning process, but they are responsible for the superior administration and the security of the whole system. The authors' concern that "readers must be able to rely on the correctness of the content" [14, p. 15] will be addressed in this article.

Considering the different system types introduced above, it becomes obvious that security requirements differ not only out of the point of view of different roles, but also that different systems have different minimal security requirements. The maximal desired security for all systems, of course, will be an invincible and everlasting system, that cannot be attacked even with infinite computational power and time, i.e., it is perfectly secure. But since perfect security is not achievable in practice, a maximal security describing a stage of security that needs so much effort that the expense of attacking exceeds the worth of the gained success by far is considered as sufficient. For our further discussion the aspect of minimal security will be focused.

As system with minimal security requirements simulation systems, for example, demand integrity of learning content, which can be supported by corresponding access control mechanisms for the server where data is stored on. Since no write-access has to be given to some user, the authentication process can be optional. As system with medium security requirements virtual universities demand secure authentication and availability for some high percentage rate of time. Non-repudiation is desirable for communication capabilities, but not necessary. Confidentiality is necessary for personal data, supported by access control mechanisms, and optional for learning content. The confidentiality of learning content depends on the financial system of the study course. If it should be available to paying students only, then confidentiality is necessary, otherwise the contents may be accessible to guests, too. In assessment systems the highest security requirements must be demanded. Here minimal security requirements tend to be equal to the maximal ones as described before. No student may be able to cheat to his advantage or to the advantage of someone else. In addition, even teachers have to be prevented from cheating for some student respectively from changing some submitted answers unintentionally. The non-repudiation security service is of high value in this case, too, since no participating student may be in the position to deny the participation, because for example he was not well prepared. Considering the uploading of assignment solutions, integrity and non-repudiation become most important if those assignments have high value for marking students. No adversary may be able to alter other solutions unrecognized and no student should be able to deny such an upload.

Geuer [5] presented a signature system for WWW applications that signs the whole data part of the HTTP stream. He proposes an extension to the HTTP protocol that requires the adjustment of web server as well as web client to support this extension. As alternative to the web client adjustments the use of a proxy server was proposed. However, since in e-learning systems not only

the integrity of data while it gets transmitted is relevant but also the integrity of every single message stored on the server, this approach is insufficient for e-learning purposes.
But how can managers be sure that the e-learning system itself was created with a secure concept in mind? For such evaluations there exist several catalogues (cf. [2, 3, 7, 12]) that give a hint how secure concepts can look like, and therefore, users can check the system against such catalogues of criteria. When considering security concepts of existing and commonly used LMS, like for example the open-source LMS MOODLE [10] (cf. Section 6), then it becomes obvious that especially integrity and non-repudiation are not protected at all. Most security aspects depend primarily on the service of authentication. If this authentication is secure enough, then no unauthorized learner or teacher can manipulate data or even read such data. From the point of view of administrators, resp. managers, the security of such authentication mechanisms should be best possible. The problem within this case is that e-learning should be possible "anytime and anywhere you like" especially from the learners' point of view. When considering strong authentication mechanisms like sophisticated biometric systems there appear contradictory goals between the portability resp. flexibility of the system as demanded by learners and security as desired by administrators. Common LMS rely primarily on password authentication mechanisms which are, unfortunately, mostly implemented without sufficient support in secure password generation and regimentation. In MOODLE, for example, there exists neither a simplicity analysis of passwords nor checking mechanisms against dictionaries. Consequently, a lot of inexperienced students will most probably choose very simple passwords without being warned by the system.
Since the authentication process as "first line of defence" is conceptually hard to manage as sketched above because of the contradictory sight of learners and administrators, we propose to implement a "second line of defence". For protecting integrity and non-repudiation aspects digital signatures can be used (cf. [11]). With respect to learners' learning process an automatism for the signing process is needed which seem to be an optimal task for a proxy servers, since they give a simple framework for altering passing packets on the network.
In the following, we regard only the case of universities using e-learning capabilities. The approaches can be adopted to, e.g., schools or companies analogously.

3 Demands and Possibilities of Signing Proxy Servers

3.1 University wide PKI

First, there is the question of how to equip every user of the e-learning system with a public-private-key pair in order to digitally sign messages. Since public keys should be verified to belong to the pretended owner in order to satisfy authenticity, we can sign such public keys after checking the identity of the owner. In universities this process can, for example, be implemented as university wide public key infrastructure (PKI) [15]. In the following we will sketch

very shortly a possible PKI implementation at a university without the demand of completeness.
Since at universities every student has to get registered at the central university administration, such an administration could take the role of the registration authority (RA) in the PKI. That means, after students have created their own pair of keys, the RA verifies the identity of every student registering in person and enables the creation of a certificate by the certification authority (CA). As CA we suggest the data processing centre or an executive of the university. Hence, every student gets a certificate that can be used for all university purposes.
For the sake of equality we have to cope with the situation that some students might not possess a computer on their own, and therefore, they need a terminal where they can generate their keys instead. Since every student needs some kind of student ID card, this can be, for example, combined with the idea of equipping every student with a smart card that contains the pair of keys on a chip and personal data of the student printed on the surface. Alternatively USB sticks could be offered by the administration for storing keys on it. This smart card or stick could then be used at all workstations in students' computer pools on the campus. The generation at terminals in the university administration would have the advantage that in case of problems competent personal is present to support. This will prevent discouragement in an early stage.
Note that there are a lot more advantages than only using digital signatures in the e-learning system, e.g., online registration for exams, which could motivate such an infrastructure additionally. However, in this work e-learning systems will be focused.

3.2 Proxy Server Architecture

The second problem is, how to establish automated security mechanisms on the client machine, i.e., how to secure the communication without disturbing the learning process. For this the use of a proxy server is sensible.
Considering the kind of messages sent to an e-learning system, i.e., learning content created by teachers or communication messages for forums and chats (by teachers and learners), it becomes obvious, that especially in the case of very short messages (like found in chats) the manually applied digital signature would mean a lot of inconveniences that enormously will interrupt the learning process and puts the sense of communication with other learners into question. The use of a proxy server as automated secretary that digitally signs all outgoing messages to the e-learning system is possible, since a proxy server runs logically on ISO/OSI (International Organization for Standardization / Open Systems Interconnection) layer 7, the application layer (cf. [9]). It is therefore able to examine and alter packets passing it, see Figure 1. The proxy server running on the client machine first has to gather access to the private key of the logged in user. This key can be, as described above, stored on a smart card, a USB stick or, if the pair of keys was created on the currently used computer, locally on

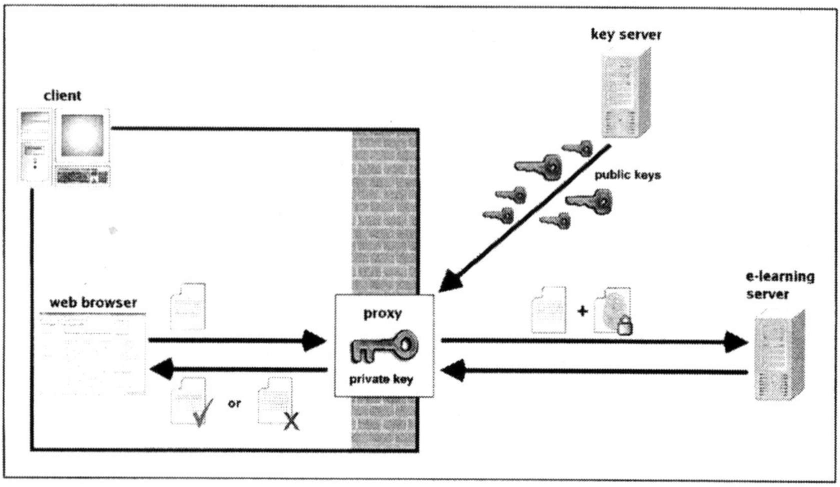

Fig. 1. Architecture with signature proxy; the LMS is running on e-learning system.

the harddisk drive. Since private keys should be protected by a pass phrase or other authentication methods, the proxy will have to demand the identification of the user. When the key could successfully be decrypted it needs to be stored in main memory to give the proxy the chance to use it several times without asking for authentication again at every access. Note that this implies some kind of security issue in favour of the learners' convenience. An attacker who can gain direct memory access would with some effort be able to extract that private key. Since direct memory access is on modern operating systems only possible by the super user account or by exploiting interface design problems (cf. [1]), this leads to administrative concerns and configuration issues that are outside the scope of this article. In the following we assume the systems to be well configured and administered to prevent the sketched attacks. To avoid this security issue even after the learner has quit the proxy server, we propose a secure deletion of the private key in main memory, i.e., in addition to freeing memory the location where the key has been stored must be overwritten (several times) by random data to scramble this information.

With holding the private key in memory the proxy can sign all messages to the e-learning system (cf. Figure 1). Of course, the proxy server needs some instructions on how to find the relevant messages and how to decide, whether the application of the signature is sensible and desired by the user. Such patterns for decision will be presented in Section 4.

For the other direction, i.e., incoming messages, the proxy server can take the role of the control instance for contained digital signatures. For evaluating embedded signatures it needs access to corresponding public keys. For this purpose a keyserver can be used that provides all known public keys of the university wide PKI.

4 Specifications

The implementation has to result in a small and fast program that is available for most platforms, i.e., a platform independent implementation is desired for not excluding some possible learners from using the more secure system. Besides this, the proxy server will have to cope with the following tasks presented more in detail below:

1. network adjustability,
2. LMS recognition,
3. LMS specific signing and verification,
4. communication with learner resp. teacher,
5. exclusion prevention.

1. Network adjustability: In association with the functionality of the network, the proxy server, of course, has to be able to cope with several simultaneous connections. That means, every connection established through the proxy server needs its own thread. Otherwise, the first connection would block the proxy server and no other connection could take place before the first one has been reset. For the sake of performance of the connection we propose the restricted storage of packets by forwarding data as fast as possible to the LMS. If storing the whole message before forwarding data to the meant target, i.e., e-learning server, then this can be very time consuming when considering sending of large file attachments. Hence, data needs to be forwarded as fast as possible while the signature can be computed on a stored copy of the whole message and afterwards be included into the stream. For being able to use the proxy server in the wide variety of networks used out there, it has to be highly configurable. For example, if the network configuration is very restrictive by using special firewall rules or demanding other proxy servers in the network, then our proxy server must be able to run on different ports of the client as well as supporting chains of proxy servers to co-operate with demanded other ones.

2. LMS recognition: Since there are a lot of different LMS available on the market, the extendability of the proxy server is highly desired. The differences in LMS can be coarsely described by the tuple `(serverURL,site)`. The first element describes the host URL (Uniform Resource Locator) for the LMS, while the second element describes the relative path on the target machine. For being able to recognize, whether a user tries to connect to a known LMS, the proxy server has to compare data like host URL and requested site from the received packet against patterns stored in its configuration files. If none of the patterns match to the currently requested page, the proxy server, of course, must not alter any detail of the request and has to forward packets without any delay, i.e., the network functionality must not be reduced in any way. Note that tasks 3 to 5 may only be applied in case of communicating with a known LMS, otherwise the communication would (at least slightly) be disturbed by unnecessary computation of received packages without giving any advantage.

3. LMS specific signing and verification: Signing and verification of embedded signatures, of course, are two different subtasks. The first, i.e., signing messages sent to an LMS, needs information about variable names contained in packets sent to a specific site on the LMS. The proxy server needs such information in order to separate content to be signed within the observed HTTP stream from that data that can be dropped. In addition, the proxy server needs to know how to combine those variables to a new simple message that finally can be digitally signed. A list of variables appears sensible to mention the relevant variables in an ordered way.
The verification process, on the other hand, needs a lot more descriptive information. Consider the case, that variables sent to the server can only be requested again in form of a flat HTML (Hypertext Markup Language) page without forms or other rather dividing structures. The messages as presented by the LMS are no longer stored in variables, but are embedded in HTML page text. In the configuration files, data about the recognition of digital signatures embedded in those pages and the possible segmentation in single message blocks needs to be given. An example is described in case study MOODLE in Section 6.

4. Communication with learner resp. teacher: The communication capability with learner resp. teacher is a main task in order to be able to inform users adequately and to support their work with the signing system. Since the proxy server has to communicate in some scenarios like warning the user if an incoming message was altered fraudulently, this should preferably take place in the language of the learner for being as comfortable as possible. Consequently, the proxy server should be dynamically adjustable to the language of the host system.
For the way of communication there exists the possibility of building a graphical user interface or the approach of modifying the HTTP stream, i.e., the proxy server can add some message text or colour bar for example on top of the requested web page to signalize the security status of this site.

5. Exclusion prevention: Since security improvements by using the proxy server demand modification and evaluation of data packets passing this proxy server, it must be able to compute received data. This means, if client and server are trying to negotiate some encrypted connection or a compression (cf. Section 5) that the proxy server does not support, then this would lead to exclusion from communication. An example is given with the use of encrypted connections based on Secure Socket Layer (SSL) resp. Transport Layer Security (TLS). Since such end-to-end encryptions take place between client, i.e., web browser, and server, i.e., web server, the proxy server will only be confronted with an encrypted HTTP stream. For being able to cope with such a situation, the proxy server has to adopt the client part for this encryption. That means, the proxy server is that party that negotiates encryption parameters with the server, and the web browser sends its data unencrypted to the (local) proxy server. Since this data will be sent only locally on the client machine, the lack of confidentiality by this now unencrypted connection is neglegible. Of course, the proxy server has to inform the user about server certificates used for the SSL/TLS encrypted connection. The proxy server must not be the deciding part, whether a certificate is trustworthy or not! But with the storage of most common certificates of certificate authorities, like web browsers do as well, it can support the user in his decision by verifying the server certificate in advance.

5 Realization

A main realization goal is the conformity to the protocol HTTP in version 1.1 (HTTP/1.1) as described in Request For Comments (RFC) 2616 [4]. There all details are described for the content of data sent from client to server and vice versa. First, the proxy server has to fulfil all requirements concerning the proxy functionality itself. The RFC 2616 describes different usage of address requests and their handling. This can be simply adopted from the standard and will therefore not further be discussed in this paper. Second, the proxy server has to be able to identify relevant parts of the HTTP stream and react appropriately. A main problem concerning the ability of recognizing relevant parts in the stream is that the stream itself is readable for the proxy server. HTTP/1.1 allows several ways of encoding and compression. Usually a web browser informs the web server about its supported compressions, the web server on the other hand compares this information to its own supported formats and decides accordingly. If the proxy server in the middle does not support the negotiated compression, then it will not be able to work with such data. Hence, the offerings of the web browser need to be considered as well and possibly be adjusted to the capabilities of the proxy server. Of course, such adjustments are only necessary and sensible if the connection does match a pattern as introduced in the former section.

Now that the proxy server can read all sent data in plain text it can search for the message to be digitally signed. For this the list of variables as described above can be used. With extracting all relevant variables and concatenating them to sign them all at once, the main task of the proxy can be fulfilled. Note that the list of variables must not be modified if it has been already used in the given way by any client, since otherwise the modification of the variable order or the number of variables would lead to another concatenated plain text, and therefore, will lead to another signature. Hence, with an altered list of variables old signatures would be falsified anytime they get checked with the new verification method description. Since HTTP supports different request methods affecting the composition of messages, we have to distinguish their handling. The most commonly used methods are POST and GET. Also relevant for the proxy server are messages encoded as multi-part messages. The proxy

server has to be able to extract the variable names and contents of all these kinds of messages. While in GET messages variables are coded into the URL, in POST messages the URL does not contain any variable, but the packet body does instead. In multi-part messages every variable gets its own field in the packet body, where these fields are separated by a boundary string introduced in the packet header. Hence, before processing the received data the type of message composition has to be determined.
To manage transparency for all users, it is sensible to store the signature in that way that it cannot be seen at first sight by a learner or teacher not using the described proxy server. For achieving this, the digital signature has to be stored in HTML tags that are not displayed. Since most LMS contain a content management system filtering user entries, there is no general solution how to hide those signatures. In the following section problems arising within MOODLE will be discussed.

6 Case Study MOODLE

Since MOODLE is now used for round about one year at the university of Siegen we could collect some experiences with its usage, implementation, and security concept. Consequently, when thinking about a prototype of the introduced proxy server we focus on the support of this LMS. It provides several learning activity capabilities like chat, forums, and polls that support learners in building social contacts within the LMS and provide platforms for discussion and exchanging messages. Of course, any of these learning activities gets controlled by a script page for reading and sending new messages. Since the functionality is still the same for, e.g., forums in different courses, the same script is used for all those courses with unique course identifier as parameter. Hence, only a finite number of sites must be observed, and therefore, the tuples representing search patterns can be easily created.
The verification of embedded signatures, e.g., in forum entries, can be handled as well. The forum gets presented as HTML page without form tags, but since forum entries have hierarchical structuring to separate main statements from their corresponding answers and comments, every entry is embedded in table data tags. Hence, starting from the digital signature the table data environment of the same hierarchical level can be extracted and be analyzed due to the entries considered in the signature. This list of entries is directly connected to the list of variables introduced in the signing process above.
When examining MOODLE the invisible embedding of digital signature turns out to be not as easy as thought at first. The client can only communicate over the interface MOODLE offers, i.e., sites for sending and storing messages. Every message sent to MOODLE gets controlled and if necessary modified. MOODLE does not allow to send HTML comments or to apply Cascading Style Sheets (CSS) instructions to some text in order to make it invisible. This, of course, is sensible from the point of view of MOODLE programmers, since the possibility

of injecting arbitrary code, e.g., in CSS definitions, means an enormous security problem. However, a possible solution to hide the signature is to add it to an URL, e.g., in an image source tag, separated from the actual URL by a question mark. The signature will be in this case interpreted as parameter to the web site given by the URL. If the site referenced by the URL does not evaluate any parameter it will not be any problem. This script could, for example, deterministically response with a transparent image. Hence, nothing can be seen by users, but the signature is still hidden in the received HTML text.

7 Conclusion

We have introduced the idea of a proxy server for automated digital signature of messages to an LMS, since most LMS on the market lack the security of integrity and non-repudiation. With the use of the presented proxy server this lack of security can be fixed. When using the formerly mentioned catalogues of criteria for checking the security of such whole e-learning systems (including the client machine, too), then the proxy server increases the security by remarkable value. Integrity and non-repudiation were in the case without proxy server not protected at all, and with the use of it these services are protected by a respectable security method like digital signature.

The LMS MOODLE, unfortunately, was more problematic than thought at first. It is a content management system, and therefore, has to filter the transmitted HTML code, since otherwise executable code could easily be injected. But filtering even commentary code and CSS directives made it a lot more difficult to embed hidden signatures. HTTP needs a lot of attention due to its set of parameters. These parameters could easily exclude the proxy server from showing its strengths. Therefore, the proxy server must not allow parameters that could prevent it from analyzing the communication.

Since the proxy server is still under development, there are a lot of adjustments to be done. After a prototype working reliably with MOODLE can be released, we will extend the set of patterns to support other commonly used LMS like ILIAS [8] or WEBCT [13], too.

Limits of our approach get obvious when considering signing large multimedia files. In this case signing and verification processes will be very time consuming, and therefore, it will no longer be an almost invisible task on the client machine without disturbing the learning process. Another concern is given by the subjective reliability of signed content. Since signatures give the feeling that the signed content has been very carefully proved before signing it, this could be misleading for learners. The main goal of protecting integrity could be misunderstood by learners as guaranteeing correctness by exhaustively prove reading content prior to signing it. This needs to be well communicated, since minor changes will be necessary with high probability.

A main problem in the current approach is, that we consider the proxy server as optional extension to an existing learning environment. This program should work nearly unnoticeable on the client machine, but as long as the usage is not obligatory, there will be most probably a lot of participants not using this system. Hence, the security improvements get unfortunately depleted. As solution an authentication method based on digital signatures is conceivable to force the usage. Since MOODLE, for example, does not provide a challenge-response authentication based on digital signatures, this still is part of further research.

References

1. Becher M, Dornseif M, Klein CN (2005) FireWire – all your memory are belong to us. CanSecWest Conference, Vancouver, Canada, `http://cansecwest.com/core05/2005-firewire-cansecwest.pdf` [02-02-2007].
2. Department of Defense (USA) (1985) Trusted Computer System Evaluation Criteria. Report DoD 5200.28-STD ("orange book").
3. Eibl CJ, von Solms BSH, Schubert S (2006) A Framework for Evaluating the Information Security of E-Learning Systems. Proc. of the 2nd International Conference on Informatics in Secondary Schools Evolution and Perspectives (ISSEP), Vilnius, Lithuania.
4. Fielding R, Gettys J, Mogul J, Frystyk H, Masinter L, Leach P, Berners-Lee T (1999) Hypertext Transfer Protocol – HTTP/1.1, Request for Comments (RFC) 2616.
5. Geuer CH (1998) Entwurf, Realisierung und Verifikation eines Signatursystems für das Word-Wide-Web. Diploma thesis (German), University of Siegen.
6. Graf F (2002) Lernspezifische Sicherheitsmechanismen in Lernumgebungen mit modularem Lernmaterial. Doctoral dissertation (German), University of Darmstadt.
7. Grobler CP (2003) A Model to assess the Information Security status of an organization with special reference to the Policy Dimension. Magister Thesis, Rand Afrikaans University.
8. Integriertes Lern-, Informations- und Arbeitskooperationssystem (ILIAS), online resource: `http://www.ilias.de/ios/index-e.html` [31-10-2006]
9. ISO/IEC 7498-1 (1996) Information Technology – Open Systems Interconnection – Basic Reference Model: The Basic Model. International Standard, corrected and reprinted version, Geneva, Switzerland.
10. Modular Object-Oriented Dynamic Learning Environment (MOODLE), online resource: `http://moodle.org` [31-10-2006]
11. Schneier B (1996) Applied Cryptography: Protocols, Algorithms, and Source Code in C. Second Edition, Wiley.
12. Swanson M (2001) Security Self-Assessment Guide for Information Technology Systems. National Institute of Standards and Technology (NIST), Special Publication 800-26.
13. WebCT, commercial LMS, online resource: `http://www.webct.com` [31-10-2006]
14. Weippl ER (2005) Security in E-Learning. Springer, New York.
15. Xenitellis S (2000) The Open-source PKI Book, online, last modified: 23-07-2000, URL: `http://ospkibook.sourceforge.net/` [17-03-2006]

Identity Theft – Empirical evidence from a Phishing exercise

T Steyn, HA Kruger, L Drevin
Computer Science & Information Systems
North-West University, Private Bag X6001, Potchefstroom, 2520
South Africa
{Tjaart.Steyn, Hennie.Kruger}@nwu.ac.za, ldrevin@acm.org

Abstract. Identity theft is an emerging threat in our networked world and more individuals and companies fall victim to this type of fraud. User training is an important part of ICT security awareness; however, IT management must know and identify where to direct and focus these awareness training efforts. A phishing exercise was conducted in an academic environment as part of an ongoing information security awareness project where system data or evidence of users' behavior was accumulated. Information security culture is influenced by amongst other aspects the behavior of users. This paper presents the findings of this phishing experiment where alarming results on the staff behavior are shown. Educational and awareness activities pertaining to email environments are of utmost importance to manage the increased risks of identity theft.

Keywords: Identity theft, phising, security awareness, education.

1 Introduction

"Beware, don't be caught!" These words serve as a warning on the website of one of the major banks in South Africa. Clients are reminded that a financial institution will never request a customer to complete personal details on a webpage-link in an email. They use the term 'phishing' to warn against this type of fraudulent emails that are most often used in conjunction with a fake website [1]. The term 'identity theft' is then used to show how the information obtained by the phishing attack can be used in fraudulent transactions. Identity theft is not a new type of crime. It has been used

---

Please use the following format when citing this chapter:

Steyn, T., Kruger, H., and Drevin, L., 2007, in IFIP International Federation for Information Processing, Volume 232, New Approaches for Security, Privacy and Trust in Complex Environments, eds. Venter, H., Eloff, M., Labuschagne, L., Eloff, J., von Solms, R., (Boston: Springer), pp. 193–203.

for centuries to impersonate someone and thereby obtaining a way of committing a crime anonymously.

The term phishing originates in the hacker community in 1996 where customer account information was stolen from AOL users. Hacked accounts were called 'phish' and were a type of electronic currency used between hackers to swap user account information for pieces of hacked software. It is a variant of the term fishing (fishing for passwords) and it is influenced by the term phreaking (exploitation of telephone systems). The meaning of the term phishing expanded over the years and the technique became more sophisticated with the resulting damages also escalating. Fake websites, key-loggers via Trojan horses and other malicious attempts are also now part of the phishing attacks [2].

One definition of phishing is given as "it is a criminal activity using social engineering techniques. Phishers attempt to fraudulently acquire sensitive information, such as passwords and credit card details, by masquerading as a trustworthy person or business in an electronic communication" [3]. Another comprehensive definition of phishing, as quoted by Granova and Eloff [4] states that it is "the act of sending an email to a user falsely claiming to be an established legitimate enterprise into an attempt to scam the user into surrendering private information that will be used for identity theft". The conduct of identity theft with this acquired sensitive information has also become easier with the use of technology and identity theft can be described as "a crime in which the impostor obtains key pieces of information such as Social Security and driver's license numbers and uses them for his or her own gain" - four common types of identity theft crime include financial ID theft, criminal ID theft, identity cloning and business identity theft [5].

According to a study done in 2004 by the Gartner group an estimated 57 million US adults received a phishing email and almost 11 million online adults have clicked on a link in phishing attacks [6]. Around 1.78 million Americans remembered giving out personal information and many more could have but did not realize it. Financial losses suffered by US financial institutions in 2003 were nearly $1.2 billion as a direct consequence from identity theft and the accompanying phishing attacks.

Awareness and training programs, technical controls and new legislation are all possibilities to handle the growing number of phishing incidents. To address ICT security awareness in an academic environment, a project was started during 2005 where a value focused approach was used to identify key areas of importance - the objective was to develop a measuring instrument for ICT security awareness levels based on the identified key areas [7]. One of the key areas identified by managers and users was the responsible use of email and the Internet. This includes awareness on phishing and identity theft. As part of the broader project, it was envisaged that system data be obtained on users' behavior regarding ICT security. To this end a practical test was designed to firstly test users' awareness levels pertaining to phishing and identity theft and secondly to make users aware of the risks of responding to these attacks. The use of such practical tests is frequently carried out by organizations and academic institutions. An example can be found in Dodge and Ferguson [8] where they described a successful exercise to evaluate students' propensity to respond to email phishing attacks.

The aim of this paper is to present a practical phishing experiment, including the planning, execution and results. The remainder of the paper is organized as follows: In section 2 the background to the exercise and the methodology used are discussed, while section 3 details the results from the experiment. Section 4 concludes the paper with a summary and possible future work.

2 Background and Methodology used

2.1 Background

As mentioned in the introduction, a project to propose a framework to measure the security awareness levels of staff was initiated in 2005. The proposed framework consists of the following phases which are described in more detail in [9]. Firstly, the key areas on which measurements will be taken need to be identified - this would form the basis of the actual measurements. Secondly, knowledge, attitude and behavior of staff, pertaining to the identified key areas, will be surveyed to determine their awareness levels. In addition to the employee surveys, it was suggested that appropriate system generated data should also be used as input to the final model as system data is expected to be more reliable (not subjective or human dependent) and fairly easy to obtain. Finally, the data should then be combined with appropriate importance factors to construct a final model to be used for improving the overall information security culture. One of the specific aspects that was identified in the initial project as an issue that should be tested by system generated data was identity theft. The verification of awareness levels that relates to identity theft would assist in covering one of the key areas viz. the responsible use of email and the Internet. These initial project phases were conducted in an academic environment [7] and it was therefore decided to design a phishing test to evaluate staff at the same academic institution.

The use of the Internet and email facilities at universities implies that universities are subjected to the same threats and vulnerabilities as other organizations. In a sense it can be argued that certain universities use electronic communication more intensively as an ordinary business because, apart from the normal communication functions, it is also used in the teaching function – both as a subject of study as well as a tool and an aid to perform teaching activities. There are a number of risks attached to the use of electronic communication systems in both organizations and universities such as spreading of viruses, using the facilities to conduct private business, routing chain emails, impersonation, eavesdropping and certainly one of the most important aspects that is dealt with in this paper, identity theft.

The university where the phishing test was conducted is a South African university that consists of three different campuses located in three different cities of which one was selected for the exercise. The selected campus is the largest of the three with eight divisions (academic faculties) and more than 26000 students. The campus is served by approximately 3400 staff members of whom about 550 are full-time academic staff. The ICT infrastructure at the campus is one of the best and staff are linked to a central network that gives access to the full spectrum of electronic communication as well as Internet access. Although a high level of security is maintained, the university has no official security awareness program in place and staff did not receive any ICT security awareness training. A general notice on where to find certain security policies are displayed during sign-on to the network. Warnings against disclosing or misuse of passwords are included in these documents.

The phishing exercise was designed with the definition of phishing in mind. An email, that claims to be legitimate, had to be constructed, sent to users and tried to convince them to surrender private information that could be used for identity theft. This explains the objective of the exercise. The reason for the test was, in the first place to obtain system generated data for the overall ICT security awareness model. Secondly, the aim was simply to gauge the reaction of staff when confronted with possible identity theft as well as to get an indication of how easy staff would give away sensitive information. Finally, the exercise itself would serve as a tool to raise security awareness and make staff aware of the dangers and risks surrounding phishing scams. All personnel were aware of a recent implementation of new systems at the university and this created the ideal opportunity to construct a credible email that most staff would be interested in opening and reading. The email asked employees to confirm their details which were necessary because of the implementation of the new administrative systems. They were then asked to click on an html link that would take them to a fake university web page that asks for their personnel number, network identification and network password. One of the advantages of asking for a password was that the usual phishing email content such as financial details were avoided – however, the password and other details requested are sufficient to commit identity theft. The implication is that adequate information would be available to get access to facilities, services, systems, etc. that could have direct adverse financial or possible other effects for the respondent, his/her division or for the university.

The design and the execution of the phishing test appear to be straightforward but there were a number of issues that needed clarification before the test could be regarded as legitimate, both from an organisational view and a research perspective. The first requirement was that the necessary permission from the appropriate level of management had to be obtained. An official request that includes a research motivation was prepared and presented to the Institutional Director (Human Resources, Students and Innovation and Research), the Institutional Director (Finance and Facilities) and the Manager Information Technology. They gave permission for the exercise on the condition that no individual staff member would be identified and that actual passwords may not be recorded during the exercise. The condition was seen as a reasonable condition that would also address possible ethical consequences such as protecting the privacy and identity of staff. The phishing program was therefore designed in such a manner that the only information recorded was whether a user opened the email, deletes it, follows the link and whether or not something was entered in the required data fields – actual data such as passwords entered was not recorded. Therefore no passwords were compromised during the exercise. The assumption was made that respondents entered their real passwords when prompted for it, however, this could not be verified. This assumption was supported by enquiries regarding passwords. Although no staff details were divulged, the results can be used by management.

Another aspect that needed careful planning was the content of the email message. The message had to be credible but the official contact details of the IT department (who normally sends out general email messages to all staff) may not be used – the reason for this was that management was of the opinion that a good relationship between users and the IT department exists and there may be a possibility of doing harm to the existing relationship by sending out fake email messages on behalf of the IT department. The authors' own contact details (phone numbers) were then added to the message. The final content of the message and the web page was again presented to the Manager Information Technology as well as the Human Resources department for approval.

Finally, a decision had to be made on whether all staff at the selected campus will receive the phishing email or whether a sample should be used. The exercise forms part of a bigger research project and it was agreed that in future there would be other exercises where it might be necessary to test users' awareness via email messages again. To prevent all staff from regularly receiving questionable email messages it was decided to use only a sample of staff members – these staff members may then be excluded in future tests. The sampling process is described in section 2.2.

2.2 Methodology used

The process followed to conduct the exercise was handled in three phases – two test runs and a final test. As an initial test, the email was sent to the authors who performed all possible actions e.g. open the message without following the link, open the message and follow the link but without entering any information, delete the message without opening it etc. The objective was purely to test the technical working of the program and to verify whether the statistics were recorded correctly.

The second test was a small pilot run where messages were sent to 20 randomly selected staff members – the aim was to determine if everything operates correctly when sending the message outside of the technical test environment and also to try and determine what reactions or enquiries could be received. An important aspect identified during the pilot run was that provision had to be made for collecting data from those people who phone or directly reply to the email message.

The final test was conducted a few days after the pilot run. As stated earlier, it was decided to send the message to a sample of staff and to assist with the sampling process the electronic campus address book, which is publicly available to all staff, was used as the population. There were approximately 2400 useable records in the address book and the sample size, n, was determined as $n = e^{-2}$, where e is the accuracy of the estimated proportion with a 95% confidence [10]. For the purpose of this study, e was chosen to be 0,05 which resulted in a sample size of 400. Once the sample size was determined, it was decided to select staff by making use of the systematic sampling method [11]. Sampling begins by randomly selecting the first observation. Thereafter subsequent observations are selected at a uniform interval relative to the first observation. The ratio N/n, where N is the population size and n the sample size, provides the interval length – for this study, N was approximately

2400 and $n = 400$ which means that every 6th element (staff member) was chosen to receive the email message.

The email message was sent to the 400 randomly selected staff members and provision was made to receive phone calls from staff. Personnel of the Help Desk were also alerted to be prepared to assist where necessary. A facility was also created to capture direct email replies. After seven days the exercise was declared closed and the recorded statistics were analysed. A discussion of the results follows in the next section.

3 Results

A response rate of 80% was received. To determine the response rate, the email messages that were not opened was ignored – these email messages were regarded as analogous to paper questionnaires that were not returned. Fourteen of these unopened email messages were immediately deleted by the recipients.

Figure 1 shows the major activities performed by all staff on the phishing email. The categories in figure 1 indicated the percentage of staff members who entered their passwords on the fake web page; the percentage of staff that reacted to the email in the form of a direct reply to the phishing email or telephonically; the percentage of staff members who opened the email, but did not follow the html link; and the percentage of staff who opened the email, followed the link but did not enter a password. It can be seen that more than half of the employees (53.4%) were willing to give their passwords away. It should be noted that the percentages do not add up to 100 as there may be overlaps between the "Replied" category and the others e.g. someone may have replied to the email but also may have entered his/her password on the web page.

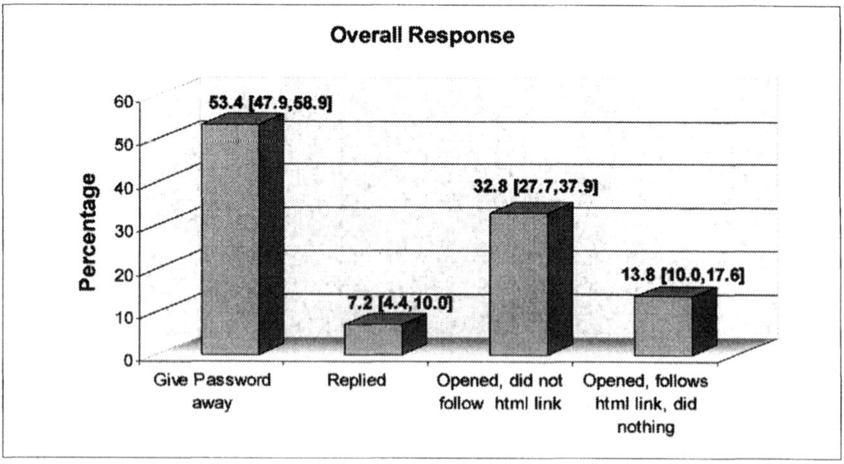

Fig. 1. Overall response

At the top of each bar in the histogram in figure 1, a 95% confidence interval for the true population proportion is given. The formula used for constructing these confidence intervals is given by $p \pm 1.96\sqrt{p(1-p)/n}$ where p is the single sample proportion and n the sample size [11]. There is therefore a 95% chance that the actual percentage of all staff on the campus that would be willing to give their passwords away is between 47.9% and 58.9%.

Figure 2 presents the distribution of the staff who responded over the different divisions, e.g. Natural Sciences, Economic and Management Sciences, etc. The graph shows that the systematic random sampling method resulted in a reflection of the proportional division sizes. There are eight divisions plus a ninth one called 'non-academic' which include all staff not working in an academic faculty e.g. student administration, human resources, technical staff, etc. Due to the protection of privacy and identity of staff it was not possible to distinguish between academic and non-academic staff within divisions – numbers per division therefore include all staff working in that specific division. Characteristics of the divisions are not disclosed due to the ethical and confidentiality considerations. The results were meaningful and could be used internally by management in training efforts to improve ICT security awareness.

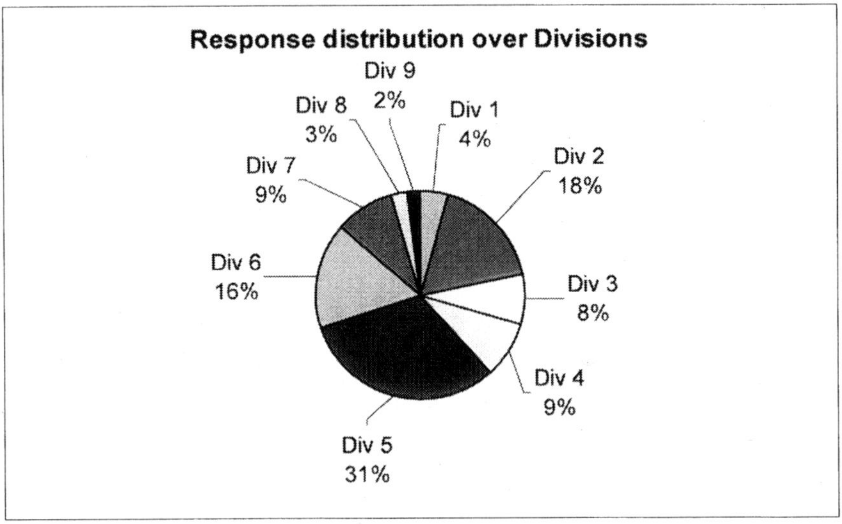

Fig. 2. Response distribution

Figure 3 shows the distribution of staff per division that was willing to give their password away, e.g. from the 171 respondents who gave their passwords away, 2% was in division 9 as opposed to the 36% in division 5. More detailed figures per division are presented in table 1.

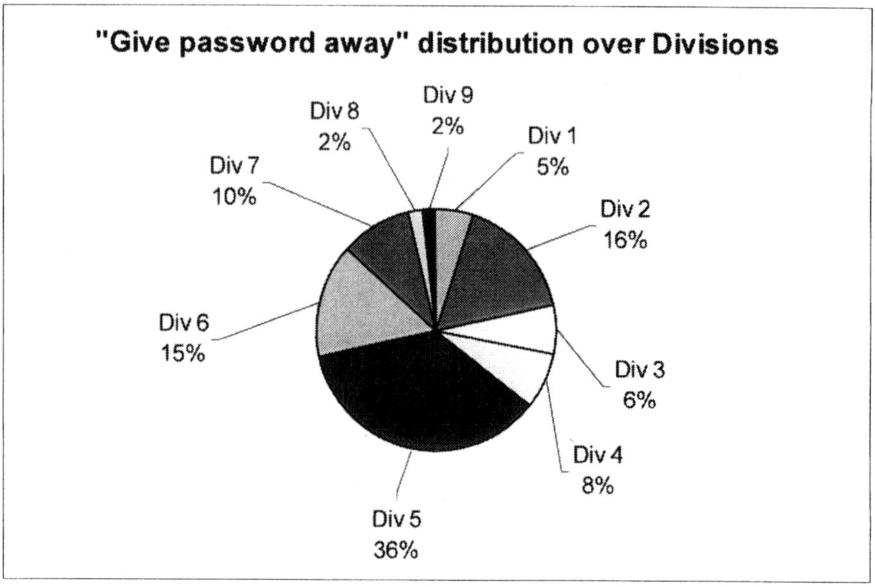

Fig. 3. "Give password away" distribution

Table 1. Information per division

Division	Number of responses	Give password away (Percentage)	Give password away (Number)	Replied	Opened, did not follow html link	Opened, follows html link, did nothing
1	13	69.2	9	1	2	2
2	56	50.0	28	3	19	9
3	25	44.0	11	1	11	3
4	29	44.8	13	3	12	4
5	101	60.4	61	11	26	14
6	52	50.0	26	3	17	9
7	30	56.7	17	0	12	1
8	8	37.5	3	1	3	2
9	6	50.0	3	0	3	0
Totals	**320**		**171**	**23**	**105**	**44**

Figure 4 shows the detailed figures from table 1 in graph form.

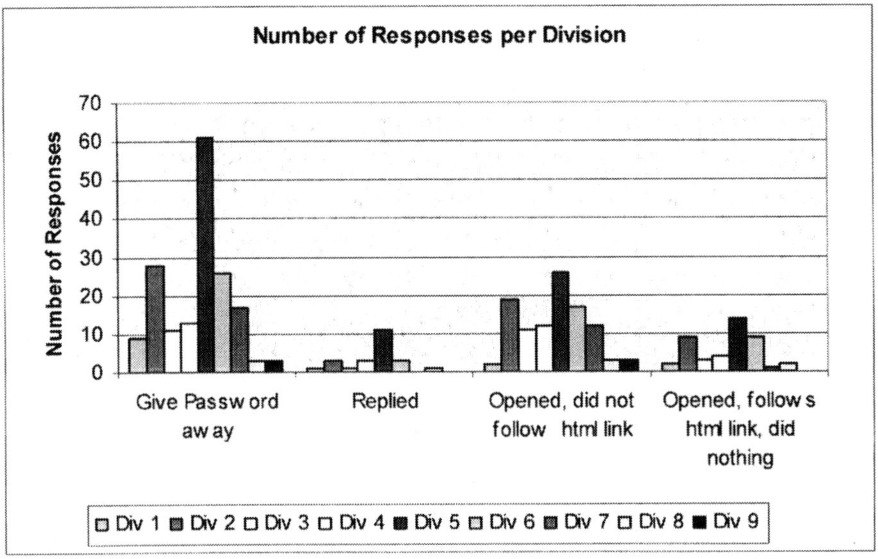

Fig. 4. Number of responses per division

The results of the experiment have indicated that the current ICT security awareness level that relates to phishing, identity theft and good management of passwords, may not be adequate with more than 50% of staff who gave their passwords away when asked for it. This figure should be considered high given the environment and the above average level of computer literacy of staff. Formal computer literacy programs for staff are in place but it is clear that these programs do not sufficiently address the ICT security risks and dangers found in the workplace. The relative low number of enquiries (replies) received (7.2%) may also be an indication of a lack of understanding on how to handle security incidents – users should be aware of *how to recognise* a security incident such as a phishing scam; be *willing to report* it and *know where to report* it. One should also expect the fourth category in Figure 1 – follows the html link but did not enter any data – to be much higher than the current 13.8%. The ideal is that when respondents see the request for personal and private information, more of them should have refused to provide it. It should therefore be worthwhile for management to consider some form of awareness training for staff or to consider the distribution of awareness material to make employees aware of the risks and dangers of phishing scams and what to do when they suspect irregularities. The statistics per division should also enable a focused and phased approach by targeting those divisions with the highest percentage of staff giving their passwords away, first. Finally, the results provided measurements that will be used in the development of a comprehensive ICT security awareness model.

4 Conclusions

In this paper a successful phishing exercise was conducted as part of an existing research project to measure ICT security awareness levels of staff in an academic environment as to raise the overall information security culture. An email message was sent to users to try and convince them to surrender their private network passwords. The results indicated that more than 50% of employees were willing to surrender their passwords – a clear indication that some form of awareness exercise may be needed.

One practical test can only provide partially insight into the awareness levels of those tested; however, the results do provide a baseline measurement for a more comprehensive measuring model as well as an opportunity for management to focus existing security awareness programs or to establish new ones. The test in itself was also useful as a tool to raise awareness amongst employees. It was shown by these results that employees are prone to phishing attacks. Therefore, potential identity theft incidents have to be managed and security awareness in email environments must be addressed in educational activities.

The intention is to expand the exercise to include the other two campuses of the university as well. The test will also be repeated after a certain period of time to determine if there was any change in awareness levels. Another possibility that is investigated is to extend the exercise in future to include the students from the different campuses.

Acknowledgement

The authors would like to thank Mr. C Muller for the technical support during this experiment. We would also like to thank the three anonymous reviewers for their useful feedback.

References

1. ABSA. Security Centre (October 25, 2006); http://www.absa.co.za/.
2. G. Ollman, The Phishing guide: Understanding & Preventing Phishing attacks, (October 25, 2006); http://www.ngssoftware.com/research/papers/.
3. Wikipedia. (October 25, 2006); http://en.wikipedia.org/wiki/Phishing.
4. A. Granova and J.H.P. Eloff, A legal overview of phishing, *Computer Fraud and Security*, 6-11, (July 2005).
5. Identity Theft Resource Center. (October 24, 2006); http://www.idtheftcenter.org/cresources.shtml.
6. A. Litan, Phishing attack victims likely targets for Identity Theft, (October 24, 2006); http://www.gartner.com 4 May 2004.
7. L. Drevin, H.A. Kruger and T. Steyn, Value-focused assessment of ICT security awareness in an academic environment, *In: IFIP International Federation for Information Processing, Volume 201, Security and Privacy in Dynamic Environments, eds. Fischer-*

Hubner, S., Ranneberg, K., Yngstrom, L., Lindskog, S. (Boston: Springer, 2006), pp. 448-453.

8. R.C. Dodge and A.J. Ferguson, Using Phishing for User Email Security Awareness, *In: IFIP International Federation for Information Processing, Volume 201, Security and Privacy in Dynamic Environments, eds. Fischer-Hubner, S., Ranneberg, K., Yngstrom, L., Lindskog, S.* (Boston: Springer, 2006), pp. 454-459.
9. H.A. Kruger, L. Drevin, and T. Steyn, A framework for evaluating ICT security awareness, *In: Proceedings of the 2006 ISSA Conference, Johannesburg, South Africa*, (5-7 July 2006, on CD).
10. A.G.W. Steyn, C.F. Smit, S.H.C. Du Toit and C. Strasheim, *Moderne Statistiek vir die Praktyk,* (Sesde uitgawe. JL van Schaik. Pretoria, 1998).
11. T. Wegner, *Applied Business Statistics,* (Juta & Co, Ltd. Kenwyn, 1993).

A practical usability evaluation of security features in end-user applications

S.M.Furnell, D.Katsabas, P.S.Dowland and F.Reid
Network Research Group, University of Plymouth, Plymouth, United Kingdom
info@network-research-group.org

Abstract. The presentation and usability of security features can represent a significant impediment to effective protection for end-user systems. In order to investigate the nature and level of problems that can be encountered during attempts to use security within standard end-user applications, this paper presents results from a series of hands-on user trials from web browsing, word-processing, and email activities. The results are based upon structured tests involving 15 participants (representing a mix of general and advanced users), revealing that in many cases users appear to have difficulties understanding and performing baseline security tasks within the applications concerned.

1 Introduction

Security-related software is now a standard provision in today's PCs, from specific tools such as anti-virus and anti-spyware utilities, through to the presence of protection features within more general applications. Although all can have a valuable role to play, the benefits can be significantly undermined if users cannot understand and make effective use of them – in some cases to the extent that they are effectively left unprotected as a result [1,2]. As such, the usability of security is a crucial factor in ensuring that it is able to serve its intended purpose. Although this requirement is now beginning to achieve much more widespread recognition [3,4], usable security remains an area in which current software is often notably lacking.

As part of a wider study into the nature of the usability problem, this paper presents the results of a hands-on trial involving the use of security-related features within a number of applications, in order to determine how well they can be understood and used by the intended end-users. Prior investigation has already established general evidence of problems, based upon the responses from over 340

Please use the following format when citing this chapter:

Furnell, S., Katsabas, D., Dowland, P., and Reid, F., 2007, in IFIP International Federation for Information Processing, Volume 232, New Approaches for Security, Privacy and Trust in Complex Environments, eds. Venter, H., Eloff, M., Labuschagne, L., Eloff, J., von Solms, R., (Boston: Springer), pp. 205–216.

users in a questionnaire-based study [5]. This survey revealed that respondents had significant difficulties understanding the language and appearance aspects of the user interfaces, suggesting that these would be an obstacle to practical usage. However, the survey had not been able to assess whether respondents would have been able to overcome their difficulties if they encountered such features in a practical context, and thus the next phase of the research aimed to get a deeper insight into users' ability to actually complete security-related tasks.

This paper begins by presenting an outline of the methodology adopted for the trial activities, followed by discussion of the results observed, with specific attention devoted to the findings from each of the applications assessed in this phase of the research. Brief conclusions and the outlook for future research are presented at the end of the paper.

2 Trial methodology

The trial involved 15 participants in a series of hands-on activities, using security features within a range of software applications. The trialists were a mixture of academic and administrative staff, and students from within the local university environment. All were regular users of IT, and familiar with the general operation of the Microsoft Windows environment in which the target applications were running. Within the group, eight participants were classed as general users, with a familiarity with using IT (and some of the applications concerned) on a regular basis, but with no specific knowledge about the detail of the technology. By contrast the other seven participants were advanced users, all with academic qualifications relating to IT and some prior knowledge in relation to security. Sampling in this study was purposeful rather than random, and was determined by the representativeness of trialists to the broader user population, the intensive nature of the think aloud methodology employed in this study, and the diminishing returns of using large samples for identifying usability problems using this method [6].

The activities were generally chosen to be representative of tasks that security-conscious users may wish to perform, as well as things that other users may find themselves needing to do as a result of the default security settings within the application, or settings that other users had applied. The required tasks were presented in writing and explained to the participants. Note that they were told what they needed to achieve, but not how to do it, and the aim of the trial was to determine whether they could understand and use the security features within the application sufficiently well to achieve the objectives. Participants were allowed to make use of any available 'help' features within the applications, as well as refer to online sources if the thought occurred to them to do so. In addition, the researcher conducting the trial was on hand to monitor their progress, provide any necessary help (as requested by participants), and to answer any questions regarding the progress of the tasks. Participants were also free to end the trial at any time.

Participants were encouraged to follow a 'think aloud' protocol, requiring them to explain their thought processes and decisions as they attempted to perform each of the tasks [7]. The intention here was to provide insights into how problem features had been interpreted, which could hopefully help to inform improvements to future implementations. However, at the time of writing, these aspects have yet to be fully analyzed, and so the information conveyed here will be restricted to the results regarding success or failure of participants to complete the tasks. Consequently, the present paper offers summary statistics that are necessary to contextualise the protocol analysis that is currently underway

The full trial required security-related tasks to be performed within six software environments. Three of these were security-specific utilities (namely the Windows Firewall, the Zone Alarm firewall, and Norton Antivirus), whereas the others were general applications that included security-related features (namely Internet Explorer, Word, and Outlook Express). The findings presented here are restricted to those from the latter three applications, as these were common to the earlier survey exercise, and the findings in relation to the security-specific tools are not directly considered in this discussion. It should be noted that the significant focus upon Microsoft applications within the trial was in no way intended to imply that Microsoft's products were particularly at fault in terms of the usability of their security when compared to alternatives from other sources. The basis was rather that they were judged to be the applications that participants were most likely to use (as was borne out, in most cases, by the findings), and thus any difficulties encountered in the trials could be more directly related back to the usability of the security aspects rather than participants' unfamiliarity with the applications in general.

Each stage of the trial ended with the completion of a brief feedback questionnaire to record the participant's views about the application they had just used. Amongst the standard questions they were asked for each application were how easy it had been to use the available security, and how long it had taken to find and use the security features required. In terms of the ease of use rating, participants were offered the following options:

- Easy (Did not encounter any difficulties at all)
- OK (with minor difficulties)
- Hard (experienced several difficulties during the tasks)
- Unable to use

Meanwhile, the options for how long participants felt it had taken to locate and use the security were as follows:

- Very quick (it was obvious where to look for the available security and what to do)
- Quick (but I would expect the process to take less time)
- Slow (I worked around the application for some time before being able to find and use the available security)
- Very slow (it took a long time to find the security and determine how to use it)

The findings from these assessments are presented for each of the applications under discussion, alongside the actual results indicating how successfully the participants performed each of the required tasks.

3 Usability trial results

The sub-sections that follow present the results observed for each of the three applications. Although the size of the participant group was too small to yield truly meaningful percentages, some of the results are nonetheless presented in this format in order to enable an easier appreciation of the proportion of users that were able to complete each task (with the calculations for general, advanced and overall users being based upon 8, 7 and 15 participants respectively). The tables also present the overall time taken to complete the trial tasks for each application (although it should be noted that this includes the time taken to complete the aforementioned feedback questionnaire, and so the actual time spent completing the hands-on task was typically two minutes less than the values shown in the tables).

3.1 Trial activities involving Internet Explorer

For this stage of the trial, participants were asked to attempt a number of tasks in relation to these elements of browser security. The first was to simply determine the current security setting of the browser, requiring users to find and understand the related options interface via the Tools menu and then recognize the current setting of the slider shown in Fig. 1. The next task involved visiting a series of four websites, and determining whether participants could recognize which ones involved secure connections (i.e. recognizing the presence or absence of 'https' in the URL and/or the padlock icon in the browser status bar). Having completed these observational tasks, the next three activities involved making changes to the security configuration. Firstly, participants had to adjust settings to permit the downloading of a file – which involved reducing the security level shown in Fig. 1 from 'high' (which had been preset for the purposes of the trial) to 'medium'. The next adjustment involved a deeper level of configuration, via the 'Custom Level' settings, to get the browser to prompt before using ActiveX controls. The final tasks involved the use and concept of Web content zones, as shown at the top of the main security settings window. Participants were firstly asked to add a website address to the 'trusted' zone and another to the 'restricted' zone, and then asked to explain their understanding of what the zones actually meant in order to determine whether they knew what they were doing.

The majority of the participants (11 of 15) used Internet Explorer as their regular web browser, and thus (in theory) many of the tasks should not have posed a major problem. The actual levels of success observed for each of the tasks (overall, and split according to the experience levels), is shown in Table 1. It is notable that even with the baseline task (determining the current security settings), a quarter of the participants were unable to complete the actions required of them, and it was particularly surprising to find that only a third were able to determine whether or not the connection to a particular site was secure. Indeed, even where some tasks were completed successfully, some participants often took a fairly long time to do so. The other notable results in the table relate to the two tasks involving web content zones – which are the only findings from the three applications under discussion in which the 'general' users were found to out-perform the 'advanced' ones. One of the main reasons for this seemed to be that some of the advanced users had pre-conceived ideas about what the 'trusted' and 'restricted' categories might mean, and consequently did not read the on-screen information closely enough (e.g. trying to add 'http' sites to the trusted list, when the browser default indicated that server verification was required, and therefore permitted only 'https' sites to be added for this zone).

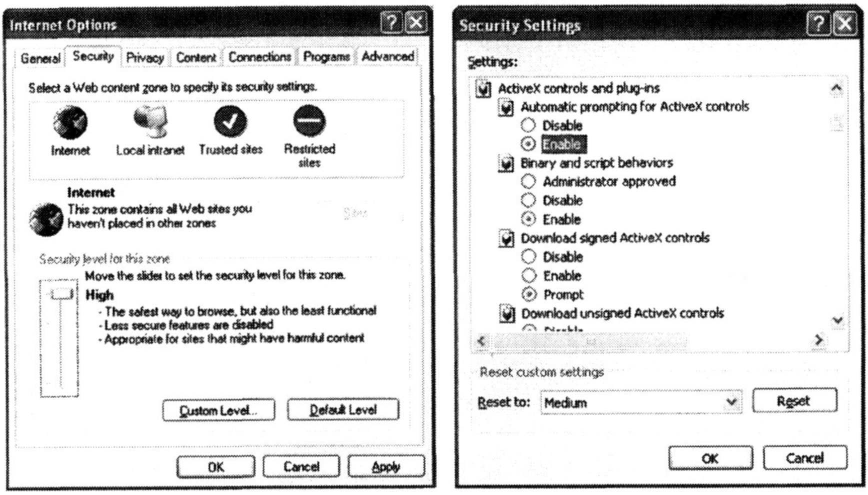

Fig. 1. Security options settings within Internet Explorer (main and custom level)

Table 1. Successful completion of user trial activities within Internet Explorer

Task	General users (%)	Advanced users (%)	Overall (%)
Determine the current security settings level within the browser	63	86	73
Determine whether communication with a specific webpage is using a secure connection	12	57	33
Customise security settings in order to permit download of a file	38	86	60
Customise security settings in order to be prompted before running ActiveX	12	71	40
Add websites to the 'trusted' and 'restricted' Web content zones	88	71	80
Explain the purpose of the Web content zones	88	43	67
Overall success	50%	69%	59%
Average time to complete all tasks	20m00s	15m50s	18m13s

Having completed the tasks, the participants were asked to express their views on how easy they had found it, and how long they felt the process had taken. The related findings are illustrated in Figs. 2 and 3, and show that in spite of the fact that many participants had been unable to complete a number of the tasks, the overall feelings were generally positive from this stage of the trial.

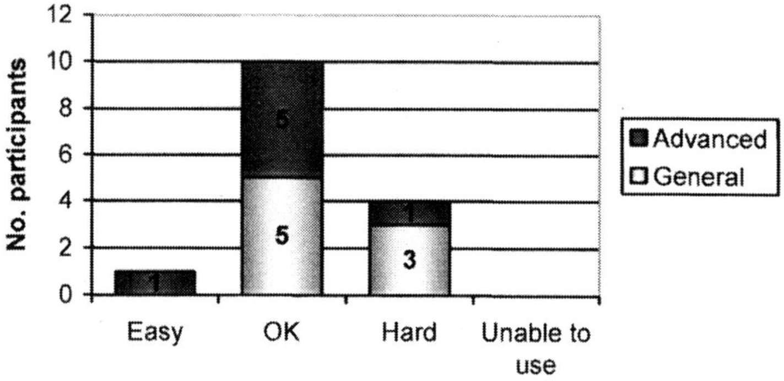

Fig. 2. Perceived ease of use of security within Internet Explorer

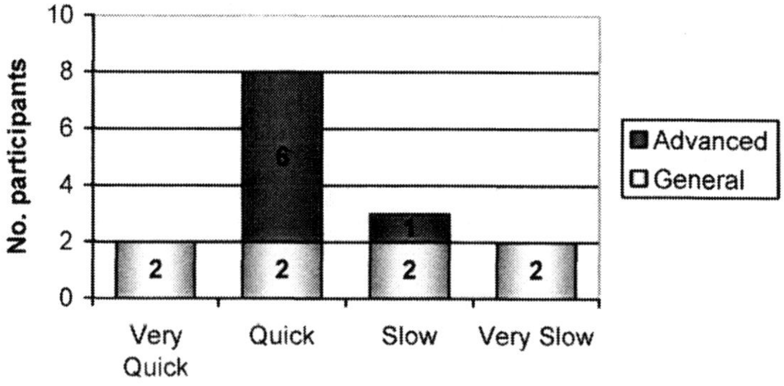

Fig. 3. Finding and using the required security features within Internet Explorer

3.2 Trial activities involving Word

As with Internet Explorer, the majority of participants were regular users of Word and so were familiar with the general interface and functionality. For the tasks in this phase, participants were provided with a sample Word document to work with and then asked to perform a number of security and privacy-related operations upon it. The first was to assign a password in order to restrict reading of the document.

This required users to locate the password protection facilities within Word (located again within options under the Tools menu), and then determine which of the two password possibilities they were meant to be setting. The two choices here are illustrated in the uppermost portion of Fig. 4, and our previous work [8] has commented upon the potential confusion that this presentation can generate. The next task required users to click on the 'Advanced' button and determine whether they could understand how the options they were then presented with (see Fig. 5) actually related to the password they had specified on the previous screen. The next task involved utilizing other features from Fig. 4 to ensure maximum privacy for their document, and then to assign a second password to prevent unauthorized changes to its content. The final activity involved inspecting and adjusting the macro security settings in order to ensure that a warning would be displayed when opening a document containing a macro. To test their decision, participants were then required to determine which document, from a pair pre-stored on the trial system, had macro content in it.

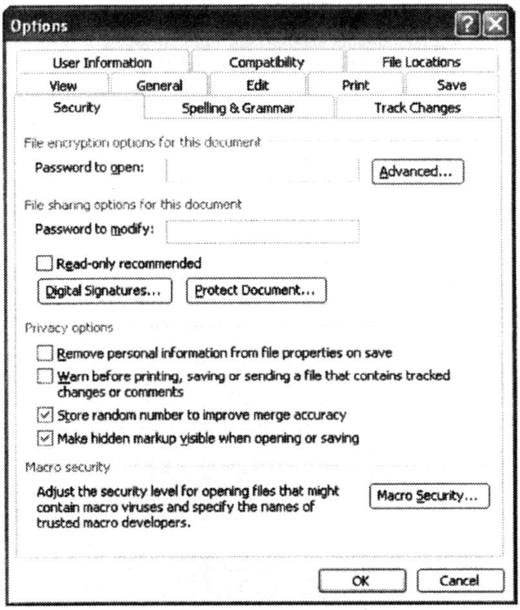

Fig. 4. Alternative password options in Microsoft Word

As the results in Table 2 illustrate, the overall findings for the Word tasks were not greatly positive, and exhibited a pronounced difference between the general and advanced users. While some of the areas of difficulty (e.g. in relation to encryption options) were anticipated, it is notable that only a third of the participants were able to successfully complete the baseline task of adding password protection to prevent a document from being read. This very much confirmed the earlier suspicions that this interface presents particular challenges for users to understand a security feature (i.e. passwords) that they would normally consider themselves familiar with.

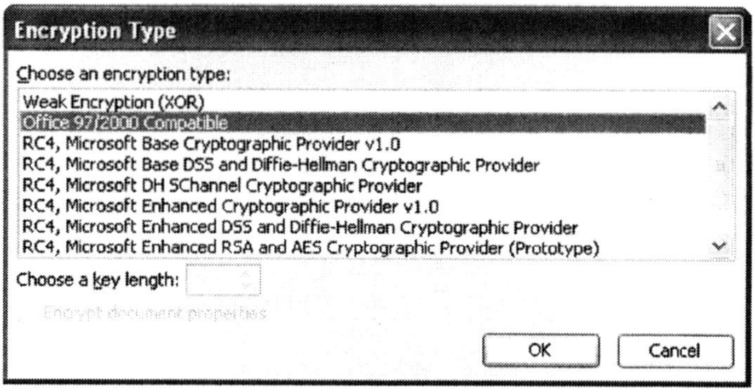

Fig. 5. The advanced encryption options in Word

Table 2. Successful completion of user trial activities within Word

Task	General users (%)	Advanced users (%)	Overall (%)
Password protect a document to prevent it being read	25	43	33
Understand how the 'advanced' (encryption-related) options relate to the password	12	43	27
Protect the privacy of the document.	75	100	87
Password protect a document to prevent changes	25	57	40
Configure the macro security settings in order to be warned when opening a document with a potentially unsafe macro	12	57	33
Overall success	30	60	44
Average time to complete all tasks	11m30s	11m50s	11m39s

Having completed the tasks, the participants' views were as shown in Figs 6 and 7. Compared to the IE findings, we can now observe a more significant split between those who found the tasks fairly straightforward and those who encountered difficulties (with the 'general' users clearly faring worse overall). Additionally, most respondents had even more negative views about the time required to find the features in the first place.

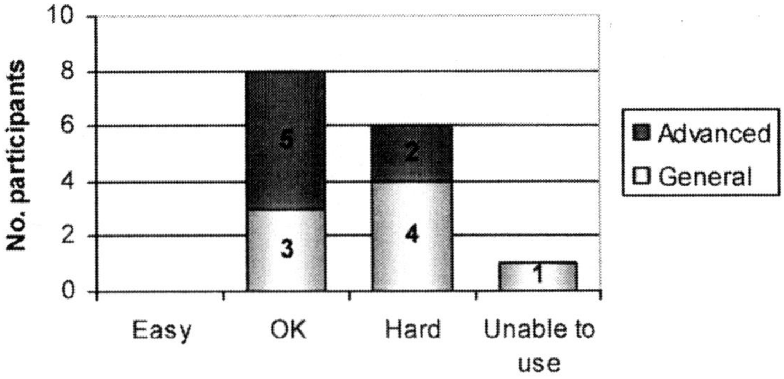

Fig. 6. Perceived ease of use of security within Word

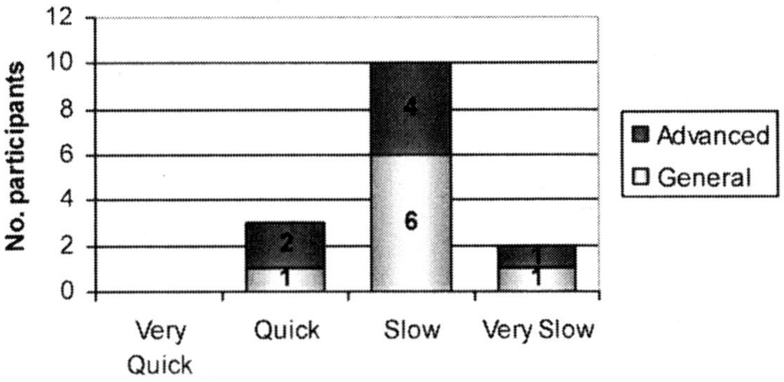

Fig. 7. Finding and using the required security features within Word

3.3 Trial activities involving Outlook Express

Whereas the other two applications were generally well-known to the participants, only four (all from the 'general' user category) indicated that they used Outlook Express as their default email client, and so in this set of tasks the participants were generally using an application that they were less familiar with. Having said this, many of the participants used the full version of Outlook and/or Outlook Web Access on a regular basis, and so were not totally unfamiliar with the general style of the interface.

For this stage of the trial, participants were asked to attempt four tasks. The first was to send an encrypted email to a given recipient, and the challenge here was for them to realize why it ultimately was not possible. Although the 'New Message' window in Outlook Express offers the apparent option to 'Encrypt' a message (see Fig. 8), to do so requires the sender and receiver to have established a DigitalID beforehand. The next task reflected the fact that, by default, Outlook Express removes access to 71 potentially unsafe categories of attachment (e.g. .exe, .mdb, and .vbs files) [9]. However, in some contexts, a user may have a genuine requirement to receive such a file from a trusted source. In this situation, they would need to determine how to configure the settings to allow access to the attachment to be regained, and this was the scenario presented to the participants. The final pair of tasks related to blocking email senders – initially requiring the user to block the receipt of email messages from a particular address, and then to locate and check the 'Blocked Senders' list to ensure that another address had not been blocked by accident.

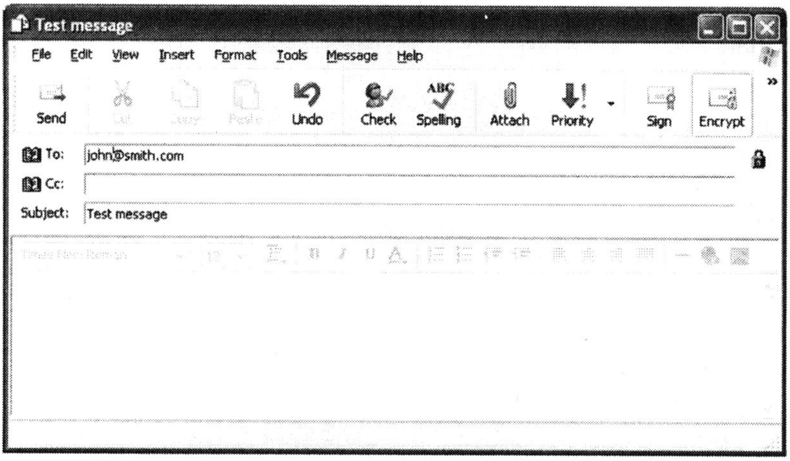

Fig. 8. Message encryption option within Outlook Express

The findings from this phase are presented in Table 3, and are notably the only set described in this paper in which less than half of the participants were able to complete any of the associated tasks. In view of the results from the table, it is perhaps unsurprising to find that the participants viewed Outlook Express as the most difficult of the three applications under discussion here (see Fig. 9). Although it could be argued that this reflects the fact that most participants did not normally use the application, it can be noted that two out of the four that *did* use it still indicated that they found it hard to use the security.

Table 3. Successful completion of user trial activities within Outlook Express

Task	General users (%)	Advanced users (%)	Overall (%)
Determine why they could not send an encrypted message.	25	71	47
Recover access to a blocked attachment	25	71	47
Block a sender who has been generating spam	12	57	33
Find the list of blocked senders	25	57	40
Overall success	22	64	42
Average time to complete all tasks	10m07s	9m20s	9m47s

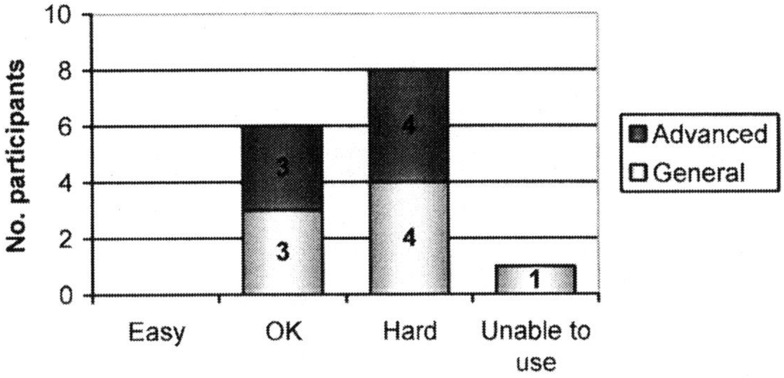

Fig. 9. Perceived ease of use of security within Outlook Express

In addition to finding it hard to complete the required tasks, the vast majority of participants clearly felt that it took too long to locate the security features and determine how to use them, as shown in Fig. 10.

4 Conclusion

The discussion here has illustrated the problems that can be encountered by users when attempting to perform security-related tasks within a number of standard PC applications. The difficulties that were encountered in the trials are particularly notable in view of the fact that all of the tests involved applications that are aimed at the general user community rather than specialists. Although it could be argued that there are other aspects of security for which usability is more critical (e.g. the ability to use authentication methods), and that some of the tasks involved in the trials would only be relevant for a subset of users, they still represent aspects of protection that some users could have a genuine desire to use.

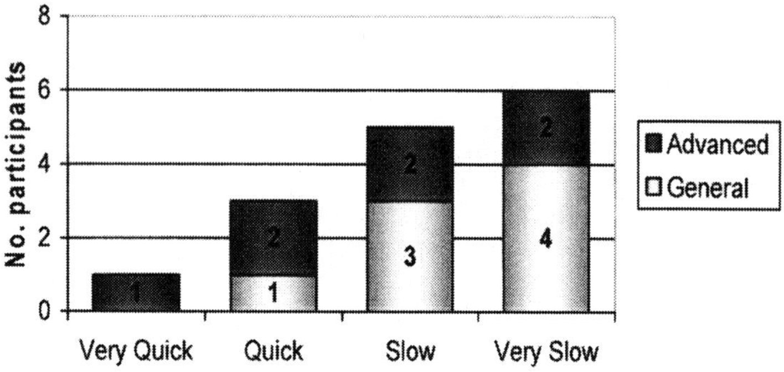

Fig. 10. Finding and using the required security features within Outlook Express

The ongoing research will use the results reported here, along with further findings from the trials, as a means of informing enhanced approaches to security interfaces and interactions. By establishing the areas in which users currently have difficulties, and more importantly the factors that contribute towards them, it is intended that enhanced alternatives can be devised and trialed in order to assess the potential for improvement.

References

1. Whitten, A. and Tygar, J. D. 1999. "Why Johnny can't Encrypt: A usability Evaluation of PGP 5.0", *Proceedings of the 8th USENIX Security Symposium*, Washington, D.C., USA, August 23–26, pp169-184.
2. DeWitt, A.J. and Kuljis, J. 2006. "Aligning usability and security: a usability study of Polaris", *Proceedings of the Second Symposium on Usable Privacy and Security (SOUPS '06)*, Pittsburgh, Pennsylvania, USA, July 12-14, pp1-7.
3. Cranor, L.F. and Garfinkel, S. 2005. *Security and Usability: Designing Secure Systems That People Can Use*. O'Reilly. ISBN 0596008279.
4. CRA. 2003. *Grand Research Challenges in Information Systems*, Computing Research Association, Washington DC, September 2003. http://www.cra.org/reports/gc.systems.pdf.
5. Furnell, S.M., Jusoh, A. and Katsabas, D. 2006. "The challenges of understanding and using security: A survey of end-users", *Computers & Security*, vol. 25, no. 1, pp27-35.
6. Nielson, J. 1994. "Estimating the number of subjects needed for a thinking aloud test", International Journal of Human-Computer Studies, vol. 41, no. 3, pp385–397.
7. Lewis, C. and Rieman, J. 1993/1994. Chapter 5 in *Task-Centred User Inferface Design – A Practical Introduction*. See http://hcibib.org/tcuid/
8. Furnell, S.M. 2005. "Why users cannot use security", *Computers & Security*, vol. 24, no. 4, pp274-279.
9. Koch, T. 2004. "Outlook Express and Windows XP Service Pack 2: Several Problems or Superior Protection?", 21 October 2004, www.microsoft.com/windows/ie/community/columns/oeandsp2.mspx.

Personal Anomaly-based Intrusion Detection Smart Card Using Behavioural Analysis

A.M. Rossudowski, H.S. Venter, and J.H.P. Eloff

Information and Computer Security Architectures Research Group (ICSA)
Department of Computer Science, University of Pretoria, South Africa
{amrossudowski, hsventer, eloff}@cs.up.ac.za

Abstract. Intrusion Detection Systems play an invaluable role within organisations by detecting attempted attacks on their IT systems. However, Intrusion Detection Systems are complex to set-up and require large quantities of memory and processing power to effectively analyse the large volumes of network traffic involved. Behavioural analysis plays an important role within Intrusion Detection Systems by looking for suspicious behaviour or behaviour out of the ordinary within the network traffic. This paper identifies several problems that decreases the overall performance of Intrusion Detection Systems. It proposes the use of a personal smart card-based Intrusion Detection System to increase the performance and effectiveness of Intrusion Detection Systems as a whole.

Key words: Intrusion Detection System, IDS, smart card, behavioural analysis, personal IDS.

1 Introduction

An Intrusion Detection System (IDS) is just one of the security tools an organisation can use to protect itself from a wide range of attacks designed to disrupt its systems or steal sensitive information. An IDS tries to detect these attacks by monitoring traffic through the organisation's network. A pattern-based IDS looks for a pre-defined pattern of traffic that could constitute an attack [1, 2]; whilst an anomaly-based IDS looks for anomalies within traffic or behaviours that exceed a certain threshold or specified base-line [1, 2]. The base-line represents the typical behaviour of the organisation's network traffic.

The problem facing an anomaly-based IDS, particularly within a large organisation, is that every employee will browse the Internet or communicate across the network in a unique way. Hence it is quite difficult—if not impossible—to determine what network behaviour constitutes the base-line. While a pattern-based IDS requires tremendous amounts of processing power and time to analyse the large quantities of information [3] passing through a network, which results in inefficiencies.

Please use the following format when citing this chapter:

Rossudowski, A.M., Venter, H., and Eloff, J., 2007, in IFIP International Federation for Information Processing, Volume 232, New Approaches for Security, Privacy and Trust in Complex Environments, eds. Venter, H., Eloff, M., Labuschagne, L., Eloff, J., von Solms, R., (Boston: Springer), pp. 217–228.

This paper proposes the use of smart card technology, in conjunction with behavioural analysis, to implement an anomaly-based Intrusion Detection System. The smart card-based IDS (SCIDS) implements several approaches, discussed later, that decrease the time taken to discover certain types of attacks. The SCIDS improves the efficiency of intrusion detection, while simultaneously reducing the complexity of anomaly detection.

Section 2 provides relevant background information concerning this study. Section 3 identifies the limitations within current IDSs and proposes solutions to these limitations. Section 4 presents the smart card-based Intrusion Detection System model. The proposed model is compared to existing IDSs within section 5 to illustrate its advantages. The paper is concluded by section 6.

2 Background

This section provides brief information on behavioural analysis, various types of Intrusion Detection Systems, and an overview of smart cards.

2.1 Behavioural Analysis

Alexander [4] states that *"the study of behaviour encompasses all of the movements and sensations by which animals and men mediate their relations with their external environment – physical, biotic and social"*. Behavioural analysis is defined in the context of this paper as *"the study of how an employee behaves under different conditions and environments, with various internal and external stimuli applied to those environments"*.

Many disparate disciplines incorporate the use of behavioural analysis. Biologists use behavioural analysis of chimpanzees as a model of early hominid behaviour [5]. Computer scientists use behavioural analysis to determine the performance and behaviour of complex systems [6]. More frequently, a cross-disciplinary approach to behavioural analysis is being applied, such as the RoboCup Initiative [7]. Researchers are also studying how humans interact with robots so they can design more socially interactive robots in the future [8].

Behavioural analysis can also be applied to the way human beings browse the Internet under changing stimuli, such as night and day and at various times of the day, week, month and/or year. Every individual will browse the Internet in a unique way, for example, at different times on different days and this pattern can be used to build a user's web browsing profile.

2.2 Intrusion Detection Systems

An Intrusion Detection System (IDS) detects unauthorised access to, or use of, a system or an application [1]. Most IDSs are passive systems using pattern-based (also known as signature-based) detection mechanisms. The most challenging IDS to implement is an active system using anomaly-based detection methods.

A pattern-based IDS detects an attack on a system by looking for a particular series of actions, commands, or events (i.e. a pattern). This pattern is usually created from the records of previous attacks [1, 2]. An anomaly-based IDS, on the other hand, looks for any actions, commands, or events that fall outside the scope of normal user behaviour (the base-line) [1, 2]. Anomaly-based IDSs are usually taught what normal system activity is and generate heuristics or rules according to this behaviour. Any actions that do not comply with these heuristics or rules are flagged as possible intrusions.

An IDS is a tool used to monitor, identify and respond to attacks on a given system and/or network. There are several different types of IDSs:

- **Host-based IDSs** are designed to run in the background on systems presumed to be critical and/or sensitive, such as web servers, mail servers and DNS servers[2].
- **Network-based IDSs** sit on the network and monitor traffic at the packet level. The system's network interface is set to *stealth* mode and *promiscuous* mode and has no IP address [9] to help hide it from the network and protect it from attacks [2].
- **Pattern-based IDSs** (also known as misuse, signature or knowledge-based IDSs) monitor the log files (host-based) or network traffic (network-based) looking for specific patterns that could indicate suspicious behaviour [1, 2].
- **Anomaly-based IDSs** (also known as behaviour-based IDSs) use statistical techniques or a trained neural-net to detect penetrations or attacks on the system. This is achieved by determining a statistical base-line of behaviour on the system. Actual behaviour on the system is then analysed and compared to the base-line and an alert issued if a certain threshold is exceeded [1, 2].

Most IDSs are *passive* systems, determining or discovering an intrusion *post factum* through the examination of log files. System and/or Network Administrators then need to determine which vulnerabilities the attack exploited and correct the problem. Unlike a passive IDS, an *active* IDS is able to detect or discover intrusions while they are occurring by monitoring the network traffic in real-time. However, the active IDS can do little to prevent the attack from proceeding.

Intrusion Prevention Systems (IPS) [10, 11] try to either prevent or mitigate the damage caused by an attack. Intrusion Prevention [10, 11] is a relatively new term and is, essentially, a combination of access control (firewall/router) and Intrusion Detection [9]. Hence, an IPS can be defined as a product that focuses on identifying and blocking malicious network activity using preventative measures in real time [9, 11].

2.3 Smart Cards

A smart card is a token that contains an Integrated Circuit Chip (ICC) and is available in a variety of shapes and sizes [12]. The ICC – stored either on the card's surface or within its structure – contains a Central Processing Unit

(CPU), non-volatile memory (RAM, ROM, and/or EEPROM) and an Operating System (OS), usually stored in the EEPROM memory. Information can be stored and retrieved from a smart card in a similar fashion to a magnetic strip card, but a smart card has certain advantages over magnetic strip cards [12, 13], such as:

- The ability to process information stored on the card or passed to it.
- The ability to encrypt the information stored on the card [14].

Moreover, certain information and functionality stored on the smart card can only be accessed if the user (owner of the card) enters an authorised Personal Identification Number (PIN). If the user enters an incorrect PIN several times, either the smart card permanently destroys itself i.e. over loads the internal circuitry, or locks itself and requires the user to enter a longer PIN to regain access [12].

The limitations of pattern-based and anomaly-based IDSs are identified in the next section, followed by a discussion of the possible ways of improving their performance.

3 IDS Limitations and Proposed Solutions

As mentioned previously, there are various problems associated with the effective implementation of different types of Intrusion Detection Systems (IDSs), especially within large organisations. These problems are elaborated on below.

A Pattern-based IDS needs to analyse all the network traffic (packets) looking for specific patterns that suggest an attack is occurring or has occurred. This can be a time consuming process if the IDS has to analyse a large quantity of network information. It is also a computationally expensive process, especially if the attacks are of a more sophisticated and complex nature. In addition, attack patterns need to be pre-recorded within the system to be discovered, especially within a real-time IDS, thus any new type of attack that has not been previously recorded will go undetected.

An Anomaly-based IDS analyses network traffic for any activity that does not fit within the "norm" i.e. base-line. The complexity and difficulty in determining what constitutes "normal" network traffic makes implementing an anomaly-based IDS particularly challenging. This is especially true in large organisations, where different departments and users are likely to generate different types of traffic, such as web traffic, SMTP traffic and telnet sessions.

As a result of the above-mentioned problems, an IDS is likely to require excessive processing power to analyse the network information in a timely manner and is rather complex to implement [3]. The authors, therefore, propose incorporating the following techniques into an IDS implementation to improve its performance: Distributed Analysis, Attack-time Isolation, and Base-line Reduction.

Distributed Analysis would accelerate the detection of attacks by distributing the computational load of analysing the network information over multiple computers, as used in a distributed processing environment and a Distributed Intrusion Detection System (DIDS) [2, 15].

Attack-time Isolation is a method for identifying the general time period during which an attack occurred, reducing the network information that needs to be analysed by allowing the IDS to "zoom-in" on network information that occurred during that specific time period. Thus, in turn, reduces the time required to isolate the actual attack information and, in the case of a real-time IDS, allows countermeasures to be deployed much quicker. Administrators can also quickly fix the security "hole" that is being exploited and mitigate the damage caused by the attack.

Base-line Reduction reduces the complexity inherent in determining a base-line for an anomaly-based IDS by creating an individual base-line for each employee (hereafter called a user) within the organisation. The following example demonstrates the advantages of individual base-lines over an organisational base-line.

Assume an organisation implements an anomaly-based IDS on an SMTP (email) server. The base-line it sets for the SMTP server is that *"no more than 50 emails are sent to the SMTP server per second, with a threshold of 5 emails per second"*. In other words, should more than 55 emails per second be sent, it should be considered a possible attack on the system.

If more than 55 legitimate emails are sent to the SMTP server by employees within the organisation—due to an internal organisational poll or survey, for example—the IDS on the SMTP server will register these events as an attack, in this instance a "false-positive". If, however, the individual base-line is that *"no more than one email is sent to the SMTP server per second"*, even if the whole organisation sends an email at exactly the same instance no attack would be registered because the event would still be within the threshold of the individual base-lines.

To facilitate the use of individual base-lines, a personal IDS must monitor a specific user's network requests. Therefore, instead of a single IDS monitoring all network requests from all users and comparing that to a single base-line, a single IDS monitors network requests from a single user and compares them to a base-line specific to that user.

The solutions mentioned above—Distributed Analysis, Attack-time Isolation and Base-line Reduction—may sound simple, but are not feasible because of the overhead involved in implementing individual IDSs and creating individual base-lines for every employee within the organisation and analysing all the data within the log files to determine the time period during which an attack occurred. Consequently, the following section proposes a smart card-based IDS implementation model that overcomes these issues.

4 A Smart Card-based IDS Model

The following sections outline the proposed model: Section 4.1 illustrates how smart cards can be used to introduce IDSs at an individual level; Section 4.2 details how user behaviour can be logged to implement effective intrusion detection; Section 4.3 outlines how the smart card detects anomalous behaviour through a request service, and in section 4.4 a feedback process that can be used to analyse the discovered anomaly in detail is discussed.

4.1 Introducing the Smart Card IDS

The model proposes an IDS environment based on the principle of Distributed Analysis and Base-line Reduction to detect anomalies within individual users' network requests. The IDS environment is implemented on a smart card and is referred to as a smart card IDS (SCIDS). Smart card technology is used within this model due to its inherent security, mobility, scalability and low manufacturing/implementation costs. However, the technical specifications of the smart card are beyond the scope of this paper. The IDS stored on the smart card is a host-based IDS. All users within an organisation are issued with a smart card. The SCIDS then monitors all network requests originating and terminating at the computer from which the user is currently working on. Figure 1 shows a UML component diagram of the SCIDS, together with the organisation's network and conventional IDS.

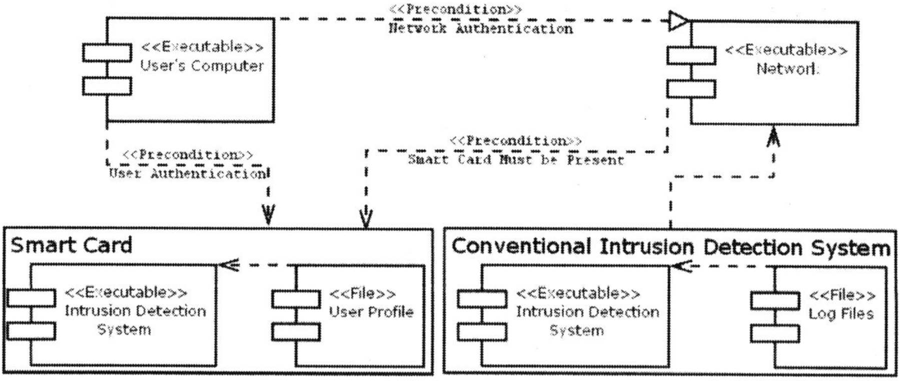

Fig. 1. UML component diagram of the Smart Card-based Intrusion Detection System.

In order to unlock the computer's network interface, the user inserts his/her smart card and authenticates his/her identity to the smart card, as shown in figure 2. While the smart card can be viewed as an authentication token, in this case its primary role is to act as an IDS. Therefore, the user still needs to authenticate him/herself to the computer network. To make certain that the SCIDS can monitor the user's network requests at all times, the smart card has to be present in the computer for the network to work, a precondition illustrated in figure 1.

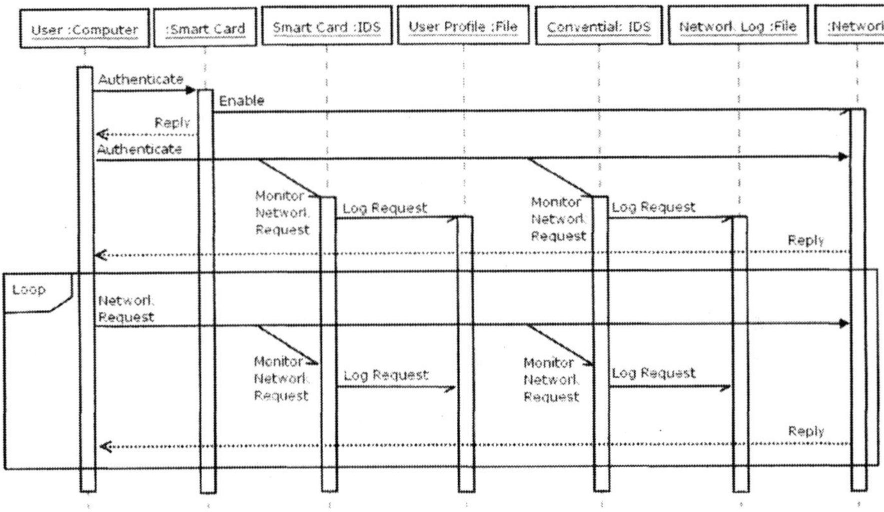

Fig. 2. UML sequence diagram illustrating the user authenticating process (both smart card and network), while the SCIDS and conventional IDS monitor the network requests.

The next section outlines how the SCIDS monitors and records user behaviour in further detail.

4.2 Tracking User Behaviour

The SCIDS tracks the network behaviour of the user, specifically, how many network requests the user makes on the network. For example, web requests, web-search requests, TCP/IP requests and UDP requests (hereafter collectively called network requests). The SCIDS creates a user network behaviour profile by monitoring the network requests made between the user's computer and the organisation's network. Due to resource limitations on the smart card, only the number of network requests a user makes per minute will be recorded by the SCIDS. Therefore, the number of network requests a user makes within a given time period, is consider a user's network behaviour profile. In addition, the organisation's network is monitored by a conventional IDS which maintains the integrity of the organisation's systems and protects the network from inside and outside attack as usual. The conventional IDS also creates a user network behaviour profile for each user on the network. Therefore, a user profile exists both locally, on the user's smart card, and centrally, on the conventional IDS. The user network behaviour profile is represented graphically as a graph in figure 3, showing the number of network requests issued by the user per quarter hour over a particular time period. This user network behaviour profile acts as the base-line that the SCIDS can then use to detect anomalies that might indicate an attack on the system. The next section discusses how this user profile can be used to discover an attack in further detail.

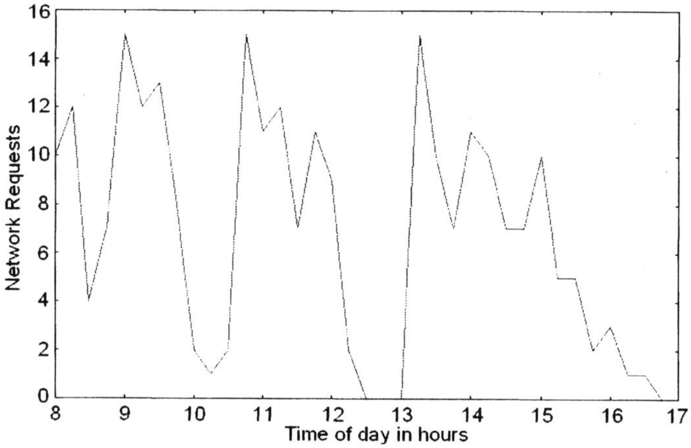

Fig. 3. Visual representation of the user's network behaviour.

4.3 Anomaly Detection

At every network log-on, the SCIDS sends a request to the organisation's conventional IDS for the user's network behaviour profile from the conventional IDS's perspective, as shown in figure 4. While the user's network behaviour profile is recorded by both the SCIDS and the organisation's conventional IDS, the network behaviour profile recorded by the SCIDS is regarded as the base-line for the user. Once the request sent by the SCIDS has been fulfilled, the SCIDS compares the network behaviour profile received from the conventional IDS to that of the user's base-line, looking for any anomalies that could suggest that an attack has occurred, as shown in figure 4. It is important to note, that the smart card does not detect intrusion on the system, but whether an anomaly between the user behaviour profile recorded by the SCIDS and the conventional IDS exists. Anomalies are any points within the network behaviour graph that do not correspond to the graph of the user's base-line, as shown in figure 5 (note the anomaly between time period 14 and 15).

These anomalous points correspond to an attack on the system using the user's network credentials. The network credentials, i.e. user ID and password,

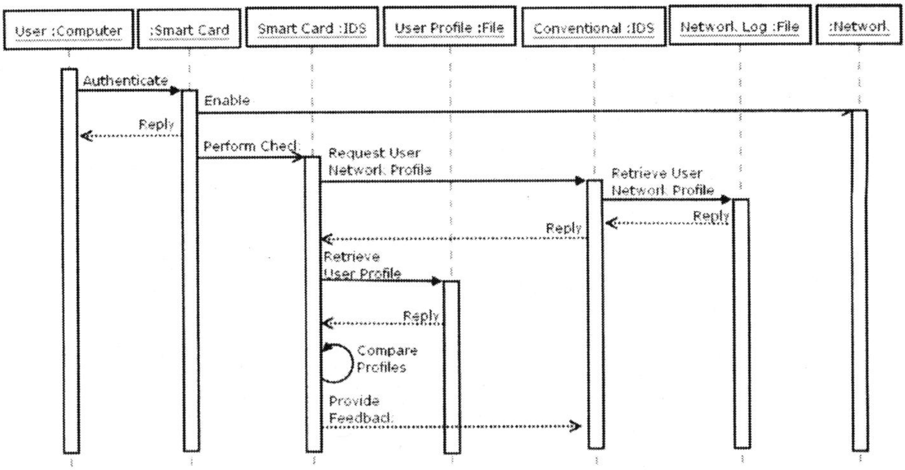

Fig. 4. UML sequence diagram depicting how the SCIDS requests the user behaviour profile from the conventional IDS, analyses the received user profile for anomalies and provides feedback.

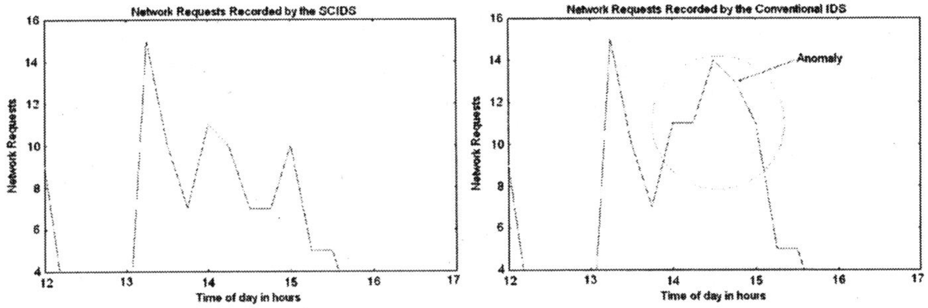

Fig. 5. Visual representation of detecting anomalous behaviour.

were stolen and used by another user (hereafter called an attacker) to commit the attack on the system. The following section details how the SCIDS handles the discovery of the attack.

4.4 Anomaly Feedback

A smart card has limited processing power, so the SCIDS cannot completely analyse the extent of the attack, the damage caused by the attack or its origin. The SCIDS has performed an important step though, it has isolated the general time period during which the attack occurred by noting the time the anomaly occurred. Therefore, the SCIDS has been able to achieve Attack-time Isolation. The SCIDS also provides feedback to the organisation's conventional

IDS regarding the anomaly that has been discovered, as shown in figure 4. This feedback informs the conventional IDS of the general time period that the attack occurred within and the network credentials that were used to perform the attack.

The conventional IDS has detailed log files of the network requests at its disposal to analyse and uncover the exact details of the attack and the attacker. The system administrator will also be able to instruct the conventional IDS to "zoom-in" on a specific time period within these log files (as specified by the information from the SCIDS). The search can be further refined by filtering out only the network requests associated with the specific user ID (again, as obtained from the SCIDS feedback information). Depending on the size of the network, log files typically have large amounts of entries, in the order of millions for large networks. Depending on the duration of the attack, the refined search of the log files could narrow down the enquiry to less than a few hundred entries that need to be analysed. This significantly smaller quantity of log file entries would make the job of applying vulnerability assessment tools and analysing the data to determine the damage that the attack has caused much easier for the conventional IDS.

At every log-on the SCIDS examines the user network behaviour profile to detect whether or not an attack has occurred, the same way a passive IDS would. However, the fact that the SCIDS can effectively isolate the time period during which an attack might have occurred, simultaneously reduces the time required to discover an attack and accelerates the reaction time required to respond. Hence, the SCIDS is defined as a semi-passive, anomaly-based IDS. Semi-passive because it does not detect attacks in real-time, but it actively decreases the time between discovery of the attack and response to the attack. Anomaly-based because, as explained in the previous section, the SCIDS discovers attacks in the same manner as an anomaly-based IDS: by looking for anomalies between the user network behaviour profile created by the SCIDS and the conventional IDS.

The following section compares the advantages and disadvantages of the SCIDS with a conventional IDSs.

5 Smart Card-based IDS versus Conventional IDSs

The smart card-based IDS (SCIDS) proposed in this paper is ideally suited to monitor network requests within an organisation and whether an employee's network credentials—such as user ID and password—have been stolen by discovering anomalies within the network requests. It is difficult for conventional IDSs to discover an attack disguised with a stolen network credential, as generally, network requests from users within the organisation should be trusted.

However, the SCIDS is not a complete IDS solution in itself, but rather compliments the entire IDS environment. For example, the SCIDS is unable to discover attacks that originate from either, other internal users or from outside the organisation. Nor is it able to discover an attack perpetrated without the use of network credentials. For example, if attacker *A* initiates a Denial-of-Service (DoS) attack on the SMTP server by flooding it with email messages—an attack that can be performed without the use of network credentials—no SCIDS would have detected it. Nor can a SCIDS discover an attack on the system if the attacker is actually a legitimate user with the organisation.

For example, assume user *B*, using his own network credentials, is able to attack the system and access information that he does not have privileged rights to access. His SCIDS is not able to discover this type of an attack because it will not discover any anomalies between the network behaviour recorded by the SCIDS and the conventional IDS, as would be the case if user *B's* network credential was stolen.

Even though a conventional IDS would be required to discover and handle such attacks, in user *B's* case, the SCIDS could prove that he perpetrated the attack. Once the conventional IDS has discovered the attack and traced it back to user *B*, he will not be able to use the theft of his network credentials as a defence. This is because the SCIDS has recorded the same network behaviour as the conventional IDS and did not detect any anomalies—verifying the conventional IDS's suspicions that user *B* committed the attacks.

6 Conclusion

The smart card-based IDS model proposed in this paper addressed the capacity problems and inefficiencies IDSs face due to the volume of network requests that need to be analysed and the complexities of implementing an anomaly-based IDS. The SCIDS is able to achieve Distributed Analysis by having a single IDS monitor the network requests of a single user. The SCIDS achieves Base-line Reduction by creating a single base-line for each user and, hence, reduces the complexity of anomaly detections. Finally, the SCIDS is able to achieve Attack-time Isolation by determining the general time period during which an attack occurred and, as a result, increase the efficiency with which attacks can be discovered and handled. Overall, the SCIDS has been shown to complement the conventional IDS environment rather than being a full-blown solution.

There are clear privacy issues that arise once a conventional IDS can generate individual user profiles from data stored in the organisation's log files. These issues need to be addressed by future work and a balance between acceptable levels of privacy and the necessary levels of IDS efficiency achieved.

7 Acknowledgement

This material is based upon work supported by the National Research Foundation under grant number 2054024. Any opinion, findings, conclusions or recommendations expressed in this material are those of the authors and the NRF does not accept any liability thereto.

References

1. Dorothy E. Denning. An intrusion-detection model. *IEEE Transactions on Software Engineering*, SE-13(2):222–232, February 1987.
2. Biswanath Mukherjee, L. Todd Herlein, and Karl N. Levitt. Network intrusion detection. *Network, IEEE*, 8(3):26–41, May 1994.
3. Wenbao Jiang, Hua Song, and Yiqi Dai. Real-time intrusion detection for high-speed networks. *Computers & security*, 24:287–294, 2005.
4. R.D. Alexander. The search for a general theory of behaviour. *Behavioural Science*, 20(2):77–100, 1975.
5. Craig B. Stanford. The social behaviour of chimpanzees and bonobos: Empirical evidence and shifting assumptions. *Current Anthropology*, 39:399–420, August 1998.
6. S. C. Cheung and J. Kramer. An integrated method for effective behaviour analysis of distributed systems. In *ICSE '94: Proceedings of the 16th International Conference on Software Engineering*, pages 309–320, Los Alamitos, CA, USA, 1994. IEEE Computer Society Press.
7. Hiroaki Kitano, Minoru Asada, Yasuo Kuniyoshi, Itsuki Noda, and Eiichi Osawa. Robocup: The robot world cup initiative. In *AGENTS '97: Proceedings of the first international conference on Autonomous agents*, pages 340–347, New York, NY, USA, 1997. ACM Press.
8. A. Kerepesi, E. Kubinyi, G.K. Jonsson, M.S. Magnussin, and Á. Miklósi. Behavioural comparison of human-animal (dog) and human-robot (aibo) interactions. *Behavioural Science*, 20(2):77–100, 1975.
9. Andreas Fuchsberger. Intrusion detection systems and intrusion prevention systems. *Information Security Technical Report*, 10:134–139, 2005.
10. John Wilander and Mariam Kamkar. A comparison of publicly available tools for static intrusion prevention. In *Proceedings of the 7th Nordic Workshop on Secure IT Systems*, pages 68–84, Karlstad, Sweden, November 2002.
11. Roberto Battistoni, Emanuele Gabrielli, and Luigi V. Mancini. A host intrusion prevention system for windows operating systems. *Lecture Notes in Computer Science*, 3193:352–368, 2004.
12. Mike Hendry. *Smart Card Security and Applications.* Artech House, April 2001.
13. Efraim Turban and Debbie McElroy. Using smart cards in electronic commerce. *International Journal of Information Management*, 18(1):61–72, February 1998.
14. Sebastian Münscher. Smartcard security. Technical report, NamITech, Giesecke & Devrient, November 2004.
15. Mauro Cesar Bernardes and Edson dos Santos Moreira. Implementation of an intrusion detection system based on mobile agents. In *Software Engineering for Parallel and Distributed Systems, 2000. Proceedings*, pages 158–164, 2000.

A Survey of Bots Used for Distributed Denial of Service Attacks

Vrizlynn L. L. Thing, Morris Sloman, and Naranker Dulay
Department of Computing, Imperial College London,
180 Queen's Gate, SW7 2AZ, London, United Kingdom.
{vlt, mss, nd}@doc.ic.ac.uk
WWW home page: http://www.doc.ic.ac.uk

Abstract. In recent years, we have seen the arrival of Distributed Denial-of-Service (DDoS) open-source bot-based attack tools facilitating easy code enhancement, and so resulting in attack tools becoming more powerful. Developing new techniques for detecting and responding to the latest DDoS attacks often entails using attack traces to determine attack signatures and to test the techniques. However, obtaining actual attack traces is difficult, because the high-profile organizations that are typically attacked will not release monitored data as it may contain sensitive information. In this paper, we present a detailed study of the source code of the popular DDoS attack bots, Agobot, SDBot, RBot and Spybot to provide an in-depth understanding of the attacks in order to facilitate the design of more effective and efficient detection and mitigation techniques.

1 Introduction

In recent years, professionalism in Internet crime has advanced with the aid of open source attack tools, higher bandwidth connections and higher processing power of desktop workstations. Distributed Denial-of-Service (DDoS) attacks on high profile organizations are becoming prevalent and have received considerable media attention [1, 2]. A recent survey [3] of 36 tier 1, tier 2 and hybrid IP network operators in North America, Europe and Asia indicated that DDoS attacks remain the foremost concern for the large network operators, with 64% indicating that DDoS attacks are the most significant operational security issue they face.

Lately, DDoS attacks have been used by extortionists and business rivals against websites of banking and financial companies, online gambling firms, web retailers and government [4-8] to cripple their operations. These attacks are launched from a large pool of compromised computers in homes, education, business and government organizations. These compromised computers, referred to as bots, typically connect automatically to a remote Internet Relay Chat (IRC) server to enable remote control

Please use the following format when citing this chapter:

Thing, V., Sloman, M., and Dulay, N., 2007, in IFIP International Federation for Information Processing, Volume 232, New Approaches for Security, Privacy and Trust in Complex Environments, eds. Venter, H., Eloff, M., Labuschagne, L., Eloff, J., von Solms, R., (Boston: Springer), pp. 229–240.

by the attacker to form a *botnet* [9, 10]. Botnets are used for generating spam emails, viruses, worms as well as DDoS attacks.

In the past, typical botnet sizes were as large as hundreds of thousands [11, 12], but, a recent report [13] has shown botnets to have "slimmed" down to an average of 20,000 in order to be less visible and make detection more difficult. It also showed that blacklisted or worn-out botnets were being resold for DDoS attacks as these did not use email or viruses and so would not be caught by the blacklists or signature-based antivirus products. A relatively small botnet comprising a few thousand bots can seriously damage a victim's website or server as their combined bandwidth (e.g. 1000 x each uplink bandwidth of 128kbps = 125 Mbps) can be higher than the Internet connection bandwidth of many corporate systems.

Developing new techniques for detecting and responding to DDoS attacks often entails using attack traces to determine attack signatures and to test the techniques. However, obtaining actual attack traces can be very difficult, particularly for the latest attacks, because the high-profile organizations which are typically attacked will not release monitored data as it may contain sensitive information. In addition, they often do not want to publicly admit to being attacked as this can damage their reputation. Analysis of the way bots behave in terms of the types of attacks they can generate, how they generate data within an attack message, the target port addresses they attack, how they generate legitimate or spoofed source addresses, can be used to formulate attack signatures and anomaly detection algorithms.

In this paper, we present a detailed study of the source code of the popular DDoS attack bots. The availability of open source for bots and their modular design has led to thousands of variants of the popular ones which require very frequent updates of signature based anti-virus products to try to prevent infections and can outwit signature-based attack detection techniques. Analyzing the attack tools based on their source code enables a more in-depth understanding and presents a clearer picture of the attacks rather than studying the attack traces. We obtained the bot source code from hacker web and forum sites. We also discuss the implications of our findings on well-known DDoS mitigation techniques and emphasize the need to acquire an understanding of the attacks before being able to design and develop more effective and efficient mitigation techniques.

Section 2 of the paper presents the related work discussing botnets. In Section 3, we describe 4 popular DDoS bots, namely Agobot, SDBot, RBot and Spybot. In Section 4, we discuss our findings and the implications on DDoS mitigation techniques. Section 5 concludes the paper.

2 Related Work

The evolution of botnets has resulted in them becoming the latest most prevalent threat on the Internet and so has resulted in significant research in the network security community to develop detection and response techniques.

A Symantec white paper [14] discusses the design, coding and structure of the source code of popular bots and looks at how they have evolved with enhancement in network propagation, communication encryption and polymorphism. Observations on botnet activities, collected using Honeypots and mwcollect is described in [15]. 180 botnets were tracked over 5 months to observe the coordinated activities within the botnets. Preventive mechanisms by identification of the activities and infiltration of the botnets to stop their operations, are proposed. In [16], an overview of the origins and structure of botnets is presented. It used data from the Internet Motion Sensor project [17] and Honeypot [18] to demonstrate the dangers of botnets due to their increase in number and their ability to exploit common system vulnerabilities such as the DCOM RPC [19] and LSASS [20]. Botnet detection by correlating data to pinpoint bots and botnet communications is also discussed. In [21], the authors studied the source code of popular bots and classified them according to their design and implementation characteristics, commands and control protocol, mechanisms to manipulate bots, propagation mechanisms, available vulnerabilities exploit, malware delivery mechanisms, obfuscation and detection evasion mechanisms. However, we could not find any existing reports providing a thorough understanding of the inner working and characteristics of the DDoS attack tools used in bots. Therefore, we conduct an in-depth study on these tools in this paper.

3 DDoS Bots

We studied the DDoS source code of 4 popular bots, namely Agobot, SDBot, RBot and Spybot [22-24] and present the details of the attacks in this section. These botnets have a few hundred to thousand variants due to multiple authors working to enhance the exploitation, propagation and communication code. We chose the version with the most advanced DDoS attack tools.

3.1 Agobot

Agobot is one of the most popular bots with the Anti-Virus vendor, Sophos [24], listing over 600 different versions. Variants of Agobot include Gaobot, Nortonbot, Phatbot and Polybot. The source code that we studied is the widely available "current" version of Phatbot, written in C++ and provides cross platform capabilities. The bot is structured in a modular way and allows new attacks to be easily added. Of all the bots studied, this has the most comprehensive set of DDoS attack tools, with the following attack commands:

- ddos.synflood <host> <time> <delay> <port>
- ddos.udpflood <host> <port> <time> <delay>
- ddos.httpflood <url> <number> <referrer> <delay> <recursive>
- ddos.phatsyn <host> <time> <delay> <port>
- ddos.phaticmp <host> <time> <delay>
- ddos.phatwonk <host> <time> <delay>
- ddos.targa3 <host> <time>
- ddos.stop

In all the above attacks, host is the IP address of the victim, time is the duration of the attack in secs, delay is the interval in msecs between sending attack packets, and port is the victim's destination port. Other dynamic or attack specific parameters are presented as follows.

In the synflood attack, if port = 0, a random port number from 1000 to 10000 will be generated for each attack packet, otherwise, the one provided will be used. In the IP header, the identification (ID) field is set to 1 and the Time-to-Live (TTL) to 128. In the TCP header, the SYN flag is set and the window size is set to 16384. The TCP sequence number for each attack packet is formed by performing a binary OR on 2 32-bit randomly generated numbers (with one been left shifted by 16 bits). For each attack packet sent, each byte of the source IP address is randomly generated from 0 to 255 and the source port is randomly generated from 1000 to 2000.

In the udpflood attack, if port = 0, the destination port number will be randomly generated from 1 to 65535 for every attack packet. The 2-byte network prefix (i.e. x1.x2) of the source IP address (i.e. x1.x2.x3.x4) is initialized to that of the attacking node (i.e. local address y1.y2.y3.y4) or "255.255" if an error occurs while retrieving the local address. y2, y3 and y4 of the local address are stored in 3 counters and incremented in nested loops for each packet. The counter for y4 is incremented and reset to 1 after 254 and the counter for y3 is incremented. The counter for y3 is reset to 0 after 254 and the counter for y2 is incremented (also reset to 0 after 254 is reached). The above mentioned process is used to generate x2 of the source IP address. x1, which is equal to y1 remains the same for all the packets. x3 and x4 of the source IP address are randomly generated from 0 to 253 and 1 to 253, respectively. The data portion of the packet is 256 bytes and is filled with the character 'A'. The attack packet source port is a random number from 1000 to 2000.

In the httpflood attack, url is the web address to be accessed and number is the number of requests to be made to the specified address. Referrer is provided by the attacker and used in the http request. If the delay = 0, a random delay in the range of 1 msec to 24 hours is generated at the end of each cycle of a request (including recursive requests) for a URL. If recursive = 0, only the URL is accessed, otherwise, a recursive request on the page's resources is performed.

In the phatsyn attack, the destination port number is randomized from 0 to 65535 for each attack packet if the one provided is 0. The SYN and URG flags in the TCP header are set. For each attack packet, the ID and TTL fields in the IP header are randomly generated from 1024 to 65535 and 200 to 255, respectively, while the TCP source port, ACK number, window size and URP (offset for computing sequence number of last byte of urgent data) field are randomly generated from 0 to 65535. The TCP sequence number is formed by adding 2 randomly generated numbers from 0 to 65535 with one number left shifted by 8 bits. The 2-byte network prefix of the source IP address is set to that of the victim's, while the lower 2 bytes are randomly generated from 1 to 254 for each attack packet.

In the phaticmp attack, the destination port is hard-coded to 0. For each attack packet, the Type-of-Service (TOS), ID, more fragmentations, total length and TTL fields in the IP header are set to 4, 1234, 1, 0 and 255, respectively. The type and code fields in the ICMP header are randomly generated from 0 to 17 and 0 to 14, respectively. The 2-byte network prefix of the source IP address is set to that of the victim's, while the lower 2 bytes are randomly generated from 1 to 254.

In the phatwonk attack, 28 victim's ports (i.e. 1025, 21, 22, 23, 25, 53, 80, 81, 88, 110, 113, 119, 135, 137, 139, 143, 443, 445, 1024, 1433, 1500, 1720, 3306, 3389,

5000, 6667, 8000, 8080) are scanned to discover open ones. The port numbers of the open ports are placed in an array of size 28. The destination port to be used in the entire attack is chosen from the array of open ports or randomly generated if any of the entries is 0. The selection process ends after 28 iterations or when the attack duration time has expired, whichever happens first. 1 TCP SYN packet and 1023 TCP ACK packets are sent to the victim per inner loop for the attack duration. The TOS, ID and TTL fields in the IP header are set to 8, a random number from 1024 to 65535, and 255, respectively, each time the outer loop is run. In each run, the most significant 2 bytes of the source IP address are randomly generated from 1 to hexadecimal FFFE and the least significant 2 bytes are set to that of the victim's IP address. Assume that x1.x2.x3.x4 represents the IP address, then, x1.x2 remains the same as the victim's IP address while x3 ranges from 1 to 254 and x4 ranges from 0 to 255. The source port, window size, sequence number and data offset fields in the TCP header are set to a random number from 0 to 65535, 16384, an addition of 2 random numbers from 0 to 65535 with one been left shifted by 8 bits, and 5, respectively, for each run of the outer loop. In the inner loop, the IP ID field and the TCP sequence number are incremented for each of the 1024 attack packets.

In the targa3 attack, the destination port number is set to 666. The IP header protocol field and fragmentation offset field are randomly chosen from a set of 14 (i.e. 0, 1, 2, 4, 6, 8, 12, 17, 22, 41, 58, 255, random number from 0 to 254) and 10 integers (i.e. 0, 0, 0, 8192, 4, 6, 16383, 1, random number from 0 to 8099), respectively, for each packet sent. The last integer in each array is randomly generated. The source IP address has the 24-bit network prefix set to that of the attacking node. The last byte of the address is randomly generated from 0 to 254. The TOS, ID and TTL fields in the IP header are set to 4, a randomly generated number from 0 to RAND_MAX (based on the compiler) and 255, respectively.

Lastly, the stop command allows the synflood, udpflood and httpflood attacks to be stopped if they are running.

3.2 SDBot

SDBot is another popular bot with over 1800 variants. The widely available version is 0.5b, but only comes with ping and udp flooding tools, whereas the "SYN Flood Edition" includes TCP SYN flooding attacks. SDBot is written in C++ and targets Windows systems. The DDoS commands are as follow:

- udp <host> <number> <packet size> <delay> <port>
- ping <host> <number> <packet size> <delay>
- syn <host> <port> <time>

In the above attacks, host is the victim IP address, number is the number of attack packets to send, packet size is the size of each attack packet in bytes, delay is the interval in msecs between every attack packet sent and is set to 1 if < 1, port is the victim's destination port number and time is the duration of the attack in secs.

In the udp attack, the code restricts the port number to be from 1 to 65535. The data contents in the packets are filled with randomly generated bytes from 0 to 254. The actual size of the packet is randomized by subtracting a random number ranging from 0 to 9 from the packet size parameter provided, for each attack packet.

In the ping attack, the ICMP.DLL API is used. The ICMP Echo Request messages are used as the attack packets. The packet size is restricted to be ≤ 65535.

In the syn attack, the bot's registry entries and executables are removed from the system if a syn attack fails and the REMOVE_NONSYNNERS macro is defined. However, it is commented out of the code. The source IP address is initialized by adding the victim's address (as unsigned long integer) to 256 and a random number from 0 to 511. The ID and TTL fields in the IP header are set to 1 and 128, respectively. The SYN flag is set in the TCP header and the window size is set to 16384. For each attack packet, the source IP address is incremented by 1 and the TCP source port is randomly generated from 1000 to 2000. The TCP sequence number is formed by performing a binary OR on 2 randomly generated numbers (with one been left shifted by 16 bits).

3.3 RBot

RBot has over 1600 variants. It is also written in C++ and targets Windows systems. The version we studied is the one with the LSASS exploit and master password for scanning and compromising Optix servers. The DDoS commands include:

- ddos.syn/ddos.ack/ddos.random <host> <port> <time>
- synflood/syn <host> <port> <time>
- tcpflood/tcp <type> <host> <port> <time> [-r]
- icmpflood/Icmp <host> <time> [-r]
- pingflood/ping <host> <number> <size> <delay>
- udpflood/udp <host> <number> <size> <delay> <port>

In the above attacks, host, port, time, number, and delay have the same meaning as for the SDBot, size is the size of each attack packet in bytes, and if the optional parameter 'r' is provided, source IP address spoofing is used.

The ddos.syn, ddos.ack and ddos.random attacks exist in the same code module. For the ddos.syn attack, the ACK number in the TCP header is set to 0 and the SYN flag is set. For the ddos.ack attack, the ACK number in the TCP header is set to 0 and the ACK flag is also set. For the ddos.random attack, the ACK number in the TCP header is set to a random number from 0 to 2 and the SYN or ACK flag is set based on a probability of 0.5. In the attack packets, the ID and TTL fields in the IP header are set to 1 and 128, respectively. The source IP address is initialized by adding the victim's address (in the unsigned long integer format) to 256 and a random number from 0 to 511. It is then incremented by 1 for each packet. The TCP source port is randomized from 1000 to 2000 and the sequence number is formed by performing a binary OR on 2 randomly generated numbers (with one been left shifted by 16 bits). The TCP window size is set to 16384.

The synflood or syn attack code is based on the one in SDBot. However, the non-synners remover code is not implemented here.

In the tcpflood or tcp attack, the parameter type allows the attacker to specify a "syn", "ack" or "random" TCP attack. It has the same settings of flag and ACK number based on the attack type as in the ddos.syn/ddos.ack/ddos.random attacks. The ID and TTL fields in the IP header are set to 1 and 128, respectively. If the parameter 'r' is used, source address spoofing is performed. Otherwise, the real source address of the attacking host will be used. The spoofed source IP address is generated by adding 4 randomly generated numbers with the 2nd, 3rd and 4th number left shifted by 8, 16 and 24 bits, respectively. Each number is in the range of 0 to RAND_MAX. The TCP source port is randomized from 0 to 1024 and the sequence number is set to the hexadecimal number 12345678. The TCP destination port is randomized from 0 to 1024 if port = 0. The TCP window size is set to 512.

In the icmpflood or icmp attack, the source IP address is generated similarly to that in the above tcpflood/tcp attack. The destination port is set to 0. The ID and TTL fields in the IP header are set to 1 and 128, respectively. For each attack packet, the ICMP type and code are random numbers from 0 to 255. The ICMP ID number is randomly generated from 1 to 240, and the ICMP sequence number is set to 1. The data portion is filled with bytes randomly generated from 0 to 254.

The pingflood or ping attack code is based on the one in the SDBot, and is similar in characteristics and functions used (i.e. ICMP.DLL API).

The udpflood or udp attack is similar to the one in the SDBot.

3.4 Spybot

Spybot is written in C and also affects Windows systems. It has over 200 variants currently and the version we studied is 2.0. It has more spreading abilities than the original version written by the author known as Mich. The DDoS commands are:

- syn <host> <port> <delay> <number>
- spoofdsyn <host> <port> <delay> <number>
- ping <host> <port> <delay> <number>

In the above attacks, the parameters have the same meaning as for the SDBot.

In the syn attack, socket connections are made to the victim and closed after the connection attempts and delay is forced to a minimum of 5 msec. The source IP address is not spoofed and the source port is randomly generated by the system.

In the spoofdsyn attack, delay is forced to a minimum of 5 msec. The ID and TTL fields in the IP header are set to 1 and 128, respectively. For each packet, each byte of the source IP address is randomized from 0 to 254. The SYN flag is set in the TCP header and the window size is set to 16384. The TCP source port is randomly generated from 1000 to 2000. The TCP sequence number is formed by performing a binary OR on 2 randomly generated numbers (with one been left shifted by 16 bits).

In the ping attack, the ICMP.DLL API is used. ICMP Echo Request messages are used as the attack packets. The destination port number is set to 65500 if greater and delay is forced to a minimum of 1 msec. Each byte of the data is set to the integer 37.

4 Analysis and Discussions

4.1 Bot Features

Most of the tools provide source IP address spoofing (either in whole or in part) and randomization of the source ports, destination ports, other header fields such as the

TCP sequence number, and the data contents of the attack packets. With a high degree of randomization, it makes mitigation such as dropping the traffic difficult due to the problem of accurately identifying the signature or pattern of the attack packets. However, if there is no restriction on the randomization of fields, this will result in more anomaly values appearing and so easing the detection of the presence of attacks. For example, performing partial source IP address spoofing reduces the randomness of the attack packets. However, if the addresses produced are within the safe range of legitimate addresses, this will reduce the chance of triggering a defense alarm mechanism. On the other hand, randomization without restrictions of destination port numbers or IP protocol types would raise alarms due to obvious anomalies such as hitting closed ports or unassigned network services. Thus, a high degree of randomization eases detection of the presence of an ongoing attack (e.g. through packet sampling). However, mitigation by means of checking the validity of each individual packet and dropping them are more difficult without a common identifiable signature.

All the attack tools that perform source IP address spoofing have different ways of forming the address from the randomly generated numbers. However, all of them prevent setting the final byte to 255 which will translate to a broadcast address. Source port randomization, though provided, is not really necessary as it will be randomly generated anyway if socket binding is not performed. Ranges of destination port numbers generated include 1000 to 10000, 0 to 65535, and 1 to 65535. However, some of these ports are still unassigned with only 0 to 1023 in the "Well-known ports" range. Therefore, most of these ports will most likely be closed at the victim. Randomization of the IP identification and fragmentation offset fields are most likely used to deter mitigation. However, it is not very useful since providing a value of 0 would allow the attack traffic to mix in well with the legitimate traffic as most Internet traffic does not require fragmentation. IP Time-to-Live field randomization could hide the actual hop counts traversed by the packets though it is not particularly useful since hop counts could not reveal the exact location of the attacking host anyway.

Agobot, SDBot and RBot all support SYN flood attacks, but RBot's ddos.random attack is the most dangerous SYN attack tool as it can randomly generate SYN and ACK packets thereby circumventing mitigation techniques which try to correlate TCP SYN and ACK according to the protocol characteristics. Next in line would be Agobot's ddos.phatsyn as it set the URG flag which allows the packet to have a high priority. When the TCP/IP stack at the server sees a packet with the URG flag set, it is duty bound to stop what it is doing and immediately send this packet to the server. RBot's ddos.syn and SDBot/RBot's syn simply provide standard SYN packets flooding with partially spoofed source IP address and randomized sequence numbers. The last five tools are Agobot's ddos.synflood and Spybot's spoofdsyn, which spoofs all 4 bytes of the source IP addresses, RBot's tcpflood syn and random, which fixes the TCP sequence number for all the packets to hexadecimal number 12345678, and Spybot's syn, which performs connection and disconnection attempts of sockets and does not provide source IP address spoofing.

For the UDP flood tools, we have the Agobot's ddos.udpflood and SDBot/RBot's udp. However, Agobot's ddos.udpflood filled its data with the character 'A' which simiplifies signature-based detection. SDBot/RBot's udp tool randomized its data but only during initialization. It also randomizes its packet size but it has no source IP address spoofing. It is possible that future versions will combine the advantageous features of both tools while also randomizing the data contents for each attack packet which would make detection difficult.

For the ICMP flood tools, we have the Agobot ddos.phaticmp and RBot icmpflood. Agobot's ddos.phaticmp is slightly superior to RBot's as it limits its ICMP type spoofing from 0 to 17 and code spoofing from 0 to 14, instead of 0 to 255 in RBot. The Type-of-Service flag is set to 4 for route selection to maximize throughput if supported. In ICMP, type 1, 2 and 7 are not assigned and most types have no code at all. Spoofing an invalid type or type/code combination would therefore trigger the DDoS detection alarm. However, the chance of Agobot triggering an alarm is less than for RBot due to its type and code spoofing restrictions, though attack signature-based detection is slightly easier for Agobot due to this restriction and the fact that the identification field is fixed to the value of 1234.

SDBot/RBot and Spybot ping tools simply provide ICMP Echo Request messages flooding. It does not have any source IP address spoofing capability and is similar in function to a common ping, though Spybot's is distinguishable from its data contents which have the value 37. Agobot is the only one with HTTP requests flooding tool to emulate legitimate requests of resources from web servers. Source IP address spoofing is not used since information of subsequent resources to be retrieved has to be known to continue the recursive attacks. It also makes the attack indistinguishable from legitimate requests.

Agobot's ddos.phatwonk attack has the advantage of scanning for a list of ports to check if they are open before attempting to flood it with SYN and ACK packets. However, a balance of 0.5 probability of generating either SYN or ACK packets would reduce anomalies rather than the 1 SYN followed by 1023 ACK packets for each round of flooding. In Agobot's targa3 attack, the destination port is set to 666, which is the designated port for a popular multiplayer PC game, Doom. However, the list of IP protocol types to use will raise anomalies as only the TCP and UDP network services are typically supported for port 666. RBot's ddos.ack and tcpflood ack attack tools simply flood the victim with TCP ACK packets. However, RBot's tcpflood ack has the same disadvantage as its tcpflood syn and random whereby the TCP sequence number is set to hexadecimal number 12345678.

The main purpose of the above analysis and discussion is not to advise on how to enhance attack tools to circumvent current mitigation techniques, but to raise the awareness to the network security research community that making changes to improve on the attack tools is possible and easy. When designing and developing network security products, we have to bear in mind the need to foresee the future attacks that the attackers would be able to come up with to "challenge" the mitigation techniques and systems.

4.2 Implications on Mitigation Techniques

We see that source IP address spoofing remains a security issue. Although it could be postulated that since bots are used in current DDoS attacks, tracing the source of attack does not lead to the attack controller, so source spoofing is not really needed. However, managing bots is not an easy task for attackers and often attackers maintain ownership of their botnets to rent out for fees. Therefore, they want to make sure the bots are not traced and neutralized. Thus, source address spoofing is still used in the DDoS attack tools to deter detection. Ingress filtering removes any traffic from a customer site to the Internet which has invalid source addresses i.e. not within the range allocated to the customer. Egress filtering on traffic from the Internet to a customer site discards traffic with "illegitimate" source addresses such as private/reserved IP addresses or addresses within the domain of the customer site. Although ingress and egress filtering [25, 26] is performed, it is not universally applied and so does not completely prevent DDoS attacks with spoofed source addresses. In addition some attack tools circumvent this filtering by spoofing source addresses from within the network of the bot. [27] is a technique used to infer hop count information from the Time-to-Live value in the IP header to determine if source IP address spoofing has been performed and thus detect if the traffic is legitimate or not. However, in the case of internal source address spoofing, it would fail to tell the difference since the hop count would not differ greatly from the legitimate source. Backscatter analysis [28] also proves that source address spoofing is indeed still widely used in current attacks while [29] shows that spoofing remains a serious problem to Internet security.

In [30], a DDoS TCP SYN flooding detection mechanism, SYN-dog, was proposed based on the protocol behavior of the TCP SYN – SYN/ACK pairs to detect source IP address spoofing, which is used in TCP SYN flood attacks. The non-parametric Cumulative Sum (CUSUM) method [31] was applied to make the scheme insensitive to site and access pattern. SYN-dog was meant to be implemented near the flooding sources as with a spoofed source address, a TCP SYN packet sent out to a server would not result in receiving a SYN/ACK packet. However, we noticed in the attack source code that it is possible for attackers to send out randomized SYN or ACK packets, imitating the three-way handshake. Therefore, this mechanism will not work at the victim end as there is unlikely to be much variation in the number of SYN and ACK packets seen by the victim or within the network.

5 Conclusion

In this paper, we presented a detailed study of the functionalities of the popular DDoS attack bots, namely Agobot, SDBot RBot and Sybot. We found that analyzing the attack tools based on their source code to give an in-depth understanding of the attacks is better than studying attack traces which are difficult to obtain. The information presented on the attack tools can be used to design both detection and attack mitigation techniques.

One of the most important characteristics is the degree of randomization of addresses, protocol fields and data contents. Greater randomization can ease detection as more anomalies are generated but can make mitigation more difficult as specifying packet signatures for filtering becomes harder. We have also given a comparison between the attack tools in the bots and provided a view of possible enhancements on the tools in the foreseeable future.

We have shown that well-known DDoS mitigation techniques can be easily bypassed. For example, partial source IP address spoofing circumvents ingress and egress filtering and hop count filtering. Randomization of SYN and ACK packet generation makes some SYN flood detection mechanisms ineffective. Therefore, we see the need to acquire an understanding of the attacks before being able to design and develop more effective and efficient mitigation techniques.

As the modular design and open source nature make modifications and implementation of additional features easy for the bot authors, there will always be a race between the attackers, and network security providers to see who can be the most innovative. Therefore, it is important that network security products are able to get a grasp on the latest attack tools in use today and possibly in the future, and incorporate learning techniques and adaptive mechanisms to provide timely responses to the new variants of attack tools.

6 Acknowledgements

We gratefully acknowledge the support from the EU funded Diadem Distributed Firewall FP6 IST-2002-002154. This research is continuing through participation in the International Technology Alliance sponsored by the U.S. Army Research Laboratory and the U.K. Ministry of Defence.

7 References

1. Diane E. Levine and Gary C. Kessler, "Chapter 11 - Denial of Service Attacks, Computer Security Handbook, 4th Edition", Editors - Seymour Bosworth, Michel E. Kabay, 2002.
2. K. J. Houle and G. M. Weaver, "Trends in Denial of Service Attack Technology", Oct. 2001, CERT Coordination Center, http://www.cert.org/archive/pdf/DoS_trends.pdf.
3. Arbor Networks, "Worldwide ISP Security Report", Sept. 2005.
4. Federal Bureau of Investigation, "THE CASE OF THE HIRED HACKER: Entrepreneur and Hacker Arrested for Online Sabotage", http://www.fbi.gov/page2/april05/hiredhacker041805.htm, Apr. 2005.
5. Dawn Kawamoto, "Blackmailers try to black out Million Dollar Homepage", CNET News, http://news.zdnet.com/2100-1009_22-6028131.html, Jan. 2006.
6. BBC Technology News, "Hacker threats to bookies probed", http://news.bbc.co.uk/1/hi/technology/3513849.stm, Feb. 2004.
7. Ashlee Vance, "Man admits to eBay DDoS attack", http://www.theregister.co.uk/2005/12/28/ebay_bots_ddos/, Dec. 2005.
8. Jan Libbenga, "Dutch hackers sentenced for attack on government sites", The Register, http://www.theregister.co.uk/2005/03/16/dutch_hackers_sentenced/, Mar. 2005.
9. Basudev Saha and Ashish Gairola, "Botnet: An Overview", CERT-In White Paper, CIWP-2005-05, Jun. 2005.

10. Laurianne McLaughlin, "Bot Software Spreads, Causes New Worries", IEEE Distributed Systems Online, Jun. 2004.
11. Drew Cullen, "Dutch smash 100,000-strong zombie army", http://www.theregister.co.uk/2005/10/07/dutch_police_smash_zombie_network/, Oct. 2005.
12. Joris Evers, "'Bot herders' may have controlled 1.5 million PCs", ZDNet News, http://news.zdnet.com/2100-1009_22-5906896.html, Oct. 2005.
13. Dawn Kawamoto, "Bots slim down to get tough", CNET News, Nov. 2005.
14. John Canavan, "The Evolution of Malicious IRC Bots", Virus Bulletin Conference, Oct. 2005.
15. Felix C. Freiling, Thorsten Holz, and Georg Wicherski, "Botnet Tracking: Exploring a Root-Cause Methodology to Prevent Distributed Denial-of-Service Attacks", 10th European Symposium on Research in Computer Security (ESORICS 2005), Sept. 2005.
16. Evan Cooke, Farnam Jahanian, and Danny McPherson, "The Zombie Roundup: Understanding, Detecting, and Disrupting Botnets", USENIX SRUTI: Steps to Reducing Unwanted Traffic on the Internet Workshop, Jul. 2005.
17. Michael Bailey, et al., "The Internet Motion Sensor: A distributed blackhole monitoring system", Network and Distributed System Security Symposium (NDSS), Feb. 2005.
18. The Honeynet Project, "Know you enemy: Tracking botnets", https://www.honeynet.org/papers/bots/, Mar. 2005.
19. Microsoft, "DCOM RPC vulnerability", http://www.microsoft.com/technet/security/bulletin/MS03-026.mspx, Jul. 2003.
20. Microsoft, "LSASS vulnerability", http://www.microsoft.com/technet/security/bulletin/MS04-011.mspx, Apr. 2004.
21. Paul Barford and Vinod Yegneswaran, "An Inside Look at Botnets", To appear in Series - Advances in Information Security, Springer, 2006.
22. McAfee Threat Center, http://vil.nai.com.
23. Symantec, http://www.symantec.com.
24. Sophos, http://www.sophos.com.
25. T. Killalea, "Recommended Internet Service Provider Security Services and Procedures", IETF BCP 46, RFC 3013, Nov. 2000.
26. P. Ferguson and D. Senie, "Network Ingress Filtering: Defeating Denial of Service Attacks which employ IP Source Address Spoofing", IETF BCP 38, RFC 2827, May 2000.
27. Cheng Jin, Haining Wang, and Kang G. Shin, "Hop-count filtering: an effective defense against spoofed DDoS traffic", 10th ACM Conference on Computer and Communications Security, Oct. 2003.
28. David Moore, et al., "Inferring Internet Denial-of-Service Activity", ACM Transactions on Computer System (TOCS), May 2006, **24**(2), pp. 115-139.
29. Robert Beverly and Steven Bauer, "The Spoofer Project: Inferring the Extent of Source Address Filtering on the Internet", USENIX SRUTI: Steps to Reducing Unwanted Traffic on the Internet Workshop, Jul. 2005.
30. Yu-Shun Wang, Danlu Zhang, and Kang G. Shin, "SYN-dog: Sniffing SYN Flooding Sources", 22nd IEEE International Conference on Distributed Computing Systems, Jul. 2002.
31. B. E. Brodsky and B. S. Darkhovsky, *"Nonparametric Methods in Change-point Problems"*. 1993: Kluwer Academic Publishers.

A Hybrid PKI-IBC Based Ephemerizer System

Srijith K. Nair[1], Mohammad T. Dashti[2],
Bruno Crispo[1 3], and Andrew S. Tanenbaum[1]

[1] Dept. Computer Science, Vrije Universiteit, Amsterdam, The Netherlands
{srijith,crispo,ast}@few.vu.nl
[2] CWI, Amsterdam, The Netherlands
dashti@cwi.nl
[3] DTI, University of Trento, Italy

Abstract. The concept of an Ephemerizer system has been introduced in earlier works as a mechanism to ensure that a file deleted from the persistent storage remains unrecoverable. The principle involved storing the data in an encrypted form in the user's machine and the key to decrypt the data in a physically separate machine. However the schemes proposed so far do not provide support for fine-grained user settings on the lifetime of the data nor support any mechanism to check the integrity of the system that is using the secret data. In addition we report the presence of a vulnerability in one version of the proposed scheme that can be exploited by an attacker to nullify the ephemeral nature of the keys. We propose and discuss in detail an alternate Identity Based cryptosystem powered scheme that overcomes the identified limitations of the original system.

1 Introduction

Privacy concerns have brought the question of reliable deletion of private data into sharp focus. One of the most effective tools used in privacy invasion is data recovery from persistent storage devices, even when the user had 'deleted' the data. To mitigate this risk, expensive secure hardware devices are sometimes used to keep information private and irrecoverable when deleted and extensive and meticulous process of erasure is followed to ensure that deleted files are indeed completely deleted. For example, US government specification calls for overwriting non-classified information three times [1]. Common users, however, do not have the resources nor the know-how to use these processes or equipments.

One of the techniques used to secure data is to encrypt the data on user's local storage device and to store the decryption key at a trusted remote storage. This way, both the local as well as the remote storage will have to be compromised before the data can be obtained. Furthermore, secure deletion of the decryption key renders the data unrecoverable. However, key management becomes a complicated issue in this approach. As a solution, Perlman [2] introduced the concept of an *Ephemerizer server* which is entrusted with the duty

Please use the following format when citing this chapter:

Nair, S., Dashti, M., Crispo, B., and Tanenbaum, A., 2007, in IFIP International Federation for Information Processing, Volume 232, New Approaches for Security, Privacy and Trust in Complex Environments, eds. Venter, H., Eloff, M., Labuschagne, L., Eloff, J., von Solms, R., (Boston: Springer), pp. 241–252.

to manage the availability and secure deletion of the keys used in decryption of the encrypted data.

To formulate the problem more precisely, assume that Alice wants to send a message M to her confidant Bob at time t_0 with following expectations: (1) only Bob will be able to read the plaintext and (2) after time t_1 ($t_1 > t_0$), no one including Bob can read the plaintext. Bob is assumed to be non-malicious and a willing party in the exchange, but is not trusted to have the capability to securely delete the message after t_1. An attacker, who wants to gain knowledge of the message exchanged, is assumed to have the capability to break into the computer system of any ordinary user and seize all equipments, extract any data from persistent storage that is presently stored or previously deleted or kept encrypted, including forcing the user to disclose passwords used to secure decryption keys. We also assume an open communication medium in which all transmissions can be intercepted, recorded, modified, and retransmitted.

We describe the basic working of the original Ephemerizer system, as proposed in [2], in Section 2 and then explain in detail one of the proposed versions of the scheme. We show the existence of a vulnerability in this protocol, which allows an attacker to subvert the ephemeral nature of the system. We also identify some shortcomings associated with the scheme, which we consider to be crucial for the security of the system. We then propose a modified Ephemerizer scheme based on Identity Based Public Key Cryptography (IB-PKC). As far as we are aware of, the scheme proposed in this paper is one of the very few systems that exploit the power of IB-PKC, without suffering the associated disadvantages. The cryptography primitive is briefly explained in Section 3 while the proposed scheme is presented in Section 4. In Section 5 the security aspects of the proposed scheme is discussed in detail and we show that our scheme can support richer security features than the original scheme. We conclude in Section 6.

2 The Ephemerizer System

The Ephemerizer as proposed in [2] acts as a central server that allows parties to keep data private for a finite time period and then make it unrecoverable after that. Alice and Bob executes the protocol steps with the participation of this trusted third party. This concept was later used in a system designed to provide assured delete [3].

The underlying idea behind the scheme's working is that Alice would send the message to Bob encrypted with a key that needs to be fetched from the Ephemerizer. The Ephemerizer would check for the expiry date associated with the key's usage before responding to the request from Bob. The original paper presented two versions of the scheme - one using triple decryption and the other using blind decryption. We discuss the triple decryption method in detail next since our analysis has identified an attack against this version of the protocol, which is presented later in Section 2.2.

2.1 Triple Encryption Method

Throughout the rest of the paper, we use $\{M\}_{K_A}$ to denote asymmetric key encryption of M with public key of entity A and $[M]_K$ to denote symmetric key encryption of M with symmetric key K. We assume the existence of a trusted public key infrastructure (PKI) from which users can obtain certified public keys of other users.

Step 1 - The Ephemerizer E creates sets of asymmetric key pairs, associate them with different expiration time and advertises tuples - (public key, key ID, expiration time).

Step 2 - Alice chooses one of the keys, K_{eph}, based on the expiration time she requires, and encrypts the data M with a random secret key S to obtain $[M]_S$. She then encrypts S with Bob's long-term public key (K_{bob}) and the result with K_{eph}.The resulting value is encrypted again with a random session key T to get $[\{\{S\}_{K_{bob}}\}_{K_{eph}}]_T$. T is then encrypted with Bob's public key and an integrity check value [4] HMAC(T,$\{\{S\}_{K_{bob}}\}_{K_{eph}}$) is calculated. Finally, Alice sends the following to Bob:

$$A \rightarrow B : \{T\}_{K_{bob}} \quad [\{\{S\}_{K_{bob}}\}_{K_{eph}}]_T \quad [M]_S \ keyID \ K_{eph} \ HMAC(T \ \{\{S\}_{K_{bob}}\}_{K_{eph}})$$

Step 3 - Bob, on receiving this message, decrypts the first part of the ciphertext using his long term private key to obtain T and uses T to decrypt and obtain $\{\{S\}_{K_{bob}}\}_{K_{eph}}$. He then verifies the HMAC value and if this check is successful, chooses a random secret key J to secure his communication with the Ephemerizer, encrypts J using K_{eph} and sends the following to the Ephemerizer:

$$B \rightarrow E : keyID \ \{J\}_{K_{eph}} \quad [\{\{S\}_{K_{bob}}\}_{K_{eph}}]_J$$

Step 4 - The Ephemerizer identifies K_{eph} using *keyID*. If K_{eph} hasn't expired, the Ephemerizer uses it to decrypt and obtain J. Using K_{eph}'s private key and J, the Ephemerizer then decrypts the third part of the message to obtain $\{S\}_{K_{bob}}$ and uses J to re-encrypt the decrypted part and sends it back to Bob.

$$E \rightarrow B : [\{S\}_{K_{bob}}]_J$$

If K_{eph} has expired, Ephemerizer sends back an error message to Bob indicating the unavailability of the key.

Step 5 - Since Bob knows the value of J and his own long-term private key, he can then decrypt the message from E and retrieve the value of S which is then used to decrypt M_E to obtain M.

The Ephemerizer periodically scans its database of asymmetric key pairs and securely delete all key pairs that have an expired time value. Therefore, after the expiry of time t_1, no one will be able to recover the plaintext M if all the participants (Alice, Bob, and the Ephemerizer) have truthfully executed the protocol.

2.2 Attack Against Triple Encryption Scheme

Our analysis showed that the triple encryption version of the Ephemerizer scheme presented in [2] is susceptible to a serious oracle attack which can be exploited by an attacker to gain access to $\{S\}_{K_{bob}}$, in effect nullifying the ephemeral nature of the system. The attack plays out as follows.

The attacker captures the message sent between Bob and Ephemerizer in *Step 3* and *Step 4*. After identifying K_{eph} using $keyID$, it then generates a random key X and encrypts it with K_{eph}. The attacker encrypts the second part of the original message in *Step 3*, $\{J\}_{eph}$, with X and sends the whole message as shown below, to the Ephemerizer.

$$Att \rightarrow E : keyID\ \{X\}_{K_{eph}}\ [\{J\}_{K_{eph}}]_X$$

As long as this attack message is sent before the expiry of the key corresponding to $keyID$, the Ephemerizer cannot differentiate it from a genuine request from an user. Hence, it decrypts X using the private key of K_{eph} and using the relevant keys it decrypts the third part of the attack message to obtain J. This value of the random session key, used by Bob to encrypt his dialog with the Ephemerizer, is then sent back to the attacker.

$$E \rightarrow Att\ : [J]_X$$

Since X is known to the attacker, he can decrypt this message from the Ephemerizer and obtain J, which in turn can be used to decrypt the message sent to Bob in *Step 4* to get $\{S\}_{K_{bob}}$. Thus, the purpose served by the ephemeral key K_{eph} is completely nullified, since $\{S\}_{K_{bob}}$ is now known to the attacker and is not protected by K_{eph} in a time-bound manner. Knowing $\{S\}_{K_{bob}}$, the attacker can wait as long as required to break into Bob and retrieve the long-term private key of Bob, and decrypts the value of S, even after K_{eph} has been deleted from the Ephemerizer's database.

Workaround This attack can be mitigated by using separate ephemeral keys to encrypt $\{S\}_{K_{bob}}$ and J. In *Step 1*, the Ephemerizer would generate 4-tuple (K_{eph1},K_{eph2}, $keyID$, expiry date) instead of the 3-tuple. In *Step 2* Alice would use K_{eph1} to encrypt $\{S\}_{K_{bob}}$ and in *Step 3*, Bob would use K_{eph2} to encrypt J. Thus the message sent by Bob to the Ephemerizer in *Step 3* would become

$$B \rightarrow E : keyID\ \{J\}_{K_{eph1}}\ [\{\{S\}_{K_{bob}}\}_{K_{eph2}}]_J$$

Since two different keys are needed to decrypt the second part and the inner encryption of part three of the message, the attack described previously will not work. However this workaround involves the generation and storage of a second asymmetric key pair for every tuple and hence is less efficient. Moreover this modified scheme still does not resolve the important shortcomings pointed out in the next section.

2.3 Shortcomings

A limitation of the proposed scheme is that Alice does not have the flexibility to define her own expiry dates for the data. Instead she has to choose an expiry date advertised by the Ephemerizer, thus constraining herself to the granularity implemented by the Ephemerizer server.

The secure working of the Ephemerizer system assumes that the recipient Bob uses volatile memory to perform all his temporary computations and that he can securely delete the symmetric key obtained from the Ephemerizer as well as the temporarily decrypted plaintext data once its use is over. This is a reasonable assumption since it is easier to securely delete data in the volatile memory than on a persistent storage device [5]. However, the schemes proposed in [2] do not provide any mechanism to *verify* that the platform used by Bob does indeed provide a secure temporary work-area for the sensitive data. Similarly, the schemes do not provide any provision for Alice to specify additional restrictions on the access of the decryption key by Bob. For example, Alice may want to restrict Bob's access to the message only when he is within, say, the company network. As such the proposed schemes do not provide any mechanism to specify additional conditions for access to the data.

We argue that these limitations cripples the system's usability and security.

In the rest of the paper we present an alternative scheme to provide the envisioned ephemeral service using IB-PKC primitive as the underlying basis. We show that this proposed scheme can address the above-mentioned limitations associated with the original scheme.

3 Identity Based Cryptography

As early as in 1984 Shamir [6] had proposed the use of an encryption scheme in which *an arbitrary string can be used as a public key*. However, it was only in 2001 that a mathematically sound and practically efficient identity-based public key cryptosystem was proposed by Boneh and Franklin [7]. An IB-PKC system, based on bilinear pairing, will be used in our proposed scheme. In this section we provide a brief introduction to the crypto-primitive.

Let P denote a generator of $\mathbb{G}_1$, an additive group of some large prime order q. Let $\mathbb{G}_2$ be a multiplicative group of the same order. A pairing is a map $e : \mathbb{G}_1 \times \mathbb{G}_1 \rightarrow \mathbb{G}_2$ with the following properties:

1. Bilinear: $e(aQ, bR) = e(Q, R)^{ab} = e(abQ, R) = e(bQ, R)^a$, where $Q, R \in \mathbb{G}_1$ and $a, b \in \mathbb{Z}_q^*$.
2. Non-degenerate: $e(P, P) \neq 1_{\mathbb{G}_2}$, where $1_{\mathbb{G}_2}$ is the identity element of $\mathbb{G}_2$.
3. Computable: There exists an efficient algorithm to compute $e(Q, R)$ for all $Q, R \in \mathbb{G}_1$

It is believed that the bilinear Diffie-Hellman problem in $\langle \mathbb{G}_1, \mathbb{G}_2, e\rangle$[1] is hard. Typically the map e is derived from either the Weil [8] or Tate [9] pairing on an elliptic curve.

An IB-PKC scheme consists of four main steps (1) **setup** in which a Key Generation Center (KGC) generates global system parameters and a system secret key, (2) **encrypt** where a message is encrypted using an arbitrary public key, (3) **extract** during which the system secret key is used by the KGC to generate the private key corresponding to the arbitrary public key chosen in the step earlier and (4) **decrypt** where the private key generated is used to decrypt the encrypted message.

Interested readers are referred to [7] for a more rigorous explanation of the mathematics, protocol steps and related proof of security behind the IB-PKC cryptosystem.

4 Proposed System

In this section we describe our proposed alternative Ephemerizer scheme that uses IB-PKC to overcome the deficiencies found in the original system.

As in the original scheme, our approach is to keep only the encrypted version of the data on the persistent storage of the user and to 'store' the key needed to decrypt the data on a different machine, the Ephemerizer server. When the user needs to access the plaintext data, he retrieves the decryption key from the server and uses it to decrypt and use the data in a secure manner. The Ephemerizer server in our scheme also functions as the KGC of the IB-PKC system.

Three properties of IB-PKC are exploited by our scheme (1) an arbitrary string can be used to derive the public key of an entity (2) the private key associated with such a public key is not computed at the same time as the public key and (3) the private key is generated not by the entity that creates the public key, but by the KGC. As explained further on, we exploit these properties by letting Alice embed her finegrained access requirements into the public key of of Bob and by ensuring that the Ephemerizer, which is also the KGC of the system, computes the corresponding private key and sends it to Bob only if the embedded checks have been successfully verified.

Note that, for the ease of explanation, the scheme described here uses the *BasicIdent* version of the IB-PKC scheme. This version is not secure against an

[1] Given $\langle P\ aP\ bP\ cP\rangle$ with uniformly random choices of $a\ b\ c \in \mathbb{Z}_q^*$, compute $e(P\ P)^{abc} \in \mathbb{G}_2$

adaptive chosen ciphertext attack and hence an actual implementation of our scheme would need to use the secure *FullIdent* version [7].

We divide our scheme into five steps:

Step 1 - As in the original IB-PKC system, the Ephemerizer E generates two groups $\mathbb{G}_1$ and $\mathbb{G}_2$, the bilinear map $e : \mathbb{G}_1 \times \mathbb{G}_1 \to \mathbb{G}_2$ for the groups and choose an arbitrary generator $P \in \mathbb{G}_1$. It also specifies two hash functions H_1, H_2 as:

$H_1 : \{0,1\}^* \to \mathbb{G}_1$
$H_2 : \mathbb{G}_2 \to \{0,1\}^n$, n being the bit-length of data to be encrypted

Message space $\mathcal{M} = \{0,1\}^n$, ciphertext $\mathcal{C} = \mathbb{G}_1 \times \{0,1\}^n$

E then computes a set of ephemeral secret keys s_{eph} uniformly at random from $\mathbb{Z}_q^*$ and the corresponding public keys $P_{eph} = s_{eph}P$ and associates each (s_{eph}, P_{eph}) pair with an expiration time and a $keyID$. It also computes another key s_E and corresponding P_E. E finally publishes the system parameters $\langle \mathbb{G}_1, \mathbb{G}_2, e, n, P, P_E, H_1, H_2 \rangle$ and the set of tuples $(keyID, P_{eph}, expiration\_time)$.

Step 2 - Alice chooses a random symmetric key K and encrypts the data M with it: $M_E = [M]_K$. K is then encrypted with Bob's long-term public key $K_E = \{K\}_{K_{bob}}$. She then chooses the most appropriate value of P_{eph} from the available set such that (needed expiry date < expiry date of key). She then chooses as Bob's IB-PKC public key $ID_b =$ '$Eph|Expiry : needed - expiry - date$', where Eph is the identity of the Ephemerizer.

For example, if the set of ephemeral keys available were $(ID_1, P_1, 2006-28-12-22:00)$, $(ID_2, P_2, 2006-28-12-22:30)$ and $(ID_3, P_3, 2006-28-12-23:00)$ and Alice wants to make the data unrecoverable after 2006-28-12-22:15, she would choose ID_2, P_2 and assign $ID_b =$ '$Eph|Expiry : 2006-28-12-22:15$'. For the rest of the paper, we will assume she chose P_{eph}. She then computes $Q_{ID_b} = H_1(ID_b)$, chooses $r_b \in \mathbb{Z}_q^*$ and encrypts K_E by computing:

$C_b = \langle U_b, V_b \rangle = \langle r_b P, K_E \oplus H_2(g_b^{r_b}) \rangle$
where $g_b = e(Q_{ID_b}, P_{eph}) \in \mathbb{G}_2$

Alice then sends the following to B:

$$A \to B : \{ID_b\ C_b\}_{K\,bob}\ M_E\ keyID$$

Step 3 - Bob uses his long-term private key to decrypt the first part of the message received from A to obtain ID_b and C_b and saves them locally with the rest of the message.

When Bob needs to decrypt and obtain M, he creates an arbitrary public key ID_e for E, a random key J and computes $Q_{ID_e} = H_1(ID_e)$ and computes

$C_e = \langle U_e, V_e \rangle = \langle r_e P, (ID_b|J) \oplus H_2(g_e^{r_e}) \rangle$
where $g_e = e(Q_{ID_e}, P_E) \in \mathbb{G}_2$

Bob then sends the following to E:

$B \rightarrow E : ID_e \; keyID \; C_e$

Step 4 - When the Ephemerizer receives the message from Bob, it first makes sure that *keyID* has not expired. If the key has expired, s_{eph} and P_{eph} are deleted from the secure database and an error message is sent back to Bob. Periodically, E also scans this database on its own and deletes all expired tuples. If the key associated with Bob's request is still valid, E calculates $Q_{ID_e} = H_1(ID_e)$, $d_e = s_E Q_{ID_e}$ and $V_e \oplus H_2(e(d_e, U_e))$, which yields '$ID_b|J$'. E then examines ID_b to check for the expiration time that A has specified. Only if this expiration time is also valid would E compute $Q_{ID_b} = H_1(ID_b)$ and $d_b = s_{eph} Q_{ID_b}$, where s_{eph} corresponds to the $keyID$ specified and generated in Step 1. E then sends to Bob:

$E \rightarrow B : [d_b]_J$

Step 5 - Since Bobs knows the value of J, he uses it to decrypt the message sent by E and obtain d_b, which is then used to calculate $V_b \oplus H_2(e(d_b, U_b)) = K_E$. He then uses his long-term private key to decrypt K_E to obtain K which is then used to decrypt M_E to finally obtain M. M, J, d_b and K are deleted securely by Bob after use.

Note that since the output of H_2 is used as a one-time pad to encrypt data, n used in the definition of H_2 should be at least |maximum length of ID_b | + |maximum length of key J|. The security of the proposed system relies on the security of the original IB-PKC system and interested readers are referred to [7] for detailed analysis.

5 Discussion

5.1 Security

IB-PKC has not gained widespread usage mainly because it suffers from an inherent key escrow problem. The KGC, knowing the secret s_{eph}, can compute the associated private key. Though several solutions have been proposed to counter the inherent key escrow problem, including threshold key issuing using multiple KGCs [7], generating the private key using multiple independent private keys issued by multiple KGCs [10], certificate-based encryption [11] and certificateless public key encryption [12], none of them can be directly used in our scheme. On one hand the schemes proposed in [11] and [12] do not allow arbitrary strings as public key and hence prevents Alice from specifying her own expiration time, while on the other, proposals like 1[10] require Bob to authenticate with multiple KGCs every time he needs to decrypt the data.

This is the reason why we do not completely replace the traditional PKI based system in favor of a system solely based on IB-PKC. Instead we use a hybrid scheme using each cryptosystem's strength to provide specific security requirements.

By encrypting K with Bob's traditional long-term public key the system completely side-steps the key escrow problem. A malicious Ephemerizer will not be able to obtain M with just its knowledge of d_b, the private key corresponding to ID_b. It will also have to compromise Bob's machine to obtain his long-term private key. This provides the same security setup as the original Ephemerizer scheme of Perlman. The use of IB-PKC allows Alice to specify her own finegrained expiration time and also help extend the scheme fairly easily, as discussed further on.

In *Step 2*, ID_b is sent to Bob encrypted with his long-term public key. This prevents an attacker from knowing the value of ID_b and using the knowledge to obtain d_b.

In *Step 4* d_b is sent by the Ephemerizer to Bob encrypted using a symmetric key J that is randomly selected by Bob just for that session of the protocol run and deleted afterward. Thus even if an attacker captures the message sent to Bob in *Step 4*, it cannot decrypt and obtain M, since J is deleted immediately after *Step 5*.

The Ephemerizer will send d_b to B only if both s_{eph} and the expiration time specified in ID_b are valid. Thus Alice is able to specify her expiry date at whatever granularity she prefers (as long as she chooses the right s_{eph}). Additionally, once Ephemerizer finds out that a particular s_{eph} has expired, it is permanently deleted from its secure database. Thus, even if the Ephemerizer and Bob is compromised after the expiry of s_{eph}, the attacker would not be able to use s_{eph} to obtain M.

Note however that there could be a time gap between the expiry specified in ID_b and that of s_{eph}, between which an attacker could compromise E and gain access to s_{eph}. We argue however that since the time gap can be made as small as possible by judicious choice of *seph*, this risk is as acceptable as the chance of Ephemerizer server being compromised before the expiry date specified by Alice. Furthermore, the access to s_{eph} does not mean that the attacker can successfully generate d_b. If the whole computational process at the Ephemerizer's end, including the IB-PKC equivalent of **decrypt** as specified in *Step 4*, is implemented in a secure coprocessor [13], the comparison between the current time and the expiration time specified in ID_b can be performed in a secure and tamper resistant manner. Thus, even if s_{eph} is valid, the computation of Q_{ID_b} will fail due to expiration time check and by extension so will the computation of d_b. As the Ephemerizer server is a dedicated machine operated solely for the purpose of managing the ephemeral keys, its use of tamper-resistant hardware is not a far-fetched assumption. A similar reasoning applies to attacks aimed at changing E's system clock.

5.2 Supporting Richer Access Control

The scheme proposed above does not explicitly describe how Alice can specify further conditions for release of d_b to Bob. This was consciously done to keep the basic protocol simple and easy to explain. In this section we explain how the basic scheme can be extended to support extra conditions that Alice may like to impose.

In the basic scheme proposed in Section 4, ID_b was used by Alice to specify her fine-grained expiration time. This was checked in the later stages of the protocol run, by the Ephemerizer, to ensure its validity before d_b was sent to Bob. Extending this to include other checks is straight forward.

In *Step 1*, along with the publication of the system parameters, the Ephemerizer could state which other conditional checks are offered by it as a service to the users. These extra checks could include, for example, IP address access check, secure system check etc.

Implementing the IP address check would be as simple as Alice stating the allowed IP address or range of addresses in ID_b. For example ID_b = '$Eph|Expiry$: 2006 − 28 − 12 − 22 : 15|IP : 132.168.2.*' would mean that Alice wants to allow Bob to access the data M only until 22:15 hrs of 2006-28-12 and only from the address range 132.168.2.1 - 132.168.2.254. In Step 4 of the protocol run, when the Ephemerizer retrieves the value of ID_b from C_e, it checks the IP address that Bob is using along with the validity of the expiry date and proceeds only if both the checks succeed. The assumption is that a spoof-proof method to determine the IP address of a remote host exists, maybe using techniques like [14]. The support for wildcards would require the use of the identity-based encryption with wildcards cryptoprimitive [15].

The original Ephemerizer scheme as well as the one proposed in this paper depends on the ability of Bob to securely delete the temporary plaintext data as well as all the data that he receives from Ephemerizer. To increase the users' faith in the system, Alice should be able to verify that Bob is indeed using a secure system when accessing the secret data. The original scheme had no mechanism to check for the presence of such a system. However our proposed scheme can be extended fairly simply to support this verification. For this extension to work, Bob would need to use special hardware like the Trusted Platform Module [16], which has the ability to perform *remote attestation* [17] or a richer semantic remote attestation [14]. Alice would specify the Platform Configuration Register (PCR) that she trusts to be that of a secure system in ID_b, ID_b = '$Eph|Expiry$: 2006 − 28 − 12 − 22 : 15|$PCR1$: $2fd4e1c67a2d28fced849ee1bb76e7391b93eb12$'. It is assumed that Alice has some mechanism to find out the correct PCR value of a trusted secure system.

Once the Ephemerizer receives the decryption request from Bob, and has decrypted the value of ID_b, it initiates a protocol similar to the 'Integrity Challenge Protocol' of [18] to verify the integrity of Bob's system.

$E \rightarrow B : ChReq(n, PCR1)$
$B \rightarrow E : sig\{PCR1, n\}_{AIK}$

The Ephemerizer sends Bob a PCR challenge request, along with a nonce to prevent replay attacks. Bob's machine's TPM uses its Attestation Identity Key (AIK) to sign the PCR value requested and then sends the signed PCR value back to the Ephemerizer along with the nonce sent with the request. At the Ephemerizer, the AIK signature is first verified and then the reported PCR value can be used in calculating Q_{ID_b} and d_b. Thus a wrongly reported PCR would create a wrong ID_b and hence a wrong Q_{ID_b} and d_b, preventing Bob from accessing the protected data.

In general, the proposed scheme can be extended to support any number of extra restrictions by specifying them appropriately in Bob's public key ID_b, as long as the Ephemerizer has the ability to perform these checks.

6 Conclusion and Future Work

In this paper we analyzed the Ephemerizer system proposed by Perlman [2] and used in [3] as a system that allows parties to securely share data, by keeping the encrypted data and the decryption key in physically separate entities, for a finite time period and then making it unrecoverable after that. However, as noted in this paper, the schemes do not allow the parties to specify more detailed and flexible usage restrictions on the data. In addition one of the version of the original scheme suffers from a fatal oracle attack as described in the paper.

We proposed an alternate scheme to implement the Ephemerizer system with none of the identified flaws and functional constraints. Our scheme exploits the properties of Identity Based cryptosystem and is one of the few systems that utilise the power of the crypto-primitive without suffering the associated disadvantages. The security of the proposed scheme and its ability to support flexible usage restrictions were then discussed in detail.

We plan on developing a formal proof of correctness of our scheme as well as an implementation of the same to prove that the scheme is indeed secure and implementable.

Acknowledgment

We thanks Chandana Gamage for his invaluable inputs. This work has been supported by NWO project ACCOUNT 612.060.319 and partially by the EU project S3MS IST-STREP-27004.

References

1. United States Department of Defense (2006) National Industrial Security Program Operating Manual. DoD 5220.22-M

2. Perlman R (2005) The Ephemerizer: Making Data Disappear. Journal of Information System Security, Vol. 1 (1), pp. 51–68
3. Perlman R (2005) File System Design with Assured Delete. Third IEEE International Security in Storage Workshop, pp. 83–88, USA
4. Bellare M, Canetti R, Krawczyk H (1996) Keying Hash Functions for Message Authentication. Advances in Cryptology - Crypto 96, LNCS 1109, Springer-Verlag, pp. 1–15
5. Crescenzo GD, Ferguson N, Impagliazzo R, Jakobsson M (1999) How to Forget a Secret. International Symposium on Theoretical Aspects of Computer Science, LNCS 1563, Springer-Verlag, pp. 500–509
6. Shamir A (1984) Identity-based Cryptosystems and Signature Schemes. Advances in Cryptology - Crypto 84, LNCS 196, Springer-Verlag, pp. 47–53
7. Boneh D, Franklin F (2001) Identity-based Encryption from Weil Pairing. Advances in Cryptology - Crypto 2001, LNCS 2139, Springer-Verlag, pp. 213–229
8. Lang S (1973) Elliptic Functions. Addision-Wesley
9. Frey G, Muller M, Ruck H (1999) The Tate Pairing and the Discrete Logarithm Applied to Elliptic Curve Cryptosystems. IEEE Transactions on Information Theory, 45(5)L1717-9
10. Chen L, Harrison K, Smart NP, Soldera D (2002) Applications of Multiple Trust Authorities in Pairing Based Cryptosystems. InfraSec 2002, LNCS 2437, Springer-Verlag, pp. 260–275
11. Gentry C (2003) Certificate-based Encryption and the Certificate Revocation Problem. Advances in Cryptology - Eurocrypt 2003, LNCS 25656, Springer-Verlag, pp. 272–293
12. Al-Riyani S, PatersonK (2003) Certificateless Public Key Cryptography. Advances in Cryptology - Asiacrypt 2003, LNCS 2894, Springer-Verlag, pp. 452–473
13. Dyer J, Lindemann M, Perez R, Sailer R, van Doorn L, Smith SW, Weingart S (2001) Building the IBM 4758 Secure Coprocessor. IEEE Computer Vol. 34, no. 10, pp. 57–66
14. Haldar V, Chandra D, Franz M (2004) Semantic Remote Attestation: A Virtual Machine Directed Approach to Trusted Computing. USENIX Virtual Machine Research and Technology Symposium, pp. 29–41
15. Abdalla M, Catalano D, Dent AW, Malone-Lee J, Neven G, Smart NP (2006) Identity-Based Encryption Gone Wild. Automata, Languages and Programming: 33rd International Colloquium, LNCS 4052, Springer-Verlag, pp. 300–311
16. Trusted Computing Group (2006) http://www.trustedcomputinggroup.org
17. Trusted Computing Group (2006) Trusted Platform Module Main Specification, Part 1: Design Principles, Part 2: TPM Structures, Part 3: Commands, Version 1.2, Revision 94. http://www.trustedcomputinggroup.org
18. Sailer R, Zhang X, Jaeger T, van Doorn L (2004), Design and Implementation of a TCG-Based Integrity Measurement Architecture. 13th Usenix Security Symposium, USENIX, pp. 223–238

Keystroke Analysis for Thumb-based Keyboards on Mobile Devices

Sevasti Karatzouni and Nathan Clarke
Network Research Group, University of Plymouth, Plymouth, PL4 8AA, United Kingdom, nrg@plymouth.ac.uk
WWW home page: http://www.network-research-group

Abstract. The evolution of mobile networking has opened the door to a wide range of service opportunities for mobile devices, increasing at the same time the sensitivity of the information stored and access through them. Current PIN-based authentication has proved to be an insufficient and an inconvenient approach. Biometrics have proven to be a reliable approach to identity verification and can provide a more robust means of security, as they rely upon personal identifiers. Amongst various biometric techniques available, keystroke analysis combines features that can offer a cost effective, non-intrusive and continuous authentication solution for mobile devices. This research has been undertaken in order to investigate the performance of keystroke analysis on thumb-based keyboards that are being widely deployed upon PDA's and Smartphone devices. The investigation sought to authenticate users whilst typing text messages, using two keystroke characteristics, the inter-keystroke latency and hold-time. The results demonstrate the approach to be promising, achieving an average EER=12.2% with the inter-keystroke latency based upon 50 participants. Uniquely to this tactile environment however, the hold-time characteristic, did not prove to be a reliable feature to be utilised.

1 Introduction

The proliferation of mobile devices and mobile networking has introduced new challenges for the protection of the subscribers' assets. The security risks are no longer associated only with safeguarding the subscriber's account. With the introduction of 3rd generation mobile networks, the services and information accessible through mobile handsets has increased in sensitivity, as micro-payments, mobile banking and location-based services are all now a reality for the mobile world [1]. Statistics show that mobile theft in the UK accounts 45% of all theft [2], a fact,

Please use the following format when citing this chapter:

Karatzouni, S. and Clarke, N., 2007, in IFIP International Federation for Information Processing, Volume 232, New Approaches for Security, Privacy and Trust in Complex Environments, eds. Venter, H., Eloff, M., Labuschagne, L., Eloff, J., von Solms, R., (Boston: Springer), pp. 253–263.

which when combined with the information that can be stored on mobile handsets and the attraction that high-tech devices can pose, presents a further concern for enhanced security.

Current authentication, principally achieved by PINs, is not enough to substantially safeguard today's mobile handsets and the data accessed through them. As a secret knowledge technique it has several well established drawbacks, such as being shared, written down or kept at factory default settings [3]. Furthermore, as survey results demonstrate, subscribers consider it an inconvenient method and as such tend not to use it in the first place, leaving their device completely unprotected [4]. This is not only limited to the general public, as the Mobile Usage Survey 2005 reveals, only 2 thirds of the IT managers surveyed have enabled password security in their mobile devices, despite acknowledging the amount of sensitive business information that is stored upon them [5].

Of the two remaining authentication approaches - tokens and biometrics, the latter can offer a more viable approach. Token-based authentication implemented to date by SIM cards does not provide any protection for the user as it is unlikely to be ever removed from the device. Biometrics could provide an enhancement on the current security, as authentication is based upon a unique characteristic of a person. This fact introduces a unique level of security that other approaches are unable to accomplish, as it relates the process to a person and not to the possession of knowledge or a token. A biometric approach that can provide a cost-effective and a non-intrusive solution for mobile handset authentication is keystroke analysis, a technique which is based on the typing dynamics of a user.

The purpose of this research is to investigate the feasibility of keystroke analysis on thumb-based keyboards based on text messaging input, looking to apply this technique as an authentication method for mobile handsets that offer that unique tactile interface. The paper proceeds with section 2 describing the unique characteristics utilised in keystroke analysis and provides an overview of keystroke analysis studies to date. Sections 3 and 4 describe the methodology and results of the study. A discussion of the results, placing them in context and areas for future research are presented in Sections 5 and 6.

2 Keystroke analysis

Keystroke analysis is a behavioural biometric that attempts to verify identity based upon the typing pattern of a user, looking at certain physical characteristics of their interaction with a keyboard. Considerable research has been undertaken on the method since first suggested by Spillane [6] in 1975, with studies identifying two main characteristics that provide valuable discriminative information:

- Inter-keystroke latency, which is the interval between two successive keystrokes, and
- Hold-time, which is the interval between the pressing and releasing of a single key

The majority of the studies to date have investigated the feasibility of keystroke analysis on full QWERTY keyboards [7 – 10], showing good results for both of the characteristics mentioned. In general, the inter-keystroke latency has demonstrated better discriminatory characteristics for classification in comparison to hold-time.

As in all biometrics the method to assess the performance of keystroke analysis, is by using the False Acceptance Rate (FAR), which indicates the probability of an impostor being granted access to the system, and the False Rejection Rate (FRR), which represents the degree to which a legitimate user is rejected. A trade-off exists between these rates, in terms of increasing security (and therefore increasing user inconvenience) and increasing user convenience (and thus decreasing the security). The point at which those two rates cross is referred to as the Equal Error Rate (%) and is used as a more objective means of comparing the performance of different biometric techniques.

The underlying classification algorithms utilized in keystroke analysis were traditionally statistically based [7, 8, 10]. However, advancements in neural networks have shown this technique to be more successful. A summary of key literature and results within the domain of keystroke analysis on PC keyboards is illustrated in Table 1.

Table 1. A summary of literature & results on keystroke analysis on PC keyboards

Study	Users	Input	Inter-key	Hold-time	Approach	FAR (%)	FRR (%)
Umpress & Williams[7]	17	Alphabetic	●		Statistical	11.7	5.8
Joyce & Gupta [8]	23	Alphabetic	●		Statistical	0.3	16.4
Brown & Rogers [9]	25	Alphabetic	●	●	Neural N.	0	12
Obaidat & Sadoun [10]	15	Alphabetic	●	●	Neural N.	0	0
Ord & Furnell [11]	14	Numerical	●		Neural N.	9.9	30

Although continuous research on keystroke analysis has been conducted since the 1980's, it was not until more recently that the method was assessed on interfaces provided on mobile phones where the tactile environment considerably differs. A series of studies accessed the method on regular mobile phone keypads with promising outcomes, achieving an EER of 8% based on numerical input [12]. Nevertheless, the performance of keystroke analysis for other tactile environments such as thumb-based keyboards is undocumented. Thumb-based keyboards constitute an interesting gap in research as they provide the extensive interface of a PC keyboard and the thumb-based properties of a mobile phone.

3 Methodology

This study looked into the feasibility of authenticating a user whilst typing text messages. Two different types of analysis were conducted in the context of this research: static analysis utilising the inter-keystroke latency and pseudo-dynamic utilising the hold-time characteristic. A total of fifty participants took part in the study, involving the largest population of participants for a study such as this and enabling more statistically significant results to be concluded. The participants were asked to enter thirty messages, with each message specifically designed to ensure that certain requirements are met.

For the static analysis six varying sized keywords were included in the text messages providing a static classification component. The varying nature of the static keywords permitted an evaluation of the word length versus performance. Thirty repetitions of each keyword were included, to ensure enough data for classification. The words selected are listed in Table 2, along with the number of inter-keystroke latencies that they involve and the number of samples used for training and testing after outliers were removed (a standard procedure for keystroke analysis studies [7-15].

Table 2. Keywords used for inter-key latency

Keyword	# Inter-keystroke latencies	#Samples after outliers' removal	Training Set	Testing Set
everything	10	27	18	9
difficult	9	26	18	8
better	6	27	18	9
night	5	27	18	9
the	3	26	18	8
and	3	27	18	9

Fig. 1. An XDA IIs thumb-based keypad

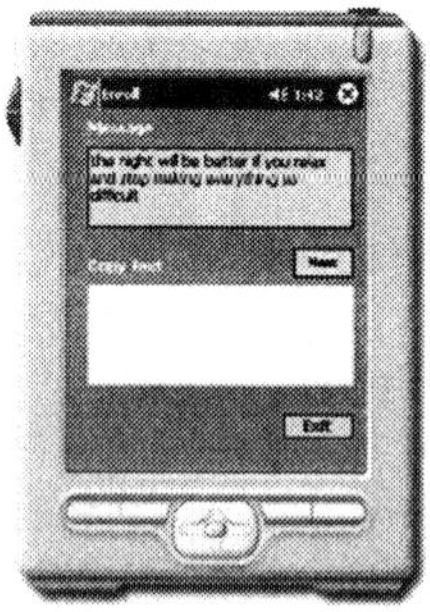

Fig.2. Screenshot from experiment software

Literature has showed that attempts to perform dynamic analysis on keystroke dynamics [13, 14] did not yield satisfactory results. As such an attempt was made to utilize a static component – the recurrent letters, in a dynamic form of analysis. The pseudo-dynamic analysis was based upon the hold-time of the six most recurrent letters in the English language – 'e', 't', 'a', 'o', 'n' and 'i' - an adequate number of repetitions of which were included within the messages.

The text messages were entered using an XDA IIs handset that deploys a representative example of today's thumb-based keyboards, as illustrated in Figure 1. In order to capture the keystroke data, appropriate software was developed using Microsoft's Visual Basic .NET, and deployed on the handset. A screenshot of the software is illustrated in Figure 2. As usual in keystroke analysis studies, corrections were not permitted in case the user misspelled a word as this would undesirably interfere with the data [7]. Instead, the whole word had to be retyped in the correct form. Although it would be preferred to collect the data during multiple sessions, as a more indicative typing profile of the users could be captured, the data collection was performed in a single session, to maximise the number of participants that completed the study.

4 Results

4.1 Inter-keystroke latency

An initial analysis of the input data showed a fairly large spread of values on the inter-keystroke latencies. Even though smaller keywords were expected to give a greater consistency in the typing pattern because of their length and commonality, that was not the case. Additionally, the difference between the values of the different users was not large. These factors put a burden on the classification algorithm, as they make the classification boundaries between users very difficult to establish successfully. Figure 3, illustrates the mean and standard deviation for the larger keyword 'everything' for all users as an example of the problem.

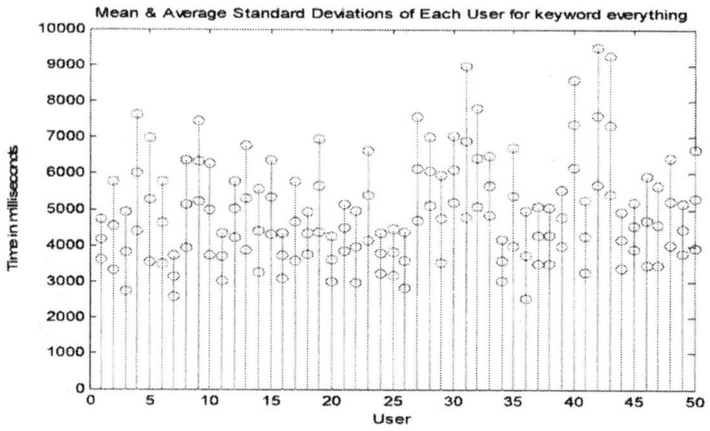

Fig. 3. Mean & Standard deviation for keyword everything

A number of analyses were undertaken, using Feed Forward Multilayer Perceptron Neural Network (FF-MLP) as it had demonstrated better performance in previous studies over other techniques [10, 12, 15, 16, 17]. Different network configurations were tested, looking for optimum performance. The best results achieved were for the keyword 'everything' with an EER of 23.4%. This was somewhat expected as the larger keywords contain more keystroke latencies and subsequently more discriminative information.

As illustrated in Table 3, the results show the FRR is much higher from the FAR which can be explained by the large number of impostors (49) extensively training the network versus the one authorised user. Furthermore, the number of samples assigned to the testing of the classification was small, resulting in the FRR encountering large steps in its transitions when being evaluated.

Although the error rate is fairly high, there were cases of users reaching an EER below 10% with the best case of user 1 achieving an EER of 0.3%, showing the ability to classify some users. The rest of the keywords resulted in higher error rates, with the error increasing as the length of the keyword was reducing. The best results for each keyword are illustrated in Table 3.

Table 3. Best results for each keyword

Keyword	FAR (%)	FRR (%)	EER(%)
everything	12.8	34.2	**23.5**
difficult	13.2	43.0	**28.1**
better	18.0	43.1	**30.5**
night	21.3	45.8	**33.5**
the	23.7	41.5	**32.6**
and	24.3	43.6	**33.9**

The average results of different networks showed minimal change in the EERs, although individual performances did vary. This suggests that the network does not optimise for individual users but rather forces a standard training scheme upon the user. To overcome this problem a different approach was utilised by Clarke & Furnell [12], which provided an improvement in performance through optimising the number of training epochs. A gradual training technique was performed, training the network for an extensive number of epochs but periodically evaluating the performance. The results showed a noticeable decrease in the error rates with best case achieving an EER of 12.2% for the larger keyword. The summary of the gradual training results are presented in Table 4.

Table 4. Gradual training results for all keywords

Keyword	**FAR (%)**	**FRR (%)**	**EER(%)**
everything	15.8	9.1	**12.2**
difficult	16.8	12.0	**14.4**
better	23.5	14.4	**18.9**
night	24.2	14.4	**19.3**
the	29.3	19.5	**24.4**
and	28.7	17.6	**23.1**

Noticeably, for the keyword "everything", 20 users achieved an FRR of 0% with a respective FAR below 10%, with the best user achieving an FAR of 0.7% and FRR of 0%. The list of best and worst case users for all keywords are illustrated in Table 5. The results underline the requirement for different training intensiveness for each user, and that the inter-keystroke latency offers the discriminative data to classify users in the specific tactile interface.

Table 5. Best & worst case results from gradual training

Keyword	Best Case		Worst Case	
	User	EER (%)	User	EER (%)
everything	2	**0.4**	6	**32.4**
difficult	11	**1.3**	46	**34.1**
better	49	**1.6**	27	**34.2**
night	34	**2.3**	25	**40.5**
the	26	**6.4**	39	**45.8**
and	11	**5.4**	5	**49.4**

4.2 Hold-time

In contrary to the inter-keystroke latency investigation, the hold-time characteristic provided little discriminative information to classify users. A series of tests on different network configurations using all six letters (as to provide the largest possible input vector) resulted in an EER of around 50%, showing little classification performance. The same error rate was achieved using different size subsets of the letters with smaller input vectors (but with the advantage of more repetitions of each letter) and also with a larger input vector of eight letters through the addition of letters 'r' and 's', as they appear next on the reoccurrence list.

In order to further assess the performance of hold-time, a group of only 20 users was utilised aiming to help the classification problem by reducing the amount and complexity of information presented to the network and thus assisting in the discrimination of authorised and unauthorised users. However, no change in the performance was experienced. Even when gradual training was applied, using the six letters set, no significant improvement was observed. Sample results from various tests are provided in Table 6. Even though there was a 10% decline on the EER using gradual training, the results are still too high to suggest that hold-time can offer any valuable discriminative information.

Table 6. Sample results from various tests on hold-time

Set	Training	Users	FAR (%)	FRR (%)	EER(%)
6 letters	normal	20	49.5	49.4	**49.5**
6 letters	normal	50	31.3	69.0	**50.2**
8 letters	normal	50	26.7	72.9	**49.8**
3 letters	normal	50	22.1	77.6	**49.9**
6 letters	gradual	50	34.2	36.8	**36.8**
6 letters	normal	20	49.5	49.4	**49.5**

5 Discussion

As the results showed the inter-keystroke latency can provide an effective means of differentiating between users. When based on a latency vector of 10, an EER of 12.2% was achieved with the gradual training approach. As was expected the use of smaller input vectors resulted in a corresponding increase in error rates, as the amount of unique discriminative information and feature space reduced.

With regards to the inter-keystroke latency, this study did not experience the very low rates in performance that have been found in previous studies based on regular keyboards. It is suggested that a number of aspects differentiate this investigation from previous studies. The keyboard utilised in this study provides a completely different tactile interface than traditional keyboards, with a more restricted keystroke interface, reduced distance between the keys and smaller key depth. In addition, the number of fingers utilised in typing has also been reduced from typically 10 fingers and thumbs to 2 thumbs. Both of these factors restrict the typing dynamics, as the combinations of the fingers in conjunction with the timing of the keystrokes and movement to achieve them, are reduced. This results in a smaller feature space for the keystrokes characteristics to reside in and subsequently making it more difficult to distinguish between them. Furthermore, although the layout was familiar to all users as it shares the same layout with a PC keyboard, some of the participants experienced difficulty in identifying the placement of the keys due to the different way of typing.

The hold-time characteristic did not provide any real evidence to suggest that it can be utilised in this specific typing interface, though there are a number of factors that may explain the inability of the keystroke feature. Firstly, the keys that the thumb-based keyboard deploys are very small related to the chunky tactile environment that a normal keyboard offers, restricting the interval length between the pressing and releasing of a key and thus not providing much differentiation in values. Although the hold-time has performed well on regular keypads [12], the keys were larger than the keyboard used in this experiment and the method of calculating the hold time was different. In the study by Clarke & Furnell [12], the hold-time was defined by the first key press down until the last key release, increasing immediately the range of values and thus the feature space (for instance, for the character 'c' the number 1 button would need to be pressed three times).

Furthermore in a thumb-based keyboard, fingers stay almost static due to the limited area. As such, the hand movement which appears in PC keyboards and may affect the pressing of a key is unlikely to happen in this case. What must also be noticed is that some participants complained about the feedback from the keyboard, as they could not at all cases be sure if they had pressed a key, which might have further complicated matters.

6 Conclusions

This research conducted a feasibility study on the utilisation of keystroke analysis as an authentication method in devices that offer the tactile environment of a thumb-based keyboard. The results showed that from the two traditionally used keystroke characteristics, the inter-keystroke latency gave promising results in-line with previous studies undertaken. However, unusually the hold-time characteristic gave no promise of a potential use in this kind of keystroke interface, though further research must be undertaken to determine this conclusively.

Future research will be conducted looking to optimise network configurations for the inter-keystroke latency to take into account the bias towards the network responding in favour of the impostor. Furthermore, the use of different keywords will be investigated, as will the concurrent use of more than one keyword within a single authentication request, the latter aspect having the potential to substantially improve performance. In respect to hold-time, further tests are required before concluding to its ineffectiveness, exploring the use of longer input vectors and different letter subsets. A future experiment will also look to utilise different thumb-based keyboards that offer a slight different tactile environments than the one utilised in this study. Additionally, future work will seek to investigate the performance of the technique in environments representing more practical situations, thereby providing more balanced results. Factors such as the user's interaction with the handset whilst they are walking and their physical condition (e.g. tired or stressed) can be investigated for their impact upon performance.

This study has demonstrated promising results for the use of keystroke analysis, using a significantly large number of participants than previous studies. Although the accuracy of the method does not compete in distinctiveness with other biometrics such as fingerprints, the nature of keystroke analysis in that it can provide a monitoring authentication mechanism, transparent to the user (which is not feasible for many other techniques) is a positive attribute. If used regularly and in conjunction with other transparent authentication techniques, keystroke analysis can be an effective means of providing a more enhanced level of security.

7 References

1. The UTMS Forum, Mobile Evolution – Shaping the future (August 1, 2003); http://www.umts-forum.org/servlet/dycon/ztumts/umts/Live/en/umts/MultiMedia_PDFs_Papers_Paper-1-August-2003.pdf.

2. British Transport Police, Mobile phone theft (August 20, 2006); http://www.btp.police.uk/issues/mobile.htm.

3. R. Lemos, Passwords: The Weakest Link? Hackers can crack most in less than a minute, CNET.com, (2002), http://news.com.com/2009-1001-916719.html.

4. N. Clarke, S.M. Furnell, P.M. Rodwell, P.L. Reynolds, Acceptance of subscriber authentication method for mobile telephony devices, *Computers & Security*, 21(**3**), pp220-228, 2002.

5. Pointsec, IT professionals turn blind eye to mobile security as survey reveals sloppy handheld habits (November 17, 2005); http://www.pointsec.com/news/release.cfm?PressId=108.

6. R. Spillane, Keyboard Apparatus for personal identification, IBM Technical Disclosure Bulletin, 17(**3346**) (1975).

7. D. Umphress, G. Williams, Identity Verification through Keyboard Characteristics, *International Journal of Man-Machine Studies*, 23, pp. 263-273 1985.

8. R. Joyce, G. Gupta, Identity Authentication Based on Keystroke Latencies, *Communications of the ACM*, 39, pp 168-176 1990.

9. M. Brown, J. Rogers, User Identification via Keystroke Characteristics of Typed Names using Neural Networks, *International Journal of Man-Machine Studies*, 39, pp. 999-1014 (1993).

10. M. S. Obaidat, B. Sadoun, Verification of Computer User Using Keystroke Dynamics, *IEEE Transactions on Systems, Man and Cybernetics – Part B: Cybernetics*, 27(**2**), (1997).

11. T. Ord, User Authentication using Keystroke Analysis with a Numerical Keypad Approach, (MSc Thesis, University of Plymouth, UK, 1999).

12. NL. Clarke, S.M. Furnell, Authenticating Mobile Phone Users Using Keystroke Analysis, *International Journal of Information Security*, ISSN:1615-5262, (2006), pp.1-14.

13. G. Leggett, J. Williams, Verifying identity via keystroke characteristics, *International Journal of Man-Machine Studies*, Vol. 28(1), (1988), pp.67-76.

14. R. Napier, W. Laverty, D. Mahar, R. Henderson, M. Hiron, M. Wagner, Keyboard User Verification: Toward an accurate, Efficient and Ecological Valid Algorithm, *International Journal of Human-Computer Studies*, 43, pp.213-222 (1995).

15. S. Cho, C. Han, D. Han, H. Kin, Web Based Keystroke Dynamics Identity Verification Using Neural Networks, *Journal of Organizational Computing & Electronic Commerce*, 10, pp. 295-307 (2000).

16. S. Haykin, *Neural networks: A Comprehensive Foundation (2nd edition)*, (Prentice Hall, New Jersey, 1999).

17. M. Bishop, *Neural Networks for Pattern Classification*, (Oxford University Press, New York, 1995).

Security Remarks on a Convertible Nominative Signature Scheme

Guilin Wang and Feng Bao

Institute for Infocomm Research (I^2R)
21 Heng Mui Keng Terrace, Singapore 119613
{glwang,baofeng}@i2r.a-star.edu.sg

Abstract. A nominative signature scheme allows a nominator (i.e. the signer) and a nominee (i.e. a designated verifier) to jointly generate and publish a signature so that *only* the nominee can check the validity of a nominative signature and further convince a third party to accept this fact. Recently, Huang and Wang proposed such a new scheme at ACISP 2004, and claimed that their scheme is secure under some standard computational assumptions. In this paper, we remark that their scheme is *not* a nominative signature in fact, since it fails to meet the crucial security requirement: *verification untransferability.* Specifically, we identify an adaptively chosen-message attack against their scheme such that the nominator can determine the validity of a new message-signature pair with some indirect help from the nominee. Moreover, we point out that using our attack the nominator is further able to demonstrate the validity of nominative signatures to a third party. Therefore, the Huang-Wang scheme does not meet *confirmation/disavowal untransferability* either.

Keywords: Nominative signature, digital signature, attacks, information security.

1 Introduction

As an important primitive in modern cryptography, digital signatures are widely used to provide integrity, authenticity, and non-repudiation for authenticating electronic messages. Standard digital signatures are *universally or publicly verifiable.* That is, according to a publicly known signature verification algorithm anybody can check whether an alleged signature-message pair is valid or not with respect to a given public key. However, this may not be a desired property in some situations, where messages to be authenticated are personally private or commercially sensitive. To restrict the universal verifiability, therefore, some variants of digital signatures have been proposed, such as undeniable signatures (US), designated confirmer signatures (DCS), and nominative signatures (NS).

In undeniable signature schemes [4, 15, 9], the validity of a signature can *only* be verified under the cooperation of the signer. Undeniable signatures find various applications, such as licensing softwares, e-cash, e-voting, e-auctions,

Please use the following format when citing this chapter:

Wang, G. and Bao, F., 2007, in IFIP International Federation for Information Processing, Volume 232, New Approaches for Security, Privacy and Trust in Complex Environments, eds. Venter, H., Eloff, M., Labuschagne, L., Eloff, J., von Solms, R., (Boston: Springer), pp. 265–275.

etc. In [6, 1, 11], designated confirmer signatures (DCS) are further proposed to guarantee that the validity of signatures can also be verified under the help of a semi-trusted party, called designated confirmer. This is a useful enhancement for verifiers, since they may need to check a signature's validity even in the case the signer is unavailable, due to some subjective or objective reasons.

Compared with these schemes, nominative signatures [14, 13] hand over the power of signature verification to the verifier. That is, without the help of a designated verifier (called *nominee*), anybody including the signer (called *nominator*) cannot determine whether an alleged signature-message pair is valid or not. Actually, nominative signatures can be considered as the dual concept of undeniable signatures. In addition, as suggested in [14, 13], nominative signatures have potential applications in the scenarios where a signed message is personally private or commercially sensitive, such as a tax bill, a medical examination report, an ID certificate, etc.

In 1996, Kim et al. [14] first introduced the concept of *nominative signatures*. Intuitively, a nominative signature scheme allows a nominator (or signer) and a nominee (or verifier) to jointly generate and publish a signature for an arbitrary message. Different from standard signatures, however, *only* the nominee (holding his/her own private key) can verify the validity of a published nominative signature. Furthermore, if necessary, the nominee can also convince a third party to accept this fact by proving (in zero-knowledge) that such a signature is indeed issued by a specific nominator.

At ACISP 2004, Huang and Wang [13] mounted an attack showing that Kim et al.'s scheme is *not* nominative, since the nominator can also verify and prove the validity of a signature to a third party. To avoid this weakness, they further proposed a new nominative signature scheme. Actually, their scheme are also *convertible*. That is, the nominee can also convert a nominative signature into a publicly verifiable one, if necessary.

Soon, Susilo and Mu [18] claimed that the Huang-Wang scheme is not nominative either. Specifically, they described three deterministic algorithms that allow the nominator alone (i.e., without any help from the nominee) to (a) verify the validity of a nominative signature, (b) convince a third party that the signature is valid, and (c) convert the signature into a publicly verifiable one. However, Guo et al. [12] pointed out that all these attacks are actually *invalid*. In particular, they showed that there exists *no deterministic algorithm* allowing the nominator to check the validity of a published nominative signature if the decisional Diffie-Hellman (DDH) problem is hard. So, it is still not clear whether the Huang-Wang scheme is a truly secure nominative signature against adaptively chosen-message attacks.

In this paper, we present a detailed security analysis of the Huang-Wang scheme [13] and show that it is indeed *not* a secure nominative signature scheme, since it fails to meet the crucial security requirement: *verification untransferability*. Specifically, we identify an adaptively chosen-message attack against their scheme such that the nominator can determine the validity of a new message-signature pair with some indirect help from the nominee. Moreover, we point out that using this attack the nominator is further able to prove the validity of nominative signatures to a third party. Therefore, the Huang-Wang scheme also *does not* satisfy the *confirmation/disavowal untransferability*, which requires that except the nominee anybody should be unable to convince a third party accepting the validity of an alleged signature. In addition, we analyze the reasons why their scheme is insecure.

This paper is organized as follows. We first review Huang-Wang scheme in Section 2, and then present our attacks in Section 3. Finally, a brief conclusion is given in Section 4.

2 Review of the Huang-Wang Scheme

2.1 Security Model of Convertible Nominative Signature

Definition 1 (Syntax of Convertible Nominative Signatures). *According to [13], a convertible nominative signature scheme consists of a six-tuple (KG, Sig, Ver, Conf, Conv, UVer) of algorithms and protocols:*

1. *KG is a probabilistic algorithm to produce public/secret key pairs* (pk_s, sk_s) *and* (pk_v, sk_v) *for a nominator S and a nominee V respectively, when a security parameter* 1^n *is given.*
2. *Sig is an interactive protocol between the nominator S and nominee V to generate a nominative signature* σ *for a given message m.*
3. *Ver is a deterministic algorithm so that the nominee V can verify the validity of a presumed signature-message pair* (σ, m) *using V's private key* x_v.
4. *Conf is an interactive confirmation/disavowal protocol between the nominee V and a third party T so that V can convince T to accept the validity or invalidity of a presumed nominative signature. Conf should satisfy the regular requirements of both completeness and soundness.*
5. *Conv is a polynomial-time algorithm that allows the nominee V to convert a nominative signature into a universally verifiable signature.*
6. *Uver is a deterministic algorithm that allows anybody to verify the validity of a converted nominative signature.*

In [13], a convertible nominative signature is called *secure* if it satisfies the following three security requirements: *unforgeability*, *verification untransferability*, and *confirmation/disavowal untransferability*. Unforgeability requires that except the nominator, anybody including the nominee cannot forge a valid nominative signature on behalf of the nominator with non-negligible probability. The essential meaning of verification untransferability is that anybody including the nominator cannot determine the validity of a presumed nominative signature with non-negligible advantage, even if he/she already checked the validity of many other signatures with the nominee. The last requirement means that anybody including the nominator cannot convince a third party to accept the validity or invalidity of a given nominative signature, even if he/she already interacted with the nominee for many times. In the following, we recall the formal definitions of those three security requirement, which are specified in [13].

Definition 2 (Unforgeability). *Let F be a probabilistic polynomial-time (PPT) algorithm, called forger, who takes input the security parameter 1^n, the nominator S's public key pk_s, the nominee V's public and private key pair (pk_v, sk_v). F can interact with the signer S by running* Sig *to request valid signatures on polynomial-many adaptively chosen messages m_i, can request the execution of* Conf *and* Conv *for polynomial-many adaptively chosen strings, and finally outputs a forged message-signature pair (m, σ) with $m \in \{m_i\}$. We say a convertible nominative signature is* **unforgeable**, *if for all such F, for any constant $c > 0$, and for sufficiently large n, the probability that F outputs (m, σ) for which at least one of* Ver *or* Conf *outputs 1 is less than n^{-c}. That is,*

$$\Pr\left[\begin{array}{l}(m,\sigma) \leftarrow F^{\mathsf{Sig},\ \mathsf{Conf},\ \mathsf{Conv}}(1^n, pk_s, pk_v, sk_v) : m \in \{m_i\} \wedge \\ (\mathsf{Ver}(1^n, m, \sigma, pk_s, pk_v, sk_v) = 1 \vee \mathsf{Conf}(1^n, m, \sigma, pk_s, pk_v, sk_v) = 1)\end{array}\right] < n^{-c}.$$

Here, the probability is taken over the coin tosses of F, S, V, m and σ.

Definition 3 (Verification Untransferability). *Let A be a PPT attacking algorithm, which takes input security parameter 1^n, the nominator S's public/private key pair (pk_s, sk_s), the nominee V's public key pk_v, and a presumed signature-message pair (m, σ) which is valid with exact probability 1/2. A can request the execution of* Conf *and* Conv *for polynomial-many adaptively chosen strings except (m, σ), and finally outputs either 0 or 1. We say a convertible nominative signature is* **verification untransferable**, *if for any such PPT algorithm A, for any positive constant $c > 0$, and for any sufficiently large n, the following inequality holds:*

$$\left|\Pr\left[\begin{array}{l}A^{\mathsf{Conf},\ \mathsf{Conv}}(1^n, m, \sigma, pk_s, sk_s, pk_v) \\ = \mathsf{Ver}(1^n, m, \sigma, pk_s, pk_v, sk_v)\end{array}\right] - \frac{1}{2}\right| < n^{-c}.$$

Here, the probability is taken over the coin tosses of A, S, V, m and σ.

Definition 4 (Confirmation/Disavowal Untransferability). *Let A be a PPT attacking algorithm, which takes input the security parameter 1^n, the nominator S's public and private key pair (pk_s, sk_s), the nominee V's public key pk_v, and a target message-signature pair (m, σ) which is valid with exact probability 1/2. A can request the execution of* Conf *and* Conv *for polynomial-many adaptively chosen strings, where A can request execution of* Conf *with the nominee V on the target pair (m, σ) but cannot request execution of* Conv *on (m, σ). Then, at some point, the attacker A as the role of prover and a honest third party T as the role of verifier engage in a confirmation/disavowal protocol* Conf', *which could be different from* Conf, *to confirm or disavow the given pair (m, σ). When they stop, the third party T outputs either 0 or 1. We say a convertible nominative signature is* **confirmation/disavowal untransferable**, *if for all such*

A and Conf', for any constant $c > 0$, and for sufficiently large n, the following inequality holds:

$$\left| \Pr \begin{bmatrix} \mathsf{Conf'}^{\mathsf{Conf},\ \mathsf{Conv}}_{(A\ T)}(1^n, m, \sigma, pk_s, sk_s, pk_v) \\ = \mathsf{Ver}(1^n, m, \sigma, pk_s, pk_v, sk_v) \end{bmatrix} - \frac{1}{2} \right| < n^{-c}.$$

Here, the probability is taken over the coin tosses of A, T, S, V, m and σ.

2.2 The Huang-Wang Scheme

We now review the concrete Huang-Wang nominative signature scheme [13], which works in the discrete logarithm setting. In the following description, notation $x \in_R X$ means that an element x is uniformly chosen from set X at random, while $\|$ denote the concatenation of strings.

1. Key Generation (KG): Let p, q be two large primes such that $q|(p-1)$, and g an element in $\mathbb{Z}_p^*$ of order q. Assume that the discrete logarithm problem (DLP) in the group $\langle g \rangle$ is hard. The nominator S and the nominee V set their public/private key pairs as (y_s, x_s) and (y_v, x_v) respectively, where $x_s, x_v \in_R \mathbb{Z}_q$, $y_s = g^{x_s} \bmod p$, and $y_v = g^{x_v} \bmod p$. In addition, a one-way hash function $H : \{0,1\}^* \rightarrow \mathbb{Z}_q$ is publicly available.

2. Signature Generation (Sig): To generate a nominative signature $\sigma = (b, c, s)$ for a message m, the nominator S and nominee V jointly perform as follows.

1) The nominee V first randomly picks $R_1, R_2 \in_R \mathbb{Z}_q^*$, then sends (a, c) to the nominator S by computing

$$a = g^{R_1} \bmod p \quad \text{and} \quad c = y_v^{R_2} \bmod p.$$

2) Upon receiving (a, c), the nominator S chooses $r \in_R \mathbb{Z}_q$, and sends (b, e, s') to V by computing

$$\begin{aligned} b &= ag^{-r} \bmod p, \\ e &= H(y_v \| b \| c \| m), \\ s' &= r - x_s \cdot e \bmod q. \end{aligned} \tag{1}$$

3) Then, nominee V checks whether both of the following equations hold:

$$e \equiv H(y_v \| b \| c \| m) \quad \text{and} \quad a \equiv g^{s'} y_s^e b \bmod p. \tag{2}$$

If not, output "False". Otherwise, nominee V outputs $\sigma = (b, c, s)$ as the nominative signature for message m by setting

$$s = s' + R_2 - R_1 \bmod q. \tag{3}$$

3. Verification (Ver): Given a signature $\sigma = (b, c, s)$ and a message m, the nominee V accepts σ as valid if and only if

$$(g^s y_s^e b)^{x_v} \equiv c \bmod p, \text{ where } e = H(y_v \| b \| c \| m). \quad (4)$$

4. Confirmation and Disavowal (Conf): For an alleged nominative signature $\sigma = (b, c, s)$ for message m, let $e = H(y_v\|b\|c\|m)$ and $d = g^s y_s^e b \bmod p$. The nominee V uses Michels-Stadler's protocol [15] to confirm or disavow the validity of σ via proving $\log_d c = \log_g y_v$ or $\log_d c \neq \log_g y_v$. Refer to Section 2.2 in [13] for the detail how this proof is conducted interactively.

5. Signature Conversion (Conv): To convert a nominative signature $\sigma = (b, c, s)$ into a universally verifiable one, V just needs to release σ together with a non-interactive proof π showing that $\log_d c = \log_g y_v$, where $d = g^s y_s^e b \bmod p$ and $e = H(y_v\|b\|c\|m)$. Please check Section 2.3 in [13] to know how to generate and verify the proof π.

6. Universal Verification (UVer): Anybody can verify the validity of (σ, π) by checking that π is a correct non-interactive proof for $\log_d c = \log_g y_v$, where $d = g^s y_s^e b \bmod p$ and $e = H(y_v\|b\|c\|m)$.

3 Security Remarks on the Huang-Wang Scheme

In [13], the authors provided some security arguments to show that their nominative signature scheme meets the three desirable security requirements: Unforgeability, verification untransferability, and confirmation/disavowal untransferability. Note that those security arguments are informal explanations instead of formal proofs, so the security of Huang-Wang scheme is *not* guaranteed in fact: It may be secure or insecure.

As pointed out in [13], it seems that the unforgeability of Huang-Wang scheme is related to that of Schnorr signature [17]. This can be informally explained as follows. Let a PPT algorithm F be a forger, who is given the security parameter 1^n, the nominator S's public key pk_s, and the nominee V's public and private key pair (pk_v, sk_v). According to Definition 2, F's goal is to forge a signature $\sigma = (b, c, s)$ for a new message m. For this purpose, F can adaptively choose messages m_i and then run the interactive protocol Sig with the signer, under the limitation that m is not equal to any m_i. If F's output $(m, \sigma = (b, c, s))$ is a valid message-signature pair, we have $(g^s y_s^e b)^{x_v} \equiv c \bmod p$, where $e = H(y_v\|b\|c\|m)$. By letting $s' = -s \bmod q$, this implies that the forger F can get a triple (b, c, s') for message m such that $g^{s'} \equiv y_s^e \cdot (bc^{-x_v^{-1}}) \bmod p$, where $e = H(y_v\|b\|c\|m)$. This triple (b, c, s') is very *similar* to a Schnorr signature (r, t) for message m so that $g^t = y_s^e \cdot r \bmod p$, where $e = H(r\|m)$. However, Schnorr signature is proved to be unforgeable if the discrete logarithm is hard [16]. So it is likely that Huang-Wang scheme is also unforgeable, though elaborated work is needed to formally prove this result by using the forking lemma proposed in [16].

For other two security requirements, however, it is another story. In the following sections, we present some direct attacks to show that the Huang-Wang scheme satisfies *neither* verification untransferability *nor* confirmation/disavowal untransferability.

3.1 Verification Untransferability

In [13], the authors argued that the Huang-Wang scheme satisfies the verification untransferability, because both of the following two statements hold:

(a) A presumed signature $\sigma = (b, c, s)$ is valid for a message $m \Longleftrightarrow \log_g y_v = \log_d c$, where $d = g^s y_s^e b \bmod p$ for $e = H(y_v||b||c||m)$. However, without the knowledge of both x_v (nominee V's private key) and R_2 (a random number selected by V) an attacker A cannot determine the validity of σ unless it resorts to nominee V's direct help on pair (m, σ) or it can solve the decisional Deffie-Hellman (DDH) problem w.r.t the tuple (g, y_v, d, c).

(b) Michels-Stadler's interactive protocol [15] is an untransferable zero knowledge proof for proving whether two discrete logarithm is equal or not.

However, we notice that neither of the above two statements are correct (and shall be explained below). Moreover, based on this observation we can mount a concrete attack on the Huang-Wang scheme so that the verification untransferability is violated.

Statement (a) is invalid, because the attacker A can "solve" the DDH problem in this scenario. This is due to the fact that according to Definition 3, an attacker A for verification untransferability is allowed to access DDH oracle by running Conf with nominee V. Hence, for given (d, c) attacker A can know whether (g, y_v, d, c) is a DH tuple by asking V whether $(g, y_v, \bar{d}, \bar{c})$ is a DH tuple, where $\bar{d} = dg^{\bar{R}_2}$ and $\bar{c} = cy_v^{\bar{R}_2} \bmod p$ are set by the attacker for some randomly chosen number $\bar{R}_2$.

Actually, using the above fact we identify an concrete attack to show that the Huang-Wang scheme is not verification untransferable. In this attack, we assume the attacker A has the knowledge of nominator S's private key sk_s. Note that this is consistent with Definition 3, which formally specified the verification untransferability. In other words, the nominator S is also allowed to be an attacker for this security requirement. Now, we describe the attack in detail.

Attack 1. To check whether an alleged nominative signature $\sigma = (b, c, s)$ is valid for a message m, the attacker A (or the nominator S) can perform as follows.

1. A first selects another message $\bar{m}$, and two random numbers $\bar{R}_1, \bar{R}_2 \in_R \mathbb{Z}_q^*$.
2. Then, using x_s the attacker A can compute a triple $\bar{\sigma} = (\bar{b}, \bar{c}, \bar{s})$ by

$$\begin{aligned}\bar{b} &= bg^{\bar{R}_1} \bmod p,\\ \bar{c} &= cy_v^{\bar{R}_2} \bmod p,\\ \bar{s} &= s + x_s(e-\bar{e}) + (\bar{R}_2 - \bar{R}_1) \bmod q,\end{aligned} \tag{5}$$

where $e = H(y_v||b||c||m)$ and $\bar{e} = H(y_v||\bar{b}||\bar{c}||\bar{m})$.

3. Finally, A interacts with the nominee V to check the validity of message-signature pair $(\bar{m}, \bar{\sigma})$. The attacker A concludes that the presumed message-signature pair (m, σ) is valid, if $(\bar{m}, \bar{\sigma})$ is valid. Otherwise, A concludes $(\bar{m}, \bar{\sigma})$ is invalid.

The correctness of Attack 1 can be justified as follows. According to Eq.(5), we have

$$\begin{aligned}g^{\bar{s}} y_s^{\bar{e}} \bar{b} &= g^s y_s^{e-\bar{e}} g^{\bar{R}_2 - \bar{R}_1} y_s^{\bar{e}} b g^{\bar{R}_1} \bmod p\\ &= (g^s y_s^e b) g^{\bar{R}_2} \bmod p.\end{aligned}$$

Therefore, (m, σ) is valid $\Leftrightarrow$ $[\exists R_2\ s.t.\ g^s y_s^e b = g^{R_2} \bmod p \wedge c = y_v^{R_2} \bmod p]$ $\Leftrightarrow$ $[g^{\bar{s}} y_s^{\bar{e}} \bar{b} = g^{\bar{R}_2 + R_2} \bmod p \wedge \bar{c} = cy_v^{\bar{R}_2} = y_v^{\bar{R}_2 + R_2} \bmod p]$ $\Leftrightarrow$ $(\bar{m}, \bar{\sigma})$ is valid.

Now, we return to Statement (b): It is also false, since Michels-Stadler's protocol [15] is *not* zero-knowledge, as first pointed out by Camenisch and Shoup (See Section 5 of [3]). Namely, (in our setting) the value of d^{x_v} is additionally revealed in the case of $\log_g y_v \neq \log_d c$ and the verifier dishonestly selects d such that he knows $\log_g d$. This weakness shall naturally affect the formal security of the Huang-Wang scheme, though we do not any find direct attack by using it [1].

3.2 Confirmation/Disavowal Untransferability

According to Definition 4, the confirmation/disavowal untransferability requires that given a presumed message-signature pair (m, σ), any PPT attacker A (including the nominator S but not the nominee V) cannot convince a third party T to accept the validity or invalidity of this pair (m, σ), where A is allowed to run Conf with V on any string and Conv with V on any string other than the target (m, σ).

However, we find out that using Attack 1 against verification untransferability as a subroutine, we can break the confirmation/disavowal untransferability as well. We now briefly present this attack.

Attack 2. To convince a third party T accepting the validity or invalidity of a target message-signature pair (m, σ), an attacker (who knows the private key x_s of the nominator S) can perform as follows.

1. From the given pair (m, σ), the attacker A first creates a new message-signature pair $(\bar{m}, \bar{\sigma})$ as in Attack 1 (see Eq. (5)).

[1] In the submission version of this paper, we did showed "an attack" by employing this flaw in the ZK protocol. However, when preparing this final version we noticed that "this attack" is actually invalid since it requires the attacker know the value of $\log_g d$, i.e., the random number R_2 selected by the nominee.

2. After that, A asks the nominee V to convert $(\bar{m}, \bar{\sigma})$. Therefore, A can get a non-interactive proof $\bar{\pi}$ that shows whether $\bar{\sigma}$ is a valid signature for message $\bar{m}$.
3. Then, the attacker A forwards $(\bar{m}, \bar{\sigma}, \bar{\pi}, \pi')$ to the third party T, where π' is a non-interactive zero-knowledge proof showing that $\bar{\sigma} = (\bar{b}, \bar{c}, \bar{s})$ is properly generated according to Eq. (5), i.e., A knows that there are two random numbers $(\bar{R}_1, \bar{R}_2)$ so that the following conditions hold simultaneously:

$$\bar{b}\ b = g^{\bar{R}_1} \bmod p \wedge \bar{c}\ \ c = y_v^{\bar{R}_2} \bmod p \wedge g^{\bar{s}} y_s^{\bar{e}} \bar{b}\ \ (g^s y_s^e b) = g^{\bar{R}_2} \bmod p. \quad (6)$$

4. Finally, the third party T validates whether π' is a correct proof for Eq. (6). If no, halt. Otherwise, T further checks whether $(\bar{\sigma}, \bar{\pi})$ is valid for message $\bar{m}$. If yes, T concludes (m, σ) is valid. Otherwise, (m, σ) is invalid.

Note that using the well-known technique called *signature proof of knowledge* [2], it is very easy for A to issue proof π' for Eq. (6). Alternatively, A can run an interactive protocol with T to prove that the conditions in Eq.(6) hold. Moreover, during this procedure it is infeasible for T to derive x_s since this proof is zero-knowledge.

The correctness of Attack 2 is almost obvious, since $(\bar{m}, \bar{\sigma})$ and (m, σ) have the same validity or invalidity and the attacker does not ask the nominee V to convert σ at all. Therefore, Attack 2 breaks the confirmation/disavowal untransferability of Huang-Wang scheme. That is, at least for the nominator the Huang-Wang is not confirmation/disavowal untransferable.

3.3 Countermeasures

As we mentioned above, the Huang-Wang scheme employs a flawed building block: Michels-Stadler's protocol, which is designed to prove whether or not two discrete logarithms are equal. However, this protocol is *not* zero-knowledge, contrary to the claims made in [15]. To avoid this weakness, we can choose two truly zero-knowledge protocols from [5] and [3] to prove the equality or inequality of two discrete logarithms, respectively.

Moreover, according to the specification of confirmation/disavowal untransferability (Definition 4), in the setting of nominative signatures one should use *concurrent zero-knowledge* (CZK) protocols rather than *special honest-verifier zero-knowledge* (SHVZK) protocols [3]. The reason is that an attacker here may act as an arbitrary cheating verifier during the execution of Conf protocol to confirm or disavow an alleged nominative signature. Fortunately, by using the techniques suggested in any of [7, 8, 10], we can easily transform SHVZK protocols from [5] and [3] to CZK protocols. Using such CZK protocols to confirm or disavow nominative signatures, the confirmation/disavowal untransferability can be guaranteed. Moreover, the formal proofs can be adapted from that given in [1, 11], where the transcripts of verifying designated confirmer signatures are also required to be untransferable.

However, we do not find any effective countermeasure to prevent Attack 1 at this moment. In fact, we believe this is the essential security flaw of Huang-Wang nominative signature scheme.

4 Conclusions

In this paper, we presented a security analysis of the Huang-Wang convertible nominative scheme [13]. According to our results, the Huang-Wang scheme is not secure, since it fails to meet two desirable security requirements: *verification untransferability* and *confirmation/disavowal untransferability*. Specifically, we identified two attacks to show that their scheme violates those two security requirements. In fact, those two attacks are due to an essential design flaw in the scheme. In addition, we also remarked that the Huang-Wang scheme employs a flawed zero-knowledge protocol. Moreover, we pointed out the reasons why their scheme is insecure. As the future work, it is interesting to consider how to prevent our Attack 1 against verification untransferability and how to design newly secure nominative signatures.

References

1. J. Camenisch, and M. Michels. Confirmer Signature Schemes Secure Against Adaptive Adversaries. In: *Proc. of Advances in Cryptology - EUROCRYPT '00*, LNCS 1870, pp. 243-258. Springer-Verlag, 2000.
2. J. Camenisch and M. Stadler. Efficient Group Signature Schemes for Large Groups. In: *Proc. of Advances in Cryptology - CRYPTO '97*, LNCS 1294, pp. 410-424. Springer-Verlag, 1997.
3. J. Camenisch and V. Shoup. Practical Verifiable Encryption and Decryption of Discrete Logarithms. In: *Proc. of Advances in Cryptology - CRYPTO '03*, LNCS 2729, pp. 126-144. Springer-Verlag, 2003.
4. D. Chaum and H. Antwerpen. Undeniable Signatures. In: *Proc. of Advances in Cryptology - CRYPTO '89*, LNCS 435, pp. 212-216. Springer-Verlag, 1989.
5. D. Chaum and T. P. Pedersen. Wallet Database with Observers. In: *Proc. of Advances in Cryptology - CRYPTO '92*, LNCS 740, pp. 89-105. Springer-Verlag, 1993.
6. D. Chaum. Designated Confirmer Signatures. In: *Proc. of Advances in Cryptology - EUROCRYPT '94*, LNCS 950, pp. 86-91. Springer-Verlag, 1994.
7. R. Cramer, I. Damgård, and P. MacKenzie. Efficient Zero-Knowledge Proofs of Knowledge Without Intractability Assumptions. In: *Proc. of PKC '00*, LNCS 1751, pp. 354-373. Springer-Verlag, 2000.
8. I. Damgård. Efficient Concurrent Zero-Knowledge in the Auxiliary String Model. In: *Proc. of Advances in Cryptology - EUROCRYPT '00*, LNCS 1807, pp. 418-430, Springer-Verlag, 2000.
9. S. D. Galbraith and W. Mao. Invisibility and Anonymity of Undeniable and Confirmer Signatures. In: *Proc. of CT-RSA '03*, LNCS 2612, pp. 80-97. Springer-Verlag, 2003.

10. R. Gennaro. Multi-trapdoor Commitments and Their Applications to Proofs of Knowledge Secure Under Concurrent Man-in-the-Middle Attacks. In: *Advances in Cryptology - CRYPTO '04*, LNCS 3152, pp. 220-236. Springer-Verlag, 2004.
11. C. Gentry, D. Molnar, and Z. Ramzan. Efficient Designated Confirmer Signatures without Random Oracles or General Zero-knowledge Proofs. In: *Advances in Cryptology - ASIACRYPT 2005*, LNCS 3788, pp. 662-681. Springer-Verlag, 2005.
12. L. Guo, G. Wang, and D. Wong. Further Discussions on the Security of a Nominative Signature Scheme. *IACR ePrint archive*, http://eprint.iacr.org/2006/007.
13. Z. Huang and Y. Wang. Convertible Nominative Signatures. In: *Proc. of Information Security and Privacy (ACISP '04)*, LNCS 3108, pp. 348-357. Springer-Verlag, 2004.
14. S.J. Kim, S.J. Park, and D.H. Won. Zero-Knowledge Nominative Signatures. In: *Proc. of PragoCrypt' 96, International Conference on the Theory and Applications of Cryptology*, pp. 380-392, 1996.
15. M. Michels and M. Stadler. Efficient Convertible Undeniable Signature Schemes. In: *Proc. of 4th Annual Workshop on Selected Areas in Cryptography (SAC'97)*, pp. 231-244, 1997.
16. D. Pointcheval and J. Stern. Security Arguments for Digital Signatures and Blind Signatures. *Journal of Cryptology*, 13(3): 361-396, 2000.
17. C.P. Schnorr. Efficient Signature Generation by Smart Cards. *Journal of Cryptology*, 4(3): 161-174, 1991.
18. W. Susilo and Y. Mu. On the Security of Nominative Signatures. In: *Proc. of Information Security and Privacy (ACISP '05)*, LNCS 3547, pp. 329-335. Springer-Verlag, 2005.

Using Payment Gateways to Maintain Privacy in Secure Electronic Transactions

Alapan Arnab and Andrew Hutchison

Data Network Architectures Group
Department of Computer Science
University of Cape Town
{aarnab, hutch}@cs.uct.ac.za

Abstract. Because many current payment systems are poorly implemented, or of incompetence, private data of consumers such as payment details, addresses and their purchase history can be compromised. Furthermore, current payment systems do not offer any non-repudiable verification to a completed transaction, which poses risks to all the parties of the transaction – the consumer, the merchant and the financial institution. One solution to this problem was SET, but it was never really a success because of its complexity and poor reception from consumers. In this paper, we introduce a third party payment system that aims to preserve privacy by severing the link between their purchase and payment records, while providing a traceable transaction that maintains its integrity and is non-repudiable. Our system also removes much of the responsibilities placed on the merchant with regards to securing sensitive data related to customer payment, thus increasing the potential of small businesses to take part in e-commerce without significant investments in computer security.

1 Introduction

In February 1996, the two leading credit card companies, Mastercard and Visa, together with a number of other companies like IBM started a process to create standardised payment processes and the security thereof [9]. Their result, Secure Electronic Transaction (SET) specification, was more than a security protocol for electronic payments, and encompassed the entire business transaction process. While technically lauded [3, 8] SET has never been a success [7, 6], for a number of reasons, including the complexity in implementation, cost of implementation and reluctance from customers.

Some of the security features offered by properly implemented SET system include:

1. end to end secure communication amongst all parties involved in the payment transaction
2. establishment of trust for all parties in a transaction
3. privacy of the consumer's payment details from the merchant
4. privacy of merchant's sale details details from the payment gateway

Please use the following format when citing this chapter:

Arnab, A. and Hutchison, A., 2007, in IFIP International Federation for Information Processing, Volume 232, New Approaches for Security, Privacy and Trust in Complex Environments, eds. Venter, H., Eloff, M., Labuschagne, L., Eloff, J., von Solms, R., (Boston: Springer), pp. 277–288.

With the absence of SET, e-commerce sites have implemented their own payment systems, and except for the spread of the use third party certified digital certificates by merchants and the use of encrypted communication channel (usually through the use of SSL or TLS) between the consumer and the merchant, nothing in the payment process can be considered standardised. This creates a great risk for consumers as their data can be compromised by the merchant due to inadequate protection or incompetence [3] or collected for sending spam to the consumer [5].

Another problem with current systems is that the consumer has to trust that the merchant will carry out the transaction correctly, and that there is adequate security in the communication links between the merchant and the bank. Furthermore, receipts produced by the merchant cannot be verified to confirm that the amount reflected on the receipt is the same as the amount actually charged. If a dispute were to arise, the consumer has to prove that the merchant's transaction service is at fault as opposed to an attempted fraud by the consumer. Thus, the status quo presents great privacy and security risk to the consumer.

In this paper, we re-examine the use of a third party payment service. A payment gateway, ideally operated by a trusted financial service for secure electronic transactions, with a main aim to promote the privacy of the parties involved.

2 Requirements

There are a number of requirements for electronic transactions, and we have identified the following key requirements, which we drafted from a number of different systems including SET and other research in this area [5, 10, 2].

2.1 Secure communication between all parties

There needs to be secure communication channels between all parties involved in a transaction. It is necessary to ensure that information is not revealed to parties not involved in the transaction regardless of the importance of the information, and that the integrity of the communication is preserved.

2.2 Minimise the sharing of data between the parties

There are two different aspects to this requirement:

1. The payment service (referred to as the payment gateway) does not need to know the details of the subject of the transaction. This is particularly important if the subject of the transaction is of sensitive nature, especially if the subject is not held in high regard in the consumer's community.
2. The merchant does not need to know the payment details of the subject other than the confirmation that the payment has succeeded. In many cases, the consumer may not want to build a relationship with the merchant, because the purchases are in-frequent (holiday travel for example). Thus, it is in the consumer's best interest

to reduce the amount of information shared with the merchant. There are also cases where the purchaser is not the end consumer of the service or product, for example in the case of gift purchases such as flowers. In such a case, it is not reasonable to collect purchaser details when they have very little in connection to the consumer.

2.3 Support a number of payment mechanisms

The credit card is the dominant payment tool on the Internet, but it is not necessarily available to everyone [5, 7]. Integrating other payment mechanisms such as debit cards, bank transfers, cheques or even other payment services such as PayPal is costly for the merchant, but a payment gateway can handle multiple payment services if there are a sufficient number of consumers spread over a number of different merchants that would be willing to use it.

2.4 Traceability and verification of transactions

In [10], the authors discuss how traceability of transactions is an important requirement in building trust. Traceability of a transaction allows for the correct auditing, provides for accountability with the implementation of associated security policies as well as a mechanism for verification of the transaction [10]. As discussed earlier, current transaction receipts offered by e-commerce sites provide neither non-repudiation nor integrity, and are thus not suitable for traceability or verification.

2.5 Merchant Authentication

It is necessary to link merchants to the payments from consumers, and there is a need to confirm that the merchant is accepted by the payment gateway. This promotes a secondary layer of trust for the consumer in that the merchant is an entity that is still operating and in business.

2.6 Minimal set up cost and infrastructure

Ideally, electronic transactions should not require large investments from any of the parties involved. One of the problems with the full implementation of SET was the requirement that every customer needed a digital certificate. This represented a sizable investment from the customer as well as third parties who needed to issue, verify and maintain these digital certificates.

3 The Payment Gateway

3.1 System Operation

Our system differs from the traditional payment mechanism by separating the sale of products and services of the merchant, and the payment transaction between the consumer and the payment gateway. The payment gateway is intended to be a financial web service, catering for a number of different merchants, but, at the same time not resembling a bank. In many cases, consumers do not need or want a relationship with the merchant or the payment system beyond their immediate transaction. Thus, the process of registering users and allowing transfers of money between registered users (like Paypal) is not the aim.

One of the main functions of a bank is to provide their clients with suitable means to conduct commercial transactions like providing a checking service or issuing credit cards. For this reason, Paypal can be seen as a bank, as they provide the means for their clients to conduct electronic transactions. In contrast, the payment gateway we present in this paper acts as an agent who helps in concluding financial transactions between the merchant and the client.

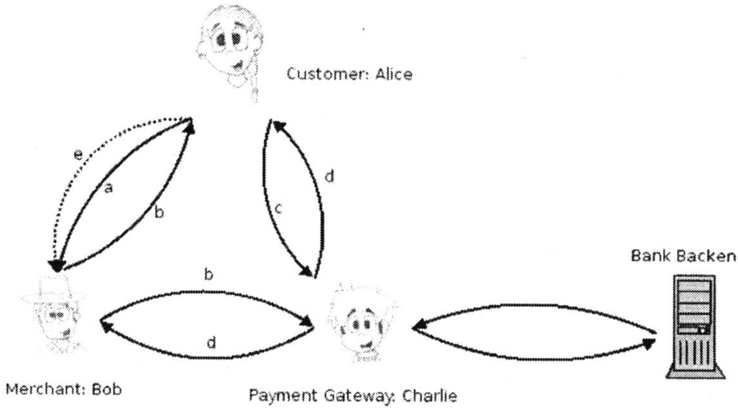

Fig. 1. Overview of the Payment Gateway System

Figure 1, gives an overview of our proposed system, comprising of four players: a bank (or similar financial institution), the payment gateway, the merchant and the consumer. The payment gateway has a secure connection to the bank which provides verification of credit cards and carry out the actual financial transaction.

After the consumer has finished shopping (step a in figure 1), the merchant creates a signed invoice for its services and products for the consumer. Another invoice with four components – a globally unique verifiable identifier (all documents will have verifiable globally unique identifiers through the use of schemes such as the one described in [1]), the amount payable (and its terms e.g. payment in full or in installments), a globally unique merchant identifier (issued by the payment gateway) and a digital signature of the invoice – is created for the payment gateway. These invoices are forwarded to the respective parties (step b). The second invoice has no details concerning the consumer, and thus the details of the sale is completely masked. The digital signature assures non-repudiation on the value of the sale and performs authentication on behalf of the merchant. Furthermore, this approach allows for non-real time communication

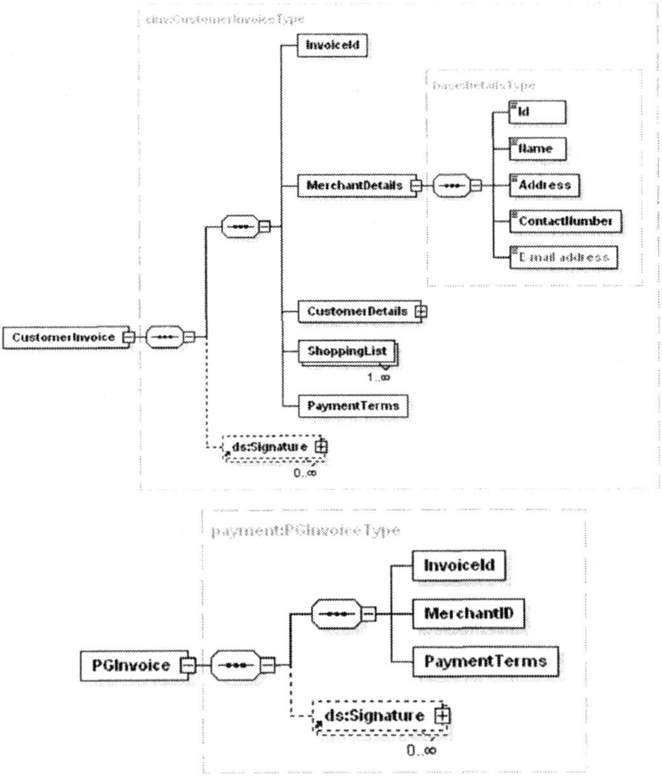

Fig. 2. XML schema diagrams for a customer invoice (left) and one for the payment gateway (right)

between the merchant and the payment gateway. XML schemas describing how such invoices could look are shown in figure 2.

The consumer is also not required to pay immediately (although the merchant is not required to perform its duties without being paid), and can shop at other merchants if they want to. The consumer can thus pay many invoices to the payment gateway within one transaction (step c), and it is the payment gateway's responsibility to allocate the receipts accordingly. Once the payment is processed, the payment gateway creates two receipts (step d). For the consumer, the payment gateway lists the terms of payment (e.g. credit card, bank transfer etc.), the identifiers of the invoices being settled and an unique identifier which is then digitally signed. For the merchants, the payment gateway creates a signed receipt listing the merchant identifier, the invoice identifier, the identifier of the consumer's receipt, an unique identifier for the merchant's invoice and the amount. Depending on the set up, this receipt could contain a number of invoices collected on the merchant's behalf since the last receipt. XML schemas describing how such receipts could look are shown in figure 3.

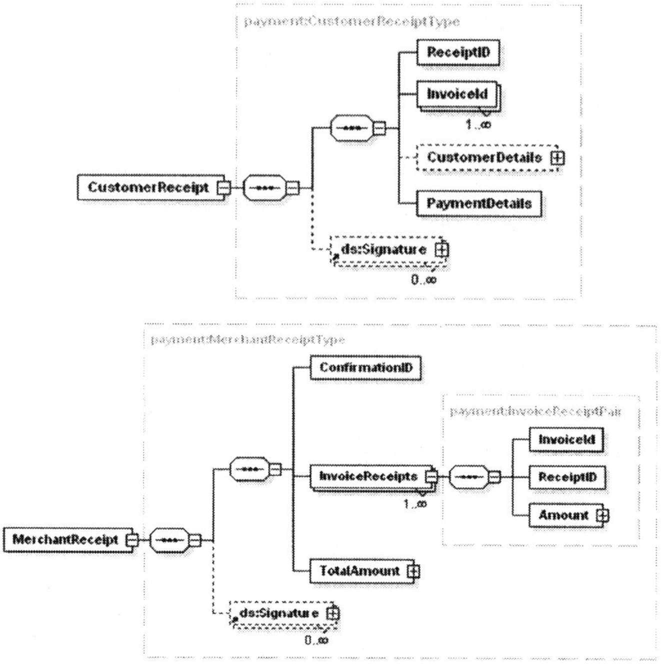

Fig. 3. XML schema diagrams for a customer receipt (left) and one for the merchant (right)

Like the invoices generated by the merchant, digital signature assures non-repudiation and authenticates the payment gateway. The merchant also does not learn any details on how the consumer paid for the goods, and in fact cannot even ascertain whether the recipient of the goods and services and the purchaser are the same. Thus the privacy of the consumer is secured. In step e, the consumer can use his/her receipt to prove that the services were paid for in the case of a dispute.

3.2 Security Considerations

Chain of Trust To provide trusted digital certificates, trusted third party certified digital certificates are required. However, unlike the full implementation of SET [3, 9], users do not require digital certificates to take full advantage of the benefits.

Secure Communication The communication between the bank backend and the payment gateway must be secure. However, it is easier to guarantee and audit one such service as opposed to every merchant wishing to perform secure transactions. SSL/TLS can be used to secure communication between the consumer and the payment gateway, and thus the consumer does not require his/her own digital certificate, although mutual authentication would be preferred. Communication between the payment gateway and the merchant can either be secured through an encrypted tunnel such as SSL/TLS or through the use of XML encryption. The later is possible as both parties have each other's public keys (to verify digital signatures).

Authentication There is no authentication of the consumer, and thus it could be possible for the consumer to be totally anonymous during a payment transaction. Merchants are authenticated using their digital signature. The merchant identifier serves as an additional layer of authentication, but is aimed more for easier administration.

Minimise Data Sharing The only data shared between the payment gateway and the merchant are identifiers to link transactions and the payment amount. Like SET's dual signature scheme, payment details and merchant's sale details remain hidden from the non-participating parties. Furthermore, unlike SET where it is not possible to prove that the payment gateway is known by the consumer [3], it is possible to show that the customer is aware of all the parties involved in the transaction, and can potentially even have a choice in the payment gateway.

Traceability and Verification The use of digital signatures allow for the verification of each step of the payment transaction. It is possible to trace the entire payment process, should it be required (during a criminal investigation for example), if both the merchant's and the payment gateway's records are matched. An examination of one party's records is not going to be enough to reveal the complete picture, thus achieving the privacy goals, without compromising traceability.

4 Potential uses of payment gateways

4.1 DRM and online services

In [4], the authors discuss how consumers expect almost no relationship between the rights holders of content and themselves, once they purchase a copy of the content. They argue that DRM breaks that mould, with the potential for the rights holder to monitor both the purchase and the use of the content. The payment gateway service was initially developed as a mechanism to break one part of such a relationship, and forms part of a wider DRM project. In the case of DRM, it is also necessary to cater for scenarios where the payment is at a future date (for example: consumer can use product until a certain date, and is then required to pay for additional usage). No current DRM system can accommodate such a scenario as they do not have any payment verification support. Since our receipts are machine readable, and verifiable, it is easy to incorporate such a mechanism.

There are also other online services for which the consumer would either like privacy due to their sensitive nature (adult entertainment for example) or would not like to establish long relationships because of their short nature (once off donations or Wi-Fi hotspot purchases while travelling for example).

4.2 Small Business

The Internet presents great opportunities for small businesses for wider market access. However, setting up and running a secure e-commerce site is a costly exercise. Because of this, less established businesses have a lower degree of trust from consumers when compared to their more well established rivals. A payment gateway system as described here has the potential to increase the trust that is placed in such a business due to two factors:

1. It is easier to conduct regular audits and ensure the security of a few payment gateways instead of auditing and securing every online payment system. Payment gateways can also publicise these audits in order to establish a higher degree of trust in the payment gateway.
2. Businesses which have a relationship with established payment gateways are less likely to be phishing scams or conduct other fraudulent activities, as there is a higher chance of being monitored.

For these reasons, payment gateways could be of great use for smaller, less established online e-ventures.

4.3 Digital Vouchers

Instead of the merchant initiating the transaction, it could be possible for the customer to pay upfront, in return for a redeemable voucher. This voucher can then be presented to the merchant as payment for services/product. To avoid duplication of vouchers, redemption of vouchers need to be real time atomic transactions; but the infrastructure described in this paper does not need to be significantly changed to accommodate vouchers.

We think that one of the main uses of vouchers could be in the realm of micro payments. The customer could buy low denomination vouchers (for example one hundred 10 cent vouchers) and then exchange these vouchers for products or services. The redeemed vouchers can be paid out in bulk at the end of the day (or even week or month), thus reducing the costs of the transaction.

5 Economics and Practicalities of running a payment gateway

In section 4, we discussed at least two areas where we think a payment gateway will be more effective that current payment systems. In this section, we briefly examine the potential business case/practicalities offered by our proposed system, as well as a few related issues.

5.1 Running a third party payment service

The main aim of a payment gateway is to serve as a payment point for a number of different merchants, and thus the payment gateway will have to charge the merchants for such a service. Thus, this service will only make sense for any merchant if this solution is cheaper when compared to implementing the payment service on their own.

There is effectively two sets of costs for any payment service, whether implemented by the gateway or the merchant: the cost of implementation and maintenance of a secure processing service and the transaction costs of processing payments.

Implementation and Maintenance Costs In either approach, a base security implementation cost is incurred, as the merchant will still be required to implement security to protect customer data. There will also be an initial set up cost to integrate the receipt/invoice system to the merchant's billing system. In either approach, we estimate that there will be no significant difference in costs, if the merchant only adopts one payment mechanism. If the merchant implements other payment mechanisms, additional costs are incurred, which are not comparable in the case of using a payment gateway.

However, one cost that is not often taken into account is the legal and regulatory costs associated with collecting data from customers. As discussed in [11], an increase in data collection from consumers increases the privacy risk ceiling for a collector, which has a significant increase in security costs. Thus, collecting and processing payment details from consumers will have an increase in costs, when compared to simply collecting data to provide the associated service, especially if the service is delivered on the Internet, thus not usually requiring the customer's private details.

Transaction Processing Costs Transaction processing costs stem from charges levied by credit card and other financial companies for completing the transaction. These charges form a significant cost for the merchant, and can be as high as 5% of the value of the transaction.

Business Case for the use of a Payment Gateway The payment gateway could take advantage of a higher volume of transactions, as they will process more transactions than a single merchant. Consequently, payment gateways can be in a position to negotiate better transaction processing charges than individual merchants. Thus, it should be possible for the payment gateway can charge the merchant lower than the financial institution, but still maintain a significant margin on their own costs.

Another value of the payment gateway is the potential to cater for different payment types. Again, with a higher volume of transactions; a higher number of merchants can cater for different payment types; without significant investment in such payment mechanisms.

Core to the success of a payment gateway will depend on the trustworthiness of the system; and thus they will need to have verifiable, well known, security audits that can be used to build customer trust. This can also be used as a marketing strategy to convince merchants to join the system.

It will still be possible to create relationships between the consumer and the merchant, through the use of customer logins etc. However, this will no longer be a requirement as it is currently for many e-commerce systems. Thus, it would be possible for merchants to device incentives for customers to maintain a long lasting relationship, but without loosing sales from consumers who do not wish to make such relationships.

5.2 Returns and Charge Backs

A direct problem with anonymous payments arises in the scenario when a product is returned or the merchant returns part (or the full) of the payment back to the customer. While receipts issued by the payment gateway can be used by the customer to prove their original payment, charge backs are not possible. One potential solution to this problem, would be the use of vouchers as explained in section 4.3. If the customer is also signed up as a merchant, then they can redeem the voucher directly. Alternate voucher redemption plans into other monetary units could also be considered.

6 Comparison to Similar Services

There are a number of payment systems used on the Internet, and in this section, we compare our system to some of these systems. Many of these systems are proprietary, and few published details are available on how their backend works.

6.1 RegNet (http://www.regnet.com)

RegNet (and other similar websites) offer secure payment solutions for digital software licenses. They offer a huge catalogue of products from a number of different vendors, and they are in effect an shopping site for software licenses, although, like our payment gateway, they do not handle the subject of the transaction. However, unlike our payment gateway, they have complete detail on what the customer purchases, and in the case of most licenses, how long the licenses are and for what purposes the licenses are being purchased.

6.2 PayPal (http://www.paypal.com/)

PayPal is one of the most established payment systems around, originating as a mechanism to pay for auction purchases on e-Bay. Like our payment gateway, PayPal also ensures dual privacy – the merchant does not know the payment details of the consumer, and PayPal does not know the sale details of the merchant.

However, PayPal is more than a payment mechanism; and can be more appropriately described as a bank. In PayPal, both the consumer and the merchant have to be registered, and with some exceptions, both parties can receive and pay money to other PayPal account holders. Because of this restriction, PayPal cannot operate in every country.

Another difference between our system and PayPal is the provision of signed receipts and invoices; although these can probably be easily added to PayPal.

6.3 Google Checkout (http://checkout.google.com/)

Google Checkout is one of the newest payment systems, released in mid 2006, and in many respects, it is similar to RegNet as opposed to PayPal and our payment gateway.

Like RegNet, Google Checkout offers a secure payment solution for multiple online stores, preserving customer payment privacy. However, unlike PayPal and our payment gateway, Google Checkout has a complete detail on what was purchased by the consumer. Thus, like RegNet, it is an electronic store that does not handle the subject of the purchase.

7 Conclusion

In current e-commerce systems for the Internet, the customer has to place a high degree of trust in the merchant, that the merchant will process the transaction correctly and handle the details of the transaction in a secure manner. Furthermore, merchants force the customers to create relationships, collecting data that is sometimes unnecessary, increasing the risks for the customer when computer security breaches occur.

In this paper, we have presented a payment gateway system that preserves privacy for all the parties involved in the transaction, as well as minimises the risks to data security for consumers. Furthermore, the system also provides traceability of all transactions, complete with signed invoices and receipts for both merchants and customers that provide integrity and non-repudiation; properties that are not possible in most of the current payment systems. The invoices and receipts are machine readable and thus can be used as payment tokens or proof of payment for various services, including DRM systems and web based services.

8 Acknowledgements

XML schema diagrams generated using XML Spy 2004.

This work is partially supported through grants from the University of Cape Town (UCT) Council and the National Research Foundation (NRF) of South Africa. Any opinions, findings, and conclusions or recommendations expressed in this paper/report are those of the author(s) and do not necessarily reflect the views of UCT, the NRF or the trustees of the UCT Council.

References

1. ARNAB, A., AND HUTCHISON, A. Verifiable digital object identity system. In *Proceedings of the Sixth ACM Workshop on Digital Rights Management, Co-Located with ACM CCS 2006, Alexandria, Virginia, USA* (2006), K. Kurosawa, R. Safavi-Naini, and M. Yung, Eds., ACM.
2. BASU, A., AND MUYLLE, S. Authentication in e-commerce. *Communications of the ACM 46*, 12 (2003), 159–166.
url: http://doi.acm.org/10.1145/953460.953496.
3. BELLA, G., PAULSON, L. C., AND MASSACCI, F. The verification of an industrial payment protocol: the set purchase phase. In *CCS '02: Proceedings of the 9th ACM conference on Computer and communications security* (New York, NY, USA, 2002), ACM Press,

pp. 12–20.
url: http://doi.acm.org/10.1145/586110.586113.
4. MULLIGAN, D., HAN, J., AND BURSTEIN, A. How DRM Based Content Delivery Systems Disrupt Expectations of "Personal Use". In *Proceedings of the 2003 ACM workshop on Digital Rights Management* (2003), ACM, pp. 77–89.
URL: http://doi.acm.org/10.1145/947380.947391.
5. PEHA, J. M., AND KHAMITOV, I. M. Paycash: a secure efficient internet payment system. In *ICEC '03: Proceedings of the 5th international conference on Electronic commerce* (New York, NY, USA, 2003), ACM Press, pp. 125–130.
url: http://doi.acm.org/10.1145/948005.948022.
6. ROBERTS, P. Strong authentication a hard sell for banks. *ComputerWorld* (02 Nov 2004).
URL: http://www.computerworld.com/action/article.do?command=viewArticleBasic&articleId=
Last accessed: 05 Aug 2006.
7. ROSENCRANCE, L. Gartner survey sparks debate on internet retail fraud. *ComputerWorld* (18 July 2000).
URL: http://www.computerworld.com/action/article.do?command=viewArticleBasic&articleId=
Last accessed: 05 Aug 2006.
8. RUIZ, M. C., CAZORLA, D., CUARTERO, F., AND PARDO, J. J. Analysis of the set e-commerce protocol using a true concurrency process algebra. In *SAC '06: Proceedings of the 2006 ACM symposium on Applied computing* (New York, NY, USA, 2006), ACM Press, pp. 879–886.
url: http://doi.acm.org/10.1145/1141277.1141480.
9. STALLINGS, W. *Network Security Essentials – Applications and Standards*, international second ed. Prentice Hall, 2003.
10. STEINAUER, D. D., WAKID, S. A., AND RASBERRY, S. Trust and traceability in electronic commerce. *StandardView 5*, 3 (1997), 118–124.
url: http://doi.acm.org/10.1145/266231.266239.
11. TSAI, J. Y., CRANOR, L. F., AND CRAVER, S. Vicarious infringement creates a privacy ceiling. In *Proceedings of the Sixth ACM Workshop on Digital Rights Management, Co-Located with ACM CCS 2006, Alexandria, Virginia, USA* (2006), K. Kurosawa, R. Safavi-Naini, and M. Yung, Eds., ACM.

A role-based architecture for seamless identity management and effective task separation

Evangelos Kotsovinos[1], Ingo Friese[2], Martin Kurze[2], and Jörg Heuer[1]

[1] Deutsche Telekom Laboratories
[2] T-Systems
{firstname.lastname}@telekom.de

Abstract. Today's on-line end user experience is compromised by the need for managing multiple redundant identities for access to various services — such as email accounts, in order to ensure a clear separation of tasks that users perform in different capacities. Approaches based on Single Sign On (SSO) have focused on the provision of interoperability and trust management solutions required to allow users to log in once and use multiple on-line services. In this paper, we argue that Single Sign On provides neither adequate privacy preservation nor sufficient fine-grained separation of tasks, as it requires that a user performs all tasks — whether e.g. personal or professional — using the same identity. We propose Identity and Role Management (IRM), a new approach to identity management, combining the benefits of SSO and user-centric frameworks: it allows a user to be authenticated as conveniently as with SSO, to still achieve an effective separation of tasks she performs in different capacities through the use of different roles, and to retain full control of her private and sensitive data. Additionally, it facilitates fine-grained service customisation, supporting a personalised on-line experience. Our experiments with real users demonstrate the effectiveness, transparency, and user acceptance of our solution.

1 Introduction

Today's on-line end user's experience is hampered by the complexity of managing identities. For instance, users often resort to maintaining multiple email identities, established with different authorities, in order to achieve a clear separation of emails they send in different capacities or what we term *roles* (such as professional email versus personal email)[3]. As another example, users are typically required to maintain a separate login/password pair for every web site they wish to register with.

[3] It is worth noting that the use of the term "role" differs from the one commonly found in other role-based systems: for us a role is one of the many sub-identities a given user may have, whereas in RBAC it denotes a class of users with common characteristics.

Please use the following format when citing this chapter:

Kotsovinos, E., Friese, I., Kurze, M. and Heuer, J., 2007, in IFIP International Federation for Information Processing, Volume 232, New Approaches for Security, Privacy and Trust in Complex Environments, eds. Venter, H., Eloff, M., Labuschagne, L., Eloff, J., von Solms, R., (Boston: Springer), pp. 289–300.

Developments in the field of Identity Management (IDM) focus on supporting Single Sign On (SSO) — the facility that allows users to log in once and access a wide range of on-line services. This is achieved by ensuring the interoperability of the various on-line accounts and by forming *federated trust relationships* to allow on-line services to delegate user authentication to reputable third-party authorities. However, while SSO removes the need for maintaining multiple identities, it does little to facilitate a clear separation of roles and to provide adequate privacy protection. Users have to maintain a single identity and use that for all their on-line interactions, whether they are professional, personal, or in any other capacity.

In this paper we propose *Identity and Role Management* (IRM), a scheme based on *roles* as a means to achieve separation of the different capacities in which a given identity can be used. Our approach is shown to combine the benefits of multiple identities and SSO; it separates tasks as effectively as multiple identities, and provides the convenience of SSO to the users.

Furthermore, our system allows users to have an *adaptable level of control* of their private data, based on their individual requirements and preferences — in full compliance with current demands for user consent. Similarly to user-centric approaches — discussed in more detail in Section 6.2, our system allows privacy-sensitive users to retain full control of their personal details. At the same time, it enables convenience-seeking users to outsource their attribute and identity storage and management to trusted third parties.

The rest of this document is structured as follows: Section 2 discuss the shortcomings of existing approaches. Section 3 describes roles as an enhancement of identity management. Section 4 presents our implementation, the experiments undertaken with real users, and the results obtained. Section 5 discusses open issues of our framework and outlines future work. Section 6 positions our work in the context of related work, and Section 7 concludes.

2 Background

The *Single Sign On* concept envisages users logging in only once, for example on a web page of an on-line service, and visiting further services or web-based applications without the need to log in again. The user can thus experience an unhindered, seamless usage of services. The key concept behind Single Sign On is federation, denoting the establishment of common references between accounts or identities in different repositories or services. Microsoft Passport[4] as well as several other systems have been developed based on this concept [16].

For services to exchange information about the user, or authenticate a user for the other service respectively, these services need to have established a trust relationship with each other. So, if a given service B trusts a given service C, users of B could be authenticated by C. In that case, C is called

[4] `http://www.passport.com`

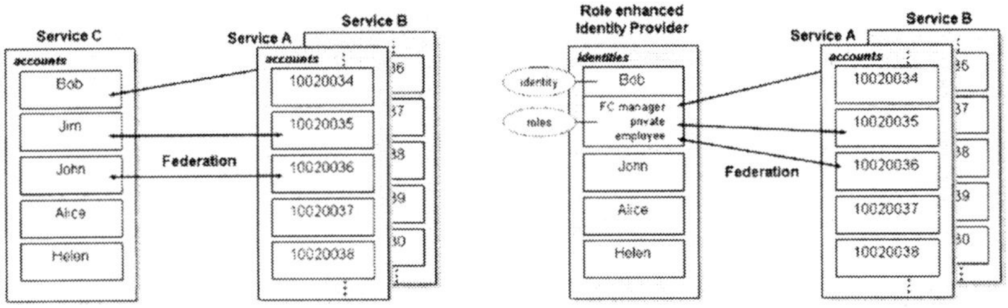

(a) (b)

Fig. 1. Identity management using a) conventional Single Sign On, and b) role-enhanced Identity Provider

an *Identity Provider* (IDP) — as shown in Figure 1(a). Longer chains of trust relationships may be established, for instance if another service C trusts service B to authenticate users, and service B trusts service A in turn to authenticate users. The concept of service federation has been described in the Security Assertion Mark-up Language specifications (SAML [13, 14]).

While SSO represents a significant progress in the way user authentication and identity management are handled over the conventional approach, we believe it provides neither adequate *separation* of tasks that users perform in different capacities nor sufficient *privacy protection*. Even using SSO, users need more than one identity to separate, for instance, private from professional email accounts, as shown in Figure 1(a): SSO associates an account with an identity, and as all accounts can be associated with the same identity this causes linkability, which compromises privacy [17]. Additionally, user data needs to be exchanged between federated services, which may not be trusted by the user for doing so. This relates to the concept of user-centric identity management, discussed in Section 6.2.

3 Framework

3.1 Overview

We propose Identity and Role Management (IRM) to enhance existing identity management approaches. IRM is based on augmenting identity management with the concept of a *role*. This is not to be confused with the meaning that the term role has in access control; here, it refers to the capacity in which a given user performs a certain action — for instance, "private", "employee of a company X", "soccer club manager".

In conventional SSO systems — as shown in Figure 1(a), a user's identity is associated with one account in each service the user is registered with. Our approach allows associating roles, not entire identities, with accounts, allowing

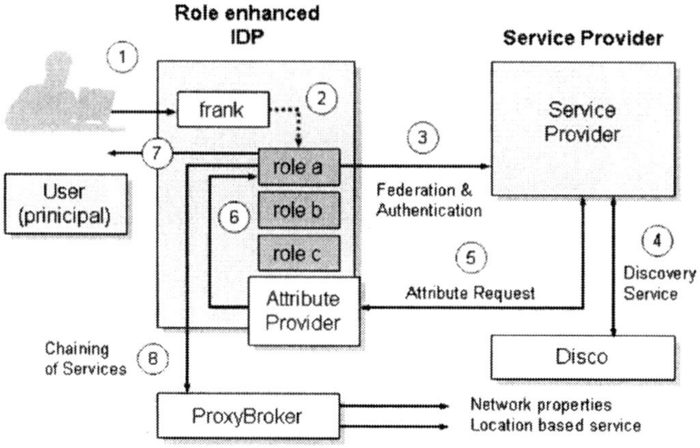

Fig. 2. Framework architecture and operation

a user to have multiple accounts with a single service in different capacities, and achieving effective task separation.

An example is shown in Figure 1(b), where a single user, Bob, is able to maintain two separate accounts in service A, each one through the use of a different role — "private" and "employee". This allows the user to achieve a clear separation of the tasks he performs using different roles. Additionally, Bob can maintain an account with service B through his "soccer club manager" role, facilitating sign-on using a single identity without compromising task separation.

When Bob reads his email using his mobile phone on the company premises he is automatically assigned the "employee" role, as long as he does not explicitly request not to, and data charges are billed directly to the company's account. When the same user chooses the role "soccer club manager", the charges are billed to his club account. Furthermore, the network is configured to provide all relevant club contacts to his device, which then displays them in his phone book application. Accordingly, the network provides the user's family contacts, when he uses the "private" role.

3.2 IRM architecture

The main parts of our IRM framework are shown in Figure 2. The core component is a trusted *Identity Provider* (IDP) module, which handles user accounts and is enhanced with role capabilities. The Identity Provider is responsible for providing authentication credentials based on the current role that a user has. It is important to note that individual services are relieved of handling user authentication themselves, as they can use the Identity Provider as an authentication service in the same way the would use a SAML enabled IDP.

A user is free to specify herself as her own IDP, if so desired, in order to maximise local control of her identity data and management.

Our role enhancement of the trusted IDP is combined with an *Attribute Provider* (AP). When a service requires information about a certain attribute of a user — such as name and email address, it submits a request to the AP, which holds the reference between the current role and the appropriate attribute. A set of user attributes can be seen as a profile that represents a role. Thus, role and profile are related concepts, closely linked to the same principal — the role referring to a user's identity and the profile referring to a user's attributes. For privacy, each user is free to select an Attribute Provider of her choice; indeed, if so desired, a user may specify herself as her provider, thus ensuring that personal details are held locally, for privacy.

The *Discovery Service* is a component that supports locating a service instance that holds certain attributes for a user with a given identifier. Upon request, the Discovery Service returns a resource offering-an endpoint and credential — for a given web service provider. The Discovery Service can be used to locate not only third-party services, but also IRM architecture services, such as the IDP and AP. This facilitates the dynamic discovery of the AP that can provide information about a certain user attribute, enabling the distribution of user attributes among different APs.

In IRM, the retrieval of user related attributes is not limited to Web Service instances, as is typically the case with a conventional attribute provider. The ProxyBroker is able to retrieve information gathered from other domains, such as the network and user properties.

IRM can be used both in a setting of transient federation — a non-permanent federation relationship, as defined in SAML 2.0 — and in a permanent federation case.

3.3 Authentication Using IRM

Let us consider a user Frank, who attempts to access a resource of a service provider, an on-line shop. Frank does not have a current log-on session on this site and is unknown to the service. The service provider sends an HTTP redirect to the role-enhanced Identity Provider. The HTTP redirect contains a SAML `<AuthnRequest>` requesting that the Identity Provider provides an assertion about the requesting user. The request asks that the Identity Provider sends back an identifier. Until this step the process is similar to those described in SAML 2.0.

From this point on, the operation of IRM in order to authenticate a user encompasses the following steps, as shown in Figure 2:

1. The user will be *challenged* by the IRM to provide valid credentials. The user provides valid credentials and identifies himself as Frank. The IRM looks up user Frank in its IDP and finds references to the various roles that Frank has created in the past.

2. The user is prompted to *choose the role*, either manually or with the help of a context-aware application framework — such as a context middleware system [2]. In our example, Frank chooses his role, named "private shopper", which he uses for shopping online. A security and session context is created for the user. The IRM creates a *name identifier* to be used for this federation, which is linked to Frank's role.
3. The IRM *redirects* the user back to the service that requested authentication. The service validates the digital signature of the SAML response and the SAML assertion. The provided name identifier is used to create a session context for Frank in his role. Frank is authenticated now through the "private shopper" role, and can be referenced via the corresponding name identifier.

3.4 Service Customization Using IRM

The on-line shopping service that Frank uses is capable of providing personalized book recommendations. In order to provide effective recommendations, the service wishes to acquire information about certain attributes of users by communication with the IRM. Additionally, information such as a user's address can be used to simplify the ordering and delivery process of goods, without requiring that the user types in the address repetitively.

For a service provider to obtain information about user attributes in the IRM framework, the following steps are taken (as shown in Figure 2):

4. The service provider requests the *discovery* of a web service instance that holds attributes for a user with a given identifier. The discovery service provides one or more references for that service — such as URLs — and credentials with which the service provider can access the service at that endpoint on behalf of the end user.
5. The service provider *requests the user attribute* in question from the Identity Provider by submitting the user identifier. The Identity Provider then maps the identifier to the appropriate user and role, and provides the value of the requested attribute. The value itself can be retrieved from a number of sources:
   - The Identity Provider's internal attribute list that is linked to the current role of the user.
   - Through direct interaction with the user, in case the attribute in question is not available through an AP, or is part of data or user information that is considered sensitive or personal.
   - From other services that are chained via interfaces, proxies or a broker — for instance, if the attribute in question is the current location the user

In our example, Frank's personal literature preferences (mystery novels) are retrieved directly from the attribute list of the "private shopper" role he has chosen. When Frank connects to the on-line bookstore using his "professional" role, the book recommendations he will be given will be related to new technology, relevant to his subject of work.

For the low-level mechanisms to facilitate all the previous steps, we use off-the-shelf protocols that are defined in standards and drafts of the Liberty Alliance. Such concepts include identity service discovery, permission-based attribute sharing, interaction service, and service chaining. This is important to allow interoperability, compatibility, and extensibility of our framework.

4 Implementation and observations

We set up a few sample services — such as an on-line shop and a messaging service based on Jabber[5] on Sun and Apache web servers, simulating the conditions of a heterogeneous platform. Two back-end Identity Providers were run in virtual machines on the same server, a Sun Fire V440 with four 1.28GHz UltraSPARC III CPUs, 8GB RAM, and 200GB SCSI HDD. Sun Access Manager[6] and RSA Security's Access Manager[7] were used for access control. These were connected to the role management extension component we implemented, which handles roles and attributes. The user interface of our system for managing roles was part of the front-end component, which communicated with the back-end over Java RMI, and run on a 3.4GHz P4 with 2GB RAM, 250GB IDE HDD, and an NVIDIA Quadro FX1400 card.

4.1 Experiments.

We conducted experiments with 36 real users to evaluate our system in three dimensions: effectiveness, robustness, and acceptance by users. Our experiments in the above setting have demonstrated that our prototype has been fully operational, successfully handling role-based identities as described in the previous sections in all tested cases. We plan to undertake further performance and scalability experiments in the future. In terms of integration challenges, we observed that in several cases existing identity management systems are not fully conformant with the Liberty Alliance's standards, and this non-conformance is not always adequately documented.

4.2 User tests.

We asked 36 users to use the sample services, while their identities were managed by our system, and describe their impressions. Initially a web-based login and password scheme was used to allow users to enter, switch, and manage

[5] `http://www.jabber.org/`
[6] `http://www.sun.com/software/products/access_mgr/`
[7] `http://www.rsasecurity.com/accessmanager`

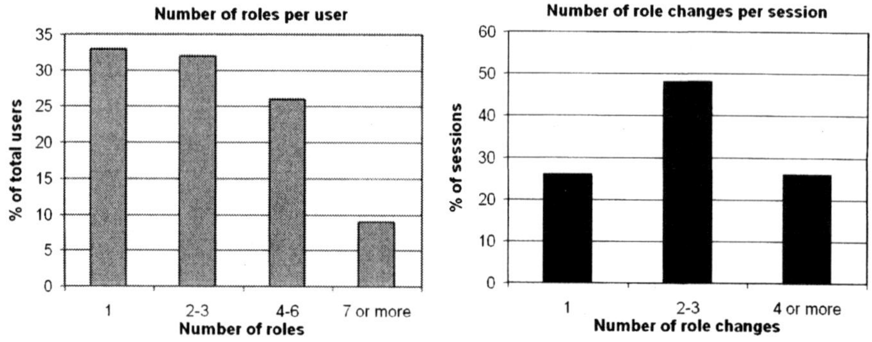

(a) Roles per user (b) Role changes per session

Fig. 3. Usage of identity and role management

roles. We measured the number of roles they opted to use (with "general user", "buyer", and "employee" being the most frequently used ones), and the number of role changes in each session. These are shown in Figure 4.1.

Users liked the role-based approach but — not surprisingly — did not want to actively change their role through an additional role-selection interface. Furthermore, they prefer not to have to select their role in advance of accessing the service. They would prefer engaging in the login process after the intended service asks for it — e.g. when the on-line bookstore browsed requests their details in the last ordering steps, after their basket has been filled. Finally, users wish to be immediately aware of the currently active role at any time, without having to request this information from our framework.

4.3 Refined interfaces and further tests.

Based on the above feedback, we developed a next version of interfaces for our prototype, which comprises a an easy-to-use role-selector that enables the following features. Firstly, it increases *awareness* of the current role by changing the desktop background every time the currently active role changes. Secondly, it communicates role changes to the user through intuitive *3D transition* metaphors, for instance by showing different roles' desktops on the different surfaces of a cube — implemented using a modified version of Project Looking Glass[8] v0.6.2. This also allows the user to work on several desktops simultaneously, each for one role. Thirdly, it reduces the manual overhead of role transition by enabling *speech-based* role selection and management.

Our users felt significantly more comfortable with the new interface. They were highly aware of their current role and were happy to be disburdened from manually managing their current login status — "who am I right now in this application?". In addition, they liked the concept of carrying their role-based set of attributes with them from application to application, still separating the individual roles from each other.

[8] `http://www.sun.com/software/looking_glass/`

5 Discussion

This document has presented our first steps towards devising a comprehensive IRM framework. However, there are a number of social and technical challenges that need to be overcome for IRM to realize its full potential.

Adoption

Although a full-scale switch to IRM would require that users gradually change familiar means of authentication, we believe that their current *frustration* with identity multiplicity and their *privacy concerns* will act as significant incentives for doing so. Additionally, our framework is built to operate in a partial deployment setting, to accommodate for its gradual adoption. Furthermore, we have successfully conducted initial user studies and are currently in the process of performing more, in order to understand and further improve the usability properties — and thus the adoption potential — of our framework.

New Requirements to User Interfaces

While we wish to provide for an abundance of roles per user, adequate to cover the different capacities in which she performs on-line activities, we also wish to *not overwhelm the user with the management of roles.* New types of user interfaces will be required to allow handling and switching between roles without placing administration burden on the user. The use of contextual information for automatic role inference could be one technique to be investigated in this area. Furthermore, the multitude and heterogeneity of devices from which a user connect to IRM places additional interface adaptation requirements.

Compatibility with Existing Services

To ensure the faster adoption of IRM and reduce the corresponding barrier to entry, we have designed our architecture to support *backward compatibility* with existing services and *interoperability* with established IDM standards. Additionally, IRM has been designed to be operational in a *partial deployment.* When an IRM-enabled user interacts with a non-IRM-enabled service that manages authentication and accounts on its own, the role of the user presented by the Identity Provider is seen as the identity of the user by the role-agnostic service.

Privacy as a Design Principle

IRM implements the following mechanisms for reassuring users about the protection of their private data. Firstly, IRM *prevents* the *association* of data referring to different roles by services and other third parties. An on-line user in different capacities is represented as two different users on the service provider side, and only the trusted IDP is able to trace back the roles to an identity. Additionally, IRM allows a user to retain *full control of her private data* by specifying herself as her Attribute Provider — or even an IDP, thus ensuring her privacy. Finally, IRM has been developed in accordance to privacy protection standards and legislation.

6 Related Work

The main areas of research related to our work are the Liberty Alliance identity specifications, the user-centric community, and (role- and attribute-based) access control.

6.1 Liberty Identity Service Interface Specification

Realizing the importance of moving towards a more fine-grained separation of on-line tasks that users perform, the Liberty Alliance has devised the Liberty Identity Service Interface specification (ID-SIS) [9] . This provides an XML schema for describing user profiles and attributes in a structured manner, and recommends a set of interfaces for querying providers of such profiles to obtain user attributes.

The approach we propose in this document is orthogonal to ID-SIS. We propose the use of roles as a key mechanism for achieving separation of tasks and privacy preservation. Furthermore, we present a comprehensive architecture for deploying IRM in an on-line setting, including facilities for IRM-based authentication, role assignment and management, and service customization. Within IRM, the ID-SIS specification can be employed as a common scheme for describing user attributes.

6.2 User-centric community

Driven by the users' growing privacy concerns regarding the handling of their authentication information, user-centric identity management approaches such as CardSpace[9], Yadis [11], SXIP [18, 6], and Persona [19] have gained popularity. These go beyond the Liberty Alliance's standards and federation concepts to allow individual users to retain full control over their own identity management, without requiring the presence of a provider of an external provider of identification information. Essentially each user manages — and is liable for — its own provider of identification information.

However, despite the thrust behind such systems at the time of writing, we believe that there are technical challenges that need to be addressed. In most such systems, it is not clear how identities can be securely *ported* between devices to allow a user to authenticate from different terminals. Additionally, protecting identities on the user side from unauthorised human users — for instance other members of the same household — needs to be done in a

[9] `http://msdn.microsoft.com/webservices/infocard/`

passwordless way. Finally, incorporating single sign-on to such systems is not trivial.

As described before, our system can support user-centric identity management functionality by registering the user herself as her attribute provider. This allows full, local control of her properties and sensitive personal data, while at the same time retaining the advantages of provider-assisted identity management such as simple Single Sign On mechanisms and ease of use.

6.3 Role- and attribute-based access control

Ferraiolo and Kuhn [4] provided an early formal description of role definition and membership for RBAC. [12] administers roles, role relationships, and access rights. [10] defines roles as sets of rights and duties. [7, 8, 5] combine roles and policies for applying RBAC to open, large-scale systems. [3] specifies positive and negative security policies associated with roles, as well as role inheritance. Attribute-based access control [1, 8] makes fine-grained access control decisions based on user attributes and their combinations. RBAC has been implemented in web-based enterprise environments [15].

Our work draws inspiration from role- and attribute-based access control systems, but at the same time is complementary to them. We focus not on the mechanisms to control which user groups have access to a given on-line resource, but rather on how such systems can be interlinked to provide an unhindered on-line experience for the user, separation of tasks, and privacy protection. We plan to evaluate the possibility of employing an off-the-shelf RBAC solution for access control on individual resources.

7 Conclusions and future work

The on-line behavior and requirements of users indicate the need for a facility to allow using a single digital identity in different capacities, thus retaining the benefits of Single Sign On while not compromising the separation of tasks achieved using multiple on-line identities. We proposed Identity and Role Management (IRM), enhancing traditional identity management approaches by introducing roles as a powerful mechanism to achieve a clean separation of tasks performed by a user in different capacities. Furthermore, we presented an architecture for implementing and deploying the IRM framework. Additionally, we described how our framework supports adaptable local control of private data and attributes, facilitating user-centric privacy preservation. Also, through experiments with real users, we demonstrated the effectiveness, transparency, and acceptance of our solution.

We believe that IRM represents a natural next step in the area of identity management, enabling the convenient use of services, ensuring fine-grained separation of tasks, protecting user privacy, and reducing the amount of authentication data that has to be administrated on the service side. Also, roles enhance personalization, by allowing the network to customize the provided services based on the current user role. Ultimately, IRM represents a step towards decreasing the barrier of using new services, by simplifying the overall on-line user experience. In the future we plan to investigate ways to make IRM intuitive and near-transparent to the users, bootstrapping issues of our identity management platform, role federation for service customisation, and role instantiation to allow a more flexible association of roles with identities.

References

1. P. Bonatti and P. Samarati. A unified framework for regulating access and information release on the web. *Journal of Comp. Sec.*, 10(3), 2002.
2. N. H. Cohen, J. Black, P. Castro, M. Ebling, B. Leiba, A. Misra, and W. Segmuller. Building Context-Aware Applications with Context Weaver. Research Report RC 23388, IBM, Oct. 2004.
3. N. Damianou, N. Dulay, E. Lupu, and M. Sloman. The Ponder Policy Specification Language. In *Proc. of the Policy2001 Workshop*, Jan. 2001.
4. D. Ferraiolo and R. Kuhn. Role-Based Access Controls. In *Proc. of the 15th NIST-NCSC Conf.*, 1992.
5. R. J. Hayton, J. M. Bacon, and K. Moody. Access Control in an Open Distributed Environment. In *Proc. of the IEEE Symp. on Sec. and Priv.*, 1998.
6. J. Merrells. DIX: Digital Identity Exchange Protocol, Mar. 2006.
7. D. Jonscher and K. R. Dittrich. Argos – A Configurable Access Control System for Interoperable Environments. In *DB Sec., IX: Status and Prospects*, 1996.
8. N. Li, J. C. Mitchell, and W. H. Winsborough. Design of a Role-Based Trust Management Framework. In *Proc. of the IEEE Symp. on Sec. and Priv.*, 2002.
9. Liberty Alliance Project. Liberty ID-SIS Personal Profile Service Spec., 2003.
10. E. C. Lupu, D. A. Marriott, M. S. Sloman, and N. Yialelis. A Policy Based Role Framework for Access Control. In *Proc. of the 1st ACM RBAC '96.*
11. J. Miller. Yadis Specification, Version 1.0, Mar. 2006.
12. M. Nyanchama and S. Osborn. Access Rights Administration in Role-Based Security Systems. In *Proc. of the 8th IFIP WG 11.3 Working Conf. on DB Sec.*, volume A-60. Elsevier, Aug. 1995.
13. Organization for the Advancement of Structured Information Standards (OASIS). Assertions and Protocol for the OASIS Security Assertion Markup Language (SAML), Apr. 2002.
14. Organization for the Advancement of Structured Information Standards (OASIS). Security Assertion Markup Language (SAML) V2.0 Technical Overview, Sept. 2005.
15. J. S. Park, R. Sandhu, and G.-J. Ahn. Role-based access control on the web. *ACM Trans. Inf. Syst. Sec.*, 4(1), 2001.
16. A. Pashalidis and C. Mitchell. A taxonomy of single sign-on systems. In *Proc. of the 8th Australasian Conf. in Inf. Sec. and Priv.*, July 2003.
17. A. Pfitzmann and M. Hansen. Anonymity, Unlinkability, Unobservability, Pseudonymity, and Identity Management — A Consolidated Proposal for Terminology. Research report, TU-Dresden, May 2006.
18. SXIP Networks. The SXIP 2.0 Overview, Mar. 2006.
19. K. Toth and M.Subramanium. Requirements for the persona concept. In *Proc. of RHAS'03*, Sept. 2003.

Extending Role Based Access Control Model for Distributed Multidomain Applications

Yuri Demchenko, Leon Gommans, Cees de Laat
University of Amsterdam, System and Network Engineering Group
Kruislaan 403, NL-1098 SJ Amsterdam, The Netherlands
{demch, lgommans, delaat}@science.uva.nl

Abstract. This paper presents the results related to the development of a flexible domain-based access control infrastructure for distributed Grid-based Collaborative Environments and Complex Resource Provisioning. The paper proposes extensions to the classical RBAC model to address typical problems and requirements in the distributed hierarchical resource management such as: hierarchical resources policy administration, user roles/attributes management, dynamic security context and authorisation session management, and others. It describes relations between the RBAC and the generic AAA access control models and defines combined RBAC-DM model for domain-based access control management and suggests mechanisms that can be used in the distributed service-oriented infrastructure for security context management. The paper provides implementation details on the use of XACML for fine-grained access control policy definition for domain based resources organisation and roles assignments in RBAC-DM. The paper is based on experiences gained from the major Grid-based and Grid-oriented projects in collaborative applications and complex resource provisioning.

1 Introduction

Role Base Access Control (RBAC) is an industry recognized and widely accepted access control model that naturally integrates with effective Identity management technologies. However, at the same time its practical implementation in complex research and industry environment for advanced collaborative and resource provisioning scenarios reveals a number of problems. Most of these problems are originated from the industry and research community gradually moving to the Grid and Web Services based Service Oriented Architecture (SOA) [1, 2]. SOA suggests service applications decomposition and decoupling including separation of different component in the traditional access control model such as Authentication,

Please use the following format when citing this chapter:

Demchenko, Y., Gommans, L., and de Laat, C., 2007, in IFIP International Federation for Information Processing, Volume 232, New Approaches for Security, Privacy and Trust in Complex Environments, eds. Venter, H., Eloff, M., Labuschagne, L., Eloff, J., von Solms, R., (Boston: Springer), pp. 301–312.

Authorisation, Identity and Attribute management. Although relying on secure network layer, all service oriented security services in SOA are bound to messages exchanged between services representing a user or requestor and a target service or resource. Classic RBAC provides a good model for internal organisational access control and scales bad in distributed and multi-organisational environment.

The generic Authentication, Authorisation, Accounting (GAAA) architecture, described in [3, 4], proposes a general model for the Authentication (AuthN), Authorisation (AuthZ), Accounting services operation and their integration with typical client/server applications. Conceptual Authorisation framework discussed in the OGSA informational document [5] suggests the GAAA-AuthZ as a basic model for the Grid service-oriented environment.

This paper describes our experiences when developing a flexible, customer-driven, security infrastructure for Grid based Collaborative Environment (GCE) and Complex Resource Provisioning (CRP) in general. These two use cases are analysed to explain specific requirements to multidomain access control and suggest RBAC extensions for multidomain applications.

The presented research and proposed solution are specifically oriented for using with the popular Grid middleware being developed in the framework of large international projects such as EGEE (http://public.eu-egee.org/) and Globus Alliance (http://www.globus.org/). The middleware provides a common communication/messaging infrastructure for all resources and services exposed as Grid services, and also allows for a uniform security configuration at the service container or messaging level.

The paper is organized as follows. Section 2 describes the Virtual Laboratory organisation in GCE as a basic use case for domain based resource organisation and management and refers to more general CRP requirements. Section 3 discusses what functionality is currently available in known RBAC implementations and identifies extensions to address specifics in controlling access to distributed hierarchical resources. Section 4 compares RBAC and GAAA access control model and identifies mechanisms to express and convey domain related dynamic security context. Section 5 provides practical suggestions and an example of using XACML for policy expression in hierarchical multidomain access control.

2 Domain Based Resource Management in GCE

The research community and processing industry makes extensive use of advanced computing resources and unique equipment which are associated and virtualised in a form of the Virtual Organisation (VO) or Virtual Laboratory (VL) [6]. VL provides a flexible framework for associating instruments, resources and users into distributed interactive collaborative environment. However, committed to the VL resource still remain in the possession and under direct administration of their original owner enterprises.

The following administrative and security domains can be defined for user, resources, policy and trust management:

1) Facility that provides administrative/legal platform for all further operational associations; may define what kind of technologies, formats, credentials can be used.

2) VL that can be created on the basis of the VL agreement that defines VL resources, common services (first of all, information/registry and security), administrative structure and a VL administrator. Trust relations can be established via PKI and/or VL Certificate population.

3) Experiment/Project defined together with the VL resources allocation, members, task/goals, stages, and additionally workflow. It is perceived that experiment related context may change during its lifetime.

4) Experiment session that may include multiple Instrument sessions and Collaborative sessions that involves experiment members into interactions.

5) Collaborative session – user interactive session.

Experiment session may include multiple Instrument sessions and Collaborative sessions that involves experiment members into interactions.

In the above provided classification domains are defined (as associations of entities) by common policy under single administration, common namespace and semantics, shared trust, etc. In this case, domain related security context may include: namespace aware names and ID's, policy references/ID's, trust anchors, authority references, and also dynamic/session related context. For the generality, domains can be hierarchical, flat or organized in the mesh, but all these cases require the same basic functionality from the access control infrastructure to manage domain and session related security context.

The Domain-based resource management model (DM) closer reflects business practice among cooperating organisations contributing their resources (instruments, other facilities and operator personal) to create a Virtual laboratory that can run complex experiments on request from customers. To become consistent the DM should be supported by corresponding organisation of the access control infrastructure.

Figure 1 illustrates relations between major components in the hierarchical DM resource management and security model. The following suggestions were used when creating this abstraction of the DM [6]:

1) physically Instruments are located at the Facility but logically they are assigned to the VL and next allocation to the Experiment. Full context Instrument name will look like:

`ResourceDM:Facility:VirtualLab:Experiment:InstrModel`

2) users/members of collaborative sessions are assigned to the Experiment, managerial and operator personnel belongs to VL and Facility and may have specific and limited functions in the Experiment;

3) particularly, domain based restrictions/policy can be applied to (dynamic) role assignment;

4) additionally, administrative rights/functions can be delegated by the superior entity/role in this hierarchical structure;

5) Trust Anchors (TA) can be assigned to hierarchical domain related entities to enable security associations and support secure communication. VL TA1 is suggested as minimum required in DM, Experiment TA2 may be included into the Experiment description. Collaborative session security association can be supported by AuthZ tickets.

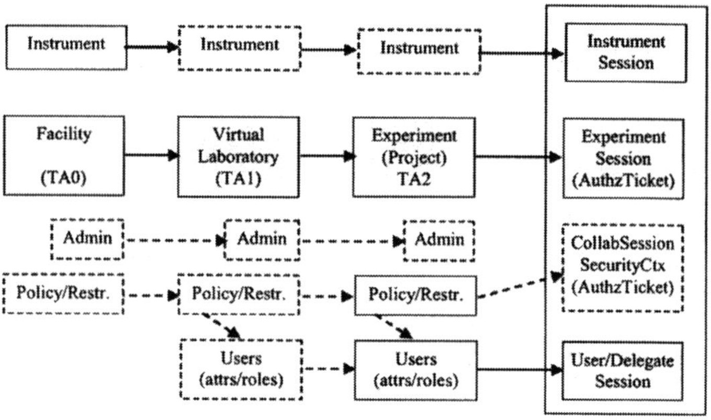

Fig. 1. Hierarchical Domain based Resource management in GCE

The Experiment description plays an important role in the DM security infrastructure, it is created by the experiment owner as a semantic object on the basis of a signed Experiment agreement (and in the context of the overall VL agreement). It contains all the information required to run the analysis, including the Experiment ID, allocated/provisioned instruments, assigned users and roles, and a trust/security anchor(s) in the form of the resource and, additionally, the customer's digital signature(s). The experiment description provides experiment-dependent configuration data for other services to run the experiment and manage the dynamic security context.

VL and Experiment/Project resources can be provisioned dynamically on-demand. In this case the VL/Experiment lifecycle or operation will include resource and service provisioning stage. The recent paper [7] by authors discusses other practical issues of implementing DM for the general CRP in Grid environment. The paper distinguishes 2 major stages in CRP: resource reservation and the reserved resource access or consumption. The reservation and allocation stage includes 4 basic steps: resource lookup, complex resource composition (including alternatives), reservation of individual resources and their association with the reservation ticket/ID, and finally delivery or deployment. The reservation stage may require execution of complex procedures that may also request individual resources authorisation in multiple administrative and access control domains.

3 Generic RBAC and Domain Based Resource Management

Generic RBAC model [8, 9, 10] provides an industry recognised solution for effective user roles/privileges management and policy based access control. It extends Discretional Access Control (DAC) and Mandatory Access Control (MAC) models with more flexible access control policy management adoptable for typical hierarchical roles and responsibilities management in organisations, but at the same time it suggest a full user access control management from user assignment to granting permissions. This can be suitable for internal organisational environment and particularly for human access rights management but reveals problems when applied to distributed service-oriented environment.

Sandhu in his two research papers [8, 9] describes 4 basic RBAC models:

- Core RBAC (RBAC0) that associates Users with Roles (U-R) and Roles with Permissions (R-P);
- Hierarchical RBAC (RBA1) that adds hierarchy to roles definition;
- Constrained RBAC (RBAC2) that extends RBAC0 with the constrains applied to U-R and R-P assignment;
- Consolidated RBAC (RBAC3) that adds role hierarchy to RBAC2.

Further RBAC development took place with publishing ANSI INCITS 359-2004 standard [10] that actually re-defined first three basic RBAC models in the context of static or dynamic separation of duties (SSD vs DSD). The standard also proposes RBAC functional specification that can be used for developing generic RBAC API.

In both models, initial Sandhu's and ANSI RBAC, there is a notion of the user session which is invoked by a user and provides instant session-based U-R association. Final result/stage of the RBAC functionality are permissions assigned to the user based on static or dynamic U-R and R-P assignment. RBAC doesn't consider (user) permissions enforcement on the resource or access object. This functionality can be attributed to other more service-oriented frameworks such as ISO/ITU PMI [11] or generic AAA [3, 4, 5].

Many studies suggest RBAC as a natural method to model the security requirements in service oriented environment but at the same time they argue for application specific extensions, e.g., for user group organisation including additional group/team defined restrictions on separation of duties, roles/attributes combinations, etc. [12, 13].

The papers [14, 15] propose an extension of the generic RBAC model the usage control (UCON) based authorisation framework for collaborative application that specifically addresses access control to the consumable resources or which access should be coordinated among a group of users. This is achieved by using obligations, resource/environmental conditions, introducing mutable resource and user attributes, and applying ongoing control. The proposed implementation uses XACML as a policy expression language with proprietary defined the Obligation element. However, detailed analysis of the proposed UCON publications and implementations revealed that the UCON framework uses centralised policy management, environment and attributes control that may have a principal problem of races when using conditions/obligations on mutable attributes. Proposed usage session doesn't allow full functionality required for generic authorisation session management in a multi-domain environment.

Generic RBAC historically was designed for centralized and autonomous access control management and inherits the following problems when applied to typical service-oriented security infrastructure:

- it is not directly applicable and integrated with/to service-oriented applications, although it is well applicable for such use cases as enterprise database/facility access control;

- doesn't separate basic functional components that have place in typical Enterprise Identity management and Access control infrastructure such as AuthN and AuthZ service, Attribute Authority, Policy Authority;
- User session, as defined in RBAC, is not present in typical PMI and AAA.

But at the same time it defines/specifies generic functional components that can be used in more service oriented access control models such as generic AAA. Practical RBAC implementation requires resolution of many other administration and security related issues left out of scope in classical RBAC such as:

- policy expression and management,
- rights/privileges delegation,
- AuthZ session management mechanisms,
- security context management in distributed dynamic scenario
- scalability in distributed and multidomain applications.

The two basic implementations of the generic RBAC model are Access Control Lists (ACL) that can be rather applications/implementation specific, and an emerging industry standard eXtensible Access Control Markup Language (XACML) that defines a rich policy expression format and simple Request/Response messages format for PEP-PDP communication [16]. XACML extensions and special profiles address most of mentioned above issues at the standard level. However, there are no widely used practical implementations for this new functionality.

The RBAC-DM (note, in most cases we will use abbreviations DM and RBAC-DM as equivalents) that combine the generic RBAC with domain based resource and roles management can address most of above mentioned issues at the practical level by introducing domain related security context that actually reflects natural for cooperating entities/enterprises administration model and separation of duties. Use of Experiment and Collaborative session allows to implement delegations and minimum privileges principle in access control management but in its own turn requires consistent authorisation session context handling. Using AuthZ ticket with full session context in DM allows for distributed access control management and decoupling access control infrastructure components in a distributed environment.

In summary, DM provides the following benefits:

1) reflects distributed hierarchical management model natural in distributed cooperative business environment;

2) multiple and hierarchical policies management that reflects hierarchical resource organisation;

3) allows for dynamic roles assignment with the domain defined restrictions;

4) supports dynamic security context management;

5) provides mechanisms for supporting multidomain authorisation sessions.

4 Relation between RBAC and GAAA Access Control Models

A Resource or Service in GCE is protected by the site access control system that relies on both AuthN of the user and/or request message and AuthZ that applies access control policies against the service request. It is essential in a service-oriented model that AuthN credentials are presented as a security context in the AuthZ request and that they can be evaluated by calling back to the AuthN service and/or Attribute Authority (AttrAuth). This also allows for loose coupling of services (providing domain independency even for hierarchical DM).

The GAAA AuthZ model includes such major functional components as: Policy Enforcement Point (PEP), Policy Decision Point (PDP), Policy Authority Point (PAP). It is naturally integrated with the RBAC separated User-Role and Role-Privilege management model that can be defined and supported by separate policies.

The Requestor requests a service by sending a service request ServReq to the Resource's PEP providing information about the Subject/Requestor, Resource, Action according to the implemented authorisation model and (should be known) service access policies.

In a simple scenario, the PEP sends the decision request to the (designated) PDP and after receiving a positive PDP decision relays a service request to the Resource. The PDP identifies the applicable policy or policy set and retrieves them from the Policy Authority, collects the required context information and evaluates the request against the policy.

In order to optimise performance of the distributed access control infrastructure, the AuthZ service may also issue AuthZ assertions in the form of AuthzTicket that are based on the positive AuthZ decision and can be used to grant access to subsequent similar requests that match the AuthzTicket. To be consistent, AuthzTicket must preserve the full context of the authorisation decision, including the AuthN context/assertion and policy reference.

A typical DM access control use-case may require a combination of multiple policies and also multi-level access control enforcement, which may take place when combining newly-developed and legacy access control systems into one integrated access control solution. The GCE experiments may apply different policies and require different user credentials depending on the stage of the experiment.

DM can improve overall services manageability but requires additional/corresponding mechanisms for dynamic security context management. It is also suggested that using AuthZ ticket with full session context will simplify distributed access control management in a hierarchical DM and allow for decoupling access control infrastructure components in a distributed environment.

Figure 2 illustrates relations between classical conceptual RBAC model and GAAA AuthN/AuthZ services. The User-Role assignment (defined in RBAC by User session) in GAAA is provided at the stage of the user authentication when a set of role are assigned to the authenticated user. It is important that the user provides sufficient identity credentials which will next define a set of assigned to his/her roles. Mapping between user Roles and Permissions in general/total are defined by the access control policy that is used to evaluate a User request to the Resource. Permitted actions relayed to the Resource by PEP and may be confirmed by the AuthZ assertion that can be used for further access during AuthZ session duration. Figure 2 helps also to understand why many authors and implementers criticise that conceptual RBAC model doesn't fit into majority of enterprise and organisational applications that actually implement another service-oriented access control model that separates AuthN, AuthZ and IdP/Attribute Authority services. The picture also illustrates difference between RBAC User session and AuthZ session.

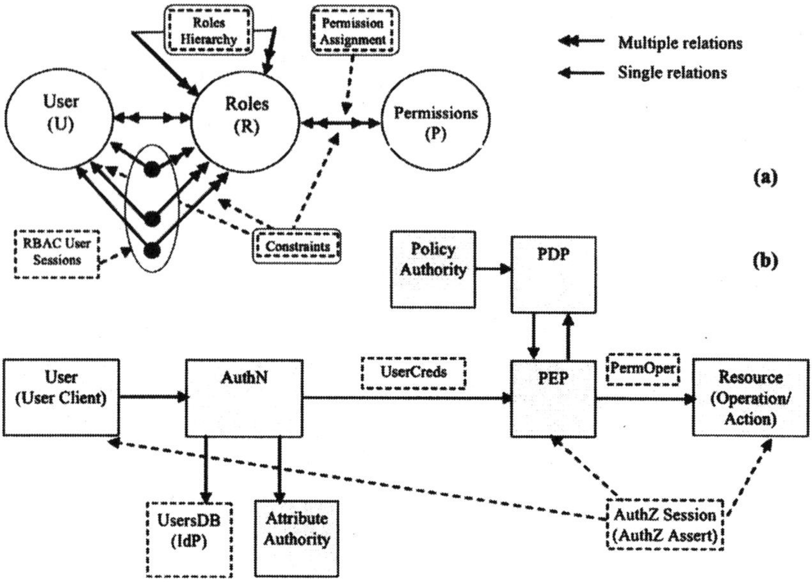

Fig. 2. Relation between (a) RBAC [9] and (b) GAAA-AuthZ/AuthN services

Detailed analysis of how dynamic security context can be managed in Grid based applications is discussed in the paper [17] that identifies the following mechanisms and components to mediate a dynamic security context:

- Service and requestor/user ID/DN format that should allow for both using namespaces and context aware names semantics.
- Attribute format (either X.509/X.521 or URN/SAML2.0 presentation).
- Context aware XACML policy definition using the Environment element of the policy Target element (see next section for detailed discussion).
- Security assertions (e.g., tickets or tokens) used for User and AuthZ session management and for provisioned resource/service identification.
- Workflow as primarily used for complex/combined services orchestration can be also used for managing dynamic security context.

5 Using XACML for Policy Expression in RBAC-DM

A XACML policy is defined for the so-called target triad "Subject-Resource-Action" which can also be completed with the Environment element to add additional context to instant policy evaluation. The XACML policy format can also specify actions that must be taken on positive or negative PDP decisions in the form of an optional Obligation element. The Environment and Obligation elements can be used for multidomain AuthZ decision combination in DM.

A decision request sent in a Request message provides context for the policy-based decision. The policy applicable to a particular decision request may be composed of a number of individual rules or policies. Few policies may be combined to form a single policy that is applicable to the request. XACML specifies a number of policy and rule combination algorithms. The Response message may contain multiple Result elements, which are related to individual Resources.

XACML policy format provides few mechanisms of adding and handling context during the policy selection and request evaluation, in particular: the policy identification using the Target element, the Environment element both in the Target and in the rules definition, and the namespace aware attributes semantics.

The DM makes extensive use of both XACML core specification and its special profiles for RBAC [18] and hierarchical resources [19]. Hierarchical policy management and dynamic rights delegation, that is considered as an important functionality in DM, can be solved with the XACML v3.0 administrative policy [20].

The XACML RBAC profile [19] provides extended functionality for managing user/subject roles and permissions by defining separate Permission `<PolicySet>`, Role `<PolicySet>`, Role Assignment `<Policy>`, and HasPrivilegeOfRole `<Policy>`. It also allows for using multiple Subject elements to add hierarchical group roles related context in handling RBAC requests and sessions, e.g., when some actions require superior subject/role approval to perform them. In such a way, RBAC profile can significantly simplify rights delegation inside the group of collaborating entities/subjects which normally requires complex credentials management.

The XACML hierarchical resource profile [19] specifies how XACML can provide access control for a Resource that is organized as a hierarchy. Examples include file systems, data repositories, XML documents and organizational resources which example is the DM. The profile introduces new Resource attributes identifiers that may refer to the "`resource-ancestor`", "`resource-parent`", or "`resource-ancestor-or-self`".

XACMLv3.0 administrative policy profile [20] introduces extensions to the XACML v2.0 to support policy administration and delegation. This is achieved by introducing the PolicyIssuer element that should be supported by related administrative policy. Dynamic delegation permits some users to create policies of limited duration to delegate certain capabilities to others. Both of these functionalities are important for the proposed DM and currently being investigated.

Figure 3 below provides an example of the XACML policy which Target and IDRef bind the policy to the Resource. There may be different matching expression for the Resource/Attribute/AttributeValue when using XACML hierarchical resource profile what should allow to create a policy for the required resource hierarchy in DM. The example also contains the PolicyIssuer element that is related to the policy administration. In our example the PolicyIssuer is declared as "`cnl:VLab031:trusted`", and the PDP will rely on already assigned PAP and established trust relations. In case, when other entity is declared as a PolicyIssuer, the PDP should initiate checking administrative policy and delegation chain.

```
<PolicySet>
 <Target/>
 <Policy PolicyId="urn:oasis:names:tc:xacml:1.0:cnl:policy:CNL2-XPS1-test"
   RuleCombiningAlgId="urn:oasis:names:tc:xacml:1.0:rule-combining-
     algorithm:deny-overrides">
  <Description>Permit access for CNL3 users with specific roles</Description>
  <PolicyIssuer>
```

```
    <Attribute AttributeId="urn:oasis:names:tc:xacml:1.0:subject:subject-id"
        DataType="http://www.w3.org/2001/XMLSchema#string">
      <AttributeValue> urn:oasis:names:tc:xacml:3.0:issuer:cnl:VLab031:trusted
        </AttributeValue>
    </Attribute>
  </PolicyIssuer>
  <Target>
   <Resources><Resource>
    <ResourceMatch MatchId="urn:oasis:names:tc:xacml:1.0:function:anyURI-equal">
      <AttributeValue DataType="http://www.w3.org/2001/XMLSchema#anyURI">
          http://resources.collaboratory.nl/Phillips_XPS1</AttributeValue>
      <ResourceAttributeDesignator
          AttributeId="urn:oasis:names:tc:xacml:1.0:resource:resource-id"
             DataType="http://www.w3.org/2001/XMLSchema#anyURI"/>
    </ResourceMatch>
   </Resource></Resources>
  </Target>
 <Rule RuleId="urn:oasis:names:tc:xacml:1.0:cnl:
              policy:CNL2-XPS1-test:rule:ViewExperiment" Effect="Permit">
  <Target>
   <Actions><Action>
    <ActionMatch MatchId="urn:oasis:names:tc:xacml:1.0:function:string-equal">
      <AttributeValue DataType="http://www.w3.org/2001/XMLSchema#string">
             ViewExperiment</AttributeValue>
      <ActionAttributeDesignator
          AttributeId="urn:oasis:names:tc:xacml:1.0:action:action-id"
               DataType="http://www.w3.org/2001/XMLSchema#string"/>
     </ActionMatch>
    </Action></Actions>
  </Target>
  <Condition FunctionId="urn:oasis:names:tc:xacml:1.0:
                   function:string-at-least-one-member-of">
    <Apply FunctionId="urn:oasis:names:tc:xacml:1.0:function:string-bag">
     <AttributeValue DataType="http://www.w3.org/2001/XMLSchema#string">
        analyst</AttributeValue>
     <AttributeValue DataType="http://www.w3.org/2001/XMLSchema#string">
        customer</AttributeValue>
    </Apply>
    <SubjectAttributeDesignator DataType=http://www.w3.org/2001/XMLSchema#string
       AttributeId="urn:oasis:names:tc:xacml:1.0:subject:role"
       Issuer="CNL2AttributeIssuer"/>
   </Condition>
  </Rule>
 </Policy>
</PolicySet>
```

Fig. 3. XACML PolicySet containing PolicyIssuer element as defined by XACML3.0.

6 Conclusion and Summary

The results presented in this paper are part of the ongoing research and development of the security infrastructure for user controlled multidomain services and its application to complex resource provisioning. This work is being conducted by the System and Network Engineering (SNE) Group in the framework of different EU and Dutch nationally and industry funded projects including EGEE, Phosphorus and GigaPort Research on Network.

The definition of the Domain based access control model RBAC-DM and proposed solutions described in this paper are based on practical experience we have gained whilst designing and developing an open collaborative environment within the Collaboratory.nl and VL-e projects. RBAC-DM reflects distributed hierarchical management model typical for industrial collaborative infrastructure and has additional features for domain related security context management. Use of Experiment and Collaborative sessions, supported by relevant session's security context management, allows for dynamic roles assignment with the domain defined restrictions, including delegation and minimum privileges principle.

The paper identifies major mechanisms that can be used for expressing and transferring dynamic security context in Grid and Web Services applications using of XML technologies. The proposed solutions are being implemented in the GAAA Toolkit [21] as a GAAAPI package that can be also used with other popular AuthZ frameworks such as GT4-AuthZ and gLite AuthZ frameworks.

Proposed RBAC-DM and its suggested implementation in GAAAPI make extensive use of XACML core specification and its special profiles for RBAC and hierarchical resources, and also XACML v3.0 administrative policy. Provided XACML policy example illustrates most of the discussed features. Practical implementation of this additional functionality will require special extension to the popular Open Source SunXACML library that is being developed as a part of the GAAAPI package.

Another important component that requires additional research and wider potential use cases analysis is the AuthZ ticket definition as a key mechanism and a component of the AuthZ session management functionality. Initial modelling with the GAAAPI package demonstrated effectiveness and sufficient increase of the AuthZ service performance when controlling remote instruments. AuthZ session support in Grid/OGSA applications was recognised as an important functionality and accepted as a work item by the OGF OGSA-AuthZ working group [22].

The authors believe that the proposed RBAC-DM access control architecture for GCE/CRP and related technical solutions will also be useful to the wider community that has similar problems with managing access control to distributed hierarchically organised resources in dynamic/on-demand services provisioning.

References

1. Foster, I. et al (2006). The Open Grid Services Architecture, Version 1.5. Global Grid Forum. Retrieved October 30, 2006, from http://www.ggf.org/documents/GFD.80.pdf

2. "Web Services Architecture". W3C Working Draft 8, August 2003. - http://www.w3.org/TR/ws-arch/

3. Vollbrecht, J., P. Calhoun, S. Farrell, L. Gommans, G. Gross, B. de Bruijn, C. de Laat, M. Holdrege, D. Spence, "AAA Authorization Framework," Informational RFC 2904, Internet Engineering Task Force, August 2000. ftp://ftp.isi.edu/in-notes/rfc2904.txt

4. RFC2903 – "Generic AAA Architecture", C. de Laat, G. Gross, L. Gommans, J. Vollbrecht, D. Spence, IETF Aug 2000, ftp://ftp.isi.edu/in-notes/rfc2903.txt

5. GFD.38 Conceptual Grid Authorization Framework and Classification. M. Lorch, B. Cowles, R. Baker, L. Gommans, P. Madsen, A. McNab, L. Ramakrishnan, K. Sankar, D. Skow, M. Thompson - http://www.ggf.org/documents/GWD-I-E/GFD-I.038.pdf

6. Demchenko, Y., L. Gommans, C. de Laat, A., van Buuren, R. Domain Based Access Control Model for Distributed Collaborative Applications". Accepted, The 2nd IEEE International Conference on e-Science and Grid Computing.

7. Using SAML and XACML for Complex Authorisation Scenarios in Dynamic Resource Provisioning, by Demchenko Y., L. Gommans, C. de Laat. The Second Internation Conference on Availability, Reliability and Security (ARES 2007), April 10-13, 200 Vienna. Accepted paper.

8. Sandhu, R. & Samarati, P., 1994. "Access Control: Principles and Practice", IEEE Communication Magazine, September 1994, pp. 40-48.

9. Sandhu, R., Coyne, E. J., Feinstein, H. L. & Youman, C.E. 1996, "Role-Based Access Control Models", IEEE Computer, February 1996, pp. 38-47.

10. Information Technology - Role Based Access Control, Document Number: ANSI/INCITS 359-2004, InterNational Committee for Information Technology Standards, February 2004, 56 p.

11. ITU-T Rec. X.812(1995) | ISO/IEC 10181-3:1996, Information technology - Open systems interconnection - Security frameworks in open systems: Access control framework.

12. Caelli W., Rhodes A., "Implementation of active role based access control in a collaborative environment", http://www.isi.qut.edu.au/research/publications/technical/ qu isrc-tr-1999-005.pdf

13. Thomas, R. K. 1997, "Team-based Access Control (TMAC): A Primitive for Applying Role-based Access Controls in Collaborative Environments", Proceeding of the Secon ACM Workshop on Role-Based Access Control, ACM, November 1997, pp. 13-19.

14. Park J.S., R Sandhu, "The UCONabc usage control model", ACM Transaction on Information and System Security, 7(1), February 2004.

15. Xinwen Zhang, Masayuki Nakae, Michael J. Covington, and Ravi Sandhu, A Usage-based Authorization Framework for Collaborative Computing Systems, in the proceedings c ACM Symposium on Access Control Models and Technologies (SACMAT), 2006.

16. Godik, S. et al, "eXtensible Access Control Markup Language (XACML) Version 2.0", OASIS Working Draft 04, 6 December 2004, available http://docs.oasis-ope org/xacml/access_control-xacml-2_0-core-spec-cd-04.pdf

17. Demchenko, Y., L. Gommans, C. de Laat, A. Taal, A. Wan, O. Mulmo, "Using Workflow for Dynamic Security Context Management in Complex Resource Provisioning" 7th IEEE/ACM International Conference on Grid Computing (Grid2006), Barcelor September 28-30, 2006, pp.72-79.

18. "Core and hierarchical role based access control (RBAC) profile of XACML v2.0", OASIS Standard, 1 February 2005, available from http://docs.oasi open.org/xacml/2.0/access_control-xacml-2.0-rbac-profile1-spec-os.pdf

19. "Hierarchical resource profile of XACML 2.0", OASIS Standard, 1 February 2005, available from http://docs.oasis-open.org/xacml/access_control-xacml-2.0-hier_profile-spe cd-01.pdf

20. "XACML 3.0 administrative policy," OASIS Draft, 10 December 2005. [Online]. Available from http://docs.oasis-open.org/access_control.

21. Generic Authorization Authentication and Accounting. [Online]. Available: http://www.science.uva.nl/research/ air/projects/aaa/

22. OGSA Authorization WG (OGSA-AUTHZ-WG). [Online]. Available: http://www.ogf.org/gf/group_info/view.php?group=ogsa-authz-wg

A Middleware Architecture for Integrating Privacy Preferences and Location Accuracy

Claudio Agostino Ardagna, Marco Cremonini, Ernesto Damiani, Sabrina De Capitani di Vimercati, and Pierangela Samarati

Università degli Studi di Milano - Dipartimento di Tecnologie dell'Informazione
Via Bramante 65, 26013 Crema (CR) - Italy
{ardagna,cremonini,damiani,decapita,samarati}@dti.unimi.it

Abstract. Location-Based Access Control (LBAC) systems support the evaluation of conditions on locations in the enforcement of access control policies. The ability to evaluate conditions on a set of authorized locations has a number of well-known advantages, including enriching access control expressiveness. However, when locations are used in combination with personal identities, users privacy must be considered. In this paper, we describe a solution to integrate a LBAC system with privacy-enhanced techniques based on location obfuscation. Our solution is based on a privacy-aware middleware component that explicitly addresses the trade-off between users privacy and location accuracy by satisfying preferences set by users and maximizing the quality of location information released to LBAC systems.

1 Introduction

In ubiquitous and mobile computing, user position is a fundamental attribute for managing location-based applications. Access to location information is achieved through a variety of sensor technologies, which recently enjoyed a relevant boost in term of precision and reliability. As a secondary effect of improved location capabilities, protection of user location privacy has become one of the hottest and most critical topics. In this paper, we address location privacy in the framework of location-based services (LBSs). Specifically, we consider *Location-Based Access Control* (LBAC) systems, which support access control policies based on the physical locations of users. Within the class of applications based on LBAC, some necessarily require the best location accuracy for their provision, like those working in mission-critical environments or aimed at providing emergency services. In these cases, privacy concerns are of lesser importance and must be treated specifically for each particular situation. Differently, many other applications based on LBAC could accept location information with sub-optimal accuracy and still offer an acceptable quality of service. In these cases, one of the most critical LBAC issue is to find a balance between *location accuracy* and *location privacy*, dealing with requirements from both business applications and user privacy. The expressive power and the granularity of LBAC

Please use the following format when citing this chapter:

Ardagna, C., Cremonini, M., Damiani, E., De Capitani di Vimercati, S., and Samarati, P., 2007, in IFIP International Federation for Information Processing, Volume 232, New Approaches for Security, Privacy and Trust in Complex Environments, eds. Venter, H., Eloff, M., Labuschagne, L., Eloff, J., von Solms, R., (Boston: Springer), pp. 313–324.

policies, in fact, heavily depend on the accuracy of the locations of users, and the disclosure of fine-grained location information to the LBAC enforcement engine must comply with user's privacy preferences and regulations.

Generally speaking, location-based services require two separate contractual agreements: *i)* between the user and a telecommunication company[1] acting as (or on behalf of) location provider, and *ii)* between the location provider and the application requiring LBAC policies. This dual agreement is critical because, as a generic subscriber to the mobile phone network, an individual may want her privacy strictly preserved, while, as a user of location-based services she may want the service provider to handle very accurate location information to receive best-quality service. To address this issue, we introduce location obfuscation techniques to protect the privacy of the location of users and a distributed architecture (built around a privacy-aware location middleware) decoupling business applications and LBAC policy enforcement from location providers. This way, location middleware can effectively and securely manage a trade-off between accuracy and privacy. The remainder of this paper is organized as follows. Section 2 describes related work. Section 3 illustrates the basic features of our LBAC system and the obfuscation techniques used to achieve user privacy. Section 4 illustrates our privacy-aware architecture, discusses different solutions for evaluating location-based predicates, and shows the working of our privacy-aware middleware. Finally, Section 5 gives our conclusions.

2 Related work

The definition of LBAC systems is an emerging research area that has not been fully investigated yet. Some papers recently present architectures, designed for pervasive environments, that incorporate mobile data for security management [2]. Others consider location information as a resource to protect against unauthorized access [3, 4, 6]. Beresford and Stajano [3] refine a method, called *mix zones*, to enhance privacy in location-based services. Their proposal uses a trusted middleware that anonymizes location information. Bettini et al. [4] present an investigation of the privacy issues raised by a location-based services scenario. Duckham and Kulik [6] investigate obfuscation techniques for protecting the privacy of the locations of users.

Other works propose special-purpose *location middleware* for managing interactions between applications and location providers, while maximizing the quality of service (QoS) [9, 10, 11]. Typically, in these proposals the location middleware *i)* receives requests from LBS components asking for location information, *ii)* collects users locations from a pool of location providers, and *iii)* produces an answer. Naguib et al. [9] present a middleware framework, called *QoSDREAM*, for managing context-aware multimedia applications. Nahrstedt

[1] This is true regardless of the specific location technology used. For instance, satellite location information like GPS is made available to applications via the mobile network.

et al. [10] present a QoS middleware for ubiquitous computing environments aimed at maximizing the QoS of distributed applications. Ranganathan et al. [11] present a middleware that provides a clear separation between business applications and location detection technologies. They also address the issue of managing location data from heterogeneous location technologies.

Although several middleware components supporting communication and negotiation between location services and applications have been presented, only a few proposals try to integrate service quality and privacy protection. For instance, Myles et al. [8] propose an architecture aimed at preserving privacy in location-based services. The architecture is based on a middleware managing the interactions between location-based applications and location providers and on the definition of policies for data release. Hong et al. [7] present an extension of the P3P language for representing user privacy preferences for context-aware applications. The main drawback of their solution is that users are seldom willing to directly manage complex preference policies. By contrast, in our approach users have only to specify a few simple and intuitive parameters. Similarly to [7, 8], our work defines an architecture centered on a middleware component aimed at balancing service accuracy and privacy protection requirements. Differently from other works, our work focuses on some obfuscation-based techniques that degrade a location accuracy and introduces a formal location privacy estimator, called *relevance*.

3 Privacy and LBAC systems

The definition of location-based conditions and their management is the first step towards the development of a privacy-aware LBAC architecture. We identify three main classes of conditions to be included in access control policies and whose evaluation is actually possible with current technology: *movement-based*, *position-based*, and *interaction-based* [2]. Starting from these classes, a set of predicates corresponding to specific conditions can be defined. For instance, predicate `inarea`(*user_term*,*area_term*) is a binary position predicate, where the first parameter represents a user and the second parameter is a geographical area. The predicate semantics is to evaluate whether a user is located within a specific area (e.g., a city, a street, a building). When evaluating location-based predicates, however, we need to consider that location-based information is radically different from other context-related knowledge inasmuch it is both *approximate* (all location systems have a margin of error) and *time-variant* (location is subject to fast changes, especially when the user is in motion).

To accommodate these peculiar characteristics of location-based predicates, we introduce the notion of *relevance* as the estimator of the accuracy of all location-based measurements and evaluations. A relevance is a number $\mathcal{R} \in [0, 1]$ that assumes value 0 when there is no accuracy in the location-based evaluation/measurement, value 1 for full accuracy, and values in (0,1) to represent various degrees of accuracy. Accordingly, the guaranteed location privacy is *(1-R)*. A LBAC system has to manage the following relevance values.

- *LBAC relevance* ($\mathcal{R}_{LBAC}$). The *minimum* accuracy required by business applications for a user location measurement or for a location-based predicate evaluation. It represents the lowest acceptable quality of a location service.
- *Privacy relevance* ($\mathcal{R}_{Priv}$). The *maximum* location relevance accepted by a user for her location information. It represents the highest acceptable location accuracy according to user's privacy preferences.
- *Technological relevance* ($\mathcal{R}_{Tech}$). The measurement accuracy provided by a location provider given a certain mobile technology and environment.

All these relevance values represent the degree of accuracy related to a location measurement. $\mathcal{R}_{Tech}$ and $\mathcal{R}_{LBAC}$ are assumed to be given, while $\mathcal{R}_{Priv}$ is the result of the application of suitable *obfuscation techniques*. Our goal is to apply an obfuscation technique to location measurements in such a way that the following relation holds: $\mathcal{R}_{LBAC} \leq \mathcal{R}_{Priv} \leq \mathcal{R}_{Tech}$. Given a location measurement with relevance $\mathcal{R}_{Tech}$, some transformations are applied to make it less accurate, so that privacy requirements can be met. The resulting location measurement retains a level of relevance ($\mathcal{R}_{Priv}$), which has to be greater than $\mathcal{R}_{LBAC}$ to be meaningful for LBAC enforcement.

3.1 Location obfuscation and user privacy

Obfuscation techniques applied to a location measurement increase the uncertainty of a user location by degrading its accuracy. In this work, we shall consider a planar (2-D) coordinate space for locations. Also, since the result of each location measurement is necessarily affected by an error, a *spatial area* is always returned, rather than a single point. We introduce two working assumptions: *i)* the area returned by a location measurement is circular, which is the actual shape resulting from many location technologies [5]; *ii)* the distribution of measurement errors within a returned area is uniform. This last assumption increases accuracy and precision, which are the main requirements for LBAC predicate evaluation. According to these two assumptions, we formally define a location measurement and the associated error as follows.

Definition 3.1 (Location measurement) *A location measurement of a user u is a circular area, denoted $Area(r, x_c, y_c)$, centered on the geographical coordinates (x_c, y_c) and with radius r, which includes the real position of u.*

Definition 3.2 (Uniform distribution) *Given a location measurement $Area(r, x_c, y_c)$, the distribution is uniform if and only if the corresponding probability density function (pdf) $f_r(x, y)$ is:*

$$f_r(x,y) = \begin{cases} \frac{1}{\pi r^2} & \text{if } x, y \in Area(r, x_c, y_c) \\ 0 & \text{otherwise.} \end{cases}$$

Since our main goal in obfuscating a location measurement is to select an area corresponding to a given relevance $\mathcal{R}_{Priv}$, we need to better specify how $\mathcal{R}_{Priv}$ is calculated. In a real world scenario, it is very unlikely that a user could explicitly specify such a value (what would a 0.6 relevance exactly mean?). Many proposals in the location privacy field assume that users specify their privacy preferences in terms of intuitive parameters such as *minimum distance* [6]. For instance, a user can require the radius of the location area to be at least 100 meters. In this case, obfuscation is achieved by increasing measurement granularity. Although minimum distance is easy to understand and implement, it has a severe drawback: an absolute distance value is only meaningful when related to a specific application context. In the previous example, the value of 100 meters is well suited to applications that provide touristic information to a user walking in a city center. Location-based applications working, for example, in smaller contexts, as inside a production plant, are likely to become ineffective if the granularity is 100 meters. Also, 100 meters can be insufficient for preserving user privacy in high sensitive contexts.

A different (and equally intuitive) way for users to specify privacy requirements is for a relative degradation of the measure with respect to the location accuracy (i.e., $\mathcal{R}_{Tech}$). In our approach, privacy preferences are therefore defined through a simple index $\lambda \in [0, \infty]$ that represents the *privacy rate* in terms of degradation applied to location accuracy. For instance, if a user asks no privacy, then $\lambda = 0$. If a user asks total privacy, $\lambda \to \infty$. Normally, a user may ask that the accuracy of her location must be decreased by a certain rate, like 100%, which implies $\lambda = 1$, or 200%, which implies $\lambda = 2$.

Both minimum distance d and rate λ are easy to specify for users. Among the two, λ is the more general index because independent from the specific application context and measurement unit.[2]

3.2 Obfuscation by scaling the radius

The first and most obvious technique for obfuscating a location measurement is to scale the radius of the circular area. The obfuscation effect directly derives from Definition 3.2: $\forall r, r_u$ with $r < r_u : f_r(x,y) > f_{r_u}(x,y)$. Fig. 1(a) shows the effect of obfuscation by scaling the radius, where the circular area of radius r is the area returned by a sensing technology and the area of radius r_u is the obfuscated area. The relevance $\mathcal{R}_{Priv}$ of the obfuscated location is calculated by dividing the pdf of the obfuscated area by the pdf of the original area multiplied by $\mathcal{R}_{Tech}$:

$$given\ r, r_u : r < r_u,\ \mathcal{R}_{Priv} = \frac{r^2}{r_u^2}\mathcal{R}_{Tech} \qquad (1)$$

[2] Parameter λ depends on the accuracy of each measurement realized with a specific location technology. In this paper, we assume that a single location technology is used and users are aware of the best accuracy that the technology can achieve. We plan to develop a more general approach in future work.

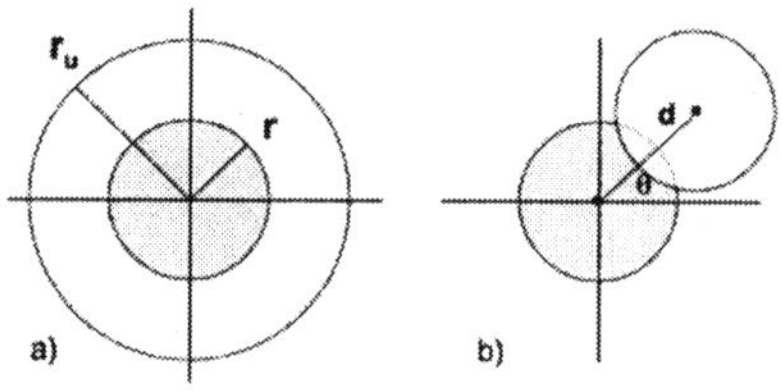

Fig. 1. Obfuscation by scaling the radius (a) and by shifting the center (b)

Otherwise, if the rate λ is used to specify the privacy preference, the new radius r_u can be derived as follows:

$$given\ \lambda \geq 0: \quad \mathcal{R}_{Priv} = (\lambda+1)^{-1}\mathcal{R}_{Tech}, \quad r_u = r\sqrt{\lambda+1}. \tag{2}$$

3.3 Obfuscation by center-shifting

Shifting the center of the location area is another way of decreasing its accuracy. The obfuscated area is derived from the original area either by setting the distance d between the two centers to the value specified by the user or by deducing d from rate λ. Let $Area(r, x_c + \Delta x, y_c + \Delta y)$ be the obfuscated area and suppose that the distance d is greater than or equal to $2r$. In this situation, the probability that the obfuscated area contains the real position of the user (i.e., (x_u, y_u)) is zero, that is, $P((x_u, y_u) \in Area(r, x_c + \Delta x, y_c + \Delta y)) = 0$. Otherwise (i.e., $0 < d < 2r$), $0 < P((x_u, y_u) \in Area(r, x_c + \Delta x, y_c + \Delta y)) < 1$.

The privacy gain can be quantitatively measured by considering the intersection of the original and the obfuscated area, denoted $Area_{Tech \cap Priv}$. Intuitively, the degree of privacy is inversely proportional to the intersection of the two areas and therefore it is directly proportional to the distance d between the two centers. In particular, if $d = 0$, there is no privacy gain; if $d \geq 2r$, there is full privacy; and if $0 < d < 2r$, there is an increment of privacy.

To derive the actual obfuscated area, the angle θ illustrated in Fig. 1(b) must be chosen too. With regard to θ, however, there is no meaning for a user to specify it, so it must be defined by the component in charge of obfuscating the location measurement. The first and obvious choice is to randomly choose θ, because in general all its values are equivalent with respect to user privacy preferences. However, in the next section, we will discuss how a reasonable choice of this parameter can be made to maximize the relevance associated with location-based evaluations, still preserving user preferences.

$\mathcal{R}_{Priv}$ can be derived from the ratio of the intersection $Area_{Tech \cap Priv}$ over the obfuscated area as follows.

$$\mathcal{R}_{Priv} = (\lambda+1)^{-1} \cdot \mathcal{R}_{Tech} = \frac{Area_{Tech \cap Priv}}{Area(r\ x_c+\Delta x\ y_c+\Delta y)} \cdot \mathcal{R}_{Tech} \tag{3}$$

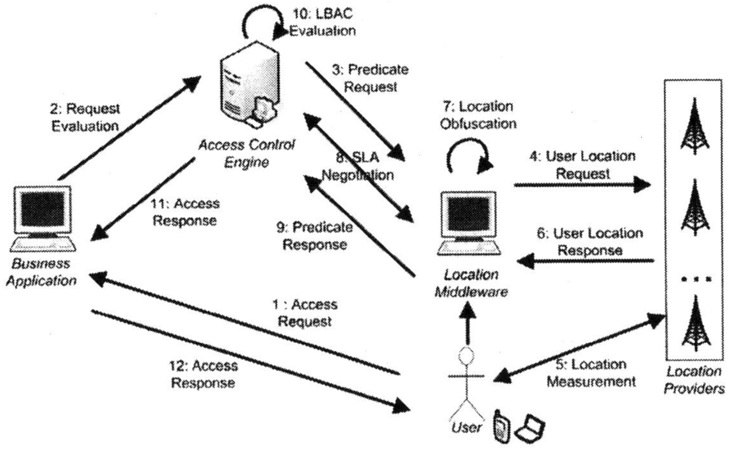

Fig. 2. Privacy-Aware LBAC Architecture

4 A privacy-aware LBAC architecture

The above concepts and techniques are at the base of the definition of our privacy-aware LBAC architecture. The logical components of the architecture are showed in Fig. 2 and can be summarized as follows.

- *User*. Individual to be located through her mobile terminal.
- *Business application*. Customer-oriented application that provides resources protected by LBAC policies.
- *Access Control Engine (ACE)*. A component that stores and enforces LBAC policies. For the enforcement, it requests location services and information from the Location Middleware.
- *Location Providers (LPs)*. Components using location sensing technologies to provide location measurements.
- *Location Middleware (LM)*. The entity that interacts with different LPs and provides location services to the ACE. It has to satisfy users privacy preferences and ACEs location accuracy needs.

Communications among these components are performed via request/response message exchanges. Basically, the interaction flow can be logically partitioned in six macro-operations: *i) initialization,* when user preferences and LBAC policies are defined; *ii) location information retrieval,* when LM collects user location information through a communication process with multiples LPs; *iii) SLA negotiation,* when a Service Level Agreement (SLA) specifying QoS attributes and corresponding service cost is agreed between an ACE and a LM; *iv) location obfuscation,* when obfuscation techniques are used to comply with both user preference and LBAC accuracy; *v) LBAC evaluation,* when the LBAC policies are evaluated; and finally *vi) access decision,* when the access request is granted or denied.

4.1 LBAC predicates evaluation

A major design issue for our privacy-aware LBAC architecture is related to the component in charge of evaluating LBAC predicates. Two choices are possible, which deeply affect how privacy is guaranteed.

- *ACE evaluation*: The ACE asks users locations to LM without disclosing LBAC predicates.
- *LM evaluation*: The ACE sends to LM a LBAC predicate for evaluation and receives a boolean answer and a relevance value.

Both choices are viable and well-suited for different set of requirements. On one side, *ACE evaluation* enforces a clear separation between applications and location services because the location service infrastructure (i.e., LMs and LPs) never deals with application-dependent location-based predicates. On the other side, *LM evaluation* avoids the exchange of user locations, although obfuscated, with applications. This second choice is also more flexible in business terms. For instance, an ACE can subscribe to a location service for a specific set of location predicates, and select different QoS according to different needs (e.g., different accuracy levels). The LM could then differentiate prices according to service quality.

Since the analysis presented so far has implicitly assumed the ACE evaluation scenario (i.e., the ACE component receives an obfuscated area with a given $\mathcal{R}_{Priv}$ value), we now describe how LM evaluation is carried out. The main difference is that now LM returns an answer for the LBAC predicate evaluation together with a relevance of that answer, which we call $\mathcal{R}_{Eval}$. This relevance is derived from $\mathcal{R}_{Priv}$ by considering both the obfuscated area and the area specified into the LBAC predicate. Since the ACE component requires a minimum acceptable relevance $\mathcal{R}_{LBAC}$, $\mathcal{R}_{Eval} \geq \mathcal{R}_{LBAC}$ must hold. For instance, let `inarea`(*JohnID*, *Room1*) be the predicate that the ACE component sends to the LM component, which asks whether the user *JohnID* is in room *Room1*. LM calculates $\mathcal{R}_{Eval}$ as follows:

$$\mathcal{R}_{Eval} = \frac{Area_{Priv \cap LBAC}}{Area_{Priv}} \cdot \mathcal{R}_{Priv} \tag{4}$$

where the scalar factor depends on the intersection, denoted $Area_{Priv \cap LBAC}$, between the obfuscated area and the area specified by the LBAC predicate.

There is, however, a subtlety to consider when center-shifting obfuscation is applied. As noted in Section 3.1, there are infinite values of angle θ that could be chosen, all equivalent with respect to the $\mathcal{R}_{Priv}$ value. When the LBAC predicate is evaluated, however, the choice of θ is relevant, because according to the position of the obfuscated area, the $\mathcal{R}_{Eval}$ value may change. This requires the following additional constraint:

$$\mathcal{R}_{Eval} \leq \frac{Area_{Tech \cap LBAC}}{Area_{Tech}} \cdot \mathcal{R}_{Tech} \tag{5}$$

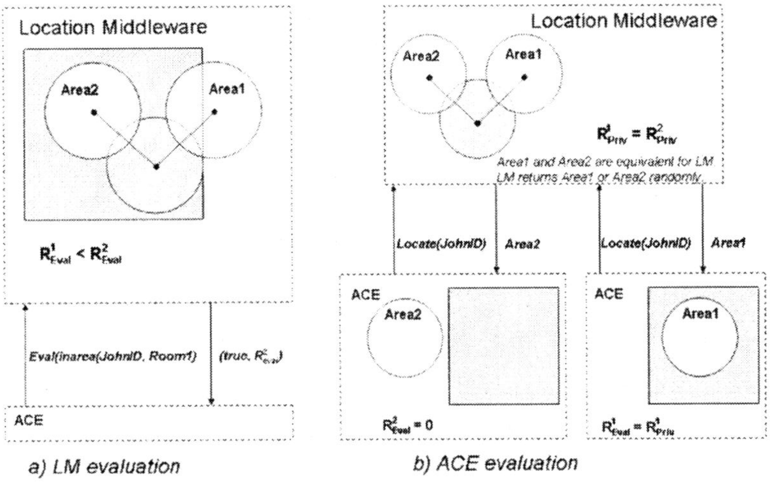

Fig. 3. An example of LM evaluation (a), and ACE evaluation (b)

The rationale for this constraint is to avoid the case of a relevance $\mathcal{R}_{Eval}$ derived from $\mathcal{R}_{Priv}$ that is greater than the one that would have provided the original area with relevance $\mathcal{R}_{Tech}$. In other terms, areas must not be manipulated with obfuscation techniques just to increase the odds of satisfying LBAC quality requirements. This case would be made possible by shifting the center in such a way that, for example, the obfuscated area is completely included into the area specified by the predicate (*Room1*, in our example), while the original area is just partially included. Our constraint ensures that, given an infinite set Θ of angles, a set $\Theta_f \subseteq \Theta$ is generated, containing all angles $\theta_1 \dots \theta_n$ that produce a relevance $\mathcal{R}_{Eval}$ at most equals to the relevance produced by considering the original area.

When center-shifting obfuscation is adopted, the ACE vs LM choice has a significant impact. To illustrate, consider the examples in Fig. 3(a) and Fig. 3(b) that show the evaluation of predicate inarea(*JohnID*, *Room1*) in case of LM evaluation and of ACE evaluation, respectively. Here, *Area1* and *Area2* are two possible obfuscated areas.

If LM evaluation is performed, LM computes $\mathcal{R}_{Eval}$ from (4) and is able to establish an ordering among obfuscated areas according to the different values of $\mathcal{R}_{Eval}$. In our example, it is easy to see that relevance $\mathcal{R}^2_{Eval}$ resulting from *Area2* is greater than relevance $\mathcal{R}^1_{Eval}$ resulting from *Area1*. This information is important for the provision of the location service, because when returned to ACE, the value $\mathcal{R}_{Eval}$ is matched with $\mathcal{R}_{LBAC}$, the minimum relevance required for LBAC evaluation. The best strategy for LM is therefore to select the angle θ that produces the obfuscated area that, given $\mathcal{R}_{Priv}$, maximizes $\mathcal{R}_{Eval}$.

If ACE evaluation is in place, LM does not calculate any $\mathcal{R}_{Eval}$ (i.e., ACE does not communicate the location predicate under evaluation), and it can only

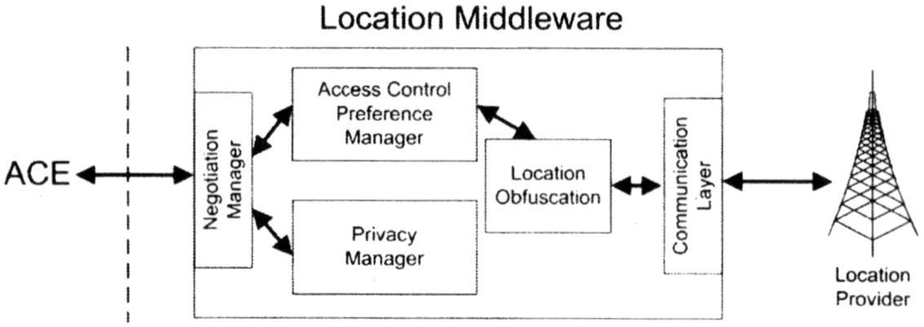

Fig. 4. Location Middleware

select randomly one value for θ among all those that produce an obfuscated area with the same $\mathcal{R}_{Priv}$. In this way, random selection of the obfuscated area (in our example, *Area1* or *Area2*) may cause an unpredictable result during ACE evaluation, ranging from relevance equal to zero (e.g., when *Area2* in Fig. 3(b) is returned) to relevance equal to $\mathcal{R}_{Priv}$ (e.g., when *Area1* in Fig. 3(b) is returned). As a consequence, also the matching with the condition over $\mathcal{R}_{LBAC}$ results in random rejection or acceptance of the predicate evaluation. Therefore, center-shifting obfuscation is incompatible with ACE evaluation. This result supports architectures including location middleware capable of autonomously evaluating LBAC predicates.

4.2 The privacy-aware middleware

As mentioned in Section 2, currently available middleware components are mostly in charge of managing interactions between applications and location providers, and managing communication and negotiation protocols aimed at maximizing the QoS. Instead, in our approach the privacy-aware middleware has to find a balance between users privacy and location-based services accuracy. To this end, our LM is responsible both for the obfuscation of user locations and for the location-based predicates evaluation. As shown in Fig. 4, LM is functionally divided into the following five logical components.

Communication Layer. It manages the communication process with LPs. Hides low-level communication details to other components.
Negotiation Manager. It acts as an interface with ACE. It provides negotiation functionalities and implements the negotiation protocols [1].
Access Control Preference Manager. It manages location service attributes and quality by interacting with the Location Obfuscation component.
Location Obfuscation. It applies obfuscation techniques for users privacy.
Privacy Manager. It manages privacy preferences and location-based predicate evaluation.

As an example of the LM operations, assume that user John subscribes to the LM by setting his privacy preference to $\lambda = 0.2$, which is meant to degrade location accuracy by 20%. After that, John uses a business application that adopts LBAC policies. In particular, one of these LBAC policies states that when a user is in *Room1*, she gains the access to an online financial service. Additionally, the ACE component is set to require a minimum evaluation relevance $\mathcal{R}_{LBAC} = 0.7$. To grant or deny John's access to the online financial service, the ACE sends to LM a predicate evaluation request for predicate `inarea`(*JohnId*,*Room1*) together with relevance $\mathcal{R}_{LBAC}$. The LM asks to the LP (for simplicity, suppose that only one LP is available) the John's position and receives as an answer a circular area together with a technology relevance $\mathcal{R}_{Tech} = 0.9$, representing the accuracy of the measurement. At this point, LM must obfuscate the location, for example, by shifting the center. It calculates $\mathcal{R}_{Priv} = (\lambda + 1)^{-1}\ \mathcal{R}_{Tech} = 0.75$. Among all possible values of angle θ that produce an obfuscated area with $\mathcal{R}_{Priv} = 0.75$, LM has to select the obfuscated area that maximizes the corresponding relevance $\mathcal{R}_{Eval}$ computed as in (4) and that satisfies the restriction defined in (5). For simplicity, we only consider *Area1* and *Area2* illustrated in Fig. 3. *Area2* falls completely into the square greyed box representing the geometry and position of *Room1*, so $\mathcal{R}^2_{Eval} = \mathcal{R}_{Priv} = 0.75$. *Area1*, instead, is partially overlapped with the grey box, so $\mathcal{R}^1_{Eval} < \mathcal{R}_{Priv}$. Both satisfy the restriction defined in (5), therefore LM can return to ACE a *true* evaluation of the `inarea` predicate together with $\mathcal{R}^2_{Eval} = 0.75$. Finally, the ACE can proceed in the enforcement of the LBAC policy having its location predicate positively evaluated, that is, the corresponding boolean value is *true* and the evaluation relevance is greater than $\mathcal{R}_{LBAC} = 0.7$.

It is important to highlight that the architecture of our location middleware can be extended to include the important case of users setting *multiple privacy preferences* according to different contexts. For instance, there could be users wishing to set: no privacy preferences for location services dedicated to the social network of their relatives and close friends; a certain level of privacy for business location services aimed at helping to find point of interests (e.g., shops, or monuments), and for location services whose goal is to find their position while at work; and strong privacy requirements in high sensitive contexts.

5 Conclusions

In this paper, we presented an architecture built around a location middleware for evaluating LBAC predicates. We have showed a solution that supports the critical issue of striking a balance between accuracy and privacy requirements. To the best of our knowledge, this is the first middleware solution that smoothly manages such aspects of a LBAC infrastructure through different obfuscation techniques and an uniform index representing a common estimator for both quality and privacy requirements. Future work to be carried out includes extending our architecture to fully support the multiple privacy preferences scenario and enriching LM with the ability to deal with contextual information.

Acknowledgments

This work was partially supported by the European Union within the PRIME Project under contract IST-2002-507591, by the Italian Ministry of Research Fund for Basic Research (FIRB) under project RBNE05FKZ2, and by the Italian MIUR under project MAPS.

References

1. C.A. Ardagna, M. Cremonini, E. Damiani, S. De Capitani di Vimercati, and P. Samarati. Location-based metadata and negotiation protocols for LBAC in a one-to-many scenario. In *Proc. of the Workshop On Security and Privacy in Mobile and Wireless Networking*, Coimbra, Portugal, May 2006.
2. C.A. Ardagna, M. Cremonini, E. Damiani, S. De Capitani di Vimercati, and P. Samarati. Supporting location-based conditions in access control policies. In *Proc. of the ACM Symposium on InformAtion, Computer and Communications Security (ASIACCS'06)*, Taipei, Taiwan, March 2006.
3. A. R. Beresford and F. Stajano. Mix zones: User privacy in location-aware services. In *Proc. of the 2nd IEEE Annual Conference on Pervasive Computing and Communications Workshops (PERCOMW'04)*, Orlando, Florida, March 2004.
4. C. Bettini, X.S. Wang, and S. Jajodia. Protecting privacy against location-based personal identification. In *Proc. of the 2nd VLDB Workshop on Secure Data Management*, Trondheim, Norway, September 2005.
5. E. Damiani, M. Anisetti, and V. Bellandi. Toward exploiting location-based and video information in negotiated access control policies. In *Proc. of the 1st International Conference on Information Systems Security (ICISS 2005)*, Kolkata, India, December 2005.
6. M. Duckham and L. Kulik. A formal model of obfuscation and negotiation for location privacy. In *Proc. of the 3rd International Conference on Pervasive Computing*, Munich, Germany, May 2005.
7. D. Hong, M. Yuan, and V. Y. Shen. Dynamic privacy management: a plug-in service for the middleware in pervasive computing. In *Proc. of the 7th International Conference on Human Computer Interaction with Mobile Devices & Services*, Salzburg, Austria, September 2005.
8. G. Myles, A. Friday, and N. Davies. Preserving privacy in environments with location-based applications. *IEEE Pervasive Computing*, 2(1):56–64, 2003.
9. H. Naguib, G. Coulouris, and S. Mitchell. Middleware support for context-aware multimedia applications. In *Proc. of the IFIP TC6 / WG6.1 3rd International Working Conference on New Developments in Distributed Applications and Interoperable Systems*, Deventer, The Netherlands, September 2001.
10. K. Nahrstedt, D. Xu, D. Wichadakul, and B. Li. QoS-aware middleware for ubiquitous and heterogeneous environments. *IEEE Communications Magazine*, pages 140–148, November 2001.
11. A. Ranganathan, J. Al-Muhtadi, S. Chetan, R. H. Campbell, and M. D. Mickunas. Middlewhere: A middleware for location awareness in ubiquitous computing applications. In *Proc. of the ACM/IFIP/USENIX 5th International Middleware Conference (Middleware 2004)*, Toronto, Ontario, Canada, October 2004.

Enabling Privacy of Real-Life LBS

A Platform for Flexible Mobile Service Provisioning

Jan Zibuschka, Lothar Fritsch, Mike Radmacher, Tobias Scherner, and Kai Rannenberg
Johann Wolfgang Goethe University Frankfurt*
Chair for Mobile Commerce & Multilateral Security
Gräfstraße 78, D-60054 Frankfurt am Main, Germany
{zibuschka, fritsch, radmacher, scherner, rannenberg}@m-lehrstuhl.de
www.whatismobile.de

Abstract. Privacy in computerized environments is perceived very differently depending on the respective point of view. Often "privacy enhancing technologies" – initiated by the user, as a measure of self-defense – are seen as conflicting with business goals such as cost-efficiency, revenue assurance, and options for further business development based on existing data. This paper presents the design and implementation of an architecture and prototype for privacy-friendly, interoperable location-based services (LBS), based on intermediation of location data via a location middleware component. The aim is to combine privacy-friendliness, efficiency, and market potential. Therefore the security interests of the stakeholders are analyzed and an architecture solution including an intermediary is introduced. Then the prototype implementation (at a mobile operator) is described and the usage of the prototype for a commercial service and product offer by the operator involved in the development is discussed.

1 Introduction

The high market penetration [1] reached by mobile phones makes these devices a highly attractive platform for the rendering of location-based services (LBS) reaching a broad user base. The mobile operator may provide the location data for specialized LBS providers or act as service provider itself.

However, location data is very sensitive. In many countries and regions there are

* This work was supported by the European Union IST PRIME project; however, it represents the view of the authors only.

Please use the following format when citing this chapter:

Zibuschka, J., Fritsch, L., Radmacher, M., Scherner, T., and Rannenberg, K., 2007, in IFIP International Federation for Information Processing, Volume 232, New Approaches for Security, Privacy and Trust in Complex Environments, eds. Venter, H., Eloff, M., Labuschagne, L., Eloff, J., von Solms, R., (Boston: Springer), pp. 325–336.

even legal requirements associated with the handling of customer data for such purposes. Typically, a mobile network operator is required to obtain permission of its customers before transmitting location information – or, more general, personal information. Also, other privacy laws and regulations, which are varying from country to country and sometimes over time, have to be taken into account. This may lead to unclear or globally inhomogeneous requirements towards the provider of a given service.

So, while mobile operators are – from a technical point of view – in a very good position to supply user location data, the actual provision of location-based services can in some cases be a legal and commercial risk. Thus, there is an incentive to outsource the rendering of location-based services to third parties under clear conditions and to ease the possibility for users to make decisions on the transfer of data. With this strategy, the operator can maintain good and trustful customer relations and get rid of potential liabilities that may arise from the specifics of a service.

However, to be widely accepted, such a system needs to be based on technology available to a broad user base. As it is highly unlikely that the system could be built to be oblivious of underlying technologies (such as WAP 1.x, 2.x, or direct TCP/IP connections) without impeding privacy guarantees, several trade-offs have to be considered during the design of the system.

This paper reports on the design of a system and architecture that try to conciliate stakeholders' interests. Section 2 presents the involved entities and their requirements; section 3 gives an overview of the architecture, followed by the presentation of implementation details in Section 4. Section 5 discusses related work and key benefits, after which section 6 wraps up.

2 Interests and Related Security Requirements

Location-based services are employed for a wide range of use cases. One widely used application are navigation services, e.g. finding the nearest pharmacy and directing the user there. Typically users open a connection to a service via their mobile phones, and then the user's position is determined by the mobile operator. The determined position is passed on to the service provider, who compares it to his database. The results – e.g. the 5 nearest pharmacies – are then returned to the user's mobile phone, where they are displayed.

So the mobile operator usually knows what kind of service the user has accessed, while the LBS provider would be able to tell which mobile operator the user is using. The service then needs to be customized for usage with a specific mobile operator's location provision interface. Additionally, precautions need to be taken to avoid that LBS providers can track users simply at their discretion. By this LBS demonstrate the also more general need for solutions that empower users to enforce privacy policies for their personal data, including their location data. Also LBS are examples of complex services that are offered by consortia; so more than just the two "classic" stakeholders (customer, provider) are involved.

For analyzing the requirements of the different stakeholders involved in the provisioning of location-based services, the concept of Multilateral Security [2, 3] was used. Multilateral Security aims at a balance between the (maybe competing)

security requirements of different stakeholders, which includes considering all involved entities as potential attackers. This is especially important for communication systems, as one cannot expect the various stakeholders to completely trust each other.
The "ideal" of Multilateral Security can be described as follows (see Figure 1):

1. Considering Conflicts:
    a. Different parties involved in a system may have different, perhaps conflicting interests and security goals.
2. Respecting Interests:
    a. Parties can specify their own interests and security goals.
    b. Conflicts can be recognized and negotiated.
    c. Negotiated results can be reliably enforced.
3. Supporting Sovereignty:
    a. Each party is only minimally required to place trust in the honesty of others.
    b. Each party is only minimally required to place trust in the technology of others.

Multilateral Security in general refers to all "classical" security goals, i.e. confidentiality, integrity, availability, or accountability can be in the interest of one party, but not necessarily in that of another. However a typical conflict occurs between the wish for privacy and the interest in cooperation. On one hand parties wish to protect their own sphere, information, and assets, on the other hand they strive for cooperation and wish to establish trust with partners, access services, transfer values, or enable enforcement of agreements.

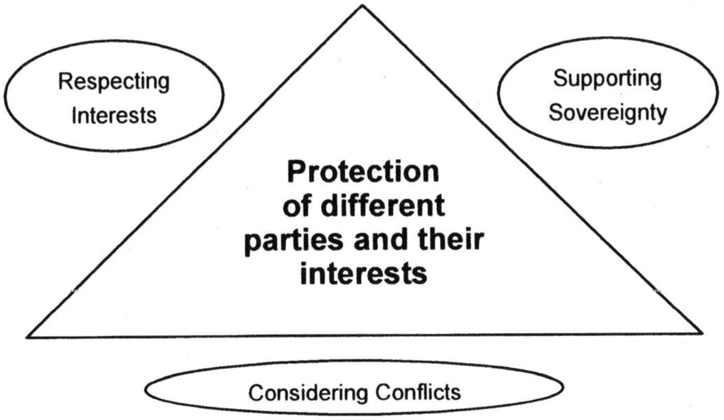

Figure 1: Multilateral Security

2.1 The Stakeholders

The investigation of the pharmacy search scenario leads on first hand to the identification of three different stakeholders:

1. A mobile operator is the owner of the mobile network infrastructure. Its business is to offer the network infrastructure that mobile subscribers use every day, including roaming between different mobile networks. Concerning the provision of location-based services, the mobile operator is often the source for the location information used, and therefore is legally responsible for the release and transfer of the respective data.
2. A service provider is offering LBSs based on the mobile network infrastructure. Classical examples are navigation and routing services such as the pharmacy search scenario illustrated earlier in this section.
3. Last but not least, the users or subscribers of the services have interests. They are often "double" customers: A subscription with the mobile operator enables them to communicate and be mobile, while for specific services they subscribe to the respective specialist service providers.

Detailed analysis of the services and their setting from the different view points and interests yields several requirements for the various entities that will be described in the sections 2.2 till 2.4.

2.2 Mobile Operators' Interests and Requirements

There are mainly five interests from the point of view of the mobile operator:

1. Legal compliance: The mobile operator requires that the interface he provides is compliant with (potentially divergent) privacy legislation.
2. Sovereignty over payment processes: The mobile operator may want to be the entity responsible for the billing of services, even when rendered externally, as this is part of the customer relation.
3. Flexible business models: As different telecommunications markets favour different organizational structures, an architecture supporting mobile operators (MOs), Mobile Virtual Network Operators (MVNOs) or independent parties as location sources is essential for international deployment of the architecture.
4. Customer loyalty: The mobile operator values customer loyalty, which may be increased by respecting each customer's privacy.
5. Standardized communication interfaces: Offering standardized interfaces can enable the mobile operator to offer a wide range of externally rendered location-based services to its users.

2.3 Service Providers' Interests and Requirements

The service provider's requirements focus on his business interests towards user and mobile operator:

1. Standardized communication interfaces: A standardized interface available at the different location sources offers flexibility and limits deployment costs.

2. Trusted payment partners: The service provider requires correct billing for service usage. This requirement also holds for the other stakeholders.

2.4 Users' Interests and Requirements

Users are the weakest of all the parties mentioned, especially if they are acting on their own. So their requirements concentrate on keeping and getting control over their data:

1. Stay anonymous: Users do not want to reveal their identity unnecessarily.
2. Being able to protect the data on one's interests: Users don't want other parties to unnecessarily know what interests they have, e.g. what services they use.
3. Sovereignty over location information: Users require facilities to configure the acceptable usage for their location information.
4. Fine-granular management of consent: Users may want to configure specific parameters concerning the handling of their personal information by different LBS providers.
5. Easy-to-use technology: Privacy functions should not impede usability, especially not the usability of mobile services, as those services are usually used in settings where users cannot simply concentrate on dealing with the user interfaces.
6. Reliable service provision: Availability of the service is a major concern, especially in critical scenarios such as search and navigate scenarios that are used to save time.
7. Confidentiality of service utilization towards mobile operator: A user's service usage patterns should not be obvious for the mobile operator, as it may involve data privileged to the user and the application service provider, e.g. for medical services.

3 Architecture

The stakeholder interests and requirements lead to several architectural requirements. First there are requirements on the controls of the information flows. These are mainly triggered by the users' privacy interests and the interests of the operators and service providers to stay legal:

- To ascertain the proper handling of personal user information by different parties, the system needs to offer a facility for managing user defined (location) privacy policies.
- In addition to enforcing users' privacy preferences, the system should aim to minimize the distribution of information regardless of the users' configured parameters. E.g., it should not be inherently necessary for the mobile operator to know which services a respective user subscribes to.
- Identity management components are needed to make sure that the flow of identity information can be controlled and still services can be accessed by users.

Figure 2 presents a UML use case diagram illustrating the basic components of the system and stakeholder interaction.

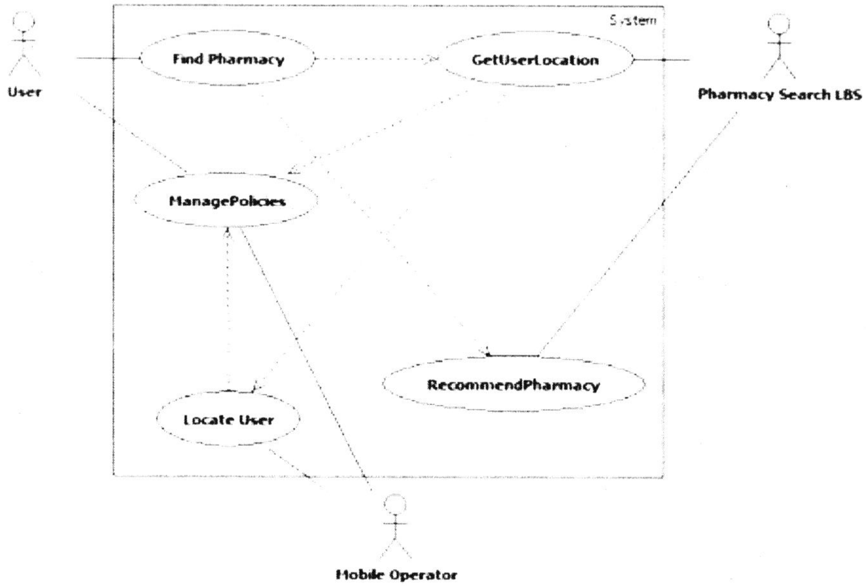

Figure 2: Pharmacy search use case diagram.

To accommodate the operator's and service provider's interests in a large customer base in the mobile market, a compromise between large scale availability of platforms and privacy requirements is needed. On the one hand, the WAP specifications do not allow end-to-end encryption and could be intercepted at the WAP-gateway, which is normally under the control of the mobile operator. Also WAP is sometimes seen as some kind of old-fashioned. However on the other hand, WAP is robust and has a high market penetration, as most mobile phones support this standard and can enable a lot of users to get into the situation of considering and defining their policies.

In addition to having a "stronger" terminal device in a later prototype and a migration path towards the use of this prototype a location middleware component for dealing with weaker devices in a flexible way was designed. The location intermediary is responsible for:

- Providing a policy management front end for clients with limited capabilities (e.g. WAP phones)
- Keeping an audit trail and so empowering subscribers to trace interactions with certain service providers
- Offering anonymization and confidentiality of service usage by providing a proxy between mobile operator and service providers

Mediating the communication between the different stakeholders, an intermediary offers anonymization of relayed traffic, if it is not deployed on the user's device and if some trust can be placed in the entity operating the intermediary (as the traffic is not anonymized against the intermediary). This can act as a fallback solution in cases where the implementation of more elaborate measures (e.g. mixes) is impractical, for example because of restricted client hardware or infrastructure capabilities. However, this will only offer meaningful security guarantees if the connections cannot be eavesdropped at the intermediary by one of the communicating stakeholders. If anonymous communication is available, the intermediary may serve as a rendezvous point for communicating entities [4]. Advanced cryptographic protocols like oblivious transfer have been proposed [5] for the privacy-friendly rendering of location-based services. However, finding a mechanism that minimizes transferred information in the case of bandwidth efficient push services is an open research question.

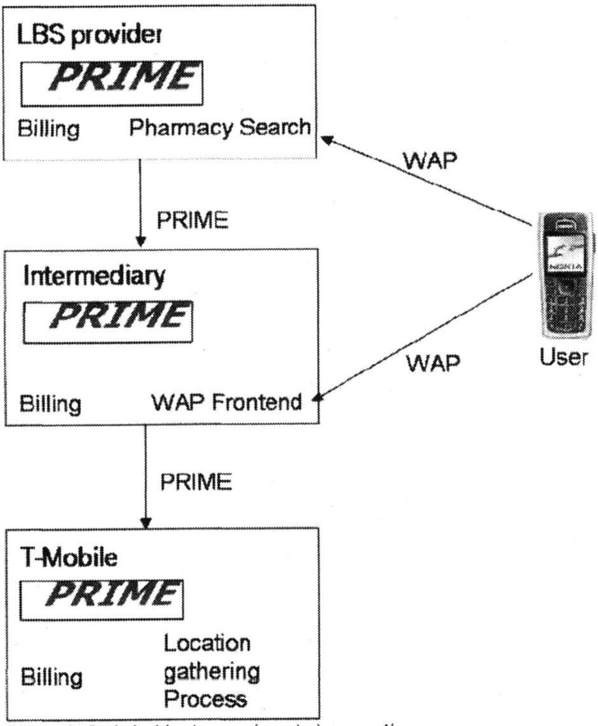

Figure 3: Stakeholder interaction via intermediary

4 Implementation

The implemented example application prototype is a mobile pharmacy search using Wireless Application Protocol 1 (see Figure 4). The usage of this widely deployed protocol enables the mobile operator to reach a maximum customer base for upcoming privacy-enhanced products based on the prototype. As it is based on a WAP infrastructure, the prototype does not offer anonymization support.

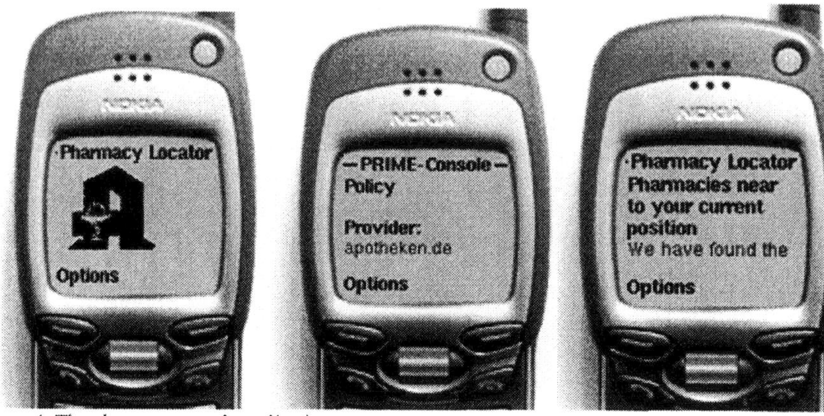

Figure 4: The pharmacy search application

When a user initiates communications with a service, he is pseudonymized and a communication channel to the MO is established, using the intermediary as a proxy. The relevant privacy policies are checked, and the service can then be rendered. The steps in detail (see Figure 5):

- The user contacts the location-based service provider
- The LBS provider requests an access handle for the current global user pseudonym (e.g. IP address, in the case of no anonymous communication infrastructure) via the location intermediary.
- The LBS provider requests user location and payment allocation from the mobile operator. Policies are managed at the location intermediary in the WAP scenario. The mobile operator may then provide user location and a payment handle to the service provider via the intermediary, if a matching policy is available. If no such policy can be found, the system proposes a policy to the user, based on the service's requirements.
- The LBS provider queries his domain logic, runs the service and provides the result to the user.
- Payment is committed at the mobile operator, again using the intermediary as a pseudonymization proxy.

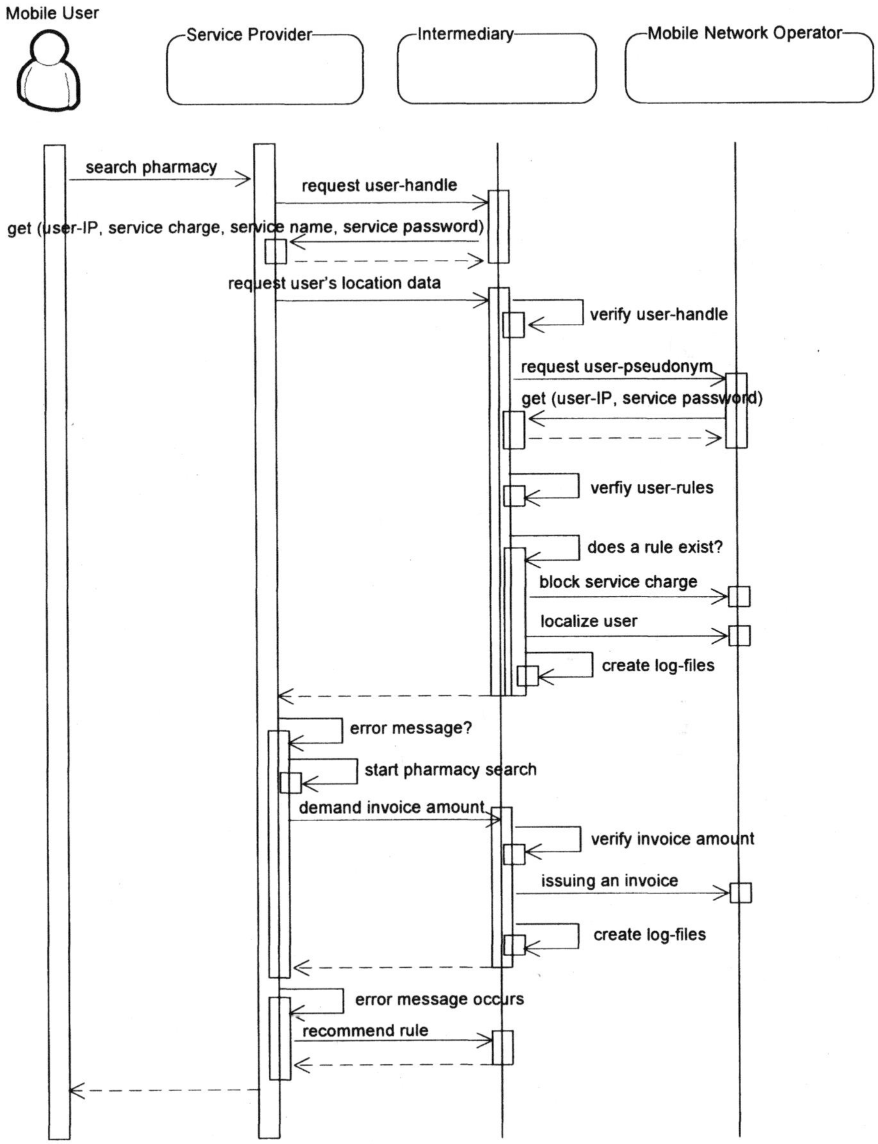

Figure 5: Pharmacy search sequence.

5 Related Work and Key Benefits

There are a wide range of technologies for protecting users' privacy in existence today, which are generally referred to as Privacy Enhancing Technologies or PETs [6]. Several protocols and architectures for the privacy-preserving handling of location information have been proposed. This section gives a quick overview of existing solutions and compares them to the implementation presented in this paper.

The Alipes platform [7] offers the possibility to control the access to location information using user-configurable privacy policies. Furthermore, location information from different sources may be aggregated. However, Alipes does not offer pseudonymization functionalities, and generally no further identity management functionality.

In [8], a system that limits the accuracy of handed-out location information based on the recipient is proposed. However, neither access control functionalities nor pseudonymization are considered.

The architecture presented in [9] proposes pseudonymization and access control functionalities for the location-based services scenario. However, no further analysis of the information flow between the communicating entities is performed.

The intermediary architecture offers several key advantages, corresponding to the requirements raised in section.

- *Interoperability:* An intermediary provides a standardized interface for LBS providers, allowing them to access location data in a unified way. This mediation of location information would then allow tapping the network effect immanent in the distributed, multi-party LBS scenario. Mobile operator independence, roaming support, and the unified interface for service providers for easy deployment and migration seem to be viable business propositions in a fast-moving marketplace. Mobility between different services, location sources, involved market players, and applications seems beneficial from users' and service providers' perspective alike. From an ordinary user's point of view, cost effectiveness, synergy effects, and convenient service usage are major issues.
- *Multi-channel strategy:* An intermediary can collect location data from various sources (GSM, WLAN, and GPS) [10].
- *Synergetic location aggregation:* An intermediary can aggregate multi-channel location information for the benefit of higher quality [11].
- *Simplification:* Intermediaries simplify process handling for LBS providers by removing the need to negotiate contracts with various location sources.
- *Cross-Operator applications:* Without an intermediary, the creation of user-to-user LBS with customers using mobile services at distinct mobile operators is much harder.
- *Pricing advantages:* Intermediaries provide many economic benefits in information markets, e.g. an intermediary buys location information from location providers in large amounts, and therefore is in a position to negotiate cheaper prices. For LBS that consume small quantities of location data, it may be cheaper to acquire location from an intermediary than from a location provider. Other benefits of information intermediaries can be found in [12].

There are different deployment scenarios for the intermediary component, reflecting different business models and organizational structures that are employed in the telecommunications industry. It may be deployed directly at the mobile operator, at a MVNO, or outsourced to a completely independent party. This also gives mobile operators the freedom to treat the intermediation of identities as either a core business or as a sideline of the business. In the first case the intermediation will stay close to the mobile operator but other entities providing a comparable intermediary function will be supported, so that the user has choice(even if many users practically don't use it). In the second case the intermediation can simply be outsourced.

6 Summary and Outlook

We presented the design of a privacy-preserving application architecture and a related prototype. The implementation was realized on a limited budget, and to the satisfaction of both project officials and industry partners. It is now being used for the development and implementation of a commercial service and product offer as well as for initialising a roadmap for further privacy enhancing services, including a second version based on a stronger terminal (with Java functionality) and using more powerful communication protocols (e.g. GPRS).

The current prototype served and still serves as a proof of concept for enabling users to manage access to their data. It demonstrated for management, business development and customer relation minded parties that privacy requirements do not need to preclude the realization of services with viable business models. It also showed that new services do not necessarily violate privacy requirements if care is taken to balance the stakeholders' interests, e.g. in the sense of multilateral security.

Further it gives some hints on possible developments in the market: Beyond a deployment of identity management functionalities at user or services side, there is also the possibility of a market dominated by independent intermediaries that chose localization and connection options dynamically from a pool of available possibilities – for example, from several MOs and MVNOs – based on the users' policies and preferences. Thus, dynamic party matching recommendations may be used to leverage network effects, building a market that offers ease-of-development and ease-of-deployment to service providers while preserving users' privacy. A further standardization of such an interface would allow LBS interoperability between operators, offering an additional incentive for service operators' acceptance of location-based services. This raises new requirements for identity management frameworks processing location information, but also presents a promising use case for advanced privacy-preserving features.

Acknowledgments: We would like to thank Georg Kramer, Tobias Koelsch, Marc Wilhelm, Klaus Kehr, and Arne Pöppel from T-Mobile, Pete Bramhall from HP Labs, and all our colleagues in PRIME for their good and fruitful cooperation and their valuable contributions.

References

1. Bundesnetzagentur: Jahresbericht. 2005.
2. K. Rannenberg, "Recent Development in Information Technology Security Evaluation – The Need for Evaluation Criteria for multilateral Security", in Richard Sizer et al.: Security and Control of Information Technology in Society – Proceedings of the IFIP TC9/WG 9.6 Working Conference August 12-17, St. Petersburg, Russia, North-Holland, Amsterdam, pp. 113-128, 1994.
3. K. Rannenberg, "Multilateral Security - A concept and examples for balanced security", *in Proceedings of the 9th ACM New Security Paradigms Workshop*, Cork, Ireland: ACM Press, 2000, pp. 151-162.
4. T. Koelsch, L. Fritsch, M. Kohlweiss, D. Kesdogan, „Privacy for Profitable Location Based Services", *Proceedings of the 2nd Intl. Conference on Security in Pervasive Computing*, Lecture Notes on Computer Science (LNCS 3450, pp.164-179), Springer; Boppard, Germany, 2005.
5. M. Kohlweiss, B. Gedrojc, "Flexible Location Based Service Protocols Using Efficient Oblivious Transfer", *Kryptowochenende*, 2006.
6. G.W. Blarkom; J. Borking; J.G. Olk: Handbook of Privacy and Privacy-Enhancing Technologies. College bescherming persoonsgegevens, The Hague. 2003.
7. K. Synnes; J. North; P. Parnes; Location Privacy in the Alipes Platform; Institutionen för Systemteknik; Lulea University of Technology; 2002.
8. R. Cheng; S. Prabhakar: Using Uncertainty to Provide-Preserving and High-Quality Location-Based Services, in: Workshop on Location Systems, Privacy and Control, 2004.
9. Jorns, O, -Bessler, S.: PRIVES: A privacy enhanced location based scheme, in: Workshop on Location Systems, Privacy and Control, 2004.
10. A. Albers, S. Figge, M. Radmacher, "LOC3 - Architecture Proposal for Efficient Subscriber Localisation in Mobile Commerce Infrastructures", *in Proceedings of 2nd IEEE International Workshop on Mobile Commerce and Services (WMCS'05)*; München, 2005.
11. T. Lindner, L. Fritsch, K. Plank, K. Rannenberg, „Exploitation of Public and Private WiFi Coverage for New Business Models", *Proceedings of the 4th IFIP Conference on E-Commerce, E-Business, and E-Government (I3E)*, 2004.
12. F. Rose, The economics, concept and design of information intermediaries. Heidelberg, Physica-Verlag, 1999.

Crafting Web Counters into Covert Channels

Xiapu Luo, Edmond W. W. Chan, and Rocky K. C. Chang

Department of Computing
The Hong Kong Polytechnic University
Hung Hom, Kowloon, Hong Kong, SAR, China
{csxluo|cswwchan|csrchang}@comp.polyu.edu.hk

Abstract. Almost all the previously proposed network storage channels write covert messages in the packets' protocol fields. In contrast, we present in this paper a new network storage channel *WebShare* that uses the plentiful, public Web counters for storage. Therefore, the physical locations of the WebShare encoder and decoder are not restricted to a single path. To make WebShare practical, we have addressed a number of thorny issues, such as the "noise" introduced by other legitimate Web requests, and synchronization between encoder and decoder. For the proof-of-concept purpose, we have experimented a WebShare prototype in the Internet, and have showed that it is practically feasible even when the Web counter and the encoder/decoder are separated by more than 20 router hops.

1 Introduction

Using a network covert channel, two Internet hosts can communicate with each other such that others are not even aware of its existence. Therefore, it is not surprising that a network covert channel has been perceived as a serious threat to the national security and enterprise security, because it can be a handy tool for data exfiltration and large-scale attack coordination. On the other hand, network covert channels have found useful applications in leaking news from some countries, and allowing privacy-concerned communities to bypass censorship and privacy intrusion devices [1, 2].

Similar to the classic covert channels in trusted computer systems, network covert channels are broadly classified into *network storage channels* and *network timing channels* [3, 4]. Since the network timing channels are not the focus of this paper, we will not further consider them in the rest of this paper. In a network storage channel, an encoder embeds messages into a storage location that can be read by a decoder. The storage locations are usually packets' header fields in the previously proposed storage channels. Moreover, to further conceal the covert channel, the encoder could send the cover traffic to a third part. Therefore the decoder has to eavesdrop the communication path from the encoder to the third party. However, eavesdropping an Internet link generally requires a special setup and is not reliable [5]. As a result, we turn to the traditional sense of storage channels investigated for multilevel secure systems [6, 7].

Please use the following format when citing this chapter:

Luo, X., Chan, E., and Chang, R., 2007, in IFIP International Federation for Information Processing, Volume 232, New Approaches for Security, Privacy and Trust in Complex Environments, eds. Venter, H., Eloff, M., Labuschagne, L., Eloff, J., von Solms, R., (Boston: Springer), pp. 337–348.

That is, we select a publicly shared state in the Internet as a storage. In this paper we use Web counters as the storage and demonstrate its practicality by presenting *WebShare*, a new network storage channel based on Web counters. Danezis [8] first mentioned the idea of using Web counters but did not provide any details to realize it.

Furthermore, there are other publicly shared states that could also be exploited for covert communications. In [9], Rowland proposes to encode into the sequence number (SN) of a TCP packet that is "bounced" to a decoder by a TCP server; thus, the SN can be considered as a TCP-layer shared state. Although this method is simple, it can be easily detected based on spoofed source IP address and an unusually large number of TCP SYN packets. As another example, Danezis has recently proposed exploiting the IPID field in the IP header as a shared state [8]. However, the global IPID counter is not supported by all systems. Moreover, the global IPID counter has been exploited for scanning idle ports since 1998 [10]; consequently, many IDSes and firewalls are able to detect and defeat it. As we will show later, the plentiful Web counters used by WebShare do not suffer from the above problems.

Although the basic idea of WebShare is simple, we will show in the rest of the paper that we have overcome many inherent technical issues in the design of WebShare. Notable ones include allowing the encoder and decoder to maintain only loose time synchronization, using multiple counters to increase the capacity, and proposing a site-hopping approach to further camouflage WebShare and boost the capacity. We have also experimented a WebShare prototype in the Internet and have evaluated its performance under different parameter settings. The initial results show that WebShare is practically feasible.

We structure the rest of this paper as follows. Section 2 introduces WebShare and details our approaches to resolving a number of design issues. In section 3, we report the experiment results and findings. Section 4 briefly summarizes the existing works on network storage channels and the defense methods. We finally conclude this paper in section 5.

2 WebShare

To communicate covertly through a WebShare channel, both the WebShare encoder and decoder agree on the start time T_0, and the Web counter to use. As will be explained in subsection 2.2, WebShare does not require strict time synchronization between the encoder and decoder. However, to simplify the discussion, we assume for the time being that the times are perfectly synchronized, and we will later propose methods to mitigate the impact of time desynchronization.

The decoder first fetches the Web counter value before T_0. After that, the encoding period T_E and decoding period T_D alternate between themselves, and the periods are also known to them beforehand. Moreover, define a *run* as $T_A = T_E + T_D$. During each T_E, the encoder requests the corresponding Web counter once for transmitting bit 1 but does not send any for bit 0. In the next T_D, the decoder fetches the Web counter value for message decoding.

In terms of the threat model, we assume that the encoder's incoming and outgoing traffic is all under a passive warden's close scrutiny for the purpose of covert channel detection. We further assume that the Web sites whose counters are used by WebShare do not conduct cooperative intrusion detection [11]. This assumption is reasonable, because the Web sites exploited by WebShare are randomly selected from a vast number of public Web sites. It is therefore very difficult, if not impossible, for them to share the Web access information. Furthermore, the WebShare traffic may not easily trigger an alarm in these Web sites, because it may not increase the counter values frequent enough.

2.1 Noise handling

As the Web counter value could also be increased by other legitimate visitors, additional *noise* will be introduced to the covert messages. Therefore, it is not sufficient to simply send 0 or 1 HTTP request as discussed before. Instead, we set a high enough threshold Q^* for determining whether the increase in the counter value is due to a covert message. The choice of Q^* obviously depends on the Webpage's popularity, and we will elaborate the impact of Q^* on the decoding accuracy in section 3.

We adopt the following notations for explaining the WebShare encoding and decoding algorithms when taking into account of the channel noise.

- VC_i: the bit (0 or 1) sent during the ith T_E.
- VW_i: the Web counter value at the end of the ith T_E.
- VE_i: the number of HTTP requests sent for VC_i.

To transmit bit 0 during the ith T_E, the encoder does not send any HTTP requests, i.e., $VE_i = 0$. To transmit bit 1, the encoder sends a number of contiguous HTTP requests, such that $VW_i - VW_{i-1} \geq Q^*$. To account for possible request losses, it is prudent to set $VE_i > Q^*$. At the end of the ith T_D, VC_i is decoded to bit 0 if $VW_i - VW_{i-1} < Q^*$, and to bit 1, otherwise. Figure 1 shows the alternating pattern of T_E and T_D, and the change in VW_i when both sides are perfectly synchronized in time.

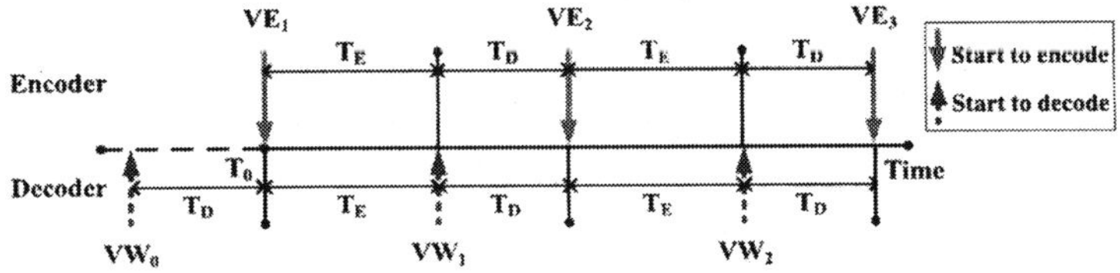

Fig. 1. The alternate encoding and decoding periods in WebShare when the encoder and decoder are perfectly synchronized in time.

To conduct a more formal analysis, let $\mu = \frac{VE_i}{T_E}$ be the encoder's average request sending rate for encoding bit 1 and λ be other visitors' average request arrival rate. Then the following inequalities must be satisfied in order to decode correctly.

$$(T_E + T_D)\lambda < Q^*. \tag{1}$$

$$(T_E + T_D)\lambda + T_E(1 - P_{loss})\mu \geq Q^*, \tag{2}$$

where P_{loss} is the probability of a request loss. Note that the encoder could dispatch all requests at the beginning of T_E or send them out with the constant rate μ.

2.2 Mitigating the effect of time desynchronization

In this subsection we show that WebShare requires only loose time synchronization which is made possible by tuning the values of T_E, T_D, and Q^*. We first let T_e (or T_d) denote the difference between the encoder's (or decoder's) local time and the standard time, and $T_i = |T_e - T_d|$. In order not to affect the next run's decoding, T_i should be less than $\min\{T_E, T_D\}$. The special case of $T_e = T_d = 0$ is therefore the same as the case of perfect synchronization. In the following, we discuss two extreme cases when $T_i = |T_e| + |T_d|$ which serves as the upper bound for the time difference between the encoder and decoder. The same result also applies to other cases, i.e. $T_i < |T_e| + |T_d|$.

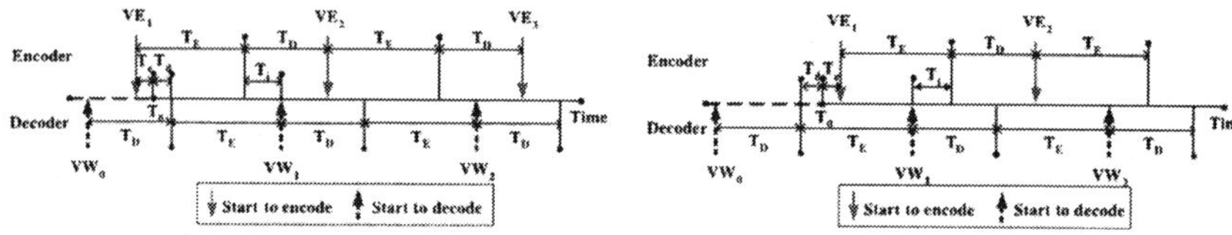

(a) $T_e < 0 < T_d$. (b) $T_d < 0 < T_e$.

Fig. 2. Two time desynchronization scenarios for WebShare.

Figure 2(a) depicts one of the desynchronization scenarios where $T_e < 0 < T_d$. As shown, the encoder starts earlier than what the decoder expects. We can also observe from the figure that each T_E is sandwiched between two consecutive decoding epoches. For example, although VE_1 requests are dispatched before $T_0 + T_d$, its effect is still registered by $VW_1 - VW_0$. Hence, it is not difficult to see that if Eqs. (1)-(2) hold, the decoding can still be done correctly.

Figure 2(b) shows an opposite scenario: $T_d < 0 < T_e$. As a result, the decoder might interpret part of the HTTP requests from the previous run as the current run's when the requests are sent out with a constant rate μ. To decode correctly, we need to consider all four possible cases for any two adjacent bits: {0 0}, {1 1}, {0 1}, and {1 0}. The same analysis can be done for the first bit in a covert message as if it were preceded by a 0.

For the case of {0 0}, since the encoder does not dispatch HTTP requests, the decoder could correctly extract the two bits if Eq. (1) is satisfied. For the case of {0 1}, Eq. (3) must also be fulfilled to decode the bit 1 correctly:

$$(T_E - T_i)(1 - P_{loss})\mu + (T_E + T_D)\lambda \geq Q^*. \tag{3}$$

For the cases of {1 1} and {1 0}, note that the first bit 1 could be correctly decoded if Eq. (3) is fulfilled. The requirements, however, are different for the second bits. For the case of {1 1}, VE_i is given by the HTTP requests leftover from the previous run and a portion of the HTTP requests from the current run. Hence, the decoder could extract the correct value if Eq. (2) is satisfied. For the case of {1 0}, Eq. (4) must be fulfilled:

$$T_i(1 - P_{loss})\mu + (T_E + T_D)\lambda < Q^*. \tag{4}$$

The remaining issue is to mitigate the adverse impact of P_{loss}, λ, and T_i on the channel quality. First, we can estimate P_{loss} from the loss rate of the normal requests and mitigate its effect by increasing the values of μ and the related parameters, i.e. T_E and Q^*. Similarly, we can also estimate λ (see section 3 for the methodology) and alleviate its impact by increasing the value of Q^*. As for T_i, we can minimize its impact by employing the network time protocol (NTP), or by exploiting the random beacons widely available in the Internet, e.g., stock indices [12]. Hence, T_i could be made as small as 100ms. To further mitigate the impact, the encoder could transmit the HTTP requests in bursts at the beginning of T_E. In this way, HTTP requests will not show up during T_i, thus minimizing the impact of T_i for the cases of {1 0}, {0 1}, and {1 1}.

2.3 Increasing the bit rate

WebShare's data rate is limited by the frequency of incrementing the Web counter. We employ three approaches to improve it. The first approach is to dispatch VE_i requests for encoding 1 through VE_i parallel HTTP connections, HTTP request pipelining in a single HTTP connection, or a mixture of the two.

The second approach is to transmit multiple bits in parallel. To do so, the encoder and decoder pre-agree on a set of ordered Web counters. During each T_E, the encoder sends 1 bit of information to each Web counter. The decoder can therefore retrieve multiple bits from the set of counters in the next T_D.

The third approach is based on *multilevel quantization*. Take a uniform quantization as an example. To convey an M-bit message, where $M > 1$, we partition the increased value of the Web counter into M intervals with an interval size of Q^*. If the increased value falls into the interval of $[iQ^*, (i+1)Q^*)$, $0 \leq i < M - 1$, then the message is decoded as i. If the number is larger than or equal to $(M-1)Q^*$, then the message is decoded as $M - 1$. As a result, the encoder could deliver $\log_2 M$ bits within a run.

2.4 Site-hopping

Recall that one of the methods of increasing WebShare's data rate is to use a set of Web counters. Using a fixed set of Web counters repeatedly, however, could increase the vulnerability of being detected. To remove this static behavior, we propose to change the set of Web counters dynamically. This idea is similar to frequency hopping in the spread spectrum communication [13]; therefore, we name it as *site-hopping*. For example, the encoder and decoder can use two sets of nonoverlapping Web counters alternately.

Besides the advantage of further camouflaging WebShare, this approach in fact helps increase the channel throughput, provided that any two consecutive sets of S counters do not have any overlap. To see why, consider the previous example again. Now it is possible to parallelize the encoding and decoding operations: while the encoder is sending S bits to the first (or second) set of Web counters, the decoder can simultaneously read S bits from the second (or first) set of Web counters.

To deploy the site-hopping approach, we have to resolve two important design issues. The first is to let both the encoder and decoder agree on the same set of Web counters each time. However, because of the additional overhead, we do not prefer to use the covert channel to communicate this information. The second is to ensure that any two adjacent sets of S Web counters do not overlap, which is required for achieving the parallelism and for reducing the decoding errors.

We propose a novel, and yet simple, approach based on enumerative combinatorics [14] to resolve the two issues. Assume that both the encoder and decoder have agreed on the list of N, where $N >> S$, available Web counters and a shared secret key K_0. We partition the N Web counters into two groups with $N_1 = LS$ counters and $N_2 > S$ counters, respectively. Therefore, for a given order of N_1 counters, we could send L S-bit segments of the message using nonoverlapped sets of counters. After sending the first L segments, we could consider a different order of the N_1 counters, and perform the similar steps. However, there may be overlapping between the last set of S counters for the ith N_1-bit block and the first set of S counters for the $(i+1)$th N_1-bit block. Our solution to this problem is to use a randomly selected set of S Web counters from the second group as a separator between the two adjacent blocks. Therefore, at least S bits of information can be transmitted before revisiting a Web counter.

To agree on the same set of counters for each S-bit message, both the encoder and decoder must first agree on the exact order of the N_1 counters to use for each N_1-bit block, and there are $NC_P = N_1!$ of them. Both must also agree on the set and order of the S counters from the second group after sending each N_1-bit block; there are a total of $NC_C = \binom{N_2}{S} S! = \frac{N_2!}{(N_2-S)!}$ such sequences. From the field of enumerative combinatorics, there exist unranking algorithms for permutations [15] (or binomial coefficients [14]) that map a positive integer uniquely to each permutation (or combination). For this purpose, we have designed an algorithm to index the NC_C sequences. Therefore, if both the encoder and decoder could come up the same indices for permutations or combinations, they could use the unranking algorithms to agree on the same set of Web counters. We use the following procedures to generate the indices securely. Let Idx_P and Idx_C be the indices for the permutations and combinations, respectively. Let H_P and H_C be good hash functions that output pseudo-random values in the range of $[1, NC_P]$ and $[1, NC_C]$, respectively. The indices can be computed randomly according to the following rules:

$$Idx_{P,i-1} = H_P(K_{i-1}) \ \ and \ \ Idx_{C,i-1} = H_C(K_{i-1}),$$
$$K_i = Idx_{P,i-1} \oplus Idx_{C,i-1}, \quad i > 0.$$

3 Experiment Results

We have prototyped WebShare encoder and decoder using Perl 5.8 under Linux kernel v2.6.8. Altogether we have conducted experiments on 220 randomly selected Web counters, whose hosting servers are located in ten different geographical locations. The Web counters increase their values on receiving an HTTP request. The encoder and decoder run on different machines in our campus network; their round-trip times (RTTs) to each Web counter are therefore very similar. Moreover, to make T_i as small as possible, we use the NTP to synchronize the encoder's and decoder's clocks. We have also examined the impact of T_i on the decoding accuracy, and the results validate our arguments in section 2.

3.1 The choice of Q^*

As recalled, one of the major factors affecting the decoding accuracy is the unavoidable noise from legitimate visitors. This factor directly affects the choice of Q^*, which determines whether the counter increment should be accepted as bit 1. To obtain a suitable value of Q^* for our target Webpages, we have performed a one-week measurement to study their popularity. During the measurement period, a node at our campus network queried the counter values of the 220 Webpages every hour. Figure 3(a) shows the empirical CDF (ECDF) of the average rate of requesting the Web counters, denoted by λ requests/second. Over 95% of the measured Web counters have their λs smaller than 0.01, while the λs for all the Web counters are no greater than 0.08. Thus, it is reasonable to choose $Q^* = 2$ to mitigate the noise-induced errors.

3.2 An evaluation of WebShare

Distribution of Web counters' write times We report the distributions of seven Web counters' *write times*, and we select these Web counters randomly from the original set. The write time is defined as the duration between a node's transmission of a TCP SYN packet (for initiating an HTTP connection) to a Web server and its reception of the counter's value from the server's responses. The write time could affect the channel accuracy, and the choices of T_E and T_D.

We measure the write times for the seven Web counters and obtain a total of 2,880 samples; each measurement is conducted with a single HTTP request. Figure 3(b) shows the box-and-whisker plot of the write time measurements, and we identify the Web counters by their geographical locations. Each box includes the lower quartile, median, and upper quartile values of the write time samples. The whiskers extended from the box represent 1.5 interquartile range of the samples. We have summarized the statistics and their respective hop counts in Table 1. Although the mean write time for each Web counter is smaller than 2s, the measured write times could range from 0.120s to 82.684s. Moreover, the variations of the write times for some Web counters, such as those in SG, AU, and US, are much larger than others. As shall see shortly, the write time variations can adversely affect Webshare's accuracy.

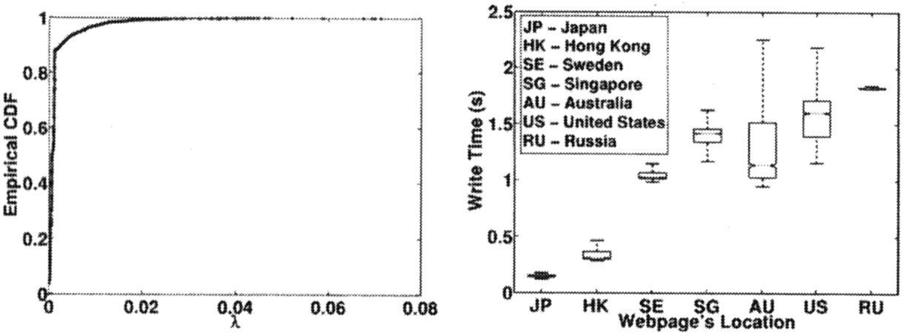

(a) ECDF of legitimate visitors' average arrival rates (λ).

(b) Distribution of the seven Web counters' write times.

Fig. 3. Some measured characteristics of the Web counters under consideration.

Choices of T_E and T_D We have measured WebShare's performance under various configurations of T_E and T_D ($T_E, T_D \in \{0.25, 0.50, 1.00\}$s) using the seven Web counters. For these experiments, we set $Q^* = 2$, and the encoder conveys a random 16-bit message to the decoder. Moreover, the encoder employs one Web server for each measurement, and sends $VE_i = 3$ requests in parallel in order to mitigate the error due to encoding delays and request losses. For each configuration of (T_E,T_D), we measure the raw bit error rate (BER) on the decoder side for 30 times, in terms of the Hamming distance. The acceptable BER depends on various factors, such as the forward error correction code in use and the application requirement.

Table 1. Measured BERs for seven Web counters under different (T_E, T_D). The four values under the column of "Write Time" represent the lower limit of and the upper limit of the 95% confidence intervals for the sample means, the sample means, and the standard deviation, respectively.

Locations	Hops	Write Time (s)	T_E with $T_D = 1$s		T_D with $T_E = 1$s		$T_E = T_D$ $= 1$s
			250ms	500ms	250ms	500ms	
JP	16	.1695/.1928/.1811/.3192	.0479	.0146	.4708	.4667	0
HK	14	.7353/.7935/.7644/.9876	.0750	.0167	.4708	.4625	.0063
SE	17	1.042/1.0582/1.0501/.2211	0	.0125	.4688	.4604	.0208
SG	16	1.5631/1.6352/1.5991/.9870	.1667	.0958	.4646	.4562	.1146
AU	23	1.6296/1.8069/1.7182/2.4280	.3083	.2875	.4813	.4250	.2604
US	18	1.6632/1.7743/1.7188/1.5214	.1500	.0333	.4729	.4292	.0729
RU	15	1.8297/1.8496/1.8397/.2713	.3979	.3521	.4604	.4396	.0531

As shown in Table 1, the channel accuracy depends greatly on the Webpages' write times. Notice that when $T_E = T_D = 1s$, WebShare performs very well with the BERs of less than 3% for some locations, such as JP, HK, and SE. We have verified that the errors are mostly due to the background legitimate requests and dropping of the encoder's and decoder's requests. However, Webshare shows poorer performance for some other locations, especially for AU, SG, and US whose write times exhibit very high variations, or whose mean write times are greater than T_E and T_D. A simple way to relieve this problem is to ensure that the values of T_E and T_D are greater than the Webpages' write times.

Besides, we observe that it is more likely to incur a higher BER for $T_D < T_E$; however, a small T_E generally has less impact on the channel performance. We conjecture that the errors may be due to the interference from the encoder's next counter update. Depending on the design of the Web counter and the Web server's program design, the server may not produce the HTTP response immediately after the counter update. On the other hand, even if T_E is small, the Web server can still produce the response for the decoder's request based on the current counter value, as long as T_D is long enough and no later request interferes the current value. Thus, it's prudent to assign a longer T_D in order to increase the decoding accuracy.

Performance gain of the site-hopping approach As discussed in Section 2.4, the site-hopping approach helps enhance both the throughput and the channel accuracy. To measure the performance gain obtained by the site-hopping approach, we adopt the same experiment settings as the last section: $Q^* = 2$ and $VE_i = 3$, and the encoder conveys a random 16-bit message to the decoder. To avoid overlapping between two adjacent sets of Web counters, the encoder and decoder agree on two distinct sets of randomly selected $S \in \{2, 4, 8, 16\}$ Web counters from the original 220 Web counters. The encoder issues HTTP requests to the S Web counters concurrently during each T_E.

Figure 4 shows the measured BERs for $T_E \in \{0.25, 0.50, 1.00, 2.00\}$s and S. As the results show, the site-hopping approach can improve the WebShare channel accuracy. For example, when $T_E \geq 1$s, all measured BERs are no greater than 1%. Even when $T_E = 250$ms, the channel's BER with $S = 2$ can stay below 5%. These results confirm that site-hopping can effectively mitigate the interference from the encoder's next counter update. Furthermore, since the encoder transmits at most S bits in parallel, and both the encoding and decoding processes are conducted in parallel, we expect that the site-hopping approach can improve the channel throughput by a factor of $[(T_E + T_D)S]/T_E$. Our experiment results are indeed close to the expected results. For instance, when $T_E = 250$ms and $T_D = 1$s, Webshare with site-hopping achieves a throughput of 57.816 bits/s, whereas that without site-hopping is only 0.789 bits/s.

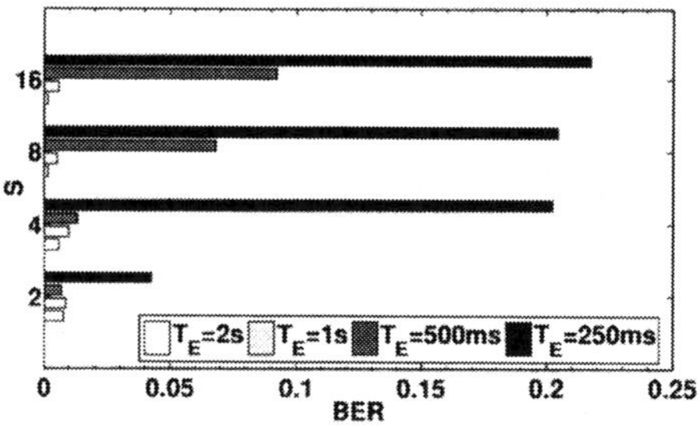

S	T_E			
	250ms	500ms	1s	2s
2	.0425	.0071	.0088	.0078
4	.2025	.0133	.0099	.0058
8	.2046	.0683	.0053	.0016
16	.2174	.0921	.0060	.0014

Fig. 4. Measured BERs for WebShare with site-hopping, $Q^* = 2$, and $VE_i = 3$ for various values of S and T_E.

4 Related Works

There have been quite a number of TCP/IP-based network storage channels proposed for the past few years. In the network layer, many methods have been proposed to hide data in the IP packets and ICMP packets. Virtually all possible fields in the IP headers have been exploited for storage covert channels [9, 16, 17, 18]. The fields in the TCP header are also equally exploited for embedding storage covert channels [9, 19, 20, 17]. On the application layer, HTTP not only has been used as a substrate for tunneling other protocols [21, ?], but also utilized to implement covert channels [1, 22, 2, 23], some of which have been deployed to facilitate anonymous communications [1, 23].

On the defense side, neural network and support vector machines have been adopted to detect storage covert channels based on the ISN of TCP flows [24, 25, 17]. Moreover, statistical approaches have been proposed to detect covert channels over HTTP [26, 2]. Besides detection, another approach is to neutralize covert channels by performing active operations on the traffic.

The basic idea of frequency-hopping has also been used in the Infranet system to avoid widespread discovery and blocking [27, 23]. However, there are important differences between our site-hopping approach and the ones in [27, 23]. First, all Web counters in WebShare are essentially "victims." In other words, the encoder and decoder just need to find and use these Web counters.

However, the proxies in the Infranet system need extra cooperation and installation. Second, our pseudo-random sequence algorithm, which is based on enumerative combinatorics, not only could generate pseudo-random sequences, but also guarantee that there are no overlapping in the consecutive sets of members. The algorithm in Infranet, however, does not provide this feature.

5 Conclusions

In this paper, we have proposed WebShare, a new network storage channel using Web counters to relay covert messages. A WebShare decoder can be located anywhere to read the messages written by an encoder. We have shown that WebShare requires only loose time synchronization between the encoder and decoder. The channel data rate can also be increased by various schemes, such as using multiple counters and the site-hopping technique. Moreover, we have demonstrated its feasibility by prototyping the WebShare encoder and decoder and performed extensive experiments in the Internet. We have measured its decoding accuracy and studied the impact of different parameters on its performance.

Besides, we have conducted an information-theoretic analysis of WebShare's capacity and have proposed a new detection system designed for WebShare. However, due to the paper limit, we could not present them in this paper. We are in the process of reporting them in the forthcoming paper.

Acknowledgment

The work described in this paper was partially supported by a grant from the Research Grant Council of the Hong Kong Special Administrative Region, China (Project No. PolyU 5080/02E) and a grant from the Cisco University Research Program Fund at Community Foundation Silicon Valley.

References

1. M. Bauer. New covert channels in HTTP: Adding unwitting Web browsers to anonymity sets. In *Proc. ACM Workshop on Privacy in the Electronic Society*, 2003.
2. K. Borders and A. Prakash. Web Tap: Detecting covert Web traffic. In *Proc. ACM CCS*, 2004.
3. DoD US. Department of defense trusted computer system evaluation criteria (orange book). Technical Report DoD 5200.28-STD, National Computer Security Center, Dec. 1985.
4. V. Gligor. A guide to understanding covert channel analysis of trusted systems (light pink book). Technical Report NCSC-TG-030, National Computer Security Center, Nov. 1993.

5. E. Cronin, M. Sherr, and M. Blaze. The eavesdropper's dilemma. Technical Report MS-CIS-05-24, University of Pennsylvania, February 2006.
6. R. Kemmerer. Shared resource matrix methodology: A practical approach to indetifying covert channels. *ACM Transactions on Computer Systems*, 1(3), 1983.
7. C. Tsai and V. Gligor. A bandwidth computation model for covert storage channels and its applications. In *Proc. IEEE Symp. Security and Privacy*, 1988.
8. G. Danezis. Covert communications despite traffic data retention. http://homes.esat.kuleuven.be/~gdanezis/cover.pdf, 2006.
9. C. Rowland. Covert channels in the TCP/IP protocol suite. *First Monday: Peer-reviewed Journal on the Internet*, 2(5), 1997.
10. Fyodor. Idle scanning and related IPID games. http://www.insecure.org/nmap/idlescan.html.
11. F. Cuppens and A. Miege. Alert correlation in a cooperative intrusion detection framework. In *Proc. IEEE Symp. Security and Privacy*, 2002.
12. H. Lee, E. Chang, and M. Chan. Pervasive random beacon in the Internet for covert coordination. In *Proc. Information Hiding Workshop*, 2005.
13. M. Simon, J. Omura, R. Scholtz, and B. Levitt. *Spread Spectrum Communications Handbook*. McGraw-Hill, 2002.
14. D. Kreher and D. Stinson. *Combinatorial Algorithms: Generation, Enumeration and Search*. CRC press, 1998.
15. W. Myrvold and F. Ruskey. Ranking and unranking permutations in linear time. *Information Processing Letters*, 79:281–284, 2001.
16. K. Ahsan and D. Kundur. Practical data hiding in TCP/IP. In *Proc. Workshop on Multimedia Security*, 2002.
17. S. Murdoch and S. Lewis. Embedding covert channels into TCP/IP. In *Proc. Information Hiding Workshop*, 2005.
18. C. Abad. IP checksum covert channels and selected hash collision. http://www.gray-world.net/papers/ipccc.pdf, 2001.
19. J. Giffen, R. Greenstadt, P. Litwack, and R. Tibbetts. Covert messaging through TCP timestamps. In *Proc. PET Workshop*, 2002.
20. J. Rutkowska. The implementation of passive covert channels in the Linux kernel. In *Proc. Chaos Communication Congress*, 2004.
21. K. Moore. On the use of HTTP as a substrate. RFC 3205, Feb. 2002.
22. Gray-World Team. Covert channel and tunneling over the HTTP protocol detection: GW implementation theoretical design. http://www.gray-world.net/projects/papers/cctde.txt, 2003.
23. N. Feamster, M. Balazinska, W. Wang, H. Balakrishnan, and D. Karger. Thwarting Web cenorship with untrusted messenger discovery. In *Proc. PET Workshop*, 2003.
24. J. Seo T. Sohn and J.Moon. A study on the covert channel detection of TCP/IP header using support vector machine. In *Proc. ICICS*, 2003.
25. E. Tumoian and M. Anikeev. Network based detection of passive covert channels in TCP/IP. In *Proc. IEEE LCN*, 2005.
26. D. Pack, W. Streilein, S. Webster, and R. Cunningham. Detecting HTTP tunneling activities. In *Proc. IEEE Annual Information Assurance Workshop*, 2002.
27. N. Feamster, M. Balazinska, G. Harfst, H. Balakrishnan, and D. Karger. Infranet: Circumventing censorship and surveillance. In *Proc. USENIX Security Symp.*, 2002.

OPA : Onion Policy Administration Model - Another approach to manage rights in DRM

Thierry Sans, Frédéric Cuppens, and Nora Cuppens-Boulahia

GET/ENST Bretagne,
2 rue de la Châtaigneraie, 35576 Cesson-Sévigné Cedex, France
{thierry.sans,frederic.cuppens,nora.cuppens}@enst-bretagne.fr

Abstract. Digital Rights Management frameworks (DRM) aim at protecting and controlling information contents widely distributed on client devices. Using a license, the content owner specifies which rights can be rendered to end-users. Basically, only the content owner must be able to define this license, but some DRM models go further. In super-distribution scenario, the content owner does not directly manage end-user's rights but rather delegate this task to a third-party called a distributor. Nevertheless, this distribution cannot be done without any control. In existing approaches, the content owner restricts the license issued by the distributors. In this paper, we provide a new approach, called the Onion Policy Administration approach (OPA). Rather than restricting licenses issued by the different distributors, OPA aims at controlling which rights are finally rendered to end-users. The main idea of OPA is to have a traceability of the content distribution. The content must keep track of all third-parties it crossed in the distribution chain. In this case, everyone can distribute the content and define a new license without any restriction. In these licenses, the content owner and distributors specify end-user's rights. Using the content traceability, the DRM controller can gather all licenses involved in the distribution chain and evaluate them. In order to be rendered, a right must be allowed by both the content owner and all distributors involved in the distribution chain.

1 Introduction

Digital Rights Management frameworks (DRM) [12, 1] aim at protecting and controlling information contents which are no longer on a server side but instead distributed on the client side. DRM frameworks provide security mechanisms in order to protect the confidentiality and the integrity of digital contents. Using a license, the content owner specifies which rights end-users can have on the protected content. The license is written according to a specific Rights Expression Languages (REL) [6, 11]. A dedicated rendering application is in charge of evaluating the corresponding license and then render the requested right to the end-user. The set of rights supported by the rendering application is defined in the Rights Data Dictionary (RDD) of the corresponding DRM framework.

Please use the following format when citing this chapter:

Sans, T., Cuppens, F., and Cuppens-Boulahia, N., 2007, in IFIP International Federation for Information Processing, Volume 232, New Approaches for Security, Privacy and Trust in Complex Environments, eds. Venter, H., Eloff, M., Labuschagne, L., Eloff, J., von Solms, R., (Boston: Springer), pp. 349–360.

Fig. 1. Super-Distribution scenario.

For each right corresponds a rendering action enforced in the rendering application. Only the given rendering application [5, 7] is able to deal with the content protection and applies a rendering action on this content. The rendering application is executed on the user's device, so it must be trustworthy and tamper resistant [4, 9].

How to ensure that anyone cannot modify or issue a valid license for a given content? At first glance, only the content owner can issue a valid license for a given content. Only the license provided by the content owner can be evaluated by the rendering application. In existing DRM frameworks, cryptographic and hashing mechanisms are used to guarantee this ownership principle. But, some distribution models go further. Rather than managing rights with end-users, the content owner might want to delegate this task to a third-party called a distributor. The latter would be in charge to manage rights with end-users or even delegate this task again to another distributor. In literature, we talk about multi-tiers distribution or super-distribution scenario [12]. Let us consider a generic example of super-distribution scenario as showed in figure 1. Art'East wants to protect and distribute its own multimedia content on the Web. Rather than dealing with distribution issue, Art'East wants to entrust its content to StoreOnline care. This is a typical B2B business model where a content owner allows a third-party to distribute multimedia contents. The owner does not allow the distributor to read the content but rather allows him or her to manage rights with end-users. This is a typical B2C business model where a distributor allows an end-user to use the content. We can even go further enabling C2C business model where a user can allow another user to use the content.

Obviously, this distribution cannot be done without any control from each party of the distribution chain. In particular, the owner wants to control how the content is used even if he or she does not directly issue the license to end-users. Art'East, as a content provider, must be able to control the rights that can be rendered to Alice even if the multimedia content is under control of the distributor StoreOnline. Similarly, a distributor might allow end-users to distribute the content. In addition to issuing the play right, Alice might be able to give the play right to her friend Brice and then become a distributor. Again, StoreOnline and Art'East must be able to control what Brice can really do with the content. In our example, Art'East wants that an end-user can play the content. The distributor StoreOnline is supposed to issue the right to play

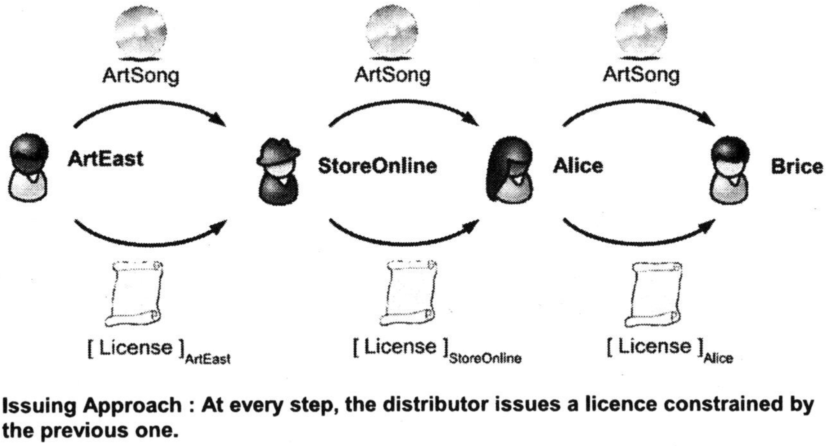

Fig. 2. The issuing approach.

only. Art'East does not restrict who can get this right and leaves StoreOnline free to define it. StoreOnline allows its members to read Art'East multimedia content. Alice, as a StoreOnline member, can read contents from Art'East. A storeOnline member can also allow a friend to play the content but the latter cannot allow someone else to play it. Here, Alice can allow Brice to read a specific content but Brice cannot allow someone else to read it.

Let us focus on how existing DRM frameworks enforce super-distribution mechanisms. We are considering here two open standards: OMA-DRM [10] and MPEG-21 [8]. The OMA-DRM specification talks about a *super-distribution mechanism.* In OMA-DRM, a third-party can redistribute a content to an end-user or to another distributor but cannot issue a new license on it. In consequence the distributor cannot restrict rights initially defined by the content owner license. The super-distribution mechanism provided in OMA-DRM does not satisfy the definition of super-distribution given above. Contrary to OMA-DRM, MPEG-REL enables a super-distribution mechanism as defined here: a third-party distributor can distribute a content and define a new license on it. In MPEG-REL, the content owner can restrict the license issued by the distributor. The content owner defines a license pattern and the license finally issued by the distributor must match this license pattern. Only this latter license is going to be evaluated by the rendering application in order to decide if a right can be exercised or not. We call this mechanism *the issuing approach.* The figure 2 shows how the issuing approach is applied to the super-distribution scenario given above. The content owner Art'East issues a license specifying that the distributor StoreOnline can "issue" a license according to a given pattern. This license pattern specifies that anyone can play the content ArtSong. Using that license, the distributor can now issue a license specifying that Alice can play the content. To be valid, this license must match the license pattern defined by the content owner license. The problem is more complex for the C2C business model. In that case, Art'East should issue a license specifying that the distributor can issue a license allowing someone else to issue the right to play.

The issuing approach aim at restricting the license issued by the different distributors involved in the distribution chain. The license finally issued is a license allowed by the content owner and by all the distributors involved in the distribution chain. In this paper, we provide a new approach, called the Onion Policy Administration approach (OPA). Rather than restricting licenses issued by the different distributors, OPA aims at controlling which rights are finally rendered to end-users. The main idea of OPA is to have a traceability of the content distribution. The content must keep track of all third-parties it crossed in the distribution chain. In this case, everyone can distribute the content and define a new license without any restriction. In these licenses, the content owner and distributors specify end-user's rights. Using the content traceability, the DRM controller can gather all licenses involved in the distribution chain and evaluate them. In order to be rendered, a right must be allowed by both the content owner and all distributors involved in the distribution chain.

In the following section, we better explain the Onion Policy Administration approach and we show how OPA enables the super-distribution scenario given previously. In section 3, we formalize the content traceability mechanism provided by OPA. We also provide a sketch of Rights Expression Language to express OPA licenses and its corresponding license interpretation algorithm. In section 4, we deal with implementation issues.

2 OPA: Onion Policy Administration model

Contrary to the issuing approach, in OPA we aim at controlling rights finally rendered to end-users rather than constraining the license issued by the different distributors. Every distributor involved in the distribution chain of a given content can issue a valid license without any restriction. The rendering application must evaluate all licenses provided by both the content owner and all distributors involved in the distribution chain. First, we provide a traceability mechanism in order to identify who is the content owner and who are the different authorized distributors involved in the distribution chain. Secondly, we provide a sketch of Rights Expression Language and its corresponding license interpretation mechanism in order to control the end-users rights. Both content owner and distributors can specify which rights can be finally rendered to end-users according to a specific sub-distribution chain.

2.1 The content traceability

Basically, only the content owner or an authorized distributors can issue a valid license for a given content. We call this principle *the ownership principle.* MPEG-21 and OMA-DRM [8, 10] have the same approach to guarantee the

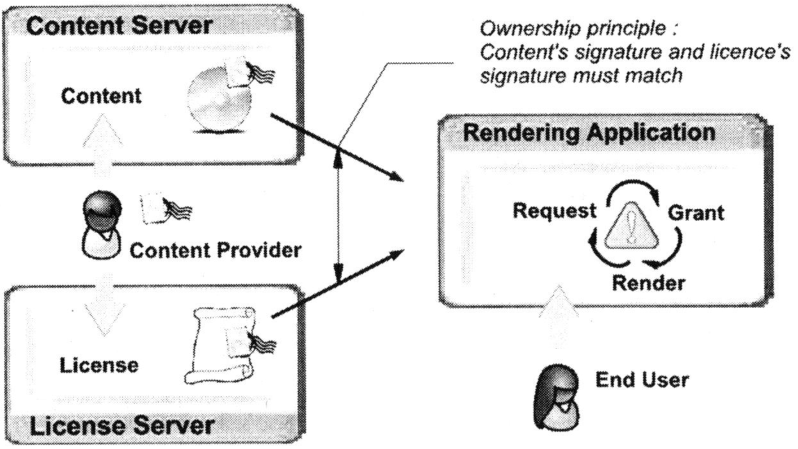

Fig. 3. The ownership principle in DRM.

ownership principle. The content and the license are tight using hashing and cryptographic mechanisms. For example in Windows Media DRM framework (Microsoft Media Player)[1] [3, 2], the content is ciphered using a symmetric key. This key is distributed to the user through the license. Obviously, this key cannot be distributed in clear in the license. The license, or the part of the license with the key, is ciphered using a session key between the license server and the rendering application. Thus, only the license issued by the content provider can be used to decipher the content. In super-distribution scenario, a distributor can issue a new license to end-users or to another distributors. In order to be valid, this new license must match a given license pattern define in a license previously issued by the content owner or the previous distributor in the distribution chain. If this license match this pattern, the cryptographic key is then transferred to the new license. This license is told to be valid because it contains the key to decipher the content.

The way to enforce the ownership principle in OPA is different. The content owner must both sign the content and the license. When the rendering application evaluates a license for a given content, these two identities must match as shown in 3. So how distributors, in super-distribution use-cases, can then issue valid licenses? Obviously, the authorized distributor must appear as the owner of the content, so the solution is to change the owner of the content, i.e. modify the signature of the content owner. To do that, the content must be repackaged in order to change the owner signature. Even if the original owner allows this repackaging operation, the solution is not acceptable as it gives the distributor a mean to issue any rights on the content. In such a configuration, the original owner totally loses control on the content. In OPA, both the owner

[1] Now named Microsoft PlaysForSure. This DRM system is told to enforce the MPEG-21 standard.

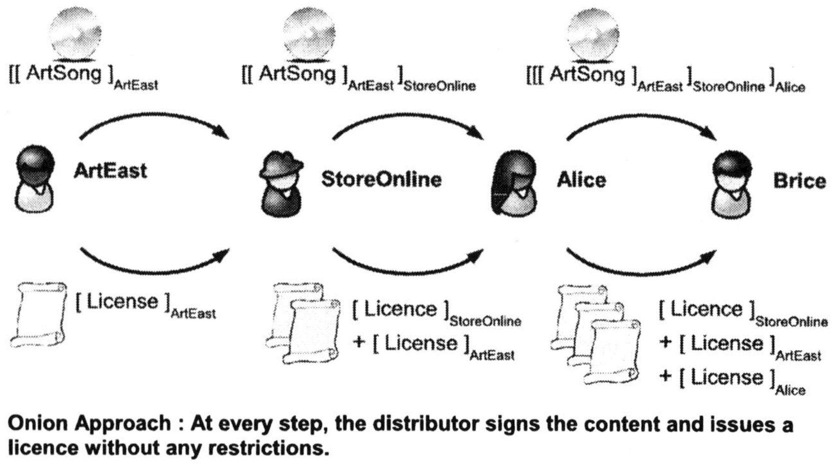

Fig. 4. Content traceability with OPA.

and distributors must be able to specify how users, and distributors if any, can use the content. If one of them does not agree, then the rendering action cannot be performed. Thus, it does not matter which rights are issued by each party but to be valid, both the owner and the distributor must allow it.

In OPA, a content provider is an entity able to specify licenses on the content, i.e. an entity allowed to add the signature to the content. Both the content owner and distributors are content providers. As showed in the figure 4, a content can be signed by several content providers depending on where is the content in the super-distribution chain. When the owner wants to allow a distributor to issue some rights, it creates a license allowing the distributor to "wrap" the content. The wrap right enables a distributor to become a content provider of the content. Once the distributor is one of the content providers, he or she can issue licenses on it.

Using this traceability mechanism, the rendering application is now able to extract the complete distribution chain of a given content. The rendering application must then evaluate all the licenses issued by the different content providers involved in this chain. In the following section, we show how content providers can control rights finally rendered to end-users and how the rendering application can decide if a right can be rendered or not.

2.2 Controlling rights with OPA

In OPA, all licenses issued by the different content providers involved in the distribution chain are evaluated. All of them must allow a right to be exercised in order to be rendered to the end-user. In our example, Art'East, as a content owner, provides a content with its signature. Art'East also delivers a license to

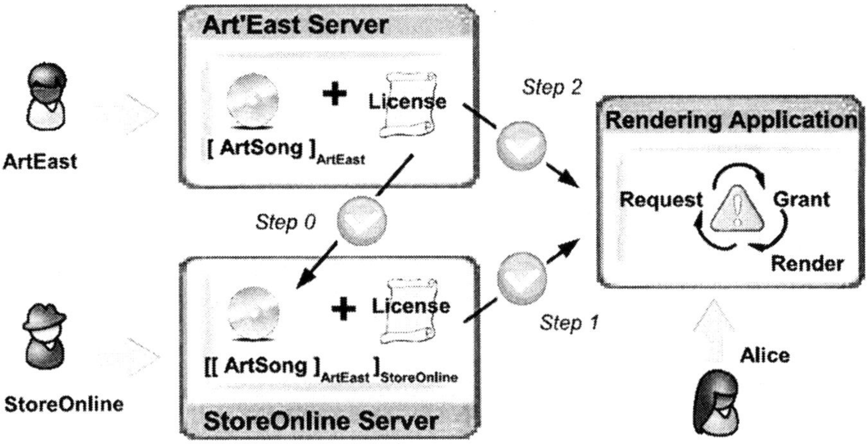

Fig. 5. Authorization mechanism with OPA.

StoreOnline allowing it to wrap the content (step 0) as showed in the figure 5. Using this license, StoreOnline adds its signature to the content and is now able to issue valid license to Alice without any restriction. Let us consider that StoreOnline first allows her to play the content. When Alice wants to read the content, she has first to get the StoreOnline license as StoreOnline is the last content provider (step 1). The license allows her to play it, but with the onion approach this is not sufficient. All content providers, involved in the distribution chain, must allow her to play it. So, she has also to get the Art'East License (step 2). For Art'East, only the play right is allowed but in practice, it does not want to specify who exactly use its content. So, why the owner does not simply specify in its license that anyone can play the content? Because this will introduce a security breach: anyone who got a content only signed by Art'East can play it. Here, Art'East wants to allow everyone to play the content only if it has been distributed by a trusted distributor, the one who got the wrap right on the content. In the onion approach, the owner can specify that everyone can play the content provided by StoreOnline. For this purpose, we introduce a parameter "from" specifying the authorized content provider. In our example, **from** *StoreOnline* is tied up to the target content of the grant.

Now let us consider that StoreOnline issues a license to Alice allowing her to modify the content. Alice can never modify the content because, even though Alice is allowed by StoreOnline, the DRM controller also checks the Art'East license. As there is no grant allowing her to modify the content when the content is provided by StoreOnline, she will fail to do any modification.

If we go further in the example, the onion approach is adequate to enable the C2C business model. When Alice wants to allow Brice to play the content, she first adds her signature to the content. She is allowed to do that because both StoreOnline and Art'East allowed her to wrap the content. StoreOnline directly allowed her to wrap the content. Art'East allowed Alice to do this wrapping because the content is distributed **from** *StoreOnline*. When Brice tries to play the content, the DRM controller first checks the license issued by the last content provider namely Alice. With this license, Alice allows Brice to play the content. Then, the DRM controller checks licenses issued by other content providers of the distribution chain. The second one is the StoreOnline license. With this license, Brice is allowed to play the content because it has been provided **from** *StoreOnline-Member*. Finally, Art'East allowed Brice to play it because the content has been provided both by StoreOnline and by someone else. In that case, Art'East allows a C2C distribution but there is no requirement on the identity.

3 The underlying model

This section formalizes the Onion Policy Administration model. We do not attempt to specify a complete DRM framework, neither to define a new Rights Expression Language covering all the expressiveness of existing ones. We rather aim at specifying the main concepts needed by a DRM framework and its corresponding REL both enabling OPA.

3.1 The content packaging

A content is a digital document wrapped in a secure container and digitally signed by the content owner as required by OPA. When a provider is allowed to redistribute a content ("wrap" right), the provider signature is appended to the previous content. Providers identities involved in the distribution chain can be seen as different onion layers wrapping the original document. The content $[ArtSong]_{Art'East}$ means that Art'East is the owner of the digital document Art'Song. This content traceability mechanism is formalized as follows:

$$\begin{array}{lll} \text{TYPE} & \multicolumn{2}{l}{Identity, Right, Document \text{ are nominal types}} \\ & Content & \triangleq [\ Document\ ]_{Provider} \mid [\ Content\ ]_{Provider} \\ & Provider & \triangleq Identity \end{array}$$

3.2 The Rights Expression Language

A license is a set of grants where a grant is a triple composed of an identity, a right and a digital document. As required in OPA, the license must contain the provider identity. This Rights Expression Language is defined as follows:

$$\begin{array}{lll} \text{TYPE} & Grant & \triangleq Identity \times Right \times Content \\ & License & \triangleq [\ \{Grant\}\ ]_{Provider} \\ & Provider & \triangleq Identity \end{array}$$

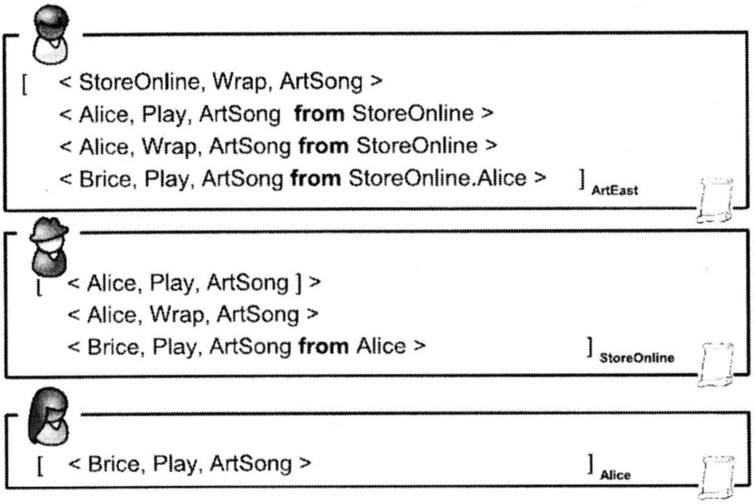

Fig. 6. Super-Distribution scenario with OPA.

Only authorized providers are allowed to append their digital signatures to the content. We define the right *Wrap*[2] enabling someone to become a content provider. If someone is allowed to *wrap* a given content then he or she is allowed to add his or her signature to the content. In our example, Art'East wants to allow StoreOnline to distribute the content. Art'East issues a license $[< StoreOnline, Wrap, ArtSong >]_{Art'East}$ allowing StoreOnline to wrap ArtSong. When StoreOnline uses this right, the rendering application creates the new content $[[ArtSong]_{Art'East}]_{StoreOnline}$. StoreOnline can then issue the valid license $[< Alice, Play, ArtSong >]_{StoreOnline}$ to Alice granting her the right to play. According to the ownership principle, the license is valid as StoreOnline is now one of the ArtSong's providers. But the license issued by StoreOnline is not enough to allow Alice to play the content. In the onion approach Art'East is still able to control which right Alice can get as an end-user of the distribution chain. Art'East must allow Alice to play the content only if this content has been distributed by StoreOnline. To do that, Art'East append a new grant $< Alice, Play, ArtSongs$ **from** $StoreOnline >$.

Let us now focus on how to enforce the C2C business model using the onion policy administration. In that business model, Alice can distribute the content to Brice. This latter can only play it but cannot distribute it. First of all, Alice must be able to wrap the ArtSong content provided by Art'East and StoreOnline. It means that both of them must allow Alice to *wrap* the content $[[ArtSong]_{Art'East}]_{StoreOnline}$. Art'East must issue the license $[< Alice, wrap, ArtSong$ **from** $StoreOnline >]_{Art'East}$ and StoreOnline must issue

[2] The Wrap right is one of the rights defined by the Right Data Dictionary of our DRM framework.

the license $[< Alice, wrap, ArtSong >]_{StoreOnline}$. Using those licenses, Alice can wrap the content and then distribute $[[[ArtSong]_{Art'East}]_{StoreOnline}]_{Alice}$ to Brice. If Brice wants to play this content then Alice, StoreOnline and Art'East must allow him to play it. Each of them must include a grant in their license allowing Brice to play the content according to who distributes it. The figure 6 shows all licenses issued by different parties enforcing all business models discussed previously in the example.

3.3 The license interpretation mechanism

In order to formalize the license interpretation mechanism, we first define the *isPermitted* predicate which is true, for a given set of license Γ, if there is a grant matching the given identity, the given right and the given document. The isPermitted predicate is formalized as follows :

$$\text{PREDICATE } isPermitted \triangleq Identity \times Right \times Content \times listOf(Provider) \rightarrow Boolean$$

$$\text{AXIOM } \Gamma \cup [\langle i, r, d \textbf{ from } plist\rangle]_{p_0} \vdash isPermitted(i, r, [d]_{p_0}, plist)$$

$$\Gamma \vdash isPermitted(i, r, [[[d]_{p_0}] \ldots]_{p_n}, (p_{n+1}|plist)) \rightarrow \Gamma \cup [\langle i, r, d \textbf{ from } plist\rangle]_{p_{n+1}} \vdash isPermitted(i, r, [[[[d]_{p_0}] \ldots]_{p_n}]_{p_{n+1}}, plist)$$

Then, we define a set of authorization predicates. These predicates are used to decide if a requested right (*request* predicate) can be allowed (*allow* predicate) or not (*deny* predicate). Such a request comes from the environment of the information system Σ. With OPA, such a request can be allowed if and only if every license in Γ, from the different content providers involved in the distribution chain, allows the request. If one content provider does not allow the request, the right cannot be rendered. These authorization predicates (*allow* and *deny*) are defined as follows:

TYPE λ is the empty list

$$\begin{aligned}\text{PREDICATE } request &\triangleq Identity \times Right \times Content \rightarrow Boolean\\ allow &\triangleq Identity \times Right \times Document \rightarrow Boolean\\ deny &\triangleq Identity \times Right \times Document \rightarrow Boolean\end{aligned}$$

$$\begin{aligned}\text{AXIOM } &\Sigma \vdash request(i, r, [[[d]_{p_0}] \ldots]_{p_n})\\ &\wedge \Gamma \vdash isPermitted(i, r, [[[d]_{p_0}] \ldots]_{p_n}, \lambda)\\ &\rightarrow \Sigma, \Gamma \vdash allow(i, r, d)\end{aligned}$$

$$\begin{aligned}&\Sigma \vdash request(i, r, [[[d]_{p_0}] \ldots]_{p_n})\\ &\wedge \Gamma \vdash \neg isPermitted(i, r, [[[d]_{p_0}] \ldots]_{p_n}, \lambda)\\ &\rightarrow \Sigma, \Gamma \vdash deny(i, r, d)\end{aligned}$$

4 Implementation

We developed a prototype as a proof of concept of a DRM framework enabling OPA. In this framework, we developed a content packager to protect a digital document and sign it. This packager enforces the wrapping mechanism defined in OPA in order to enable the content traceability. XML envelopes are used to wrap the content and XML digital signatures [13] are used to sign XML envelopes. Secondly, we defined our own XML-based REL enabling OPA. XML Signatures are also used to sign the licenses. Finally, we developed the rendering application in charge of interacting with a physical user (Graphical User Interface) or an external application (service). Through this interaction layer, a request can be made and the corresponding rendering can be delivered. The DRM controller embedded in the rendering application is able to interpret the licenses and give a decision if the right can be granted or not. The DRM controller algorithm is compliant with the OPA decision mechanism as shown in figure 5.

5 Conclusion

In super-distribution scenario, the content owner does not directly manage end-user's rights but rather delegate this task to a third-party: a distributor. Existing DRM approach, enforcing super-distribution, are based on *the issuing approach* where a content owner or a distributor restricts the license issued by the next distributor in the distribution chain. This paper provides a new approach called OPA (Onion Policy Administration) to manage rights in super-distribution models. OPA aims at controlling which rights are finally rendered to end-users rather than restricting the licenses issued by the different distributors in the distribution chain. With OPA, distributors are free to issue a license without any restriction. In these license, the content owner and the distributors specify which rights can be rendered to the end-users according to how this content was distributed, i.e. the content owner and the distributors specify that a given content must have been distributed according to a specific sub-distribution chain. The rendering application, in charge of deciding if a right can be rendered or not, must evaluate all licenses involved in the distribution chain of a given content. All of them must allow the requested right in order to be rendered.

Compared with the issuing approach, we assume that OPA has two main advantages. First, OPA provides a content traceability mechanism in order to identify the distribution chain of a given content. Each time a content is redistributed by a third party, the distributor signature is stored in the content. This traceability mechanism can be required by critical DRM applications. Indeed, we believe that DRM techniques can be used in critical information systems such as medical, administrative or military applications and not only in commercial application. The second main advantage is that OPA simplifies rights management in super-distribution. With the issuing approach, the distribution chain is defining using overlapping grants, so there are as many overlapping grants as there are distributors in the distribution chain. The more third parties there are in the chain, the more difficult is to write license. In the onion approach, there is only two grants : one specifying if someone can be a content provider (using the *Wrap* right) and another one specifying what the end-user can do with the content according to a valid sub-distribution chain. Thus, OPA is more adequate for DRM application involving many third-parties in content super-distribution.

Acknowledgement: This work was supported by funding from the French ministry for research under "ACI Sécurité Informatique: CASC Project"

References

1. Eberhard Becker, Willems Buhse, Dirk Gnnewig, and Niels Rump, editors. *Digital Rights Management: Technological, Economic, Legal and Political Aspects.* Lecture Notes in Computer Science - Springer Berlin / Heidelberg, 2003.
2. Microsoft Corporation. Using windows media encoder to protect content. Technical report, March 2003.
3. Microsoft Corporation. Architecture of windows media rights manager. Technical report, May 2004.
4. John S. Erickson. Fair Use, DRM and Trusted Computing. *Communication of the ACM*, 46(4), April 2003.
5. Richard Gooch. *Requirements for DRM Systems Introduction - The Requirement for DRM*, volume 2770. January 2003.
6. Susanne Guth. *Rights Expression Languages*, volume 2770. January 2003.
7. Susanne Guth. *A Sample DRM System*, volume 2770. January 2003.
8. International Organization for Standardization (ISO). *ISO/IEC 21000:2004 Information technology - Multimedia framework (MPEG-21)* , 2004.
9. Dirk Kuhlmann and Robert A. Gehring. *Trusted Platforms, DRM, and Beyond*, volume 2770. January 2003.
10. Open Mobile Alliance (OMA). *OMA Digital Rights Management V2.0*, 2006. http://www.openmobilealliance.org/release_program/drm_v2_0.html.
11. David Parott. Requirements for a Rights Data Dictonary and Rights Expression Language. Technical report, Reuters, June 2001.
12. Bill Rosenblatt, Bill Trippe, and Stephen Mooney. *Digital Rights Management: Business and Technology.* Wiley, Decembre 2001.
13. World Wide Web Consortium (W3C). *XML-Signature Syntax and Processing*, 2002. www.w3.org/TR/xmldsig-core/.

Non-Repudiation in Internet Telephony

Nicolai Kuntze[1], Andreas U. Schmidt[1], and Christian Hett[2]

[1] Fraunhofer–Institute for Secure Information Technology SIT
Rheinstraße 75, 64295 Darmstadt, Germany
{andreas.u.schmidt,nicolai.kuntze}@sit.fraunhofer.de
[2] ARTEC Computer GmbH
Robert-Bosch Straße 38, 61184 Karben, Germany
christian.hett@artec-it.de

Abstract. We present a concept to achieve non-repudiation for natural language conversations over the Internet. The method rests on chained electronic signatures applied to pieces of packet-based, digital, voice communication. It establishes the integrity and authenticity of the bidirectional data stream and its temporal sequence and thus the security context of a conversation. The concept is close to the protocols for Voice over the Internet (VoIP), provides a high level of inherent security, and extends naturally to multilateral non-repudiation, e.g., for conferences. Signatures over conversations can become true declarations of will in analogy to electronically signed, digital documents. This enables binding verbal contracts, in principle between unacquainted speakers, and in particular without witnesses. A reference implementation of a secure VoIP archive is exists.

1 Introduction

The latest successful example for the ever ongoing convergence of information technologies is Internet based telephony, transporting voice over the Internet protocol (VoIP). Analysts estimate a rate of growth in a range of 20% to 45% annually, expecting that VoIP will carry more than fifty percent of business voice traffic (UK) in a few years [1]. The success of VoIP will not be limited to cable networks, convergent speech and data transmission will affect next generation mobile networks as well. The new technology raises some security issues. For eavesdropping traditional, switched analogue or digital phone calls, an attacker needs physical access to the transport medium. Digital networks are generally more amenable to attacks, as holds already for ISDN and to a yet greater extent for IP networks. Efforts to add security features to VoIP products are generally insufficient, though proposals exist for the protection of confidentiality and privacy. Secure VoIP protocols, using cryptographic protection of a call, would even be at an advantage compared to traditional telephony systems. Protocols like SRTP [2] can provide end-to-end security to phone calls, independently of the security of transport medium and communication provider.

With VoIP maturing, it becomes natural to ask for application-level security in the context of IP telephony. Our purpose is to achieve non-repudiation in this context, i.e., for speech over packet-oriented, digital channels, and in particular for VoIP conversations. This means the capability to produce tenable evidence

Please use the following format when citing this chapter:

Kuntze, N., Schmidt, A.U., and Hett, C., 2007, in IFIP International Federation for Information Processing, Volume 232, New Approaches for Security, Privacy and Trust in Complex Environments, eds. Venter, H., Eloff, M., Labuschagne, L., Eloff, J., von Solms, R., (Boston: Springer), pp. 361–372.

that a conversation with the alleged contents has taken place between two or more parties. Ancillary information, e.g., that the conversation partners have designated, personal identities, and the time at which the conversation has taken place, may be of utmost importance in this regard, either to establish a supporting plausibility, e.g., 'caller was not absent during the alleged call', or to express relevant semantic information, e.g., 'telephonic order came in before stock price rose'. For electronic documents this kind of non-repudiation is commonly achieved by applying electronic signatures based on asymmetric cryptography. In the communication between several parties, the desired result is a binding contract, and in analogy the central goal of the present contribution is a technology to establish binding verbal contracts without witnesses.

This subject has a long pre-history: As early as 1905, Edison proposed the recording of voice, which was patented 1911 [3]. With the advent of digital signature technology, Merkle [4] envisioned, referring to Diffie and Hellman that "Digital signatures promise to revolutionize business by phone". However, work on non-repudiation of digital voice communication is scarce. The work most closely related to ours is the proposal in [5], resting on the theory of contracts and multi-lateral security [6]. It comprises a trusted third party ('Tele-Witness') that is invoked by communicating parties to securely record conversations and make them available as evidence at any later point in time.

Non-repudiation of inter-personal communication is interesting because of its inherent evidentiary value, exposed by forensic evaluation of the contained biometric data, e.g., as an independent means of speaker identification [7, 8]. Methods for the latter are advanced [9], yielding to recorded voice a high probative force, e.g., in a court of law. In comparison to other media, specific features of voice contribute to non-repudiation. Voice communication is interactive [10] and enables partners to make further enquiries in case of insufficient understanding. This mitigates to some extent problems to which signed digital documents are prone, e.g., misinterpretations due to misrepresentation, lack of uniqueness of presentation, and inadvertent or malicious hiding of content [11].

We set out requirements for non-repudiation which are very particular in the case of VoIP and other multi-media communication over IP, in Section 2 and propose the method to meet them in Section 3. Section 4 analyses the security of the method by listing and assessing the auditable information secured by it. A section which describes the implementation of a secure VoIP archive could, unfortunately, not be included for space restrictions. It may be found in [27] and at `http://arxiv.org/abs/cs.CR/0701145`. Conclusions and an outlook are found in Section 5.

2 Requirements for non-repudiation of conversations

From the schematic characterisation of non-repudiation in the standards [12, 13], we focus on the secure creation of evidence for later forensic inspection. This overlaps with the basic information security targets integrity and availability of the well-known CIA triad. To account for the particularities of the channel, we here take a communication-theoretical approach to derive requirements for non-repudiation. The general characteristics of the class of electronic communication that we address are the same for a wide media range, comprising audio, video, and multi-media. In essence it is always a full duplex or multiplex channel operating in real time using data packets, and we subsume communication over those under the term *conversation*. Generic requirements for the non-repudiation of conversations can be profiled for specific media, and we sometimes exemplary allude to the case of speech and VoIP. They are grouped around the top level protection targets *congruence* and *cohesion*. We describe the latter and devise for each a minimal set of specific, but application- and technology-neutral requirements. The requirements are necessary preconditions to achieve the protection targets, and are ordered by ascending complexity.

T1 Congruence. Communication theory and linguistics have established that the attributions of meanings can vary between a sender and a receiver of a message [14, Chapter 6], [15] — a basic problem for non-repudiation. Apart from the ambiguity of language, this implies particular problems for electronic communication channels and media. For digital documents bearing electronic signatures, the presentation problem is addressed by invoking the 'What You See is What You Sign' (WYSIWYS [11]) principle. It is often tacitly assumed that presentation environments can be brought into agreement for sender and receiver of a signed document [16]. We term this fundamental target *'congruence'*. It has special traits in the case of telephony. Essential for non-repudiation is the receiver's understanding, which leads in analogy to the principle 'What Is Heard Is What Is Signed'. But additionally it is indispensable to assure senders (speakers) about what precisely was received (heard).

R1.1 Integrity of the data in transmission, including technical environments for sending and receiving them. For VoIP, this is to be addressed at the level of single RTP packets and their payloads *and* of an entire conversation.

R1.2 Treatment of losses in the channel must enable information of senders about actually received information. This is independent of methods for *avoidance* or *compensation* of losses, such as Packet Loss Concealment (PLC). Rather it means a secure detection of losses (enabled by fulfilled R1.1), enabling a proper handling on the application level as well as a later (forensic) inspection.

R1.3 User interaction policies and their enforcement finally use fulfilled R1.1 and 1.2 to ensure congruence in the inter-personal conversation. For electronic documents this can simply amount to prescriptions about the technical environments in which a electronically signed document must be displayed. Or it can be an involved scheme to guarantee the agreement of contents of documents undergoing complex transformations [17, 18], e.g., between data formats. For speech, it can be realised in various ways taking into account the interactive nature of the medium. This is elaborated on in Section 3.5.

T2 Cohesion regards the temporal dimension of conversations. It means in particular the protection and preservation of the sequence the information flows in all directions of the channel. Again this is at variance with signed documents, where temporal sequence of communication is immaterial. Cohesion means to establish a complete temporal context of a conversation usually even *in absolute time*, since the temporal reference frame of a conversation can be meaningful.

R2.1 Start times of conversations must be determined and recorded. This is analogous to the signing time of documents (the assignment of which is a requirement for qualified signatures according to the EU Signature Directive).

R2.2 Temporal sequencing of conversations must be protected and related to the reference time frame established by fulfilling R2.1.

R2.3 Continual authentication of communication devices and if possible even communication partners is necessary, e.g., to prevent hijacking.

R2.4 Determined break points must allow for non-repudiation of conversations until they are terminated intentionally or inadvertently.

From the requirements analysis it is apparent that congruence and cohesion are complementary but not orthogonal categories. A specific profile for VoIP is not formulated here for brevity, but rather included in the development of the method below. It is understood that additionally the known standard requirements for electronic signatures as declarations of will and for non-repudiation of electronically signed documents, which are rooted in the theory of multilateral security [19], must be taken into account. We do not address details of user authentication, consent to recording, general privacy, confidentiality, and interaction with respect to the signing as a declaration of will proper. Nonetheless, the method proposed below enables the secure recording and archiving to preserve the probative value of a conversation, as demonstrated in [27].

3 The method

The requirements (R2.4) entail that signing a entire conversation with a single RSA signature by A is not viable, since this yields full disposal to determine (maliciously) the end time of signing of a conversation, and deprives B of any possibility to control and verify this *during conversation*. The opposite approach to secure single packets does not assure cohesion (R2.2 in conjunction with R1.1), since single RTP-packets contain only little audio data which may then easily be reordered. Apart from that, it would be computationally expensive. This is the prime motivation for the method we now present in general for the case of a bilateral conversation between A and B, using, e.g., the SIP/RTP protocol combination [20, 21]. In a basic model A secures the conversation as an unilateral declaration of will. We proceed in a bottom-up fashion from the base concept of intervals of VoIP data, over securing their integrity by a cryptographic chain, to coping with inevitable packet loss. For later reference we call the technique presented in 3.1— 3.4 below the *interval-chaining* method.

3.1 Building intervals

Intervals are the logical units on which the protection method operates. Intervals span certain amounts, which may be nil, of RTP packets for only one direction. As bi-directional communication needs formation of intervals for both directions, A and B hold buffers for packets both sent and received. Since directions are handled differently w.r.t. packet loss, as described in Section 3.3, directionally homogeneous intervals are advantageous from a protocol design viewpoint. To resolve the full duplex audio stream into an interval sequence we determine that intervals in the directions from and to A alternate. Intervals are enumerated as I_{2k-1}, I_{2k}, $k = 1, \ldots, N$ for directions $A \to B$ and $B \to A$, respectively. Interval I_l comprises RTP packets $(p_{l\,j})$, $j = 1, \ldots, K_l$, sent or received by A. For the moment we assume that there is no packet loss.

The length of an interval (in appropriate units) is a main adjustable parameter, and an important degree of freedom. Adjustable sizes of, e.g., data frames are not very common in communication technology, but recent proposals [23] show that they can be advantageous in certain situations, like the present one. We determine that interval boundaries are triggered by the elapse of a certain time, called *interval duration* and denoted by D. If T is the duration of the conversation then $N = \lceil T \; D \rceil$. Basing intervals on time necessitates the formation of intervals without voice data payload when a silence period exceeds D. This design choice entails some signalling, transport, and cryptographic overhead. This is however outweighed by some favourable properties. In particular, the maximum buffer length is known from the outset, and control of the interval duration is a direct means to cope with the (known) slowness of (public key) cryptographic soft- and hardware. Adjustment of D therefore allows for an, even dynamical, trade-off between security and performance, as it controls the ratio of security data to payload data. The alternative of triggering intervals by full-run of packet buffers at both sides causes concurrency problems.

Since the communication channel is fully duplex, the sequence of intervals does not reflect the temporal sequence of audio data, rather I_{2k-1} and I_{2k} comprise approximately concurrent data sent in both directions. But this is immaterial since intervals are only logical units and security data for intervals can be stored separately from the RTP streams. This is a key feature of our method. It does not affect the VoIP communication at all but can be run in complete — logical and even physical (extra hardware) — separation from it. VoIP communication is therefore not impeded by our method.

3.2 Cryptographic chaining

The basic idea is to cryptographically secure the payload contained in each interval and include the generated security data in the subsequent interval to form a cryptographic chain. We use the shorthand $(\cdot)_X \stackrel{\text{def}}{=} \text{Priv}_X(h(\cdot))$ for entity X' digital signature by applying a private key Priv_X and a hash algorithm $h(\cdot)$. TS is a time-stamping authority. The notation $\longrightarrow$ signifies the sending of some data. To sign a conversation A performs the following operations.

$$\begin{aligned}
\text{Sec}_I:\; & M_I \stackrel{\text{def}}{=} (D, \mathsf{SIP_Data}, \mathsf{Auth_Data}, \mathsf{nonce}, \ldots) \longrightarrow B; \\
& S_0 \stackrel{\text{def}}{=} \big((M_I)_A\big)_{TS} \longrightarrow B; \\
\text{Sec}_l:\; & S_l \stackrel{\text{def}}{=} (I_l, S_{l-1})_A \longrightarrow B; \quad l = 1, \ldots, 2N \\
\text{Sec}_F:\; & M_F \stackrel{\text{def}}{=} (\mathsf{termination_condition}, \ldots) \longrightarrow B; \\
& S_F \stackrel{\text{def}}{=} \big((M_F, S_{2N})_A\big)_{TS} \longrightarrow B;
\end{aligned}$$

In the initial step Sec_I, $(\cdot)_{TS}$ means a time-stamp applied by TS, e.g., according to RFC 3161 [22], and is enveloping the meta-data M_I signed by A (R2.1). This may include some authentication data Auth_Data , e.g., A's digital certificates. To provide a broad audit trail for later inspection, data from the call negotiation and connection establishment, here subsumed under SIP_Data, should be included. The final time-stamp can be used optionally to detect drift, and narrows down the conversation in time. Since this is sufficient to secure the temporal context required for cohesion, the application of time-stamps in every step, which may be costly, is not proposed. A nonce is included in M_I to prevent replay attacks. By including S_{l-1} in the signed data S_l and S_{2N-1} in S_F, and alternation of interval directions, R1.1 and R2.2 are satisfied. Signatures of A and additional authentication data in M_I support R2.3. If communication breaks inadvertently, interval chaining is verifiable up to the last interval, thus R2.4 is satisfied, with a loss of at most one interval duration of conversation at its end. A controls interval timing and the operations Sec_I, Sec_l, and Sec_F occur at times 0, $\lfloor l \;\, 2 \rfloor \cdot D$, and $N \cdot D$, respectively.

3.3 Treatment of packet loss

Digital voice communication offers a rather high reliability leading generally to a higher understandability of VoIP communication in comparison with all predecessors. However, packet loss may occur and must be treated as explained in R1.2. Denote by $\delta_l \subset \{1, \ldots, K_l\}$ the sequence of identifiers of packets actually received by A respectively B. Intervals are reduced accordingly to $I'_l \stackrel{\mathrm{def}}{=} (p_{l\ j})_{j \in \delta_l}$. The steps Sec_l are modified by a protocol to report received packages.

$$
\begin{aligned}
\mathrm{Sec}'_{2k-1}:\ & \mathsf{repeat} \\
& \qquad \mathsf{repeat} \\
& \qquad\quad \mathsf{interval\_termination} \longrightarrow B; \\
& \qquad \mathsf{until}\ \delta_{2k-1} \longrightarrow A; \\
& \mathsf{until}\ S_{2k-1} \stackrel{\mathrm{def}}{=} (I'_{2k-1}, S_{2k-2})_A \longrightarrow B; \\
\mathrm{Sec}'_{2k}:\ & \mathsf{repeat} \\
& \qquad S_{2k} \stackrel{\mathrm{def}}{=} (I'_{2k}, S_{2k-1})_A \longrightarrow B; \\
& \qquad \delta_{2k} \longrightarrow B; \\
& \mathsf{until\ success};
\end{aligned}
$$

This accounts for losses in the VoIP (RTP) channel as well as failures in the channel for transmission of signing data. The loop conditions can be evaluated by explicit (Sec'_{2k}) or implicit (Sec'_{2k-1}) acknowledgements by receivers.

3.4 Extension to multilateral conversations

Here we present the simplest way to extend the method above to conference-like situations. Multilateral non-repudiation means mutual agreement about the contents of a conversation between all parties. For implementing it for M participants $A_0, \ldots, A_{M-1}$ a round-robin scheme [24] can be used to produce the required chain of signatures as in Lemma 1. Round-robin is a simple algorithm to distribute the required security data between the participants of the conference. Other base algorithms of distributed systems like flooding, echo, or broadcast might be used, depending, for instance, on the particular topology of the conference network. During the round, a token is passed from participant to participant, signalling the signer role. If participant A_m carries the token, he waits for time D and buffers packets sent by himself. When A_m terminates the interval a signalling and signing protocol is processed, which, in contrast to the scheme above, only concerns data *sent* by A_m. The numbering of intervals is as follows. In the time span from 0 to D the packets $(p_{m;j})$ sent by A_m are in the interval I_m. The packets emitted by A_m during $[D, 2D]$ are in I_{M+m}, and so on. It is here not feasible to sign merely the packets received by *everyone*, because cumulative packet loss could be too high. Instead, an additional hashing indirection is included and hashes $H_k^\theta \stackrel{\text{def}}{=} (h(p_{k;j}))_{j\in\theta}$ of all packets θ received by at least one person from A_m in interval k are distributed and can be used to check the signature in spite of packet loss. Let δ_k^σ denote the list of packets sent by A_m and received by A_σ in interval k. Set $R_m \stackrel{\text{def}}{=} \{0,..,M-1\}\backslash m$ and let $r \geq 0$ be the round number. In order to account for latencies in reporting of packet loss, computing hashes, and signing, we introduce a parallel offset in the round-robin scheme. In round r participant A_m carrying the token terminates interval with number $\widehat{k}(r,m) \stackrel{\text{def}}{=} rM^2 + (M+1)m + 1$. He secures the set of intervals $\widehat{I}(r,m) \stackrel{\text{def}}{=} (\widehat{k}(r,m) - M \cdot \{0,\dots,M-1\}) \cap \mathbb{N}$.

$$
\begin{array}{l}
\text{Sec\_mult}_{r\,m}: \forall\sigma \in R_m \ \textsf{do} \\
\qquad \textsf{repeat} \\
\qquad\qquad \textsf{interval\_termination} \longrightarrow A_\sigma; \\
\qquad \textsf{until}\ (\delta_k^\sigma)_{k\in\widehat{I}(r\,m)} \longrightarrow A_m; \\
\quad \textsf{od}; \\
\quad \theta_k \stackrel{\text{def}}{=} \cup_{\sigma\in R_m} \delta_k^\sigma \ \textsf{for}\ k \in \widehat{I}(r,m); \\
\quad D_{r\,m} \stackrel{\text{def}}{=} \left((\delta_k^\sigma)_{\sigma\in R_m}, H_k^{\theta_k}\right)_{k\in\widehat{I}(r\,m)}; \\
\quad S_{r\,m} \stackrel{\text{def}}{=} (D_{r\,m}, S_{\text{pred}(r\,m)})_{A_m}; \\
\quad \forall\sigma' \in R_m \ \textsf{do} \\
\qquad \textsf{repeat} \\
\qquad\qquad (S_{r\,m}, D_{r\,m}) \longrightarrow A_{\sigma'}; \\
\qquad \textsf{until success}; \\
\quad \textsf{od};
\end{array}
$$

The preceding security value $S_{\text{pred}(r\,m)}$ bears indices

$$
\text{pred}(r,m) = \begin{cases} (r, m-1) & \text{if } m \geq 1; \\ (r-1, M-1) & \text{if } r \geq 1,\ m = 0; \\ I & \text{otherwise,} \end{cases}
$$

where I stands for the initialisation interval which can be constructed as in the preceding sections, replacing single sending by broadcast with acknowledgements. The numbering scheme for Intervals and the evolving sequence of

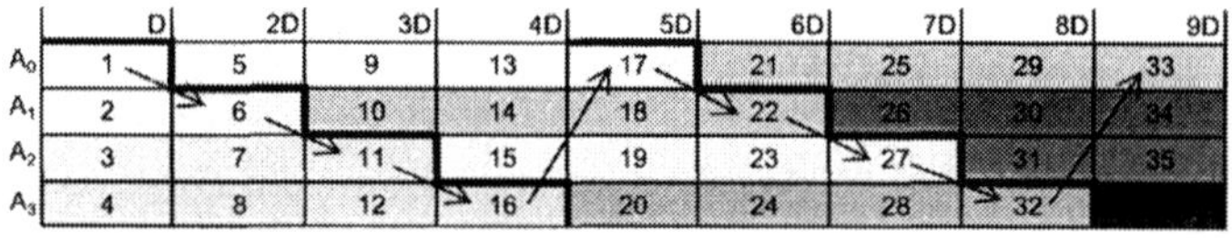

Fig. 1. Numbering of intervals in the case of 4 participants along the time axis. Arrows indicate the sequence of security values S. Thicker borders separate rounds. Equally coloured intervals are secured in a single operation $\text{Sec\_mult}_{r,m}$.

security values is shown in Figure 1 below. In effect, A_m broadcasts (with acknowledgement) a signature over hashes of all packets received by at least one other participant. This is the *common* security data with which the chain can be continued. According to Lemma 1, non-repudiation of the total, multilateral conversation for the first interval duration from time 0 to D is achieved after execution of $\text{Sec\_mult}_{2\,M-1}$ at time $2M \cdot D$. With each further execution of Sec_mult a subsequent piece of conversation of length D obtains multilateral non-repudiation.

In case of call termination, $2M+1$ finalisation steps without audio data (two final rounds plus finishing by the participant carrying the token at the time of termination) are required to obtain non-repudiation of the last interval in time. Joining and leaving a signed multilateral call while the signature is created by the participants can be enabled through finalisation. If participant B requests to join the call, A_m, who posses the token, initiates a finalisation and B can join after this (inserted as $m+1$). In the case that a participant likes to leave he awaits the token and finalises including a leave message.

3.5 Operational policies

We do not lay out a complete set of rules for the operation of a system using the non-repudiation method above. Rather we list the most obvious ones and stress the most important point of monitoring and treatment of packet loss, or rather understandability.

To account for requirement R1.3, users should be signalled at any time during a conversation about the signature status of it. This necessitates to an extent specified by application-specific policies the cryptographic verification of the interval chaining, and continual evaluation of relevant information, see Section 4.1. Additionally a *secure voice signing terminal* should control every aspect of user interaction and data transmission. This is elucidated in [25].

To maintain congruence and mitigate attacks aiming at mutilating a conversation, packet loss and the ensuing level of understandability must permanently be monitored. When the packet loss is above a configurable threshold, an action should be triggered according to determined policies. The principle possibilities are: 1. ignore; 2. notify users while continuing signing; 3. abort the signing; and 4. terminate call. The first two options open the path for attacks. Termination of the call is the option for maximum security. From a practical viewpoint, the loss threshold is seldom reached without breakdown of the connection anyway due to insufficient understandability or timeouts.

Options 3 and 4 provide a 'Sollbruchstelle' (predetermined break point) for the probative value of the conversation. In contrast, most other schemes for securing the integrity of streamed data, e.g., the signing method of [26] aim at loss-tolerance, for instance allowing for the verification of the stream signature with some probability in the presence of packet loss. We suggest that for the probative value of conversations, the former is advantageous. A signed call with an intermediate gap can give rise to speculations over alternatives to fill it, which are restricted by syntax and grammar, but can lead to different semantics. Using this, a clever and manipulative attacker could delete parts of the communication to claim with certain credibility that the remnants have another meaning than intended by the communication partner(s). If the contents of a conversation after such an intentional deletion are unverifiable and thus cannot be used to prove anything, this kind of attack is effectively impeded.

4 Security considerations

We corroborate the statement that interval chaining can achieve non-repudiation for VoIP conversations, based on the information generally secured by interval chaining. An analysis based on an instance of a system architecture and possible attacks is contained in [27].

4.1 Auditable information

In this section we analyse the information that can be gained and proved to have integrity in a call secured by interval chaining. Table 1 gives a, perhaps incomplete, overview over this audit data, which may be amenable to forensic inspection, e.g., by an expert witness in court, or, on the other extreme, applicable during the ongoing conversation, or both.

4.2 Comparison with SRTP and IPsec

The well-known security methods SRTP and IPsec address the protection of confidentiality, authenticity and data integrity on the application, respectively network layer, and can be applied to VoIP and as well in parallel with interval-chaining. We want to show salient features of interval-chaining, which distinguishes it from both standards and in our view provides a higher level of non-repudiation and even practicality. On the fundamental level, both SRTP and IPsec necessarily operate on the packet level and do not by themselves provide protection of the temporal sequence and cohesion of a VoIP conversation. While it is true that pertinent information can be reconstructed from the RTP sequence numbers, in turn protected by hash values, such an approach would have some weaknesses, which taken together do not allow full non-repudiation. In particular, RTP sequence numbers can suffer from roll-overs and though their integrity is secured in transmission, they can still be rather easily be forged by the sender, since they belong to protocol stacks which are not especially secured in common systems. While packet loss can be detected or reconstructed using sequence numbers, interval chaining yields a well-defined, tunable, *and cryptographically secured* means to deal with it during an ongoing conversation,

Auditable item	Req.	Protection target	Verifies/indicates	When applicable
Initial time stamp	2.1	Cohesion	Start time	Always
Initial signature & certificate	2.3	Cohesion	Identity of signer	Always
Interval Chaining	2.2, 1.1	Cohesion	Interval integr. & order	Always
Packet loss in intervals	1.2, 2.4	Congruence	QoS, understandability	Always
Monotonic increase of RTP-sequence numbers	1.1, 2.2	Integrity & cohesion	RTP-stream plausibility	Always
Relative drift of RTP-time marks against system time	2.2	Cohesion	RTP-stream plausibility	During convers.
Relative drift of RTP-time marks against $\lfloor l \; 2 \rfloor \cdot D$	2.2	Cohesion	Packet & stream plausibility	Ex post
No overlaps of RTP-time marks at interval boundaries	2.2	Cohesion	Packet & stream plausibility	Always
Replay-window		Integrity	Uniqueness of recorded audio stream	Always
Final time stamp	2.2	Cohesion	Conversation duration	Ex post
Forensic analysis of recorded conversation		(Semantic) authenticity	Speaker identity, mood, lying, stress, etc.	Ex post, forensic

Table 1. Auditable information of a conversation secured with interval chaining. Columns: Secured data item audited, Non-repudiation requirement addressed, Protection target supported, Actual information indicated or verified, and when is the check applicable.

significantly limiting potential attack vectors. In essence, RTP sequence numbers are not designed to ensure a conversation's integrity and thus have lower evidentiary value in comparison to chained intervals. From the viewpoint of electronic signatures, their level of message, respectively, conversation authentication can only be achieved with an protocol-independent means to manage authentication data such as asymmetric keys, i.e., a Public Key Infrastructure. The connection and session dependent key handling of IPsec and SRTP, relying on HMACs and merely allowing for symmetric keys deprived of authentication semantics, are generally insufficient for non-repudiation. Interval chaining is an independent means to control the cryptographic workload benefiting scalability. Finally, NAT traversal is a problem for network layer integrity protection like IPsec since rewriting IP headers invalidates corresponding hash values (a solution has been proposed by TISPAN [28]). This problem does not occur with the interval chaining method, since only RTP headers, not IP headers of packets need to be (and are in the implementation below) signed.

5 Conclusions

IP-based multimedia communication is not restricted to VoIP, for instance by now, several video conferencing systems are maturing, some of which are based on sophisticated peer-to-peer communication [29]. Moreover the service quality and availability of the new communication channels is constantly increasing through developments like packet loss concealment (PLC) for audio [30] and even video [31] streams. Our proposed method for non-repudiation is applicable in all these contexts. Its adoption would pave the way for a new paradigm for trustworthy, inter-personal communication. An efficient self-signed archive for VoIP calls and its system architecture was implemented as a prototype together with a verification and playback tool. It requires no modification to the terminal equipment, and secures the ongoing conversations 'on the fly' [27].

The next steps in our research are to i) implement the operational context for electronic signatures over speech, i.e., user interaction and signalling, ii) devise a trustworthy signature terminal for that purpose, preferably using Trusted Computing technology on mobile devices, e.g., to secure audio I/O and processing, iii) extend the method to conferences and other media than VoIP.

References

1. Kavanagh, J.: Voice over IP special report: From dial to click. `http://www.computerweekly.com/Articles/2006/02/14/214129/VoiceoverIPspecialreportFromdialtoclick.html`, visited 1.3.2006.
2. Baugher, M., et al.: The Secure Real-time Transport Protocol (SRTP). RFC 3711, IETF, March 2004. `http://www.ietf.org/rfc/rfc3711.txt`
3. Edison, T.A.: Recording-telephone. United States Patent P.No.:1,012,250, United States Patent Office, Washington, DC (1911) Patented Dec. 19, 1911.
4. Merkle, R.C.: A certified digital signature. In Brassard, G., ed.: Advances in Cryptology (CRYPTO '89). Number 435 in LNCS, Springer-Verlag (1989) 218–238 Republication of the 1979 original.
5. Strasser, M.: Möglichkeiten zur Gestaltung verbindlicher Telekooperation. Master's thesis, Universität Freiburg, Institut für Informatik und Gesellschaft (2001)
6. Kabatnik, M., Keck, D.O., M. Kreutzer, A.Z.: Multilateral security in intelligent networks. In: Proceedings of the IEEE Intelligent Network Workshop. (2000) 59–65
7. Poh, N., Bengio, S.: Noise-Robust Multi-Stream Fusion for Text-Independent Speaker Authentication. In: Proceedings of The Speaker and Language Recognition Workshop (Odyssey). (2004)
8. Rodriguez-Linares, L., Garcia-Mateo, C.: Application of fusion techniques to speaker authentication over IP networks. IEEE Proceedings-Vision Image and Signal Processing **150** (2003) 377–382
9. Hollien, H.: Forensic Voice Identification. Academic Press, London (2001)
10. Goodwin, C.: Conversational organization: Interaction between speakers and hearers. Academic Press, New York (1981)
11. Landrock, P., Pedersen, T.: WYSIWYS? What You See Is What You Sign? Information Security Technical Report, **3** (1998) 55–61
12. ISO: Information Technology: Security Frameworks for Open Systems: Non-Repudiation Framework. Technical Report ISO10181-4, ISO (1997)
13. ISO: Information Technology: Security Techniques - Non Repudiation - Part 1: General. Technical Report ISO13888-1, ISO (1997)
14. Searle, J.R.: Mind, Language and Society. Basic Books, New York (1999)
15. Austin, J.L.: How to Do Things with Words. Harvard University Press, Cambridge, Mass. (1962)
16. Schmidt, A.U.: Signiertes XML und das Präsentationsproblem. Datenschutz und Datensicherheit **24** (2000) 153–158

17. Schmidt, A.U., Loebl, Z.: Legal security for transformations of signed documents: Fundamental concepts. In Chadwick, D., Zhao, G., eds.: EuroPKI 2005. Volume 3545 of Lecture Notes in Computer Science., Springer-Verlag (2005) 255–270
18. Piechalski, J., Schmidt, A.U.: Authorised translations of electronic documents. In Venter, H.S., Eloff, J.H.P., Labuschagne, L., Eloff, M.M., eds.: Proceedings of the ISSA 2006 From Insight to Foresight Conference, Information Security South Africa (ISSA) (2006)
19. Rannenberg, K., Pfitzmann, A., Müller, G.: IT Security and Multilateral Security. In Müller, G., Rannenberg, K., eds.: Multilateral Security in Communications. Volume 3 of Technology, Infrastructure, Economy., Addison-Wesley (1999) 21–29
20. Rosenberg, J., et al.: SIP: Session Initiation Protocol. RFC 3261, IETF, June 2002. `http://www.ietf.org/rfc/rfc3261.txt`
21. Schulzrinne, H., et al.: RTP: A Transport Protocol for Real-Time Applications. RFC 1889, IETF, January 1996. `http://www.ietf.org/rfc/rfc1889.txt`
22. Adams, C., et al.: Internet X.509 Public Key Infrastructure Time-Stamp Protocol (TSP). RFC 3161, IETF, August 2001. `http://www.ietf.org/rfc/rfc3161.txt`
23. Choi, E.C., Huh, J.D., Kim, K.S., Cho, M.H.: Frame-size adaptive MAC protocol in high-rate wireless personal area networks. ETRI Journal **28** (2006) 660–663
24. Shreedhar, M., Varghese, G.: Efficient fair queuing using deficit round-robin. IEEE/ACM Transactions on Networking **4** (1996) 375–385
25. Hett, Ch., Kuntze, N., Schmidt, A. U.: Security and non repudiation of Voice-over-IP conversations. To appear in: Proceedings of the Wireless World Research Forum (WWRF17), Heidelberg, Germany, 15-17 November 2006.
26. Perrig, A., Tygar, J.D., Song, D., Canetti, R.: Efficient authentication and signing of multicast streams over lossy channels. In: SP '00: Proceedings of the 2000 IEEE Symposium on Security and Privacy, Washington, DC, USA, IEEE Computer Society (2000) 56–75
27. Hett, C., Kuntze, N., Schmidt, A.U.: A secure archive for Voice-over-IP conversations. In et al., D.S., ed.: To appear in the Proceedings of the 3rd Annual VoIP Security Workshop (VSW06), ACM (2006) `http://arxiv.org/abs/cs.CR/0606032`
28. Telecoms & Internet converged Services & Protocols for Advanced Networks (TISPAN) `http://www.tispan.org/`, see also the Whitepaper `http://www.newport-networks.com/cust-docs/91-IPSec-and-VoIP.pdf`
29. Zühlke, M., König, H.: A signaling protocol for small closed dynamic multi-peer groups. In: Proceedings of High Speed Networks and Multimedia Communications, 7th IEEE International Conference (HSNMC 2004), Toulouse, France. Volume 3079 of LNCS., Springer-Verlag (2004) 973–984
30. Perkins, C., Hodson, O., Hardman, V.: A survey of packet loss recovery techniques for streaming audio. IEEE Network **12** (1998) 40–48
31. Zhu, Q.F., Kerofsky, L.: Joint source coding, transport processing, and error concealment for H.323-based packet video. In Aizawa, K., Stevenson, R.L., Zhang, Y.Q., eds.: Visual Communications and Image Processing '99. Volume 3653 of Proceedings of SPIE., SPIE (1998) 52–62
32. Kolletzki, S.: Secure internet banking with privacy enhanced mail - a protocol for reliable exchange of secured order forms. Computer Networks and ISDN Systems **28** (1996) 1891–1899
33. Grimm, R., Ochsenschläger, P.: Binding Cooperation. A Formal Model for Electronic Commerce. Computer Networks **37** (2001) 171–193

FirePatch: Secure and Time-Critical Dissemination of Software Patches*

Håvard Johansen[1], Dag Johansen[1], and Robbert van Renesse[2]

[1] University of Tromsø, Norway. `haavardj|dag@cs.uit.no`
[2] Cornell University, USA. `rvr@cs.cornell.edu`

Abstract. Because software security patches contain information about vulnerabilities, they can be reverse engineered into exploits. Tools for doing this already exist. As a result, there is a race between hackers and end-users to obtain patches first. In this paper we present and evaluate *FirePatch*, an intrusion-tolerant dissemination mechanism that combines encryption, replication, and sandboxing such that end-users are able to win the security patch race.

1 Introduction

Automatic software updates for bug fixes are essential for Internet applications. It is particularly important when a software update fixes a security hole. Software vendors, for fear of liability, release patches for security holes as soon as possible. They do so without publicizing what the bug is, for fear that hackers will exploit the vulnerability before end-users have an opportunity to install the patch.

In practice the time between when a patch is released to the time that it is installed is long and typically measured in days [1, 6]. A counterintuitive observation is that a long patching cycle is worse than no patching cycle at all. This paradox stems from the fact that a security patch can be reverse-engineered to reveal the vulnerable code. In other words, if the software vendor cannot provide the mechanism to distribute *and* install a patch quickly, the end user might be better of if the patch is not released at all.

Even if users are notified about a vulnerability and are able to download a patch in time, installing a patch is an inconvenience and might lead to downtime of critical services. Patches might also contain bugs that break system configuration or introduce new vulnerabilities. It has even been suggested that patch installation should be delayed until the risk of penetration is greater than the risk of installing a broken patch [2].

Fortunately, protection against security vulnerabilities can be done in the network layer by installing stateful packet filters like Shields [14], Self-Certifying Alerts [4], or vulnerability-specific predicates [9] that inspect and modify incoming packets. Such patches do not interrupt the execution of applications and

* This work is supported in part by the Research Council of Norway (IKT 2010 program), AFOSR, AFRL/IFSE, NSF, and Intel Corporation.

Please use the following format when citing this chapter:

Johansen, H., Johansen, D., and van Renesse, R., 2007, in IFIP International Federation for Information Processing, Volume 232, New Approaches for Security, Privacy and Trust in Complex Environments, eds. Venter, H., Eloff, M., Labuschagne, L., Eloff, J., von Solms, R., (Boston: Springer), pp. 373–384.

are a viable intermediate solution until the user is able to install a permanent fix to the software. Also, automatic patching infrastructures have emerged that greatly reduce the time software is left vulnerable. For instance, a recent study on the Microsoft Windows Update mechanism [6] shows that the automation of notification, downloading, and installation of patches ensures that as much as 80% of the end-clients are updated within one day of patch release.

This still gives a malicious agent ample time to construct and execute an attack. For instance, by examining the binary difference between a vulnerable version of the Microsoft Secure Socket Layer (SSL) library and a corresponding patch, Flake [5] constructed a program that reliably exploited this vulnerability within 10 hours. Marketplaces for buying and selling exploits already exist [12]. It is therefore imperative that software vendors disseminate patches with low end-to-end latency. Such a patch dissemination service must be resilient to *denial-of-service* (DoS) attacks and intrusions as hackers might target the service to increase their opportunity to exploit the vulnerabilities exposed by the patches.

This paper describes *FirePatch*, a scalable and secure overlay network for disseminating security patches. *FirePatch* employs the following three techniques:

1. A patch is disseminated in two phases. First, an encrypted version of the patch, which cannot be reverse engineered, is disseminated. Some time later, the decryption key is disseminated. As the key will typically be significantly smaller than the patch, it can be disseminated much faster to a large collection of machines.
2. In order to deal with DoS attacks against dissemination of patches, attempting to increase the time during which a vulnerability can be exploited, we have developed a distributed software mirroring service. While replication makes DoS attacks more difficult, it increases the likelihood that individual servers are compromised—a highly undesirable situation for a server that disseminates security patches to clients. Therefore, our service is also made tolerant of Byzantine failures.
3. For machines that are not on-line at the time that a patch is disseminated, we have developed a simple protocol for secure download and installation of patches, run each time a machine goes on-line. While this goes on, a packet filter prevents the machine from participating in other network communication.

The rest of this paper is organized as follows. In the next section we present related work. In Section 3 we outline the architecture of *FirePatch* and state our assumptions. Section 4 describes our two-phase dissemination protocol which we use in our dissemination overlay described in Section 5. *FirePatch* is evaluated in Section 6. Section 7 concludes.

2 Background and Related Work

A study done on several software vulnerabilities appearing in the last half of the 1990's [1] found that almost all intrusions can be attributed to vulnerabilities known by both the software vendor and by the general public and to which patches existed. The study found that vulnerable software remained unpatched for months or even years. The primary reason for such long patching cycles was, the authors claim, that the studied software was not enrolled with an automatic updating service. Instead, end-users were required to discover the existence of both vulnerabilities and patches on their own by browsing the vendors web-sites, visiting bulletin-boards, etc.

With approximately 300 million clients, Microsoft Windows Update is currently the world's largest software update service [6]. The service consists of a (presumably large) pool of servers that clients periodically pull for updates. Other commercial patch management products like ScriptLogic's Patch Authority Plus[2] and PatchLink Update[3] enable centralized management of patch deployment on the Windows platform. However, it is unclear how any of these systems protect themselves from intrusion and if they address the possibility that hackers reverse-engineer patches into exploits.

Open-source communities, like the Debian GNU/Linux Project[4], organize their software update services similarly to Windows Update as a pool of servers that clients periodically pull for updates. Clients can freely choose which server to pull. The servers are organized into a hierarchy with children periodically querying their parent for updates. As these communities rely on donated third party hosting capacity, an attacker can easily intrude into the server pool.

The ratio of how often a patch is released and how quickly it must be received by clients implies substantial overhead for pull-based retrieval mechanisms like those used in the above systems. Pushing is better suited for this type of messaging, but incurs overhead to maintain an up-to-date list of clients. Peer-to-peer content distribution systems, like SplitStream, Bullet, and Chainsaw [3, 10, 11] approach this by spreading both maintenance and forwarding load to all clients. Although the elimination of dissemination trees in Chainsaw makes it more robust to certain failures than SplitStream and Bullet, these systems do not tolerate Byzantine failures. SecureStream [7] provides Byzantine tolerant dissemination by layering a Chainsaw-style gossip mesh on top of our *Fireflies* membership protocol [8] similarly to *FirePatch*. However, SecureStream targets multimedia streaming, which allows for certain packet loss.

A promising approach to detecting vulnerabilities in existing software is to use machine clusters that emulates a large number of independent hosts in order to attract attacks. Such "honeyfarms" have been shown to be able to emulate the execution of real Internet hosts in an scalable manner [13] and can be used

[2] `http://www.scriptlogic.com/products/patchauthorityplus/`

[3] `http://www.patchlink.com/`

[4] `http://www.debian.org/`

to generate self-certifying alerts (SCAs) [4] automatically upon detection of intrusion.

3 Architecture and Assumptions

We distinguish three roles: *patchers*, *clients*, and *mirrors*. Patchers are typically software providers that issue patches. For simplicity, we will assume a single patcher in this paper, although any number of patchers is supported. Clients are machines that run software distributed by the patcher, mirrors are servers that store patches for clients to download, and notify clients when a new patch is available.

We assume that the patcher is correct and is trusted by all correct clients. In particular, using public key cryptography clients can ascertain the authenticity of patches. In our system, clients are passive participants, and in particular do not participate in the dissemination system. Thus we do not have to assume that clients are correct.

In order to increase the patcher's upload capacity and ability to fight attacks, we employ a distributed network of mirror servers. The more mirrors, the harder it is to mount a DoS attack against the network. However, the easier it is to compromise one or more mirrors. We allow a subset of mirrors to become compromised, but assume that individual compromises are independent of one another, and that the probability that a mirror is compromised is bounded by a certain P_{byz}. However, we do allow compromised mirrors to collude when mounting an attack.

The patcher publishes (and signs) the list of servers that it considers mirrors for its patches. This list contains a version number so the patcher can securely update this list when necessary.

We assume that all communication goes over the Internet, the shortcomings of which are well-known. In order to deal with spoofing attacks, all data from the patcher is cryptographically signed, and we assume that the cryptographic building blocks are correct and the private key is securely kept by the patcher.

4 Two-Phase Dissemination

We refer to the time from when a software vulnerability is first made public to when the number of exploitable systems shrinks to insignificance as the *window of vulnerability*, or WOV for short. We have devised a dissemination protocol that, when layered on top of a secure broadcast channel, makes the WOV independent of message size. The net result of such an invariant is that the WOV can be kept fixed and small despite the fact that voluminous data has to be transferred over the wire.

We disseminate patches (or any data) in two phases. In phase one, we distribute an encrypted patch, and in the second phase, we disseminate the small

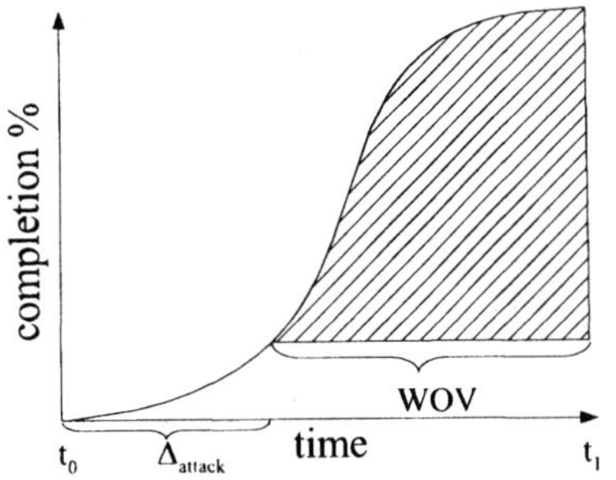

Fig. 1. Cleartext dissemination

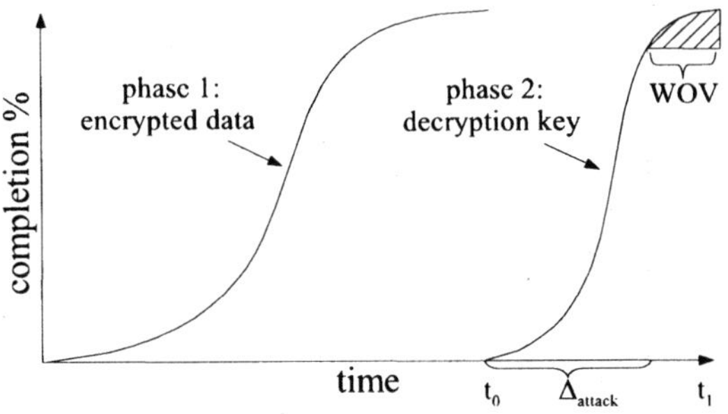

Fig. 2. Two-Phase dissemination

fixed size decryption key. More formally, our general applicable protocol is specified as follows. Let d be a message that a source s wants to disseminate to a set of clients. In the first phase, s generates a symmetrical encryption key K and a unique identifier UID, and broadcasts a ⟨ENVELOPE, UID, K(d)⟩ message, signed by s. Upon receipt and verification of the signature, a client stores this message locally. In the second phase, s broadcasts ⟨KEY, UID, K⟩ to all clients. Upon receipt, clients can decrypt the ENVELOPE message. The UID contains a version number so clients can distinguish newer from older versions of patches.

If t_0 is the time when the first client receives a patch p, if t_1 is the time when the last client receives p, and if Δ_{attack} is the time needed by an attacker to reverse engineer p into a workable exploit, then, as illustrated in Fig. 1, the WOV opens at time $t_0 + \Delta_{\mathrm{attack}}$ and closes at time t_1. In traditional dissemination the size of the patch determines the length of the WOV. The advantage of the two-phase dissemination scheme is, as illustrated in Fig. 2, that the WOV only depends on phase two. That is, the dissemination of a small fixed size decryption key.

The time between the two phases is a policy decision. One extreme is to do the second phase immediately when the first phase completes. This would require a mechanism by which the patcher detects when all recipients have received the encrypted patch and are ready to install it. However, this is not a viable approach as disconnected clients can delay the completion arbitrarily. More alarmingly, malicious clients can prevent the second phase for happening by never acknowledging receipt. A better scheme is to start phase two some configured time after phase one is initiated. For instance, in the Windows Update system, a 24 hour time period between the phases would allow at least 80% of the clients to receive the encrypted patch [6].

5 Secure Dissemination Overlay

As mentioned before, *FirePatch* employs a network of mirrors to increase the patcher's upload capacity and to fight DoS attacks. The mirrors form a superpeer-like network structure [15] to which clients connect. Thus, the patcher

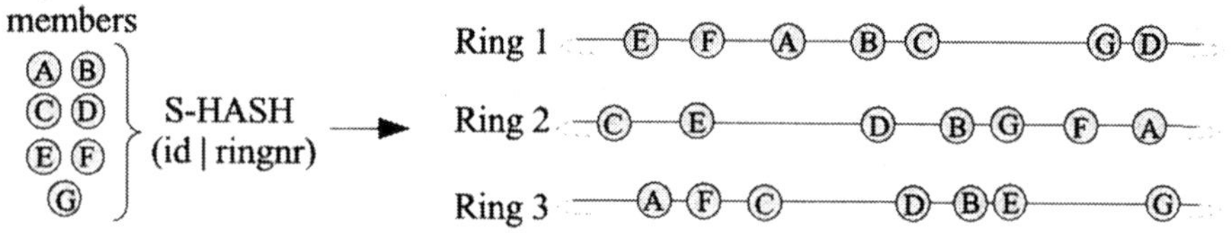

Fig. 3. *Fireflies* membership with three rings

does not broadcast patches and keys directly to the clients, but instead to the collection of mirrors. The mirrors forward this information to all clients that are currently connected to the Internet, and provides it on demand to clients that connect to the Internet at a later time. Each client connects to a minimum number of mirrors such that at least one mirror is correct with high probability.

5.1 Mirror Mesh

An attacker might be in control of one or more mirrors. Such Byzantine mirrors are not bound to any overlay protocol and might display arbitrary and malicious behavior. Although cryptographic signatures prevent Byzantine mirrors from modifying or inserting patches, they can still mount a DoS attack by neglecting to forward data. Our approach to fight such attacks is to ensure that the dissemination overlay contains sufficient link redundancy and link diversity such that, with high probability, there exists at least one path of only correct mirrors from the patcher to each correct mirror and to each correct client.

For this we build on *Fireflies* [8]—our intrusion-tolerant membership protocol that provides to each member a reasonably current view of all live members. *Fireflies* ensures, with high probability, that malicious members cannot keep crashed members in the view of live members, or live members out of these views. For this, members monitor one another and issue *accusations* (failure notices) whenever a member is suspected to have failed. If a member is falsely accused, it has the opportunity to issue an *rebuttal* before it is removed from the views of correct members.

Accusations and rebuttals are disseminated to all member using a *secure broadcast channel*, which is constructed by organizing the members in k circular address spaces, or rings. Each ring is a pseudo-random permutation of the membership list and is calculated deterministically from the secure hash of the members' identities in combination with a ring identifier. A ring defines successor and predecessor relationships between the members such that each member has k successors and k predecessors. As an example, consider the seven members A through G in Fig. 3 hashed into three rings. The successors of C are $\{G, E, D\}$, and its predecessors are $\{B, A, F\}$. Each member exchanges notes and accusations with its successor in each ring.

The number of rings, k, determines the probability that the resulting submesh of correct members is connected such that Byzantine members cannot successfully execute omission attacks. It turns out that k grows logarithmically with the number of members [8]. For instance, if one-third of the members are Byzantine in a network of 1000 members, then k should be at least 14. With $1,000,000$ members, k should be at least 19.

5.2 Data Dissemination

FirePatch reliably disseminates patches by an efficient flooding protocol on the neighbor mesh created by *Fireflies*, much like ChainSaw [11]. First, a patch is split into a set of fixed sized blocks that are individually signed by the patcher and disseminated through the mesh. A mirror m_1, upon receiving block b, notifies all of its neighbors by sending them a ⟨BLOCK-NOTIFY, block-id⟩ message, where block-id is the signature of the block. Upon receiving this notification, m_2 can request this block by issuing a ⟨BLOCK-REQUEST, block-id⟩ message to m_1. m_1 then responds with a ⟨BLOCK, block⟩ message containing the requested block. Upon receiving the block, m_2 verifies the signature and stores the block locally. m_2 then notifies all its neighbors, except m_1 that it has received the block.

To enable clients to reassemble the patch from the blocks, the patcher disseminates a signed ⟨PATCH, UID, block-id list⟩ message, where UID is the unique patch identifier. Upon receiving such a message for the first time, a mirror forwards it immediately to all its neighbors except the neighbor from which the message was received. Finally, after some time, the patcher reveals the content of the patch by disseminating a signed ⟨KEY, UID, key⟩ message. These messages are disseminated similarly to the BLOCK-NOTIFY and PATCH messages. Figure 4 summarizes the *FirePatch* dissemination protocol.

To run this protocol, each mirror maintains a TCP connection to each of its neighbors. Mirrors strive to keep all connections busy downloading missing blocks while trying to minimize the number of redundant blocks that they both send and receive. For this we use two techniques. The first technique is to randomize the order in which BLOCK-NOTIFICATION messages are sent. This helps disperse the block randomly upstream from the patcher such that mirrors are able to request different blocks from different neighbors. This is particularly important during the initial phase of the dissemination. The second technique is to schedule block requests randomly such that a request for the same block is not made to more than one neighbor unless some timeout has expired and the other connections are not busy.

5.3 Disconnected Nodes

A problem with the approach so far is that not all clients may be up and connected to the Internet at the time that the patch is being disseminated. When at some later time such a client connects to the Internet, it is vulnerable as hackers have now had ample time to create an exploit and may be lurking on such clients. We thus need a protocol for connecting clients to get the patches it is missing without being compromised.

```
on receive ⟨BLOCK, block⟩ from m:
  blockid = block.signature
  if  blockid in missingBlocks:
    blockStore.add(blockid, block)
    missingBlocks.remove(blockid)
    for patch in patches:
      if patch.completed(): decrypt_and_install(patch)
    for n in neighbors:
      if n != m: send ⟨BLOCK-NOTIFY, blockid⟩ to n
  schedule_next_request(m)

on receive ⟨BLOCK-NOTIFY, blockid⟩ from m:
  if not blockid in blockStore: availableBlocks[m].add(blockid)

on receive ⟨BLOCK-REQUEST, blockid⟩ from m:
  if blockid in blockStore:
      send ⟨BLOCK, blockStore[blockid]⟩ to m

on receive ⟨PATCH, uid, blockList⟩ from m:
   if not uid in patches:
     patches.add(uid, blockList)
     for blockid in blockList: missingBlocks.add(blockid)
     for n in neighbors:
       if n != m: send ⟨PATCH, uid, blockList⟩ to n

on receive ⟨KEY, uid, key⟩ from m:
   patches[uid].setKey(key)
   if patches[uid].completed(): decrypt_and_install(patches[uid])
   for n in neighbors:
       if n != m: send ⟨KEY, uid, key⟩ to n

proc schedule_next_request(m)
  queue = randomize( missingBlocks ∩ availableBlocks[m])
  next_request = queue[0]
  for blockid in queue:
    if blockid not requested: next_request = blockid; break
  send ⟨BLOCK-REQUEST, next_request⟩ to m
```

Fig. 4. Pseudo-code for the *FirePatch* dissemination protocol

Our approach is as follows. When running, clients store the list of all mirrors (disseminated by the patcher just like patches and keys) on disk. When a client connects, a local firewall is initially configured to block all network traffic except certain message formats to and from the mirrors selected at random from the stored list. A client connects to a minimum number of mirrors in order to make it likely that at least one of the mirrors is correct . If all clients connect to all mirrors an unreasonable load might ensue on the mirrors.

First, the client sends a ⟨RECOVER, v⟩ message to each selected mirror, where v is the version of the latest installed patch at the client. Each mirror responds with notifications of the missing patches as in the protocol described above for connected clients, and the client proceeds to download the necessary patches and keys while all other messages are ignored and dropped. When completed, the client reconfigures its firewall to allow arbitrary communication.

6 Evaluation

Our prototype implementation[5] is written in Python and has been evaluated on a local cluster consisting of 36 3.2 GHz Intel Prescott 64 machines with 2 GB of RAM. The machines were connected by a 1 Gbit Ethernet network. We ran 10 mirrors on each machine for a total 360 mirrors. In addition, one dedicated machine was used to run a mirror that acted as the patcher. To limit the effect of network congestion, the outbound bandwidth of each agent was, using a hierarchical token bucket, limited to a rate of 500 kB/s with a max burst size of 1 MB. In addition, each agent divided its total bandwidth equally amongst all its active neighbors. In all experiments we used $k = 9$ rings, resulting in each mirror having 18 neighbors. Hence, bandwidth between two mirrors was approximately 28 kB/s.

In our first experiment we measured the effect of the block size on the end-to-end latency. Our experiment consisted of injecting 2 MB patches with block sizes varying between 4 kB and 2 MB. We used a 240 second delay between consecutive patches to prevent interference. A 20 B decryption key was released after a fixed delay of 180 seconds after each patch. To achieve acceptable 95% confidence intervals, we repeated each experiment 20 times.

Figure 5 shows the resulting average total dissemination time[6]. As can be seen from the figure, the block size has a significant impact on the end-to-end latency. As expected, the messaging overhead increases with the number of blocks. Also, as the block size increases, the efficiency of our randomized block selection algorithm decreases, producing more duplicate messages and hence a longer dissemination time. We observe that in our set-up the optimal block size is between 16 kB and 64 kB.

Next we tested *FirePatch*'s resilience to attacks from an increasing fraction of Byzantine mirrors in both phase-one and in phase-two of our dissemination protocol. We fixed the block size at 32 kB and repeated the previous experiment with the fractions of Byzantine mirrors varying between 0% and 20%. Each Byzantine mirror was configured to execute omission attacks by notifying block arrivals but not responding to block requests from neighbors. Byzantine mirrors were chosen randomly from the list of all mirrors. In all our experiments Byzantine mirrors were not able to prevent correct mirrors from completing either phase-one or phase-two.

[5] The source code is available on `http://sourceforge.net/projects/fireflies`.

[6] The measured 95% confidence intervals were small and are left out for clarity.

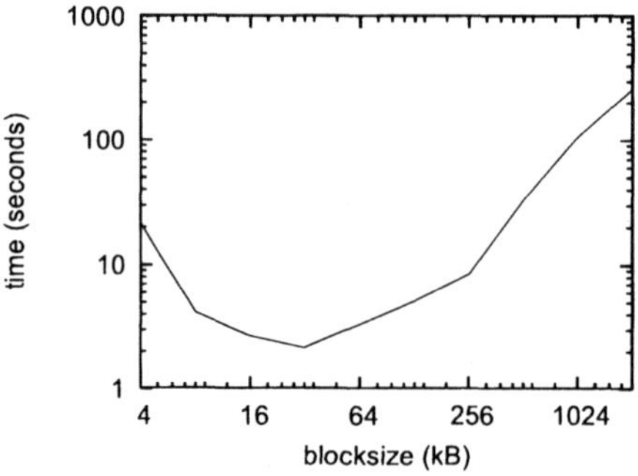

Fig. 5. Effect of the block size on dissemination

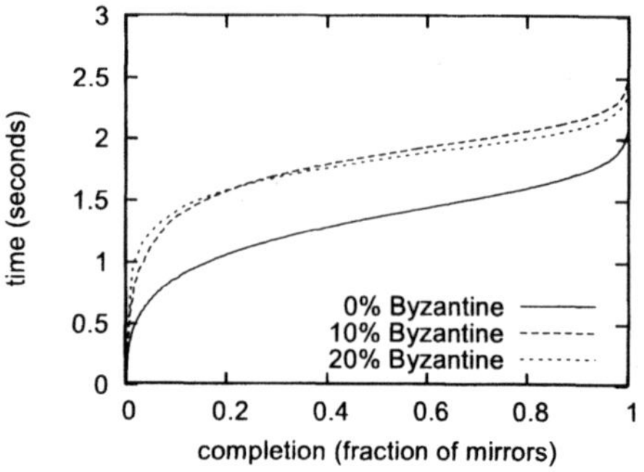

Fig. 6. Time to complete phase-one

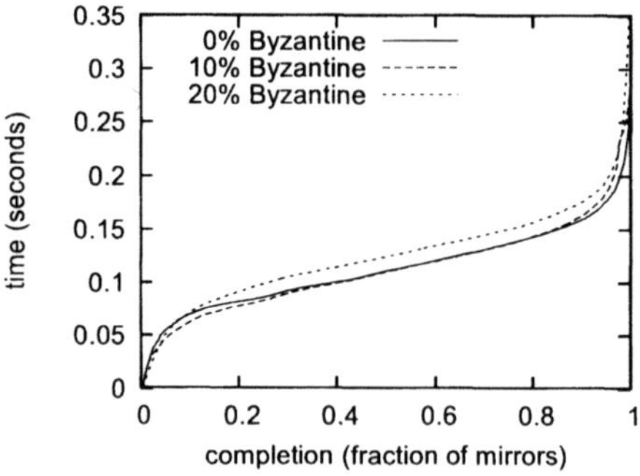

Fig. 7. Time to complete phase-two

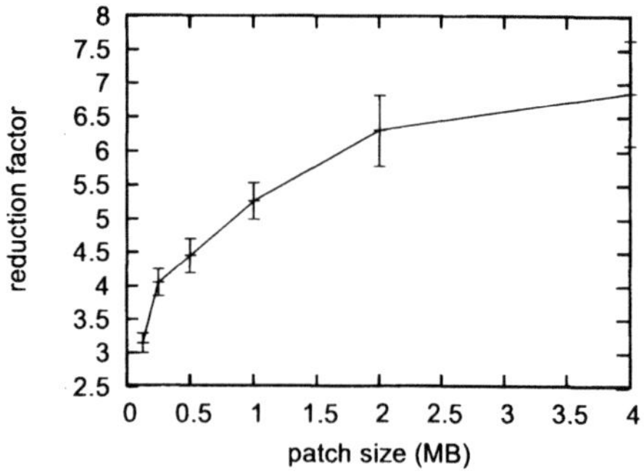

Fig. 8. WOV reduction due to two-phase dissemination

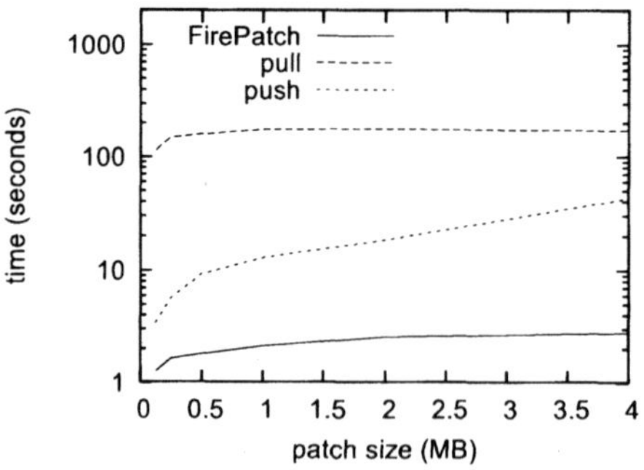

Fig. 9. Comparing naïve pull and push

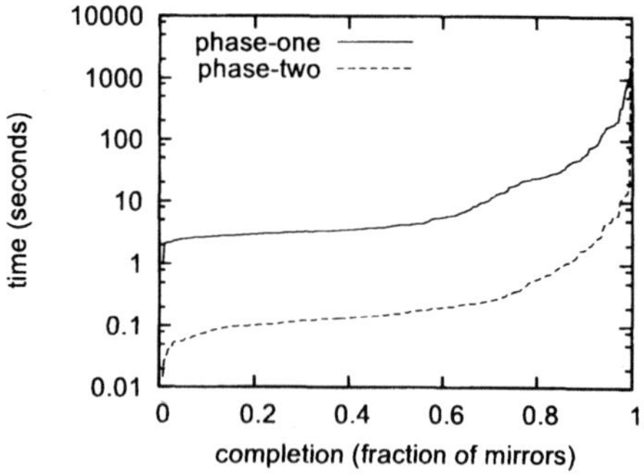

Fig. 10. Dissemination on PlanetLab

Figure 6 shows the resulting average time for an increasing fraction of the mirrors to complete phase-one of our protocol. As expected, the graph displays a clear gossip-like behavior by starting slow, speeding up, then ending slow. When under attack by 20% of the mirrors, we observed a delay of less than 1 second compared to when all mirrors were correct. This indicates that *FirePatch* is highly resilient to omission attacks. Note that for larger systems we expect the dissemination time to grow logarithmically in the number of mirrors because the diameter of the *Fireflies* mesh grows logarithmically.

Figure 7 shows a similar graph of the completion of phase-two. As expected, the dissemination of the smaller decryption key in phase-two is significantly faster than for the larger sized patch in phase-one. Also, omission attacks had little impact. Figure 8 shows the reduction of the WOV size due to our two-phase dissemination protocol when the patch size varies between 128 kB and 4 MB.

Next we compare our phase-one dissemination protocol with naïve push and pull mechanisms. For the push mechanism we modified our code such that mirrors transmitted the blocks instead of block notifications. To implement a pull mechanism we modified our block request scheduler such that it would not make more than one request for a block unless a static timeout of 20 seconds had expired. The performance of pull, push, and *FirePatch* dissemination for varying patch sizes is shown in Fig. 9.

To test *FirePatch* in a more realistic environment, we deployed our code on PlanetLab[7]. We set the fraction of Byzantine mirrors to 20% and removed the bandwidth limitation. Figure 10 shows the result of one experiment that we ran on the 30th of October 2006 where a 2 MB patch and a 20 B key were disseminated in a mesh of 279 mirrors. In this particular setup 80% of the mirrors had completed phase-one within 24 seconds and phase-two within 0.58 seconds. However, we also observed that a few mirrors used a significantly longer time. It turned out that these mirrors had become unresponsive due to heavy CPU and network load from other projects. This was particularly noticeable during phase-two where all but two mirrors received the key within 19 seconds. The last two mirrors became unresponsive between the phases but reintegrated themselves into the mesh and completed phase-two one hour later. Because each client connects to multiple mirrors, such outages will not prevent clients from receiving updates.

7 Conclusion

We have investigated a secure approach to distribute software security updates in a partially connected Internet environment, combining encryption, replication, and sandboxing upon reconnection of disconnected computers. Our findings are intuitive, but are highly effective.

We have demonstrated that an intrusion-tolerant overlay substrate can be used to scale the system without adding trusted mirrors. Notice that our two-phase dissemination protocol has wide and general applicability. We conjecture that the protocol can be incorporated easily into existing large-scale software patching schemes. It also enables secure peer-to-peer distribution of virus definition files.

[7] `http://www.planet-lab.org/`

References

1. William A. Arbaugh, William L. Fithen, and John McHugh. Windows of Vulnerability: A case study analysis. *IEEE Computer*, 33(12):52–59, 2000.
2. Hilary K. Browne, William A. Arbaugh, John McHugh, and William L. Fithen. A trend analysis of exploitations. In *Proc. of the 2001 IEEE Symp. on Security and Privacy*, pages 214–229, 2001.
3. Miguel Castro, Peter Druschel, Anne-Marie Kermarrec, Animesh Nandi, Antony Rowstron, and Atul Singh. SplitStream: High-bandwidth multicast in cooperative environments. In *Proc. of the 19th ACM Symp. on Operating Systems Principles*, pages 298–313, 2003.
4. Manuel Costa, Jon Crowcroft, Miguel Castro, Antony Rowstron, Lidong Zhou, Lintao Zhang, and Paul Barham. Vigilante: End-to-end containment of Internet worms. In *Proc. of the 20th ACM Symp. on Operating Systems Principles*, pages 133–147, 2005.
5. Halvar Flake. Structural comparison of executable objects. In *Proc. of the 2004 Conf. on Detection of Intrusions and Malware & Vulnerability Assessment*, Lecture Notes in Informatics, pages 161–173, 2004.
6. Christos Gkantsidis, Thomas Karagiannis, Pablo Rodriguez, and Milan Vojnović. Planet scale software updates. *ACM SIGCOMM Computer Communication Review*, 36(4):423–434, 2006.
7. Maya Haridasan and Robbert van Renesse. Defense against intrusion in a live streaming multicast system. In *Proc. of the 6th IEEE Int. Conf. on Peer-to-Peer Computing*, pages 185–192, 2006.
8. Håvard Johansen, André Allavena, and Robbert van Renesse. Fireflies: Scalable support for intrusion-tolerant network overlays. In *Proc. of the 1th ACM Eurosys*, pages 3–13, 2006.
9. Ashlesha Joshi, Samuel T. King, George W. Dunlap, and Peter M. Chen. Detecting past and present intrusions through vulnerability-specific predicates. In *Proc. of the 20th ACM Symp. on Operating Systems Principles*, pages 91–104, 2005.
10. Dejan Kostić, Adolfo Rodriguez, Jeannie Albrecht, and Amin Vahdat. Bullet: High bandwidth data dissemination using an overlay mesh. In *Proc. of the 19th ACM Symp. on Operating Systems Principles*, pages 282–297, 2003.
11. Vinay S. Pai, Kapil Kumar, Karthik Tamilmani, Vinay Sambamurthy, and Alexander E. Mohr. Chainsaw: Eliminating trees from overlay multicast. In *Proc. of the 4th Int. Workshop on Peer-to-Peer Systems*, volume 3640 of *Lecture Notes in Computer Science*, pages 127–140, 2005.
12. Brad Stone. A lively market, legal and not, for software bugs. *The New York Times*, online, January 30 2007. `http://www.nytimes.com/2007/01/30/technology/30bugs.html`.
13. Michael Vrable, Justin Ma, Jay Chen, David Moore, Erik Vandekieft, Alex C. Snoeren, Geoffrey M. Voelker, and Stefan Savage. Scalability, fidelity, and containment in the Potemkin virtual honeyfarm. In *Proc. of the 20th ACM Symp. on Operating Systems Principles*, pages 148–162, 2005.
14. Helen J. Wang, Chuanxiong Guo, Daniel R. Simon, and Alf Zugenmaier. Shield: vulnerability-driven network filters for preventing known vulnerability exploits. In *Proc. of the 2004 Conf. on Applications, Technologies, Architectures, and Protocols for Computer Communications*, pages 193–204, 2004.
15. Beverly Yang and Hector Garcia-Molina. Designing a super-peer network. In *Proc. of the 19th IEEE Int. Conf. on Data Engineering*, pages 49–60, 2003.

An Experimental Evaluation of Multi-key Strategies for Data Outsourcing

E. Damiani[1], S. De Capitani di Vimercati[1], S. Foresti[1], S. Jajodia[2], S. Paraboschi[3], and P. Samarati[1]

[1] Università degli Studi di Milano, 26013 Crema - Italy {damiani,decapita,foresti,samarati}@dti.unimi.it
[2] George Mason University, Fairfax, VA 22030-4444 jajodia@gmu.edu
[3] Università di Bergamo, 24044 Dalmine - Italy parabosc@unibg.it

Abstract. Data outsourcing is emerging today as a successful solution for organizations looking for a cost-effective way to make their data available for on-line querying. To protect outsourced data from unauthorized accesses, even from the (honest but curious) host server, data are encrypted and indexes associated with them enable the server to execute queries without the need of accessing cleartext. Current solutions consider the whole database as encrypted with a *single key* known only to the data owner, which therefore has to be kept involved in the query execution process. In this paper, we propose different *multi-key data encryption* strategies for enforcing access privileges. Our strategies exploit different keys, which are distributed to the users, corresponding to the different authorizations. We then present some experiments evaluating the quality of the proposed strategies with respect to the amount of cryptographic information to be produced and maintained.

1 Introduction

Data outsourcing has become increasingly popular in recent years. Its intended purpose is enabling data owners to outsource distribution of data on the open Net to *service providers* following a "database-as-a-service" paradigm. Data outsourcing promises higher availability and more effective disaster protection than in-house operations. However, since data owners physically release their information to service providers, data confidentiality and even integrity may be put at risk. Methods that protect outsourced data from unauthorized accesses are therefore needed, and data encryption techniques together with indexes associated with the data have been often used for this purpose [4, 7, 9, 10]. These techniques guarantee data confidentiality, even from (honest but curious) service providers, enabling providers to execute queries without accessing cleartext data.

Although different security aspects of the outsourced scenario have been addressed (e.g., integrity [11], inference exposure [6], physical security measures [5]), most current solutions still consider the whole database as encrypted with a single key known only to the data owner, which therefore has to be

Please use the following format when citing this chapter:

Damiani, E., De Capitani di Vimercati, S., Foresti, S., Jajodia, S., Paraboschi, S., and Samarati, P., 2007, in IFIP International Federation for Information Processing, Volume 232, New Approaches for Security, Privacy and Trust in Complex Environments, eds. Venter, H., Eloff, M., Labuschagne, L., Eloff, J., von Solms, R., (Boston: Springer), pp. 385–396 kept involved in the query execution process. This is indeed a severe limitation, since a desirable feature of database outsourcing is a full delegation of query management to the hosting environment. In this paper, we put forward the idea of using a multi-key solution for enforcing different access privileges for different users without necessarily involving the data owner in the query processing. To this purpose, we propose to use different *multi-key data encryption* strategies that can be used for implementing access control. We then evaluate the quality of these strategies in terms of the amount of cryptographic information that needs to be stored and managed. We illustrate some experimental results, which clearly demonstrate that the use of the techniques described in the paper offers significant savings in the amount of access control information to be maintained, with a considerable increase in overall system efficiency.

The remainder of this paper is organized as follows. Section 2 describes the different approaches that can be applied to enforce selective access in an outsourced scenario. Section 3 describes the experimental setup. Section 4 presents our experiments and discusses the quality of the different approaches in terms of the amount of (public) information that needs to be managed by the system to enforce the access control policies. Section 5 concludes the paper.

2 Access Control in the Outsourced Scenario

Given a system with a set $\mathcal{U}$ of users and a set $\mathcal{T}$ of resources, the policies regulating the accesses of users on resources can be modeled via the traditional *access matrix* $\mathcal{A}$ with $|\mathcal{U}|$ rows, one for each user, and $|\mathcal{T}|$ columns, one for each resource.

For simplicity and to strengthen the relationship with previous proposals on the "database-as-a-service" paradigm, in this paper we consider tuples as resources, allowing row level access control enforcement. Note, however, that the technique presented in this paper is applicable to many scenarios, since it can support authorization at different granularity (e.g, table, column, row, or cell) and it can be used to manage access to resources stored outside the DBMS (e.g., a file service hosted by a third party).

Each entry $\mathcal{A}[\mathtt{u},\mathtt{t}]$ in the matrix contains the list of actions that user u is authorized to execute over resource t. Since we take into consideration `read` actions only, each entry in the access matrix can simply assume two values: $\mathcal{A}[\mathtt{u},\mathtt{t}]=1$ if u can read t; 0 otherwise. Figure 1 reports an example of access matrix for a system with 7 tuples ($\mathtt{t}_1 \ldots \mathtt{t}_7$) and 5 users (**A**, **B**, **C**, **D**, and **E**). Given an access matrix $\mathcal{A}$, $\mathit{acl}_\mathtt{t}$ denotes the access control list for tuple t, that is, the set of users that can read t; $\mathit{cap}_\mathtt{u}$ denotes the capability list of user u, that is, the set of resources u can read. For instance, with reference to Fig. 1, $\mathit{acl}_{\mathtt{t}_1}=\{\mathbf{A},\mathbf{B},\mathbf{C}\}$ and $\mathit{cap}_\mathbf{A}=\{\mathtt{t}_1,\mathtt{t}_2,\mathtt{t}_3,\mathtt{t}_5,\mathtt{t}_7\}$.

In the above scenario, the enforcement of access control policies cannot be delegated to the remote server, which is not trusted for accessing neither database content nor the access control policies themselves. To tackle this issue,

	t_1	t_2	t_3	t_4	t_5	t_6	t_7
A	1	1	1	0	1	0	1
B	1	1	1	0	1	1	1
C	1	0	0	1	1	1	1
D	0	1	0	1	1	1	0
E	0	0	1	1	0	1	0

Fig. 1. An example of access matrix

we propose to enforce access control by using *multi-key* techniques [3, 13–15]. Basically, these techniques consist in using different keys for encrypting data and in giving to each user a *key set* such that she can access all and only the resources she is authorized to access.

A straightforward solution for adopting these approaches consists in encrypting each tuple t with a different key and communicating to each user u the set of keys used to encrypt the tuples in cap_u. This solution correctly implements the policy represented by access matrix $\mathcal{A}$, but it is expensive to manage, due to the high number of keys that users are required to manage. We therefore combine a multi-key technique together with *key derivation methods* [1,2,8,12]. These methods operate on a hierarchy where each of its elements is associated with a key; the keys of lower-level elements can be computed based on the keys of their predecessors and on information publicly available. In our context, these methods permit to reduce the number of keys that need to be directly communicated to each user. Among the different key derivation methods proposed in the literature, Atallah's method [2] is well adapted to our context. This method is based on the concept of *token*, which is defined as follows. Given two keys, k_i and k_j, and a public label l_j associated with k_j, a token from k_i to k_j is defined as $T_{i\,j}=k_j \oplus h(k_i,l_j)$, where $\oplus$ is the n-ary *xor* operator and h is a secure hash function. Given $T_{i\,j}$, any user from the knowledge of k_i and with access to public label l_j can compute (derive) k_j. All tokens $T_{i\,j}$ in the system are stored in a *public catalog*. The combination of a multi-key technique with this key derivation method can be performed according to different strategies, which we generically call *multi-key data encryption* strategies. Implementing these strategies involves several technicalities; for the sake of clarity, in the remainder of this section we shall outline the algorithms we have designed at the level of detail needed to carry out a comparison between the approaches.

The first and simplest strategy assigns a label and a key to each tuple $t \in \mathcal{T}$ and a key to each user $u \in \mathcal{U}$. For each entry $\mathcal{A}[u,t]$ such that $\mathcal{A}[u,t]=1$, token $T_{u\,t}$ is computed and stored in the public catalog. This strategy drastically reduces the number of keys that each user has in her key set (each user has exactly one key), but introduces a huge public catalog of tokens. For instance, with respect to the access matrix in Fig. 1, the public catalog contains 23 tokens because the access matrix contains 23 entries equal to 1. Every time user u_i has to access tuple t_j, u_i retrieves t_j, l_j, and $T_{i\,j}$ from the public catalog. Tuple t_j can then be decrypted using the key obtained computing $T_{i\,j} \oplus h(k_i,l_j)$, where

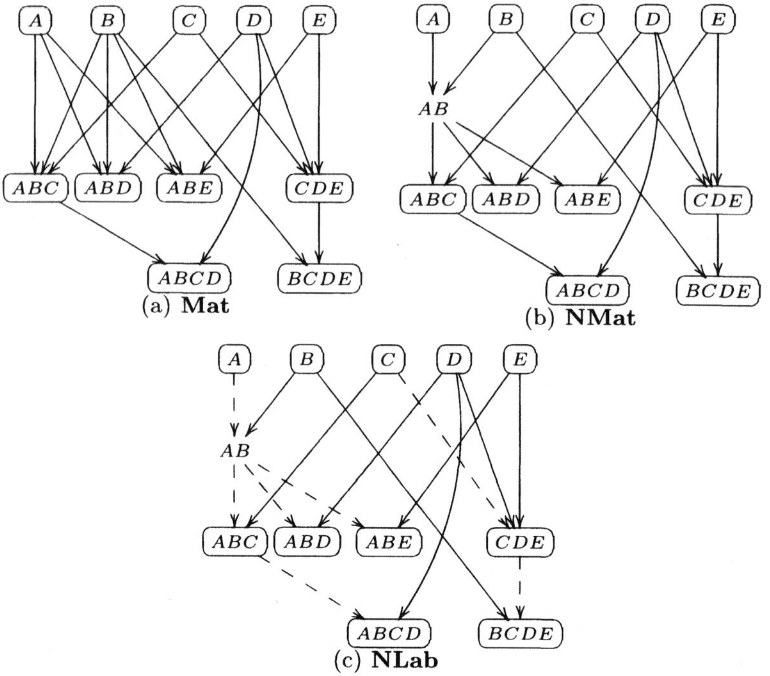

Fig. 2. Examples of UH hierarchies based on the access matrix in Fig. 1

k_i is the key assigned to user u_i. Due to the high number of tokens, we do not consider further this strategy. Instead, we propose to use other approaches described in the remainder of this section.

AM approach. The first approach we propose improves on the direct representation of the access matrix by encrypting with the same key all the tuples having the same *acl* (e.g., tuples t_1 and t_7 in Fig. 1). The reduction in the number of tokens provided by this approach depends on the number of resources that share the same access profile. In the example, the use of this strategy reduces the number of tokens to 20, because the same tokens can be used to access t_1 and t_7. To access a tuple, user u_i will have to retrieve the encrypted tuple, its label l_j (which characterizes all the tuples with the same *acl*) and token $T_{i\,j}$.

To further reduce the number of tokens in the public catalog, we propose to apply the Atallah's approach to a *user key derivation hierarchy* UH, where the elements correspond to sets of users in the system (i.e., *acls* that can be defined on $\mathcal{U}$) and the partial order is naturally induced on it by the subset containment relationship. Each element in the hierarchy has its own key, while each arc has its token in the public catalog. Each tuple is then encrypted with the key associated with the element representing its *acl*, and each user is associated with an element (and therefore a key) representing herself in the hierarchy.

Since the number of tokens in the public catalog depends on the number of arcs in the hierarchy, we need to carefully select the elements and the arcs in the hierarchy. To this purpose, we develop an algorithm that takes an access matrix as input and returns a user key derivation hierarchy as output. This hierarchy can be computed in different ways.

Mat approach. A first hierarchy-based approach consists in selecting a set M of elements, called *material*, that contains the elements representing single users and the elements corresponding to *acls* in $\mathcal{A}$. The algorithm then connects the material elements using a set of arcs (i.e., tokens) with no redundant arcs (e.g., if we consider node ABCD in Fig. 2(a), we observe that among its 6 potential ancestors, only ABC and D have an outgoing arc reaching it). Figure 2(a) represents the UH obtained by applying the **Mat** approach to the access matrix in Fig. 1. In this case the public catalog contains 16 tokens, one token for each arc in the hierarchy. As an example of key derivation, suppose that user **A** needs to read tuple t_5, which is encrypted with key k_{ABCD} (acl_{t_5}={**A**,**B**,**C**,**D**}). User **A** can use her key k_A and token $T_{A\ ABC}$ to derive key k_{ABC}, which in turn can be used together with token $T_{ABC\ ABCD}$ to derive key k_{ABCD}.

NMat approach. Another hierarchy-based approach consists in using other elements in addition to the material ones. To this purpose, our algorithm selects a set NM of elements, called *non material*, that are useful to reduce the number of tokens. Intuitively, a non material element can reduce the total number of tokens if it allows to have different paths in the hierarchy with a common node. Figure 2(b) represents the UH obtained by applying the **NMat** approach to the access matrix in Fig. 1. In this case, the public catalog contains 15 tokens.

NLab approach. A third hierarchy-based approach consists in allowing the presence of arcs in UH without a corresponding token. In this case, the hierarchy obtained by applying the **NMat** approach is modified by assigning a randomly chosen key only to *root elements*, that is, elements without incoming arcs. For each non root element, the algorithm chooses an incoming arc and computes the key of the element through a traditional key derivation method operating on trees [12]. For instance, given the arc (v_i,v_j) for element v_j, key k_j is computed by applying a predefined hash function to k_i. The remaining arcs are associated with tokens. Figure 2(c) illustrates the same hierarchy obtained with the **NMat** approach, where the arcs without a token are represented with a dashed line. In this case, the public catalog contains 8 tokens.

3 Experimental Setup

We perform some experiments aimed at assessing the quality of the different approaches in terms of the number of tokens that need to be managed. We

Category of Users	Notation	Cardinality
Team Managers	$TM_1 \quad TM_t$	t
Players	$P_1 \quad P_p$	$p = t \cdot pt$
Writers	$W_1 \quad W_w$	$w = \lceil t \ tw \rceil$
Managers of writers	$WM_1 \quad WM_m$	$m = \lceil w \ wm \rceil$
Subscribers	$S_1 \quad S_s$	s

pt: number of players of each team
tw: number of teams assigned to a writer
wm: number of writers in a group

Fig. 3. Categories of users in the system

consider a sport news database, with t *teams* of pt *players* each and s *subscribers* (i.e., team supporters). The league is also followed by a number of *writers*, each working with tw teams. The writers are grouped into sets of wm elements and one *manager* is assigned to each set. The set of users $\mathcal{U}$ is partitioned into five categories summarized in Fig. 3.

Analogously, the set of resources $\mathcal{T}$ in the database is partitioned into two subsets: *player news* $PN_1 \dots PN_p$ (tuples describing players); and *team news* $TN_1 \dots TN_t$ (tuples describing teams).
We then define two classes of authorizations. The first set contains authorizations assigned to users on the basis of the tuples that they need to access for playing their role (e.g., each team manager needs to access the team news for the teams she follows; we omit the formal description of this authorization set).

The second set of authorizations contains access rights assigned on the basis of subscribers' requests (e.g., each subscriber can choose the teams and players she wants to follow). In particular, we define two different configurations to better evaluate the scalability of the different approaches. The first configuration, denoted C_1, is characterized by a great variability in the authorization set because each subject can subscribe to whatever resource she wants to. The second configuration, denoted C_2, is instead more static because each subject cannot choose to subscribe to a single resource, but can only be associated with a predefined set of access rights, defined by the data owner. The second configuration is more similar to a real-life application, where it is required to manage subscriptions to news. The first scenario has been designed with the goal to be difficult to manage by the approaches we have designed, in order to put them to a significant test.

3.1 Configuration of Scenario C_1

In scenario C_1 the set of authorizations associated with subscribers is completely random, as well as some authorizations associated with team managers. These authorizations are formally defined as follows.

- $\mathcal{A}[TM_{2i}, TN_j] = 1, i = 1 \dots \lceil t \ 2 \rceil, j = 1 \dots t$: half team managers can access all the team news of the league.

$\mathcal{A}[TM_{2i-1}, TN_j] = 1$, $i = 1 \ldots \lceil t \;\, 2\rceil$, for each value of i, j is randomly chosen in $\{1, \ldots, t\}$: half team managers (the ones that cannot access all the team news) can access the team news of another team of the league.

$\mathcal{A}[TM_{2i-1}, PN_l] = 1$, $i = 1 \ldots \lceil t \;\, 2\rceil$, $l = ((j-1) \cdot pt + 1) \ldots (j \cdot pt)$: these team managers have also access to the player news of the same team, that is, for each i, the corresponding j is the one chosen for the previous item.

Each subscriber S_i in the system can access $f(i)$ team news, and player news of the players of the same team. Function f is a *Zipf* distribution that increases with the number s of subscribers. In our experiments, the first $s \;\, 3$ subscribers can view just a team news, $2s \;\, 9$ subscribers can access two team news, and so on. For each subscriber S_i, once computed $f(i)$, we randomly choose the team news that she can access. It is important to note here that we avoid to assign the same subscriber twice to the same team.

Each subscriber S_i in the system can access also $f(i) \cdot pt$ player news, randomly chosen from the set of player news in the system that she cannot access.

3.2 Configuration of Scenario C_2

Scenario C_2 is characterized by pre-defined sets of authorizations to which team managers and subscribers can subscribe. We define two sets for team managers, and two sets for subscribers. The two sets for team managers contain a team news and all the player news associated with the players of the considered team. The first set for subscribers contains the news of two teams together with their player news and twelve other player news; the second set contains three team news together with their player news and twelve other player news. These authorizations are formally defined as follows.

$\mathcal{A}[TM_{2i}, TN_j] = 1, i = 1 \ldots \lceil t \;\, 2\rceil$, $j = 1 \ldots t$: half team managers can access all the team news of the league.

Half team managers (the ones that cannot access all team news) can subscribe to one of the two sets defined for them.

Each subscriber S_i in the system can subscribe to one of the two sets defined for them.

Although in C_1 and C_2 authorizations are differently distributed among users and resources, their total number is nearly the same.

4 Experimental Results

The main goal of this set of experiments is that of analyzing the behavior of the different approaches for creating a key derivation hierarchy when the size of the system grows, that is, when both $\mathcal{T}$ and $\mathcal{U}$ increase. We ran experiments by varying the number t of teams from 5 to 50 and by considering the following different cases: 0, 10, 20, and 30 subscribers (s), $pt = 5$ players per team, $tw = 5$ teams followed by each writer, and $wm = 5$ writers followed by each manager.

Note that we focus our investigation more on the increase in the number of team rather than on the number of subscribers, because in this way we are able to increase at the same time the number of users and the number of resources. With 50 teams, the model creates more than 300 distinct users, in the roles of team players, team managers, and writers.

For each combination of values for t and s, we evaluate: the number of tokens in the public catalog; and the number of elements in the hierarchy, distinguishing between material and non material. We decide to measure these two parameters since they have a great impact in the access control enforcement: a huge catalog causes great key derivation costs. The number of material and non material elements in the hierarchy is also important to evaluate the quality of UH because its structure determines the number of tokens in the public catalog. The same experimental setup has been adopted in configuration C_1 and configuration C_2, where the approaches described in Sect. 2 (i.e., **AM**, **Mat**, **NMat**, and **NLab**) have been evaluated.

4.1 Number of Tokens in the Public Catalog

Figure 4(a) illustrates the number of tokens in the public catalog according to the four approaches **AM**, **Mat**, **NMat**, and **NLab** in configuration C_1, as the number of teams varies and the number of subscribers s is equal to 20. As the graph shows, there is a substantial gap between **AM** curve and the other curves. The curves **NMat** and **NLab** are very close and the gap between them is relatively constant, because in these two cases UH contains the same set of elements; the only difference is that **NLab** suppresses some tokens. By contrast, **Mat** is based on a different set of elements, which contains only material elements, and therefore UH is different from the hierarchy obtained by applying **NMat** and **NLab**.

Note that in Fig. 4(a) we consider only the case where the number of subscribers is equal to 20, because the graphs associated with all the other configurations (i.e., with a number of subscribers equal to 0, 10, and 30, respectively) exhibit an almost identical behavior. As a proof of this statement, consider, for example, the **NLab** approach: Fig. 4(b) reports the number of tokens in the public catalog according to the four different values of s in C_1, as the number of teams varies. Here, the curves have exactly the same trend and, as expected, the number of tokens increases with the number of teams in the system. We observe that **Mat**, **NMat**, and **NLab** scale well with the system size and, as expected, the best solution is obtained with the **NLab** approach. These experiments have also been performed with configuration C_2 and they confirm the considerations above-mentioned. In particular, by comparing the number of tokens in C_1 and C_2 we observe that, as expected, configuration C_2 is significantly more frugal than configuration C_1. Figure 4(c) compares the number of tokens in C_1 and C_2 when the **NLab** approach is applied and the number of subscribers is equal to 30. As the graph shows, the number of tokens, as well as the gap between the two curves, increase with the number of teams. This is because in C_2 au-

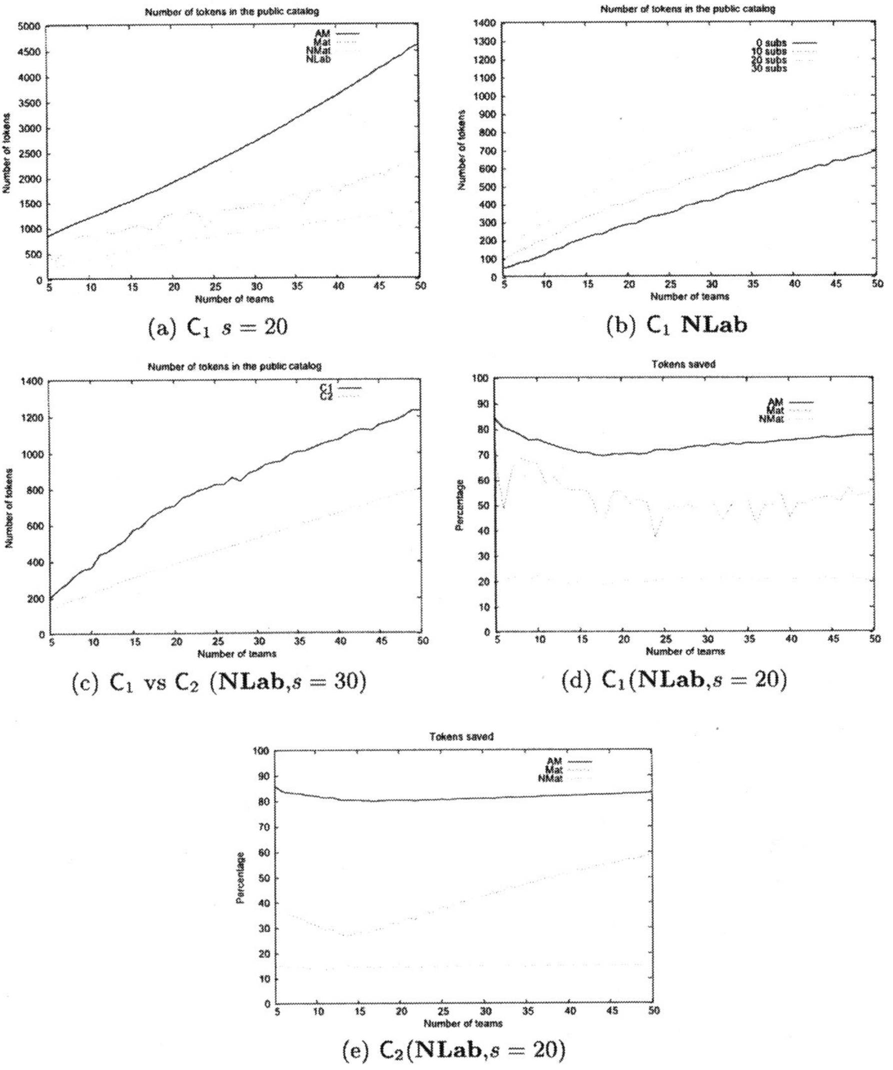

(a) C_1 $s = 20$ (b) C_1 **NLab**

(c) C_1 vs C_2 (**NLab**,$s = 30$) (d) C_1(**NLab**,$s = 20$)

(e) C_2(**NLab**,$s = 20$)

Fig. 4. Number of tokens in the public catalog (a)-(c) and percentage of tokens saved with **NLab** (d)-(e)

thorizations are less variable than in C_1 and therefore it is easier to determine a good solution in terms of the hierarchy that the algorithm is able to create.

The advantage of approach **NLab** compared with the other three approaches **AM**, **Mat**, and **NMat** is much more visible in Fig. 4(d) and Fig. 4(e), which report the percentage of tokens saved with the **NLab** approach in C_1 and C_2, respectively, and when the number of subscribers is equal to 20. As the graphs

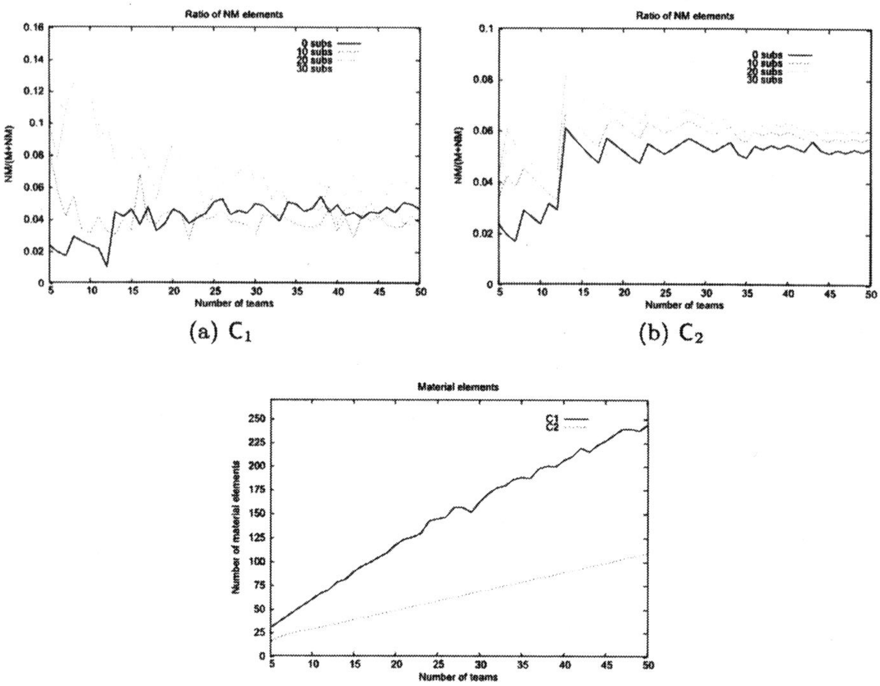

(a) C_1 (b) C_2

(c) C_1 vs C_2 ($s = 20$)

Fig. 5. Ratio of the number of non material elements in the system (a)-(b) and number of non material elements as the number of teams varies (c)

show, this percentage has a slow but growing trend with respect to the **AM** approach while it is quite constant with respect to the **NMat** approach (around 20% in C_1 and 15% in C_2). With respect to the **Mat** approach, the percentage is variable in C_1 and has a well defined increasing trend in C_2. The main reason for this is that the hierarchy in the **NMat** and **NLab** approach is exactly the same, while it may be very different in the **Mat** approach, depending on how authorizations are distributed in the system.

4.2 Number of Material and Non Material Elements in UH

Another important aspect that should be considered in evaluating and comparing the different approaches proposed is the number of elements in the final hierarchy. In particular, it is relevant the ratio between non material and material elements in the structure to better understand whether non material elements are useful to reduce the number of tokens. Figure 5(a) and Fig. 5(b) show the ratio between the number of non material elements and the total number of elements of the hierarchy obtained for C_1 and C_2, respectively, as the number of teams increases. Note that this measure is available when the hierarchy is built by applying the **NMat** or **NLab** approaches only (**AM** and **Mat** do not consider non material elements), which are characterized by the same hierarchy. By comparing the graphs in Fig. 5(a) and Fig. 5(b), we can immediately note that they are very different. Configuration C_1 presents a great variability with respect to the considered measure. More precisely, when the number of subscribers is equal to 0 or 10, the ratio increases with the number of teams; it decreases when the number of subscribers is equal to 20 or 30. This behavior is mainly due to the fact that material elements vary on the basis of the authorizations initially defined. By contrast, in configuration C_2 the considered measure follows a trend that is similar for the different values of s and this ratio decreases with the number of teams. As it is also visible from these graphs, both C_1 and C_2 present a ratio that tends to converge to a value between 4% and 6%, and the gaps among the different curves in each configuration decrease with the number of teams.

Figure 5(c) illustrates the number of material elements in C_1 and C_2, as the number of teams varies and the number of subscribers s is equal to 20 (note that the graphs that we can obtain for the other possible values of s have basically the same trend). As the graph shows, the number of material elements increases with the number of teams and the curve increases more rapidly in C_1. This is because the number of material elements in a hierarchy depends on the different *acl* values. Therefore, if the resources to be protected are characterized by similar access profiles, the corresponding *acls* will be the same and the number of material elements will be low. Since in C_1 authorizations are randomly chosen, it is more likely to have a lot of different *acl* values and consequently a lot of material elements. By contrast, in C_2 authorizations follow pre-defined patterns, and the number of different *acl* values is lower. In addition, in C_2 the number of material elements follows the same trend for all possible values of s; it varies in C_1.

5 Conclusions

In this paper, we presented different strategies for enforcing selective access in an outsourced database scenario. We then performed some experiments to evaluate their quality with respect to the amount of cryptographic information to be produced and maintained. The results of the experiments demonstrate the significant savings produced by the use of **NLab** compared to **AM** approach. We designed two experimental scenarios that, even if based on the same data, present significantly distinct access profiles; the fact that good results have been obtained in the two scenarios, and specifically in scenario C_1, is a strong indication that the savings produced by the **NLab** approach can be achieved in most applications.

Acknowledgements

This work was supported in part by the European Union under contract IST-2002-507591, by the Italian Ministry of Research Fund for Basic Research (FIRB) under project "RBNE05FKZ2", and by the Italian MIUR under project 2006099978. The work of Sushil Jajodia was partially supported by the National Science Foundation under grants CT-0627493, IIS-0242237, and IIS-0430402.

References

1. S. Akl and P. Taylor. Cryptographic solution to a problem of access control in a hierarchy. *ACM Transactions on Computer System*, **1**(3), 239–248 (August 1983).
2. M.J. Atallah, K.B. Frikken, and M. Blanton. Dynamic and efficient key management for access hierarchies. In *Proc. of the ACM CCS*, Alexandria, VA, USA (November 2005).
3. J.C. Birget, X. Zou, G. Noubir, and B. Ramamurthy. Hierarchy-based access control in distributed environments. In *Proc. of the IEEE International Conference on Communications*, Helsinki, Finland (June 2002).
4. D. Boneh, G.D. Crescenzo, R. Ostrovsky, and G. Persiano. Public-key encryption with keyword search. In *Proc. Eurocrypt 2004*, Interlaken, Switzerland (May 2004).
5. L. Bouganim and P. Pucheral. Chip-secured data access: confidential data on untrusted servers. In *Proc. of the 28th VLDB Conference*, Hong Kong, China (August 2002).
6. A. Ceselli, E. Damiani, S. De Capitani di Vimercati, S. Jajodia, S. Paraboschi, and P. Samarati. Modeling and assessing inference exposure in encrypted databases. *ACM TISSEC*, **8**(1), 119–152 (February 2005).
7. E. Damiani, S. De Capitani di Vimercati, S. Jajodia, S. Paraboschi, and P. Samarati. Balancing confidentiality and efficiency in untrusted relational DBMSs. In *Proc. of the ACM CCS*, Washington, DC, USA (October 2003).
8. E. Gudes. The design of a cryptography based secure file system. *IEEE Transactions on Software Engineering*, **6**(5), 411–420 (September 1980).
9. H. Hacigümüs, B. Iyer, and S. Mehrotra. Providing database as a service. In *Proc. of the ICDE*, San Jose, CA, USA (February 2002).
10. H. Hacigümüs, B. Iyer, S. Mehrotra, and C. Li. Executing SQL over encrypted data in the database-service-provider model. In *Proc. of the ACM SIGMOD*, Madison, Wisconsin, USA (June 2002).
11. E. Mykletun, M. Narasimha, and G. Tsudik. Authentication and integrity in outsourced database. In *Proc. of the 11th Annual Network and Distributed System Security Symposium*, San Diego, California, USA (February 2004).
12. R.S. Sandhu. Cryptographic implementation of a tree hierarchy for access control. *Information Processing Letters*, **27**(2), 95–98 (April 1988).
13. Y. Sun and K.J.R. Liu. Scalable hierarchical access control in secure group communications. In *Proc. of the IEEE Infocom*, Hong Kong, China (March 2004).
14. H. Tsai and C. Chang. A cryptographic implementation for dynamic access control in a user hierarchy. *Computer and Security*, **14**(2), 159–166 (September 1995).
15. C.K. Wong, M. Gouda, and S.S. Lam. Secure group communications using key graphs. In *Proc. of the ACM SIGCOMM*, Vancouver, British Columbia (September 1998).

Building a Distributed Semantic-aware Security Architecture

Jan Kolter, Rolf Schillinger, Günther Pernul

Department of Information Systems, University of Regensburg, D-93040 Regensburg
{jan.kolter,rolf.schillinger,guenther.pernul}@wiwi.uni-regensburg.de

Abstract. Enhancing the service-oriented architecture paradigm with semantic components is a new field of research and goal of many ongoing projects. The results lead to more powerful web applications with less development effort and better user support. While some of these advantages are without doubt novel, challenges and opportunities for the security arise. In this paper we introduce a security architecture built in a semantic service-oriented architecture. Focusing on an attribute-based access control approach, we present an access control model that facilitates semantic attribute matching and ontology mapping. Furthermore, our security architecture is capable of distributing the Policy Decision Point (PDP) from the service provider to different locations in the platform, eliminating the need of disclosing privacy-sensitive user attributes to the service provider. With respect to privacy preferences of the user and trust settings of the service provider, our approach allows for dynamically selecting a PDP. With more advanced trusted computing technology in the future it is possible to place the PDP on user side, reaching a maximum level of privacy.

1 Introduction

Over the last years information systems developed from large monolithic systems to dynamic distributed networks. Aside from performance factors, expected economic benefits are the main reasons for this development. More and more companies outsource parts of their production chain, which is only possible with flexible communication infrastructures that provide techniques for distributed processing. Such infrastructures may be based on the emerging service-oriented architecture paradigm [1] that allows the registration and discovery of remote applications which are wrapped into web services.

Along with the development of distributed systems comes the demand for a flexible security infrastructure which suits the complex concepts of the underlying distributed architecture. Apart from privacy, integrity, availability and non-repudiation, access control plays a central role in information systems. Due to the heterogeneous and open character of distributed architectures, access control is not only a major security component; it emerges to a decisive factor in developing a trustworthy architecture.

Please use the following format when citing this chapter:

Kolter, J., Schillinger, R., and Pernul, G., 2007, in IFIP International Federation for Information Processing, Volume 232, New Approaches for Security, Privacy and Trust in Complex Environments, eds. Venter, H., Eloff, M., Labuschagne, L., Eloff, J., von Solms, R., (Boston: Springer), pp. 397–408.

In this paper our focus is on the development of a distributed security architecture that facilitates flexible semantic access control. Our goal is to employ the existing attribute-based access control (ABAC) and enrich it with semantic components residing in the architecture. The architecture further provides the option of moving the privacy and trust-sensitive Policy Decision Point to a suitable location.

Our work is carried out in the project Access-eGov[1]. The project's goal is to employ Semantic Web and Peer-to-Peer technologies to build a service-oriented e-Government architecture that provides distributed registries and semantic discovery of annotated web services. An integral part of this semantic architecture is a security infrastructure, providing a flexible access control component and protecting citizens' privacy.

The remainder of this paper is organized as follows: In Sect. 2 we discuss the development and existing approaches of ABAC. We continue with introducing the concept of semantic service-oriented architectures in Sect. 3. In Sect. 4, we present a dynamic, semantic-aware security architecture, the main contribution of this paper. Finally, Sect. 5 describes the building blocks and implementation details of our prototype system. Section 6 concludes this paper and gives an outlook on our future work.

2 Attribute-based Access Control

As the attribute-based access control (ABAC) component is the key component of our security architecture, we lay out the development and give an overview of ABAC in this section. Furthermore, we pinpoint existing approaches of ABAC in service-oriented and semantically-enriched settings.

2.1 Access Control

Lopez et al. define access control as "the prevention of unauthorized use of a resource, including the prevention of use of a resource in an unauthorized manner" [2]. Generally, the question of which subject owns permissions to access a set of objects occurs whenever a number of subjects have to use a number of objects to fulfill certain tasks. From the early days of multi-user computing access control emerged to a central security issue and is still a major concern of modern distributed information systems.

A general access control architecture is introduced by Sandhu and Samarati [3]. Main actors of this architecture are a subject wanting to access an object, a database with access policies called the authorization database, and a reference monitor, that either allows or disallows a subject's access to an object, based on data from the authorization database. This architecture is generic enough to serve as basis for every modern access control system and generally follows one

[1] Supported by the European Union, IST Programme, Contract No. FP6-2004-27020

of the three following security models, namely the Discretionary Access Control (DAC) model, the Mandatory Access Control (MAC) model or the Role Based Access Control (RBAC) model [2].

All three of these access control models, however, bear shortcomings that conflict with certain requirements of modern information systems.

2.2 Development of Attribute-based Access Control

As opposed to aforementioned access control models with static mappings, concepts focusing on subjects' and objects' dynamic properties are of importance in large-scale distributed systems. Those attribute-based access control (ABAC) policies gained increasing popularity in the last years.

The basic idea of ABAC is based on the comparison of values of selected subject attributes and object properties (so called subject and object descriptors) [4]. Descriptors are a construct to "group" objects and subjects dynamically, not explicitly by an administrator but implicitly by their attribute or property values. As an example consider that access may depend on the age of a user. In this case, privilege assignments to the user cannot be done statically by a security administrator but have to be dynamically evaluated by the system based on the value of some of the attributes, e.g. "DateOfBirth". As the user gets older, his authorization state changes automatically. Access permissions might even depend on an external attribute, such as "physical location" of a user in a mobile environment.

While ABAC cannot be seen in many production environments, it has been taken up for research several times. Early work by McCollum et al. suggested a move away from discretionary access control and mandatory access control to "user attribute based access control" in the context of access to classified documents [5]. Throughout the 1990s, a number of researchers explained various forms of ABAC.

One widespread approach, the attribute certificate-based access control, encompasses work with practical implementations which are usually very close to efforts related to the X.509 / ITU-T [6] notion of attribute certificates, as presented by Farrell and Housley [7]. Most of the work in this field does not move too far away from a RBAC approach. Certified attributes are mainly used as assertions of the presence of certain roles. The main difference to RBAC is the decentralized management given by the concept of privilege management infrastructures as is for example explained in [2]. It is important to note that those approaches do usually not include the concept of the accessed objects bearing attributes. The interested reader is referred to [8, 9, 10] for a selection of research in this area.

A further reaching approach in the generic attribute-based access control propose the move away from the strong RBAC foundations, also including subject and object attributes in the access decision. Adam et al. showed that digital libraries need an access control which is not based on roles but on "qualifications and characteristics of users" [11]. The XACML specification [12] is a policy language already supporting both subject and resource attributes. This idea was also taken up in [13] with the ultimate goal of allowing access control decisions without creating rules for every single resource.

3 Semantic Service-oriented Architecture

The security infrastructure presented in Sect. 4 is built in a semantically-enriched service-oriented architecture (SOA). As we employ the semantic components of this architecture, this section points out the weaknesses of plain SOAs and introduces the idea of the Semantic Web, resulting in the Semantic SOA (SSOA) paradigm.

SOAs are considerably flexible with regards to composition of different services. The discovery of services, however, is still a tough task. The service user has to search for relevant services using keywords, if the exact location of a needed service is not known in advance. Only in rare cases the location of the service is known from the start, e.g. if it is cached from previous executions or if it is known at implementation time of a SOA-based application. Consequently, if the location of a service is neither cached nor agreed upon, the architecture has to provide means to find matching services.

This discovery process in SOAs is equivalent to information retrieval in the World Wide Web or other networks, with all its problems and proposed solutions [14]. The current state of the World Wide Web shows that the widespread mechanisms of using spiders to fetch web pages, indexing them and calculating a matching score for each query, bears many problems. Most of them are related to the issue of choosing the correct index terms. While many advanced matching scores and techniques already exist, the selection of the index terms remains a big issue. There are many vocabularies to choose from; different organizations are prone to having different vocabularies.

That is where Tim Berners-Lee's notion of the Semantic Web comes into play [15]. His idea was to annotate human-readable web resources with metadata bearing a precise semantic. This enables so called web agents to process web content automatically without any interaction with the user. Aside from metadata models and a common syntax, a main collar of Tim Berners-Lee's Semantic Web was the definition of a standardized vocabulary. Such a vocabulary can be a plain list, a taxonomy - already capable of representing a hierarchy - or an ontology which features a set of elements with complex relationships among them.

Applied to the SOA paradigm the Semantic Web approach leads to a semantic service-oriented architecture. The underlying idea is the same as already proposed by Berners-Lee. Web services are annotated using certain taxonomies or ontologies to make them machine-readable. Without this machine readability, there would be no possibility for a matching based on semantics instead of plain keywords.

4 Security Architecture

In the following we introduce our distributed security architecture based on attribute-based access control (ABAC) and the semantic service-oriented architecture paradigm (SSOA). We start this section with a short outline of the underlying system.

4.1 System Architecture

As mentioned in Sect. 1, the service-oriented architecture (SOA) is a popular technology to outsource processes to remote locations providing a standardized representation of services and common mechanisms to register and discover them. In Sect. 3 we pointed out that SOAs still need to face the issue of different local vocabularies and index terms. Tim Berners-Lee's Semantic Web targets this issue and provides means to define common, machine-readable vocabularies like taxonomies and ontologies. These concepts are employed by SSOAs to combine the advantages of SOA and the Semantic Web.

Within the scope of the project Access-eGov (see Sect. 1) we developed a SSOA for a European-wide e-Government scenario. The overall system architecture of Access-eGov is depicted in Fig. 1. The Access-eGov architecture represents a Peer-to-Peer network with physically separated service providers and a set of supporting nodes. The employment of a Peer-to-Peer network satisfies the demand for a scalable and well maintainable platform of European e-Government systems.

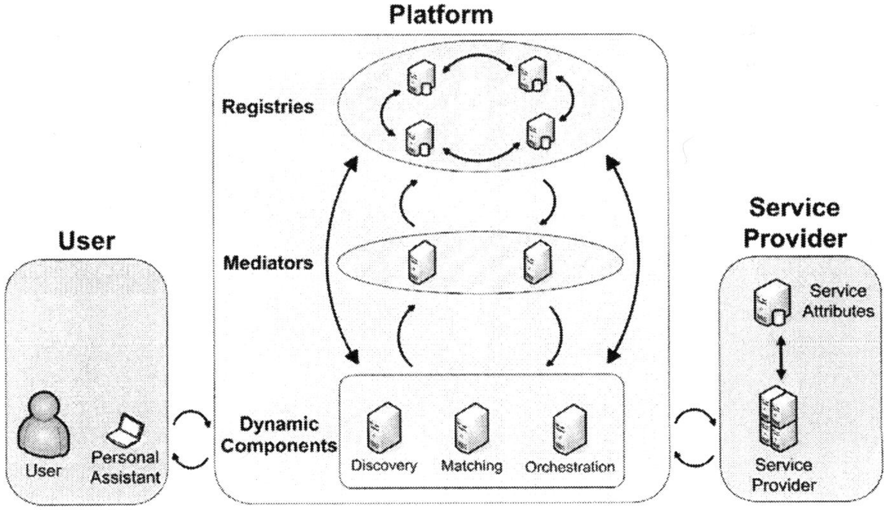

Fig. 1. Structural view of the Access-eGov architecture

Core components of the architecture are the dynamic modules for the discovery, matching and orchestration of services [16]. Supporting components of the platform are distributed storage facilities. These service and ontology repositories facilitate the semantic discovery of services. Annotated services of the service provider are registered in the service repository. The corresponding vocabulary used for the annotation is stored in the ontology repositories. For the semantic discovery the user query is matched with the service attributes using the corresponding "local" ontologies. The platform provides so-called ontology mediators that enable the mapping of ontologies. It also facilitates the composition of atomic services into complex scenarios, offering full coverage of citizens' life events.

The user communicates with the platform via a digital personal assistant. This user interface accesses the infrastructure functionality via standardized interfaces and communicates with the above mentioned components.

4.2 Security Architecture

As the Access-eGov platform deals to a high degree with personal information and brokers this information between a large base of services, special care has to be taken in the development of a security architecture. Examining a set of pilot scenarios we defined the following requirements [17]:

The most important requirement for a security architecture in the described scenario is that personal information stored and processed in the system is secured from unauthorized access. Furthermore, the architecture has to be scalable, as it has to cater for an unspecified but possibly large number of services in the system. The possibility of adding new dedicated security nodes without reconfiguration of the whole network is very important in this context. A fundamental requirement of the end users is privacy, especially since the system deals with sensitive personal data. The administrators on the other hand need a system that can be handled with low administrative overhead. If more than one entity is allowed to issue user credentials, not only the administrative overhead will be minimized but also competence conflicts among competing administration authorities can be eliminated.

Implementing these requirements, the following paragraphs will present our security architecture.

Distributed, Semantically-enriched ABAC To overcome the issue of different vocabularies we target to develop an ABAC approach that processes semantically-enriched attributes and performs a semantic mapping of attributes from different vocabularies. Figure 2 presents a picture of our security architecture. The picture resembles the already presented system architecture with a focus on the involved security components.

We build our architecture on the ABAC approach standardized by [12]. After the discovery of a queried service the user's personal assistant tries to access a service on the service provider's premises. The request is diverted to a Policy Enforcement Point (PEP) which - after consulting a Policy Decision Point

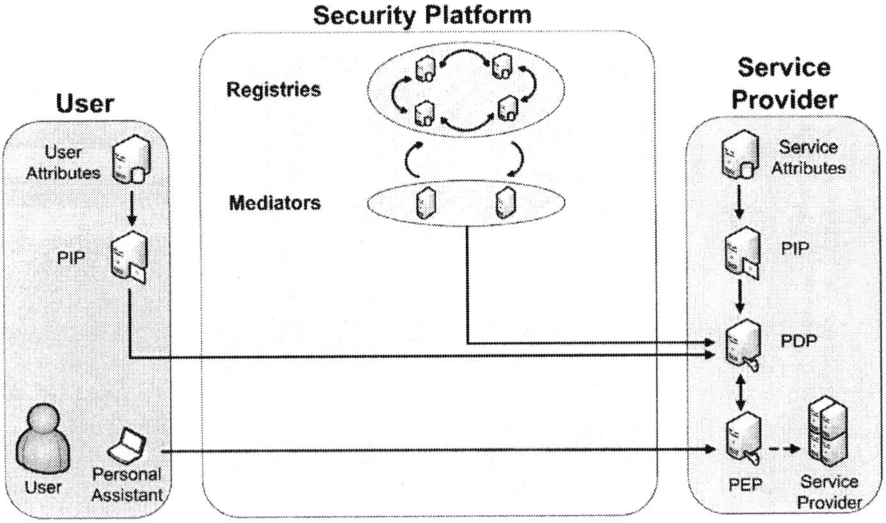

Fig. 2. Distributed security architecture with semantic components

(PDP) - grants or rejects access to the resource. To make an access decision, the PDP retrieves the service provider's access policy and collects attributes from both the user and the service, accessing the corresponding Policy Information Points (PIP). If attributes from the service requester and the provider come from domains using the same ontology, the PDP looks up the local ontology and performs a semantic matching. If attributes come from sources with different vocabularies, the PDP accesses the semantic components of the system architecture collecting the unknown vocabularies and employing ontology mediators for the semantic mapping.

An inference engine in the ABAC model, as introduced by Priebe et al. [18], is a step towards utilizing the potential of Semantic Web technologies in access control. A first notion of semantic mapping in [13] extends this approach by introducing the possibility of defining access-control relevant attributes in the Web Ontology Language (OWL). Domain independence is achieved through brokering the semantic descriptions using different ontologies. We extend this approach to encompass many different domains and their respective attribute combinations. Large-scale SSOAs like Access-eGov benefit from such a semantic attribute processing, even though the task of mapping attributes given in many different ontologies is complex.

Privacy and Trust As ABAC approaches usually deal with sensitive user attributes, we enhance our security architecture with mechanisms protecting privacy. In our architecture the Policy Decision Point (PDP) gathers all necessary attributes for an access decision. Protecting privacy, we do not consider user and service attributes to be stored in the platform. The PDP rather accesses the involved Policy Information Points (PIP) to collect only the data needed for a particular access decision. As the PDP in our generic approach resides in the domain of the service provider, this controlled disclosure of attributes guarantees that other information about the user is not transmitted in any way. This is a first step towards a privacy-sensitive ABAC.

We further this approach by introducing the notion of privacy preferences in our security architecture. A user can fine-tune his digital personal assistant with regards to the attributes he wants to transfer under which circumstances and under which constraints. Circumstances and constraints can for example involve the context of transmission: A user might rather disclose a social security number to a bank than to an e-commerce shop. Also technical aspects can influence user preferences. For certain attributes the user might only approve a transmission to trusted authorities or via a SSL encrypted connection. A candidate for a proper language for defining privacy preferences is APPEL (A P3P Preference Exchange Language) [19], designed within the scope of the Platform for Privacy Preferences project[2] (P3P).

Extending the concept of user privacy preferences, we introduce the idea of flexible locations of the PDP. As the PDP's location is generally considered to be in the service provider's domain, a distributed ABAC always faces the issue of service providers reliant on attributes for the access decision and users not willing to disclose certain attributes, even if they are solely used for the access decision.

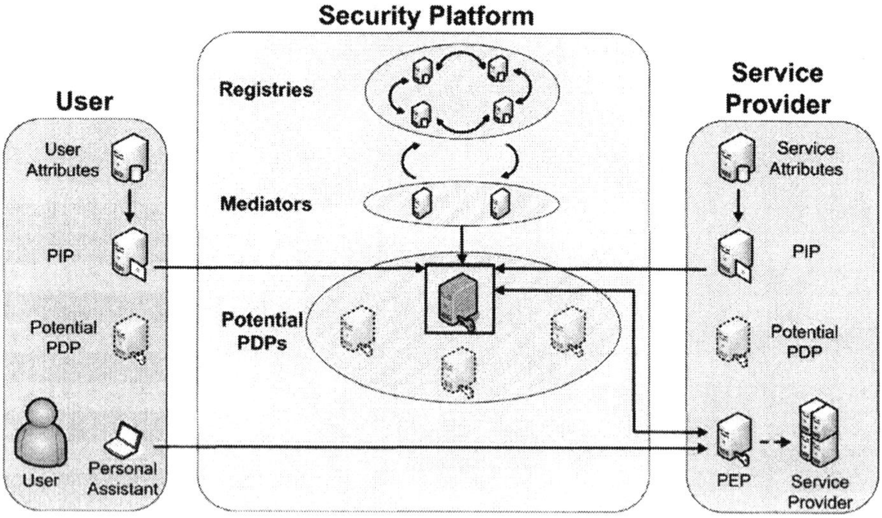

Fig. 3. Security architecture with flexible locations of the Policy Decision Point

[2] http://www.w3.org/P3P/

Our security architecture resolves this issue by giving users and service providers the possibility to choose from a set of PDPs. There are numerous potential positions for a PDP, from which we will describe three to show the extremes that limit the PDP positions. As mentioned above, the most common location of the PDP is a node of the service provider. This is the best alternative for the service provider, as it solely controls the entity deciding on the access control. However, this choice is prone to conflicting with privacy preferences of the user, as personal information needs to be handed out.

If the PDP is placed on a node between the user and the service provider, we have the classic concept of a trusted third party, both entities have to rely on. Based on user's privacy preferences and the service provider's trust settings both parties need to negotiate and agree about an acceptable position of the PDP in the platform. In this case user attributes for the access decision are transferred to a third party that does not conflict with his privacy preferences. The attributes are not disclosed to the service provider itself. As the service provider loses total control of the access decision, it needs to trust the third party to a certain level. Figure 3 depicts the scenario of a PDP between the user and the service provider.

The third and most extreme possibility is to place the PDP on the user side. This is only possible, if a correct execution of the PDP can be guaranteed to the service provider. Obviously, this is not viable with current hardware and operating systems. For this approach ideas of the Trusted Computing Group[3] initiative on hardware-secured platforms are of use. Such a platform is able to execute a PDP in a trusted environment enabling maximum privacy for the user, as no privacy-sensitive attributes are given away. On the other hand the necessary level of trust for the provider is guaranteed, as its interests are secured through the trusted platform. [20, 21, 22] present research in the trusted computing field.

It is noteworthy that a security architecture flexible enough for arbitrarily placing PDPs on platform nodes is able to handle the addition of new PDPs without reconfiguration of the whole network, resulting in improved scalability of the architecture.

5 Implentation

In the previous sections we laid out a security architecture built in the project Access-eGov (see Sect. 1). For the evaluation of our architecture we are in the process of building a prototype security system that is intended to serve as security facility of the Access-eGov platform. A lively open source community allows us to reuse existing and proven solutions like the following, which are at the same time our main building blocks.

Attribute certificates according to the ITU-T Recommendation [6] are a promising way of relating identities and attributes. [23] proposes an approach

[3] https://www.trustedcomputinggroup.org/home

to a complete attribute certificate framework. In a previous project the authors have implemented initial X.509 attribute certificate support for the widely used crypto provider bouncycastle[4] which was the main reason for choosing it for this project. The specific task of attribute certificates in the Access-eGov architecture is to link attributes to users. A user with a set of attributes and some additional metadata is what we refer to as a user profile.

The concept of the flexible placement of the Policy Decision Point (PDP) establishes the need to pass on authorization decisions between requesters and enforcers of those decisions. The idea of Single Sign On (SSO) ideally fits to this concept of distribution, as in SSO models the entity doing the access control decision (the PDP) and the entity making use of the result of that decision (the Policy Enforcement Point) are not identical as well. The Security Assertion Markup Language (SAML) [24], used in many SSO projects, is our choice for the task of passing the authorization decisions between the nodes in our platform.

Before even being able to pass SSO tokens around, the system first needs to arrive at an access control decision. As previously mentioned, our architecture partially follows the XACML specification [12]. For this reason, it is a logical choice to use XACML as the language for our authorization requests and access control results.

It is not necessary to reinvent ontologies for semantic service-oriented architectures, because there is a number of promising projects in this area. After a careful evaluation and selection process, we picked the Web Service Modeling Ontology (WSMO) [25], including WSMO's ontology language WSML, for semantically describing our services and the Web Service Execution Environment (WSMX)[5] as the underlying technology platform. While there are very good reasons for choosing WSMO and WMSX, neither one has any special preparations for security concepts. Therefore the Access-eGov project will extend WSMX and to a certain extent WSMO to be able to accommodate our security infrastructure.

6 Conclusions

Due to the distributed character of modern information systems the requirements of a suitable security architecture have changed significantly. Modern distributed architectures favor security concepts focusing on dynamic attributes rather than static information. Furthermore, users' privacy concerns move to the center of attention, as users are not willing to pass personal information to every service provider.

In this paper we presented a distributed security architecture in a semantic service-oriented architecture (SSOA) focusing on dynamic access control. We built the access control component upon the existing attribute-based access

[4] http://www.bouncycastle.org

[5] http://www.wsmx.org

control model. In order to overcome the issue of diverging attribute vocabularies in a distributed environment, we integrated semantic components of the underlying SSOA for semantic attribute matching and the mapping of different ontologies. Furthermore, our approach facilitates the movement of the Policy Decision Point (PDP) from the service provider to a trusted location in the architecture. Based on the user's privacy preferences and the service provider's trust settings a PDP can be chosen dynamically.

Future work will involve ways to express and edit privacy preferences on user side as well as trust settings of the service provider. We further want to pursue the technical possibility of creating a trusted environment on user side in order to move the PDP to the user, the ultimate privacy solution.

Acknowledgment

The work reported in this paper is done within the Access-eGov project which is funded by the European Union under the Sixth Framework Program (Contract No. FP6-2004-27020). We would like to thank our project partners for helpful comments and stimulating discussions.

References

1. MacKenzie, C. M. and Laskey, K. and McCabe, F. and Brown, P. F. and Metz, R. Reference Model for Service Oriented Architecture 1.0. *OASIS Standard*, October 2006.
2. J. Lopez, R. Oppliger, and G. Pernul. Authentication and Authorization Infrastructures (AAIs): A Comparative Survey. *Computers & Security*, 23(7):578–590, 2004.
3. R. Sandhu and P. Samarati. Access Control: Principle and Practice. *Communications Magazine, IEEE*, 32(9):40–48, 1994.
4. E.B. Fernandez and G. Pernul. Patterns for Session-Based Access Control. In *Proc. of the Pattern Languages of Programming conference (PLoP '06)*, October 2006.
5. C.J. McCollum, J.R. Messing, and L. Notargiacomo. Beyond the Pale of MAC and DAC - Defining New Forms of Access Control. In *IEEE Symposium on Security and Privacy*, pages 190–200, 1990.
6. ITU-T Recommendation. X.509: The Directory – Public Key and Attribute Certificate Frameworks, March 2000.
7. S. Farrell and R. Housley. RFC3281: An Internet Attribute Certificate Profile for Authorization. *Internet RFCs*, 2002.
8. W. Johnston, S. Mudumbai, and M. Thompson. Authorization and Attribute Certificates for Widely Distributed Access Control. In *Proc. of the 7th Workshop on Enabling Technologies (WETICE '98)*, pages 340–345, Washington, DC, United States, 1998. IEEE Computer Society.
9. J.S. Park and R. Sandhu. Smart Certificates: Extending X.509 for Secure Attribute Services on the Web. In *Proceedings of the 22nd National Information Systems Security Conference (NISSC)*, October 1999.

10. D. Chadwick, A. Otenko, and E. Ball. Role-based Access Control with X.509 Attribute Certificates. *IEEE Internet Computing*, 7(2):62–69, 2003.
11. N.R. Adam, V. Atluri, E. Bertino, and E. Ferrari. A Content-based Authorization Model for Digital Libraries. *IEEE Transactions on Knowledge and Data Engineering*, 14(2):296–315, 2002.
12. T. Moses. eXtensible Access Control Markup Language (XACML) Version 2.0. *OASIS Standard*, February 2005.
13. T. Priebe, W. Dobmeier, and N. Kamprath. Supporting Attribute-based Access Control with Ontologies. In *Proc. of the 1st International Conference on Availability, Reliability and Security (ARES '06)*, pages 465–472, Los Alamitos, CA, United States, 2006. IEEE Computer Society.
14. R. Baeza-Yates and B. Ribeiro-Neto. *Modern Information Retrieval*. Addison-Wesley Longman Publishing Co., Inc., Boston, MA, United States, 1999.
15. T. Berners-Lee, J. Hendler, and O. Lassila. The Semantic Web. *Scientific American*, May 2001.
16. P. Bednar, S. Dürbeck, J. Hreno, M. Mach, R. Lukasz, and R. Schillinger. Access-eGov Platform Architecture. Access-eGov deliverable D3.1, October 2006.
17. R. Klischewski, S. Ukena, and D. Wozniak. User Requirements Analysis & Development/Test Recommendation. Access-eGov deliverable D2.2, July 2006.
18. T. Priebe, W. Dobmeier, B. Muschall, and G. Pernul. ABAC - Ein Referenzmodell für attributbasierte Zugriffskontrolle. In *Proc. of the 2nd Jahrestagung Fachbereich Sicherheit der Gesellschaft für Informatik (Sicherheit '05)*, pages 285–296, 2005.
19. L. Cranor, M. Langheinrich, and M. Marchiori. A P3P Preference Exchange Language 1.0 (APPEL 1.0). *World Wide Web Consortium Working Draft*, April 2002.
20. B. Balacheff, L. Chen, S. Pearson, D. Plaquin, and G. Proudler. *Trusted Computing Platforms: TCPA Technology in Context*. Prentice Hall PTR, Upper Saddle River, NJ, United States, 2002.
21. T. Garfinkel, B. Pfaff, J. Chow, M. Rosenblum, and D. Boneh. Terra: A Virtual Machine-based Platform for Trusted Computing. In *Proc. of the nineteenth ACM symposium on Operating systems principles (SOSP '03)*, pages 193–206, New York, NY, United States, 2003. ACM Press.
22. R. Sandhu and X. Zhang. Peer-to-Peer Access Control Architecture Using Trusted Computing Technology. In *Proc. of the tenth ACM symposium on Access control models and technologies*, pages 147–158, New York, NY, United States, 2005. ACM Press.
23. J.A. Montenegro and F. Moya. A Practical Approach of X.509 Attribute Certificate Framework as Support to Obtain Privilege Delegation. In *Proc. of the 1st European PKI Workshop (EuroPKI '04)*, pages 160–172. Lecture Notes in Computer Science (LNCS), 2004.
24. John Hughes, Eve Maler, and Rob Philpott. Technical Overview of the OASIS Security Assertion Markup Language (SAML), Version 1.1, May 2004.
25. D. Roman, H. Lausen, and U. Keller. Web Service Modeling Ontology (WSMO). WSMO deliverable D2v1.3, October 2006.

Using Trust to Resist Censorship in the Presence of Collusion

Andriy Panchenko and Lexi Pimenidis*

RWTH Aachen University,
Computer Science Department - Informatik IV,
Ahornstr. 55, D-52074 Aachen, Germany
{panchenko,lexi}@i4.informatik.rwth-aachen.de

Abstract. Censorship resistance deals with an attempt to prevent censors from the acquaintance of distribution of a particular content through the network. Providing resistance against censoring is a very challenging and difficult task to achieve. However it is vital for the purpose of freedom of speech, mind and achievement of democratic principles in todays society.
In this paper we define a model of a censorship resistant system. Thereafter we propose to split the problem of resisting censorship into the following two sub-problems: a trusted directory and steganographic data transfer. The directory is used in order to prolong contacts among peers based on their reputation in a way, that honest members get contacts only to other honest peers and colluded members remain isolated. Furthermore, we aim to provide an analysis of a trusted directory for reputation and its implications on censorship resistant systems. To this end we define a set of properties that such a directory has to fulfill and develop a proposal for the implementation. Finally we provide a simulation-based validation of our approach.

1 Introduction

According to the Universal Declaration of Human Rights, everyone has the right to freedom of opinion and expression, including receiving and imparting information and ideas through any media regardless of frontiers [9]. In todays world, however, an increasing number of organizations, companies and even countries block the free access to parts of the Internet [10]. The censors try to impede accessing some special political, ethical or religious content. For example, Saudi Arabia runs a country-wide Internet Service Unit (all ISPs must, by law, route through it), which provides an infamous web-censoring system that is supposed to defend Saudi citizens from "those pages of an offensive or harmful nature to the society, and which violate the tenants of the Islamic religion or societal norms"[2]. Another well known example is the "Great Firewall of China", where

* The authors are funded by the European Commission's 6th Framework Program.
[2] http://www.newsforge.com/article.pl?sid=04/01/12/2147220

Please use the following format when citing this chapter:

Panchenko, A. and Pimenidis, L., 2007, in IFIP International Federation for Information Processing, Volume 232, New Approaches for Security, Privacy and Trust in Complex Environments, eds. Venter, H., Eloff, M., Labuschagne, L., Eloff, J., von Solms, R., (Boston: Springer), pp. 409–420.

strict censoring is provided at the governmental level. Lots of web pages like the British radio station BBC, human rights organizations, or the free encyclopedia Wikipedia are blocked. According to an Amnesty International report there are 54 people in jail in China because of illegal content distribution[3]. International Internet search engines like Google, Yahoo and Microsoft's MSN were recently criticized for censoring search results according to China's guidelines. Moreover, content filtering is also a subject in democratic nations. So, for example, US Marines Corps censors web access for troops in Iraq[4 5]. European Union considers filtering and ranking according to the Internet Action Plan [4].

For the purpose of freedom of speech, mind and achievement of democratic principles there is a great demand to withstand filtering and censoring of information access and dissemination. Blocking resistant[6] systems try to provide as much reachability and availability as possible, even to users in countries where the free flow of information is organizationally or physically restricted [6].

Censorship resistant systems often have to provide anonymity to its users in order to grant their protection (especially from the blocker) and therewith to achieve desired properties of the system. Providing resistance usually requires distributed, peer-to-peer systems in order to overcome the blocking of the central server entity. Distributing functionality across many network nodes allows to avoid an obvious single point of failure where an attacker can clog the entire network. Using peer-to-peer based systems, though, requires the need to place trust on peers in the network. For this purpose reputation can be introduced. However, if the main objective of the network is to provide support for anonymity, the realization of the reputation itself becomes very problematic. Hiding the real identity gives a possibility for an attacker to easily throw away a pseudonym that has acquired a bad reputation. Furthermore, it is difficult to verify a member's behavior while keeping his status anonymous as these are two contradictorary things. However, to the favor of blocking resistance blocker and "normal" users have different objectives which can serve as an incentive for the classification.

2 Related Works

Zittrain and Edelman present their research results about Internet filtering practices by different countries and organizations worldwide in [10]. This includes country-specific results as well as studies of the concrete filtering software.

Perng et al. [7] define a term of *censorship susceptibility* (probability that an adversary can block a targeted document while allowing at least one other to be retrieved from the same server). Thereafter the authors analyze current implementation of censorship resistant schemes with respect to the defined model of

[3] http://www.heise.de/newsticker/meldung/70800
[4] http://yro.slashdot.org/article.pl?sid=06/03/07/1613236
[5] http://wonkette.com/politics/wonkette/our-boys-need-gossip-158687.php
[6] We use terms "blocking resistance" and "censorship resistance" as synonyms.

censorship susceptibility. They call a system resistant to censoring if the censor must disable access to the entire host in order to filter the selected content. Further they show that existing systems fail to meet the above provided strong adversary definition. Authors claim that Private Information Retrieval (PIR) is necessary, though not sufficient to achieve the definition. Moreover, they propose to use PIR in combination with digital signatures in order to reach the required properties [7].

Danezis and Anderson [2] propose an economic model of censorship resistance inspired by economics and conflicts theory. They assess how two different design philosophies – random and discretionary (encouraging nodes to serve content they are interested in) distribution of content in peer-to-peer network – resist censorship regarding to the model. The main finding was that a discretionary distribution is better suited to solve the problem.

Köpsell and Hillig [6] have proposed mechanisms in order to extend blocking resistance properties of their anonymity service AN.ON. The proposed principles are not technically mature in the sense that they do not solve the entire problem, but rather can only be used to make the job of the blocker more difficult. The work gives, though, a very good overview of the problematic and possible directions that solutions should strive for.

Infranet [5] is a system developed at the MIT that enables surreptitiously retrieval of the censored information via cooperating distributed web servers. The system uses a tunnel protocol that provides a covert communication channel between clients and servers. The latter also provides normal uncensored content. The requests are hidden by associating meaning to the sequence of HTTP request, and the results are placed into uncensored images using steganographic techniques.

Some other examples of censorship resistant systems are Freenet [1], Free Haven [3], Publius [13], Tangler [12], etc. Generally it is possible to say, that all known systems try to establish as many entry nodes to the blocked network as possible [6]. The idea is to hope that the blocker is not able to block all those nodes.

3 Model

In this section we explain our view on censorship resistant systems and explain in detail the model and level of abstraction that we want to use in the following parts of the paper.

For the simplicity of explanation we call all regular users that are part of a censored system *Alices*, those on the side which is not subject to filtering – *Bobs*, and the guardian entity – *warden*. Let $\mathcal{A}$ be the set of Alices and there exists a subset $\mathcal{A}' \subseteq \mathcal{A}$ that cooperates with warden $\mathcal{W}$. Let $\mathcal{B}$ be the set of Bobs. There also exists a subset $\mathcal{B}' \subseteq \mathcal{B}$ that cooperates with warden $\mathcal{W}$. The adversary can thus be seen as $\mathcal{W}' = \mathcal{W} \cup \mathcal{A}' \cup \mathcal{B}'$. Finally, there exists a group of users $\mathcal{A}^* \subseteq \mathcal{A} - \mathcal{A}'$ that are interested in communication with entities from the set $\mathcal{B}^* \subseteq \mathcal{B} - \mathcal{B}'$ on some specific topic that the warden wants to censor. Initially there exist neither $a \in \mathcal{A}$ nor $w \in \mathcal{W}'$ that knows which $b \in \mathcal{B}$ are also in $\mathcal{B}^*$.

All users $a \in \mathcal{A}$ and $b \in \mathcal{B}$ relay messages to each other through $\mathcal{W}$. These messages can be of two types:

- *"good"* - those that do not include information that the warden is interested to censor;
- *"bad"* - are those the warden wants to filter.

It should be mentioned, that the guardian only profits from filtering "bad" messages, since blocking "good" has negative impact on his utility (e.g. consider losses of the Chinese economy from blocking trading transactions).

Based on educated guesses regarding the type of the message and its sender and receiver, the warden can choose to do one of the following actions:

- forward original data;
- forward modified data;
- drop data.

Moreover, he may store messages in order to collect enough evidence about his suspicions regarding some Alices. Furthermore, based on his suspicions he may (possibly even physically) punish the sender. The risk of $a \in \mathcal{A}^*$ to send messages of type "bad" to $b \in \mathcal{B}$ rises with the probability of correct classification of messages by the warden (if the warden can correctly classify messages the risk of detectibility is 100%, if he cannot do the classification there is only a marginal risk).

We call a system that allows any $a \in \mathcal{A}^*$ to communicate with $b \in \mathcal{B}^*$ despite the existence of $\mathcal{W}'$ *'blocking resistant'* with respect to the properties of $\mathcal{W}'$. Note that the probability of messages of type "bad" being blocked is not necessarily linked to the probability of being correctly classified by the warden (and vice-versa: not being blocked is not a sign for not being detectable). This is due to the fact that messages can be stored and analyzed off-line by the guardian. Thus the communication can take place but the evidence remains.

4 Our Approach

One way to achieve blocking resistance is to split the problem into two parts which can be solved separately:

- finding $b \in \mathcal{B}^*$;
- communicating with $b \in \mathcal{B}^*$.

The latter can be achieved by means of steganography [6]. It is possible to use one of the following for the first part — finding $b \in \mathcal{B}^*$:

- extensive search - this is a basic discovery technique that can be applied in the address space of $\mathcal{B}$;

secret channel - it is possible to assume that there exists some small bandwidth information flow from Bobs to Alices. This can be provided e.g. by means of a satellite broadcast channel or some other channel that is not controlled by the warden but whose costs are much more expensive. This information can be especially effectively used for bootstrapping a censorship resistant system;
- a collusion resistant probabilistic directory for answering contact queries.

Extensive search is a very time and resource consuming procedure. Moreover, it is very problematic to place trust on newly discovered nodes since these can be warden's agents. The secret channel approach has additionally scalability issues, i.e. consider the dissemination of information about the channel on both communication sides. A collusion resistant directory to find peers to communicate with seems to have obvious advantages against the other two techniques. However, it should be investigated whether it is possible to build a directory that protects the presence of honest users from the warden and its agents and at the same time prolongs contacts among system users.

It should be noted that the warden possibly has a huge amount of resources at his disposal, however, the human ones remain most expensive and cannot be raised as easily as e.g. computational power. For this reason it is possible to generate tests by $\mathcal{B}^*$ that most humans can pass but are infeasible for automatic programs (in order to tell humans and computers apart) as described in [11]. This could be used in order to distinguish regular users from the warden's automated attempts to get contacts.

Blocking Resistant Technique

We propose to split the problem of creation of a censorship resistant network into the following two sub-problems:

- net of trust;
- steganography.

The net of trust can be implemented as a directory and can then be used by $a \in \mathcal{A}^*$ to find communication partners in $\mathcal{B}^*$. This puts some degree of trustworthiness on the contacts from directory: if it works as it should and can distinguish honest users from colluded ones, the contacts that are provided by the directory to the honest users are much more trustworthy than e.g. some random addresses. Steganographic communication is necessary to hide the traffic to and from the system, as well as between users.

Up from now we assume that all communication takes places in some steganographic form. This is necessary to thwart the threat that the warden can distinguish between ordinary messages and those belonging to the censorship resisting system. Given some sufficiently stealthy technique, the warden remains with only two ways to compromise the system: either he owns the directory or he tries to subvert the directory by inserting colluded members.

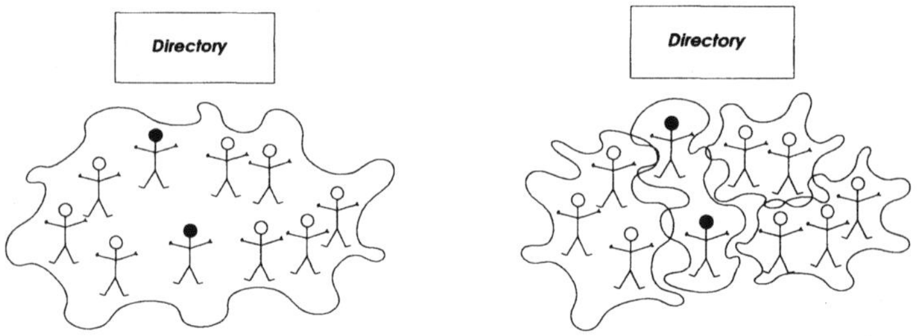

(a) Initial Setup (b) Situation After Some Epochs

Fig. 1. The Effect of Clustering by Directory

While we can exclude the first possibility as uninteresting (w.l.o.g. it is possible to assume the presence of the directory at the side of Bobs; digital signatures can be used in order to prevent impersonating), the latter remains a threat.

Collusion Resistant Directory: Properties

The directory should be distributed (in order to provide protection against denial-of-service attack and single point of failures) and to make it difficult for the warden to block the access to the directory. At first, however, we want to investigate the applicability of the approach with the help of a central directory. If the centralized directory cannot provide protection for the net of trust and is not resistant against the *"domino"* effect (having detected some user $u \in \mathcal{A}^* \cup \mathcal{B}^*$ the warden must learn as little information as possible from this fact about the other users in $\mathcal{A}^* \cup \mathcal{B}^*$ and their communication), it is most probable neither will be a distributed directory. One of the reasons for this is that the centralized directory has a global view on all members in the system and receives a feedback from all communication partners, thus gives agents less possibilities to have unnoticed dual behavior. Due to the fact that constructing a distributed directory requires much more effort, we make an analysis for the centralized one first. If it is not possible to build a centralized directory with the above mentioned properties, we suppose that neither would be a distributed one suitable to satisfy the requirements.

The directory will need to support the following functionalities in order to fulfill its duties:

Join Users must be able to establish new identities in this directory. There is no need for the directory to either limit the number of accounts per user, or to know the user's real identity. However, users must be in possession of a proof of the claiming identity if they want to reuse it.

Poll Once a user has an account on the system, he is allowed to query the directory for addresses of other users. To thwart the possibility that users drain the system's resources, they receive only a single address per time interval, e.g. a day.

Push Users may return feedback to the directory, expressing to which extend they "trust" a peer. The directory should take care that users and their communication partners only submit feedback for peers for which they received the address from the directory. It must be possible to change the trust value at any point in time if users make new experiences.

After receiving a pseudonymous address of a contact from the directory the user makes an experience with the negotiated peer and both parties send feedback back to the directory. Based on this feedback the directory should distinguish users in the way that the probability of finding (getting contact to) $b \in \mathcal{B}^*$ should be

high for $a \in \mathcal{A}^*$;
low for $w \in \mathcal{W}'$.

We claim that in order to be resistant against collusion it suffices to have steganographic communication and a directory with the properties as mentioned above. At this point, we will not go into steganography, but rather assume that there are systems that allow hidden communication like e.g. [5].

Collusion Resistant Directory: Methodology

In order to achieve collusion resistance, the directory must make sure that either no colluded user is able to harvest many of the honest users' addresses, or that the cost of doing so is prohibitive high such that it is not worth doing so.

To this end, we propose that the directory clusters its users into disjunct sets, where each user will only be able to receive addresses from other users within the same set. Therewith, if the directory manages to correctly classify different groups of users, e.g. honest Alices, Bobs and those cooperating with the warden, the honest users will be able to find each other, while the colluded members will only be referred to other colluded members.

One method of grouping its users into disjunct sets is to run a clustering algorithm using the users' trust vectors as an input. In the next section we will describe the procedure in detail and show the results of the evaluation that are produced by our technique (in order to test its suitability for the purpose of trusworthy contacts' dissemination). The desired result is depicted in Figure 1. As already mentioned, the warden's agents are depicted with black heads. In the beginning (*a*) all system participants belong to the same cluster. After some initialization epochs, the warden's agents are isolated (*b*) and only get contact to each other.

5 Evaluation and Analysis

In this section we will show the findings of using cluster algorithms for directories in order to achieve collusion resistance.

Before investing effort in design and deployment of a real system and gathering data in the real world, we wrote a simulation to check the properties and applicability of this approach. The simulation was written in Python using the library `pycluster` from the University of Tokyo [8].

In the simulation we had an overall number of U users of the directory. The users arrived equally distributed over the complete time interval of the simulation and consisted of $U_h < U$ honest users and $U_c = U - U_h$ colluded users. The directory clustered the users into k disjunct clusters using the $k-means$ clustering algorithm [8] based on the Euclidean distance of the users' trust vectors (how they are trusted by the others).

Social Model

All users had a fixed "social intelligence" factor $\mathcal{I}(user)$ that was used to calculate how well they were able to distinguish other users' intentions, as well as to hide their own identity. The values ranged from zero to ten, where ten was used for simulated persons that were able to pretty good understand other person's intentions after several rounds of interactions. We interpreted the value of five in the way that the user would be of average intelligence, while the value zero would denote complete sillies.

The "level of trust" between two users started out being neutral, i.e. five on a scale from zero to ten, where zero denotes absolute distrust and ten absolute trust. We denote it as $\mathcal{T}_i(u,p)$ and calculate the level of trust that an honest user u places on his communication partner p after the i-th round of interaction by:

$$\mathcal{T}_i(u,p) = \begin{cases} \mathcal{T}_{i-1} \cdot \lambda + (1-\lambda) \cdot \xi \cdot \theta_h : \text{if } p \text{ is honest} \\ \mathcal{T}_{i-1} \cdot \lambda + (1-\lambda) \cdot \xi \cdot \theta_c : \text{if } p \text{ is colluded} \end{cases} \quad (1)$$

where

$$\theta_h = (\mathcal{I}(p) + \mathcal{I}(u))\ 2, \quad (2)$$

$$\theta_c = (\mathcal{I}(p) - \mathcal{I}(u) + 10)\ 2, \quad (3)$$

and λ is a factor that determines the influence of the previous trust value (before an experience of the last interaction), ξ is a fuzziness factor. We used a random value within the range of $[0.8, 1.2]$ for ξ.

In contrast to these, colluded members have always applied the following formula in order to make the trust vectors of other colluded users similar to those of honest members:

$$\mathcal{T}_i(u,p) = \mathcal{T}_{i-1} \cdot \lambda + (1-\lambda) \cdot \xi \cdot \theta_h. \quad (4)$$

User notified the directory after each contact about the changes of their trust vector. This way, the directory could cluster users based on the way they were trusted by others. We define a trust vector of user j as:

$$\mathcal{T}^j = (\mathcal{T}(u_1, u_j), \ldots, \mathcal{T}(u_n, u_j)), \quad (5)$$

where $\mathcal{T}(u_j, u_j) = \mathcal{T}_{max}$.

Simulation Workflow

Each time interval the simulation first checked whether new users had to join the network and, if it is the case, initialized new entities. It then simulated the directory and clustered the users based on their trust vectors (how they are trusted by the others) and according to the main simulation parameters (like e.g. number of cluster). Each user then queried the directory for an address of another user (which possibly returns an address he already knew). Immediately afterwards the users returned their feedback, i.e. inserted a new trust value for their peers or refined the existing value based on the interaction experience according to the formulas shown above. After a fixed amount of time slices we collected the final results and those from intermediate slices. The simulation was repeated several times in order to get rid of random noise and to pinpoint the deviation of the results, which yielded to be very small.

Results

The main results are shown in Figure 2. In that series of simulations we used $U_h = 100$ honest users, $U_c = 5$ on (a) and (b), $U_c = 7$ agents on (c) and ran each simulation over 1000 time slices. Users have joined the system equally distributed over the entire time interval.

Part (a) shows on one axis the value of honest users' "social intelligence", while the second axis displays the time slice at which the users had joined the system. The z-axis displays the average number of distinct agent contacts for the honest users that joined the system at the corresponding time slice. Of great interest is the finding that the longer a user stays in the system, the less contacts to colluded members he gets with the time.

Part (b) of Figure 2 displays the effect of rising the number of clusters on the average number of distinct colluded users that each honest user communicated with. While two clusters were obviously not enough and nearly all users were seen by all five colluded members, the number dropped significantly for ten clusters and dropped even further for fifty. The small hill in the middle of picture (b) is due to the fact that the agents actively dislike honest users with a low intelligence, while honest users with a higher intelligence dislike agents.

Picture (c) shows an example clustering at the end of a simulation run with 5 clusters: while nearly all agents (red dots) are in the same cluster, there are two main clusters each with roughly half of the more intelligent honest users (large green dots), and two clusters for those with less social intelligence (small green dots). The size of the circle reflects the intelligence of the agent. The blue lines denote trust between peers (trust level is not smaller than 8.5), the red one – distrust (trust level is not greater than 0.5).

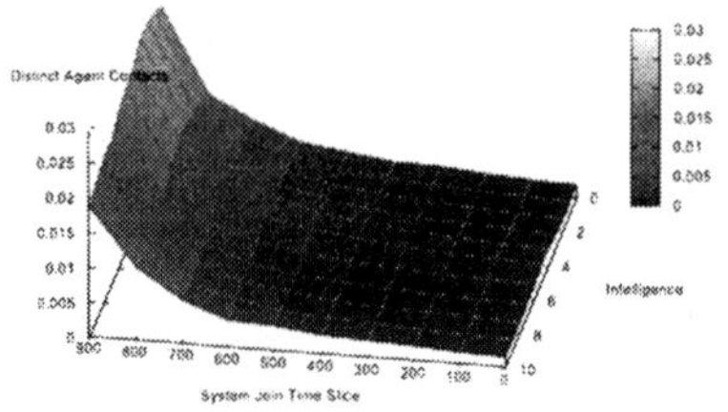

(a) Average Distinct Contacts With Agents

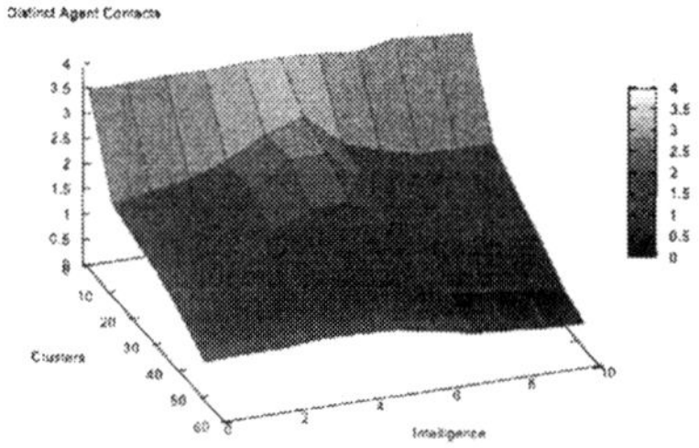

(b) Average Distinct Contacts With Agents

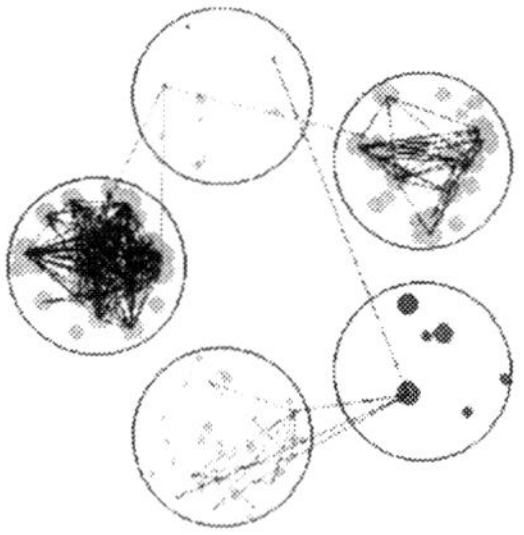

(c) Simulation Outcome: Trust Network and Clusters

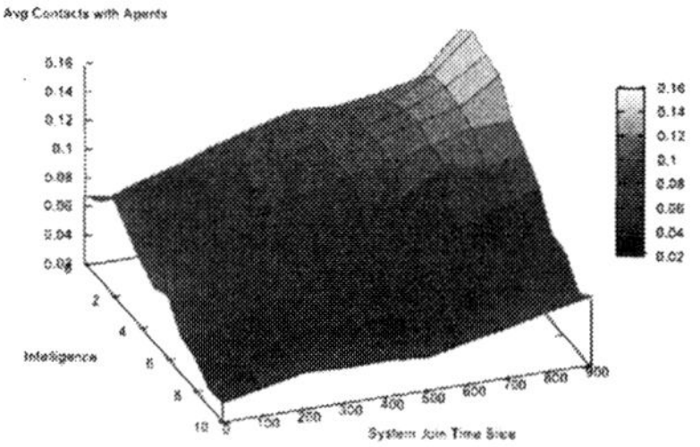

(d) Average Contacts With Agents

Fig. 2. Results

Discussion

With the above provided results we have shown that clustering users based on their mutual trust seems to be a promising method for building a collusion resistant directory.

Besides clustering users on basis of the vector of how they were trusted, we also experimented with clustering users on basis of how they trust the others. While the results were similar, we finally chose the vector of how a user was trusted because this way it is much harder for colluded users to successfully attack the clustering algorithm. An evil node may try to guess the values that are assigned by the honest members. Moreover, colluded nodes may cooperate and place "catches" – having produced different values for the trust vectors they will be able to catch different classes of honest system users. Clustering based solely on the single value of (dis-)trust between two persons was not significantly better than choosing random contacts. Moreover, in order to change the default trust value in this case, users have to communicate with each other at least once, which is not desired.

There are two major different ways to attack this scheme: the first way is to poison the database with a lot of different entries. But as long as real users act sufficiently different from automated entries, and as long as users do not really interact with the poisoned entries[7], this does not seem like an easy way to subvert the scheme. The seconds way is to convince other users that a colluded user is an honest one. In order to achieve this, an agent has to behave like an honest user over a long period of time, i.e. in interests of honest users. Therefore agents have to provide service that is not in their interest over a continuous period of time for "catching" dissidents with a high intelligence. Further research on the economics of playing double role for agents has to be performed. Also the impact of agents to honest users ratio on the system behavior has to be investigated.

6 Conclusion

In this work we have defined our model of censorship resistant system and proposed to split the problem into a net of trust and steganographic data transfer. Steganographic communication is necessary to hide the traffic to and from the system as well as between the users. The net of trust is needed in order to find peers for communication and prolong contacts among them. We have proposed to realize it as a collusion resistant, probabilistic directory. A definition of a set of properties has been given that this directory must fulfill. With the simulation based evaluation we have shown that clustering users based on their trust vectors is a very promising method to build a directory with the defined before properties. With the help of the clustering algorithm, the trusted directory has become a powerful tool to distinct between different user classes *without* classifying them as *"good"* or *"bad"*. We achieve this by clustering the system users into disjoint sets, instead of calculating a global value of trustworthiness.

To ease the implementation we have investigated the approach of a centralized directory. In order to provide protection against denial-of-service attack, single point of failures and, not less important, to make it difficult for the warden to block the access to the central entity, switching to distributed directory and its implications must be researched and implemented.

All in all it is hard to say at this point to which extent our results are applicable to real systems. Even though we took care to choose powerful social model, it is very difficult to sufficiently abstract and simulate the human behavior and interpersonal trust. Therefore, in order to make final conclusion statements about our approach, evaluation in real world settings are necessary.

References

1. Ian Clarke, Oskar Sandberg, Brandon Wiley, and Theodore W. Hong. Freenet: A distributed anonymous information storage and retrieval system. In *Proceed-*

[7] It is as difficult as solving the Turing Test to create a program that interacts as humans.

ings of Designing Privacy Enhancing Technologies: Workshop on Design Issues in Anonymity and Unobservability, pages 46–66, July 2000.
2. George Danezis and Ross Anderson. The economics of censorship resistance. In *Proceedings of Workshop on Economics and Information Security (WEIS04)*, May 2004.
3. Roger Dingledine, Michael J. Freedman, and David Molnar. The free haven project: Distributed anonymous storage service. In H. Federrath, editor, *Proceedings of Designing Privacy Enhancing Technologies: Workshop on Design Issues in Anonymity and Unobservability*. Springer-Verlag, LNCS 2009, July 2000.
4. European Union Internet Action Plan: Filtering & Rating. http://europa.eu.int/information_society/activities/sip/projects/filtering/, 2006. visited March 2006.
5. Nick Feamster, Magdalena Balazinska, Greg Harfst, Hari Balakrishnan, and David Karger. Infranet: Circumventing web censorship and surveillance. In *Proceedings of the 11th USENIX Security Symposium*, August 2002.
6. Stefan Köpsell and Ulf Hillig. How to achieve blocking resistance for existing systems enabling anonymous web surfing. In *Proceedings of the Workshop on Privacy in the Electronic Society (WPES 2004)*, Washington, DC, USA, October 2004.
7. Ginger Perng, Michael K. Reiter, and Chenxi Wang. Censorship resistance revisited. In *Proceedings of Information Hiding Workshop (IH 2005)*, June 2005.
8. Pycluster - Clustering Library. http://bonsai.ims.u-tokyo.ac.jp/~mdehoon/software/cluster/software.htm, 2005. visited March 2006.
9. Universal Declaration of Human Rights. http://www.un.org/Overview/rights.html, 1998. visited March 2006.
10. Documentation of Internet Filtering Worldwide. http://cyber.law.harvard.edu/filtering/, 2003. visited March 2006.
11. L. von Ahn, M. Blum, N. Hopper, and J. Langford. Captcha: Using hard ai problems for security. In *Proceedings of Eurocrypt*, pages 294–311, 2003.
12. Marc Waldman and David Mazières. Tangler: a censorship-resistant publishing system based on document entanglements. In *Proceedings of the 8th ACM Conference on Computer and Communications Security (CCS 2001)*, pages 126–135, November 2001.
13. Marc Waldman, Aviel Rubin, and Lorrie Cranor. Publius: A robust, tamper-evident, censorship-resistant and source-anonymous web publishing system. In *Proceedings of the 9th USENIX Security Symposium*, pages 59–72, August 2000.

Evaluating the Effects of Model Generalization on Intrusion Detection Performance

Zhuowei Li[1 2], Amitabha Das[2] and Jianying Zhou[3]

[1] Indiana University, USA. zholi@indiana.edu
[2] Nanyang Technological University, Singapore. asadas@ntu.edu.sg
[3] Institute of Infocomm Research, Singapore. jyzhou@i2r.a-star.edu.sg

Abstract. An intrusion detection system usually infers the status of an unknown behavior from limited available ones via model generalization, but the generalization is not perfect. Most existing techniques use it blindly (or only based on specific datasets at least) without considering the difference among various application scenarios. For example, signature-based ones use signatures generated from specific occurrence environments, anomaly-based ones are usually evaluated by a specific dataset. To make matters worse, various techniques have been introduced recently to exploit too stingy or too generous generalization that causes intrusion detection invalid, for example, mimicry attacks, automatic signature variation generation etc. Therefore, a critical task in intrusion detection is to evaluate the effects of model generalization. In this paper, we try to meet the task. First, we divide model generalization into several levels, which are evaluated one by one to identify their significance on intrusion detection. Among our experimental results, the significance of different levels is much different. Under-generalization will sacrifice the detection performance, but over-generalization will not lead to any benefit. Moreover, model generalization is necessary to identify more behaviors in detection, but its implications for normal behaviors are different from those for intrusive ones.

1 Introduction

There exist two general approaches for detecting intrusions: *signature-based intrusion detection* (SID, a.k.a. misuse detection), where an intrusion is detected if its behavior matches existing intrusion signatures, and *anomaly-based intrusion detection* (AID), where an intrusion is detected if the resource behavior deviates from normal behaviors significantly. From another aspect, there are two behavior spaces for intrusion detection (Figure 1): *normal behavior space* and *intrusive behavior space*, and they are complementary to each other. Conceptually, SID is based on knowledge in intrusive behavior space, and AID is based on knowledge in normal behavior space [2]. Perfect detection of intrusions can be achieved only if we have a complete model of any one of the two behavior spaces, because what is not bad is good and vice versa ideally. Figure 1 (a) and (b) illustrate the behavior models for SID (i.e., *intrusive behavior model*) and for AID (i.e., *normal behavior model*) in the real applications.

A critical problem. There are two quality factors within the behavior models: *inaccuracy* and *incompleteness*. For example, a part of the intrusive behavior

Please use the following format when citing this chapter:

Li, Z., Das, A., and Zhou, J., 2007, in IFIP International Federation for Information Processing, Volume 232, New Approaches for Security, Privacy and Trust in Complex Environments, eds. Venter, H., Eloff, M., Labuschagne, L., Eloff, J., von Solms, R., (Boston: Springer), pp. 421–432.

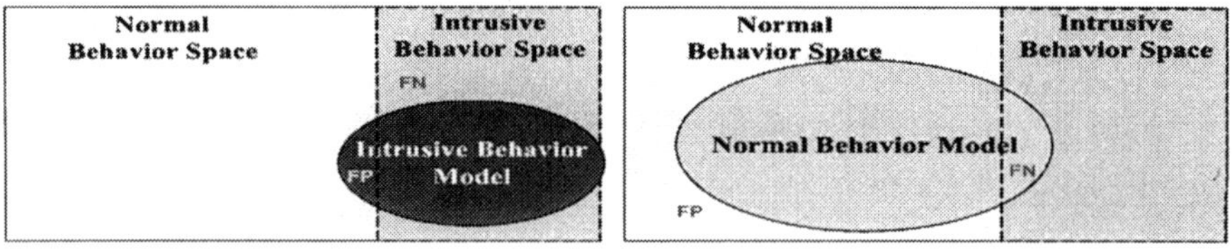

(a) Intrusive Behavior Model. (b) Normal Behavior Model.

Fig. 1. Behavior spaces and models.

model falling into the normal behavior space leads to the *inaccuracy*. Due to incompleteness, the intrusive behavior model cannot cover all intrusive behavior space, and the normal behavior model cannot cover all the normal behavior space either. In SID (Figure 1.a), model inaccuracy will lead to false positives (FP) and model incompleteness in it will lead to false negatives (FN). In contrast, model inaccuracy in the normal behavior model will lead to FNs and model incompleteness in it will cause FPs (Figure 1.b). To build a practical intrusion detection system, *it is critical to reduce the model inaccuracy and incompleteness, and thus to lower FPs and FNs in the detection phase.*

Past addressings. To make up for the incompleteness, most existing '*model building*' techniques try to infer the unknown behaviors via *model generalization* (defined in Section 3), which is able to eliminate FNs in SID and to reduce FPs in AID. However, as indicated in Figure 1, it can also lead to more FPs in SID and more FNs in AID. In other words, *model generalization is two-edged for intrusion detection in principle* [9]. Various techniques have been introduced recently to exploit too stingy or too generous model generalization (*Section 2*), for example, mimicry attacks[11], mutate exploits[10], automatic signature variation generation[7] etc.

Evaluation. Thus, it is very useful to identify the utility of model generalization. We can envision at least four of its applications.

- Determine deployment conditions for an intrusion detection technique, as well as proper techniques to detect intrusions into a specific environment.
- Guide the development of an adaptive intrusion detection technique by adjusting the generalization extent.
- Alleviate concept drifting. Intrusion and application evolution patterns can determine the extent of generalization in an ad hoc deployment.
- Perform intrusion detection evaluation. According to different generalization extents, we can generate appropriate artificial datasets, which can identify the generic detection capability of a SID/AID technique.

Our contributions. We believe that our evaluation advances the research on intrusion detection in two perspectives. First, we design *a framework to evaluate the effect of model generalization*, in which model generalization is achieved at different levels according to the reasonableness of the underlying assumptions. Secondly, on a typical dataset, our experiments are performed to verify the evaluation framework, and to identify the utility of model generalization.

The remaining parts are organized as follows. Section 2 reviews the related work on model generalization. In section 3, an evaluation framework for model generalization is designed. As a case study, experiments in section 4 reveal the implications of model generalization on intrusion detection. Lastly, we draw conclusions and lay out the future work in section 5.

2 Related Work

To our knowledge, we are the first to evaluate model generalization for intrusion detection while there are two existing implicit applications of model generalization: extending behavior models and evade detection.

First, the intrusion signatures can be generalized to cover more intrusion variations. Anchor et al. [1] applied the evolutionary programming to optimize the generalization in an intrusion signature, and thus to detect more intrusion variants. Rubin et al. [8] presented a method to construct more robust signatures from existing intrusion signatures. Secondly, the normal behavior model of AID can be generalized as well. In [5, 12], existing audit trails are modeled *inexactly* to accommodate more behaviors, and thus to achieve model generalization.

Several work is proposed to utilize the false negatives introduced by model generalization. In AID techniques, mimicry attacks [11] are designed to misuse the generalization by mimicking its normal behaviors, and thus to avoid being detected. In SID techniques, model generalization is also exploited [10, 7] to generate intrusion variations, which cannot be detected either.

In summary, too generous generalization in AID will make mimicry attacks successful [11], while too stingy generalization in SID will make some attack variations undetectable [8, 10]. In our research, we try to identify the relations between the extent of generalization and detection performance.

3 An Evaluation Framework for Model Generalization

In this section, we proposed the evaluation framework for model generalization based on a theoretical basis for intrusion detection [6].

3.1 Theoretical Basis for Intrusion Detection

In a nutshell, the basis introduces three new concepts to formalize the process of intrusion detection: `feature range`, `NSA label` and `compound feature`. Every instance in a training audit trail can be represented as a feature range of a high-order compound feature, and every feature range has a NSA label, which is used to detect behaviors in test audit trails. In detail, the value of every feature in an instance can be replaced with a feature range, which is gotten by extending its value so that the extension does not conflict with other existing values. The feature ranges of all features are compounded using cartesian products to build a (training or test) behavior signature for intrusion detection.

In this framework, it is supposed that there is a training audit trail and a feature vector $FV = \{F_1, F_2, \ldots, F_n\}$. For every feature F_i, a series of feature ranges $R^1_{F_i}, R^2_{F_i}, \ldots, R^m_{F_i}$ is first mined from the training audit trails. Using feature ranges of all features, the behavior signatures $Sig_1, Sig_2 \ldots, Sig_l$ are constructed for intrusion detection. In the detection phase, a test instance is formalized as a signature Sig_t, and it is detected in accordance with whether it matches any existing behavior signature.

3.2 Model Generalization

We first define model generalization within the context of intrusion detection.

Definition 1 (Model Generalization). *Suppose that there exists a set of behaviors associated with a resource.* ***Model generalization*** *is an operation that tries to identify a new behavior associated with the same resource based on the existing set of behavior instances.*

Model generalization can improve the detection rate by identifying more novel behaviors (e.g., normal behaviors) but may also degrade the detection performance by mis-identifying novel behaviors because of generalization errors [9]. This influence of model generalization on detection performance is generally determined by its underlying assumptions per se. In our evaluation, we first pinpoint three phases of our framework where we can use various assumptions to apply three levels of generalization, and then evaluate them one by one for model generalization. We also include a level without any generalization in which the behaviors in the training audit trails are represented precisely.

In the follow-up subsections, we describe the methods to evaluate the three levels of generalizations which moves the model from most specialized to most generalized as we move down the level (from L0 to L3).

3.3 L0 Without Generalization

Suppose that for a feature F, there exists a series of feature values, $v_1, v_2, \ldots, v_l$. Without generalization, every feature value v_i is regarded as a feature range with its upper and lower bounds equal to v_i. In this way, the instances in the training audit trails are represented *precisely* by the signatures generated from these feature ranges. Note that, for F, we have not inferred the NSA label of unknown feature subspace between any two feature values.

3.4 L1 Model Generalization

For every feature, to achieve L1 generalization, we assume that the unknown parts in its feature space have the same NSA label as its neighboring feature values. Obviously, inherent in this assumption is a concept of distance. Therefore, due to the lack of distance concept in nominal features, we will only discuss the L1 generalization on numerical (discrete and continuous) features, and regard every feature value of a nominal feature as a feature range. For convenience, we use two more notations on a feature range R_F^i: $Upp(R_F^i)$ is its upper bound and $Low(R_F^i)$ is its lower bound. With respect to a feature value v_i, an initial feature range R_F^i will be formed with $Upp(R_F^i) = Low(R_F^i) = v_i$.

L1 generalization is described in algorithm 1. In this generalization, one critical step is to split the unknown subspace $(v_i, v_{i+1}) = (Upp(R_F^i), Low(R_F^{i+1}))$ $(i+1 \le l)$, and allocate the two parts to existing neighboring ranges R_F^i and R_F^{i+1}. We use several strategies and evaluate them in our framework. These are:

Algorithm 1 L1 model generalization for a discrete/continuous feature F.

Require: (1) R^1_F, R^2_F,... R^l_F. (2)ε (ε_d for discrete features and ε_c for continuous features).
1: **for** $i = 1$ to $l - 1$ **do**
2: Determine a splitting border S within $(Upp(R^i_F)\ Low(R^{i+1}_F))$;
3: Split $(Upp(R^i_F)\ Low(R^{i+1}_F))$ into two parts $(Upp(R^i_F)\ S]$ and $(S\ Low(R^{i+1}_F))$;
4: $R^i_F = (Low(R^i_F)\ S]$; $R^{i+1}_F = (S\ Upp(R^{i+1}_F))$;
5: **end for**
6: i=1;
7: **while** $i < l$ **do**
8: **if** $Low(R^{i+1}_F) - Upp(R^i_F) \leq \varepsilon$, and $L(R^i_F) = L(R^{i+1}_F)$ **then**
9: Merge R^{i+1}_F into R^i_F; Delete R^{i+1}_F; $l = l - 1$;
10: **else**
11: $i = i + 1$;
12: **end if**
13: **end while**

(1) no splitting (2) equal splitting, (3) frequency-based splitting, (4) intrusion-specific splitting. Note that, in Algorithm 1, the merging step for feature ranges (i.e., lines 6-12) is selective after the splitting step (i.e., lines 1-5). This step for merging range is also a generalization operation in L1 generalization.

1. **L1.1: No splitting**. If we do not conduct the merging step either, the L1.1 generalization actually becomes same as L0, i.e., no generalization.
2. **L1.2: Splitting it equally**. The unknown interval between v_i and v_{i+1} is split at the midpoint $S = \frac{v_i+v_{i+1}}{2}$. That is, $(v_i, S]$ is assigned the same NSA label as v_i, and (S, v_{i+1}) is assigned the same NSA label as v_{i+1}.
3. **L1.3: Frequency-based Splitting**. Let the frequency of v_i in the training audit trails be f_{v_i}. Then, the splitting point is $S = v_i + (v_{i+1} - v_i) * \frac{f_{v_i}}{f_{v_i}+f_{v_{i+1}}}$. $(v_i, S]$ is assigned as $L(v_i)$, and (S, v_{i+1}) is assigned as $L(v_{i+1})$.
4. **L1.4: Intrusion specific splitting**. Given a predefined generalization parameter G_{in} for intrusions. For a pair of neighboring values v_i and v_{i+1}, if $L(v_i) = \mathtt{N}$ and $L(v_{i+1}) = \mathtt{A}$, $S = v_{i+1} - G_{in}$. If $L(v_i) = \mathtt{A}$ and $L(v_{i+1}) = \mathtt{N}$, $S = v_i + G_{in}$. Otherwise, $S = \frac{v_i+v_{i+1}}{2}$. $(v_i, S]$ is assigned as $L(v_i)$, and (S, v_{i+1}) is assigned as $L(v_{i+1})$.

In addition, we also evaluate the merging step for every splitting strategy.

In the detection phase, every instance is formalized as Sig_t by replacing every value with its feature range. Finally, we evaluate whether Sig_t matches any signature in $\Omega(F_1\ _n)$. If matched, it is identified by that signature. Otherwise, Sig_t will further be evaluated by L2 generalization evaluation processes.

3.5 L2 Model Generalization

After the L1 model generalization, all the (nominal, discrete, and/or continuous) features are uniformly represented by a series of feature ranges. In L2 model generalization, we will utilize the relations between feature ranges rather than values, which are measured by the distance of two signatures. To this end, let us first define a distance function of two signatures in the behavior models.

Signature distance. Let $R(Sig_1, F_i)$ denote the feature range of F_i in a signature Sig_1. For any two signatures, Sig_1 and Sig_2, their distance is:

$$D(Sig_1, Sig_2) = \sum_{i=1}^{n} \delta(Sig_1, Sig_2, F_i)$$

Where, $\delta(Sig_1, Sig_2, F_i) = \begin{cases} 0, \text{ if } R(Sig_1, F_i) = R(Sig_2, F_i); \\ 1, \text{ otherwise.} \end{cases}$

Evaluating L2 generalization. L2 generalization is achieved by the following two generalization operations. `L2.1: grouping feature ranges`. If several feature ranges of a feature are interchangeable in $\Omega(F_{1\ldots n})$ without loss of signature distinguishability, they will be combined into a group. `L2.2: mutating feature ranges`. For a feature, its feature range in a signature can be mutated to any of its other feature ranges without loss of signature distinguishability.

Grouping feature ranges. For a feature F_i, if a feature range in $\Omega(F_{1\ldots n})$ is interchangeable with another feature range without loss of signature distinguishability (i.e. without changing its NSA label), their significance is equal to each other. We can group these feature ranges in constructing behavior models. As a special case, a feature range can form a group by itself. In this way, we can form a series of groups for F_i, $G_{F_i} = \{G^1_{F_i}, G^2_{F_i}, \ldots\}$ such that for any feature range $R^j_{F_i}$, there is a group $G^k_{F_i}$, $R^j_{F_i} \in G^k_{F_i}$. Finally, we achieve a grouping scheme for all features in the feature vector: $G_{FV} = \langle G_{F_1}, G_{F_2}, \ldots, G_{F_n} \rangle$.

For two signatures Sig_1 and Sig_2 in $\Omega(F_{1\ldots n})$, they are *equivalent* to each other with respect to G_{FV} based on the following rule.

$$Sig_1 \overset{G_{FV}}{=} Sig_2 \Leftrightarrow \exists i(\delta(Sig_1, Sig_2, F_i) = 1) \\ \wedge(\exists j\{R(Sig_1, F_i), R(Sig_2, F_i)\} \subset G^j_{F_i}) \tag{1}$$

For any two equivalent signatures, they are *compatible* if they have the same NSA label. Otherwise, they are *conflict* to each other in the behavior models.

The behavior models can be generalized by grouping feature ranges. For example, for signatures "$\langle a, 1, E\rangle$" and "$\langle b, 2, F\rangle$", if 'a' and 'b' are grouped, the behavior models can be enlarged by two additional signatures "$\langle b, 1, E\rangle$" and "$\langle a, 2, F\rangle$". Essentially, like in Genetic Algorithm [4] we are allowing *crossover* operation between signatures by interchanging the feature ranges in a group.

Algorithm 2 Evaluating a test signature via grouping.

Require: (1) $\Omega(F_{1\ldots n})$; (2) Sig_t; and (3) np_g.
```
Initialization, StatusList = ∅
for every signature Sig_1 ∈ Ω(F_1...n) do
    calculate D(Sig_t, Sig_1)
    if D(Sig_t, Sig_1) ≤ np_g then
        /* if R(Sig_1, F_i) ≠ R(Sig_t, F_i), P = {R(Sig_1, F_i), R(Sig_t, F_i)} */
        Enumerate all feature range pairs P_1 ... P_k (k ≤ np_g);
        if no conflicting signatures w.r.t. P_1, P_2 ... P_k then
            Append status(es) of Sig_1 into StatusList; /*Lemma 3*/
        end if
    end if
end for
determine the detection results based on StatusList;
```

Moreover, to measure the diversity in G_{FV}, the number of grouping points np_g is utilized in the detection phase. In other words, if the grouping scheme does not exist, there are at least $n - np_g$ equivalent feature ranges between Sig_t and any signature Sig_i in the behavior models. The larger the parameter np_g is, the more diverse the group operation is. Given np_g and $\Omega(F_{1\ldots n})$, a test instance is evaluated as in Algorithm 2.

If the output is an anomaly, we will evaluate Sig_t using mutation operation.

Mutating feature ranges. Neglecting some features will cause a signature to identify more behaviors. For example, suppose that there is a signature "*height* $\in$ *(156cm, 189cm], weight* $\in$ *(45kg, 75kg], and Nationality* $=$ *USA*". If all three features are used, it cannot identify the instance '*height* $=$ *174cm, weight* $=$ *65kg, and Nationality* $=$ *China*' will not be identified. But if '*Nationality*' is ignored, the signature will identify the instance. Essentially, ignoring features is equal to the mutation operation in Genetic Algorithms[4]. One condition of the mutation is that it should not lead to any contradiction in the existing signatures. For example, if we let F_1 and F_2 mutate, signatures "$\langle a, b, c, d\rangle$" in $N(F_{1\ldots 4})$ and "$\langle x, y, c, d\rangle$" in $A(F_{1\ldots 4})$ will contradict to each other.

Furthermore, we use a mutation point number np_m to measure the diversity of the mutation process. In the detection phase, given np_m and $\Omega(F_{1\ldots n})$, the unidentified test signature Sig_t will be evaluated as in Algorithm 3.

Algorithm 3 Evaluating a test signature via mutation.

Require: (1) $\Omega(F_{1\ldots n})$; (2) Sig_t; and (3) np_m.
```
Initialization, StatusList = ∅
for every signature Sig_1 ∈ Ω(F_1...n) do
   calculate D(Sig_t, Sig_1)
   if D(Sig_t, Sig_1) ≤ np_m then
      /*if R(Sig_1, F_i) ≠ R(Sig_t, F_i), F_i will be mutated*/
      Enumerate all mutated features F_m1, ..., F_mk (k ≤ np_m);
      if no conflicting signatures w.r.t. F_m1, F_m2, ..., F_mk then
         Append the status(es) of Sig_1 into StatusList;
      end if
   end if
end for
Determine the detection results based on StatusList;
```

3.6 L3 Model Generalization

If the test signature Sig_t cannot be identified by L1 and L2 generalization, it will be identified by the signature(s) with the minimum distance to it.

Nearest signatures. We assume that the test signature has the same NSA label as its nearest signature(s) in the behavior models, which is measured by its minimum distance to all signatures in $\Omega_{F_{1\ldots n}}$,

$$D_{min}(Sig_t, \Omega(F_{1\ldots n})) = \min_{Sig_i \in \Omega(F_{1\ldots n})} D(Sig_i, Sig_t)$$

3.7 Measuring the Detection Performance

We assign a cost scheme as in Table 1 to quantify the detection performance, and calculate the average detection cost of an instance in the test audit trails. If the behavior is identified correctly, the cost is 0. Otherwise, we can assign some penalty for the detection result. In our cost scheme, we assume that the detection of an intrusion as an anomaly is useful but it is less useful than identifying an intrusion. Specifically, suppose that there are T instances in the test audit trails. The number of false positives is $\#_{NA}$, and for false negatives, it is $\#_{IN}$. The average cost of a test instance is defined

INDEX	NOTATIONS	ORIGINAL CLASS	DETECTION RESULTS	COST
1	$\#_{NN}$	normal	normal	0
2	$\#_{NA}$	normal	anomaly	3
3	$\#_{II}$	intrusion	original intrusion	0
4	$\#_{IA}$	intrusion	anomaly	1
5	$\#_{IN}$	intrusion	normal	3

Table 1. Detection results and their costs.

as: $cost = \#_{NA} \times 3 + \#_{IN} \times 3 + \#_{IA} \times 1 \times \frac{1}{T}$. In addition, the average cost in absence of any generalization gives the reference baseline, $cost_{base}$, of the detection performance. In practice, the usefulness of model generalization is reflected in the relation between its average cost and $cost_{base}$. If $cost > cost_{base}$, its performance has been degraded by such model generalization. Otherwise, the model generalization can be assumed to be useful for intrusion detection.

4 Experiments: A Case Study

We have chosen a typical dataset from KDD CUP 1999 contest [3], which meets the requirements of our framework: *labeled audit trails* and *an intrusion-specific feature vector*, in which $\varepsilon_d = 1$ and $\varepsilon_c = 0.01$. In order to keep the computation within reasonable limits, we sample instances from the datasets: 10000 instances from the total 4898431 training instances and 500 instances from 311029 test instances randomly. For convincing, we give three pairs of such training and test samples. We have performed our experiments on larger samples, but the experimental results on our larger samples have the same characteristics to the results on the current samples.

4.1 Without Model Generalization

Table 2 lists the detection results when there is no generalization, and they are regarded as the baseline $cost_{base}$. Also in this table, the 2nd and 3rd columns give the numbers of normal and intrusive instances in every sample pair.

Sample	Norm.	Intru.	$\#_{NN}$	$\#_{NA}$	$\#_{II}$	$\#_{IA}$	$\#_{IN}$	*cost*
Pair 1	103	397	0	103	203	193	1	1.01
Pair 2	91	409	0	91	216	193	0	0.932
Pair 3	108	392	5	103	193	198	1	1.02

Table 2. L0: without model generalization.

Among the detection results, more than half of intrusive instances are identified correctly (denoted by $\#_{II}$), but, in comparison, almost all normal instances are detected incorrectly. To some extent, it indicates that the normal behaviors are of great variety, and more generalization is needed to infer their statuses.

		with the range merging step:						without the range merging step:					
L1	G_{in}	$\#_{NN}$	$\#_{NA}$	$\#_{II}$	$\#_{IA}$	$\#_{IN}$	*cost*	$\#_{NN}$	$\#_{NA}$	$\#_{II}$	$\#_{IA}$	$\#_{IN}$	*cost*
L1.4	0	35	68	280	115	2	0.65	6	97	278	118	1	0.824
L1.4	1	35	68	280	115	2	0.65	6	97	278	118	1	0.824
L1.4	2	35	68	281	114	2	0.648	6	97	278	118	1	0.824
L1.4	3	35	68	280	115	2	0.65	6	97	279	117	1	0.822
L1.4	4	35	68	281	114	2	0.648	6	97	279	117	1	0.822
L1.4	5	35	68	281	114	2	0.648	6	97	278	118	1	0.824
L1.4	10	35	68	280	115	2	0.65	6	97	279	117	1	0.822
L1.4	20	35	68	281	114	2	0.648	6	97	278	118	1	0.824

Table 3. L1.4 generalization on the 1st sample pair.

4.2 Evaluating L1 Model Generalization

Table 3 gives the detection performance on the 1st sample pair with L1.4 generalization, where $G_{in} \in \{0, 1, 2, 3, 4, 5, 10, 20\}$. Obviously, the value of G_{in} has no influence on the detection performance in all aspects. The same phenomenon is held in the other two sample pairs of our experiments as well. Thus, we let $G_{in} = 0$ in the following experiments.

The utility of the range merging step. In Table 3, the range merging step has contributed much to the performance enhancement by identifying more normal behaviors. Note that the range merging step has little effect on the identification ability for intrusive behaviors.

Table 4 gives the evaluation results on the four scenarios of L1 generalization. We analyze their utility for intrusion detection, and their difference.

	with the range merging step						without the range merging step					
L1	$\#_{NN}$	$\#_{NA}$	$\#_{II}$	$\#_{IA}$	$\#_{IN}$	*cost*	$\#_{NN}$	$\#_{NA}$	$\#_{II}$	$\#_{IA}$	$\#_{IN}$	*cost*
(Pair 1) Normal:Intrusion=103:397												
L1.1	6	97	241	155	1	0.898	0	103	203	193	1	1.01
L1.2	35	68	281	114	2	0.648	6	97	279	117	1	0.822
L1.3	35	68	280	115	2	0.65	6	97	278	118	1	0.824
L1.4	35	68	280	115	2	0.65	6	97	278	118	1	0.824
(Pair 2) Normal:Intrusion=91:409												
L1.1	3	88	263	144	2	0.828	0	91	216	193	0	0.932
L1.2	39	52	294	113	2	0.55	7	84	294	113	2	0.742
L1.3	39	52	292	115	2	0.554	7	84	294	113	2	0.742
L1.4	39	52	290	117	2	0.558	7	84	290	117	2	0.75
(Pair 3) Normal:Intrusion=108:392												
L1.1	9	99	234	154	4	0.926	5	103	193	198	1	1.02
L1.2	45	63	273	115	4	0.632	10	98	273	115	4	0.842
L1.3	45	63	273	115	4	0.632	10	98	273	115	4	0.842
L1.4	45	63	273	115	4	0.632	10	98	273	115	4	0.842

Table 4. L1 model generalization (L1.1~4,$G_{in} = 0$).

The utility of the unknown subspace splitting step. L1.1 generalization without the range merging step is L0, which has no generalization at all. Comparing the detection results in Table 4 and Table 2, it is apparent that the generalization led to by the unknown subspace splitting step is useful to identify more instances, and significantly so for intrusive behaviors.

The difference between L1.2/3/4. The new false negatives caused by L1 generalization is negligible in all three sample pairs (with 1, 2 and 3 additional ones). Overall, L1.2/3/4 have little difference on the detection results.

In summary, L1 generalization with L1.2/3/4 and range merging is useful but the detection results are not sensitive to the splitting strategies. Therefore, we arbitrarily select L1.4 with $G_{in} = 0$ in the following experiments.

4.3 Evaluating L2 Model Generalization

Figures 2 and 3 list the evaluation results highlighting the influence of grouping and mutation operations on intrusion detection. In both figures, we only illustrate $\#_{NA}$, $\#_{IA}$ and $\#_{IN}$ but the numbers of $\#_{NN}$ and $\#_{II}$ can be deduced with ease since the total of normal and intrusive behaviors remains constant.

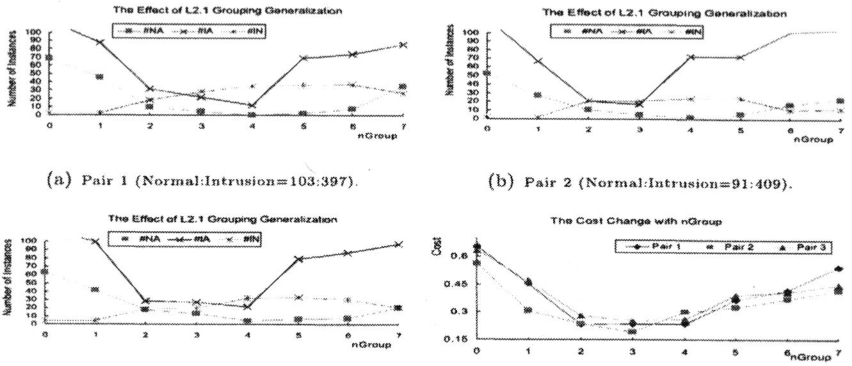

(a) Pair 1 (Normal:Intrusion=103:397). (b) Pair 2 (Normal:Intrusion=91:409).

(c) Pair 3 (Normal:Intrusion=108:392). (d) Overall Performance w.r.t. nGroup

Fig. 2. L2 generalization-grouping (nMutate=0).

L2.1 grouping generalization. As indicated in Figure 2, the grouping operation enhances intrusion detection, and the detection performance on the three samples have the same characteristics. Specifically, the overall detection performance improves because of a reduction in the detection cost. With the increase of *nGroup*, $\#_{NN}$ and $\#_{II}$ increase while $\#_{NA}$ and $\#_{IA}$ decrease, all of which are desirable. One negative aspect of grouping generalization is the increase of $\#_{IN}$ with the increase of *nGroup*.

Overall, the generalization from the grouping mechanism is useful for intrusion detection even though it will lead to a few more false negatives. We choose $nGroup = 3$ in the following experiments.

L2.2 mutation generalization. In Figure 3, the improvements caused by L2.2 mutation generalization is not that significant as L2.1 or L1 generalization. The decreased extent of false positives, $\#_{NA}$, is neutralized by the increased extent of false negatives, $\#_{IN}$. This fact is also reflected by the overall detection cost in subfigure 3.d, which is reduced only by a very small extent. The mutation operation will further worsen the negative aspects in grouping generalization.

In our case study, the L2.2 mutation generalization is useful but it is not that significant. We select $nMutate = 5$ in evaluating L3 model generalization.

4.4 Evaluating L3 Model Generalization

In evaluating L3 generalization (Table 5), $nGroup = 3$ and $nMutate = 5$. In the sample pair 1, all the normal behaviors are identified correctly, and most intrusions are also identified correctly (88.7%=352/397). In pair 1/2/3, most normal behaviors can be identified correctly with fewer false positives (i.e., $\#_{NA}$, which decreases with more generalization) after the model generalization (from L1 to

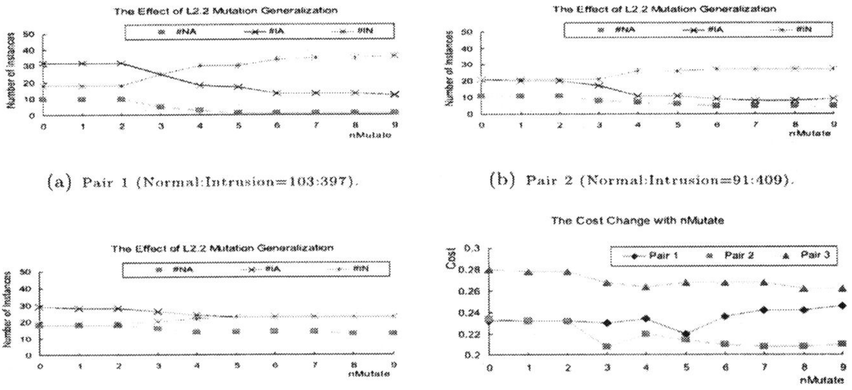

(a) Pair 1 (Normal:Intrusion=103:397). (b) Pair 2 (Normal:Intrusion=91:409).

(c) Pair 3 (Normal:Intrusion=108:392). (d) Overall Performance w.r.t nMutate

Fig. 3. L2 generalization-mutation (nGroup=3).

Sample	$\#_{NN}$	$\#_{NA}$	$\#_{II}$	$\#_{IA}$	$\#_{IN}$	*cost*
Pair 1	103	0	352	4	41	0.254
Pair 2	89	2	375	9	25	0.18
Pair 3	105	3	353	2	37	0.244

Table 5. L3 generalization (nGroup=3,nMutate=5).

L3). In contrast, even though more intrusive behaviors are identified correctly as well with more generalization, the false negatives (i.e., $\#_{IN}$) increase to a large extent (in comparison with Table 2).

4.5 The Implications of Model Generalization

In summary, model generalization is necessary for intrusion detection for identifying more behaviors correctly. The significance of every level of model generalization for intrusion detection is summarized in Table 6.

Levels	FP	FN	**Utility**
L0, L1.1	-	-	they act as an evaluation baseline to indicate whether model generalization is necessary for intrusion detection. We also found that most intrusions are identified even without generalization.
L1.2/3/4	↓	-	They improve the detection performance in our case study, significantly for intrusive behaviors. Most importantly, they lead to only a few more false negatives. Their difference are negligible.
Range Merging in L1	↓	-	It is very useful to infer the statuses for normal behaviors, but it contributes less in identifying intrusive behaviors. Another good point is that it does not lead to more false negatives.
L2.1	↓	↑	The identification capability is significantly lifted with decreasing anomalies. However, there is an optimal value for the number of grouping points, which should be determined in advance.
L2.2 /L3	↓	↑	The identification capability is slightly lifted with decreasing anomalies. But the increase of false negatives is so large that we should neglect the increase of identification capabilities.

Table 6. The significance of different levels of model generalization. The symbol '↓' represents '`decrease`' and the symbol '↑' represents '`increase`'. '-' denotes that it will not affect the parameter.

5 Conclusions and Future Work

In this paper, we designed a formal framework to evaluate the effect of various model generalization on intrusion detection in accordance with the reasonableness of its underlying assumptions. In a case study, we applied it to identify the implications of model generalization. We found that L1 generalization is generally useful to identify more 'novel' behaviors, especially for normal behaviors. L2.1 generalization will benefit intrusion detection by significantly improving the identification capability with slight increase of false negatives. The gains and losses from applying L2.2 and L3 generalization should be considered seriously under different application scenarios.

Even though our evaluation framework is generally applied to most scenarios for intrusion detection, it should be pointed out that our conclusions are only based on our case study on a typical dataset for intrusion detection. Our further work is to collect datasets to further evaluate the utility of model generalization in other areas, such as bioinformatics.

References

1. K.P. Anchor, J.B. Zydallis, G.H. Gunsch, and G.B. Lamont. Extending the computer defense immune system: Network intrusion detection with a multiobjective evolutionary programming approach. In *ICARIS 2002: 1st International Conference on Artificial Immune Systems Conference Proceedings*, 2002.
2. S.N. Chari and P. Cheng. BlueBox: A Policy-Driven, Host-based Intrusion Detection System. *ACM Transaction on Infomation and System Security*, 6(2):173–200, May 2003.
3. The KDD CUP 1999 Contest Dataset. As of january, 2006. http://www-cse.ucsd.edu/users/elkan/clresults.html, 1999.
4. David E. Goldberg. *Genetic algorithms in search, optimization, and machine learning*. Addison-Wesley Pub. Co., 1989.
5. W. Lee and S.J. Stolfo. A framework for contructing features and models for intrusion detection systems. *ACM Transactions on Information and System Security*, 3(4):227–261, Nov. 2000.
6. Zhuowei Li, Amitabha Das, and Jianying Zhou. Theoretical basis for intrusion detection. In *Proceedings of 6th IEEE Information Assurance Workshop (IAW)*, West Point, NY, USA, June 2005. IEEE SMC Society.
7. Shai Rubin, Somesh Jha, and Barton P. Miller. Automatic generation and analysis of nids attacks. In *Proceedings of the 20th Annual Computer Security Applications Conference (ACSAC'04)*, pages 28–38, 2004.
8. Shai Rubin, Somesh Jha, and Barton P. Miller. Language-based generation and evaluation of nids signatures. In *Proceedings of S&P'05*, pages 3–17, 2005.
9. Alfonso Valdes and Keith Skinner. Adaptive, model-based monitoring for cyber attack detection. In *Proceedings of RAID'00*, pages 80–92, October 2000.
10. Giovanni Vigna, William Robertson, and Davide Balzarotti. Testing network-based intrusion detection signatures using mutant exploits. In *Proceedings of CCS'04*, pages 21–30, 2004.
11. David Wagner and Paolo Soto. Mimicry attacks on host-based intrusion detection systems. In *Proceedings of CCS'02*, pages 255–264, 2002.
12. K. Wang and S.J. Stolfo. Anomalyous payload-based network intrusion detection. In *Proceedings of RAID*, 2004.

Modernising MAC: New Forms for Mandatory Access Control in an Era of DRM

William J Caelli
1 Information Security Institute, Queensland University of Technology,
GPO Box 2434, Brisbane. Queensland. 4001. Australia.
w.caelli@qut.edu.au
and
International Information Security Consultants Pty Ltd,
21 Castle Hill Drive South, Gaven. Queensland. 4211. Australia.
w.caelli@iisec.com.au

Abstract. By its definition "discretionary access control" or "DAC" was not designed or intended for use in the untrusted environment of current globally connected information systems. In addition, DAC assumed control and responsibility for all programs vested in the user; a situation now largely obsolete with the rapid development of the software industry itself. However, the superior "mandatory access control" or "MAC" specifications and resulting implementations proved to be unacceptable for commercially oriented systems and their managers. For example, the USA's National Security Agency's (NSA) "Secure LINUX" or *"SELinux"*, program made available under open source arrangements in 2000, aims at changing this state so that the benefits of MAC technology could be used to "harden" commodity ICT products. This paper analyses the need to abandon DAC, suggests variations and enhancements to basic access control concepts and relates the technology to the particular requirements of the "home computer". However, the potential for this technology to be used to limit competition must also be considered as a new participant is considered, i.e. the "owner" of software or allied systems wishing to impose digital rights management (DRM) requirements on the legitimate user.

Please use the following format when citing this chapter:

Caelli, W., 2007, in IFIP International Federation for Information Processing, Volume 232, New Approaches for Security, Privacy and Trust in Complex Environments, eds. Venter, H., Eloff, M., Labuschagne, L., Eloff, J., von Solms, R., (Boston: Springer), pp. 433–442.

1 Introduction

The microcomputer revolution [1] not only introduced the world to the commoditization of the computer hardware industry but it also heralded the rapid and accelerating growth of the overall software industry including, most notably, the "packaged software" sector. From the earliest days of use of computer systems for business and commerce applications, such as the LEO system of the mid-1950s, commercial software systems had been largely developed, tested, deployed and managed by "in-house" systems analysis and software development teams. Indeed, as large time-sharing/batch processing operating systems came into commercial usage in the early 1960s, e.g. the IBM System/360's OS/360 system, the realization that information security was becoming a concern started to arise. The USA's "Ware Report" of 1970 [2] illustrates this trend most notably. By the early 1970s computer usage had started to outgrow the physical security boundaries of the well established "computer" or "data processing" centre of the previous 20 years. Timesharing introduced the "end-user" to computer systems, e.g. firstly the creation of the FORTRAN programming language, largely used in batch processing form at the time, and then the development of the BASIC programming language for use by scientists and engineers to create their own software systems in an on-line, real-time, terminal oriented environment. In this emerging situation, it became essential that users could be protected from each other and the basic operating system and allied library structures of the main system protected from all users. The MULTICS project of the late 1960s and on till the 1980s emphasized the development of protection/security architectures and structures to achieve these goals.

In 1985, IBM sent out a *"security questionnaire"* which set out a number of pertinent questions. These included:

"21. Do operating systems provide adequate user-to-user isolation for the intended applications and environments ?

Are they able to protect themselves from disorderly behaviour by users ?

22. Are applications free from outside interference ?

23. Is data free from outside contamination ?

24. Are authorized changes to the operating systems controlled to maintain the ability to protect themselves from users ?

..... etc. "

The questions pointed to growing concern about the very security environment that was emerging by that time as commodity personal computer systems started to have an influence on the IT marketplace and such systems had started to be adopted for mission critical commercial level applications. Interestingly, this questionnaire is from the same year as the release of the final version of the USA's "Trusted Computer Systems Evaluation Criteria (TCSEC)", i.e. the *"Orange Book"*. This famous document had three major aims that are equally applicable today, as follows:

"(a) to provide users with a yardstick with which to assess the degree of trust that can be placed in computer systems for the secure processing of classified or other sensitive information;

(b) to provide guidance to manufacturers as to what to build into their new, widely-available trusted commercial products in order to satisfy trust requirements for sensitive applications; and
(c) to provide a basis for specifying security requirements in acquisition specifications."
From the outset it can be seen that a clear commercial emphasis is placed on the creation and propagation of such security parameters.

However, even by 1994 the impression, and indeed the reality, of a decline in computer systems security from the 1970s was widespread despite the existence of the "orange Book" and its allied documents that formed the so-called "Rainbow Series" of specifications. By this time the microcomputer/PC revolution dominated the ICT industry and Internet based global connectivity of these untrusted systems emerged. The feeling was summed up by Kay [3] in 1994 as follows:

"... Security is an issue because the majority of today's operating systems – both stand alone and networked – were developed without any consideration for security capability whatsoever, or security and control features were tacked on as an afterthought..."

1.1 Access Control

Corbato [4] clearly set out a major parameter for what was to become known as time-sharing operations on a central computer in a 1965 paper on the MULTICS system with the following requirements statement:

"Finally, as noted earlier, the value of a timesharing system lies not only in providing, in effect, a ***private computer*** *to a number of people simultaneously, but, above all, in the services that the system places at the fingertips of the users."*

(The emphasis is from this author.) This system became operational and in use at M.I.T. by 1969 and was later commercialized. Now, this concept of user separation, in essence a private (personal) computer, is fundamental to all forms of "trusted" usage in computer systems and forms the base of what has become known as the lowest form of control for a computer system, i.e. *"discretionary access control (DAC)"*. However, there are very severe limits to this paradigm as the Orange Book explained.

Therefore, before continuing it is worthwhile to consider the overall and general requirements that were set by the Orange Book as bases for any secure system. These were as follows, in abridged form:

"Fundamental Computer Security Requirements
Any discussion of computer security necessarily starts from a statement of requirements, i.e., what it really means to call a computer system "secure."
In general, secure systems will control, through use of specific security features, access to information such that only properly authorized individuals, or processes operating on their behalf, will have access to read, write, create, or delete information. Six fundamental requirements are derived from this basic statement of objective...

Policy

Requirement 1 - SECURITY POLICY - There must be an explicit and well-defined security policy enforced by the system... ...

Requirement 2 - MARKING - Access control labels must be associated with objects....

Accountability

Requirement 3 - IDENTIFICATION - Individual subjects must be identified...

Requirement 4 - ACCOUNTABILITY - Audit information must be selectively kept and protected so that actions affecting security can be traced to the responsible party... ...

Assurance

Requirement 5 - ASSURANCE - The computer system must contain hardware/software mechanisms that can be independently evaluated to provide sufficient assurance that the system enforces requirements 1 through 4 above....

Requirement 6 - CONTINUOUS PROTECTION - The trusted mechanisms that enforce these basic requirements must be continuously protected against tampering and/or unauthorized changes..... "

The Orange Book went on to define some four hierarchical "divisions", viz. D, C, B and A, with divisions C and B being further divided up into "classes", viz. C1, C2, B1, B2, B3. Division A was the "highest" security specification and D the lowest or "minimal" division. Today, almost all commercial operating systems lie in the "C1/C2" class providing *"discretionary access control"*. These provide simply *"separation of users and data."* Moreover, these classes are intended to have *"some form of credible controls capable of enforcing access limitations on an individual basis, i.e., ostensibly suitable for allowing users to be able to protect project or private information and to keep other users from accidentally reading or destroying their data."* However, and most importantly, the operating "environment" for these "C1/C2" systems is *"expected to be one of cooperating users processing data at the same level(s) of sensitivity."* In the age of global interconnection of host servers and client systems via the Internet, with unknown and even hostile users in existence willing to attack other systems, the concept of "cooperating users" is no longer relevant and these classes of systems should have long ago been clearly seen as unsafe and obsolete in the new interconnected environment. However, this is clearly not the case.

Moving to a higher, more secure division, the "B" or "mandatory access control (MAC)" division the parameters suddenly change. Starting at Class B1 the following applies:

"Class (B1) systems require all the features required for class (C2). In addition, an informal statement of the security policy model, data labelling, and mandatory access control over named subjects and objects must be present. The capability must exist for accurately labelling exported information."

At last some form of acknowledgement of the needs for connected security comes to the fore. By Class B2, the Class that seems to most reliably represent the situation in 2007, the security features of a modern operating systems and allied components can be clearly seen. Indeed the Orange Book itself contrasted discretionary access control (DAC) and mandatory access control (MAC) as follows:

"Discretionary security is the principal type of access control available in computer systems today. The basis of this kind of security is that an individual user, or program operating on his behalf, is allowed to specify explicitly the types of access other users may have to information under his control. Discretionary security differs from mandatory security in that it implements an access control policy on the basis of an individual's need-to-know as opposed to mandatory controls which are driven by the classification or sensitivity designation of the information. Discretionary controls are not a replacement for mandatory controls."

Even later attempts by the USA to force, or at least influence, its Department of Defence to enter into purchase of systems designed and evaluated around the Orange Book's "C2" specification achieved little, as Ryan [5] points out as follows:

"The Computer Security Act of 1987 was interpreted into policy by the DoD as requiring all computer systems to be C2-compliant by 1992, a policy known as 'C2 by '92.' "

There was also discussion at the time of making an even higher bid for computer security in the USA's Department of Defense with another, unheeded call for *"B2 by '95"* to surpass that 1992 deadline. In summary, the basic admonition of the Orange Book never really came to reality, i.e. *"to encourage the Computer Industry to develop trusted computer systems and products, making them widely available in the commercial market place. Achievement of this goal will require recognition and articulation by both the public and private sectors of a need and demand for such products."*

2 Rethinking MAC

2.1 Problem Description

In simple terms, the requirements at the enterprise level for efficient and effective access control can be paraphrased from the 4th of the USA's Computing Research Association's (CRA) *"Grand Challenges"* in computer and information security [6] set out in 2003. The 4th challenge stated as follows, and can be regarded as still being significant today:

"Give end-users security controls they can understand and privacy they can control for the dynamic, pervasive computing environments of the future."

From an enterprise perspective a "new MAC" paradigm could be proposed based on the CRA challenge above, as follows;

"Give the CIO security controls they can understand and enforcement they can control for the dynamic, pervasive computing environments of the future."

At the same time Microsoft has introduced a next generation of operating system, Windows Vista, that, according to BusinessWeek [7] *"shakes up the ecosystem"*. In particular the BusinessWeek article cited above clearly identifies the "hardening" of security in the system as a major factor; a factor of particular note to producers of commodity product level software to operate on this platform. The article presents the challenge to these companies in the following way;

"Vista also introduces big changes in the way programs install files on a PC's hard drive, log users in, and handle security functions. That could cost software companies lots of engineering time and support calls—and sap profits, says Simon Heap, a partner at consultancy Bain & Co., which advises makers of business software."

Some new and important factors have now arisen. The rapid rise of the software industry also led to questions of "software piracy" and the legitimate usage of purchased packaged systems. This meant that a new "user", so to speak, now entered the computer system; one whose interests were allied to "digital rights management (DRM)", i.e. the enforcement of whatever terms and conditions of use had been placed on the software in use, and whose "enemy" may actually be the "customer" who had purchased a license to use the software. Indeed, this development is not considered at all in the earlier "Orange Book" case where, it would appear, the model in use is one where all software systems, particularly application systems, have been designed, developed, tested and installed by the "owner" of the system who now also manages the operation of these systems.

Many enterprises no longer maintain any internal ICT professional group in the sense that such a group is chartered with the design and development of application or sub-system software for use by the enterprise. Software is now a purchased commodity, installed and operated by end-users in most cases.

2.2 The Trouble with DAC.

Figure 1 : Microsoft Inc "XENIX" system – 1984. (Source: Wikipedia – Feb 2007)

Into the 1990s attempts were made to make "B-level" trusted systems with MAC capability commercial realities. An example is *"Trusted XENIX"*, a special version from "Trusted Information Systems Inc." of Microsoft's "XENIX" operating system developed for the Intel x86 CPU chip set from an AT&T UNIX licence in the late 1970s. Other activities included research projects aimed at a similar level of trusted system behaviour. These included the "Trusted MACH (TMach)" project aimed at a high trust version of the Mach micro-kernel system. In addition the "SEVMS", by

Digital Equipment Corporation [8] implemented *"..a mandatory (i.e. non-discretionary) access control mechanism"* with the claimed property that it *"..is an implementation of a security policy which is beyond direct user control. This security policy is centrally and uniformly established by the system security manager (often the system manager). SEVMS is responsible for enforcing the security policy established by the security manager."* Similarly "Trusted Solaris" [9] from SUN Microsystems aimed at the same philosophy. This is summarized in the Trusted Solaris data sheet as follows: *"MAC hierarchical and compartmentalized labels correspond to the sensitivity of information that must be kept separate, even when it is stored on a single system. Because information labeling happens automatically, MAC is mandatory. Ordinary users cannot change labels unless the system administrator gives them special authorization. In fact, users with labels in separate compartments are not allowed to share information. By enhancing and extending security mechanisms, Trusted Solaris 8 software provides additional protection for servers and desktop systems that process highly sensitive information."*

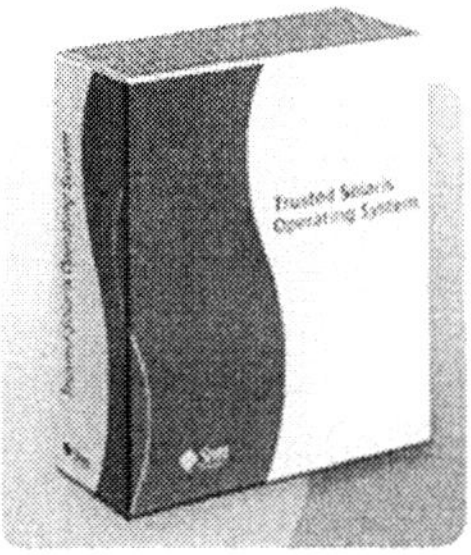

2.3 Themes and Challenges

The past thirty years or more has seen a number of security models developed, meeting complementary requirements for security in computer systems. [10, 11] Experimental and "small run" operating systems have been developed and deployed using these models but none, outside the basic "access control list (ACL)" structure has really been accepted in mass market operating systems and allied software products.

Thus, the challenge of "modernizing MAC" can best be considered in the light of four distinct themes or broad categorizations of information systems usage. These are:

a. Large enterprises, both public and private,
b. Small to medium enterprises,
c. Micro-businesses, and
d. Individual or home users.

Within each of these broad categories a number of challenges can be set out, as follows.

2.3.1 Large Enterprises, Public and Private

The challenges here are mainly personnel based. These may be summarized as follows:

- comprehensibility to the normal enterprise CIO,
- mapping of commercial enterprise parameters and risk assessment processes to a new paradigm,
- incorporating risk assessment and management processes into the mandatory-style regime,

- development of assessment methods for the system definition and procurement stages,
- appropriate "profile" definition and management packages aligned to enterprise realities and integrated into enterprise level systems,
- appropriate education and training for the CIO,
- education and training for application system developers, and
- appropriate cost evaluation parameters for senior management, including any necessary retraining and allied expenses.

2.3.2 Small to Medium Enterprise

In this case it must be assumed that some ICT professional resources are available to the enterprise, either "in-house" or by contract. The challenges become a sub-set of the ones above:

- availability of appropriate security/profiling definition tools mapped to medium enterprise needs,
- incorporation of MAC "awareness" into packaged systems relevant to this class of enterprise, and
- higher levels of education and training tools.

2.3.3 Micro-enterprises

This category of enterprise covers the normal "small-office, home-office (SOHO)" category of enterprise consisting of under 10 staff members, for example. This business profile means that the enterprise does not have any "in-house" ICT professional assistance and, as needed, will normally employ appropriate contractors in the necessary area. The challenges here are quite different and important since this class of enterprise which, once connected to the global Internet using commodity level hardware and software products, becomes a target for attack and compromise. Some challenges in this situation are:

- incorporation of MAC facilities into popular business information systems used by this class of enterprise,
- simplified schemes for the installation and management of MAC oriented operating systems and relevant software systems, and
- education and training of the application software enterprises catering to this class of user.

2.3.4 Home User

This, the largest category of user, has unique requirements. The DAC paradigm has meant that computer programs loaded into a home computer from other computer systems connected to the global Internet have largely "inherited" the access parameters of the user and software system used to load such packages, e.g. the "browser", email handler, etc. recent attempts, e.g. by Microsoft Inc of the USA with its "Windows/Mandatory Integrity Control (W/MIC)" concept has started on path towards the need to separate the information environment of the home user from that assumed by software packages "invited" into the system. The challenges for MAC in this environment appear to include:

- transparency of the underlying MAC level complexity from the end-user/administrator,
- simplification of the labeling requirements inherent in MAC design,
- provision of understandable and easily administered "profiles" covering the normal processes undertaken on a "personal/home" computer system.

2.4 Digital Rights Management and Encryption

A string new role "player" has come to the fore in the 21st century. This is the role of the software/content "owner" whose "enemy", in a way, is its very own customer. Digital rights management (DRM) introduces in to the MAC paradigm a parameter not normally considered in the past in defining the appropriate access control models, e.g. read/write/append/delete permissions, etc. Today, DRM systems may be required to limit legitimate and authorized systems users from certain activities within their own computer systems, e.g. read from one file and write to another such as is required to "copy" data from a "source" to a "target". At present, DRM enforcement schemes at the operating systems level appear to be limited to the following incomplete list of methods and schemes,

- use of encryption/decryption processes to restrict access to data,
- control of the encryption/decryption processes themselves through restrictions on access to operating systems components, such as device drivers, etc., an example being access to the device driver sub-systems for high density DVD units,
- control of the necessary cryptographic "key" structures required by the encryption/decryption processes, and
- use of "privilege" restrictions to separate access rights of legitimate users from those which are claimed by the "owner" of the data, e.g. copyright holder, etc.

An open research question exists in relation to the most appropriate technologies required to integrate cryptographic sub-systems into MAC operating system architecture. While such systems as "SELinux" have started to address this problem with appropriate interface definitions and appropriate kernel level architectures, the high level relationships between such cryptographic sub-systems and end-user/process profiles is still largely unresolved.

3. Conclusions.

This paper has proposed that there are many challenges to the goal of making MAC security architectures relevant and useful at the commercial and commodity computer system level. These challenges are both technical and administrative. At the same time, the lack of and need for appropriate information security education and training is seen as a barrier to the commercial acceptance of "hardened" MAC-based operating systems and allied structures.

Acknowledgments

This overall research program has been supported by a grant from the Australian Research Council (ARC).

References

1. Caelli, W., The Microcomputer Revolution: Some Social Implications of Advanced Technology, (Monograph No. 1, Australian Computer Society, Sydney, 1979. ISBN 0-909925-21-6).
2. Ware, W. H., ed., Security Controls for Computer Systems: Report of Defense Science Board Task Force on Computer Security, AD # A076617/0, Rand Corporation, Santa Monica, Calif., February 1970, reissued October 1979.
3. Kay. R., Distributed and Secure, BYTE Vol. 19, No. 6, June 1994, Pg. 165.
4. F. J. Corbato and V. A. Vyssotsky, Introduction and Overview of the Multics System, Fall Joint Computer Conference 1965; http://www.multicians.org/fjcc1.html.
5. Ryan J., The Effect of Public Budgetary and Policy Decisions on Development of Trusted Systems, http://www.gwu.edu/~asem_dc/RyanASEM02.html.
6. http://www.cra.org/Activities/grand.challenges/security/home.html.
7. http://www.businessweek.com/technology/content/feb2007/tc20070222_677788.htm?link_position=link1 Accessed at 24 Feb 2007.
8. SEVMS User's Guide, Order Number: AA-QC05A-TE, November 1994, Digital Equipment Corporation, Massachusetts. USA.
9. http://www.sun.com/software/solaris/trustedsolaris/ds-ts8/index.xml.
10. Summers, R, C., An overview of computer security, IBM Systems Journal, Vol. 23, No. 4, 1984.
11. Ames, S. R. and Neumann, P., Guest Editors' Introduction: Computer Security Technology, Computer, Vol. 16, No. 7. July 1983.

Covert Identity Information in Direct Anonymous Attestation (DAA)

Carsten Rudolph

Fraunhofer Institute for Secure Information Technology – SIT,
Rheinstrasse 75, Darmstadt, Germany, Carsten.Rudolph@sit.fraunhofer.de

Abstract. Direct anonymous attestation (DAA) is a practical and efficient protocol for authenticated attestation with satisfaction of strong privacy requirements. This recently developed protocol is already adopted by the Trusted Computing Group and included in the standardized trusted platform module TPM. This paper shows that the main privacy goal of DAA can be violated by the inclusion of covert identity information. This problem is very relevant, as the privacy attack is both efficient and very difficult to detect.

1 Introduction

Authenticity and strong privacy seem to be obviously contradictory requirements. One cannot remain anonymous and authenticate oneself at the same time. Pseudonymous authentication based on certification authorities require strong trust into these authorities, as they can link pseudonymous identities to real identities. Recently sophisticated approaches have been developed in order to achieve pseudonymous authentication while preserving the privacy of the entity to be authenticated and relying on weaker trust assumptions for the certification authorities involved in the process. One practical and efficient protocol is called *direct anonymous authentication (DAA)* and was proposed by Brickell, Camenisch and Chen [2, 3]. A straightforward application for DAA lies in the area of *trusted computing*, where a platform is said to be trusted when it can attest to comply with a particular standard and runs with a particular configuration. The consequences to the privacy of the platform owner have been widely discussed (e.g. [6, 1]). Among other things, the TPM is criticised as being a tool for collecting personal information and for supporting data miners in generating consumer profiles.

The DAA protocol is based on Camenisch-Lysyanskaya signatures [4]. The main goal of DAA is to provide strong authentication and privacy even if the certification authority (here called *DAA issuer*) and the verifier collude. The issuer and the verifier could even be the same entity. By using DAA a prover can remain anonymous (or pseudonymous), and nevertheless, provide evidence by which is attested that it is using certified trusted hardware (e.g. a TPM protected platform) and pseudonymous identification without the possibility of tracing and linking actions of one particular TPM. DAA seems to provide a

Please use the following format when citing this chapter:

Rudolph, C., 2007, in IFIP International Federation for Information Processing, Volume 232, New Approaches for Security, Privacy and Trust in Complex Environments, eds. Venter, H., Eloff, M., Labuschagne, L., Eloff, J., von Solms, R., (Boston: Springer), pp. 443–448.

reasonable solution for the privacy problems associated with TPMs. DAA was quickly adopted by the Trusted Computing Group (TCG) and included in the TCG standard for the trusted platform module (TPM) [5].

In this paper we show that the issuer can use the join protocol of DAA to include covert identity information into the public key used for certification and DAA signature verification. This inclusion of identity information does not constitute an attack on the cryptographic mechanisms used by DAA. The security proofs for DAA rely on the (implicit) assumption that no data in the DAA protocol contains covert identity information. The presented privacy attack nicely shows that even such a highly sophisticated protocol can be easily misused to successfully undermine the security requirements. Furthermore, the attack cannot be detected by any honest participant of the protocol.

2 Direct anonymous attestation

We give a high level description of DAA. This description contains only those details required to understand the privacy problem explained in the subsequent section. In particular, all details concerned with the detection of rogue TPMs and revocation are not relevant for the attack and therefore omitted. More details of the scheme, explanation of the underlying cryptographic algorithms and security proofs can be found in the original publication [2] and in a full version of [2] available at http://eprint.iacr.org/2004.

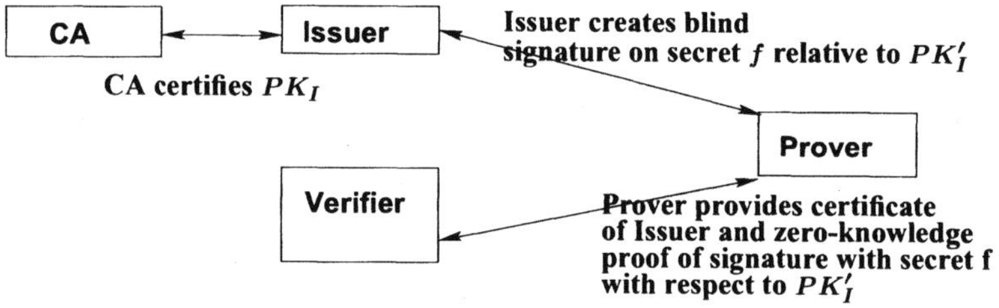

Fig. 1. DAA overview

The scenario for DAA requires four actors as depicted in Figure 1 showing an overview of the DAA protocol. A certification authority CA certifies long-term public keys (PK_I). The role of this CA corresponds to the role of certification authorities in standard public key infrastructures. A second (low-security) certification instance, the issuer, provides blindly signed credentials to be used for DAA signatures with respect to a DAA public key (PK'_I). The main actors in the DAA scheme are prover and verifier. In a trusted computing scenario the verifier might require that a prover provides evidence that its platform is equipped with a trusted platform module TPM and is in conformity with the particular standard. Further, the verifier might request an authentic report on the current configuration of the platform. In this process, it can be in the interest of the prover to stay anonymous or at least to provide only pseudonymous identification. It shall not be possible for different verifiers to link actions by the prover using the same platform, i.e. initiated using a particular TPM. Furthermore, no verifier should learn any identity information from the DAA signature, apart from the pseudonym used for this DAA exchange. Please note that DAA allows for different modes distinguished by the level of privacy for the prover. This level ranges from total anonymity to a pseudonymous authentication that allows the verifier to link different actions. The verifier decides on the level of privacy.

The DAA scheme consists of two main phases, the join protocol and the actual sign/verify protocol.

The goal of the join protocol as shown in Figure 2 is that the issuer provides to the prover a blind signature that can be used to prove that a secret f was generated by the prover (e.g. by the prover's TPM). In the context of trusted computing, this credential is a critical component in the scheme, as with knowledge of the credential one can "impersonate" TCG-compliant hardware. Therefore, the credential must stay inside the TPM, even during the signature verification process.

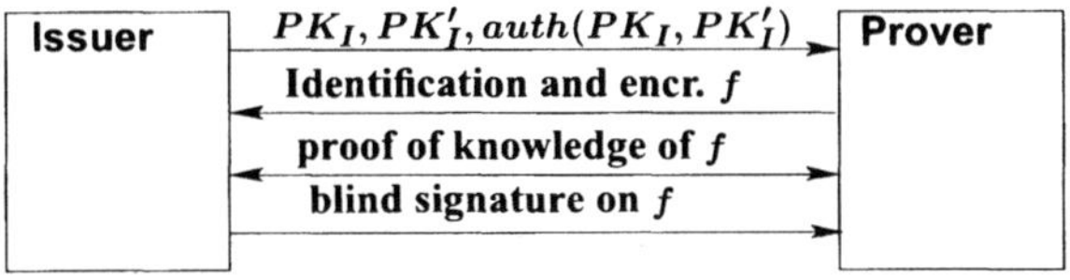

Fig. 2. DAA join protocol

The main steps of the join protocol can be summarized as follows:

1. Issuer generates a public key PK_I' and authorises this key with its own long-term public key PK_I which is certified by the CA.
2. Issuer proves to the prover that PK_I' is correctly generated to satisfy the conditions for secure use in DAA (see [2] for details).
3. Prover provides identity information to the issuer and authenticates itself. A TPM, for example, uses its endorsement key EK that uniquely identifies a particular TPM.
4. Prover chooses secret f and sends f encrypted for blind signature to issuer.
5. Issuer generates a blind signature on f and sends it to the prover.

In the DAA sign protocol, the prover (i.e. the prover's platform and TPM) signs a message m, (in the trusted computing context this might be an anonymous attestation identity key AIK). The following description shows the principal steps of the sign protocol.

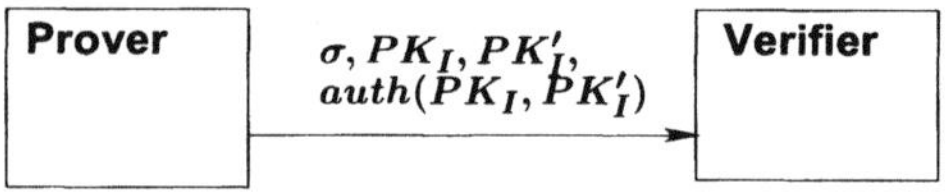

Fig. 3. DAA sign protocol

1. The prover and verifier agree on the parameters to be signed. One of the parameters is the *name* of the platform in the protocol. If this name computed from a random number, the sign is completely anonymous, if the name is computed from a number chosen by the verifier, the sign constitutes a pseudonymous identification and the verifier can link different instances of the sign protocol by the same platform. However, the verifier cannot link these with DAA instances the platform has run with other verifiers.
2. The prover produces a signature of knowledge σ over the name and a few other parameters expressing that σ was computed using the secret f blindly certified by the issuer.
3. The verifier receives PK'_I and σ and can now verify this signature w.r.t PK'_I. In the context of trusted computing the verifier can now conclude that the issuer has checked the endorsement key EK (and conformance credentials), that secret F is stored within this TPM, and that message m belongs to this TPM.

3 Insertion of covert identity information into the issuer's DAA public key

A central security proposition of DAA is that nobody can link DAA signatures to particular instances of the join protocol, i.e. the identity of the TPM is protected and different actions of one TPM with different verifiers cannot be linked even when verifiers and issuer collude. In the remainder of this paper the term *identity information* denotes all information that weakens this property.

Before the start of the join phase, the issuer computes the DAA public key PK'_I. During the join protocol the TPM's endorsement key EK is used to identify the TPM. This endorsement key uniquely identifies a TPM. Obviously, if the issuer is able to create a unique public key for each TPM, every DAA signature of the TPM can be linked back by the issuer to the TPM's EK. As the DAA public keys are self-certified by the issuer using its long-term key PK_I, the issuer can generate these keys without the help of any other entity. Thus, by using different keys PK'_I for different TPMs the issuer has effectively included identity information into the public keys. Every entity taking part in the protocol can now link a PK'_I to a particular TPM. The DAA protocol itself remains totally unchanged and neither the platform nor the TPM is able to tell whether the issuer has associated the public key with any identity information. However, if verifiers are aware that the issuer has generated unique public keys for each TPM they can match this information and tell which transactions where made using the same TPM. By colluding with the issuer a verifier can even match particular actions with a TPM's public endorsement key, thus totally breaking the pseudonymity or anonymity of the protocol.

4 Relevance of the attack

The relevance of the attack depends on several factors, most importantly: plausibility of the attack scenario, difficulty of detection by honest participants, efficiency of the attack, and availability of fixes to prevent the attack.

First, the attack scenario is very plausible. It attacks one of the main advantages of DAA. The issuer is not supposed to be as secure as a "classical" PKI certification authority. The only trust required is that the issuer will not issue wrong certificates, but there are no privacy requirements. Issuer and verifier could even be the same entity. Thus, the issuer can indeed be interested in including covered identity information into the DAA public key. Furthermore, one can imagine a situation where an issuer generates a completely new public key for each DAA join protocol without the intention to provide any identity information. In principal, such a behaviour should increase the security of the protocol. However, by being able to distinguish different instances of DAA join, verifiers are able to identify actions by particular provers even without any malicious behaviour of the issuer or any collusion between issuer and verifier.

Second, the issuer does not act in contradiction to the DAA protocol. Consequently, nobody can tell whether any of the components of the DAA public key is linked to any identity information. Only verifiers with access to many DAA public keys from the same issuer can detect the embedded information. However, verifiers might be interested in collecting identity information or might collude with the issuer. Therefore, detection of the privacy attack is very difficult.

Third, the generation of a large number of public keys can be done very efficiently. During the setup stage the issuer first selects a RSA modulus $n = pq$ with $p = 2p' + 1, q = 2q' + 1$. Then a random generator g' of the group of quadratic residues modulo n is chosen. Next it chooses six random integers $x_0, x_1, x_z, x_s, x_h, x_g \in [1, p'q']$ and computes

$$g := g'^{x_g} \bmod n,\ h := g'^{x_h} \bmod n,\quad S := h^{x_s} \bmod n,$$
$$Z := h^{x_z} \bmod n,\ R_0 := S^{x_0} \bmod n,\ R_1 := S^{x_1} \bmod n.$$

The values g, h, S, Z, R_0, R_1 are components of the issuer's DAA public key and can therefore be used by the issuer to link the key to the identity information. The issuer only needs to go through the setup process once and then independently compute, for example, a unique value $R_1 := S^{x_1} \bmod n$ for each TPM. Thus, only a minimal amount of additional computation (one modular exponentiation) is required for each join protocol.

Finally, there is no obvious change to DAA that can prevent the attack. One possibility is to require higher security from the issuer (audits, control, etc) losing one big advantage of the protocol. However, even if only a small number of public keys is used, it is still possible for the issuer and the verifiers to distinguish several groups of users by using a specific key for each particular group.

For the trusted computing scenario the consequences have to be considered very problematic. All DAA signatures by a particular TPM could be linked to the identity of this TPM. The TPM has no control over the issuer's public key. Thus, the TPM cannot detect and consequently cannot prevent the inclusion of covert identity information. If verifiers are aware of this covert identity information, they can track TPM actions and several verifiers can tell which actions where executed by the same TPM without actively colluding with the issuer.

5 Conclusions

DAA is a very sophisticated approach to achieve some kind of authenticity and security without violating privacy requirements. However, as the example in this paper shows covert identity information can be easily embedded by the DAA issuer. This breaks the main privacy goals of the protocol. The consequences for a TPM owner's privacy largely depends on the particular applications and circumstances in which the protocol is used. Nevertheless, the relevance of the problem is increased by the fact that the degree of required collusion between verifier and DAA issuer is quite small. As soon as the verifier realises that the issuer uses a unique public key for every EK, all actions by the same TPM can be linked by the verifier without any contribution of the issuer. Only if the platform of the prover shall be identified by its EK, issuer and verifier have to collude as this information can only be provided by the issuer. However, this kind of collusion is realistic in the case of DAA, because DAA was explicitly developed to also support business scenarios where issuer and verifier are the same entity.

References

1. R. Anderson. 'trusted computing' frequently asked questions. http://www.cl.cam.ac.uk/~rja14/tcpa-faq.html, 2003.
2. E. Brickell, J. Camenisch, and L. Chen. Direct anonymous attestation. In *11th ACM Conference on Computer and Communications Security*. ACM Press, 2004.
3. J. Camenisch. Better privacy for trusted computing platforms. In *9th European Symposium On Research in Computer Security (ESORICS 2004)*, 2004.
4. J. Camenisch and A. Lysyanskaya. A signature scheme with efficient protocols. In *Security in Communication Networks, Third International Conference, SCN 2003*, volume 2576 of *Lecture Notes in Computer Science*, pages 268–289. Springer Verlag, 2003.
5. Trusted Computing Group. TCG TPM Specification 1.2 revision 94. www.trustedcomputing.org, 2006.
6. M. Hansen. A double-edged blade - on trusted computing's impact on privacy. In *Datenschutz und Datensicherheit*, pages 525–528, 2004.

Safeguarding Personal Data using Rights Management in Distributed Applications

Adolf Hohl[1] and Alf Zugenmaier[2]

[1] University of Freiburg, adolf.hohl@iig.uni-freiburg.de,
[2] DoCoMo Euro-Labs, zugenmaier@docomolab-euro.com

Abstract. Privacy includes the right to determine the use of personal information after it has been released. Some compliance solutions have been proposed already. However, they are usually monolithic systems operating only within one database system or requiring a customized infrastructure. This paper explores the possibility to use an off-the-shelf document rights management platform to enable enforcement of usage policies. First experiences from a building a demonstration application are encouraging.

1 Introduction

Fears of users about misuse of their personal data can prevent acceptance of new services and technologies. This is especially the case, when software acting on behalf of the user can autonomously release sensitive information to communicating partners or services. Nearly everybody has had experience of misused personal information in the Internet such as unwanted advertisements and spam. This is only the tip of the iceberg. More serious abuse of the information may involve selling it to rating agencies, resulting in unwanted "personalization" of prices, interest rates, denial of credit, etc.

Therefore, it is essential that services handle their users' personal data with care and can communicate this fact to the service users. If it is not possible to ensure this, fear of misuse and privacy concerns remain with the user.

In this paper, we address the problem of giving service users more control over their data after they are transmitted, e.g., during the use of a service or an application. As a running example, we make use of a sales scenario in which a person is interested in buying a car. To improve the service quality to the user the car dealer can combine his car offering with a suitable car insurance and provide a finance offering.

We assume a very simple policy to avoid misuse: use the data only for providing an offer and delete the data afterwards. This policy is also called oblivion[1, 2].

Part of this work was funded by the DFG / Gottlieb Daimler and Carl Benz Foundation. We would like to thank Caspar Bowden of Microsoft EMEA for his comments on an earlier version of this paper.

Please use the following format when citing this chapter:

Hohl, A. and Zugenmaier, A., 2007, in IFIP International Federation for Information Processing, Volume 232, New Approaches for Security, Privacy and Trust in Complex Environments, eds. Venter, H., Eloff, M., Labuschagne, L., Eloff, J., von Solms, R., (Boston: Springer), pp. 449–456.

The contribution of this paper is to show the feasibility and explore the practical problems of using rights management for privacy aware managing of personal data as proposed by Korba and Kenny [3].

The paper is structured as follows: The next section discusses an overview of the approach. Section 3 describes the application implementation. We briefly evaluate the performance in Section 4. A discussion of these results takes place in Section 5. Related work is described in Section 6. Conclusions conclude the paper.

2 The Approach

Korba and Kenny observed in in [3] that the interests a service user has in dealing with sensitive data are similar to those of providers of copyrighted digital contents. Both, the copyrighted content provider and the service user, i.e., the personal data provider, are interested in making data available only for limited use and processing. Furthermore, unauthorized onward transmission and use should be prevented. Subsequently, control over transmitted data or contents has to be enforced.

Sensitive personal data is therefore sent in a protected way to the service provider thus preventing unauthorized usage and information leakage. This encrypted data has a license attached to it when communicated to the service providers. The license limits the use of this personal data. The service user now takes the role of a content provider and license issuer. Because it would be unmanageable if every service user had her own slightly different license attached to her data interest groups should act as liaison and offer standardized licenses.

This is an orthogonal approach to classical anonymization techniques with the concepts of data minimality and data obfuscation. This attacker model assumed here is weaker than the model usually assumed for privacy enhancing technologies. We expect some level of cooperation by some service providers. The service user needs to find out which service providers are willing to cooperate. Another new aspect of this attacker model is that the service provider is not seen as one atomic entity. There may be parts of the service providers organization that could be more trustworthy than others.

3 Technical Solution

In our proof of concept implementation we built a client – server application for the car sales scenario to make and serve a request using rights protected personal data while at the same time adhering to policies. The personal data is encrypted and the usage license for the service provider is created and issued. It is the duty of the application, respective the developer of it that it adheres to the semantic of a specified right or a corresponding policy. To ensure this property, a review by an independent party should certify the source code. The source code could also be published to give somebody the chance to do this task.

Despite the obvious need for a hardware root of trust such as a Trusted Computing Platform[4], they are not widely deployed.

Therefore, we have chosen a rights management framework on the Windows platform which currently does not support the level of security as hardware based approaches but is widely available. In addition to dealing with digital rights, this framework provides similar primitives as realized by TC-Platforms by using a hardened software implementation[1]. At this point we don't focus on the security of this hardened implementation. Instead we speculate that with the availability of Trusted Computing Platforms this could be improved easily. We focus on the services the framework provides and how they can be used for privacy protecting applications.

The framework implements necessary requirements for distributed access control on an application level. This includes the *application identification and signing* to detect if a rights managed application is tampered with. This is necessary to prevent a tampered application making use of a granted right. A *secure storage* is realized by binding keys and licenses to the platform by encrypting it with a platform specific key. Data could be bound to dedicated platform configurations and users. This is realized by *authentication framework* for *platform attributes*(e.g. the absence of a screen-grabber) and the *user*.

3.1 The Used Rights

In the selected scenario, we implement two rights. The right *VIEW* is based on a built in right of the framework and decrypts protected content. The semantic interpretation of this right here is to view personal data and use it for the calculation of a car offer. Despite the fact that the right is called view, the application does not allow a sales clerk to view the personal information. The right *ANONYMIZE:* is specified by our own. It is introduced because there is no delegation feature in the rights management (RM) framework. From a functional point of view, the framework treats it as the *VIEW* right and provides decryption solely. Special functionality must be defined in the conforming application. If *ANONYMize* is specified as a right, the car dealer is allowed to transmit user data only after removing identifying information.

3.2 The User's Application

The user's application protects the personal information for use by the service application. While the representation of the data similar to a *vcard* address form remains, this content is encrypted and suitable licenses for the consumers are issued. A detailed description of this procedure is in [5]. In Figure 1 the necessary

[1] Because of the limitations in protecting code this is mainly done by security through obscurity such as anti-debugging techniques and embedded secret keys in libraries

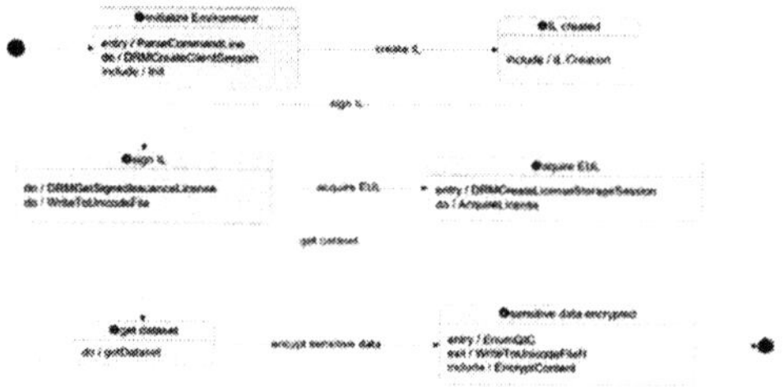

Fig. 1. State chart of the user's application

steps are visualized in a state chart of the application. After the initialization of the environment and the RM-framework (step 1) the application prepares an *Issuance License, IL* and grants rights with a validation date to the principal under whose ID the server application is running (step 2). The Issuance License is signed. Therefore a prior acquired *Client Licensor Certificate, CLC* from the license server is loaded to sign the Issuance License and make it to a *Signed Issuance License, SIL* (step 3). To encrypt the content an *End User License, EUL* is derived from the IL which allows to extract the encryption key (step 4). After this step, the personal data is read in (step 5) and encrypted by the framework (step 6). It is ready for transmission to the service together with its SIL.

3.3 The Service Application

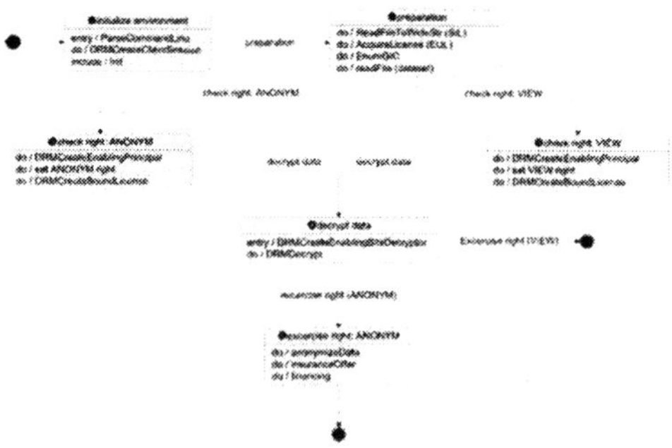

Fig. 2. State chart of the service application

The service acts from a rights management viewpoint as a consumer of protected content and licenses. Therefore the service application uses the RM-framework for decrypting and consuming content in a granted context. The service application logic has to ensure that it does not leak any personal data.

The user has to rely on the assurance that a particular application really adheres to the specified rights. Figure 2 visualizes the states of the service application. First, the environment and the RM-framework is initialized (step 1) and the protected personal data set and the SIL is loaded. The license server is contacted and a EUL, corresponding to the SIL is requested (step 2). The application checks the EUL for the granted rights *VIEW* and *ANONYMIZE* (step 3). Using a granted right, the content is decrypted and processed with the method implementing the purpose for the right specified (step 4,5).

4 Implementation Evaluation

Because the evaluation of the security of the rights management framework is out of scope for this paper, the performance of our implementation was measured basically in order to figure out very time consuming phases. This is important if one envisions large number of transactions privacy protected with rights management. We could not identify such a time consuming phase which would make it unfeasible to use. When a service supports several users at the same time the time consumption of step 2, 3 and 4 on the service side are of special interest. Processing of these steps are necessary for each user.

For our measurement, the code of our application was instrumented with a time reporting procedure at important phases.

Issuing of the license took just under two seconds, while consumption (steps 2, 3 and 4) took 0.7 seconds. The issuing part of the application contacts the license server via the network when it acquires a CLC, accounting for 1.3 seconds of this time. Therefore this value depends on the round-trip-time of the network and the workload of the license server. The same appears when the consuming application acquires an EUL. Under heavy load of the license server this time can increase. However, our test setup was not designed to stress test the server.

5 Discussion

The implementation represents a first step towards using cooperative mechanisms to protect the privacy of users which are reported and enforced technically by the service provider. The operating system provides a rights management framework for distributed access control at the application level. Currently the root of trust of the framework is software based, but will hopefully support a hardware attested *Trusted Computing Base* in the future.

Limitations by design is the effort necessary for a check of an implementation for processing a certain right is compliant with the semantic meaning of this right. Currently the rights *VIEW* and *ANONYMIZE* can be granted by a service user. Their compliance has to checked by the service user or a trusted independent party. If the code of the service application is publicly available, everybody can check that it does what it claims. Our implementation could easily be extended to rely on third party certification of the code. Another alternative that can also handle legacy applications would be to sandbox the service application, to grant the license to the sandbox, which then limits the capabilities of the application to store or communicate data. Programming languages with information flow tracking capabilities can simplify this procedure, because they detect inferences between confidential data and unclassified data.

The performance data as measured is not great. However, one can expect service pack 1 of the rights management platform to massively improve performance as the platform verification is optimized and does not require Internet connectivity any more. In addition, as rights management performs distributed access control, there is only one central performance bottleneck: the rights management server. Under the assumption that rights management is also used for other digital content (such as music), it would be surprising if this infrastructure could not scale similarly for privacy protection.

6 Related Work

There has been lots of work on the regulatory aspects of privacy, such as EU data protection legislation, HIPAA, Gram-Leach-Bliley Act, or the safe harbor agreement. All of these regulations set the backdrop against which all technical work will be evaluated by the marketplace. Related technical work covers three main areas: expression of privacy policies, negotiation of policies and enforcement of policies. The World Wide Web Consortium standardized in its platform for privacy preferences (P3P) project an exchange format for privacy preferences of web server users [6]. It also defines a protocol by which the users preferences can be compared with those of the server and support for negotiation. A big drawback of the original P3P specification was that the policies were described on a level of detail that was not understandable to the general public. Even for an expert it is difficult to determine what the effect of a given policy can be. Compact policies [7] try to remedy this situation by defining default settings that can be given a meaningful name.

To remedy the fact that P3P policy specifications are very web centric, E-P3P [8, 9] tried to generalize the policies to enterprise applications. It then evolved to EPAL [10] which was submitted to W3C.

Negotiation can take place over policies expressed in P3P or E-P3P. The fundamental reason for this is that their underlying framework permits comparison of policies. The language APPEL [11] was designed to enable preference specification for negotiation of P3P policies.

Our work does not try to design a new privacy policy language. For our prototype we stated the policy in self defined terms. However, our design allows to include any policy interpretation engine.

On the enforcement side, hippocratic databases [12] were a first step towards enabling privacy aware data processing. The concept of a hippocratic database is that every information element in the database is tagged with a privacy policy.

Whenever data is retrieved form the database, the privacy policy is returned as metadata. It is then up to the application retrieving the data to adhere to the policy. The hippocratic database concept also includes the idea of doing an audit module to trace privacy breaches. This work restricts itself to database level, dealing only with one database.

Work at HP [13] adds the aspect of tracing data access by encrypting the returned data, which includes the privacy policy, with identity based encryption. An audit trail can be built up by logging the requests for keys and where access to the data was required. By using a tagging OS they propose to limit the flow of information marked as sensitive. An implementation of this concept is described in later papers [14, 15]. In these papers the architecture described contains a reference monitor doing access control at the database server and an enforcer module which is not described to greater detail. This work again is focussed on a single large enterprise.

An approach to dispose of this central reference monitor is described by Korba and Kenny [3]. The key observation is that digital rights management and management of personal information are very similar. Their paper gives an analysis of the entities involved in DRM and in data processing of personal data and the relation between them.

Our work shows the feasibility of the approach of Korba and Kenny by presenting an implementation. We chose the Microsoft information rights management framework which has a widely available software development kit. Enforcement of privacy policy is done at the application level in a distributed fashion. It is therefore possible to implement this approach across multiple domains. We also have the advantage over the HP approach that we do not leak information about accesses to the personal data which would produce privacy sensitive information at the IBE key server. If audit trails are required the application in question can produce the required information directly. Another aspect that is not mentioned in the work done at IBM and only mentioned in passing in the work done at HP is the concept of attestation.

Langheinrich's work [16] tries to tackle the problem in extremely distributed settings such as pervasive computing. His approach relies on cooperation of the entities being asked to refrain from recording or keeping personal information.

7 Conclusions

The results from the first trials are encouraging and lead us to believe that mechanisms similar to rights management can be used to enforce privacy. Because service application certification does not scale well, it seems not to be a general approach but to provide solutions in cases where certified privacy conforming components can be reused, e.g. for sandboxes. It is also thinkable to use certified modules for querying servers in client/server-scenarios where a client has obligations concerning to the usage of his submitted data.

Additionally, this approach can be used to shift the work of ensuring the correct handling of data from the person installing and maintaining the computing environment to the software vendor for the service application.

We believe it was a useful exercise to try to validate the proposal by Korba and Kenny by implementation. Only in this way the missing links (such as delegation) became obvious. In conclusion, it can be said that the fundamental idea may work, but the rights management platforms need to be tailored accordingly.

References

1. Zugenmaier, A., Claessens, J.: Privacy in Eletronic Communications. In: Network Security. IEEE Press (to appear)
2. Stajano, F.: Will your digital butlers betray you? In: WPES '04: Proceedings of the 2004 ACM workshop on Privacy in the electronic society, New York, NY, USA, ACM Press (2004) 37–38
3. Korba, L., Kenny, S.: Towards Meeting the Privacy Challenge: Adapting DRM. (2002) ACM Workshop on Digital Rights Management.
4. Trusted Computing Group: TCG Backgrounder. (2003)
5. Hohl, A., Zugenmaier, A.: Safeguarding personal data using rights management in pervasive computing for distributed applications (to appear)
6. Clarke, R.: P3p re-visited. In: Privacy Law and Policy Reporter. (2001) 81–83
7. Cranor, L.F., Lessig, L.: Web Privacy with P3p. O'Reilly & Associates, Inc., Sebastopol, CA, USA (2002)
8. Ashley, P., Hada, S., Karjoth, G., Schunter, M.: E-P3P Privacy Policies and Privacy Authorization. In: Proc. 1st ACM Workshop on Privacy in the Electronic Society (WPES). (2002) 103–109
9. Karjoth, G., Schunter, M., Waidner, M.: The platform for enterprise privacy practices - privacy enabled management of customer data. In: 2nd Workshop on Privacy Enhancing Technologies (PET 2002). LNCS, Springer (2003) 69–84
10. Karjoth, G., Schunter, M., Waidner, M.: Privacy-enabled services for enterprises. In: DEXA Workshops. (2002) 483–487
11. Langheinrich, M., Cranor, L., Marchiori, M.: APPEL: A P3P preference exchange language. W3C Working Draft (2002)
12. Agrawal, R., Kiernan, J., Srikant, R., Xu, Y.: Hippocratic Databases. In: 28th Int'l Conf. on Very Large Databases (VLDB), Hong Kong. (2002)
13. Mont, M., Pearson, S., Bramhall, P.: Towards Accountable Management of Identity and Privacy: Sticky Policies and Enforceable Tracing Services. (2003) HPL-2003-49.
14. Mont, M., Thyne, R., Chan, K., Bramhall, P.: Extending HP Identity Management Solutions to Enforce Privacy Policies and Obligations for Regulatory Compliance by Enterprises. Technical Report HPL-2005-110, HP Laboratories Bristol (2005)
15. Mont, M., Thyne, R., Bramhall, P.: Privacy Enforcement with HP Select Access for Regulatory Compliance. Technical Report HPL-2005-10, HP Laboratories Bristol (2005)
16. Langheinrich, M.: A Privacy Awareness System for Ubiquitous Computing Environments. (2001)

Identification Now and in the Future: Social Grant Distribution Process in South Africa

Stephen Flowerday and Gideon Ranga
Information Systems Department, University of Fort Hare,
P. O. Box 7426, East London, 5200, South Africa.
sflowerday@ufh.ac.za; rangags@gmail.com

Abstract. This paper seeks to apply Identity Management (IDM) principles to the social grant distribution process in South Africa, which has been prone to fraud and corruption. It discusses the social grant distribution process and the problems encountered. Suggested solutions to the problems are highlighted and these include moving from an Isolated IDM architecture to either a Federated and/or Centralised IDM architecture.

1 Introduction

The government of South Africa, under the Ministry of Social Development, has formed the South African Social Security Agency (SASSA) which is responsible for the distribution of social grants to ten million underprivileged citizens. Of the three billion Rand invested in social grants per month, more than five percent is lost to fraud [1]. Much of the fraud is attributed to Identity Management problems. This paper begins by discussing the social grant distribution process in South Africa. It then states the problems experienced in the process. Finally, the paper discusses how the process could function in the future so as to minimise the fraud caused by the Identity Management problems.

2 Social grant distribution process

SASSA subcontracts the issuing of social grants to distribution companies which carry out the identification and the verification processes in different parts of the country. SASSA and the distribution companies obtain a list of eligible recipients from local government and enrol the beneficiaries onto the system. The distribution companies identify and verify a social grant beneficiary using biometrics and smart cards and then issue the grant to the eligible recipient [2]. The process involves

Please use the following format when citing this chapter:

Flowerday, S. and Ranga, G., 2007, in IFIP International Federation for Information Processing, Volume 232, New Approaches for Security, Privacy and Trust in Complex Environments, eds. Venter, H., Eloff, M., Labuschagne, L., Eloff, J., von Solms, R., (Boston: Springer), pp. 457–459.

checking an individual's fingerprints against templates in a local database and verifying it against a template encoded onto a smart card. The social grant distribution process is an IDM system in that it seeks to allow certain rights (in this case social grants) to certain people (users) and currently adopts an Isolated IDM architecture [2].

3 Problems associated with the social grant distribution process

The following points are identified as problems encountered during the social grant distribution process.

1. Since the templates are tested in local databases, there have been cases where people have more than one smart card and a fake ID number, which allows them to obtain grants at different locations. Presently there is no central database which verifies all the fingerprints that are existent in order to detect duplicity [3].
2. Most of the beneficiaries are in rural areas and this introduces additional challenges in that many rural areas are outside the telecommunications and electrical grid. This results in the transactions being conducted offline rather than in real-time where automatic updating of databases occur. Updating of data therefore takes place at night and often occurs more than twenty-four hours after the transactions have been performed. This results in fraud occurring within this twenty-four hour window period [3].
3. There are cases whereby different people may erroneously have the same ID number and this complicates the enrolment stage because the recipients may all be eligible to receive the grant yet the system identifies them as one entity and therefore pays out only once [4].
4. Another problem identified is the use of fingerprints in the enrolment process. As people age their fingerprints are no longer clearly defined due to the nature of the work many of the people participate in, especially in the rural areas [2].
5. Finally, when people travel they are required to go back to their districts where they originally registered because the system does not allow an individual to receive a grant at different locations. This causes inconvenience including the cost implications of returning to the original district in order to receive one's grant [3].

4 Suggested solutions and conclusion

There should be a federation between the various distribution companies and databases of different geographical locations. This will enable users to sign in wherever they are and monitoring between the companies will become more effective. The system should consider incorporating a Federated Identity Management (FIDM) model which manages identities across policy and/or application domains in which the identity data is distributed [6, 7]. In addition it should ensure that there is proper authentication and authorisation of individuals in order to address points 1, 3 and 5 [5]. As SASSA is one organisation it could consider incorporating a centralised model for easy administration and audit. Furthermore a Centralised IDM model has strong Single Sign-On (SSO) capabilities which enables users access to their resources (grants) anywhere which assists with point 5 [8]. IDM solutions and architectures however will fail to solve point 2 because this is a rural development and telecommunications problem and not necessarily an IDM issue. Additionally biometric mechanisms such as face, voice and iris recognition could be used as an alternative to the fingerprint method in cases where this method does not suffice in order to address point 4 [9]. The central database however has its own security, privacy, cost implications and administrative risks.

References

1. InfoSA. (2005). About South Africa, 2005. Available from :<http://www. southafrica. info/ess_info/sa_glance/social_delivery/social_grants.htm> [Accessed: 15 August 2006].
2. Rusere, L. (2006). AllPay Social Grant Distribution Company. East London, South Africa.
3. de Jongh, A. (2006). AllPay Distribution Company. East London, South Africa
4. Macocozoma, B. (2006). Deal House Social Grant Distribution Company. East London, South Africa.
5. Fidis, (2006). ID-related Crime: Towards a Common Ground for Interdisciplinary Research. *Future of Identity in the Information Society.* White Paper, fidis-wp5-del5-2b.ID-related.crime.doc.
6. Madsen, P. Koga, Y. & Takahashi, K. (2005). Federated Identity Management For Protecting Users from ID Theft. *Computer-Communications Networks.*
7. Ahn, G. & Lam, J. (2005). Managing Privacy for Federated Identity Management. *Communications of ACM.*
8. Josang, A. Fabre, J. Hay, B. Dalziel, J. & Pope, S. (2004). Trust Requirements in Identity Management. *Distributed Systems Technology.*
9. Wayman, J. (2000). Picking the best Biometric Authentication Technologies. *National Biometric Test Center Collected Works.* vol. 1, pg, 269-275.

Hard-drive Disposal and Identity Fraud

Paula Thomas and Theodore Tryfonas
Information Security Research Group
Faculty of Advanced Technology
University of Glamorgan
Wales, UK
pthomas@glam.ac.uk, ttryfona@glam.ac.uk

Abstract. A personal computer is often used to store personal information about the user. This information may be intentionally kept by the user or information maybe automatically stored as the result of the user's activities. In this paper we investigate whether it is possible for identity fraud to occur as a result of post-disposal access to the residual data stored on a personal computer's hard drive. We provide indicative types of information required to commit an identify fraud and examine the personal information contained in a series of second-hand personal computer hard disk drives, purchased as part of a wider research study.

1 Introduction

A large amount of personal information can be found available on the Internet today. Public access documents found online, such as the voting register, used by themselves or in combination with other documents, can give an amount of information that may be more than enough for a fraudster to commit various criminal activities [1]. This availability of personal information is one of the main enablers for the crime that can be identified as Identity (ID) Fraud. The US Federal Trade Commission defines ID fraud as "a fraud committed or attempted using the identifying information of another person without authority" [2].

This can be accomplished in a number of ways depending on the information available to the perpetrator and the objective of the ID fraud. From the perspective of the perpetrator, identity fraud has to provide some form of gain that is usually, but not always, financial. Therefore, the identity fraud perpetrator is interested in acquiring specific pieces of personal information, some of which may need to be combined with other personal information in order to be of value. Some of the most common types of personal information that may be useful and the purpose for its collection are indicatively highlighted in Table 1 below.

Please use the following format when citing this chapter:

Thomas, P. and Tryfonas, T., 2007, in IFIP International Federation for Information Processing, Volume 232, New Approaches for Security, Privacy and Trust in Complex Environments, eds. Venter, H., Eloff, M., Labuschagne, L., Eloff, J., von Solms, R., (Boston: Springer), pp. 461–466.

Table 1. Examples of the use of various types of personal information for identity fraud

Type of personal info use	**Information required**	**Impact on the individual**
Registering for mail / on-line services	Name (surname, first names, possibly maiden / previous names), Address / postcode	Reputation
Phishing	Email Address, Possible passwords	Financial
Taking control of existing bank accounts / Obtaining Loans	Name (surname, first names, possibly maiden / previous names), Address / postcode, Other family details e.g. mother's maiden name, photographs, Bank Account Information (Bank, Account Number, etc)	Financial
Opening New Bank accounts Requesting loans	Name (surname, first names, possibly maiden / previous names), Address / postcode	Financial

Personal information could be used in a number of ways to commit different forms of identity fraud and could range from taking over an existing bank account to opening a new account or obtaining a loan in the victim's name. For example, in order to apply for a loan in a U.K. context, the ID fraud perpetrator would require someone's full name, other family details, a bank account number, branch details etc.

Information items listed in Table 1 may well exist in electronic form within a personal computer. Computer security countermeasures are deployed exactly in order to protect those, amongst other information assets. Despite a lot can be done to secure this information in its early and mid life cycle stages (e.g. password protection, encryption), it is interesting to examine if there are enough provisions in place for protecting such information at the end of its lifecycle.

Such measures can be of significant importance in the light of the growing popularity of e-commerce sites that facilitate the exchange of data storage, e.g. used disks and flash memories. Electronic marketplaces or on-line auction sites provide the means for a profitable disposal of unwanted memory capacities. By analysing the disk drive of a personal computer (PC) acquired in such a manner, it is possible to identify personal and sensitive data that could be used for a potential criminal activity. The personal data that is left behind on a PC's hard drive seems to pose a very realistic risk of identity fraud.

The purpose of this paper is to illustrate the level of risk associated with the disposal of media that could contain personal data and to bring to a wider audience the discussion on the necessary provisions that would need to be in place for its successful mitigation.

2 Second-hand Hard Disk Acquisition and Recovery of Personal Data Remaining on Disposed of Drives

One of the most common ways of acquiring storage that possibly contains personal identifiable information is via the purchase of second hand equipment. Especially if this happens via an on-line facility (e.g. via an Internet e-auction site), as it provides anonymity and introduces complexity in the tracing of a potential fraudster. An article reported e.g., that a research group had purchased a hard disk for £5 through an auction site that contained a customer database as well as the current access codes to what was supposed to be a secure Intranet of a large European financial services group [3]. This fact illustrates how improperly recycled equipment that is intended to be reused, needs to be considered within a safe recycling strategy.

Another way for storage media acquisition is through conventional dumpster diving. Equipment that is not intended to be reused, often ends up unprocessed in bin bags at the doorsteps of individuals or organisations. Such disposal may occur for hard discs that are believed to be old or faulty, optical discs that may contain user backups etc. all of which may provide information useful to perform an ID fraud. Social engineering may be employed to acquire the disk as well; the fraudster may foil a scenario for the collection of unwanted discs for a supposedly charity or other fictional occasion.

In order to discuss on the level of perceived risk against the individual, we shall examine in this section the results from Jones et al. [4, 5] study on the forensic analysis of residual data, in relation to the method of examination used and the effort allocated to achieve those. In their study, Jones et al. analysed a large number of second hand discs. In terms of the methodology used, as far as the sample is concerned, those were purchased at computer auctions, computer fairs or on-line and were supplied 'blindly' to a research laboratory for analysis. The study looked at the residual data on the disk drives and determined whether there was any information on the disk that was easily recoverable and possibly might allow corporations or individuals to be identified.

The research involved the discs' forensic imaging, which was followed by an analysis aiming at determining what information remained and whether it could be easily recovered. Forensic imaging is the making of an exact duplicate of the entire hard drive and there are a number of proprietary tools that can perform this procedure. This copy of the hard drive or image is then used for analysis, ensuring that the original drive is not altered. The tools used to carry out the disc analysis included similar functions to the MS Windows Unformat and Undelete commands and to a hex editor, which can be used to view any information that existed in the unallocated portion of the disk. Besides commercial data recovery and forensic analysis suites, there are also freely available applications, such as the open source Sleuth Kit, as well as freeware toolsets such as the Windows Forensic Toolchest [6]. These types of tools are in essence available to anyone who could obtain the disks.

Fragkos et al. [7] have proposed an empirical methodology as a result of their work on Jones et al.'s study. Their proposed methodology is concerned with the identification and extraction of the most important repositories for information on a disk drive. The methodology starts with the exclusion of faulty disks then an automated procedure is used to check for wiped drives ie disk drives that do not contain any data. The next step is to locate all image files on the disk drive and to extract all the thumb.db files which are then used to extract the actual images. The thumb.db files store a backup/preview of image files even if that image file has been deleted or wiped. The next stage of the proposed methodology suggests that the directory names be extracted from index.dat file in order to access the cache of the user's activity. The final stage is to extract the registry file of the user in order to identify information that may help to profile the user.

Of the disks analysed, over 40% contained a range of personal information including addresses, phone numbers, bank accounts and credit cards, other personal details, photographs, email and various on-line discussions.

3 Level of Exposure, Risk Mitigation and Challenges

Examples of the recovered data that could relate to acquisition of enough personal information to commit an identity fraud include the following [5]. From a major automotive company, there was payroll information, internal telephone contact details including mobile phone numbers, details of the internal network configuration and copies of invoices and orders. There were also emails between the company and its customers, meeting minutes and communications that were intended as written warnings to staff relating to poor performance. Other data from a disk recovered from an academic institute, included the names and web surfing habits of the users, the names of teachers, some confidential emails etc. There was also data that is thought to be test scores for individual students that was held in a database.

Similar data may well be used to commit an ID fraud; payroll records and personal contact information such as mobile phone numbers may provide enough data for a fraudster to attempt a request for a personal loan, on the financial details of an existing employee, under their own address. The availability of both employee and customer contacts may provide the grounds for social engineering attacks that will damage a company's reputation, if, for example, an attacker contacts customers using the credentials of real, existing employees.

An analysis of residual data on the grounds discussed in the previous section requires for the time being a significant amount of effort and expertise. However the tools required to perform such a task are freely accessible and know-how on their use is readily available over the Internet. And as on-line defences mature and become stronger (e.g. the move towards two-factor authentication systems driven by the banking sector), potential perpetrators of ID fraud may viably resort in off-line ways for committing an attack.

Users of personal computers do not necessarily have the knowledge, or the tools, available to forensically wipe their hard disk drives prior their disposal. Failure to adequately remove such data may result in the personal data being exploited for criminal gain in the form of identity fraud.

Therefore there is a clear requirement for the *education and training* of the relevant staff within organisations and of home users to inform them of the potential problems that arise from the failure to properly remove the information from disks and systems that are leaving their control. When organisations dispose of obsolete computers and hard disks, they must ensure that, whether they are handled by internal resources or through a third party contractor, adequate procedures are in place to destroy any data and also to check that the procedures that are in place are effective.

In this direction future releases of Apple's operating systems for example, will embody functions for secure erasure of the disposable medium. The recent AppleMac OS X operating system includes a file erasure facility that immediately overwrites the file with erroneous data, so that the file disappears and cannot be reconstructed.

Individuals and organisations should also consider the full encryption of hard disks so that if the disk is lost or the data is not effectively removed on disposal, it will not be easily recoverable. This would provide adequate protection in most situations. In this respect Microsoft planned the next generation of their operating systems (Windows Vista) to provide capabilities for full disk encryption. The new Windows Vista operating system has improved support for data protection at all levels with a full volume encryption of the system volume, including Windows system files and the hibernation file, which helps protect data from being compromised on a lost or stolen machine. The Encrypting File System has also been enhanced to allow storage of encryption keys on smart cards, providing better protection of encryption keys.

Both of these accommodations (disc erasure and encryption) are necessary to mitigate the level of anticipated risk, however they do not come without controversy. Law enforcement and the regulatory environment in countries where full encryption is not permitted in an unrestricted fashion (e.g. the French crypto legislation or the U.S. export controls) will need to reflect on these new technological developments.

4 Conclusions

Much of the focus on the protection from ID fraud has been given to its on-line form (e.g. [8]). However, there is another electronic-based form that fraudsters may employ, as more sophisticated on-line defences are used: the off-line route. In this paper we outlined the nature of personal data which may be found on personal computer hard drives that, once it has been uncovered may be used to commit an identity theft.

In the light of the growing popularity of electronic marketplaces and auction sites, the exchange of technology items that contain some form of storage capacity is booming. But such exchange could lead to exposure of personal information to potential fraudsters. Another off-line route may be the acquisition of improperly disposed of hardware. Indeed, there seems to be limited awareness in relation to the protection of information assets at the later stages of their life cycle.

The findings of relevant empirical studies [9, 10] demonstrate the feasibility of such off-line attacks and the methods and tools used provide an estimate of the effort required and the profile of a potential perpetrator. At the minute, considerable expertise and effort is required to perform such a task, however in the light of the availability of toolsets for forensic analysis and data recovery and the documentation of the research experiences and the knowledge in the public domain, this method poses as a significant emergent threat of the near future.

Therefore, there is a realistic risk associated with the incorrect recycling or disposal of personal information contained on computer hard disk drives. The recent

European Waste from Electrical and Electronic (WEEE) directive requires computer manufacturers to have recycling and refurbishment programmes in place [11]. There are many specialist waste disposal companies who will handle electronics and computer disposal on behalf of the manufacturers who need to comply with the EU directive. In the future, the recycling and disposal of computer hard disk drives should become less of a risk as this EU directive should go some way to preventing the current ad-hoc disposal of disk drives and thus will reduce the risk of theft of personal information from such drives.

Computer manufacturers and software vendors are incorporating enhanced security features in their products. The new Operating System countermeasures have been strategically positioned within the future releases of popular products, however it will be interesting to examine their impact in terms of effectiveness, user acceptance and the reaction of communities of interest such as law enforcement.

References

1. Tryfonas T., Thomas P., Owen P. (2006), "ID Theft: Fraudsters' techniques for Personal Data Collection, the Related digital Evidence and Investigation Issues", *Information Systems Control Journal,* (JOnline) Vol. 1.
2. Federal Trade Commission (2003), Fair and Accurate Credit Transactions Act of 2003 Revision, www.ftc.gov/os/2004/10/041029idtheftdefsfrsm.pdf
3. Leyden, J., "Oops! Firm accidentally eBays customer database", The Register, 7 June 2004.
4. Jones A., Mee V., Meyler C., Gooch J., "Analysis of Data Recovered from Computer Disks released for Resale by Organisations", *Journal of Information Warfare,* 2005.
5. Jones A., Valli C., Sutherland I., Thomas P. (2006), "An Analysis of Information Remaining on Disks offered for sale on the second hand market", *Journal of Digital Security, Forensics & Law,* Vol. 1 No 3.
6. Windows Forensic Toolchest, freeware tool available for download at http://www.foolmoon.net/security/wft/ (last accessed January 2007).
7. Fragkos, G., et al. (2006), "An empirical methodology derived from the analysis of information remaining on second hand hard disks", in Blyth, A., Sutherland, I., *WDFIA 2006, Proceedings of the First Workshop in Digital Forensics and Incident Analysis.*
8. Marshall, A.M. and Tompsett, B.C. (2005), "Identity theft in an online world", *Computer Law & Security Report,* Vol. 2005, Issue 2, Page 128 – 137.
9. Garfinkel, S.L., Shelat A., "Remembrance of Data Passed: A Study of Disk Sanitization Practices", *IEEE Security & Privacy,* Vol. 1, No 1, 2003.
10. Valli, C. (2004), "Throwing out the Enterprise with the Hard Disk", In *Proceedings of 2nd Australian Computer, Information and Network Forensics Conference,* We-BCentre.COM, Fremantle Western Australia.
11. Department for Trade and Industry, on-line (latest accessed 20-01-2007) http://www.dti.gov.uk/innovation/sustainability/weee/page30269.html.

An analysis of security and privacy issues relating to RFID enabled ePassports

Eleni Kosta[1], Martin Meints[2], Marit Hansen[2], Mark Gasson[3]
1 K.U.Leuven, Interdisciplinary Centre for Law and ICT, Sint-Michielsstraat 6, B-3000 Leuven, Belgium, eleni.kosta@law.kuleuven.be
2 Independent Centre for Privacy Protection, Holstenstr. 98, 24103 Kiel, Germany, {meints,hansen}@datenschutzzentrum.de
3 University of Reading, Department of Cybernetics, Reading, Berkshire, UK, m.n.gasson@reading.ac.uk

Abstract. The European Union sees the introduction of the ePassport as a step towards rendering passports more secure against forgery while facilitating more reliable border controls. In this paper we take an interdisciplinary approach to the key security and privacy issues arising from the use of ePassports. We further analyse how European data protection legislation must be respected and what additional security measures must be integrated in order to safeguard the privacy of the EU ePassport holder.

1 The ePassport

Electronic ID documents are seen by the European Union as a necessary upgrade for important paper ID documents and consequently one of the first to become 'electronic' was the passport. Based on the international technical ICAO [1] standards defined in Document 9303 [2] and following Council Regulation EC 2252/2004 [3] in European legislation, the implementation of the European electronic passport (ePassport) began in 2005[1]. The ePassport is an internationally accepted Machine Readable Travel Document (MRTD) and has already been rolled out in several EU Member States.

The ICAO's Document 9303 has been adopted globally as the standard for new ePassports which ensures interoperability between regions and countries. However, adoption of the ICAO standard means that ePassports differ from the traditional passport in several ways. In order to comply with the standard, new ePassports must

1 Note that Belgium has issued ePassports since November 2004, cf. the press release available at http://diplobel.fgov.be/en/press/homedetails.asp?TEXTID=26303

Please use the following format when citing this chapter:

Kosta, E., Meints, M., Hansen, M., and Gasson, M., 2007, in IFIP International Federation for Information Processing, Volume 232, New Approaches for Security, Privacy and Trust in Complex Environments, eds. Venter, H., Eloff, M., Labuschagne, L., Eloff, J., von Solms, R., (Boston: Springer), pp. 467–472.

have a microprocessor (chip) embedded in the paper passport as well as a contactless mechanism for data transmission. For MRTDs, the ICAO specifies the use of the ISO 14443[2] standard that enables contactless data communication between the microprocessor of the ePassport and a remote reader, i.e. Radio Frequency Identification (RFID). The standard also specifies an operating frequency of 13.56 MHz and an 'intended' read range [4] of 10 to 15 cm.

For EU Member States, Art 1(2) of the Council Regulation EC 2252/2004 obliges the storage of the ePassport holder's facial image in the RFID enabled chip, whilst allowing them to "optionally also include fingerprints in interoperable formats". The biometric data are stored in the Common Biometric Exchange File Format (CBEFF), according to the standards ISO CD 19794-2 to ISO CD 19794-6.

The mechanism implemented to prevent unauthorised disclosure of digital data stored in the ePassport is Basic Access Control (BAC). The reader first acquires the Machine Readable Zone (MRZ) from the data page of the ePassport, usually via a manual optical scanner. From the MRZ data, the passport holder's birth date, the passport number and passport expiry date are used to calculate a 'session key'. This key is used to encrypt the information exchanged between reader and ePassport in order to prevent skimming of data. By using information printed on the ePassport, the intention of BAC is to restrict digitised data access to those parties who have direct physical access to the document. To prevent manipulation of the digital data, the ePassport is digitally signed by the issuing country and these signatures, which are also stored in the ePassport, can be checked during the validation of the document to ensure data integrity. Once BAC has been successfully completed, active authentication is employed to verify that the RFID enabled chip itself has not been substituted.

2 Failings of the ePassport

In short, no coherent and integrated security framework for MRTDs has been disclosed. The publicly available documentation for such a framework is currently limited to '*Protection Profiles for Biometric Verification Mechanisms and MRTDs including Basic Access Control (BAC)* [5]' and '*Technical Guideline v1.0 for Extended Access Control (EAC)*'.[3] This documentation falls short because it does not necessarily consider existing ePassport implementations[4], it consists mostly of suggestions rather than obligations and it fails to include the necessary organisational aspects of an integrated security concept. Several theoretical and scientifically demonstrated threats and conceptual flaws of ePassports have already been published, yet countermeasures have not been analysed nor specified by Protection Profiles or any appropriate technical guidelines. The most significant of these issues are further described below.

[2] Note that the ISO 14443 standard specifically refers to contactless smartcards, i.e., proximity cards which utilise RFID.

[3] Issued by the German Federal Office for Information Security (BSI) in August 2006 and announced at http://www.bsi.bund.de/fachthem/epass/eac.htm

[4] For example only the Belgian ePassports issued after July 2006 supports BAC.

Although ISO 14443 states that the distance from which the RFID enabled chip is readable should be between 10 and 15 cm, in the ePassport this can be extended [6] up to 50 or 60 cm for active communication with the ePassport and up to 5 m for eavesdropping on the ePassport / reader communication. However, most European countries have chosen not to physically shield the ePassport using a so called Faraday cage, in contrast to countries such as the U.S.

Even if the ePassport itself is physically protected, the MRZ can be easily read and copied. This is especially of concern in several countries (e.g., Italy, Slovakia and Czech Republic), where besides public authorities the passport has to be provided to private organisations, e.g., when registering in a hotel. Furthermore, BAC shows severe cryptographic weaknesses, especially the use of very low-entropy input when deriving the secret keys [7]. It has already been demonstrated that BAC in the Dutch ePassport can be circumvented (hacked) within 2 hours [6]. ISO 14443 specifies the communication protocol used between RFID enabled devices and readers. However, this communication depends on a pseudo-unique 32 bit RFID enabled chip identifier which is fixed for some implementations of the ePassport and can easily be abused to track it. Additionally, cloning of the actual RFID enabled chip in MRTDs has also been demonstrated [8].

Extended Access Control (EAC) has been proposed as an improvement to BAC, but even EAC only partially fulfils the security requirements. EAC allows an ePassport to verify the authenticity of the reader before disclosing selected elements of the personal data (notably those categorised as privacy-sensitive such as biometric fingerprint data), while data such as the digital face, name, date of birth, and so on are not covered. Furthermore, since ICAO has not accepted EAC as an international standard yet, it cannot be enforced internationally and thus non-European countries will only support BAC. Future versions of the ePassport need to be downward compatible.

Biometrics as currently implemented in MRTDs cannot be revoked. Since biometric features of the users, such as fingerprints and facial features, cannot be changed easily, 'stolen' biometrics can be abused for a long period of time. In addition, a number of methods which spoof biometric sensors have already been demonstrated [9], in some cases even without the cooperation of the person the biometric feature belongs to. The intention of European governments to further use such technologies and standards for national ID cards [10] causes additional concerns.

In summary, the use of ePassports enables tracking of citizens under certain circumstances, e.g., by equipping door frames with RFID readers, and exposes raw biometric data for additional purposes in the private and public sector. Moreover, BAC does not adequately protect the ePassport's content, while EAC is also flawed and only primarily relevant for European ePassports. Furthermore, the transfer of the ePassport's technical concept to national ID cards may well create an authentication infrastructure that is extremely vulnerable to identity theft.

3 Privacy and data protection implications of RFID in MRTDs

The data that are to be included in ePassports and that are saved on the RFID enabled chip are *information relating to an identified or identifiable natural person*, i.e., the ePassport owner, and are therefore considered as personal data according to the definition of the Data Protection Directive (hereafter DPD) [11]. This means that the European data protection legislation applies in the case of ePassports and the data protection principles must be respected. Pursuant to the data minimisation principle[5] the data stored in the RFID enabled chip shall only be those necessary for the identification of the ePassport owner.

When the ePassport is read by authorised personnel, the processing of the data stored within is legitimate since authorised personnel – and only they [12] – 'exercise official authority' (Art. 7(e) DPD). In cases of unauthorised reading of the information stored in the ePassport, such as skimming or eavesdropping, the data subject is not aware that his data are being collected. Since the data subject cannot consent to something of which he has no knowledge [13] the processing of the data is consequently not legitimate.

The ePassport owner needs to be informed about the data that will be included in the ePassport and about the ways in which he can *access, rectify, erase or block incorrect data* that are stored. Furthermore, personal data needs to be processed *fairly and lawfully* (Art. 6.1(a) DPD). The data shall be collected for specified, explicit and legitimate purposes and be further processed only in a way compatible with those purposes (finality principle) (Art. 6.1(b) DPD).

The Data Protection Directive calls the Member States to impose a security obligation on the data controller, who must implement "[...] *appropriate technical and organisational measures* to protect personal data against accidental or unlawful destruction or accidental loss, alteration, unauthorised disclosure or access, in particular where the processing involves the transmission of data over a network, and against all other unlawful forms of processing" (Art. 17.1 DPD). The processing of personal data must be done in a maximum security environment [14].

When considering controls carried out by authorities outside of the European Union, the use of RFID enabled chips as the storage medium on ePassports raises significant privacy concerns. When personal data are undergoing processing in a third country, this country should 'ensure an adequate level of protection', which is determined by the European Union on the basis of Article 25 (6) of the Data Protection Directive or by means of international agreements on the administrative procedures to be followed.

[5] The data shall be '*adequate, relevant and not excessive* in relation to the purposes for which they are collected and/or further processed', Art. 6.1(c) Data Protection Directive.

4 Proposed solutions

Since ePassports with the described weaknesses have already been introduced and will inevitably be used in the future, we recommend the following measures for immediate integration to reduce the risk of security failure and identity theft.

Organisational integration and enforcement of the finality principle is required, especially for biometrics used in ePassports, where the defined purpose is identification of international travellers. ePassports should not be used for authentication purposes, e.g., in the private sector. Citizens need to be informed of the risks inherent in owning, carrying and using their ePassports and the corresponding security measures which can be undertaken by them (e.g., avoiding the release of the documents to anyone, especially private organisations such as hotels, in cases when not required by law). Security measures such as Faraday cages, which are available but not widely integrated, should be integrated into newly issued ePassports immediately. In addition organisational and technical procedures are required to prevent abuse of personal data from ePassports, including tracking and identity theft.

For the next generation of the ePassport, a new convincing and integrated security framework covering MRTDs and related systems needs to be developed. It should be investigated how the integration of technologies utilised can be improved, e.g., on-card matching and on-card sensors for biometrics and it should be considered whether inherently more secure and privacy-preserving technologies such as contact instead of contactless mechanisms should in fact be used.

5 Conclusions

By failing to integrate an appropriate security architecture, European governments have effectively forced citizens to adopt new international Machine Readable Travel Documents which dramatically decrease their security and privacy and increases risk of identity theft. Simply put, the current implementation of the European passport utilises technologies and standards that are poorly conceived for its purpose. This is especially true considering the international usage and long lifetime (up to ten years) of current MRTDs. For the next generation of the ePassport a redesign including a convincing integrated security framework is needed, where most notably the use of biometrics and RFID should be reconsidered.

Acknowledgements

This paper is based in part on the 'Budapest declaration' [15] produced by the authors and other researchers from the multidisciplinary 'Future of Identity in the Information Society' (FIDIS) Network of Excellence. More detail can be found at http://www.fidis.net/. The authors would like to extend special gratitude to Danny de Cock for his valuable input to this paper.

References

1. ICAO = International Civil Aviation Organization, http://www.icao.int/.
2. Information available via http://www.icao.int/mrtd/publications/doc.cfm.
3. http://europa.eu.int/eur-lex/lex/LexUriServ/site/en/oj/2004/l_385/ l_38520041229en00010006.pdf.
4. A. Juels, D. Molnar, and D. Wagner, Security and Privacy Issues in E-passports, IEEE SecureComm 2005; available online at http://www.cs.berkeley.edu/~dmolnar/papers/RFID-passports.pdf. The term 'intended' indicates the range of vendor-standard readers.
5. Protection Profile BSI-PP-0016-2005 and BSI-PP-0017-2005, certified in August and October 2005 respectively by the German Federal Office for Information Security; available via http://www.bsi.de/zertifiz/zert/report.htm.
6. This has recently been analysed and demonstrated with a Dutch passport (see H. Robroch, ePassport Privacy Attack, 2006, which also details reading and eavesdropping distances; see http://www.riscure.com/2_news/ 200604%20CardsAsiaSing%20ePassport%20Privacy.pdf.)
7. J. Beel and B. Gipp, *ePass – der neue biometrische Reisepass,* Shaker Verlag, Aachen 2005. Download of chapter 6 "Fazit": http://www.beel.org/epass/epass-kapitel6-fazit.pdf). In most ePassports the effective key length is far lower than 56 bits, typically 35 bits, and in some cases even as low as 28 bits.
8. See, e.g., K. Zetter, Hackers Clone E-Passports, Wired News, August 3, 2006; http://www.wired.com/news/technology/1,71521-0.html.
9. Among others see Z. Geradts (ed.), *FIDIS Deliverable D6.1: Forensic Implications of Identity Management Systems*, Frankfurt 2006; http://www.fidis.net/fidis-del/period-2-20052006/#c822 / Starbug, How to fake fingerprints?, October 26, 2004; http://www.ccc.de/biometrie/fingerabdruck_kopieren.xml?language=en.
10. In France: e.g., the project INES (identité nationale électronique sécurisée), January 31, 2005; http://www.foruminternet.org/telechargement/forum/pres-prog-ines-20050201.pdf; in Germany: C. Engel, Auf dem Weg zum elektronischen Personalausweis, Datenschutz und Datensicherheit 4/2006, pp. 207-210, Vieweg, Wiesbaden 2006.
11. Directive 95/46/EC of the European Parliament and of the Council of 24 October 1995 on the protection of individuals with regard to the processing of personal data and on the free movement of such data, OJ L 281 , 23/11/1995 pp. 0031-0050.
12. Article 29 Data Protection Working Party, Opinion on implementing the Council Regulation (EC) No 2252/2004 of 13 December 2004 on standards for security features and biometrics in passports and travel documents issued by Member States, adopted on 30 September 2001, 1710/05/EN (WP 112).
13. R. Jay and A. Hamilton, *Data protection – Law and practice*, London Sweet & Maxwell 2003, p. 91.
14. P. van Eecke and G. Skouma, RFID and Privacy: A difficult Marriage?, in: S. Paulus, N. Pohlmann, and H. Reimer (eds.), ISSE 2005 Securing Electronic Business Processes – Highlights of the Information Security Solutions Europe 2005 Conference (pp. 169-178), Vieweg, Wiesbaden 2005, p. 173.
15. http://www.fidis.net/press-events/press-releases/budapest-declaration/ (2006).

Toward User Evaluation of IT Security Certification Schemes: A Preliminary Framework

Nicholas Tate[1], Sharman Lichtenstein[2],and Matthew J. Warren[2]
1 Faculty of Science and Technology, Deakin University
221 Burwood Highway, Burwood, 3125 Australia
n.tate@its.uq.edu.au
2 School of Information Systems, Deakin University
221 Burwood Highway, Burwood, 3125 Australia
{sharman.lichtenstein,matthew.warren}@deakin.edu.au

Abstract. This paper reports a preliminary framework that supports stakeholder evaluation, comparison and selection of IT Security Certification schemes. The framework may assist users in the selection of the most appropriate scheme to meet their particular needs.

1 Introduction

Information technology (IT) security certification is of increasing importance to organisations seeking a professional approach to information security management [1]. In the Western world, employers are increasingly relying on IT security certifications - and higher education (HE) qualifications based on such certifications - as key selection criteria in the recruitment of IT security professionals. However, by September 2006 there were around 100 vendor-neutral certifications and around 40 vendor-specific certifications [2]. While these numbers include a broad range of certifications and are, therefore, not always equivalent - they present a bewildering array of schemes from which key stakeholders (such as IT security practitioners and their employers) must select the most appropriate scheme to meet their individual needs.

Currently, such selection must rely only on information available from expert accounts such as [2] or on classifications and approaches such as [3, 4, 5, 6, 7]. Such approaches are not systematic, however. This paper develops a preliminary framework of categories and characteristics to support an evaluation and comparison of IT security certification schemes. The framework is intended for use by the four

Please use the following format when citing this chapter:

Tate, N., Lichtenstein, S., and Warren, M., 2007, in IFIP International Federation for Information Processing, Volume 232, New Approaches for Security, Privacy and Trust in Complex Environments, eds. Venter, H., Eloff, M., Labuschagne, L., Eloff, J., von Solms, R., (Boston: Springer), pp. 473–478.

key constituent audiences – IT security practitioners, employers, HE institutes and government agencies (hereafter termed "users"). It aims to assist users in understanding the relative merits and positioning of each scheme, and assist in the selection of the most appropriate scheme for individual needs. The framework was developed from a literature review and focus group of industry, academic and government stakeholders, held at the AusCERT2006 conference in Australia in May 2006. Next, we review a set of categories and characteristics that underpin the framework.

2 Categories and Characteristics

2.1 Credibility

For a scheme to be accepted by a user, it must be perceived as credible [12]. Three characteristics for credibility are: *governance*, *assessment* and *curriculum definition.* First, if the *governance* of an organisation that offers a particular certification scheme is not open and transparent - with few, if any, conflicts of interest - the scheme is unlikely to gain sufficient user credibility. In addition, if governance of the scheme is not seen to guarantee its independence from any particular commercial, government or national interests, the scheme is likely to suffer diminished credibility. The importance of scheme governance is illustrated by the proportion of the ISO/IEC 17024 standard - ISO/IEC 17024 [16] - devoted to the rules for governing bodies of certification schemes. This standard also states: "The certification body shall be structured so as to give confidence to interested parties in its competence, impartiality and integrity."

Second, the credibility of a certification scheme is linked to its *assessment.* Schultz [15] suggests that many schemes are too simplistic in their assessment requirements. Third, the IT security *curriculum definition* underpins the Body of Knowledge for an IT security professional and is therefore an important credibility characteristic [1, 15]. In particular, the body of knowledge should include discussion and assessment of technological, legal and ethical aspects of IT security [11]. It must also be current and based on relevant international standards.

2.2 Accessibility

It is important that an IT security certification scheme is accessible to potential users. The accessibility of the scheme and the extent to which there are financial or other constraints may be a differentiating factor between schemes when an inclusive approach to evaluation of educational programs is adopted [9] and, for some users, will form an important aspect of evaluation. Three characteristics of accessibility are: *access restrictions*, *cost* and *national restrictions*.

First, in respect of *access restrictions*, an open certification scheme enables individuals to demonstrate their IT security capabilities, irrespective of training. Access restrictions are in place when it is mandatory that a candidate for certification examination first undertake a particular training course, thereby increasing costs and imposing further constraints. Second, user selection of a certification scheme is likely to be linked to the financial *cost* of access. In the case of international schemes, the notion of affordability varies by economy. It is suggested that a scheme which does not account for such variability is likely to limit user access to the scheme. The increasing importance of all the elements comprising the cost is, as reported in [14], amply illustrated by the practice of determining a Return on Investment (ROI) for the certification.

Third, as cybersecurity becomes increasingly important and linked, in the perception of many, to national security, there has been some debate as to whether *national restrictions* should be applied to the selection of candidates for IT security courses. Frincke [13] poses the question, "Who should be allowed to listen?" and observes that "Many security programs already segregate their audiences to a certain extent, for certain material. There are many examples. Some US agencies limit participation to those with US citizenship". In other words, only US citizens may be taught in some IT security courses. An interesting and important question can therefore be posed: is it possible to have a global IT Security certification scheme if certain aspects of it are limited to citizens of a particular country?

2.3 Relevance

For a scheme to be accepted it must be perceived as relevant by (a) IT security professionals who will seek to be certified under it, (b) the employers who may wish to rely on it for selecting staff, and (c) the national jurisdiction in which it operates. Five key relevance-oriented characteristics are: *vendor neutrality, academic credentials and experience, ethical code, market acceptance* and *localisation.*

First, regarding *vendor neutrality*, certification schemes may be differentiated by the providing organisations. There are schemes provided by vendors, which concentrate on certifying that the certification holder has knowledge relating to a particular product from a vendor. There are also schemes which certify broad knowledge of a particular domain, that are generally run by an industry or "not-for-profit" group. Second, regarding *academic credentials and experience*, a key question for a certification scheme is "What are its objectives?" and how does the scheme relate to an academic degree in IT security? Experts suggest that vendor-neutral certification is both complementary to, and an extension of, a degree in IT security by generally requiring a degree, a level of experience and some specific knowledge of professional practise in IT security, which would not normally be included in a degree. Vendor-specific certification is generally regarded as not directly linked to either, but rather, skills training for particular equipment.

Third, most established professions have adopted an *ethical code*. With IT security, a code of ethics can assume particular importance since the knowledge that is needed to defend systems and networks against attack is the same knowledge that could be used to attack them [14]. The need for a code of ethics appears to be met by vendor-neutral certification schemes that mandate agreement to their code. Fourth, if a scheme does not gain *market acceptance* from employers and governments, the scheme will lose relevance and use [10]. Fifth, *localisation* is important as if a scheme does not account for local variations in law, culture, regulation and market development, it is unlikely to be relevant to the jurisdiction in which it operates. The APEC IT skill Report [3] identifies local requirements as key to the relevance of a scheme. It is noted that a number of certifications originate in the USA and, in some cases, their curriculum is based on US legal practice rather than international needs.

3 Toward an Evaluation Framework

A preliminary evaluation framework was synthesised from a literature review and focus group. A fragment of the ten-page framework is provided in the Appendix. The framework is organised by Category, Characteristic and Criterion, and suggests a method for quantitatively assessing each criterion to enable comparisons between schemes, as well as a column for a user to document qualitative assessment. The rationale explains to users why a specific characteristic is important, while the criteria provide ways that the characteristics can be assessed. Four columns in the framework indicate the relevance of a criterion to the four key user types.

In constructing the preliminary framework, it emerged that the credibility of an IT security certification scheme is substantially linked to (1) the credibility of the organisation that issues it and (2) factors which relate more specifically to the certification. The existence of this relationship transfers the requirement for certification scheme rigor and transparency to the governing body for a given certification scheme. There has been validation of this point by the recently released ISO standard 17024, which specifically addresses this area.

The preliminary framework offers important advantages for users aiming to select an IT security certification scheme. By providing the criteria for assessing the characteristics and the rationale for their inclusion, it is possible for a user to better understand the relative importance of a particular criterion in their particular circumstances. In addition, by providing a standard set of criteria, it is possible to make a genuine comparison between certifications. A drawback of the framework in its current form is that weightings for each criterion to express individual preference for certain criteria are missing and this weakness reduces the level of customisation that is immediately available. A future development of the framework will include weightings with the aim of producing a scheme which would associate a numerical value with the relevance of a certification scheme to a particular group of security specialists.

4 Conclusion

A preliminary IT security certification evaluation framework has been developed in this paper. The framework is extensible and sufficiently flexible to allow different categories of users to identify those characteristics which are of greatest importance. Such flexibility will allow a user to make a more informed choice and will also allow customisation of the framework to individual user needs. Issues of governance emerged as significant contributors to the credibility of an IT Security Certification and this point has been underscored by both the recent trend to conformance with ISO 17024 by a number of schemes such as CISSP and CISM, and considerable feedback from the focus group participants. Future development of the framework will allow for the addition of user-defined weightings to be applied to each criterion together with a diagrammatic representation of the profile of each certification to allow for a greater level of comparison. A further focus group is planned to validate the final framework. The development of an automated tool to assist in evaluation and comparison presents another potentially useful direction to pursue.

References

1. M. Hentea, and H.S. Dhillon, Towards Changes in Information Security Education, *Journal of Information Technology Education* **5**, 221-223 (2006).
2. E. Tittel and K. Lindros, Analysis: The Vendor-neutral Security Certification Landscape, SearchSecurity.com, 26 September (2006).
3. APECTEL, IT Skills Report, Asia-Pacific Economic Cooperation Telecommunications & Information Working Group e-Security Task Group, (March 2004); http://www.apectelwg.org Document number: telwg29/ESTG/05.
4. E. Tittel, Building a Career in Information Security, *Certification Magazine* April (2004).
5. M. Bean, The Quest for the IT Security Professional, *Certification Magazine* November (2004).
6. E. Tittel, Security Certification: A Marketplace Overview, *Certification Magazine* February (2003).
7. M.E. Whitman, and H.J. Mattord, A Draft Model Curriculum for Programs of Study in Information Security and Assurance, Kennesaw State University, Georgia, 1 – 83 (2003).
8. M. Bishop and D. Frincke, Academic Degrees and Professional Certification, *IEEE Security & Privacy Magazine* November, **2**(6), 56 – 58 (2004).
9. K.L. Bledsoe and J.A. Graham, The Use of Multiple Evaluation Approaches in Program Evaluation, *American Journal of Evaluation* **26**(3), 302-319 (2005).
10. T. Claburn, Security Pros get their Due, *Information Week*, 16 January, (2006).
11. B. Endicott-Popovsky, Ethics and Teaching Information Assurance, *IEEE Security & Privacy Magazine*, July/August, 65-67 (2003).
12. T. Facklam, Certification of Persons – ISO/IEC DIS 17024, *ISO Bulletin* October, 31 – 34 (2002).
13. D. Frincke, Who Watches the Security Educators? *IEEE Security & Privacy Magazine*, May/June, 56 – 58 (2003).
14. P.Y. Logan and A. Clarkson, Teaching Students to Hack: Curriculum Issues in Information Security, ACM SIGCSE Bulletin, *Proceedings of the 36th SIGCSE Technical Symposium on Computer Science Education SIGCSE '05* **37**(1), 157-161 (2005).
15. E. Schultz, Infosec Certification: Which way do we turn from here? *Computers & Security* **24**(8), 587-588 (2005).
16. ISO/IEC 17024, Conformity Assessment—General Requirements for Bodies Operating Certification of Persons, 1-10 (2003).

Appendix: Fragment of Preliminary Framework for User Evaluation of IT Security Certification Schemes

Legend: PRO - IT Security Professionals; EMP - Employers of IT Security Professionals
DEV - Developers of IT security courses; GOV - Governments

Categ-ory	Characteristic	Criterion	Rationale	PRO	EMP	DEV	GOV	Method of Quant. Assess-ment	Quali-tative Assess-ment (user)
Credibility	Governance	With which Governance standards does the Certification Scheme conform? (e.g. ISO standard 17024)	If the governance of the organisation which is behind a particular IT security certification scheme is not open and transparent with few, if any, conflicts of interest, then the scheme is unlikely to attract the credibility necessary to be successful.	x	x	x	x	None = 0 At least one recognise d standard = 1	

Teaching of Information Security in the "Health Care and Nursing" Postgraduate program

Tatjana Welzer[1], Marko Hölbl[1], Ana Habjanič[2], Boštjan Brumen[1], Marjan Družovec[1]
[1]University of Maribor, Faculty of Electrical Engineering and Computer Science, Smetanova 17, SI-2000 Maribor, Slovenia, {welzer, marko.holbl, bostjan.brumen, marjan.druzovec }@uni-mb.si
[2]University of Maribor, University College of nursing studies, ana.habjanic@uni-mb.si

Abstract. Informatics plays an increasing role in the area of health care services. Not only will the patient's satisfaction with the medical treatment depend on the cooperation and communication between the nurse and the doctor, but also on the nurse and her way of dealing with and usage of IT technology. Although having become a part of daily routines in the meantime, the question arises if nurses are aware of the importance of IT technology for their work duties. How many of the nurses will have probably ever thought about the importance and sensitivity of the data they daily use? Without doubt, computer-literacy among members of all professional groups within society has increased enormously in the last years. Nevertheless, especially the area of health care service demands some more specific knowledge and awareness by the concerned staff related to topics of possibilities, benefits, possible mistakes and theirs consequences, especially from the security point of view, including the sensitivity of the working area, as well as ethical issues. The aim of this paper is to present, the postgraduate program in general as well as the actual handling of providing lectures on information security for nurses. Furthermore, the paper will focus on (gained) experience, and the formative assessment of the postgraduate program.

1 Introduction

An essential part of every modern information technology (IT) environment is the issue of security. Security considerations include, fast and secure information processing, data gathering, decision support applications, data mining, and information generation either in the health care centers, pharmacies, hospitals or any other health care institutions. These considerations demand employing suitably educated personnel for activities where IT and information security (IS) are part of

Please use the following format when citing this chapter:

Welzer, T., Hölbl, M., Habjanič, A., Brumen, B., and Družovec, M., 2007, in IFIP International Federation for Information Processing, Volume 232, New Approaches for Security, Privacy and Trust in Complex Environments, eds. Venter, H., Eloff, M., Labuschagne, L., Eloff, J., von Solms, R., (Boston: Springer), pp. 479–484.

everyday work and life. To cope with this situation, nurses have to be trained in a proper way [7], [14].

Taking into consideration the required knowledge from IT and IS, we are convinced that the proper way is to achieve an undergraduate or post graduate education where student nurses play an active role in the lecture phase. This participatory learning model increases the capability for students to use this knowledge when using IT systems in the workplace. To reach these goals, we developed a postgraduate nursing curriculum within the frame of the EU Phare Tempus [14] project called NICE - Nursing Informatics and Computer Aided Education [1], [7] in which, as the name already reveals, informatics and IT as well as IS will be addressed and taught.

In the paper we will give a brief overview on the NICE curriculum. Besides this, we will concentrate on some details derived from the security lecture, which will be followed by experience which we acquired in the last years by teaching the mentioned lecture. Experience is very important for a further upgrading of the lectures, for the curriculum development and for keeping up with up-to-date lecture material accessible via webpage. The paper will be concluded by addressing teaching results and final remarks given in the conclusion.

2 The NICE curriculum

At the end of the 1990's (1996-1999), the NICE project was established with the aim to develop and introduce new short cycle degree courses from nursing informatics at the university colleges. The project partners came from Austria, France, Greece, Italy and Slovenia [1]. The team who developed the curriculum consisted of members of various professions like nurses, engineers, computer scientists, medical doctors and administrators. These participants have very different views, opinions and beliefs on nursing informatics in general and in particular on the content of the nursing informatics curriculum [4]. In Slovenia, this postgraduate program was the first one of his kind who integrated IT lectures to the curriculum for educating people for the health care and nursing domain. One of the top priority goals of the program was, besides integrating informatics and computer science knowledge to the program, the integration of experts from the mentioned fields to the lecturing of nurses and health care domain staff.

After discussing various approaches that had been used in education [5], [6] as well as talking about other system approaches [6], we agreed on the common definition of nursing informatics [2], [3] and teaching nursing informatics as follows [1]: Teaching nursing informatics is a process in which students obtain basic knowledge in the following areas:

- informatics and computer science,
- informatics in health care (medical informatics),
- informatics in care and nursery (nursing informatics),
- computer communications and security (internet),
- medical instrumentation and simulation supported by computers with the aim to support nursing care processes as well as making nursing work more visible and enjoyable.

Additionally the goals of the program are to provide and enable better health care for all. On this foundation the postgraduate nursing and health care informatics curriculum was developed and approved to by Slovenian authorities.

The program is, like all other study programs for postgraduate students at our university, offered as a part time study. Most of students are part time students (regular matriculation is also possible, but is not the normal case), working as nurses or keeping other similar positions. These students already have a background knowledge from the nursing area duties or closely related to it. Some of the students have a technical background in computer science and informatics and are working in health care institutions, pharmacies, hospitals and similar institutions. The program started in 2001 with one student. Currently the number of students in the program has reached 10-12 students starting every year. The postgraduate program can be finished within 1.5 year (3 semesters). During the program, two semesters are dedicated to attending classes (theories, practices, tools). The students will spend the last semester preparing their research and thesis. Within the two semesters of classes, students have to pass 18 exams.

The offered lectures of the program are divided into three modules: Nursing informatics, informatics in health care, and search for information in computer networks. In the following we will focus on the first module and give insight to the single lectures: "Information systems", "Telematics in health care", "Databases", "Intelligent Systems", "Ethics" and "Security of computerized data." Already the titles of lectures reveal the multidisciplinary content of the curriculum. Knowledge from nursing is combined with knowledge from the informatics and computer science and is added by electrical engineering cognition. The teachers of the individual lectures have high competence in their subject as they have achieved their expertise in this specific field of knowledge. Lectures like "Information Systems", "Databases", "Intelligent systems" and "Ethics and security for computerized data" are given either only by a lecturer from informatics and computer science or by lecturers from two or three areas who will then cooperate in the same lecture.

For each single lecture in the previously mentioned courses, teaching materials were produced, including a NICE book series [9] and PowerPoint presentations. Books published in the NICE series, cover all lectures and provide the basic knowledge required to finish the obligations of the program. Additionally, in response to the achieved feedback, the PowerPoint presentations and other electronic materials and tools [13] from lectures of the last years are available [7].

3 The security lecture

When developing the NICE curriculum, we followed the "Backward Curriculum Design Process" [8]. This process begins with desired outcomes and goals and goes back to learning objectives which are then divided into courses and modules. This approach was used also when developing single courses. The following section will provide details on the security lecture in the NICE program called "Ethics and security for computerized data" [9]. This lecture series is broken into 6 sessions:

Introduction and history: This part briefly introduces the importance of security in and for health care, gives some definitions and general historical overview on the security including understanding information security, positions and roles.

Information Security: For successful information security, also some other topics of security have to be presented such as issues of security in computational systems, physical security (natural disasters, un-authorized access), users' security, technical security (data encryption, algorithmic systems, cryptography) and viruses, just to mention the most important topics.

Sensitive data: Sensitive data is data that should not be made public [12]. We are discussing which data are sensitive and what is their cause of being so sensitive. We are having a closer look at solutions of how to protect a database if only some pieces of data are sensitive. Furthermore, the role of data mining is pointed out.

Information Security in health care and medical systems: This part discusses the range of topics in which information security is used. Also available to the students are commercial and research projects and possible guidelines are presented [10].

Ethics: Special professional areas like medicine, health and pharmacies are closely related to the issue of ethics. Ethics is complex term and sometimes also confused with religion because many religions provide a framework in which they make ethical choices [9]. Besides giving a basic definition of the term, also the question of ethics versus relation, ethical principals and ethical reasoning are presented. Very important parts of the lecture are examples of ethical principles and case studies of ethics. Each case study is presented in detail and analyzed. Furthermore, alternative solutions or extensions are offered. A complementary topic is also the code of ethics as they are stated by IEEE, ACM and Computer Ethics Institute.

Practical work: Essential for students is the possibility of transferring their theoretical knowledge concerning information security to practical work and gaining practical experience with this issue. Instructors guide students to approach the topic of information security from their own field. The enterprise is defined by each student for his/her seminar work and information security is presented and developed. Results are presented and discussed with other students, the instructors and the lecturer. Final conclusions are done after having gained practical experience.

4 Experience

In general, educational assessment is the process of gathering, describing or quantifying information about the learning performance. The lecture being evaluated can range from the performance of students and instructors to the evaluation of lecture materials, courses and or the entire study program. Educational evaluation could be arranged during or after lectures and with different purposes. Generally speaking, assessment can be defined as the systematic process used to obtain information about study achievements [8].

After having provided a brief overview on the NICE nursing and health care postgraduate program and having presented the security lecture with some details, we would like to address some assessment results which were acquired during the last years. Most of them are obtained in informal discussions with students after having concluded the exam of the Security lecture (formative evaluation). More formal assessment (summative evaluation) was not possible because the groups of participating students are very small and ranging between 5 and 12 students. Besides this, assessment is much more difficult if new teaching methods and experimenting are introduced.

One of the goals of the lectures is to prepare students to be actively involved into the developing process of information security, while they will have probably the role of domain (nursing, health care) expert consultant. Therefore they have to acquire knowledge and practice how to do this. Consequently, they have to select their own domain to develop information security. Very important is also that we put attention to the session about ethics and integrate it to the everyday work of the students (mostly nurses).

How do students tend to react when first being confronted with the issue of IS? There are no special requests for IT or IS by matriculation. So, they are mostly still quite unfamiliar with the topic (except those students with a non-nursing background or undergraduate study). They feel motivated to "reject" the lecture and to pass it as fast as possible, not paying attention to the importance of the topic and the knowledge they could actually gain.

After having experienced the first "shock" ("we are not able to do this"), they start gradually understanding the importance of information security and ethics. After having prepared the seminar work, they have developed a feeling for the importance of this particular lecture. This is maybe a surprising result as the students had already been working close to or in the selected domain before they had started the postgraduate program.

In the formative assessment, students explain their own story. We assist the student by providing formative questions (What is the biggest problem within information security in your domain? What is your opinion on the best method to solve your problem? Open questions, such as: What skills are lacking? What methods do you use to increase information security awareness?). The pedagogy of participatory learning is somewhat unfamiliar playing an active role in selecting and forming the content of their seminar work (they select the domain as well as a possible application for which the security/ethics needs to be developed) prepares the student to address unfamiliar problems when in the workplace.

In the summative evaluation, a secondary emphasis is used to assess students' achievement at the end of the lecture. The assessment data which was collected can also be used to provide feedback about lecture materials, the approach, and adjustment of the whole lecture, and gives response on the adequacy of the lecture in the presented program.

5 Conclusion

The main idea of this paper was to emphasize and prove the importance of both IS and IT in the nursing and health care educational programs – staff with this knowledge is more and more wanted. Actually, IS and IT are now part of every day life, starting with shopping experience up to working place conditions and visiting a doctor. Whenever things fail, are disliked, or experienced as being uncomfortable, we are unsatisfied and complain either to the shop assistant or vendor or both or to our webmaster, IT engineer and also to the nurse or even the doctor. Quite often we blame the wrong person because the system is either not good or not working correctly. Sometimes the reason for dissatisfaction is due to the lack of knowledge by people who are using these systems. The NICE program was created to avoid this misunderstanding. We can report that employers are reacting positive on first graduates [7].

We have decided to implement the knowledge of IS to the nursing educational program, independent to the fact that for the majority of students this issue will be a new, unfamiliar domain. The presented curriculum provides the postgraduate students with the opportunity to compensate for the before mentioned lack of knowledge. By offering lectures in computer science and informatics, we are motivating our students also to play more active role in real projects at daily work using new IT and IS products for the mentioned domains. We are putting our graduates opposite the IT experts who have lack of health care and nursing knowledge and need much more additional work to come closer to mentioned areas as our students from opposite background.

References

1. Kokol, P., Micetic Turk, D. (2004); Soft System Methodology in development and implementation of a new nursing informatics curricula, Faculty of Electrical Engineering and Computer Science, University College of Nursing studies, Internal report.
2. Hovega E.J.S. (1998); Global Health Informatics Education, Proceedings of HTE 98, ed. J. Mantas, University of Athens.
3. Ball M.J. et al. (1995); Nursing Informatics, Springer, New York.
4. Kokol P. et all (1998); New Nursing Informatics Curriculum – an Outcome from the Nice Project, Proceedings of HTE 98, ed. J. Mantas, University of Athens.
5. Gregory W.J. (2000); Designing Educational Systems: A critical System Approach. System Practice Vol 6, No 2.
6. Bathany B.H.(ed.)(2002); Transforming Education by Design,System Practice Vol 6, No 2.
7. Welzer T. et all (2006); Teaching IT in the postgraduate health care and nursing program; Proceedings of international symposium on health information management research, (iSHIMR'06), (ed.) Abidi R., Bath P., Keselj V., Dalhousie University, Halifax, Canada.
8. Whitman M.E., Mattord H..J. (2004); Designing and Teaching Information Security Curriculum, Proceedings of InfoSecCD Conference, Kennesaw, USA.
9. Kokol P. (ed) (1999); Health care Informatics (in Slovenian), University of Maribor, Sl.
10. SEISMED Consortium (ed) (1996); Data Security in Health Care, Guidelines, IOS Press.
11. Yu H. et all (2006);Teaching a Web Security Course to Practice Information Assurance, Proceedings of SIGCSE'2006, Huston, Texas, USA.
12. Pfleeger C.P., Lawrence Pfleeger (2007); Security in Computing, Prentice Hall.
13. Habjanic A. et all (1999); A tutor for nursing process education; Medical Informatics Europe '99, (ed.) Kokol P., Zupan B., Stare J., Premik, M., Engelbrecht R., IOS Press.
14. http://ec.europa.eu/education/programmes/tempus/, Last visit: February 2, 2007.

Remote Virtual Information Assurance Network

Ronald C Dodge JR[1] , Corey Bertram[2], Daniel Ragsdale[3]
1,3 Department of Electrical Engineerig and Computer Science, United States Military Academy, West Point, NY, ronald.dodge@usma.edu, daniel.ragsdale@usma.edu
2 George Washington Universtiy, Washington DC, qr7@gwu.edu

Abstract. The use of virtualization technologies to increase the capacity and utilization of laboratory resources is widely used in classroom environments using several workstation based virtualization products. These virtual networks are often "air gapped" to prevent the inadvertent release of malware. This implementation however requires users to be in the classroom. A novel extension on this concept is to design the infrastructure to support remote access to the virtual machine(s) using virtual server applications, while maintaining the complete isolation of the virtual networks.

1 Introduction

In 2000, virtualization started to become a popular tool to enable the development of innovative instructional techniques. Many universities have adopted the use of virtual machines to provide students with an environment to understand how systems interact, demonstrate communication protocols, experiment with malware for exploit understanding, and provide more scalable lab environments. These systems are traditionally implemented using workstation based virtualization applications that are accessible only from the workstation they reside on. Students in this environment must come into the lab to access the virtual machines since they are bound to a physical host. The architecture described in this paper frees the student from needing to go into the lab and also reduces the likelihood that no lab resources are available by consolidating the virtualization application onto a server platform. While the discussion here is focused on information assurance, the architecture described supports other requirements like network fundamentals and operating systems.

The paper continues as follows: in section 2 we describe differing virtualization environments and previous work in virtual lab implementations. In section 3 we describe a web services oriented architecture implemented by the authors and conclude in section 4.

Please use the following format when citing this chapter:

Dodge, R., Bertram, C., and Ragsdale, D., 2007, in IFIP International Federation for Information Processing, Volume 232, New Approaches for Security, Privacy and Trust in Complex Environments, eds. Venter, H., Eloff, M., Labuschagne, L., Eloff, J., von Solms, R., (Boston: Springer), pp. 485–490.

2 Background and Previous Work

Starting in the 1960's large main frame systems used virtualization to provide individual computing environments for users (for example, the IBM System 360). As platforms evolved to make personal computers relatively commonplace, the need for virtualization decreased; to the point where it became rarely implemented. As the personal computer became increasingly more capable, system resources began to exceed computing requirements and the opportunity to instantiate multiple virtual machines on a single personal computing platform emerged. [1, 2] Virtualization products include open source projects such as OpenVX and Xen; and commercial products, VMware, VirtualPC, and Parallels.

Virtualization essentially decouples the physical machine hardware from the operating system by inserting a software virtualization layer. The following discussion focuses on the VMware Workstation and VMware Server product implementation. The virtualization application forms a normalized representation of the physical hardware that each "guest" operating system utilizes. This normalization layer sits on top of the host operating system. This virtualization layer presents each guest operating system with its own set of virtual hardware (CPU, RAM, Hard Drive...). The guest operating system (and data) is a file on the host system. This architecture makes it trivial to move virtual machines from one physical system to another. This capability is very important to the deployment described in section 3. The virtual machines' network card can be bridged to the host's network card (enabling the virtual machine to be connected to the physical network) or connected to a virtual switch (enabling communication with other virtual machines).

The past 5 years have seen various employments of virtual infrastructures to facilitate education and training. This is in response to a realization that students must practice the concepts and theories discussed in lecture to fully understand the material. This point has been well argued in many papers [3, 4] and evidenced by the growth in virtual and remote access labs used by education institutions and industry. The general architecture agued for in the referenced literature dictates that an optimal lab provides an "air gapped" system environment to prevent malware or malicious activity (scanning) from interacting with non-lab systems. Additionally, the lab should present the user with a robust suit of operating systems and applications that communicate over an air gapped network that is also separate from other air gapped networks. The advancement offered in this paper is to provide an architecture that satisfies these requirements while permitting access to the lab to remote users. The design of the architecture described in this paper is builds on the experience of leading institutions in the deployment of IA/CS environments, such as the University of Alaska Fairbanks, Brooklyn Polytechnic University, the Universitaet Trier in Germany, and the University of Milan in Italy. The architectures currently adopted by these institutions for use in their IA/CS research and education programs is similar in intent but vary in implementation; each having unique advantages and disadvantages.

The University of Alaska Fairbanks built a virtual infrastructure where VMware workstation is employed in an isolated network where the guest operating system files are stored on a central file server. Students log into a machine in the lab and access their virtual machine files on the file server. The CPU and other non-file system resources on the local machine are used, however all file I/O is accomplished on the file server. The lab has strength in that it is air gapped from any production network and the Internet; preventing any of the security tools or malware from unintentionally interacting with other networks. This architecture however requires the student be in the lab.

An alternative architecture is used at the Brooklyn Polytechnic University. [6] Here, the infrastructure is built on a combination of physical switches and routers and the VMware ESX virtualization platform. Instructors create a collection of hosts (on the ESX server) and switches/routers that are shared by groups of students. The students accessing the lab are presented with a diagram of the network and by clicking on each of the devices receive a console session (over an applet in the browser). The lab uses a VPN concentrator to provide connectivity between the networks over the public network. The strength of the ISIS environment is that students do not need to be in the lab to use the resources. However the VPN concentrator breaks the "air gap" network philosophy, leaving open the opportunity (and challenge to some) to subvert the established controls. The sharing of hosts by a number of simultaneous users is a second drawback.

A third virtual lab is the IT security Tele-lab at the Universitaet Trier, Germany. [7] The Tele-lab implements architecture built using User-Mode Linux. The users interact with the virtual machines directly using a Virtual Network Computing (VNC) client application. This presents a significant drawback as the virtual machines are connected to the physical network; leaving open the possibility of potential for use misuse by exposing the security lab to an external network. Additionally, User-Mode Linux only supports a virtual machine based on the kernel of the host machine. This greatly limits the type of operating systems users can interact with.

A final comparative lab is the Open Source Virtual Lab hosted at University of Milan, Italy. [8] This lab offers remote access to a collection of XEN virtual machines. The open source nature of the lab (and XEN 2.0 limitations) permits only the use of Linux virtual machines. This lab architecture permits users to log into the system through a web interface to enable the system to start the requested virtual machine. Once the virtual machine is started a direct SSH connection between the user and the virtual machine is provided through a terminal shell. Currently, the documented implemented system only supports Linux virtual machines; however XEN 3.0 will support Windows operating systems. The current architecture however still only supports terminal shell interaction. Additionally, while the infrastructure used in the Open Source Virtual Lab differs from the others previously discussed the same disadvantage of user access to local networks and limited operating system interaction.

The solution described in the following section implements a remote accessible architecture that provides the benefits available to the ASSERT and the United States Military Academy's Information Warfare Analysis and Research (IWAR) lab. [4] The Remote Access Virtual Information Assurance Network provides an architecture where it is not possible to communicate with external networks, while providing a robust suite of Windows and Linux hosts controlled through a VNC session.

3 System Architecture

The objective of the Remote Access Virtual Information Assurance Network (RVIAN) is to provide users with a lab experience – only not in the lab. The laboratories described in the previous section all attempt to provide this environment and recognize that the optimal configuration would provide:

Realistic Heterogeneity: The operating systems used should represent the full spectrum of operating systems that a user should understand from a security perspective.
Configurability: The hosts the user has access to should be as configurable as a system in a physical lab.
Isolation: The network the users control is air gapped from external networks. This is to prevent any accidental exposure of malware and malicious activity to external network.
Scalable: The virtual lab should provide a scalable solution that provides the same if not more capability of a physical lab. For instance, in a physical lab if a student requires two systems to conduct a network sniffing lab, then the designed architecture should not require more than two physical systems.
Cost Effective: The virtual lab should be affordable to implement and not require excessive system administration/maintenance.
In the following sections, we describe the implementation of the RVIAN, and then readdress the five configuration requirements and how they are met.

3.1 Physical/Software Infrastructure

The RVIAN is implemented using a web services architecture, as shown in figure 1

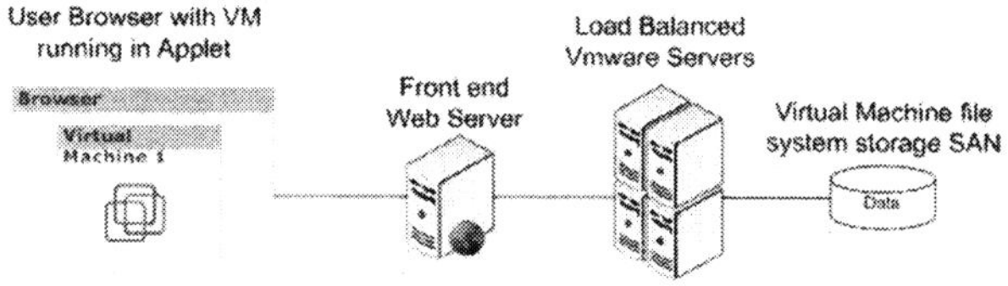

Figure 1: RVIAN Architecture

The user enters the system through a web browser and authenticates using a userID and password. The front end web server provides information on the RVIAN environment, links to required software, load balancing for the backend virtual machine servers and the authentication logic to allow access to the virtual machines, as shown in Figure 2 The Web server is powered by Apache 2.2 and PHP. Behind the server, a collection of servers running VMware server run virtual machines for each user. The VMware servers use a storage area network to hold the virtual machine file systems.

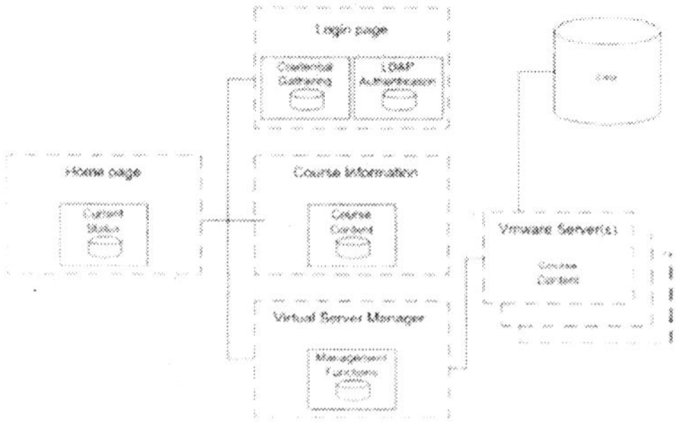

Figure 2: RVIAN Web page layout

Access control is implemented through LDAP credential authentication. Users are initially provided an account on the system. Along with the credentials, users are provided a user directory on the storage area network. The user directory stores the file system for each virtual machine allocated to the user.

Using a menu driven system, the user selects which virtual machine(s) to launch. The selected virtual machines can be based on a predefined selection to be used for a specific lesson module or the user's desire to experiment. The available virtual machines are typically copied over to the user directory on the storage area network by the system manager in advance; however the system can support copying new virtual machines dynamically, assuming the user disk quota is sufficient. The virtual machine manager selects which server to host the virtual machines on and uses port forwarding to return to the user's browser the virtual machine using TightVNC through a Java applet. The Virtual Server Manager load balances the workload using performance statistics from the Virtual Servers to determine which server to host the user's virtual machines.

3.2 Remote Lab Requirements

This architecture supports each requirement previously discussed.

Realistic Heterogeneity: Vmware Server supports a wide range of operating systems in full graphic interaction mode. The operating systems supported include any version of Windows, most distributions of Linux, and Solaris X86. This full interaction capability and robust suite of guest operating systems provides an unmatched flexibility in virtual labs.

Configurability: The VMware server virtual machines can be configured by the instructor to meet a variety of instructional and training needs. Instructors can configure the network infrastructure to consist of many (ranging from 1 to 99) virtual switches that have no external connectivity. Users have full control over the operating system of the virtual machine – the environment is what contains the user.

Isolation: The Virtual Machine Networks (or VMnets) implemented by VMware provide an environment where virtual machines can connect to up to 99 virtual networks (actually each virtual machine limited to a maximum of four network interface cards). These virtual networks can be configured such that there is no connection to a physical network (even though the supporting virtualization software, VMserver, provides a connection through which the user interacts with the virtual machine). This environment provides separates the virtual network from the external networks the users communicate on with the instances of VMware Server. For example, if VMware server were running on three backend servers, the VM manager would determine which server to run the user's virtual machines and also determine what virtual networks they would use. This segregation keeps virtual machines from interacting with both external networks and other user's networks.

Scalable: Depending on how the virtual machines are built, each virtual server we are using (dual 3.2 processor, 8 GB RAM) can support 12~14 virtual machines. In the modules we have developed each user needs approximately four virtual machines. The system scales with the number of virtual servers used. In our lab we have a 10 blade enclosure running VMware server; allowing for approximately 25 simultaneous users.

Cost Effective: Laboratory equipment is costly. A student workstation capable of running a standard suite of virtual machines needed for the modules we implement is roughly equivalent to 50% the cost of a server running VMware server. (VMware server itself is free.) This cost however is outweighed by the flexibility the server based system provides.

4 Conclusion

Literature strongly supports the benefits of experience based learning and the development of laboratories to provide that exposure. The examples discussed in the opening of this paper represent a few of the examples of efforts to provide a laboratory experience; only without the physical lab. The greatest difficulty in providing the capability for remote users interact with and control networks designed for security training and education is the requirement to ensure the networks remain isolated. The benefit of the solution described in this paper rests on the robust virtual networking supported by VMware server. The capability provided allows for students to interact with the virtual machines using TightVNC presented in a Web Browser Java Applet; however the networks the virtual machines use are completely isolated from the external network and the networks of other users. Future work includes the development of a physical hardware management system that allow for the inclusion of physical routing and switching equipment into the environment while still providing separation between the students virtual network and the underlying support network.

References

1. M. Rosenblum, “The Reincarnation of Virtual Machines,” ACM Queue, Vol. 2 No. 5 - July/August 2004.
2. B. Supnik, “Simulators: Virtual Machines of the Past (and Future)”, ACM Queue, Vol. 2 No. 5 - July/August 2004.
3. Cynthia E. Irvine, “Amplifying Security Education in the Laboratory,” Proceedings IFIP TC11 WC 11.8 First World Conference on Information Security Education, pp 139 -146, Kista, Sweden, June 1999.
4. D. J. Ragsdale, S. D. Lathrop, and R. C. Dodge," Enhancing Information Warfare Education Through the Use of Virtual and Isolated Networks," The Journal of Information Warfare, Volume 2, Issue 3, pp. 47-59 August 2003.
5. B. Hay and K. Nance, “Evolution of the ASSERT Computer Security Lab,” Proceedings of the 10th Colloquium for Information Systems Security Education, page 150-156, Adelphi MD, June 5-8, 2006.
6. V. Padman and N. Memon, “Design of a Virtual Laboratory for Information Assurance Education and Research,” Proceedings of the 5th IEEE Information Assurance Workshop, West Point, NY, 17-19 June 2002.
7. J. Hu, D. Cordel, and C. Meinel, “A Virtual Laboratory for IT Security Education,” Proceedings of the Conference on Information Systems in E-Business and EGovernment (EMISA), pp. 60-7, Luxembourg, 6-8 Oct 20041.
8. E. Damiani, F. Frati, and D. Rebeccani, “The Open Source Virtual Lab: a Case Study,” Workshop on Free and open Cource Learning Environments and Tools, Como, Italy, 10 June 2006.

Certifying the Computer Security Professional Using the Project Management Institute's PMP Model

Kara L. Nance and Brian Hay
ASSERT Center, University of Alaska Fairbanks
210 Chapman, Fairbanks, AK 99708 U.S.A.
ffkln@uaf.edu brian.hay@uaf.edu
WWW home page: http://assert.uaf.edu

Abstract. While many organizations offer certifications associated with information technology (IT) security, there is no single overarching accrediting organization that has identified the body of knowledge and experience necessary for success in the IT security field. In order for an IT security workforce to be acknowledged and recognized throughout the world as possessing a proven level of education, knowledge, and experience in IT security, a formal process for certifying IT security professionals must be developed. This research effort suggests that the IT security community use the Project Management Institute's process for certifying Project Management Professionals (PMPs) as a model for developing an open and easily accessible IT Security Body Of Knowledge (ITSBOK) and an associated international certification process for IT security professionals.

1 Introduction

Information security has become an increasingly important issue, and the repercussions of a failure in information security have become much more serious as the level of public, corporate, and governmental awareness of such issues has been raised. Twenty years ago the loss of bank backup tapes or university student records may not even have been reported to law enforcement agencies, whereas today such losses not only have legal implications, but are likely to be publicized by national news organizations. As such, the need for excellence in IT security is apparent not only within the IT community, but at all levels of the corporate and governmental hierarchies. The problem, however, is there currently is no suitable, vendor-neutral, standard by which to judge the competence of a potential IT security employee. While there are many certifications related to the information security field, many

Please use the following format when citing this chapter:

Nance, K. and Hay, B., 2007, in IFIP International Federation for Information Processing, Volume 232, New Approaches for Security, Privacy and Trust in Complex Environments, eds. Venter, H., Eloff, M., Labuschagne, L., Eloff, J., von Solms, R., (Boston: Springer), pp. 491–496.

have such a narrow or vendor-specific focus that they have little value in determining how an employee could adapt to new threats and technologies in this rapidly developing field. In many cases, IT security professionals have simply evolved into their current roles, often because they were system administrators who realized there was a need to "secure" the systems they were responsible for. However, when an individual evolves into such a position, the full breadth of information assurance issues is often missed, and is replaced by a focus on the threats that the employee in question is either aware of or can imagine. In addition, one need not search long to find any number of ill-conceived IT security plans, such as many of the current digital rights management (DRM) schemes, which most truly competent information assurance professionals know are doomed to failure. As IT security becomes increasingly important in all aspects of life, including those, such as RFID embedding in passports, which are not within the realm of traditional computer security, there must be a mechanism by which those truly qualified to design, implement, and manage such systems can be identified. In addition, there must be a roadmap for those without the in-depth experience or a wide ranging understanding of the information security discipline, including students, to develop throughout their careers into the IT security leaders of the future.

2 Background

In order to assess the training and certification needs of the computer security professional, one first must determine the background of the personnel who tend to hold security positions in IT fields. The rapid technological advances of the information age have resulted in a large number of IT workers who have evolved into their positions as well as those who have been trained for their positions. In many cases, the individual at the organization who knew the most about computers became the system administrator, without any formal training in system administration or computer security. In other cases, system administrators have a strong background in general computer science, but not specific training in computer security. ABET, Inc., the recognized accreditor for college and university programs in applied science, computing, engineering, and technology [1] does not currently include computer security as a required topic in a computer science or information technology curriculum.

To address the lack of trained computer security professionals, the National Security Agency (NSA) developed the Center of Academic Excellence in Information Assurance Education (CAE) program in response to Presidential Decision Directive 63 [2], with the goal of increasing the number of graduates with experience in information assurance. As of February 2003, the CAEIAE program is co-sponsored by the NSA and the Department of Homeland Security (DHS) [3]. There are currently approximately 70 academic institutions from across the United States that currently hold the CAE designation. This credential is intended to indicate that the institution is capable of producing graduates who have some minimal information assurance skills upon entry into the workforce. This is based on the national standards set by the Committee on National Security Systems and indicates that the institution has mapped its courses to the NSTISSI standards such as 4011 [4].

There are, however, weaknesses associated with the current CAE model. One weakness is that the depth to which the topics are covered varies greatly across the certified programs. Another is the lack of mandatory association between the course mapping process and the IA certification process, given that there is no requirement in the CAE application process to demonstrate that students receiving IA certification have completed a comprehensive set of the courses mapped to a particular NSTISSI. While CAE institutions have been successful in raising the level of security awareness among students, nothing in this process addresses the continued development of skills beyond the academic setting, which is necessary to transition from the level of college graduate to that of a well-rounded, highly experienced IT security practitioner. While there are certainly many other bodies who currently offer various levels of security certification [10, 11, 12], the lack of standardization across this wide field is readily apparent as each responds to the needs of its identified target audience. Many, if not all, of the courses currently available were developed by the training organizations without conducting an industry-wide needs assessment, resulting in certifications which tend to target specific or current products and issues, rather than those which address the long term or higher level needs of the IT community.

IT is such a rapidly changing field that vendor or product-specific skills acquired in such courses either quickly become obsolete, or serve as a method by which organizations become dependant on specific vendors, simply because the costs involved in retraining for alternate products is prohibitively high in the short term. Thus it is important that certified professionals possess the underlying foundational knowledge necessary to allow them to adapt to the wide range of IT security threats that they are likely to encounter now, as well those future threats that have not yet been imagined. Crowley conducted a survey of current literature discussing information systems security training and education in industry, government and academia. [13] There is a clear lack of standardization across the many self-designated bodies that have chosen to offer certifications in computer security. The result is that the IT security community has not identified a dominant standards organization with an open and easily accessible body of knowledge to certify professionals in IT security.

3 PMI Model

3.1 Problem Description

The challenges regarding standardizing IT security professionals are very similar to the challenges that were successfully addressed in certifying project management professionals. The Project Management Institute is an international organization that has identified five process areas and nine knowledge areas as well as metrics for certifying individuals as Project Management Professionals (PMPs). The program administers a "globally recognized, rigorous, education, and/or professional experience and examination-based professional credentialing program that maintains an ISO 9001 certification in Quality Management Systems."[5] Certified Project Management Professionals have demonstrated that they have met the education and/or professional experience requirements; have passed the rigorous PMP examination, have agreed to follow the PMP Code of Professional Conduct; and have committed to maintaining their status through continuing certification requirements. [6]

3.2 PMBOK

In addition to professional magazines, a refereed journal, and monthly newsletter, the Project Management Institute publishes A Guide to the Project Management Body of Knowledge (PMBOK Guide) [7]. This publication is currently in its third edition and has been translated into numerous languages to allow standardization of the field of project management across cultural and language barriers. The PMBOK was developed twenty years ago by PMI volunteers through a substantial research project, who worked together to identify the project management body of knowledge. [8] It is updated on a four-year cycle to ensure that it continually reflects the current state of the art in project management, based on input from its readers, and other project management professionals.

3.3 Experiential Requirement

The option to achieve the requisite training either through a bachelor's degree combined with some verified experience (>4,500 hours) or through more substantial verified experience (>7,500 hours) provides an excellent mechanism that opens the certification opportunity to those who have evolved into their positions in addition to those who have specifically been trained into the position. Both paths require experience so that the individual has proven themselves as a competent project manager. In addition, both tracks require at least 35 contact hours of formal education in project management. This experiential requirement would not be sufficient for certification on its own as this requirement would not provide a consistent measure of experience for all candidates nor ensure that the individual demonstrate comprehension of the body of knowledge necessary for success in the field. PMP candidates must complete an extensive application to verify that their background is consistent with the PMP eligibility requirements. Once approved, eligible candidates have one year to take the PMP examination. [9]

3.4 Examination

The four hour examination consists of questions that have been developed and validated by global work groups of experts in the content; each is referenced to at least one project management publication; they are monitored through psychometric analysis; and they satisfy the test specifications of a job analysis. [6] In addition, the breakdown for the exam topics is consistent with the performance domains. The examination is available in 10 languages and is offered only through approved test centers under a very strict examination process. Passing the examination is the final step in becoming a certified Project Management Professional, although keeping the certification current requires a commitment to meeting the continuing education requirements to keep current in the field.

4 IT Security Solution

IT Security professional could be certified using a similar process, building on the success of the PMP certification process and adopting their model. To oversee this effort, an organization similar to the PMI would need to take leadership in the effort. A similar approach has been used by the International Information Systems Security Certification Consortium for Certified Information Systems Security Professional (CISSP), but the related body of knowledge and the test which covers the CBK, has been criticized as demonstrating only lower levels of Bloom's taxonomy of educational objectives rather than true understanding of the underlying concepts necessary for success in the IT security field. One of the first objectives for this organization would be to develop a concise Guide to the IT Security Body of Knowledge (ITSBOK). Similar to the PMBOK, this publication would be easily available and vendor-neutral, and could easily build on the existing NSTISSI standards.

A poll of IT security professionals could help determine the experiential components that would be required in order for individuals to be eligible for the certification. Much of this work has been done, especially through the identification of the formal requirements for an institution to be certified as a CAEIAE. Like the PMP content, the content would need to be presented in a consistent, evolutionary, and vendor-neutral format, with sufficient depth to guarantee mastery of content rather than mere memorization of facts. The criteria could be reevaluated in compliance with a set revision schedule to ensure that it continually reflected a consensus body of knowledge that was evident of best practices in the field of IT security. An examination over the content should be a mandatory component in the certification process in order to ensure that all certified individuals demonstrated competence in the IT security body of knowledge. Like the PMP candidates, an ITSP should be prequalified based on a combination of education, verified experience, and IT security training prior to becoming eligible to take the examination.

While the ITSBOK would form the basis for the ITSP certification process, it could also be used as a guide for the development of training programs, such as those offered by technical colleges, or internal corporate training programs. While these programs may or may not culminate in ITSP certification, they can still benefit from the clear designation of the goals defined in the ITSBOK. This approach would enable a scaleable solution to meet the needs of government, industry and academia.

5 Conclusion

To create a certification in IT Security that is accepted internationally is a lofty, but necessary and worthwhile goal. In order to accomplish this, an accrediting body must be identified or established, the IT Security Body of Knowledge must be defined, and the formal process for certification must be developed and published. The creation of an Information Technology Security Professional (ITSP) certification following the highly successful model of the Project Management Institute's Project Management Professional (PMP) certification would guarantee that the IT security arena would have a population that would be widely recognized and accepted throughout the world as possessing a proven level of education, knowledge and experience in IT security.

References

1. ABET. Retrieved November 1, 2006 from www.abet.org
2. Department of Justice. White Paper - The Clinton Administration's Policy on Critical Infrastructure Protection: Presidential Decision Directive 63. May 22, 1998. Retrieved November 1, 2006 from http://www.usdoj.gov/criminal/cybercrime/white_pr.htm
3. National Security Agency. Centers of Academic Excellence. Retrieved November 1, 2006 from http://www.nsa.gov/ia/academia/caeiae.cfm
4. National Security Telecommunications and Information Systems Security. National Training Standard for Information Systems Security (INFOSEC) Professionals. NSTISSI No. 4011 20 June 1994.
5. Project Management Institute. PMI Home Page Retrieved November 1, 2006 from www.pmi.org
6. Project Management Institute. PMI Certification Program. Retrieved November 1, 2006 from http://www.pmi.org/info/PDC_CertificationsOverview.asp
7. Project Management Institute. A Guide to the Project Management Body of Knowledge – Third Edition. 2005.
8. Project Management Institute. Book Descriptions. Retrieved November 1, 2006 from http://www.pmibookstore.org/PMIBookStore/productDetails.aspx?itemID=358&varID=1
9. Project Management Institute. PMP Credential Handbook. PMI. 2000.
10. SANS Institute. Retrieved November 1, 2006 from http://www.sans.org/training/
11. ICS^2 Retrieved November 1, 2006 from https://www.isc2.org/cgi-bin/index.cgi
12. Global Information Assurance Certification. Retrieved November 1, 2006 from http://www.giac.org/
13. Crowley, E. 2003. Information system security curricula development. In Proceedings of the 4th Conference on information Technology Curriculum (Lafayette, Indiana, USA, October 16 - 18, 2003). CITC4 '03. ACM Press, New York, NY, 249-255.

Author Index

Printed in the USA